"Theory is one thing; practice quite another. This book is about the doing, not the talking. As such, it provides new and important insights into the practical challenges of religious peacemaking. It also helps define the art of the possible in this burgeoning, yet largely unexplored, field."

Dr. Douglas Johnston
Founder and President, International Center for Religion and Diplomacy
Coeditor of *Religion: The Missing Dimension of Statecraft*

"I strongly commend *Peacemakers in Action* at this time when religion's leaders and its positive role are being questioned.

"This book illustrates the successful work actually being done on the ground – at the micro level – by many religious leaders of differing faiths who work to diminish the darkness. They are all united in using their moral suasion to further the peace and justice that arises from their beliefs, and to build bridges of coexistence and community. It also illustrates the importance for all leaders at the macro level to support these religious leaders who wish to unify, instead of divide, and to assist in furthering their visions and dreams of a world where common values of a peaceful community are universally respected."

Alan Slifka
Board Chairman of The Abraham Fund Initiatives

"*Peacemakers in Action* persuasively makes the case for the positive role people of religion can play in those parts of the world that have seen devastating destruction of innocent life. Each personal journey toward conflict resolution and peace reveals the unspoken quality of each anonymous servant of God, male or female, without whose sincere efforts on the path to peace, the suffering of the people in those regions would have continued unabatedly.

"Needless to say, without the efforts of the Tanenbaum Center, the present volume mapping the constructive role religion can serve as a resource for peacemaking would have remained inaccessible. The beautifully written narrative of real people engaged in peacemaking provides a plan of action for those who want to emulate peacemakers like Pastor Wuye, Imam Ashafa, Father Reid, Rabbi Froman, Sakena Yacoobi, and many others, who stand out as beacons of light in the darkness of injustice and violence. A rare and unique addition to the literature on what people of religion can deliver in action today."

Dr. Abdulaziz Sachedina
Author of *Islamic Roots of Democratic Pluralism*

PEACEMAKERS IN ACTION

Just a quick look at your local media on any given day is a powerful reminder that devastating armed conflicts worldwide are destroying lives and whole communities – often in the name of religion. Hidden in the news, if reported on at all, are the brave religious leaders in these zones of violence, working to bring peace and reconciliation to their people. These inspiring men and women offer critical insights and skills for addressing today's most urgent conflicts. But their stories are rarely told.

Peacemakers in Action: Profiles of Religion in Conflict Resolution shares the experiences of 16 such remarkable religious peacemakers who have put their lives on the line in conflicts around the world – from Israel-Palestine to Northern Ireland, the Balkans, Sudan, South Africa, El Salvador, Indonesia – and beyond. For each of these men and women, religious texts and traditions have served both as a source of inspiration and as a practical resource in resolving conflict. These grassroots peacemakers are powerful – but underutilized – actors for resolving some of the world's most horrifying conflicts. As such, this book contains timely information for diplomats, government officials, conflict resolution practitioners, as well as today's students of religion and international affairs – our future peacemakers. And in a world where religion-based conflict affects us all, this book provides critical lessons and much-needed hope for each of us.

David Little is the T. J. Dermot Dunphy Professor of the Practice in Religion, Ethnicity, and International Conflict at Harvard Divinity School and an associate Fellow at the Weatherhead Center for International Affairs, Harvard University. Previously, he was Senior Scholar in Religion, Ethics, and Human Rights at the United States Institute of Peace in Washington, DC. There, he co-authored a book on Islamic activism and U.S. foreign policy and two books and several articles in the Institute series on Religion, Nationalism, and Intolerance. From 1996 to 1998, Dr. Little was a member of the U.S. State Department Committee on Religious Freedom Abroad. Previously, he taught at a number of other schools, including Yale Divinity School, the Universities of Virginia and Colorado, and Amherst and Haverford Colleges. Dr. Little's writings are in the fields of comparative ethics, human rights and religious freedom, religion and peacemaking, sociology of religion, and the study of nationalism.

The Tanenbaum Center is a leader in providing practical programs urgently needed to prevent verbal and physical conflict perpetrated in the name of religion. As a non-sectarian not-for-profit organization, the Tanenbaum Center addresses unresolved – and often unrecognized – tensions by helping to change behaviors in areas of armed conflict, schools, and workplaces. *Religion and Conflict Resolution*, one of the Tanenbaum Center's core programs, runs the *Peacemakers in Action* initiative. In a world where religion is increasingly misused to fuel conflict, this initiative identifies and supports the work of relatively unknown men and women who use religion as an effective resource to resolve conflicts. The Tanenbaum Center is a pioneer in the field in its study of the unique techniques of these individual religious peacemakers, the expert training it provides them in order to strengthen their impact, and its commitment to widely disseminating its findings to bring attention to these *Peacemakers* and other religious leaders as urgently needed resources for resolving today's conflicts.

Peacemakers in Action

Profiles of Religion in Conflict Resolution

Edited by
David Little

with the
**Tanenbaum Center
for Interreligious Understanding**

Foreword by
Ambassador Richard C. Holbrooke

CAMBRIDGE
UNIVERSITY PRESS

CAMBRIDGE UNIVERSITY PRESS
Cambridge, New York, Melbourne, Madrid, Cape Town, Singapore, São Paulo

Cambridge University Press
32 Avenue of the Americas, New York, NY 10013-2473, USA

www.cambridge.org
Information on this title: www.cambridge.org/9780521853583

First published 2007

Printed in the United States of America

A catalog record for this publication is available from the British Library.

Library of Congress Cataloging in Publication Data

Peacemakers in action : Profiles of religion in conflict resolution / Tanenbaum
Center for Interreligious Understanding ; edited by David Little ; foreword
by Richard C. Holbrooke.
    p.   cm.
Includes bibliographical references and index.
ISBN 0-521-85358-3 (hardcover) – ISBN 0-521-61894-0 (pbk.)
1. Conflict management – Religious aspects – Case studies.   2. Tanenbaum
Center for Interreligious Understanding – Case studies.   I. Little, David, 1933–
II. Tanenbaum Center for Interreligious Understanding.
BL629.5.C66P43   2006
201'.7273 – dc22   2006031156

ISBN   978-0-521-85358-3 hardback
ISBN   978-0-521-61894-6 paperback

Contents

Acknowledgments   *page* vii

Foreword by Ambassador Richard C. Holbrooke   xi

Preface   xv

PART I. INTRODUCTION

1   The *Peacemakers* in Action, by the Tanenbaum Center for
    Interreligious Understanding Program on Religion and
    Conflict Resolution   3

PART II. CASE STUDIES

2   Peasant Power: José Inocencio Alas, *El Salvador*   25

3   Men Who Walked the Street: Father Alex Reid and the Rev.
    Dr. Roy Magee, *Northern Ireland*   53

4   "Would You Shoot Me, You Idiot?": Friar Ivo Markovic,
    Bosnia and Herzegovina   97

5   The Cybermonk: Father Sava Janjic, *Kosovo*   123

6   The Elder: Ephraim Isaac, *Eritrea/Ethiopia*   151

7   The Power of Ritual: The Rev. Dr. William O. Lowrey,
    Sudan   186

8   The Nonviolent Deputy Minister of Defense: Nozizwe
    Madlala-Routledge, *South Africa*   215

9   Warriors and Brothers: Imam Muhammad Ashafa and
    Pastor James Wuye, *Nigeria*   247

10   The Power of Organization: Alimamy Koroma,
     Sierra Leone   278

11   Israel and Palestine: A History   302

     "I am Palestinian, Arab, Christian, and Israeli": *Abuna
     Elias Chacour*   321

     The Settler Who Spoke with Arafat: *Rabbi Menachem
     Froman*   341

     An Open House: *Yehezkel Landau*   356

12   Underground Woman: Sakena Yacoobi and the Afghan
     Institute of Learning, *Afghanistan*   382

13   Toward a Zone of Peace: The Rev. Benny Giay,
     West Papua, Indonesia   402

PART III. CONCLUSION

14   Religion, Violent Conflict, and Peacemaking
     Dr. David Little   429

Notes   449
Bibliography   471
Index   475

Acknowledgments

In the course of developing a book such as this, you inevitably have occasion to work with many people without whom the book would not have been possible. And although you always want to take a moment to express your gratitude for their help, in this case, I must begin by thanking the men and women who are the subject of this book – the Tanenbaum Center *Peacemakers in Action*. These men and women are true heroes. They inspire us. And we owe them a vast debt of gratitude for allowing us into their worlds and work – usually kept so private and out of the public eye – so that we can better understand what they do, how they do it, and how they keep going.

It is an honor to have the opportunity to tell the stories of these sixteen diverse individuals. Together, the Tanenbaum Center *Peacemakers* represent a global network of often isolated local leaders. Their devotion to resolving violent conflict (including those fueled in part by religious differences), and their use of religion as a tool for peace provide a roadmap for activist religious peacemaking. I thank each of the *Peacemakers* for all that you do and for allowing us to tell your stories.

Although it is the *Peacemakers* themselves who are the centerpiece of this book, in shaping this project another community of individuals has emerged; one dedicated to the power of the religiously motivated peacemaker and to the vital importance of telling his or her story. I would like to thank all those whose imagination, dedication, and tireless effort brought about the publication of this volume.

First, I have to express my appreciation to Dr. Georgette Bennett, the founder and President of the Tanenbaum Center for Interreligious Understanding, for her vision and unflagging commitment to making religion a resource for resolving conflicts and transforming societies. Without her ability to translate ideas into action, this book would never have come to be. I am deeply grateful to Georgette for having the opportunity to work on this important project.

All books require someone to guide them and their content. This book would not have been possible without the dynamic dedication of Joyce Dubensky, Executive Vice President of the Tanenbaum Center. Her keen appreciation of the timeliness and importance of this project to the global community, as well as her deep understanding of the work of the religiously motivated peacemaker, has provided us with unmatched guidance and leadership, vital to the success of such a formidable undertaking. Thank you, Joyce, for everything.

Throughout the process of writing this book, the members of the Tanenbaum Center for Religion and Conflict Resolution Advisory Council were a constant source of inspiration. Special thanks are due to Ambassador Richard C. Holbrooke, Honorary Chair of the Advisory Council and the inspiration for the Peacemakers in Action Award. The growing community of Tanenbaum Center *Peacemakers* is a living testament to him.

I also owe a great debt of gratitude to Ambassador Nancy E. Soderberg, member and former Chair of the Advisory Council, who designed the strategic plan for the Program on Religion and Conflict Resolution that affirmed the publication of these stories and the growth of our work with the *Peacemakers* Nancy is a great friend to the Tanenbaum Center, and her support of this project was invaluable.

Indispensable as well have been HRH Prince El Hassan bin Talal, who convened the *Peacemakers* for their first retreat in Amman, Jordan, and from which many of the learnings in this book emerged, and Dr. Marc Gopin, current Chair of the Advisory Council, whose work with the *Peacemakers* at the recent Tanenbaum Center working retreat deepened our understanding of how they address some difficult issues involving religious differences. Additionally, I am proud to credit Joseph Coffey, Senior Consultant to the Tanenbaum Center at the time of the program's inception, for his foresight in developing the early structure of the *Peacemakers'* case studies and identifying the initial criteria for the Peacemakers in Action Award, which is given each year to a newly identified religiously motivated peacemaker.

Likewise, I am indebted to the insightful research and adept writing of those who created the initial versions of some of our early case studies: Dr. David A. Steele, Program Manager, Civil Society and Conflict

Management Group, Mercy Corps (Markovic); Phillip Berryman, author and Catholic scholar (Alas); Dr. Katharina P. Coleman, Assistant Professor, University of British Columbia (Wuye and Ashafa); and Atalia Omer, Ph.D. candidate in Religion and Society at Harvard University (Froman). I thank each of you for your help in moving this project from idea to reality. It was your work that set the standard for this book and the case studies that were to follow.

Additionally, I want to thank the Tanenbaum Center staff, whose tireless efforts over the past several years have made our *Peacemakers* stories come to life.

Special thanks go to Tara Sugiyama and Natalie M. Carnes, whose prescience, commitment, intellectual creativity, and hard work transformed a collection of personal anecdotes and historical facts into detailed case studies that today have become the chapters of this book. Tara and Natalie's ability to articulate the special contributions of grassroots individuals motivated by religion to the field of conflict resolution was essential to telling their stories.

This book would not have been completed without the dedication of Sheherazade Jafari, who took over the leadership of this project and brought to this book uncommon intellect, insights, and the ability to translate complex ideas into language. Thank you for your professionalism and unrelenting commitment to excellence as you saw this project through to its final stages.

I also extend my sincere appreciation to Jonah Geffen for his dedication to this project, his ability to tackle delicate subjects with great care, his willingness to assist wherever needed, and his humor when we all needed a laugh. Also, thank you to Zachary Larson for his focus, his sharp editorial eye, and his readiness to do all the large and small tasks that had to be done during the closing stages of this project.

I also want to thank the others who contributed to this effort, especially Yasmin Hamidi and Josh Segal for their assistance in negotiating some of the more politically sensitive sections of the book, as well as former Tanenbaum Center colleagues whose efforts at various stages of this project are still appreciated: Nahide Bayrasli, Jason Biros, David Passiak, and Larry Rosales.

Throughout the creation of this book, there has been one other member of our *Peacemakers'* book-community who stood with us, encouraging and chiding us on. I thank John Berger, Senior Editor at Cambridge University Press, for his extraordinary belief in our cause. John's partnership, commitment to getting it right, and profound patience are without parallel. And his ability to chuckle as we proceeded has kept us all going.

Dr. David Little
T. J. Dermot Dunphy Professor of the Practice in Religion, Ethnicity, and International Conflict
Harvard Divinity School and Tanenbaum Center for Religion and Conflict Resolution
Advisory Council Member

Foreword

Ambassador Richard C. Holbrooke

At least one thing has become clear in the last few years: if you are interested in peace in the twenty-first century, you cannot ignore religion.

Today's conflicts look different from the conflicts of the Cold War, when I started my career in international diplomacy. In those days, the threat of nuclear war conducted by nation states hung over us. The United States was fighting a war in Southeast Asia in which religion was not a factor. Today, religious and ethnic identity plays a huge role in setting the world's agenda. Indeed, at the end of the last century, the brutality and violence conducted in the name of religion was profoundly shocking. If today's leaders are going to be effective, they must learn how to respond to personal and group religious identity.

But focusing on religion as an instigator of conflict is only half the story and, quite frankly, dangerously inaccurate. Throughout my career, from the Indo-China wars, to the Bosnian war, to my work today, I have had occasion to witness the positive and powerful force of religion in promoting peace in communities torn apart by intractable conflicts. Amidst the violence were unsung heroes: religious men and women who put their lives at risk to bring stability to their communities. Their work and insights were crucial to ending human suffering. But they never made the headlines.

Some years ago, I sat with the president of the Tanenbaum Center for Interreligious Understanding, Dr. Georgette Bennett, and discussed the importance of publicly identifying religious peacemakers for recognition, support, and training. My idea was that these men and women would gain some protection from the public recognition and would be harder to marginalize – or kill – once the public became aware of their work. I already appreciated the Tanenbaum Center's readiness to tackle religious intolerance in ways that others had not done before. Dr. Bennett and her team have dedicated enormous vision and energy to this effort. In only eight years, the Tanenbaum Center has identified *Peacemakers in Action* working in conflicts throughout the world, convened them for expert training, and learned of their incredible stories, which they have captured for the public in this book.

It is, therefore, a personal privilege to write this Foreword, and to have the opportunity to acknowledge the Tanenbaum Center *Peacemakers*. This is their book, full of the stories of men and women who are driven by the peaceful teachings of their faith to work tirelessly toward ending some of the world's deadliest conflicts. They work within communities, on the ground, and are generally unknown outside their personal circles. They work within their religious institutions and outside of them, with those who are victims and those who kill. And they do this with one shared impulse: to create an environment for lasting peace and stability. In today's political climate, religiously motivated men and women are a necessary component of Track Two diplomacy. They are the answer to other people who, in the name of their religion, preach race-hatred, assassination, the killing of innocent bystanders, and war. We must encourage them.

We have much to learn about the role of religion in peacemaking. Thankfully, the field of religious conflict resolution is growing, and currently it offers a handful of useful publications, which primarily concentrate on the work of religious communities and institutions. This groundbreaking book pushes the field, providing a much-needed focus on *individuals* and an in-depth glimpse into the impact that individual religious and lay leaders can have. But *Peacemakers in Action: Profiles of Religion in Conflict Resolution* does even more. By analyzing the ways religion motivates and creates a distinct set of conflict resolution techniques, this book shows how others might follow in their footsteps. Such a study is critical to understanding how we can further promote the efforts of these individuals – and utilize a key tool for diplomacy today.

In my almost forty-five years working in international affairs and diplomacy, I have seen firsthand the efforts of hundreds of religiously motivated men and women. Nearly always, they were working alongside the people – long before, and long after the diplomats arrived. Many had keen insights about what was transpiring around them, and they frequently displayed an insider's perspective on how to convince key actors to move toward reconciliation. Above all, they had credibility. Whether or not a particular conflict revolved around religion, I saw how these religious peacemakers often had a legitimacy that allowed them to reach out to parties in a conflict, especially at times when the diplomats, politicians, and other Track One actors could not.

The individuals in this book are stellar examples of religiously motivated peacemakers from around the world. Each of the Tanenbaum Center *Peacemakers* is unique, as they hail from different religious traditions and carry out their work in vastly different settings. And yet their efforts are motivated by a shared moral conviction and a religious calling to work until peace and justice are a reality.

One of the first things I learned as a diplomat is that success in peacemaking takes a number of qualities: diligence and persistence, unique insight, credibility, passion, and a commitment to the idea that peace is possible. The Tanenbaum Center *Peacemakers* display all of these attributes, and in today's world, they are one of the strongest links to communities throughout the world. As the misuse of religion continues to kill, devastating the lives of generations and escalating tensions to new heights, I fear what will happen if we ignore the impact of these individuals – and what they teach us about resolving today's conflicts – any longer. These heroes must no longer remain an underutilized resource.

This book poses a unique opportunity for diplomats and students of religion, as well as politicians, academics, religious and lay leaders, conflict resolution practitioners, community activists, young people – in short, all of us. I urge you, as someone concerned about violent conflict and the countless lives lost, to read carefully these *Peacemakers'* accounts. We need to engage their insights and skills and support their crucial role in Track Two diplomacy. For students of religion, let these men and women serve as examples of how even one person's religious motivation can move us closer to peace. I urge you to learn and be our future peacemakers, and I hope the rest of us will find ways to support your vital work into a more peaceful future.

Preface

Religion is a powerful force in societies around the world and in the lives of people everywhere. However, its impact, whether international or local, is too often associated with violent conflict. Recognizing this, the Tanenbaum Center for Interreligious Understanding promotes practical programs aimed at reducing verbal and physical violence perpetrated in the name of religion. We are a nonsectarian organization and our goal is simple: to encourage the practice of interreligious respect in daily experiences – in school, at work, and in areas of armed conflict.

This book is a product of one Tanenbaum Center program: *Religion and Conflict Resolution.* As part of this program, every year we conduct a global search for religiously motivated men and women working on the ground to end violent conflicts. Those individuals most clearly exemplifying Tanenbaum Center ideals are then selected as *Peacemakers in Action* by the experts who comprise our Religion and Conflict Resolution Advisory Council.

Today there are nineteen *Peacemakers,* and sixteen are the subject of this book. In all likelihood, you have never heard of most of them. That is by design. Our objective is to discover unheralded and religiously motivated grassroots leaders who, with limited resources and little publicity, regularly risk their lives and freedom in an effort to end violent conflicts.

But the Tanenbaum Center does much more than simply identify and write about these compelling individuals. We also bring them together for intensive working sessions designed to enhance their effectiveness. The *Peacemakers* were first convened in Amman, Jordan, in 2004 at the invitation of His Royal Highness Prince El Hassan bin Talal of Jordan. More recently, in 2005, they were assembled for a six-day working retreat in New York City. There, they shared their life stories and insights and worked with expert trainers to strengthen their skills and enhance their ability to address the conflicts that they work to resolve. In New York, they personally met His Holiness the Dalai Lama, who publicly affirmed the importance of their work. And as they departed, they declared that they were leaving with renewed strength to continue their peacemaking efforts.

To meet the *Peacemakers* and hear their stories is to recognize their unique and crucial role in conflict resolution. This book makes that point, by tracing "who" they are and "how" they do their work. In this, the book is inspirational, and we are confident that it will move religiously motivated people of action worldwide to follow in the *Peacemakers'* footsteps. The Tanenbaum Center *Peacemakers* prove that religious peacemaking *is* a vocation. And if this book helps to stimulate the professionalization of Religious Peacemaking, it will have fulfilled another goal of the Tanenbaum Center, while aptly honoring the lives of the *Peacemakers in Action* to whom it is dedicated.

Additionally, the Tanenbaum Center believes that – if people pay attention – they will find men and women like our *Peacemakers* at work all over the world, endeavoring to resolve armed conflicts. Having studied the great impact that they have in transforming their communities, we are convinced that these anonymous individuals are a critical resource for diplomats and others working to transform the more than fifty religiously affected conflicts around the world today. If this book encourages diplomats and government officials to engage religiously motivated grassroots peacemakers in the task of mitigating violent conflicts, then, again, the Tanenbaum Center will have begun to meet another of its core goals.

The one thing these stories have in common is their power. In their details and the way they are told, they are very different. Involved are sixteen distinct individuals, all of whom have unique ways of narrating and communicating their experiences. Some are effusive, others more reserved. Some are expansive and natural storytellers, while others are impatient to get on with their chosen vocations. Some *Peacemakers* were ready respondents no matter where they were located, whereas others could seldom be reached because they work in remote villages, where contact is often impossible.

In all cases, effort was made to fill in gaps with extensive research and additional information obtained from friends and associates. And although the *Peacemakers'* stories differ in structure and, in part, reflect constraints faced in assembling the book, what each of them have told us only whets our appetite to know more about them.

It also will be noted that the *Peacemakers* are not referred to in a uniform way throughout the book. Sometimes they are mentioned by religious titles, sometimes not; sometimes by last names, sometimes by first names; and occasionally by a title of endearment. An effort was made, depending on the *Peacemaker*, to reflect in one case the way they refer to themselves, in another, the way their community speaks of them and, in still another, the way we at the Tanenbaum Center have come to know them after years of collaboration and friendship.

Finally, we have sought to present a balanced and accurate account of the dangerous and highly complex situations to which the *Peacemakers* have responded. It can be argued that "balanced accuracy" is unattainable because of the sensitivity of interpreting the conflicts represented in this book. Yet, in our view, we must do the best we can. The settings in which the *Peacemakers* work, however complicated and controversial, must be described in order to appreciate the nature of the contribution these men and women make. Accordingly, the level of detail, as well as the complexity of description, varies in the history section of each case (note that at the end of each chapter are a summary of facts and, when appropriate, definitions for each conflict location).

This work tells the stories of heroic individuals, who are finding ways to use their religious traditions as a resource for building peace. Our fervent hope is that those who read these stories will be inspired to pick up where they leave off.

Georgette Bennett, Ph.D.   Joyce S. Dubensky, Esq.
Founder and President   Executive Vice President
Tanenbaum Center for Interreligious
    Understanding

PART I

INTRODUCTION

1 The *Peacemakers* in Action

Tanenbaum Center for Interreligious Understanding Program on Religion and Conflict Resolution

I really admire the Tanenbaum Center *Peacemakers* in Action. They work courageously for the greater good under the most difficult circumstances. In order to build world peace through inner peace, I think the world's religious traditions have a special role. We should all learn from and follow their great example.
      – His Holiness the Dalai Lama, September 26, 2005, Riverside Church, New York City

On September 25, 2005, a group of religiously motivated peacemakers gathered in New York City to meet for the second time in a working retreat. Some came wearing a cross around their neck, some came with a yarmulke or scarf on their head, some with traditional dress from a homeland thousands of miles away, and some came in jeans. They hailed from some of the world's worst contemporary conflicts. Collectively, they have survived torture, seen family and friends murdered, endured death threats, and fought to stop the destruction of their communities. Yet, in the midst of devastation, they found within their individual religious teachings a call for action. Driven, they have wrestled with violence and sought to restore peace and stability for their communities. To the people for whom they work, these men and women are local heroes. For the Tanenbaum Center, they are *Peacemakers in Action*. And for all of us, these individuals are one of the most potent resources for peace today.

Today, it is widely accepted that religion is a cause – rather than a solution – to many of the world's violent conflicts. This should not be surprising. Almost daily, the media are filled with news of growing religious radicalism and religiously charged wars. The majority of contemporary conflicts involve issues of religious, national, or ethnic identity (less than

10 percent actually begin among state actors).[1] And religious teachings are being used to legitimize wars and all forms of brutality and violence. Not to be overlooked, September 11, 2001, stands as evidence for the conviction that religious fervor can lead to violence.

Conversely, the role of religion in resolving armed conflicts has gone unheralded. But, it is now starting to receive the attention it deserves. To date, most of the focus has been on the work of faith-based organizations, religious peacemaking movements, established churches, and religious institutions. In his 2002 report on the prevention of armed conflict, for example, UN Secretary-General Kofi Annan affirmed: "Religious organizations can play a role in preventing armed conflict because of the moral authority that they carry in many communities." He went on to note that certain religious groups and leaders "possess a culturally-based comparative advantage in conflict prevention" and can help to "emphasize the common humanity of all parties...[and] mobilize non-violent alternative ways of expressing dissent prior to the outbreak of conflict."[2]

Kofi Annan's observations have been validated in recent years by a handful of groundbreaking books and initiatives. Works by such scholars as Scott R. Appleby, Douglas Johnston and Cynthia Sampson, Marc Gopin, and David Smock of the United States Institute of Peace have focused on the power of religion as a resource for addressing conflicts. The activities of well-known organizations such as the World Council of Religions for Peace are likewise proving this point.

This book offers a different perspective. It fills a void in the field of religious peacemaking by presenting the work of religiously motivated *individuals*. The religious men and women who make up the Tanenbaum Center *Peacemakers* have dedicated themselves to bringing intractable conflicts to a peaceful end. Usually situated in local communities among the people, their religious identities help them reach diverse audiences: militants, tribal heads, leaders from other religious communities, local actors, victims, and sometimes government officials. They achieve practical results and have earned the right to describe themselves as *practitioners* of religious peacemaking.

To fully understand the impact, and the potential, of religious peacemaking, it is critical to explore the work of these individuals. What quickly becomes evident is that religiously motivated *Peacemakers* have unique stature precisely because of their religious identities. And they use this stature in different ways. Some of them worked in their individual capacity outside their religious institutions – as lone witnesses to their faith. Others also worked as individuals but felt that they were supported by their religious institutions. Still others have founded, and today lead, highly effective faith-based organizations dedicated to actualizing peace and reconciliation. It thus becomes clear that religious peacemaking, as a field, is not limited to the work of institutions. We also must understand the individuals, who are a driving force behind so many forms of religious peacemaking.

The *Peacemakers* in the following chapters are active in vastly different conflicts and settings. When we first began to study them, our operating thesis was that patterns and generalizations would emerge. We expected to extract invaluable and replicable methods for using religion in the resolution of conflicts. Ultimately, our thesis proved correct. However, in the course of working with the *Peacemakers*, it also became clear that there were other things to learn. In particular, we realized that there are similarities in the role that religion plays in their lives. For these individual practitioners, religion is far more than just a valuable resource and tool for peacemaking. It is also a powerful personal force that defines them and everything they do.

Community Peacemakers: The Influence of Local Religious Leadership

In great part, the *Peacemakers'* effectiveness derives from the positions they hold in their communities. Most are religious leaders or are respected as religious individuals. This gives them stature in the community and credibility to lead. It also gives them the standing to draw on religious resources in a call to forgive and to recognize the humanity of the "other."

Perhaps equally important, most of these practitioners obtain credibility because they are indigenous to the communities they serve. Those who are not tend to stay for long periods, and their commitment to the community helps them to achieve high levels of respect and integration within it. The central identity of all the *Peacemakers*, therefore, is as a committed neighbor who intimately understands the human experience and suffering of the community – sometimes as a witness and, often, as someone who has suffered personal loss in the local conflict.

As religious leaders living in the community, the *Peacemakers* are trusted to have the long-term interests of the people at heart. They are seen as authentic and, therefore, have standing to speak with all sides. And when they do so, the expectation is that they can be trusted to act with integrity and fairness, even though they may have strong views one way or the other on the conflict. Alimamy P. Koroma, a religious leader and *Peacemaker* in Sierra Leone, explained it this way:

> I am influenced by confidence and hope in ordinary people and religious leaders. The United Nations and other organizations disappoint people: they do not deliver. But religious leaders, churches, and mosques did not flee in Sierra Leone during the war. They remained behind to inspire us that all was not lost. And today we still work with people to say that all is not lost.

Working from their unique vantage point, the *Peacemakers* have been able to exercise authority in different arenas. Nearly all have worked at the grassroots level. (As examples, consider the work of José "Chencho" Alas with the peasants in El Salvador and Sakena Yacoobi's work with educators and students in Afghanistan.) Several have worked with government leaders, including the Israeli settler Rabbi Menachem Froman, who developed a close working relationship with Yasser Arafat. Some have even worked directly with militants. As an example, one of the Tanenbaum Center's newest *Peacemakers,* Ricardo Esquivia Ballestas (his story will be told in a future publication), attended the New York retreat in September 2005 but, immediately after it ended, rushed back to the jungles of Colombia to meet with local guerrilla leaders on a humanitarian basis, as a representative of his community.

In coming to understand our *Peacemakers* and how their public stature enables them to do their work, we were struck by a sad irony. They are effective because of their religious identity and their membership in the local community. And yet, almost all the *Peacemakers* experience a profound sense of being isolated, even when they enjoy support from families or religious communities. This aloneness was particularly striking during the working retreats conducted by the Tanenbaum Center, where the *Peacemakers* had an opportunity to meet, learn, and network together.

Another of our more recently named *Peacemakers,* Canon Andrew P. B. White, is working in Iraq, Israel, and the Palestinian Territories. Although he will be the subject of a future case study and is not represented in this book, his comments about the aloneness of this type of work bear repeating here:

> The Tanenbaum Center [*Peacemakers in Action* Working] Retreat is the only event that I have ever been to where the other peacemakers were people really searching and working for peace in traumatic circumstances. It was wonderful just to spend time with others who really knew the challenges and difficulties of peacemaking. They have experienced the same as me in equally difficult places. They knew the pain involved in this search.

For the first time ever, I was with others who really knew the pain of my daily life.

Religion and Personal Identity

The *Peacemakers* are extroverts and introverts, all with very different personalities (some are funny; several are arm-waving, boisterous, and vocal; and others speak in even tones and listen intently). However, when one is with them, it quickly becomes clear that, regardless of the range of their personal styles, most share a personal quality beyond their aloneness that makes them somehow different. The quality is hard to define but very real. In trying to parse it out for the reader, the place to start is their relationship with religion.

For the *Peacemakers*, religion is deeply personal and only sometimes institutionally based. To a person, they see humanity in all people, a value that defines them and is reinforced by their conviction that every person reflects the divinity of God. This belief derives from a religious doctrine common to the three Abrahamic faiths of which, as it happens, all the *Peacemakers* in this book are members.*

The *Peacemakers* are propelled by their faith, but their religious beliefs, alone, do not fully explain this elusive quality. It also involves emotional intelligence. By this, we are referring to the *Peacemakers'* unusual capacity for deeply understanding others and experiencing, with great compassion, their hopes and their pain. All the *Peacemakers* seem to share this quality. It is evident in their visceral reaction to injustice and cruelty, and to their profound revulsion in the face of violent conflict. But rather than run from what they find painful – as is the common temptation – they are compelled to confront it and become activists.

One can see this in all their stories. Consider Nozizwe Madlala-Routledge, who fought apartheid in South Africa and paid dearly with time in solitary confinement. Since the overthrow of apartheid, she

---

* Although this book happens to be focused on religiously motivated individuals who come from the Abrahamic traditions, it is important to note that the Tanenbaum Center's Peacemakers in Action program is open to peacemakers from all traditions. To date, we have received few nominations for individuals outside the Abrahamic faiths. Accordingly, we have expanded our outreach in an attempt to encourage more nominations for individuals from other traditions. In the future, we expect that we will have an even more diverse group of *Peacemakers*, and we look forward to learning from them and documenting how their work aligns with our findings and the work of their colleagues from across the religious spectrum. From our work with religiously motivated peacemakers worldwide, our thesis is that the findings presented in this book will hold true across various other traditions.

has continued her activism, initially as the nation's first female Quaker Deputy Minister of Defense and currently as its Deputy Minister of Health.

Likewise, there is Dr. Ephraim Isaac, known for his work in Ethiopia and Eritrea. Ephraim was present during the most recent working retreat with his fellow *Peacemakers,* although he repeatedly ran from the room to call the President of Ethiopia and local opposition leaders. A respected elder from the community even though he now resides in the United States, Ephraim was single-handedly trying to alleviate the risk of a threatened political protest erupting into devastating violence.

The power of their religiously inspired emotional intelligence is also evident in the *Peacemakers'* capacity for deep personal awareness and self-reflection. This is clear in the case of the Nigerian *Peacemakers* Pastor James Wuye and Imam Muhammed Ashafa. Former enemies, each felt called to religious leadership and found within his traditions the justification for fighting the other. It was only years afterward that both again were called by their faith, but this time to the forgiveness of each other for the horrible violence and losses that they both experienced. As their powerful story shows, it was this transformation that has become the foundation of their collaboration today.

To meet the *Peacemakers* and talk with them is to be impressed by the depth of their commitment toward making peace a living reality. Their goal is clear, and clarity of purpose permeates all their communications. This clarity helps them to influence others, and helps explain their personal and spiritual charisma. Although they conduct themselves in very different ways, all share this inner quality. *Peacemaker* Sakena Yacoobi from Afghanistan explained it this way, "If you live what you believe, other people will come to you. . . . I believe in the power of inner peace."

In addition to these qualities, we were struck by the *Peacemakers'* extraordinary intellectual abilities, which come through in their thoughtful comments and openness to creative ideas. Their intellect is also present in their work. Consider Father Sava Janjic, who worked by day to save lives and feed the people caught on all sides of the Kosovo War, and worked every night on the Internet in an effort to mobilize the outside world to stop the conflict devastating his homeland.

The *Peacemakers* are driven by, and often rely on, their religious beliefs and texts for motivation. These resources sustain them when their life's work becomes physically and emotionally overwhelming. For them, religion is the reservoir from which they draw strength to keep going and take action. The Rev. Dr. Benny Giay of West Papua described this phe-nomenon when he explained that his faith is a source of hope, helping him to overcome despondency and remember that peace is possible. This also was true of Father Sava and Father Reid, who turned to religion after becoming so overcome by their work that they became ill. It is also true of Nozizwe, who draws strength for her work in South Africa from her Quaker beliefs, and of Abuna Elias Chacour in Israel, who finds his inspi-ration in the Beatitudes.

Just as the *Peacemakers* relate to the eternal nature of their religious truths, their sense of responsibility knows no bounds. They are in the struggle for the long haul. While some have changed the way they work over the years, none has abandoned the effort to build sustainable peace for their communities and, sometimes, for communities across the globe.

One just has to look at the Rev. Dr. William Lowrey, who was in the thick of ending an on-the-ground conflict in the Sudan, and who now works out of the United States to develop educational tools and build regional networks of peace and advocacy. Likewise, Yehezkel Landau, having spent most of his adult life proactively creating opportunities for Israeli Jews and Arabs to reconnect in a spirit of compassion, is now pro-moting his message among Jews, Muslims, and Christians in the United States, and teaching the next generation about peacemaking.

As a group, the religious men and women in this book practice peace and cannot tolerate injustice. They are committed to their work because they are responsible to their religious beliefs and to the generations that will follow. They are intellectually and emotionally gifted. For these reli-giously motivated individuals, peacemaking is simply not a choice. It is a sacred duty – one that they are compelled to undertake despite the seemingly insurmountable challenges and grave risks.

The *Peacemakers'* Techniques

Most of the religiously motivated *Peacemakers* in this book did not receive formal training in what was to become their life's work. Rather, their peacemaking approaches were developed mostly through trial and error. They drew on their personal strengths, on community religious beliefs, and on the methods of "secular" and highly-trained conflict resolution practitioners. Indeed, many of the *Peacemakers'* techniques are compara-ble to the methodologies employed by secular social justice workers. They frequently use dialogue, facilitation skills, and active listening as compo-nents of their work. But what ultimately distinguishes the *Peacemakers* is their ability to use religion, as a source of motivation and as a practical tool.

In studying their techniques and methodologies, several things are apparent. Most striking is that these religious *Peacemakers* who had never met – or even heard of one another – were using similar approaches in diverse conflicts across the globe. Also significant is that their peacemaking techniques sometimes involve active efforts to address and stop ongoing conflicts; sometimes focus on creating the societal preconditions for achieving a sustainable peace; and sometimes do both simultaneously.

The most frequently used of the *Peacemakers'* unique and remarkably effective techniques are described in the following sections. As the reader will soon note, this is not a complete list of every technique that is present in their stories. Instead, it represents an effort to analyze their most common techniques. This is not as straightforward a task as it might appear. There is considerable overlap among the techniques, and many of the *Peacemakers'* activities do not fall neatly into just one category. Nonetheless, this review is critically important. It provides us with a roadmap for following in the *Peacemakers'* footsteps and establishes them as full partners with their secular counterparts in the difficult work of stopping violent conflicts and creating communities of reconciliation worldwide.

The Use of Religious Texts

As religiously motivated individuals, the *Peacemakers* weave religious texts into their work to great effect. This practice is a critical element of many of the techniques detailed later. In the section on peace education, for example, note the way the Qu'ran was used as a resource to help women become empowered; and in the section on the use of religion in transforming debates and resolving conflicts, note how religious concepts of forgiveness are being used effectively in mediation work.

One arresting example of the use of religious texts is in the work of the Rev. Roy Magee in Northern Ireland. A trusted advisor to the Protestant paramilitary, the Rev. Magee talked with the militants about the legacy they wanted to leave for their children and, pointing to religious texts, reminded them to live according to the laws of God. He often exhorted them, saying, "You may escape the court of the land, but you will not escape the judgment of God." By drawing on his listeners' religious traditions and family values, and by persisting in this approach over time, the Rev. Magee was able to get the men to start listening. And this was the prerequisite for them to agree to embark on the path of ending the violent conflict in their communities.

The Power of the Pulpit

Several of the *Peacemakers* worked within their religious institutions and made use of their influence as parish leaders. Again, the Rev. Magee is a good example. His involvement with the paramilitaries actually developed after one of his parishioners (a leader of one of the largest paramilitaries in Northern Ireland) asked him to meet with the militants. His daily presence in the parish and the message of his sermons defined him as someone who could be trusted. And this led to the Rev. Magee's invitation to become a confidant and counselor to local militants.

Similarly, in El Salvador, Chencho Alas used his Sunday sermons to mobilize support for the cause of peasant rights. Citing biblical passages from such books as Genesis and Isaiah, Chencho was known to mobilize thousands and inspire them to seek justice through nonviolence. In fact, on one occasion when several peasants were threatened with injustice in the courts, he addressed the situation during his evening sermon. And when he spoke on behalf of the peasants in the court shortly thereafter, hundreds of his parishioners gathered outside in solidarity.

The power of the pulpit is not a force in all of the *Peacemakers'* stories, but it remains a tool for those who claim its mandate. In a related vein, some *Peacemakers* made use of their religious institutions in other ways. Several used their church, mosque, or other religious building as an organizing base or as a place of personal refuge. Some *Peacemakers* used their religious edifices as neutral territory where opposing groups could meet. And others used their religious homes as safe havens for those being threatened or displaced by conflicts raging across their communities.

Using Religious and Cultural Rituals and Traditions

As religious members of their communities, the practitioners in this book have sometimes taken liberties with their religious beliefs by adapting the local religious and cultural rituals to their traditional doctrines. This was often effective because there is symmetry between the indigenous belief systems and many of the core values of institutional religions. (Consider the work being done in West Papua and El Salvador, as described in the section "Creating Philosophies of Nonviolence and Zones of Peace.")

At other times, the *Peacemakers* simply drew on local religious practices as a method of encouraging trust and reconciliation. An example is the work of the Rev. William Lowrey with the Nuer and Dinka tribes in

Sudan. Originally from the American south, the Rev. Lowrey spent years observing and studying the tribal cultures. Recognizing the power that rituals and symbolism held for both peoples, he was able to effectively adapt their traditional practices as tools for peacemaking.

Because he appreciated that leadership among both tribes is decentralized, the Rev. Lowrey organized groundbreaking, time-intensive conferences that allowed for broad participation. Held in a neutral physical environment, the conferences used rituals and truth-telling to build empathy and trust among the participants. The details of his work, which are unique to the Nuer and Dinka, may not be universally applicable. But the technique of using symbols and rituals that are religiously or culturally potent to both sides is replicable and can be a particularly powerful tool in peacemaking, even in the hands of a respected religious outsider.

Similarly, one of Dr. Ephraim Isaac's most effective peacemaking methods in Ethiopia has been to call upon one of the country's indigenous resources: the social system of elders. In a culture in which elders are viewed as the traditional leaders and are deeply respected, Ephraim frequently organizes and leads community elders to collaborate in efforts to stop violence and facilitate peacemaking processes.

Many of these elders have lived through Ethiopia's years of human suffering, and with their authoritative societal roles, command the attention of those with the power to inflict violence. Through his own experience as an elder and community leader, Ephraim has concluded that Ethiopia's tradition of eldership can bring communities to peace in a way that politicians or "professionals" – with their frequent lack of understanding of key local traditions – never can.

The Use of Religion in Debate and Finding Common Ground

When Nigerian *Peacemakers* Pastor Wuye and Imam Ashafa were still bitter enemies leading militant religious groups, a mutual friend called on them to use their positions of leadership to stop the violence. Convinced that the other was wrong in his beliefs, they agreed to organize a debate between their respective Christian and Muslim communities, in which each had every intention of proving that his beliefs were the one, right path. In the process of organizing this event, however, the men had to cooperate. And over time, they came to a surprising realization – that their religions had more similarities than differences, including shared values and teachings on peace and forgiveness.

Today, as co-leaders of the Interfaith Mediation Centre, they work to break stereotypes of the religious "other" and use shared religious precepts to resolve conflicts and establish common ground for interreligious reconciliation. Their success can be seen by the groups of former religious militants who are today rebuilding some of the churches and mosques they once fought so hard to destroy.

Peace Education as the Foundation for Ending Conflict and Sustaining Peace

A technique employed by all the *Peacemakers,* in one form or another, is to empower and encourage new understandings that lead to peace through education. Although each does this informally when interacting with multiple parties to the conflict, some have formalized this method by building educational institutions.

Abuna (Father) Elias Chacour, a Palestinian Christian Israeli citizen living in the Galilee, founded the Mar Elias Educational Institutions to educate a new generation on the possibility of coexistence in a land as diverse as the religious and ethnic identity he himself represents. The students of his schools hail from different religious and cultural backgrounds spanning the whole spectrum of Israel/Palestine: Jewish, Muslim, Christian, Druze, Arab, and Palestinian. All are taught to be model citizens of peace in a land they all love and to which they all belong.

Almost two thousand miles away in Afghanistan, hundreds of thousands of women and their families have gained an understanding of Islam's peaceful teachings and doctrines, thanks to the leadership of *Peacemaker* Sakena Yacoobi and her Afghan Institute of Learning. During Taliban rule, Sakena secretly taught literacy to women (an illegal and dangerous undertaking) through reading the Qu'ran, the religious text that was being abused to justify the harsh regime under which they were living. From Sakena, girls and women of all ages learned about their religion, how the actual text differed from many of the Taliban's practices, and how Islam embraces women's rights. Today, her organization continues to educate on health, family planning, and skills training, in order to prepare her people to create a stable environment characterized by respect and equality.

Both Abuna and Sakena have created sustainable institutions that are transforming communities through training a new generation in peace and reconciliation. Both gained strength from their religious teachings – Christianity and Islam, respectively. Their institutions are similarly fueled by an understanding that the core of all religions is the embrace of peace and the mandate to treat others as one would want to be treated. And in both countries, where religion so powerfully intermingles with all aspects of society, they are equipping their students to recreate their societies and to end conflict.

Even though many of the *Peacemakers* have not created institutions like Abuna and Sakena have, they do educate and promote an understanding that all people deserve to be valued. All of them, in one way or the other, teach their communities how to see the human in the other, how to forgive, and how to seek justice nonviolently.

Religious Peacemaking through the Use of Communication Skills

The *Peacemakers'* vast intellect is reflected in how they use communication vehicles in religious peacemaking. Some have written documents behind the scenes that move the peace process forward, whereas others have been responsible for producing final public pronouncements.

One example is Father Alex Reid of Northern Ireland. During the violent times known as the Troubles, he wrote a series of documents that set out a strategy for peace. In them, he laid out a process that included dialogue, negotiation, and an agreement to end the cycle of retaliation and adopt nonviolence. And because he was a religious leader with a proven commitment to the community, his words carried great weight. Paramilitary leaders and government officials were his audience, and eventually his writings helped to bring about the IRA ceasefire and the negotiations leading to the 1998 Good Friday Agreement.

Like Father Reid, Chencho Alas has written a peacemaking roadmap for MesoAmerica that he has begun to implement in recent years. Other *Peacemakers* use the written word for other purposes. Several have formalized commitments to end conflict by authoring peace declarations, accords, and agreements. Nigerian *Peacemakers* Pastor Wuye and Imam Ashafa led a team of Christian and Muslim leaders to draft and sign the Kaduna Peace Agreement, helping to calm years of widespread violence perpetrated in Kaduna State in the name of religion. To demonstrate publicly their agreement to renounce violence, these religious leaders together unveiled a centrally located plaque of their agreement for all community members to read and celebrate.

Several of the *Peacemakers in Action* have independently developed communiqués and papers to encourage religious peacemaking. In 1998, Father Sava published a paper on how religious communities can and should be involved in Track Two diplomacy and conflict resolution. Similarly, Father Ivo Markovic in Bosnia has written both for newspapers and theological texts about the role of the church in the Bosnian War, delineating ways that religious and cultural approaches can help in the reconciliation process, in particular, by treating war trauma.

Creating Philosophies of Nonviolence and Zones of Peace

Of all the techniques used by the *Peacemakers,* there is one particularly compelling series of approaches used by Benny Giay in West Papua and simultaneously used by Chencho Alas in El Salvador, halfway around the world. At the time that they began implementing this technique, the two had not met and did not know of one another. But they followed remarkably similar paths, and we have much to learn from them.

Both Chencho and Benny are men of the people, deeply committed to their indigenous neighbors. Chencho's lifelong commitment has always involved bringing justice to the peasants. And Benny, an evangelical minister, now seeks the same for his fellow West Papuans. They both understand the spiritual and practical significance of the land in their people's lives. And each promotes nonviolence based on a philosophy that incorporates religious and indigenous understandings on peace, justice, and a people in harmony with a sustainable environment.

Chencho first consulted with his people through a participatory democracy process to understand what a "culture of peace" would look like. After two years of workshops involving thousands of people, he and his organization inaugurated a "zone of peace." Through his consultative process, local leaders had agreed to establish the zone and, within it, to collaborate and resolve all conflicts nonviolently for a community characterized by a sustainable peace.

In a very different community fighting a different conflict, Benny led the Papua Peace Commission to create a zone of peace in West Papua. As with Chencho's emphasis on participatory democracy, the Commission first built a coalition from all segments of Papuan society by holding peace seminars throughout the land. Enthusiasm for the idea resulted, and many West Papuans support Benny's vision of maintaining their land as a zone of peace. The effort remains a work in progress, however, because they are meeting resistance from the Indonesian military, which has not supported the concept.

The stories of other *Peacemakers* show a similar propensity for nonviolence. Indeed, with only a few exceptions, the *Peacemakers* are personally inclined to adopting this philosophy. In pursuing it, a few have actually been able to stop violent conflicts and get agreements for ceasefires, which were then followed by negotiations and sometimes peace agreements.

Interfaith Mobilization as a Tool in Peacebuilding

As religious leaders, the *Peacemakers* are positioned to lead cooperative action with people of other faiths. As we see in their stories, several are involved in serious interreligious efforts, which they use as a platform for pursuing a shared goal of peace, and to reinforce the message that peaceful coexistence among different peoples is attainable.

Interfaith mobilization can be a powerful peacemaking technique even when religion is not a factor in the conflict, as demonstrated by Sierra Leone *Peacemaker* Alimamy Koroma. Alimamy successfully harnessed the already positive relationships between Christians and Muslims in his country to create a platform for peaceful action through his Inter-Religious Council of Sierra Leone. He understood the role of religion in the people's lives and the history of coexistence among them. By mobilizing religious leaders from both traditions to act as neutral mediators and negotiators, Alimamy created a force for confronting the rebels, who were killing, kidnapping, and terrorizing his country.

In a very different setting, where religious and ethnic difference had been used to justify horrendous crimes against humanity, Bosnian *Peacemaker* Friar Ivo Markovic took an interreligious approach to healing. After the Bosnian War, he brought together men and women from the different religions of his country to found the Interreligious Service Oci u Oci (Face to Face) and to create the multiethnic and multireligious Pontanima Choir. After years of risking his life to save others during the war (and risking his religious standing among peers who disapproved of his work), Friar Markovic knew that a stable peace for Bosnians required that all members of the community be able to work cooperatively, notwithstanding their religious differences. His choir has become a platform for interreligious cooperation, and in 2006 celebrated its ten-year anniversary. The choir now performs around the world.

Rabbi Menachem Froman works to quell the Israeli-Palestinian conflict based on an understanding that the region's religions share a common goal of peace and can indeed coexist on a shared land. As a leading religious figure in his settler community, Rabbi Froman has built well-established, trusted relationships with Arab Muslim and other regional leaders. Although their religions are different, they relate to each other through a shared understanding of what it means to have a strong faith. This common recognition of the power of religion in their own lives, as well as within their communities, provides a platform of understanding for fruitful dialogue not easily recognized, let alone utilized, by secular leaders.

Awakening the Global Community

The religious *Peacemakers* in this book live and work in the midst of armed conflicts. Yet, they have demonstrated a capacity to see all sides of the conflict, in part because they start with the premise that all the players share a common humanity. As a result, through the media and other communication vehicles, several of them sought to influence the global community and encourage it to become involved. In all cases, they shared truths that were often missing from media accounts.

Known as "the Cybermonk," Father Sava Janjic worked night and day during the Kosovo War, to the point of exhaustion, to reach the international community. Countering the media's biased portrayal of the war's devastation, which was further inflaming the hatred and intolerance on both sides, Father Sava utilized the Internet. Every night, he provided real-time data on the escalating humanitarian crisis and insight on the true factors fueling the violence. His understanding of the conflict and its causes proved particularly useful. Father Sava's voice helped the outside world understand that, although religion had a visible role in the conflict, the real cause was the clash between two extremist nationalist ideologies.

Because of his balanced coverage and commitment to truth-telling during the war, he received recognition and was able to access policy makers, including some NATO officials and U.S. diplomats, with whom he pressed his perspective that both sides were responsible for the suffering, and that post-conflict efforts must achieve forgiveness and reconciliation.

Other *Peacemakers* have also engaged the outside world. After living and working for peace in Israel for nearly twenty-five years, Yehezkhel Landau moved back to the United States to teach seminarians how to foster reconciliation and peaceful coexistence in the Middle East. In addition, he is dedicating his time to meeting with policy leaders in order to cajole the United States to serve as an active peace builder in the region. As such, he meets with American policy makers in Washington, D.C. about on-the-ground realities in the Israeli-Palestinian conflict. In these conversations, Yehezkel focuses on the daily needs that motivate the people (security, but, more important, dignity, honor, and freedom), thereby encouraging an activism that will honor all people in the region and a resolution that accomplishes this aim.

Despite having his work frequently banned by the Indonesian government, the Rev. Benny Giay in West Papua writes and publishes extensively to communicate the Papuan plight to his own people and the international community. Benny is a theologian and educator on West Papua's indigenous roots. As such, many consider him to be one of the few individuals with the scholarly, cultural, and religious background necessary to understand and effectively communicate the realities in West Papua, while simultaneously defining a roadmap for peace.

Adapting Secular and Western Practices for Religious Peacemaking

Although motivated by faith and recognized by the local people as religious, many of the *Peacemakers* also successfully adapt "secular" peacemaking methods. As noted earlier, they exhibit many of the same qualities and use some of the same techniques that make secular conflict resolution practitioners effective. They are good listeners, act nonjudgmentally, identify human rights abuses, and search for the common ground. They hold skills training workshops, utilize the media, build institutions, network and partner with secular and religious actors, and document the factors in, and the solutions to, their regional conflicts.

A number of *Peacemakers* have demonstrated impressive skills in mediation and negotiation. Often working behind the scenes to bring fighting factions together, they have kept the parties focused even when talks proved difficult. Their stories demonstrate that the negotiation and mediation methods they use are very similar to secular conflict resolution practices. Like their secular colleagues, they are often perceived as neutral (or at least, as fair), and they know when to listen and when to respond. However, their religious identity, which sets them apart from their secular counterparts, plays a role. It reinforces their credibility as trusted leaders in the community and allows them to bring in religious concepts such as forgiveness that might otherwise be harder to utilize in tense negotiations.

The *Peacemakers* also draw on various internationally recognized tools. Nozizwe Madlala-Routledge in South Africa has been a strong advocate and example of the role of women at the negotiating table. She proudly uses her role as a political leader to emphasize UN Security Council Resolution 1325, which calls for the full participation of women at all levels of security and peacemaking. Similarly, the creation of zones of peace in West Papua and El Salvador, though born out of local realities, is a technique that has been used in conflict situations by the UN and other international institutions around the world.

Other *Peacemakers* have actually studied secular conflict resolution theory in order to master known skills and then adapt them through their religious lens. In particular, Imam Ashafa and Pastor Wuye of Nigeria did this by seeking out and attending intensive trainings in conflict resolution and mediation. And when Friar Ivo Markovic of Bosnia visited the United States in 1994, he purchased forty kilograms of books on conflict resolution. He then translated lessons on pacifism and conflict resolution into Croatian, in order to introduce methods once unknown and unavailable under the communist educational system.

New Applications for Religious Peacemaking

The *Peacemakers* represented in this book do not dabble in religious peacemaking. Rather, it is central to their lives and defines their work. We have much to learn from them. They demonstrate that religious peacemaking transforms conflicts and have created new peacemaking methodologies that can be adapted elsewhere. For example, when the Rev. Lowrey used a "people-to-people peace process" with the tribes in Sudan, his use of local tribal practices were unique to the situation and not generally applicable elsewhere. In contrast, his process (i.e., using local rituals and shared symbols) are replicable and can be adapted for other grassroots efforts.

More recently, the *Peacemakers* themselves have begun to show how their techniques can be applied in new places and in new ways. Father Alex Reid immediately comes to mind. The architect of the IRA cease-fire in Northern Ireland, he moved across borders and, for more than four years, worked in the Basque region in Spain. There, he once again worked behind-the-scenes as an architect for ETA's cease-fire. And other *Peacemakers* are planning additional new applications. After their most recent Working Retreat, the Tanenbaum Center's African *Peacemakers* began looking at how they can collaborate to replicate our *Peacemakers* program on a regional level. Their goal is aligned with ours: to create a network of religious peacemakers who can be mobilized across the continent.

Religious Peacemaking: A Vocation

There are other things to learn from the *Peacemakers* and their stories. Perhaps the most obvious is that, for these practitioners, religious peacemaking is a *vocation,* not an avocation or a sideline to their other work. Even though they are called educators, politicians, mediators, or members of the clergy, religious peacemaking is what these men and women do. We are inspired by them and, as we have seen, they are modeling a range of techniques that can be replicated for practicing their craft. The conclusion readily follows. It is time to recognize religious peacemaking as a vocation.

Today's students of religion, including seminarians, future rabbis, imams, young practicing Buddhists, and others, are our future peacemakers. Today, they are studying religion, and tomorrow, they will choose how to apply what they have learned. This presents seminaries, divinity schools, religious educators, and leaders with an opportunity.

If religious peacemaking were to be recognized as an accredited line of study leading to a recognized vocation, our future religious leaders would be better prepared to decide whether to choose the pulpit, the hospital, or a zone of armed conflict for their future work. For this to occur, religious institutions would have to recognize the vocation of religious peacemaking, develop the programs to prepare their students to become practitioners of peace, and then apply resources to support this course of study and the work that follows it.

But religious institutions cannot stop there. They also must include training in religious peacemaking for all students of religion, whether they opt to assume the mantle of peacemaker or not. Today's students will undoubtedly be confronted by tension, and disputes in which they will be asked, or will want, to intervene. All will benefit when religious peacemaking and conflict resolution skills are understood as a necessary component of in the religious life. And when tomorrows religious leaders acquire these skills, they will be better able to address conflicts – whether they occur in a congregation, an inner-city neighborhood, or a rural village.

One important conclusion drawn from the lives and work of the *Peacemakers* is that they have a critical impact on the peacemaking efforts of government officials and diplomats. Operating behind the scenes, these religious *Peacemakers,* and others like them who remain unrecognized, are unique in Track Two (citizen) diplomacy. It is high time to recognize that they are a valuable resource for the diplomats charged with Track One (official) diplomacy and peacemaking. Religiously motivated peacemakers offer necessary perspectives and trusted grassroots ties. Their insights into the religious, cultural, and political situation, from the ground, can be crucial to understanding how to foster sustainable peace and security. They often are able and willing to work behind the scenes, without recognition. And their commitment to the community assures that they are likely to be a more stable resource than the international bodies whose staying power is at times limited. As such, religious peacemakers can be an important partner for their diplomatic colleagues.

It is our hope that they will become increasingly part of the solution to armed conflicts and will find their seats at the table.

Toward Reconciliation

As we conclude this chapter, we wish to emphasize the one, shared perspective that ultimately defines the work of our *Peacemakers* and the power of their impact. They are not working for peace, as the absence of war. Instead, they share a far grander goal.

In communities suffering from intractable conflicts, the *Peacemakers* understand that bringing about peace today will not ensure a peaceful tomorrow. Thus, they seek the more challenging and time-consuming goal of creating sustainable communities. Many of their techniques demonstrate this commitment. They educate the next generation, develop programs for widows and orphans of conflict, share song and traditions among young people, and build libraries.

In so doing, they are changing communities and behavior over the long term, as they put in place cultures of nonviolence, forgiveness, and mutual respect. In the truest sense, the *Peacemakers in Action* who comprise this book are practitioners of peace. They relentlessly seek reconciliation among divided and hostile peoples – an irreducibly religious undertaking.

PART II

CASE STUDIES

2 **Peasant Power**

José Inocencio Alas

El Salvador

It was the middle of the night when Chencho Alas gradually awoke from a drug-induced coma on a hilltop in El Salvador. Naked and shivering, he was able to summon help and ultimately was taken to a hospital for treatment. Alas had been abducted earlier that day, likely by the military. Dragged into a car, he had been blindfolded, brutally beaten, and eventually thrown out of the vehicle as the car drove off. Unlike so many others, Alas's life was spared, but only because Archbishop Luis Chavez y Gonzalez had personally intervened with the Minister of Defense, and because the peasants in Alas's home region of Suchitoto had organized and protested the abduction.

José Inocencio "Chencho" Alas, then a Catholic priest, was a threat to the status quo. His proactive efforts to improve the lot of peasants through education and land reform had put him at risk, and he was unpopular among some of the more powerful groups in El Salvador. Indeed, the event on the hilltop was only one of several attempts to silence him. Yet each time, Alas persevered, turning to his faith to give him strength.

As a *Peacemaker*, Alas began with a focus on land reform at the local level, and eventually moved to the broader goal he espouses today – the establishment of a "Culture of Peace." To build greater stability in El Salvador, Alas helps local peasants learn how to organize and work together to move from war and a "culture of violence," to its opposite. To Chencho, people only need the tools and initiative to accomplish this transformation – and he has dedicated his life to providing both.

Toward this end, he has spent a lifetime conducting workshops in which he uses biblical passages to develop skills in leadership, nonviolence, appreciation of the environment, and agriculture. In place of inertia and passivity, Alas offers hope and strategies for promoting peace. In so doing, he has moved historically powerless communities of peasants in

El Salvador to action – even in the face of threats posed by the military, the government, and right-wing death squads. With new skills learned from working with Chencho, they, too, are pursuing a "Culture of Peace."

The Context: An Overview of El Salvador

El Salvador [the Savior] is the smallest country in Central America. From San Salvador, the capital, it is possible to reach the Pacific Coast in half an hour, the Guatemalan border to the west in an hour and a half, and the Honduran border to the north and east in about two hours. El Salvador is largely agricultural, relying mostly on the production of coffee, cotton, and sugar, all of which are under the control of a traditional oligarchy.

From its first contact with colonialism almost five hundred years ago, El Salvador has been linked to Catholicism. In 1492, Christopher Columbus named the first island he encountered San Salvador, or Blessed Savior, symbolizing the central objectives of the Spanish empire and the Catholic Church, namely conquest, colonization, and conversion.

For most Spanish colonialists, conversion to Christianity presumed wholesale adoption of Spanish culture. In practice, however, indigenous peoples were often reluctant converts, subjugated by force under the auspices of evangelization. Two notable exceptions to the practice of coerced conversion were the Dominican friar Antonio de Montesinos and the Spanish priest Bartholomew de las Casas, both of whom denounced the practice of forcing one's beliefs on others. Taking this stand was risky. Some who shared their views were persecuted and even murdered by the Spanish, including Bishop Antonio de Valdivieso of Nicaragua who was killed in 1550 along with twenty others for their loyalty to the indigenous peoples.

When the Spanish initially entered the land they called San Salvador, they were engaged in a futile search for gold. As that effort failed, the country turned to agriculture under a system of *encomienda* in which the Spanish government placed select individuals in charge of particular lands and granted them the right to extract tribute from the inhabitants. This placed the indigenous peoples in a position of involuntary servitude.[1] At the same time, given the deep connection between Catholicism and the expanding Spanish empire, bishops appointed to the colonies by Spain assumed political as well as religious power. The result was an economy and society characterized by a vastly unequal distribution of power, land, and wealth. Perhaps not surprisingly, over time it was persistent force and persuasion that compelled many indigenous peoples to convert to Christianity, similar to what occurred in most Central and South American countries.

Independence

Even though the influence of Spain as a global power diminished over time, particularly after the Napoleonic conquest of the Iberian Peninsula in 1808, land ownership by an oligarchy remained the pattern in El Salvador. The country continued to be stratified largely by class and ethnicity, dividing the native populations and the more powerful Spanish.

In the years before independence, many of the priests came to resent what they perceived to be the arrogance of Spanish bishops and officials and aligned with the *criollo* population (those of Spanish heritage born in Central America, many of whom inherited large land holdings from their parents) against the Spanish crown. In practice, this ultimately lodged power in a new criollo oligarchy that expanded its dominion over the indigenous peoples and the *mestizos* (people of mixed ancestry).

When El Salvador gained independence in 1821, societal divisions persisted. But independence did bring some changes. The purely indigenous population gradually disappeared as a significant identifiable group because of disease and intermarriage. In their stead, the mestizo farm laborers, known as *campesinos,* came to dominate the lower economic and social classes.

At the same time, ecclesiastical structures began to deteriorate with the loss of support from Spain. Then, when Francisco Morazan rose to power in 1829, he further eroded the church's power by immediately expelling Bishop Causaus y Torres, who later died in exile in Cuba. Although Catholicism remained the official state religion, under Morazan it lost much of its clout. He prohibited the publication of papal documents, declared freedom of worship, permitted divorce, and suppressed monasteries and the payment of tithes.

Persecution of the church persisted through the nineteenth century, and in 1861, then President Barrios made it obligatory for all priests to swear unconditional alliance to the government and its laws. Bishop Tomas Miguel Pineda y Saldana responded that the oath could only be administered if the canonical laws would be respected. That November, he got his answer. He was exiled together with a number of other priests.

Coffee became El Salvador's major export product during these years, and its value rose rapidly during the thirty-four years between 1880 and 1914, up more than 1,100 percent. The coffee economy perpetuated the divisions within the country. A few of the coffee-producing elite monopolized most of the income in the country and were able to wield substantial power over the government and military. Communal lands that belonged to the remnants of the indigenous populations were expropriated, as were small communal farms. When the coffee producers became concerned about the possibility of uprisings from the disenfranchised campesinos, they turned to the military which shifted its priorities from a focus on national security to the maintenance of internal order.[2]

Depression and Oppression

The worldwide depression of the 1930s led to sharp cutbacks in global coffee consumption and a rapid decline in coffee export prices, which dropped 54 percent between 1928 and 1931. The impact on the El Salvadoran economy was severe, particularly on the campesinos, who were already living under conditions of extreme poverty. Because most of El Salvador's land was dedicated to coffee production, the bulk of the country's food had been imported. When the depression hit, most of the population were unable to grow or buy food. The relatively peaceful rule of the coffee republic came to an end with clashes between the government and ruling elite and the poor, disenfranchised masses of campesinos.[3]

From 1927 to 1931, Pio Romero Bosque served as the country's president. In contrast to his predecessors, he democratized the political system by including some of the historically less powerful groups, and turned on his predecessor President Quiñonez, forcing him out of the country. Bosque also kept members of the landowning elite out of the government and, in 1931, instituted presidential and municipal elections in which all but the radical left parties were allowed to participate.[4]

Arturo Araujo won that election and assumed power over a country in the midst of a major economic crisis and growing unrest. Support for numerous Marxist organizations was growing, and the seeds of rebellion among farm-laboring campesinos were being sown. In the midst of these troubled times, Agustin Farabundo Marti emerged as a leader of the campesinos. Already known to law enforcement for his antigovernment activities (he had been jailed several times), Marti was head of the Salvadoran branch of the Marxist organization called the Red Aid International (SRI) and became the leader of a popular uprising by the peasants.[5]

Araujo came from a wealthy family and people expected that he would cater to the needs of the rich land owners. When the leftist groups and their growing legions of campesino followers began pushing for reform, he first acted to appease the ruling class by using military force to quell the unrest, but demonstrations continued. He then decided to schedule municipal elections for December of 1931 to try to quiet the protests and made the controversial decision to allow the Communist Party of El Salvador to participate.[6]

The elite landowners and military were outraged by the thought of the communist party controlling political seats in their country. A large contingent of military officers collaborated to oust Araujo before the elections could take place, thereby ushering in an age of military rule that would last for fifty years. General Maximiliano Hernández Martínez, who had been vice president under Araujo, assumed the presidency. In what appeared to be a surprise move, he allowed the municipal elections to be held. However, Communist Party candidates who won were not allowed to take office, thereby securing the power of the ruling military and rendering the elections far from democratic.[7]

General Hernández's intervention became a catalyst for more rebellion. A violent uprising was planned, but before it could be carried out, the government caught wind of the rebels' plot and intervened. Marti of Red Aid International and numerous other leaders were arrested. Four days later, the rebels attempted to overthrow the government but were quickly – and violently – defeated by the military.[8]

The chaos that followed came to be known as "the slaughter." Infuriated by the uprising, General Hernández ordered his troops to continue killing people until the lesson that the government would not tolerate rebellion had been driven home. The total number killed has never been determined, but the figure of thirty thousand is now generally accepted.[9]

Hernández ruled as a dictator until 1944, when he was overthrown in a coup after attempting to circumvent direct elections to extend his reign. Hernández's ten-year tenure as president would be the longest in the nation's recent history, and he would later become a celebrated figure among the political right. In fact, years later, a death squad in the 1970s actually bore his name. From the 1930s until 1979, the country's presidents were nearly all military men who ruled as dictators. During this period, the Catholic Church engaged in some diplomatic work with the government to help alleviate the suffering of the poor, but under these repressive regimes, the church's power was severely limited.[10]

It was not until the 1960s that politically left organizations became more involved and began participating actively in the direct elections. One of the parties on the left was the Christian Democratic movement, which drew inspiration from similar movements in Chile and Venezuela. It called for moral principles to be applied to the legislative process and for working on issues such as extreme poverty and land redistribution.

The movement toward Christian democracy should be understood within a broader context of reforms within the Catholic Church that resulted from the Second Vatican Council (1962–1965), the landmark worldwide meeting of Catholic bishops that launched contemporary Catholicism.[11] By making certain changes in the church (especially the change from Latin to vernacular languages in the liturgy), and by accepting a greater "opening to the world" in general, the Second Vatican Council effectively encouraged local bishops to assume greater authority to help alleviate injustices in their respective communities. In Central and South America, these developments led Catholic clergy such as Chencho Alas to become advocates and leaders in the political struggles to redistribute resources to the poor.

In 1969, El Salvador and Honduras went to war in what came to be called the Football War, primarily over the issue of Salvadorans settling illegally on Honduran land. The border between Honduras and El Salvador previously had not been policed or enforced, and an estimated three hundred thousand Salvadorans had settled and were working illegally in Honduras by 1969. Fighting did not last long, but the repercussions in El Salvador were significant. Ties with Honduras were severed, and land shortages again became a serious problem when the Salvadorans were forced to return to their native country.[12]

The Christian Democratic Party (PDC) – which had increasingly gained support during the 1960s – advocated land redistribution and made a strong push to win the presidential elections in 1972 as part of a United National Opposition (UNO). The elections were tense. UNO leaders complained of kidnappings and harassment by the elite-backed government. When the elections were eventually held, the UNO poll watchers claimed to have won with a vote of 327,000 versus 318,000, but the government claimed that the ruling party had won by 10,000 votes.[13]

Frustrated by the democracy-thwarting efforts of the ruling party, a coup again was attempted just after the election. But many in the military were still loyal to the government, and the coup failed. Ever since, the country has been plagued by violence and military confrontations between the right and left. Death squads funded by the oligarchic elite emerged to suppress those identified as communist threats to the government. Many of these death squads specifically targeted religious leaders, who were seen as a threat to the elite's control of the land because many were publicly preaching equality and holding Bible studies. At the same time, leftist communist guerrilla groups also adopted societally disruptive tactics such as kidnappings in an attempt to push the country into a state of chaos.[14]

As all of this was happening, movement in the Catholic Church was further stirring young priests to action. Starting years before in the 1940s, Archbishop Luis Chavez y Gonzalez had begun an initiative to send hundreds of young Salvadoran priests to study in Europe. Many of these young priests were from lower-middle-class, rural families. When they returned by the 1960s and early 1970s, they were well trained, and many were focused on creating greater social justice at home. As a result, during this period the Catholic Church in El Salvador claimed many priests, who empathized with the poor campesinos and were ready to actively risk their lives to pursue justice for their people. Many died in the process. But the courageous efforts of priests such as José Inocencio Alas made an enduring difference, despite the climate of violence and oppression in which they worked.

José Inocencio Alas – "Chencho"

José Inocencio Alas, known to almost everyone as "Chencho," is not very tall, and when his broad face breaks into a warm smile, his eyes light up almost impishly. Usually dressed in casual attire, Chencho's appearance is warm and affable, belying his great intellect and skill in five languages. That he was to have the opportunity for such learning was not a foregone conclusion. Born to campesino parents in 1934 in the small village of Chiapas, Alas entered the seminary at age thirteen. However, in 1956, he was sent to the Grant Seminary of Sherbrook, Canada to study theology and was ordained four years later in Rome. After further study in Brussels, he returned home to El Salvador in 1961.[15]

As a young priest, Alas founded the Cursillo Movement in El Salvador and worked to establish and spread it throughout the country. This spiritual movement, which he had first encountered in Spain, was designed to bring about the religious conversion of men by means of highly emotional weekend retreats that focused on personal and family morality. Many extremely wealthy Salvadorans were drawn to these retreats, including people from the business community and, over the six years he was involved with this work, Alas came to know many of them well. Reflecting on this experience, he now notes that it "gave me deep insight about wealth in El Salvador and the culture that is attached to it."[16] As such, it gave Alas an understanding that would help him to be more effective in his later work.

After leaving this assignment in 1968, Alas spent seven months at the Latin American Pastoral Institute (IPLA) in Ecuador. In addition to being a year of worldwide political activism, this was also the year when Latin American Catholic bishops met at Medellin, Colombia to consider the implications of Vatican II for their region. The documents they produced in August 1968 became a *magna carta* for a generation of Latin American church activists – including Chencho Alas. Inspired by his time at IPLA, Alas notes that he developed a broad perspective on the economic, political, religious, cultural, and societal forces affecting the region and had access to a number of the theologians, social scientists, and bishops who helped shape the Medellin documents. In addition, he was able to observe firsthand the implementation of land reform in Ecuador, where church-owned land was being redistributed to peasants.

Stirred to Action: Alas – The Priest in Suchitoto

On his return to El Salvador, Archbishop Chavez y Gonzalez assigned Alas to the parish in Suchitoto, a district of about forty-five thousand people (mostly campesinos) about an hour's bus ride from San Salvador. The town itself has twelve thousand people, with the rest spread among some thirty-three rural villages. Two huge plantations dominate the landscape and most of the people in the region either work on these farms or tend to their own small plots.

Although not confrontational by nature, it was shortly after his arrival that Alas's work began to provoke controversy. In April 1969, five peasants came to tell Alas about their dispute with a wealthy landholder, Dr. Quiñonez. They had signed a contract with the powerful doctor in which they agreed to clear some of his land and plant corn on it for one year, after which Quiñonez would use it as pastureland. However, while their crops were growing, Dr. Quiñonez had the peasants removed from the land and – because of his connections – made sure that their efforts to seek redress in the courts came to naught.

Alas listened to their story, and in a Sunday evening sermon, he cited the Bible as a source for discussing and denouncing the practice of cheating peasants. Quiñonez's wife and the judge responsible for the case were at the mass. As soon as it was over, Quiñonez's wife confronted Alas, angrily denying that her husband had done anything wrong. In response, Chencho noted that his sermon had not specifically mentioned her husband. Rather, it had focused on a not uncommon practice in which landowners hired – but unjustly failed to pay – their campesino workers.

When the judge heard this exchange, he announced that he was a "just judge" and that he would reconsider the case. Alas sought help from a young law student, and two weeks later – when the judge opened the case – four hundred peasants were outside the courtroom demonstrating for agrarian reform. Alas spoke on behalf of the peasants before the court, and the judge ruled that the peasants could return to use the land so long as they did not remove any wood from it.

This led to an exchange in which Alas's deep passion for the people overruled his regard for his own well-being. When the judge made the ruling about the wood, Chencho spoke up, "That's good. The devil will need all that wood to burn you when you go to hell." The judge responded that Alas had to show respect for the court. But Alas retorted, "We must have respect for the people." Looking back, Alas explains that he was trying to get the judge to think about justice and not only the laws. He also says that this experience was pivotal for him: "this case opened my eyes to the land problem."[17] And it also helps to explain why he then centered his ministry on this issue.[18]

The Suchitoto Town Council was not amused by Alas's activism. It declared him *persona non grata* and pressured the bishop to remove him. Newspapers in San Salvador reported on the situation. A large demonstration in support of Alas was planned, and President Sanchez Hernandez himself came to town in case he was needed to make a decision about quelling the demonstrators. Archbishop Chavez y Gonzalez also came to Suchitoto but his raison d'être was to demonstrate his support for the young Alas. There, the archbishop was greeted by ten thousand campesinos who showed their solidarity for Chencho and demanded that the rights of peasants be recognized. National Guard troops were on hand, and there were reports that an ambulance – supposedly standing ready to help the people – was actually equipped with machine guns, ready to be used on the crowd if necessary. After Sunday morning mass, Chencho spoke encouragingly to the peasants, and they then marched peacefully through the town. Fortunately, the National Guard showed restraint and the demonstration proceeded smoothly.

Alas quickly recognized the power of such peaceful demonstrations and learned how to use them. Soon afterward, a group of peasants asked Alas to help them deal with a company that was charging very high prices for lands the peasants hoped to purchase but could not afford. In this instance, peasants from different areas made their case by marching through the streets of the capital, San Salvador. Aligned with their cause, Alas appealed to his fellow priests for support at a clergy meeting. But he received a mixed response. Older members criticized his activism, and younger priests took up a collection for the cause. The peasants' march made an impact. Soon thereafter, some sympathetic politicians took action, and the government ordered that the prices be lowered to a more just level.

Alas was committed to bringing his ministry to the scattered thirty-three rural villages in his parish. To do this, he needed help from their leaders. Drawing from his studies in Equador, therefore, Alas began an initiative to train nineteen campesino leaders chosen by their communities. He brought them together for an intensive two-month course called "Theology of Community Organization," which used the Bible as the basic reference for learning how to organize community action for social justice. In the evenings, he taught them public speaking skills. And after a predawn mass every Sunday morning, the student-leaders would return to their villages and take communion to their neighbors, after which they would hold community meetings to discuss local issues.[19]

Within his first months in Suchitoto, many features of what has become "the Alas approach" had taken shape: intensive workshop courses for leaders who would then be partners in creating a social movement; the use of the Bible as a basic text for inspiration; nonviolent action among the poor to achieve social reform; incorporating a passion for the land and the value of Mother Earth; and teaching practical skills like public speaking that helped to put the vision of greater justice into practice.

Abduction and Progression

Chencho's activism was getting noticed. In January 1970, the head of the Salvadoran legislature initiated a meeting to discuss land reform in El Salvador. This idea was not entirely radical – the U.S. government had been promoting land reform in Latin America since the early 1960s – but for years the landowners had successfully resisted. The meeting was tense. Alas was present and vocal. During a break in the meeting, as he walked across a parking lot, Chencho was forced into a car by a group of men, blindfolded, made to lie on the floor, and driven away. He recalls: "Because of [my] ministry, I was kidnapped . . . , tortured, and beaten almost to death."[20]

But he had committed friends. As soon as Archbishop Chavez y Gonzalez heard of the abduction, he assumed it had been ordered, and possibly carried out, by the military. He went immediately to the Minister of Defense and demanded that Alas be returned. Meanwhile, peasants in Suchitoto gathered to ring church bells and light candles in protest, an outpouring of support that ultimately helped secure Alas's release.

Alas's captors, who periodically stopped for telephone or radio consultations, eventually informed him that his life would be spared. Forcing him at gunpoint to drink a bottle of alcohol and to take a pill, he quickly lost consciousness. Around midnight, he awoke needing to vomit and feeling very weak. Not knowing where he was, Alas stood up and stumbled down a path, barefoot and naked. As dawn began to break, he made his way to a peasant home. They gave him coffee and a hemp bag to use as a makeshift robe. Later, accompanied by two policemen, Alas was able to reach the nearest town – Texistepeque – and to telephone Archbishop Chavez y Gonzalez. Following the abduction, Alas had to be hospitalized for eleven days. He then left the country for a time, before returning to his parish.

Alas suspected that a local member of the paramilitary group ORDEN (Nationalist Democratic Organization) orchestrated his kidnapping. Such groups often worked under the direction of the military to combat insurgencies. As part of the death squads financed by elite landowners, they sought to suppress land redistribution efforts and leftist political activity. The result of the kidnapping was not what the paramilitary men had planned. Chencho Alas's kidnapping increased his profile even further, and leftist organizers began inviting him to speak throughout the country.

This was not to be the last time that Alas would be targeted. But he continued his work, even though in the ensuing years, his house was bombed and burned and he was arrested several times by the police.[21]

The National Teacher's Strike of 1971

Alas's activism was again evident during a national teacher's strike held in 1971. His intervention on behalf of the teachers provides a powerful example of what one person can do to mobilize public support against unjust persecution. It also shows how an organized community can collectively act to actualize social justice. Alas sets the scene:

> The teachers were demanding better salaries, social security, better infrastructure for the schools, etc. As the Ministry of Education did not hear their demands, they went on strike. In order to maintain the level of awareness

and commitment, they organized inter-city visits. Thirty-three teachers decided to visit their colleagues in Suchitoto. Four kilometers before their arrival, the National Guard stopped them and accused them of carrying subversive literature. However, the only printed material they had were the newspapers printed that very day, all conservative newspapers. As soon as the teachers in Suchitoto learned about what was happening to their colleagues, four of them, all women, went to support them. The National Guard arrested them too and took all of them to the town's prison.[22]

In the early afternoon, as he returned to Suchitoto from a meeting in San Salvador, Alas found some supporters of the thirty-seven striking teachers in front of the local jail shouting slogans of encouragement. He invited three of them to come to his house to discuss what could be done. They talked about alerting radio stations in the capital and continuing to demonstrate outside the prison with loudspeakers to keep up the spirits of those inside. If the prisoners were transferred to the capital, they planned to follow.

Alas proposed that people be convened to celebrate a mass in the evening, but the union members were skeptical about whether people would actually come on such short notice. Alas told them that "it was my problem to get the peasants [from the countryside] there" and then assigned to them the task of convening the townspeople from Suchitoto.[23]

I got in my jeep and went to the agricultural school. At that time we were giving a course to a group of forty young men. I went right to Toribio Flamenco, the director, and I asked him to let me have fifteen young people to go to the hamlets. He asked me what was happening, and I told him about the teachers being in jail and that we had to find a way to get them out. Then we asked for fifteen volunteers, and as might be expected, they all wanted to go. I asked six of them who knew how to ride a horse to go to six hamlets and asked the rest to come with me. I told them that they simply had to go ring the church bells as hard as they could, talk with the first people they encountered, and pass on to them the urgent situation we had on our hands.

By seven P.M. we had an enormous crowd in Suchitoto. We rang the church bells and then we began the celebration of the mystery of life, the Holy Eucharist. Of course the sermon was aimed at giving hope in the struggles we undertake in the name of justice. Before finishing mass, I announced that there would be a march through the city and that it was very important that everyone take part. We had to demand that our innocent teachers be set free.

As soon as we left the church, the celebrants of the Word and a good number of teachers set out to organize the crowd to start the march. According to our plan, we first headed toward the Calvario neighborhood at the main entrance to the town, passing in front of the jail, and then to the Concepción neighborhood [that] leads to the Lempa River, toward the north. Our aim was to go through the town from one end to the other. Finally, we planned to go and set ourselves up in front of the jail, all night if we had to.

As people lined up ten by ten, filling the street, people kept coming from the countryside and the city. The lines were unending. After going by the jail we came to the National Guard post. I looked at the entry gate and was surprised to find it closed. What was going on? Were they afraid? I asked Toño Valte and Amadeo Acosta to count the number of participants, simply to count a row and multiply by ten. About an hour later they came back and said, "We've got approximately ten thousand people marching here." So then I realized why the Guardia had closed the gate. They were afraid!

The atmosphere was one of joy and triumph. People were singing, shouting their slogans, encouraging one another. And why not? We were all surprised to find so many people in this march that was organized in such a short time!

Once we had gone over our planned route, we headed to the jail. There, people let their feelings go full blast. Some were yelling the names of the teachers inside, encouraging them, filling them with joy and the hope of freedom. Others were dancing. Since the entry gate to the jail was closed, we couldn't see what was going on inside. Only later did we learn that the prisoners also had their own rally in the prison yard.

We didn't sleep that night. Some brought firewood from their houses, and we lit a beautiful fire. Some women got the idea that it was a nice time to make a little money and three or four of them set up shop with their fires, oil, plantains, and other things to sell food to the four hundred of us who were holding vigil. . . . The night air was cool, and we were both tired and happy. We were standing before an organized people.

At about 5:00 A.M. the judge came to the jail and ordered the teachers to be let out in groups of five [with security escorts] to hear their cases. Of course, there was no justification for keeping them in jail. The Guard had simply overstepped its power – as they almost always do! By 11:00 A.M. all had been processed and were free. But no one had left – everyone waited until the end, and everyone was free.[24]

Alas later claimed triumphantly, "That day the campesinos and towns-people learned the power of being organized."[25]

Further Organizing

These first years in Suchitoto were busy ones, during which Alas developed his academic approach to land reform. With a $10,000 donation from the U.S. Catholic Bishops Secretariat for Latin America, he set up the agricultural school from which he recruited help to organize the peasant protest over the teachers' incarcerations. The agricultural school allowed young rural campesinos to receive intensive training in leadership, approaches for tackling social issues, and to learn enhanced farming practices.

Alas located a plot of land near the Lempa River and chose a local land use planner to head the school. Alas and others went to work designing and building a facility for forty students. They made their own cement blocks, and Alas hauled building materials in his jeep. The surrounding land was used for experimenting with crops and agricultural techniques. However, the long term results of this experiment were not fully anticipated in the early days. Alas explains,

> The most permanent result that we obtained was to have a large number of young people who were familiar with social analysis and were willing to become organized to liberate the country. We later found a good number of them in leadership positions in the guerrillas.[26]

The school had a short life. El Salvador's recently inaugurated president, Colonial Armando Molina, announced a major project to dam the Lempa River to supply hydroelectric power and provide a new water source for irrigation. The river, El Salvador's largest, runs through the country from the northeast and empties into the Pacific. Project proponents claimed that the dam would improve the lives of the poor in the area. The most immediate and inevitable effect, however, was that the dam would flood a large area and deprive many people living in the Suchitoto parish of their homes and land.

In presenting the project, the government asserted that the people would be paid a fair price and would be assisted in obtaining land of equal quality nearby. They were also promised credit, technical assistance, and health and education services to rebuild their settlements and reforest the area. Skeptical that the government would deliver, Alas and the parish created a series of ten three-day courses to prepare participants to organize and take collective action, if the time came to do so. At the same time, they began establishing links with other peasant organizations to present a united front. Alas joined peasant leaders who went to meet with President Molina. He must have made an impression, because within two days, Chencho was traveling around the country by helicopter with the president to facilitate discussion between villagers and the president on local concerns regarding the hydroelectric project.

Nevertheless, the dam was built with all the anticipated land loss. Homes and farms were lost, and Alas's school, which had operated only for a few years, closed when the Lempa River flooded the area. However, Chencho's organizing efforts did provide his people with some relief. Adequate compensation was paid to those who lost their property.

As Alas organized and educated the peasants against the existing power structure, his prominence as a local religious leader grew, increasingly making him a threat to the country's power structure. When a rightwing politician became mayor of Suchitoto, therefore, it was not surprising that he organized a campaign to force Chencho and his brother to leave town. Given that the law made it illegal to organize the campesinos, arrest warrants were issued for Alas and his brother based on allegations that they were inciting a revolt. Fortunately, the judge in charge of the case tipped Alas off, and he promptly took refuge in San Salvador. Only when the charges were later dropped did Alas return to Suchitoto, where crowds gave him a hero's welcome. Celebrating mass with him that week was his mentor and friend, Bishop Oscar Romero, whose timid demeanor gave no hint of the role he would later play as the Archbishop of San Salvador and a vocal defender of the poor.

These experiences confirmed for Alas that conventional electoral politics could not offer the kind of change the country needed. Rather, he focused his energies even more on creating grassroots movements as stimuli for change. He pursued important partners – including labor unions, the powerful teachers union ANDES, the National University, and the Catholic University. Working with them, Chencho sought to create an "alliance to struggle for the rights of the people." They began with organizational meetings. The first were held in Suchitoto, but when they attracted too much attention, the meetings were moved to churches in San Salvador. At one such meeting of nearly two hundred people, Alas and one of the teachers' union leaders presented their idea of establishing a national network of grassroots organizations, United Popular Action Front (FAPU).

FAPU included peasant organizations, unions, students, politicians, and priests, and they began their work by protesting a government massacre of demonstrators in San Salvador in 1977. Although the FAPU did not ultimately remain cohesive, its creation stirred a movement in which "popular organizations" became active, conducting countless demonstrations, marches, and other actions in San Salvador throughout this time. Using classic nonviolent tactics such as those espoused by Alas (including street marches and vigils), these political fronts fought for the issues about which Alas is passionate: land reform, labor rights, and fair housing.

Through all of this, Alas stood with the peasants and the people of his country. But while continuing to denounce oppression and violence, he also reached out to those he opposed, meeting with government and army officials and urging them to seek compromise without violence.[27]

Increased Unrest, Violence, and Repression

Alas persisted in his fight for reform, but increasing political tensions were making it harder and harder to continue. Conflicts escalated during the mid-1970s, when President Molina proposed moderate land reform in two provinces. Molina's aim was to provide peasants with land by motivating landholders to sell their property and move into manufacturing and trade. The U.S. Embassy, the Catholic University, and the Communist Party all supported the plan, but others from the left and the powerful oligarchy (albeit for opposite reasons) furiously opposed the reforms. Perhaps predictably, the landholding oligarchy forced the government to back down and rallied around General Humberto Romero, the opposition presidential candidate for the moderate-left coalition of Christian Democrats and others.

It was within this environment in December 1975 that peasants gathered adjacent to Suchitoto to try to resolve a dispute with two landholders, who were also brothers. The discussion turned violent, and one of the landholders was shot and killed accidentally by his brother, according to the peasants. The landholding oligarchy blamed the peasants and accused the Jesuits of inciting them to violence. The landowners then took action against the church. Several priests were arrested, beaten, and deported.

Violence escalated. The February 1976 Legislative Assembly and municipal election raised claims of fraud and a coalition opposing the government's misconduct rallied in a plaza in San Salvador outside a church. When the protest showed no signs of ending, official troops moved in, breaking up the rally in the middle of the night, killing dozens, and then using fire hoses to clean the streets of their blood. At about the same time, rival guerrilla groups kidnapped two prominent Salvadorans and in exchange demanded the release of some of their members from jail.

Tensions were exacerbated when, only a month later, Father Rutilio Grande, pastor of the parish next to Suchitoto, was shot and killed while on his way to say mass. This was the first political murder of a priest in El Salvador, executed at the behest of a landholder and with the involvement of a government death squad. Archbishop Oscar Romero, who had been hastily installed as Archbishop of San Salvador, faced these multiple crises. In his first major decision, he ordered that an outdoor mass be celebrated, and to highlight its importance, all regular Sunday masses for that day were canceled. The mass brought El Salvador's Catholic community together in a time of turmoil and uncertainty.

The growing repression in El Salvador was typical of what was occurring throughout Latin America at that time. In Brazil, Chile, Argentina, and Uruguay, activist priests, nuns, pastors, and bishops were being murdered and tortured to suppress political opposition to their repressive military governments. As one of the most visible and public of all the young Salvadoran priests, Alas had every reason to fear that he might be next. For safety, he avoided his own bed, sleeping in the sacristy or at the house of Dominican sisters who taught in the school. But when a warning came from Archbishop Romero about a death threat, he escaped from Suchitoto, concealed in a compartment of a large truck.

Chencho spent the next three months hiding out in a seminary in San Salvador and serving as an advisor to Archbishop Romero, whom Chencho now refers to as "our martyr and prophet."[28] When a second priest, Alfonso Navarro, was gunned down in May, Alas was persuaded to take refuge in the Vatican embassy. Two weeks later, he left the country.

Chencho Alas had been in Suchitoto for eight years. While there, he sought to implement a new kind of pastoral work along the lines developed by the Catholic bishops at Medellin. In doing so, he became a central figure in the region's struggles during the 1970s. His effectiveness as a rural parish pastor who could mobilize people brought Alas national attention, making him a thorn in the side of those in power: the oligarchy and the government.

A Life in Exile

When Alas left El Salvador on May 27, 1977, he had little idea of what would become of him or his country. He set out for Quebec, where he thought he would teach. But on his way, he stopped in Washington, D.C., where he visited Hispanic churches and shared his experiences with violence and repression at home. This led to Alas being asked to testify on human rights violations in El Salvador to a congressional committee. He ended up staying in Washington, D.C. and taking a job at the

Inter-American Development Bank, where he worked from 1979 to 1983 overseeing a variety of different projects.

Meanwhile, tensions in El Salvador were getting even worse. As mass demonstrations became increasingly confrontational, the streets of San Salvador were plagued with scenes of violence. More priests were killed. When the Sandinistas overthrew the Somoza dictatorship in Nicaragua, it was therefore assumed that an uprising in El Salvador was inevitable. But it did not materialize.

Then, in October 1979, a group of young military officers overthrew President Humberto Romero and proclaimed their intention to carry out progressive changes. Instead, the level of violence against unarmed civilians increased. By early 1980, approximately one thousand civilians per month were being killed by official forces and elite-backed death squads. And in March 1980, Archbishop Romero was murdered while leading mass. Months later, three U.S. nuns and one volunteer were raped and murdered. Peaceful public opposition to government repression turned violent, as organizers and activists fled the country or joined the guerrilla movement.

Alas watched these developments from abroad. Meanwhile, in his new home, Ronald Reagan had been elected president and vowed to prevent the spread of Marxism in Central America. El Salvador was one country where President Reagan soon took action. The recently united Salvadoran guerrilla forces formally began an offensive in January 1981, seeking a Marxist overthrow of the government. But when they failed to ignite a widespread insurrection in the capital (similar to the one in Nicaragua a year and a half earlier), they retreated to rural outposts, primarily near the Honduran border in the north, from which they continued their campaign. The country became engulfed in a brutal civil war in which thousands of civilians lost their lives. Despite massive amounts of American aid, the Salvadoran military was unable to defeat the guerrillas, and the situation remained at an impasse throughout the 1980s.

Going Home – The Work of Rebuilding

During his fifteen years in exile, life changed dramatically for Chencho Alas. He asked the Bishop of Arlington, Virginia to be permitted to serve the community as a priest. While the request was pending, Alas celebrated a mass for someone from the Inter-American Development Bank who had died. Alas spoke of the man, saying that he was now with God and that God would judge him. He went on to note that all present would one day

die and would then be called to account for their lives. Alas then challenged the listeners to consider what they were doing for their neighbors
in Latin America. He described the situation there and challenged them
to action. Among the listeners was a Spanish priest who worked for and
subsequently spoke to the Arlington bishop about this mass. And shortly
thereafter, Chencho received the letter that would define his future. The
bishop refused to allow Alas to serve as a parish priest because of his
outspoken advocacy.

Alas left the priesthood. Without the constraints of a parish, he found
new freedom to serve his people. But even as Chencho ended his official
tenure with the church, he did not leave his faith. Indeed, the people
to whom he had devoted himself continue to see him as a leader of the
faith community. To them, he is still "Father Alas." Chencho describes
the phenomenon this way: "People in El Savador, in San Salvador and
also in the community, they approach me and call me Father, even if they
know that I [now] have a wife and children. For the majority of them, I
am a Father."[29]

Throughout his exile, Alas's heart was always with his people, and he
remained in contact with his friends in El Salvador through occasional
meetings in the United States and elsewhere. In 1983, he returned to
his beloved Central America, moving to Nicaragua where he worked
with the San Francisco–based Capp Street Foundation to administer
funds for small projects, especially in food production. Seeing the continued need to provide resources, he set up the Central American Foundation three years later to channel funds to projects throughout the
region.

But it was not until the civil war was officially over in 1992 that Alas
ventured back to El Salvador and then, only in the company of five Americans who served as his "bodyguards." The country to which he returned
was quite different from the one he had left. Although coffee was still
the country's main export, agriculture was declining in economic importance. It amounted to only 15 percent of the GDP, despite the fact that 40
percent of the population still worked in the agricultural sector.[30] Most
Salvadorans had moved to cities and towns, and criminal violence had
increased significantly. Approximately one-fifth of all Salvadorans were
now living outside the country – many of them in the United States.
Driven out by the violence of war, they had established firm footholds
in Los Angeles, Washington, D.C., and other cities. Indeed, remittances
from Salvadoran expatriates were now the country's single largest source
of income.

It was clear that much needed to be done, to actualize social justice and to sustain the land and the environment. Alas renewed contact with people he had known from his Suchitoto days and sought to channel development aid to them as he had been doing in Nicaragua. Discussions that he had started years earlier with other Salvadoran exiles, including a leader of the FMLN (Farabundo Marti National Liberation) leftist movement in the civil war, Commander Mario Lopez, and the rector of the National University, Fabio Castillo, proved fruitful and led to the creation of a foundation called Institute for Technology, Environment and Self-Sufficiency (the "Institute"), which opened an office in San Salvador. Knowing that the Institute's financial health would depend on American support, Alas moved to Texas to facilitate fundraising for the initiative.

The Institute focused its efforts on an area along the Pacific Coast where the Lempa River empties into the ocean. Relatively unpopulated, much of the land had been occupied by the military under the country's land reform policies. It was beginning to be resettled by the early 1990s, largely by people escaping from war zones – including about four thousand former guerrilla combatants who moved in with their families. The government also settled some of its own former army combatants in the locale. The Institute began to work on a few projects in the area, and from 1992 to 1995, Alas devoted himself largely to raising funds for the work of building this community.

The "Zone of Peace"

In 1995, government officials released waters from the same large dam on the Lempa River that had flooded lands in Suchitoto twenty years earlier. Without any warning, the dam was opened, the region in which the Institute was working was devastated by floods, and ten thousand people were displaced. Afterward, leaders from seven communities met to identify strategies for preventing such disasters in the future. They named themselves the Coordinadora del Bajo Lempa (the Coordinating Committee of the Lower Lempa River and Bay of Jiquilisco) and together went to address the National Congress. Although they succeeded in having the Bajo Lempa declared a disaster area, little help actually arrived.

Alas was instrumental in the creation of the Coordinadora, which served as an umbrella organization dedicated to low-income communities. It eventually formed an executive committee of fourteen and an assembly of elected leaders from eighty-six communities who represent approximately thirty-five thousand people. With Chencho serving as an adviser, facilitator, and fundraiser, they worked to achieve: environmental sustainability (including flood disaster programs), economic self-sufficiency (including community farms and businesses), social justice, and peace. In fact, Alas is proud that among the executive committee members, there are former enemies who work together – members of the national guard and the government, and members from the opposing FMLN.[31]

Among the key challenges still facing the Coordinadora is a legacy of violence in El Salvador and particularly in the area where it is active, the Usulután province. Alas describes the dire situation in the years after the war had ended, "[There] was street crime. And that had been growing and growing and growing. . . . [There were kidnappings.] . . . Some were killed and tortured. There were robberies every day."[32] Youth gang members returning to the country from Los Angeles brought their violent gang practices, whereas local youth reflected a culture where guns had been commonplace during their formative years. Things were so serious that business people in the town of Jiquilisco organized a two-day "strike" to protest their lack of security. Summing up the situation, Chencho says:

> We have a culture of violence. Due to the military rule in El Salvador for sixty years and people trying to overthrow the military. [A percentage of the people own guns]. And certainly if you have a large percentage of people who are living impoverished or are in misery . . . then they are trying, to do what is possible in order to at least have what is needed. . . .
>
> Also there is a problem of migration from the rural sector to the city. In the cities they are not known. There are very few things they can do because they are rural people . . . And that was especially [true] during the war, [when] many, many, many of our villages disappeared and people went to San Salvador or to other places to live.
>
> Then there is the policy that our government has been following since 1990 – the privatization of everything. . . . And instead of trying to support the agricultural sector, our government has been supporting the financial sector . . . [in which] very few people participate.[33]

To create a much needed sanctuary, Alas and others from the Coordinadora conceived of the idea of declaring the Lower Lempa a "Local Zone of Peace" – a region committed to changing the culture of violence to one of collaboration, mutual problem solving, and peace. Others were already trying the idea: Central American presidents had declared all of Central America as a "Zone of Peace," while UNESCO also was developing programs around the notion of a "Culture of Peace" in various regions of the world. Alas and others sought to apply this concept, which until then had been used for much larger regions, to the smaller local region over which they had influence.

But before this could be done, the people had to be consulted. The responsibility for laying the groundwork fell to Alas. Trying to develop momentum for implementing the vision, he held dozens of weekend workshops for the peasants and people of the region on the theme of a "Culture of Peace." Alas believes that such involvement is critical for evolving a shared vision from the people themselves. Through such a process, true participatory democracy is practiced and problem solving emerges. He notes: "People need to be, you know, to be a nation. So, democratic participation is important at all levels. The community level and the national level."[34]

Each workshop would begin with a session in which Chencho asked participants to discuss the reality of human rights and conflict in their communities. They discussed their experiences in small groups and reported back to the larger group to share their conclusions. Alas would then lead a discussion based on the opening chapters of the Book of Genesis dealing with conflict, such as the story of Cain and Abel in Genesis 4, and discuss New Testament passages such as the Sermon on the Mount. The emphasis on the first day of the workshop was managing – rather than resolving – conflicts.

The second day was devoted to developing a vision of peace. Alas used biblical passages from books including Genesis and Isaiah, and facilitated discussion on having respect for the earth, forming local organizations, and democratic participation. In many ways, these workshops were an evolved version of Alas's early work in Suchitoto two decades earlier.[35] And they led to a shared vision.

By 1998, after nearly two years of work and workshops involving several thousand people, the Coordinadora was ready to inaugurate the "Zone of Peace." On August 4, nearly two thousand people from the region joined supporters from all over El Salvador, the United States, and Europe to march the eight miles from San Marcos Lempa to Ciudad Romero. There, in the presence of government representatives, diplomats, and nongovernmental organizations (NGOs), the Lower Lempa was formally declared a local "Zone of Peace," signifying the commitment of all the local communities to collaborate and work together to resolve all future conflicts for the sake of a real and long-lasting peace.

In his *Guidebook for Peacemakers,* Alas describes this effort and the declaration as "the beginning of a new way of community life ..." Indeed, the Coordinadora and the people in the local Zone of Peace are working to transform "problems like poverty, hunger, violence and the lack of education, training, and skills." Alas explains that the "vision is holistic" because it includes the full range of issues that need to be addressed to reach true peace, and not merely the absence of war. Alas writes, the vision "includes human rights as well as obligations, conflict transformation, democratic participation, and sustainable economic development." And, not surprisingly, in the vision for the Lower Lempa's Zone of Peace, "the Earth has a value in itself."[36]

To ensure the success of the Coordinadora, resources were needed. Chencho therefore created the Foundation for Self-Sufficiency in Central America (FSSCA) in 1996 to raise funds in the United States to provide financial, technical, and moral support to the Coordinadora. To do this, Alas split his time between El Salvador and the United States. While in the United States, he traveled widely to educate people and potential funders on the situation and the need in El Salvador.

In his meetings, Alas speaks powerfully of the need to help the peasants and protect the earth. He also voices concerns over "new economic policies [that] insist on converting Central America and the south into a giant sweat shop where peasants, workers and indigenous people are employed by transnational corporations."[37] And, as he travels around the United States, Alas also predictably calls for a new paradigm in which peace becomes a reality.

Religiously Motivated Peacemaking

Chencho Alas's tireless work continues. Until just before this book went to publication, he was still serving as the President and Executive Director of FSSCA. But in the organization's Winter 2005 newsletter, he announced that he would step down and assume the role of Peace Project Coordinator to devote himself full-time to "something that is very close to my heart and very important to the people we serve: the Mesoamerican Peace Project."[38] In this capacity, Alas is building on his work with the local Zone of Peace. He wants to expand the vision and take it to a more impactful level – to all the Mesoamerican countries (i.e., the region from southern Mexico to Panama) and the United States.

Although Alas is no longer in the priesthood, religion continues to play an integral role in his life and is central to his work. When asked if the importance of religion and spirituality in his work has diminished since his time in the clergy, he responds "certainly not!" If anything, he says, it has only deepened and expanded over the years. During his years as a priest before El Salvador's civil war, Alas found himself working almost exclusively with other Catholics. Moreover, as a priest he often encountered difficulties in working with Marxists, whose atheist ideology often inhibited cooperation with the church even on issues of common interest.

Today, Alas works with many people from different religions (and from no religion), including Jews, Catholics, Evangelicals, and Buddhists and is therefore able to assume a much broader approach to his mission. Of his work with people from different faiths, Alas says that it has helped him to realize that "all religions can contribute to peace and help to teach people to appreciate our differences." The goal is not to find within one faith the inspiration for peace alone. Rather, it is to find within multiple religious, faith, and spiritual traditions shared values that inspire and direct us to peace and to a new way of living that accords justice for all people and care for the earth and the environment.

Moving Forward: Alas's "Theology of Peace"

Alas's role as an activist has evolved since his early days in the parish of Suchitoto. Through it all, he has been steadfast in his commitment to helping the peasants, promoting justice, and using the power of community organizing to achieve shared goals. Expanding on the original issues he confronted in Suchitoto, where he mobilized people around more equitable land reform, Alas today focuses on a broadly defined concept of peace that includes those concerns but far more as well. Peace, as he defines it, "is a state of harmony between body and soul, at the individual and community level, within an environment that is politically, economically, socially, and environmentally good and beautiful." Theologically speaking, Alas explains the same vision, "Peace is the constant recreation of the harmony between God and humans, among human beings, and between human beings and the earth."[39]

This is the ideal that Alas is pursuing today in his Mesoamerican Peace Project. Alas describes his work as a "Theology of Peace." Based on values and principles, the Mesoamerican Peace Project is designed to develop a peaceful response to globalization from the bottom up. In one recent workshop, Alas trained peasant participants from every country in Central America to create community stores. His goal is to economically empower local communities through these stores, which will later open the way for political empowerment. This, in turn, will create a force that can be an answer to globalization.

Working with grassroots communities, Alas's approach still starts with his deep respect for people and appreciation for what motivates them. For some, shared values are defined through their culture. For others, it is through their cosmological vision and spirituality. And for still others, it is through the inspiration in their theology. Using all of these motivators, Alas now works to reach people and create a network of peacemakers who share a large vision of peace that starts with a deep appreciation of the importance of our shared earth. When Alas describes the process for achieving his vision, he lists concrete steps for organizing meetings and running workshops. But under these practical details, it is evident that he has a strong belief that we can all grow spiritually and, as we grow, new possibilities for a lived peace will be discovered. Thus, when Alas describes the anticipated result of his newest – and most ambitious – project, it is really quite simple. He wants us to recognize that "[W]e all need to be peacemakers."[40]

To achieve peace, Chencho Alas believes that it is necessary for people to be good in their heart. But this alone is not enough. To be peacemakers, people are required not only to be kind to others, but also to act and try to change the injustices around them. This is how Chencho Alas lives. And given his great contributions for so many in El Salvador and elsewhere, this is how he will always be known – as a *Peacemaker* for El Salvador, its people, and its land.

EL SALVADOR FACT SHEET[41]

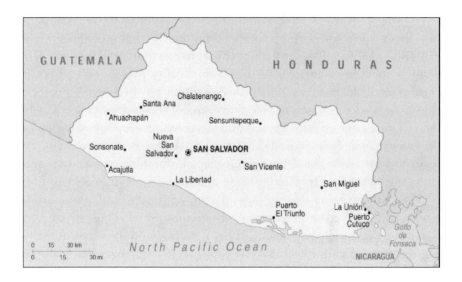

Geography

Location: Central America, bordering the North Pacific Ocean, between Guatemala and Honduras.

Area: *Total:* 21,040 sq km
Land: 20,720 sq km
Water: 320 sq km

Area comparative: Slightly smaller than Massachusetts.

Climate: Tropical; rainy season (May to October); dry season (November to April); temperate in uplands.

Geography note: Smallest Central American country and only one without a coastline on Caribbean Sea.

Population

Population: 6,704,932 (July 2005 est.)

Racial/ethnic groups:

Mestizo:	90%
White:	9%
American Indian:	1%

Religions:

Roman Catholic:	86%
Protestant:	14%

Languages: Spanish, Nahua

Government

Government type:	Republic
Capital:	San Salvador
Legal system:	Based on civil and Roman law, with traces of common law; judicial review of legislative acts in the Supreme Court.

Background

El Salvador gained its independence from Spain in 1821 and from the Central American Federation in 1839. Since the time of the Spanish occupation, land in El Salvador has been owned by a few elite, who have possessed most of the country's wealth. They have also largely shaped government policies in their own interest and at the expense of the majority of the population of farmers, a condition that has led to sharp divisions in society along class lines.

A twelve-year civil war, which cost the lives of some seventy-five thousand people, ended in 1992 with the signing of a peace treaty that provided for military and political reforms by the government and leftist rebels. At the end of the 1970s, the Salvadoran government's repression of its people increased significantly and a civil war seemed inevitable. Peaceful rallies were turning violent and news footage of attacks on unarmed demonstrators began circulating around the world. By the beginning of the 1980s, the opposition of the Salvadoran Left began to join together to coordinate their struggle against the government, eventually forming the Farabundo Martí National Liberation Front (FMLN). The group began an offensive in 1981 and – despite its failure to defeat the government outright – was able to retain certain military strongholds in parts of the country.

In the United States, the 1980 election of Ronald Reagan brought significant changes to American foreign policy. Although the United States had already been involved in the Salvadoran conflict under President Carter, the new administration placed a higher priority on preventing the spread of Marxism in Latin America, and increased aid to the Salvadoran military considerably.

The civil war persisted throughout the 1980s, and many parts of the country were locked in a bloody stalemate that cost tens of thousands of civilian lives. In 1989, six Jesuit priests, their housekeeper, and her daughter were murdered at the University of Central America, which finally prompted the international community to act.[42]

The U.S. Congress created a special task force to analyze the conflict and the American role in it. The task force's report, which revealed the Salvadoran government's brutality, initiated an international peace process that culminated in United Nations peace talks and the signing of the 1992 Peace Accords that ended the twelve-year war.

Economic Overview

Since the signing of the Peace Accords, El Salvador's economy has improved significantly, especially on the macro level with improved fiscal management and free market initiatives. However, unequal income distribution continues to be a problem. The country also suffers from a weak tax collection system, factory closings, and low world coffee prices. On the bright side, in recent years inflation has fallen to single digit levels, and total exports have grown substantially. In 2001, El Salvador adopted the U.S. dollar as its currency, thus losing control over its monetary policy. The substantial trade deficit has been offset by remittances from the large number of Salvadorans living abroad and from foreign aid.

3 Men Who Walked the Street

Father Alex Reid and the Rev. Dr. Roy Magee

Northern Ireland

Political and religious affiliations in Northern Ireland are closely aligned. Consequently, religious leaders were well positioned to influence public policy and the direction of its conflict. But although most resisted that opportunity, two men in particular have embraced peacemaking as a religious duty. On opposite sides of the dispute, Father Alex Reid and the Reverend Dr. Roy Magee each risked their lives and reputations in the search for peace. It was the history of their land that called each of them to peacemaking, and it was their deeply held religious convictions that helped them to answer the call.

For over twenty-five years, these men worked in their respective communities to bring their people together for a shared effort to establish peace. As their stories show, both Reid and Magee were key behind-the-scenes actors. Their efforts to halt deadly violence and ultimate success in negotiating cease-fires with the paramilitaries opened the way for the diplomats and the historic Belfast Agreement in 1998. More popularly known as the Good Friday Agreement, its multiparty collaboration was such an achievement that its primary architects, David Trimble and John Hume, later won the Nobel Peace Prize.

But although diplomatic achievements are often the more recognized part of the conflict's story, they do not reflect the lives of Northern Ireland's ordinary people, their experiences, their unsung heroes, and their lasting memories, including these recalled by a reporter after thirty years covering the intractable conflict:

> A farmer's wife in County Tyrone telling me how she prayed night after night for the strength to forgive the men who had blown her son to bits. The children of an IRA hunger striker clutching their mother's hands as they walked behind his coffin, trying not to cry because their father had died for Ireland. . . .

The two soldiers lying on a patch of waste ground who had been stripped to their underpants before the IRA shot them, although the gunmen had left their socks on.[1]

These are the stories of the people. And these were daily experiences for Father Alex Reid and the Rev. Roy Magee – two of the unsung heroes. Not widely recognized outside their communities, they are best remembered by their neighbors as the priest and the minister who were always there, working for peace, even at great risk to their personal safety.

Historical Overview

Unionists and nationalists understand the history of Northern Ireland differently, and their diverging interpretations make it difficult to tell the conflict's history free of bias (for definitions of unionist, nationalist, and other parties in this conflict, see the Fact Sheet at the end of this chapter). As R. Scott Appleby notes in *The Ambivalence of the Sacred: Religion, Violence, and Reconciliation:*

> An impartial or "objective" summary of what actually happened . . . is difficult, if not impossible, to provide. Nationalists begin their histories with the first Norman invasions in 1169–70, while the Unionist myth opens with the plantation of Ulster in 1609. "The Catholic story" recounts centuries of uninterrupted English brutality in Ireland, while "the Protestant story" emphasizes the courageous survival of British settlers facing overwhelming odds and a series of barbaric sieges.[2]

The following attempt at inclusive storytelling begins in 1169, when the ancestors of the nationalists first came to the island of Ireland.

History of Ireland: 1169–1609

The Gaelic-speaking Iberian Celts who first inhabited Ireland survived several attacks before the Normans of England successfully invaded in 1169 and spread out over the fertile island. But England's King Henry II feared that this would lead to an independent Norman state, and invaded just a couple of years later.[3] At the time, England's presence in Ireland was limited primarily to a small area near present-day Dublin, where it attempted to import English administration, customs, and language. Seeing the English as a threat to their sovereignty and culture, most Irish clans actively resisted these invasions, successfully containing the

English until the sixteenth century and preserving the Gaelic identity for hundreds of years. During these centuries, Ireland's native Gaelic population retained allegiance to a sovereign Ireland, whereas the Anglo-Irish, who continued to consider themselves English, maintained allegiance to England.

With the Protestant Reformation of the sixteenth century, the face of religion changed throughout Europe. Henry VIII decreed all of England (including Wales, Scotland, and Ireland) a Protestant nation, established the Church of England (later known as the Anglican Church), and named himself its head. He resolved to bring all of Catholic Ireland under Protestant English control, and after his daughter, Queen Elizabeth, assumed power, she followed in his bold footsteps. After much bloodshed, she succeeded in extending England's control to all of Ireland, with the exception of the northern province of Ulster, where local clans succeeded in fighting off her armies.[4]

Nonetheless, by 1606, the English-appointed attorney general of Ireland imposed English law on Ulster, the region he referred to as "the most rude and unreformed part of Ireland, and the seat and nest of the last great rebellion."[5] Rather than accept diminished authority and English redistribution of their land, in 1607 the once powerful earls of Ulster opted to sail to Europe and eventually, to settle in Rome. Choosing never again to return to Ireland, their departure would later become known as the "Flight of the Earls."[6] Recognizing the void, just a few years later, the British founded a plantation in Ulster and began colonizing the region. Mass migrations followed, marking the beginning of the Protestant experience in Northern Ireland.

Laying the Foundation for Future Discord: 1609–1801

The British colonists came from all levels of society, including many Protestants from England, Scotland, and Wales. The new inhabitants quickly assumed the former earls' power and land, and the native, predominantly Catholic Irish were driven from their homes.[7] In the words of John Darby, a scholar on the Northern Ireland conflict, Protestants built new towns that functioned as "fortresses against the armed resentment of the Irish," and were viewed by the native population as foreigners who "spoke differently, worshiped apart, and represented an alien culture and way of life."[8] In short order, the British established themselves economically, legislatively, and militarily. Within less than one hundred years, Ulster Catholics owned only 5 percent of the land in Ulster[9] and many were reduced to servility. The seeds of conflict were sown, and an economic fault line has since divided Protestants and Catholics.

The year 1641 marked a violent turning point. Beginning in Ulster, Catholics rebelled, massacring thousands of Protestant settlers. Looking back, the Catholic community tends to recount this uprising as an example of righteous revenge against unjust oppressors, whereas Protestants tend to view the massacre as the impetus for Oliver Cromwell's English reconquest a decade later.[10]

Ireland was ruled by Protestants until James II, a Catholic, assumed power. Faced with almost unanimous resistance from the British population, James II was quickly forced from the English throne and replaced by his Protestant son-in-law, William of Orange.[11] William's legacy continues today through the Orange Order, which was founded in 1795 and is the largest Protestant organization in Northern Ireland. Boasting some one hundred thousand members, its annual marches celebrate the victory of William of Orange over Catholics and have served as a source of sectarian tension.[12]

By the end of the seventeenth century, the British government imposed penal laws that assured Protestant political control. All members of the Irish government were required to take an Oath of Allegiance and officially denounce the Pope and mass – acts that observant Catholics would not do.[13] Catholics were similarly excluded from the legal professions and local corporations, and Catholic children were forced to go to Protestant schools.[14]

Less than one century later, responding to the French Revolution – and its call for democratic reforms – Irish Catholics and other dissenters of colonial rule took action, especially in Ulster. They formed the Society of United Irishmen, but were defeated in trying to rid Ireland of British control.[15]

Belfast and the Changing Dynamics of Ulster:
Nineteenth Century

In the heart of Ulster lies Belfast, a Victorian city whose main thoroughfares radiate from its center like the spokes of a bicycle wheel, seemingly inviting people to it from every direction. Unlike the rest of the island, in which the majority of the population remained Catholic and agrarian despite colonial rule, Ulster had a substantial Protestant and Scottish Presbyterian population. As Belfast's industries expanded in the mid-nineteenth century, more people came to work in the new factories, including Catholics from faraway regions of Ireland. Many came during the great Potato Famine of 1845–1849, in which over one million Irish died of starvation and the British were blamed for not doing more to prevent these deaths while the rest of England was prospering.[16]

Practicing their indigenous religious and cultural traditions, Belfast's newcomers changed the face of the city seemingly overnight. They settled along the main roads of the city, often living in small ghettos whose religious makeup could change from street to street. Such widespread diversity was new to Belfast, and the adjustment to this reality proved difficult, particularly for the migrants from rural areas.

With ardently Protestant and Catholic populations living in such close proximity, nineteenth-century Belfast was characterized by an uneasy coexistence marked by sporadic sectarian riots. Religion and local politics were intertwined, with competition for scarce resources, religious tensions, and violence becoming the foundation for modern political life in Northern Ireland.

The Irish Independence Movement: 1801–1921

In 1801, the United Kingdom of Great Britain and Ireland was created by an Act of Union passed by both the British and Irish parliaments. In effect, this act abolished the colonial Irish government and explicitly gave Westminster direct control over Ireland. When George III, then King of the United Kingdom of Great Britain and Ireland, refused to authorize simultaneous legislation emancipating the Catholics of Ireland, many politicians, including British Prime Minister William Pitt, resigned in protest.[17] Anti-British sentiments in Ireland grew throughout the century and debates on home rule divided the unionist Protestants (predominantly residing in the northeast) and the nationalist Catholics, who populated most of Ireland.[18]

By the time World War I diverted Britain's attention, the paramilitary group the Irish Republican Army (IRA), with the help of large stockpiles of arms supplied by the Germans, was ready to act and attempted a military uprising seeking a united Ireland in 1916. When it failed, the leaders were executed for treason, stimulating anger among the Catholic Irish population and sympathy for the IRA and Sinn Féin, its political wing at the time. Those who died were memorialized as Christlike martyrs, with anti-British leaders subsequently drawing heavily on religious imagery to win popular support. Two years later, Sinn Féin ("We Ourselves" in Gaelic) won the majority of Ireland's seats in the parliament of the United Kingdom of Great Britain and Ireland. The victory bolstered support for the IRA and led to the Anglo-Irish War (or the Irish War of Independence). Depicted as a conflict between Protestants and Catholics, the violence on both sides was brutal and great numbers of people died. By 1920, the war ended in a truce, and the Anglo-Irish Treaty of 1921 delineated the terms of the ensuing peace.[19]

The History of Northern Ireland: 1921–1969

Under the Anglo-Irish Treaty, twenty-six of the thirty-two counties of Ireland became independent, and are now known as the Republic of Ireland. Britain retained the remaining six counties – the primarily Protestant Ulster – whose majority favored union with Britain. Ulster officially became Northern Ireland, the newest addition to the United Kingdom. In Belfast, a government subordinate to Britain was established, and the Northern Ireland government sent representatives to Westminster to participate in Britain's Parliament.

Following the Treaty, the religiopolitical tensions that had previously characterized the whole of Ireland focused in Northern Ireland. There, the Protestants continued to hold most positions of power, whereas many Catholics left the north to cross into the newly independent Republic of Ireland. This left an even more marginalized Northern Ireland Catholic community to face the daily discrimination.

By the 1960s, however, a Catholic middle class emerged in part because Britain had granted all citizens the right to a free education.[20] More educated, the Catholics became a more potent political force. Inspired by the Civil Rights Movement in the United States, Catholics and some Protestants founded the Northern Ireland Civil Rights Association in 1967 to seek social justice and reforms that would improve life for all. The activists demonstrated, demanding the establishment of public authorities charged with stopping discrimination, allocating housing more fairly, and ending gerrymandering so that each person had one vote.[21] Although government concessions initially seemed possible, hardline unionist extremists refused to accept any compromise and staged counter-demonstrations.

At first, the civil rights protests took the form of marches, sit-ins, and media engagement. But as extremists became more involved, civil disobedience turned to riots, with marchers and police directly confronting one another. The situation deteriorated, eventually leading to a constant state of civil unrest and violence that came to be known simply as the Troubles.[22]

The Troubles Break Out: 1969

The Troubles were a state of not quite war, but not quite peace, between Protestants and Catholics. Characterized by bombings, murders, oppressive fear, and constant uncertainty, the violence penetrated daily life and divisions ran deep. Particularly poignant were the local expressions seen in murals painted on neighborhood buildings and walls, including the "peace lines" (a term coined by the British Army to describe the tall barriers that were erected to divide Catholic and Protestant neighborhoods to minimize violent confrontations[23]). On the nationalist side, pictures of nationalist martyrs were displayed along with slogans such as "Free Ireland." But just down the road, the very same figures were depicted by Protestants as black-hooded terrorists with machine guns.[24]

The Troubles escalated rapidly. The summer of 1969 saw angry protests and Protestant marches, including one by the Orange Order held in Londonderry* to commemorate the victory of William of Orange.[25] Another march by a Protestant group called the Apprentice Boys went by Bogside, a predominantly Catholic area of Londonderry, with predictable results. The BBC described what transpired next:

> The RUC [Royal Ulster Constabulary, the police force answerable to Britain] intervened and, assisted by a Protestant mob, charged at the Nationalists forcing them into William Street. Within hours rioting had escalated into what local priest Fr. Mulvey described as a "community in revolt." The police were stoned and petrol bombed as they made their way in riot gear into the Bogside. After two days and nights of continuous rioting the police were exhausted.[26]

As nationalists drove the British police back with bottles and stones in Londonderry, Protestant mobs in Belfast invaded Catholic districts. Riots erupted, houses were burned,[27] and rumors abounded that the loyalists planned to burn down Clonard Monastery, where Father Alex Reid lived. One priest actually gave two armed Catholics permission to defend the monastery. But although rioters attacked nearby streets and homes, the monastery was not harmed.[28]

The fighting ended when England sent the British Army to intervene directly. Catholics initially welcomed them, believing that the army would secure their rights and safety. But relations quickly soured.[29]

---

* The official name of the city is Londonderry, but many of its inhabitants call it Derry. The name is a contentious issue, in which nationalists prefer Derry and unionists prefer Londonderry.

It was during these days of bloodshed that Father Alex Reid thought about the parishioners gathered in his church to worship with their spouses, children, and parents. Many were involved – and even responsible for – the violence. As he looked at them one Sunday, Father Reid came to the difficult realization that simply condemning terrorist violence would be an easy but ineffective response. It would not bring the Troubles to an end. At about the same time, in another part of town, the Rev. Dr. Roy Magee faced his protestant congregation and reached a similar conclusion. It was a moment of decision for both men. Each vowed to respond – but not with empty words. Rather, each resolved to work directly with his flock, even though that would mean working with family men and women who were also murderers.

In the ensuing months, the violence persisted and more extreme elements emerged, causing intragroup tensions that complicated the already tense region. Militants blamed the IRA for failing to protect Catholics and republicans in Northern Ireland. Breaking away, they formed the highly influential Provisional Irish Republican Army (PIRA, IRA, or Provos). Thereafter, the original Irish Republican Army became known as the Official IRA, and most references to the IRA actually came to refer to the more militant PIRA.

By 1970, the Provisional IRA had begun its campaign of violence and quickly gained in power and membership. When the Official IRA tried to declare a cease-fire in 1972, the Provisional IRA quickly marginalized them. This early feuding among the paramilitaries was just the beginning. It would plague the nationalist cause for years.

Internment and Direct Rule

In a desperate move to regain control, the unionist-controlled government of Northern Ireland introduced a policy of internment in 1971. But those whom the government "interned" were almost always Catholic men and women, who were arrested, often without trial, and treated brutally. The European Commission for Human Rights found Britain guilty of torture, although the European Court of Human Rights later ruled that the treatment was inhumane and degrading but did not in fact constitute torture.

However the behavior was officially defined, the people of Northern Ireland were outraged. England again turned to the British Army, but this only caused greater problems.[30] On January 30, 1972, the infamous day now known as "Bloody Sunday," British soldiers shot thirteen unarmed Catholic men and youth, who were illegally protesting internment without trial on the streets of Londonderry. The resulting British investigation found that the soldiers had fired only after first being fired on, and that they were not guilty of any wrongdoing – even though there was no evidence that the dead had been holding or firing weapons. The Londonderry coroner refuted the report's findings and accused the British soldiers of "sheer unadulterated murder."[31]

Violence bred more violence, including the burning of the British embassy in Dublin, an Official IRA bombing that killed three civilians, and an assassination attempt on a Northern Ireland government minister. In response, British Prime Minister Edward Heath imposed a system of "direct rule" from Westminster, stripping the parliament of Northern Ireland of its power. The British government articulated its two aims: first, to maintain security in Northern Ireland, and, second, to ameliorate the existing social and economic discrimination that Catholic citizens were experiencing.

Although Westminster intended the arrangement to be an effective but temporary response, the violence persisted, reaching a tragic peak on "Bloody Friday" (July 21, 1972) – a day that the Provisional IRA exploded nineteen bombs, killing nine and wounding 130 people. In all, direct rule would last for more than twenty-five years, until the signing of the Good Friday Agreement.[32]

The Efforts of Reid and Magee

From the time of the Troubles to the Good Friday Agreement, the history of Northern Ireland is inextricably linked to the lives of Father Alex Reid and the Rev. Dr. Roy Magee. Their experiences show how religiously motivated individuals, working on the ground and ready to put themselves at risk, can help people move beyond conflict toward peace. In fact, because their lives and work provide such a clear example of Track Two diplomacy, it is especially useful to tell their stories in the context of the seemingly intractable conflict they each strived so hard to resolve.

The Reverend Dr. Roy Magee: Mediating for Lives and Souls

Born into a Presbyterian family, Magee grew up in the Shankill Road area of working-class Protestants, right alongside Belfast's largest Catholic enclave. His father was a proud man, who worked as a fitter in a actory on Falls Road and "was saving for a rainy day, which, thankfully, in his time, didn't come about."[33] As a child, Magee knew those who lived nearby, and many of his closest friends were Catholic. Although religion was not

then central to his family life, Magee's parents, as people deeply respectful of the Lord, made sure to send him to Sunday school. Although he
became tied to his Protestant heritage, it was only as a young teenager
that religion took on a more central role in his life. He recalls:

> I had a very personal experience. I was a young man who was involved in
> soccer and sport. I was looking after my body and it occurred to me that
> here I was in possession of something that was very precious and it was
> inside a "box" . . . a worthless "box," and I was looking after the "box" and
> neglecting the precious part – the spiritual end of my life. I began to think
> about a more spiritual dimension and I came to a very personal faith in
> Christ.[34]

Soon after, Magee became an Evangelical Christian by conviction and
was accepted into the Presbyterian Ministry. By the time the Troubles
first gathered momentum in the early 1970s, the Rev. Magee was serving
as a young pastor of the working-class Sinclair Seaman Presbyterian
Church in the midst of neighboring Catholic and Protestant areas north
of Belfast city center.

It was from this vantage point that the Rev. Magee watched: as paramilitary groups on both sides turned to violence; as "vigilantes" roamed the
streets to protect their homes; and as the people all around him became
engulfed by fear. Noting that the combination of walking sticks ("there's
nothing more lethal!" Magee notes) and assembled crowds was likely
to produce riots, Magee became proactive. In an effort to limit deadly
violence, he approached the men in his community who were out each
night prepared to ward off threats. The Rev. Magee talked them into staying home by promising to personally walk those streets every night and
assure their protection.[35]

Looking back, Magee ignores the magnitude of his undertaking, min-
imizing his role with self-deprecating humor: "Now what I could have
done if the area had been attacked was probably run faster than any of
them at that time, but beyond that I couldn't have done anything."[36] More
reflectively, Magee also notes that this was a time in which key relationships began. "In a strange way, I look back and think that God was forging
relationships that He could use."[37] Magee earned the trust of the men,
some of whom were then becoming active in the paramilitary, and others
of whom would ultimately emerge as its leaders. "I don't think they saw
me as a minister of religion *per se*," Magee explains, "but . . . as someone
whom they could . . . depend on, rely on thoroughly."[38] The experience
and associations paved the way for Magee to later become an effective
peacemaker.

Many of the Rev. Magee's important relationships began when he aligned with the unionists and joined the new Vanguard movement, led by the strong Protestant leader, William Craig, previously Northern Ireland's Minister of Home Affairs. Craig's movement considered seeking an independent state of Northern Ireland, to be ruled by its Protestant majority. After witnessing what Magee describes as "the awful atrocities being perpetrated by the IRA," he saw Vanguard as a potential answer and a vehicle for speaking in a "united Unionist voice."[39]

Craig moved into the spotlight shortly after Bloody Sunday. Refuting the idea – at least officially – that all Roman Catholic citizens should be viewed as the enemy, his rhetoric was nonetheless inflammatory. Craig demanded revenge and called for all "terrorists" to be identified and punished. In one of his most memorable – and controversial – statements, Craig declared, "We must build up dossiers on those men and women who are a menace to this country, because, if and when the politicians fail us, it may be our job to liquidate the enemy."[40]

Responding to British Prime Minister Edward Heath's decision to dissolve the parliament of Northern Ireland and impose direct rule in 1972, Craig led a two-day strike against the British policy. Although the strike stirred the local populace, Craig appeared to have a change of heart after the two days. Instead of urging the assembled thousands to continue protesting, he called for an orderly end to the strike. Shortly thereafter, he turned Vanguard into a political party, but within six years it had disappeared altogether. In the meantime, Magee resigned from Vanguard, disappointed because his goal of a united unionist voice clearly was "not imminent."[41]

The Vanguard Movement, in its early and more aggressive phase, was widely opposed. Nationalists viewed it as a group of vigilantes eager to inflict violence, whereas some unionists rejected it as simply too extreme. It is therefore not surprising that Magee's association with the movement made him a figure of suspicion in some circles.

He was well received elsewhere. His image as a strong defender of Ulster Unionism generated what he describes as "loose" friendships with many of the people who would later become leaders of the unionist movement.[42] Among them was David Trimble, who, after serving in the Ulster Unionist Party (UUP) and working on the 1998 Good Friday Agreement, became the First Minister of Northern Ireland. Another was Reg Empey, also a member of the UUP, twice mayor of Belfast, then Minister of Enterprise for Northern Ireland, and later another participant in the Good Friday negotiations. And there was also the Rev. Robert Bradford, who served in Westminster beginning in 1974 but was assassinated by the Provisional IRA just a few years later, an event that was devastating for Magee.[43]

Unlike these and other individuals, the Rev. Magee never pursued an active career in politics. Instead, he remained committed to the ministry, and all his associations with politics were in this capacity. Loyal to his calling and his parishioners, Magee nonetheless ultimately left the Sinclair Seaman parish to become pastor of a church in Dundonald, a predominantly Protestant town on the outskirts of East Belfast, where he was known for his "fire and brimstone" sermons.[44] In many ways, the parishioners there were similar to those of Sinclair Seaman, with many working-class families who lived in public housing.

But Dundonald was also home to the two largest loyalist paramilitaries in Northern Ireland, the Ulster Defense Association (UDA; also known as the Ulster Freedom Fighters), and the Ulster Volunteer Force (UVF). The UDA leader, Andy Tyrie, attended the Rev. Magee's church and used the opportunity to ask the young Reverend to talk with his men. Magee agreed, and thus began his early work with members of the loyalist paramilitary movement. Magee spent his time with Tyrie's men speaking about spiritual matters. When he later reflected on these sessions, however, it was not the spiritual content that seemed core to the experience. Rather, for Magee, the most important result from these meetings were the relationships he formed – once again, relationships that would later prove invaluable. As he notes, "I believe you've got to gain the right to tell people that they're wrong."[45]

Father Alex Reid: The Heart of the Peace Process

Like his counterpart the Rev. Magee, Father Reid was clear about his future vocation quite early in life. After completing his primary and secondary schooling in County Tipperary in 1949, he joined the Most Holy Redeemer, a Roman Catholic order known popularly as the Redemptorists, which ministered to the poor and downtrodden. Only a year later, he took his vows of Religious Life, and after becoming ordained, was appointed to the Redemptorist Clonard Monastery in Belfast, located along the "peace line." Since 1962, this has been where Reid lives and works. Again like the Rev. Magee, Father Reid became active during the Troubles, which broke out just behind the monastery. And around the same time that Magee began his first conversations with the paramilitaries in Dundonald, Father Reid entered the fragmented world of nationalist politics, a world in which he remained integrally and often secretly involved for over twenty years.

When a dispute in 1975 between the Official IRA and the Provisional IRA turned violent – ultimately leaving six dead – Father Reid reached out to "get the situation off the streets and around the conference table."[46] Successful, he was able to mediate an end to the violence. This was not to be the last time he would do so. Two years later, this time at the behest of Sinn Féin's President Gerry Adams, Father Reid again intervened when the Official IRA accused the Provisional IRA of bombing its Easter parade (it later turned out that loyalists were responsible for the attack).[47] Although his immediate goal was to mitigate the violence, these occasions ultimately served a greater purpose. Like the Rev. Magee, Father Reid was developing important relationships. Gerry Adams fondly recalls their relationship and how Father Reid came to be known simply and endearingly as "the Sagart," an Irish world for Priest.[48] It was during these days that the foundation for Reid's future work was laid.

Working with paramilitary groups was risky enough, but it was only one of the ways in which Father Reid sought to minimize violence during the Troubles. He also worked with prisoners of the Westminster government. In 1976, the political prisoner status of the republican prisoners was changed so that they no longer had rights similar to prisoners of war (i.e., that they did not have to wear prison uniforms or do prison work, and were allowed extra visits). The prisoners' responded by going on strike. But by 1980, their tactics took a deadly turn. Instead of wearing blankets in lieu of prison garb or refusing showers (the strategies of their earlier strikes), this time, they determined to conduct a hunger strike.

The first hunger strike began October 27, 1980, in Maze Prison. Brendan Hughes, leader of the Maze Prison's branch of the IRA, was the first to strike, and others followed at staggered intervals. Recognizing that he would soon be too weak to lead, Hughes turned to Bobby Sands to take over the leadership of the Maze Prison IRA.

Father Reid was distraught that the strike and the conditions in the prison put human life at risk. Desperately seeking a solution, he met with the strikers and tried to convince them to call off the strike – but to no avail. Determined, he sought allies and turned to Cardinal O' Fiaich, an Irish Cardinal and Roman Catholic Archbishop of Armagh, who was popular among the Catholic community. Reid updated him on the deadly consequences at stake and encouraged him to get involved. After a visit to the prisons, Cardinal O'Fiaich was dismayed: "One could hardly allow an animal to remain in such conditions, let alone a human being ... The problems of these prisoners is one of the great obstacles to peace in our community ... it is only sowing the seeds of future conflict." At Father Reid's urging, Cardinal O'Fiaich agreed to speak with both Sinn Féin and the British government in an attempt to bring a mediated end to the strike.[49]

In the meantime, however, the day in and day out work of warding off death and violence, as well as his work amid the paramilitaries, the strikers, and the people in his congregation, took a toll on Father Reid. He became physically and emotionally exhausted. Then, one day, while waiting for the minibus to take him away from the prison, he began to feel worse. Shortly thereafter, he collapsed and was rushed to the hospital, where he nearly died. Father Reid's recovery was slow. Unable to continue with his work, he went to Rome and spent months convalescing.

It was while he was not active that Father Reid learned that his efforts in the prison had not been in vain. The British government had announced concessions, and Cardinal O' Fiaich had directly appealed to the striking prisoners. The strikers called off the hunger strike, but the British government did not honor its promises. Bobby Sands therefore called a second hunger strike in early 1981, again implemented at staggered intervals to maximize publicity. Convinced that someone would have to die before the prisoners' demands would be met, Sands actually started his own hunger strike two weeks before the other prisoners, effectively positioning himself to become a martyr.

The striking prisoners evoked sympathy from the nationalist community, and the political party Sinn Féin rode a wave of popular support into elections. Large blocks of voters from Belfast's Catholic working-class communities turned out. Bobby Sands, then a local hero, received a majority of the vote for a seat in Parliament, but died weeks later on the sixty-sixth day of his strike. Estimates vary, but between seventy-five and one hundred thousand people followed his funeral procession.[50]

Notwithstanding Sinn Féin's rising popularity and the growing sympathy for the IRA strikers, British Prime Minister Margaret Thatcher refused to back down. Only after nine other prisoners died from starvation, and the families of the remaining strikers made it clear that they were ready to seek medical intervention to prevent more deaths, was the standoff resolved. On October 3, 1981, the prisoners ended the strike, and shortly thereafter, Prime Minister Thatcher made concessions to their demands.

As all this evolved, Father Reid was recovering from the exhaustion and the deep-seated distress he had felt as he faced the strikers. He felt personally close with many of the prisoners and their families, and his intense involvement had left its mark. Father Reid was now – more than ever – convinced that the Church had to use its influence to prevent further suffering. He therefore pressed his superiors until they allowed him to return to work.[51] Looking back, some report that the peace process among the nationalists quietly started at this time, thanks to Father Reid's subtle efforts.[52]

Soon after returning to the monastery, a series of killings pushed Father Reid back into action. When the IRA captured a unionist sergeant, a unionist gang, known as the "Shankill Butchers," retaliated by kidnapping a Catholic man in Belfast. Father Reid immediately reached out to a republican leader whom he first met almost a decade earlier. Together, they traveled to the site where the unionist sergeant was being held hostage to try to stop the killing, but they were too late. The soldier had died, and the Shankill Butchers had in the meantime brutally killed the captured Catholic man. Father Reid was pained. As he explained a few years later: "My only aim is to help those who, if the present situation continues, will be killed, injured or imprisoned over the next few weeks and months and whose personal tragedies will blight, not only their own lives, but also the lives of those to whom they are near and dear."[53]

The daily tragedy of death and loss only strengthened his resolve, and Father Reid focused on forging communications among nationalist leaders, who historically held very different ideas on how to reach a nationalist solution. It was at this very early stage of the conflict that Father Reid composed a paper outlining possible conditions that could lead to a cease-fire. He sent his paper to the IRA, and even consulted with a senior unionist lawyer, who, to Reid's surprise, responded positively. However, he found that although the nationalist leaders were responsive, not all were ready to join forces and collaborate. Instead, they were focused on the outcome of concurrent Anglo-Irish negotiations.[54]

The Anglo-Irish Agreement of 1985 and Reactions to It

At the same time that the Hunger Strikes dominated the news, Prime Minister Margaret Thatcher and Taoiseach* of Ireland Charles Haughey appointed a commission to study and report on the status and future relationship of the United Kingdom, the Republic of Ireland, and Northern Ireland. The findings indirectly led to the new Anglo-Irish Agreement, which for the first time in Britain's history recognized the legitimacy of

---

* Taoiseach is the Gaelic word for prime minister.

an Irish interest in Northern Ireland (but, as Haughey unhappily pointed out, also confirmed the legitimacy of Britain's presence there). Signed in 1985, both Britain and Ireland agreed that the status of Northern Ireland could change, but only if a majority of its citizens favored that outcome.[55]

The agreement sparked outrage in the loyalist community. Feeling betrayed, a crowd of loyalists physically attacked Tom King, Northern Ireland's Secretary of State (the British cabinet minister responsible for Northern Ireland), during a visit to Belfast shortly after the signing. A few days later, one hundred thousand publicly demonstrated their anger at Belfast's City Hall. Two thousand shipyard workers staged a protest march, and all fifteen loyalist members of the Westminster Parliament resigned. Over the next two years, continuing riots, protests, and marches opposing the agreement created a political stalemate – ultimately causing the dissolution of the Northern Ireland Assembly.

The growing violence not only made Magee uneasy but demonstrated for him the conflict's tragic consequences on a very personal level:

> As well as having to conduct the funerals of innocent people, one of my closest friends was murdered in cold blood by the Republican movement. This brought me to the place where I realized that REVENGE is not the solution and in order to try to establish a better future for my Grandchildren, I should do all in my power to help end the bloodshed. I am not what might be defined as a pacifist; believing that in DEFENCE of my FAMILY, my FATHERLAND or my FAITH, as a very last resort and only then, I may be compelled to take up arms.[56]

Even though he was no longer active in Vanguard or its unionist politics, Magee understood how someone could be moved to violence and decided to turn to his former contacts with this insight, coupled with his passion for the Judeo-Christian commandment not to kill.[57] Picking up the phone after one terrible atrocity, he called a man whom he knew was involved with the Ulster Defence Association (UDA). The Rev. Magee explains:

> I didn't realize at the time that he was the top military man, but I soon found out. And I said, "I need to talk to you." I met with him, and his response was, when I told him they were breaking the law of God, as well as the law of man, and that one day they would be held accountable for that, his response was: "Well, you had better speak to the military people about this."[58]

Magee understood what this paramilitary leader was saying. He did not want to repeat Magee's message to his men for fear that he would be viewed as a traitor to the military command structure. Instead, he had made an opening, and Magee stepped up to the challenge.

> So I appeared to the inner council and I said to them, "You may escape the court of the land but you will not escape the judgment of God." After this long silence, they said, to my surprise, "You know, you're right – will you come and talk to us?"[59]

One meeting followed another, and the Rev. Magee kept returning to themes about core religious beliefs, the members' religious traditions, their sense of honor, and the legacy they hoped to leave their children. Magee recognized that religious leaders can be effective "not only [through] their message from their particular pulpits...but [through] their lifestyle and their contact with the people that they are set up to pastor. They should be creating a climate whereby things are done without violence."[60] After every atrocity, he reached for the phone and repeated his message, challenging those he viewed as part of his parish to live in accordance with the laws of God and to break the cycle of violence.

Although Magee viewed his involvement as an extension of his pastoral duties, his Church did not agree. As Magee explains, the church did not "want to get its hands soiled [by] being in contact with people who were committing murder and bombing and creating terrible mayhem within the province."[61] In fact, many of his fellow Protestant clergy considered communication with organizations and groups responsible for violence to be a conflict of interest. Speaking of his own involvement in such controversial, behind-the-scenes negotiating, Magee says:

> Because those with whom I was dealing had so blatantly broken both the law of man and God, many misunderstood and some misrepresented what I was trying to do. Many argued that by my contact with such people I was merely justifying the crimes they were committing. This meant that many of my colleagues isolated me. On two particular occasions, I approached colleagues to come alongside but they refused. What I was doing only became acceptable and respectable when the Cease Fire was announced.[62]

These were hard times for the Rev. Magee. "I felt very isolated," he explains. "I couldn't talk to anyone...It was a price I had to pay."[63]

From the opposite perspective, many who supported the violence saw Magee's peacemaking efforts as putting into question his true commitment to unionism and Protestant Christianity. In their eyes, the government did not protect working-class Protestants, and the paramilitaries were the only true defenders of the downtrodden Protestant. Still, shortly after he began his efforts to convince the paramilitaries to stop the violence, the BBC conducted a poll to see how the community felt about their minister "talking to terrorists." Magee was surprised – and encouraged – when 100 percent of the people interviewed supported him.[64]

Father Reid found more support in this lonely work than the Rev. Magee but not *per se* from the Catholic Church, whose distant disapproval of the paramilitaries actually created tensions between the people and the church. During these years, many republicans became alienated from their church, angered at its condemnation of the IRA and what they saw as a failure to equally denounce British violence.[65] Father Reid notes that the official church failed to reach the republican paramilitaries with a clear message, "this is *why* you're wrong."[66] The church voiced its contempt, but never offered a solution.

But notwithstanding its official position, church leaders who officially condemned involvement in "this kind of behavior" gave Reid the space to do his work. One such leader actually told him, "If you come up to me, I am going to say to you, this is the official position. Don't come up to me . . . if you think you can do something to help, go and do it. But don't be coming to me about it, it's up to yourself." As Father Reid wryly noted, "sometimes the official church doesn't wish to know."[67]

But the monastery did. In fact, along with some of his fellow priests, Reid created a ministry within the Redemptorist Order specifically for peacemaking and thereby took action with his community but outside of official church policy. The ministry was not to have a political role, except in ensuring that "God-like compassion for people [was] the first principle of all human relationships, including those of politics."[68] As a result, political and paramilitary leaders report that Father Reid and the Redemptorist Order provided a crucial, neutral environment for many private meetings.[69] Reflectively, Reid talks about his fellow priests in the monastery: "We have our own peers, we have our own structure. We decide our own policy. So anything I did would have the full support of . . . my order . . . I am actually doing it in their name. Which means that I am . . . a representative in a sense."[70]

Father Reid's approach differed from the greater Catholic Church. He did not just preach and talk about why violence is wrong. Rather, he got into the trenches, actually trying to stop killings and human suffering. He contemplates, "I often thought to myself that if Jesus Christ came himself, the first place he would have gone to would be the Troubles."[71] And, thankfully, within his Redemptorist Order, Father Reid had the independence to follow this example.

As Magee was working to redirect loyalists toward peace, Father Reid was toiling undercover with the republican movement. But by 1986, he decided to try a new tactic and wrote a fifteen-page letter to Charles Haughey, Fianna Fail* leader and past Taoiseach, and John Hume, the leader of the more moderately nationalist Social Democratic and Labour Party (SDLP). "I decided this was the last throw of the dice," recalls Reid, "that I would put it all on paper so that the opportunity that was there to end the armed struggle would be known . . . "[72] In his letter, Reid began by emphasizing his own pastoral and moral duty to work toward peace. He then proposed that a partnership among the nationalist parties in Northern Ireland and in the Republic of Ireland be created as a necessary step to resolving the Troubles.

Father Reid's letter served as a catalyst for change. He was able to meet with Haughey, who listened as Reid described how face-to-face meetings could ultimately result in an IRA cease-fire. As Reid saw it, such meetings would demonstrate to the republican leadership in the north that they were not alone and that, if they made a commitment to nonviolence, they would become part of a larger constitutional and nationalist family working together to unite Ireland. Reid urged Haughey to meet Sinn Féin's Gerry Adams. Although Haughey refused so long as republican-led violence continued, he nonetheless proved helpful.

Haughey introduced Reid to Fianna Fail's Head of Research, Dr. Martin Mansergh. As Reid later recalled: "What does the Bible say, 'There was a man sent by God'; I thought 'Cometh the hour, cometh the man.' Martin was the ideal person for conducting a debate with the Republican Movement. . . . "[73] Reid became the link between Mansergh and Adams, a connection that would require nurturing but would ultimately prove crucial in the heated negotiations of the coming years.

In the meantime, Father Reid also succeeded in getting SDLP's nationalist leader John Hume – who had responded immediately to Father Reid's original letter – to confidentially meet with Adams, beginning what was to become a lengthy dialogue. This was a significant departure from the historically troubled relationship between Sinn Féin and the more moderate SDLP, who maintained that Sinn Féin was the political arm of the IRA and therefore officially refused to engage with them. The link that Reid forged between Hume (who had relationships with the Republic of Ireland's government) and Adams (who could brief the IRA leadership) was thus a new line of communication within the nationalist movement.

* Although Fianna Fail is not a party in Northern Ireland, it is the party with the most representation in the Republic of Ireland. "Soldiers of destiny" in Gaelic, Fianna Fail was founded in 1926 as an opposition group to the Anglo-Irish Treaty of 1922.

In the meantime, Father Reid strategically maintained his own connections with the Irish government, republican political parties, and the
IRA by informing them at opportune moments of the evolving nationalist strategy.[74] The meetings between Hume and Adams continued and,
by the end of 1987, were public knowledge.[75] Years later, journalist John
Mullins would describe Reid's success in connecting Adams and Hume
as "arguably the single most important step towards the Good Friday
Agreement."[76]

But during these early talks, the violence continued. In November 1987,
the world was again rocked when an IRA bomb exploded during a service
on Remembrance Day (the day the United Kingdom remembers its fallen
soldiers), killing eleven and injuring sixty-three.[77] Outraged, Father Reid
again turned his keen intellect to the written word, this time producing
position papers that detailed realistic principles of self-determination
and consent as core steps to attaining a peaceful political solution. To
achieve this, Reid stressed that both nationalists and unionists would
need to dialogue, negotiate, and ultimately agree to be bound by the
results. Father Reid's papers were prophetic:

> It was a remarkably prescient document. . . . It anticipated the statement
> made by Peter Brooke, the UK Secretary of State, in November 1990 as well
> as the repeal of the Government of Ireland Act 1920 (which formed part
> of the Belfast [or Good Friday] Agreement) and the eventual multi-party
> talks process of 1996–1998 in its idea of a constitutional conference. There
> was not yet a clear recognition that in republican terms any settlement at
> this stage could only be an "interim" one. The unspoken premise of the
> entire paper was an understanding that an IRA ceasefire was necessary for
> all-party talks to take place.[78]

Father Reid was identifying workable solutions that others on the ground
were just beginning to understand, but had not yet begun to implement.

Just a few months after the IRA bombing, Charles Haughey finally –
albeit uneasily – approved a secret meeting between Fianna Fail representatives and Sinn Féin. With Father Reid as the intermediary, this first
face-to-face meeting took place in the Redemptorist monastery in
Dundalk. Father Reid introduced Mansergh and Adams, who were
sitting across from each other for the first time. He led them in a prayer,
as he explained, "to help you in your deliberations." And then he left the
room.[79]

Although progress in the peace process was not yet publicly apparent,
this first secret meeting, and a second that followed that year, mirrored
the initial steps laid out in Father Reid's position papers. As he explains:

"It was a big thing for Sinn Féin to say they had met representatives of Fianna Fail, in brackets the Irish Government. That created credibility with the military side of their movement, that they were actually being taken seriously and engaging at the highest level. . . . "[80] For perhaps the first time, common ground was being laid between this government party of the Republic of Ireland and the republican movement of the north.

In the meantime, with Reid again working as the conduit, Gerry Adams continued his discussions with SDLP's John Hume, eventually beginning formal party-to-party meetings. Like the meetings between Mansergh and Adams, Reid led the two republican parties in prayer asking for success in finding a common understanding.[81] The Reid, Hume, and Adams meetings led to a series of published papers, in which they shared with their constituents ideas on how the nationalists could work together peacefully, involve unionists, and come to a peaceful solution to the British presence. The discussions created a positive buzz among nationalists, who began to feel more confident that change was possible.[82]

Most of Father Reid's work went unseen. But in March 1988, for just a brief moment, a wider audience was able to witness him in action. During a week in which a series of revenge attacks culminated in the killing of two undercover British soldiers during the funeral of an IRA member, Father Reid was caught on camera kneeling and praying over the soldiers. His image of giving the British soldiers their last rites was published and broadcast worldwide.[83] For many, it became the image of the Troubles in Northern Ireland. Years later, Mary Holland, a reporter for the *Guardian*, described what she saw that day:

> The eyes of a dying soldier in West Belfast as Father Alex Reid said to me: *"This one is still breathing, do you know how to give the kiss of life?"*[84]

For just a moment, the public got a fleeting view of Father Reid's essential principle of peace, in which human dignity reigns regardless of what side of the battle one is on.

From Violence to Hope in the 1990s: Cease-Fires and the Good Friday Agreement

In unofficial and secretive settings during the early 1990s, Father Reid maintained constant contact with representatives from the government of Northern Ireland, Sinn Féin, the IRA, and the SDLP. Their leaders recall this as a time of some hope for the nationalists, when all of them came "tantalizingly close to reaching an understanding of the potential bases for a political settlement [to the conflict]."[85] In 1991, Reid drafted another proposal on a democratic strategy for justice, peace, and reconciliation. Gerry Adams recalls: "In essence, he was proposing a peace convention. John Hume and I incorporated his ideas into our ongoing discussion."[86] The meetings between Hume, Adams, and Reid continued to move forward. They produced new position papers on a nonviolent alternative, which were secretly presented at various points to the IRA and the Republic of Ireland's government. Now known as the Hume-Adams statements, the papers called for a joint declaration by the British and Irish governments.

Reid's proposals also informed the ongoing work of Martin Mansergh with Adams. Still working as the liaison between the two men, Reid would meet with each of them separately at Dublin coffee shops. After Albert Reynolds replaced Charles Haughey as Taoiseach in 1992, these negotiations became more serious, and Reid was increasingly seen frequenting Dublin's government buildings. As one Fianna Fail advisor observed, "There was the man Reynolds referred to only as 'the priest.' Slightly built, almost wraith-like, he would 'appear' and invariably make a bee-line for Mansergh's room."[87] After each of his meetings with either Mansergh or Adams, Reid would send to the other a typed summary of his discussion with his own commentary. Although this kept the conversation going, it was a slow-moving process, sometimes twelve weeks between exchanges. But, over time, these communiqués resulted in newer versions of a joint position paper.[88]

As progress continued, Mansergh and Adams met again in person at the Redemptorist monastery in Dundalk. But this time, Reid decided to remain in the room during their discussions. He realized that his presence eased tensions and reminded the two men of the reasons they were meeting: to convince the IRA to agree to a cease-fire and, eventually, to reach common ground with the British government. With Reid as the constant and trusted intermediary, the Mansergh-Adams joint declaration evolved, ultimately incorporating compromises from various perspectives, including from the British and Irish governments, republicans, and unionists.[89]

Simultaneously, Magee was immersed in dialogues in the loyalist camp. But as the situation on the ground evolved, he felt compelled to do more. When the large Protestant paramilitary group the Ulster Volunteer Force (UVF) began initiating violence against their Catholic neighbors (transitioning to "active rather than reactive" attacks), Magee felt compelled to turn to activist peacemaking.[90] Within two years, he was personally meeting with the UVF and again with the UDA, urging both to leave violence behind and agree to a cease-fire. Trusted because of his former ties, he was able to secure promises that both would reciprocate if the IRA announced a cease-fire. Magee decided to make these promises public in 1993 and 1994, despite the obvious risks.

Generally careful about working with the media, Magee found it to be a useful tool at this critical moment. He decided to be open with the paramilitaries and pragmatic with the media. Thus, Magee explicitly told his loyalist paramilitary contacts that he would not discuss details of their negotiations with the media, but that he would be forthcoming about his contact with them. For Magee, this meant that he was interpreting "the Loyalists' paramilitary mind for the people so that they would understand what was happening."[91] He did not see himself as a media spokesperson for the paramilitary organizations, though some insisted on doing so.

Magee strategically used the media to send signals. For example, he sometimes made statements just so that they would be reported and the opposition would know that their positions had been heard and understood. This in turn fostered a sense that there was an ongoing dialogue, even when the unionist parties were not directly negotiating. Speaking of this innovative approach to peacemaking, Magee describes his methods as practical, breaking lots of rules, and as tactics that worked. He says:

> [M]y method of conflict resolution would be totally scorned, I'm sure by the academic conflict analysts, because I used directive methods. My whole training is in directive counselling, not indirect. And it wasn't enough for me [to participate in a process and then have] people . . . come out of the process at the end of the day wanting to take more lives. . . .
>
> I tried to get the road blocks dealt with and demolished and kept on the path. Maybe you had to tour around it but come back onto the path to get to the place where the guns are silent, where the bomb making material is set aside. That's to me what the conflict resolution process was. Now okay, academics will criticize that. But it worked. It worked in the situation.[92]

Notwithstanding such hypothetical criticisms, Magee moved the peace process forward, helping to create a climate conducive to a cease-fire.

Other than Magee's strategic exchanges with the media, much of his work was outside the limelight. Quite isolated, he pushed forward despite frequent setbacks, more death, and, at times, despair. When an IRA bomb exploded in a store located along Shankill Road in October, 1993, the bomb missed its intended target – a UDA leadership meeting upstairs – but claimed nine civilians, including four women and two girls, aged seven and thirteen. Outrage was universal, and the loyalist community was especially incensed.

The Rev. Magee hurried over to Shankill Road to comfort the community. He expected to find rage and momentum for revenge. "I was there helping with the rubble, dealing with people whose loved ones were blown to smithereens,"[93] he recalls. But as he walked along Shankill Road, the reactions were not what he expected. He remembers:

> A couple of ladies of that area came to me and they said, "The killing has got to stop. There should be no retaliation for this." Now remember... all the people [were] Protestant people. [But they said,] "There's got to be no response of a negative nature to this bomb." [This is what you would expect people to] say to a minister. The difference was this. Standing beside me was the military commander.... [And] that was a turning point.[94]

The general populace, and even members of paramilitary organizations, were tired. There had been too many random deaths. It appeared that some were beginning to believe that a diplomatic resolution to the conflict might be possible, or at least that somehow it was necessary if the violence was ever going to be stopped.

Moved, Magee went to the paramilitaries as a voice of the people and conveyed their demand that the killing stop. Perhaps the tragedy had also transformed his listeners. In any event, Magee found a new responsiveness within loyalist leadership to his argument that violence would not result in success, either for them or their opponents: neither a unified, independent Ireland nor a strengthened union with the United Kingdom could be achieved by more bloodshed.

Unfortunately, just when it seemed that diplomatic progress was possible, a unit of the Ulster Defence Association near Londonderry retaliated. Seven civilians in a public house were shot and killed. A new cycle of violence had begun. Disgusted and despairing, Magee moved to sever his contact with the loyalist paramilitaries. But many of their leaders were disillusioned with the paramilitary tit-for-tat and were ready to hear Magee's message. They pursued him, imploring him to reopen discussions among the loyalist opposition groups.

Magee agreed – with conditions. If he was going to work with the paramilitaries, he wanted a firm commitment. He therefore demanded that all their future agreements be in writing. If the paramilitaries wanted Magee, he insisted that they set forth their desire for peace unequivocally and publicly commit to participating in a dialogue.

It was around this time that the Downing Street Declaration was adopted, and it proved a perfect vehicle for Magee to push the loyalists for a commitment. Officially known as The Joint Declaration for Peace, the document was issued on December 15, 1993, after a series of meetings and phone calls between U.K. Prime Minister John Major and Taoiseach Albert Reynolds, in which they urgently sought a joint solution. Their efforts were informed by the complicated web of both secret and official meetings among parties on both sides during the preceding years. Magee's efforts had readied the loyalists. And Reid's groundwork with the Adams-Mansergh and Hume-Adams dialogues – and the joint position papers from these extensive discussions – informed the Declaration.[95] Unrecognized at the time, Father Reid's earlier position papers were also a crucial predecessor to the Declaration, as essential components of his strategy were incorporated into the document.[96]

The Downing Street Declaration affirmed the right of the people of Northern Ireland to self-determination: Northern Ireland would be transferred to the Republic of Ireland if the majority of the island's population favored this move; and parties associated with paramilitaries could play a role with the governments in seeking a peaceful solution, if they renounced violence. The Declaration was designed to stimulate a diplomatic political dialogue, but ultimately required significant compromise by both republicans and unionists. The following year saw extensive discussion within parties on all sides of the conflict. They debated how to respond. And they demanded clarifications. Magee facilitated a conversation on the Declaration among the loyalist groups and the men and women on the ground. He recalls:

> I arranged a conference for Loyalist organizations to discuss the Downing Street Declaration. We invited all Unionist parties to attend to speak for or against [it.] The Democratic Unionists (DUP) refused to send a delegate, complaining that the groups were too undisciplined. The top brass of the military wings did attend, however. After hearing the pro-Declaration Unionists, they issued a new statement saying that they weren't disturbed, although they weren't yet convinced.[97]

It became clear that though the loyalist paramilitary groups still viewed the Declaration with some scepticism, they were not rejecting its goal of ending the violence.

Meanwhile, Father Reid was "constantly on the road between Belfast and Dublin,"[98] conducting parallel conversations with Mansergh, the SDLP, Sinn Féin, and the nationalist paramilitaries. He was similarly seeking clarifications and keeping lines of communication continuously open as the various parties debated the Declaration. Referring to Father Reid as "the heart of the peace process," Adams noted that "his determination and commitment to dialogue, to inclusiveness and to never giving up, even in the worst of times, is an example of courage and integrity to all."[99]

The on-the-ground efforts of Father Reid and the Rev. Magee may appear easier in hindsight than they were at the time. There was great mistrust within the two communities, and deep-seated fears about communicating with their deadly enemies. Magee reflects:

> When you have trust you don't have fear. I remember when any [Irish] government official came up from Dublin, I always informed the [Unionist] organizations. I remember at one stage that they told me not to make contact with the Irish [government's representative]. But I just said to them, "I feel that this guy is really genuine and I must go." I was given this police escort, because they feared what would happen ....
>
> [O]ver time, there was a building up of relationships. They [the paramilitary Loyalists] [eventually] appointed the top two military commanders to come with me to seek answers to questions.[100]

Father Reid also talks about how he built relationships with individuals in the paramilitaries. The key was that he saw them as regular people and got involved with their lives, and with their battles. But perhaps more important, he recognized that they had multiple identities. They might be associated with violence as members of the IRA, but they were also parents, sons, brothers, wage earners, and members of the church. By seeing them as complex individuals and talking about the things that were important to them in their different roles, Father Reid established mutual trust and respect. Reflecting on these personal relationships, Reid says:

> You knock at the first door [in the local neighbourhood] ... walk down that street there ... they're the neighbor's children, you know? The boy next door, the girl next door. Which makes you wonder, why did they get involved?
>
> If there is a riot going on, especially if you are a priest, and you are looking out the window ... well the natural thing to do is go down and brawl in the street, and see what is going on here, who started this fight and this kind of thing ... That is an example of actually finding out what is going on ... the fact that you were interested enough to go down and get into the moment, and get into the midst of it, and listen to them and talk to them, that gains respect. ... And when you gain their respect, then you become a kind of almost part of their crowd ... you become one of them, in a sense.
>
> The interesting thing was that when you started to talk to them, you found that the people who were most interested in stopping the violence were the people who used the violence. I would say, "you are caught, you are going to get ten or fifteen or twenty years in jail. You were married last year, you have a young baby ... your wife." ... So who wants war, who

wants to live this kind of life? And so in a way, the people who most want to stop the violence are the people who are engaging in it . . .[101]

With military commanders on both sides ready, Magee and Reid crossed paths. It was at a meeting, in which Magee served as the channel of communication between the Republic of Ireland and the loyalists, and Father Reid represented the republicans. This led to other meetings, where the Rev. Magee moderated between the Republic of Ireland and the military leadership of the loyalist paramilitaries, the UDA and UVF. Gradually, a web of communications emerged.

These were tense times and both men sought to bring their communities to the table and to a cease-fire. As he had always done before, Father Reid relied on the presence of the Holy Spirit for support. But he also used the Holy Spirit as a metaphor in his conversations with Gerry Adams of Sinn Féin. As Adams explains, when he and the "Sagart" (as he called Father Reid) wanted to talk but were concerned that their phone lines were tapped, they used the Holy Spirit – as envisioned on the football field no less – as their code. Adams recalls how the Holy Spirit's "position on the field indicated the state of play. So if he was in backs, we were on the defensive. Forwards, we were on the attack . . . Once I told the Sagart the Holy Spirit had transferred to the other team. Another time he, or she as the Sagart reminded me, was injured. . . . These conversations invariably occurred at points of great tension after crisis meetings."[102]

By August 1994, the IRA declared a cease-fire. Father Reid's years of determined work – bringing together and encouraging the key players to stay committed when hope seemed futile – had brought the peace process to this moment. As he was never interested in fame, Father Reid's role did not receive much public attention, but those involved in the process knew just how crucial he had been. Speaking to the BBC, Gerry Adams said: "we would not have even the possibility of a peace process if it wasn't for the unstinting, patient, diligent work of a third party [Father Reid]. There is no doubt that he was the constant . . . in the development of relationships between the key players. He was the key to it and he brought a very special quality to it."[103]

When the IRA called the cease-fire, the heavily Catholic Falls Road filled with songs of celebration and jubilee. The Rev. Roy Magee seized the moment. The Former Taoiseach Albert Reynolds, knowing the power of Magee's influence on the loyalist paramilitaries, had actually told Magee about the IRA cease-fire forty-eight hours before it was announced.[104] Holding them to their word, Magee worked to secure a responding cease-fire by the loyalist UVF. He relayed to them Reynolds's reassurance that the principle of consent had been secured, which was as crucial to unionists as the principle of self-determination was for the nationalists. Calming loyalist fears and urging the paramilitaries to publicly accept the republican cease-fire, Magee stimulated a local conversation, which was soon reflected in the local graffiti on the walls of Shankill's Protestant community.

Meanwhile, paramilitary organizations continued settling old scores. Indeed, before the IRA cease-fire had been announced, Trevor King, a top Protestant UVF leader, was killed by nationalists, predictably causing anguish among the loyalists. Despite Magee's efforts, the UVF retaliated with a rain of gunfire in a local pub during a World Cup football match.

The loyalists did not immediately announce a reciprocal cease-fire, wanting to be sure that the IRA cease-fire was permanent and that their constitutional position within the United Kingdom remained secure. Before publicly agreeing to a cease-fire, they first wanted to speak with their prisoners. Magee quickly secured key meetings with influential loyalists being held at the Maze prison. Afterward, the prisoners sent a message to the Protestant UDA leadership, stating that a continuation of the military campaign would be "counterproductive" and a cease-fire would be "seen by our long-suffering community as a contributing factor in establishing a lasting peace."[105]

Six weeks after the IRA cease-fire – weeks full of widespread unionist scepticism and nonstop work by Magee – the Combined Loyalist Military Command (a cooperative organization built from a collaboration of the UDA and the UVF) acted. Calling for a complete loyalist cease-fire, they declared, "The Union is safe," and asked forgiveness from the relatives of "innocent victims." Unfortunately, this was not to be the end of paramilitary violence. Almost eighteen months later in February 1996, the IRA called off the cease-fire, declaring that there had been no breakthroughs in the negotiations.

Nevertheless, the year-and-a-half reprieve from violence had allowed for inroads. It helped to restore some loyalist-republican relationships, paving the road for another cease-fire the next year and, thereafter, the 1998 Good Friday Agreement – arguably the most significant step toward establishing peace in Northern Ireland.

The Good Friday Agreement was based on the principle that the citizens of Northern Ireland should determine their constitutional future. The Agreement thus established Northern Ireland's government and simultaneously upheld both the principle integral to the loyalist cause – that the people of Northern Ireland must give their consent to a change in the status of Northern Ireland – and the nationalist principle of self-determination. Signed on April 10, 1998, the Agreement was endorsed in separate referenda by voters of Northern Ireland and the Republic of Ireland in May of the same year.[106] After hundreds of years of violence between Catholics and Protestants, the nationalist and unionist parties of Northern Ireland (with the exception of the Democratic Unionist Party) declared support for the agreement:

> The Tragedies of the past have left a deep and profoundly regrettable legacy of suffering. We must never forget those who have died or been injured, and their families. But we can best honor them through a fresh start....
>
> We reaffirm our total and absolute commitment to exclusively democratic and peaceful means of resolving differences on political issues, and our opposition to any use or threat of force by others for any political purpose, whether in regard to this agreement or otherwise.[107]

For their respective roles in securing the original cease-fires, Reid and Magee later became corecipients of the Tipperary International Peace Prize, whose honorees over the years have included Nelson Mandela, Mikhail Gorbachev, William J. Clinton, and Bob Geldof. The Good Friday Agreement contemplated that all of the paramilitaries would disarm within two years. But there were dissenters within the parties and intrafaction tensions eventually turned violent, as those opposed to disarmament formed splinter groups.

In August 1998, the dissident republican paramilitary called the Real IRA – which had opposed peace talks and the 1997 cease-fire, and therefore had split from the IRA – bombed Omagh, a largely Protestant town in southwest Northern Ireland. Father Reid's efforts to stop the bombing had failed, and twenty-nine people, including nine children and one pregnant woman, died.[108] Father Reid showed resilience as he pressed on. He continued meeting with the paramilitaries even though he was briefly questioned (but ultimately highly praised) by the authorities about his connection to the violent perpetrators. Shortly after Omagh, thanks to Father Reid's dedication to the continuing dialogue, the Real IRA joined in the cease-fire.

Loyalist infighting was also intense. In the midst of murders and accusations being hurled between March 1999 and June 2000, Magee offered to mediate among the groups with strong bases in or near Dundonald. Assessing the tense situation, the BBC commented:

> [I]t is unclear, with deep divisions between the member of the [Combined Loyalist Military Command] and the political parties they are linked to,

whether even Roy Magee, with nearly 30 years of experience talking to the Loyalist paramilitaries, would be an acceptable go-between.[109]

But life was changing in Northern Ireland. Notably, throughout the 1990s, and particularly following the signing of the Good Friday Agreement in 1998, Northern Ireland's economy began to rebound from a three-decade long slump. Unemployment and poverty rates dropped, and Catholics made significant gains that narrowed their economic gap with the Protestants. The number of Catholics (historically about one-third of the population of Northern Ireland) swelled to 40 percent during the 1990s, with the majority of the balance identifying with various Protestant faiths.[110] In practice, therefore, both economically and demographically, Catholics and Protestants came closer to becoming equals than ever before in the history of Northern Ireland.

Hope after the Good Friday Agreement: The Slow Road to Peace

Today, these economic and demographic changes, combined with diplomatic breakthroughs – in particular the Good Friday Agreement – collectively foster a sense that long-standing peace may become a twenty-first-century reality in Northern Ireland. Yet a larger constituency and greater wealth for Catholics are not a guarantee that conflict is a thing of the past. As Father Reid and the Rev. Magee point out, both the conflict and the peace remain complicated.

The Rev. Magee maintains that various factors combine to cause and sustain the country's divisions. He elaborates:

> Culture, Ethnicity, Nationality, and Religion are all part of the mix which causes the division in Northern Ireland. Unfortunately, when these elements exist together people are prepared to take and lose lives. Religion is one of the components but not the only one. The problem is that the vast majority of Roman Catholics are Nationalists . . . while the vast majority of Protestants are Unionists. . . . This exacerbates the situation by adding a Political dimension to the problem.[111]

Religion may be only one aspect of the conflict, but it is often described as its major axis, with Protestants in one camp and Catholics in another. Most scholars agree, in fact, that religion and politics are inseparable in the Northern Ireland conflict. As resources and the population demographics become more evenly distributed, therefore, religious leaders are uniquely positioned to help establish peace, especially at the local level where residential segregation leaves many people reluctant to travel or work in areas predominately populated by the other community.

Father Alex Reid maintains that the republicans have strong religious and political beliefs, which are both separate and intertwined. He notes how they have handed down from generation to generation a belief in the right to determine their own fate and to take up arms with a fervor that is "like a religious faith."[112] One need only consider a centuries-old phrase to encapsulate Catholic republican attitudes: "We take our religion from Rome but our politics from home."[113] Yet, when Father Reid discusses the conflict, he focuses, not on religion or ethnicity or even politics but, rather, on inequities and human rights that stimulate conflict and are also capable of being identified and addressed. At the Tanenbaum Center's *Peacemakers in Action* Retreat in Amman, Jordan, Father Reid elaborated:

> People thought the IRA were romantic fanatics who were fighting for a united Ireland. While this was important, the whole reality of it was that the Nationalist community was an oppressed community. They believed they would never get justice under the British, so they wanted the British out. When they saw they could get justice and equality under the British, they supported the Good Friday Agreement.[114]

Although Father Reid does not deny that the nationalist community wanted a united Ireland, he believes that something much more funda-mental drove the nationalist effort: they longed for respect and dignity. Father Reid's decades-long dedication to bringing peace to his commu-nity gave him the opportunity to know, work with, and understand the people he served. Thus, he saw that for nationalists, it was oppression and the lack of power and self-determination in their own land that fed the call for violence in the name of religion. As Reid came to understand, the underlying issue was not religion itself, but feelings of anger and frustration that could be addressed through dialogue.

Reflections on Religiously Motivated Peacemaking

Both the Rev. Roy Magee and Father Alex Reid are men of religion driven by their faith to work with the most violent of individuals to bring peace to Northern Ireland. Although they spent most of their lives on opposite sides of that intractable conflict, they sound remarkably similar when they talk about what drove them to religious peacemaking.

Indeed, it was Jesus who inspired both men. "As I read the Gospels, the attitude of the Lord Jesus Christ toward those who hated him burned itself into my mind," Magee explains of his decision to pursue what became his life's work. "My actions were established when I examined in detail the example of the Lord Jesus Christ as recorded in the Gospels."[115]

In fact, it was this example that Magee was emulating when he put himself in dangerous and violent environments. As he saw it, he had taken risks because it was the only way he might reach – and redeem – those responsible for perpetrating the conflict. He looked to Jesus as his model: "God...became human and befriended sinners in order to redeem them."[116] For Magee, this was a religious and moral imperative:

> I saw it as a calling. If the church said, "Thou shalt not kill," and they were killing, I had to go. I didn't make that law. I was like a policeman trying to enforce it. [I] was going to them from a religious perspective.[117]

Father Reid's motivation for working with paramilitaries is similar. He also points to Jesus, who descended into the messiness of the world to become involved with all of humankind:

> [W]e can learn from the pastoral example of Jesus Himself. He is always "the Lord who is with us," the Saviour who is "in the midst," the Friend who is there not to condemn but to save. He went among the people, stood where they stood, sat where they sat and was "like unto them in all things except sin."
>
> He communicated directly with those whom He wished to influence, including people who were condemned by the official Church of the time as the worst of sinners and outlaws. He sat down to the table with them and engaged them in personal dialogue so often and so much that He became known by what I believe is His greatest title – "The Companion of Sinners"....
>
> This was the method, the pastoral approach of Jesus, and I believe that the Church in Ireland must follow it if she wants to persuade those who are using the tactics of armed force to change over completely to the tactics of politics and diplomacy.[118]

For Father Reid, modeling Jesus's pastoral leadership means being willing to be the "Friend and Companion of Sinners."[119] He says, "We are all sinners, right? What would the Lord do? He spoke to the sinners, you know? The key to the whole [conflict in Northern Ireland] was to speak with [paramilitaries]."[120] But Reid does not limit his responsibility to the paramilitary groups. He recognizes that all must be involved in a resolution of conflict, and he purposely built relationships both with the perpetrators of violence and its victims. Reid turns to the Gospel of John ("The Word became flesh and dwelt amongst us") noting, "Jesus exercised His pastoral leadership by dwelling in the midst of those whom He wished to influence so that they could experience His company and He could experience theirs."[121]

Father Reid and the Rev. Magee thus both draw on remarkably similar religious imagery, language, and symbols as they explain their motivation and commitment to peacemaking. Both also speak of religion as a resource in sustaining them as they pursued their peacemaking work. Magee shares that he often turned to scripture for support, when confronted with the loneliness of acting without the organizational and communal support of the Presbyterian Church. Father Reid was sustained by the Holy Spirit:

> [W]hatever the problems, setbacks, deadlocks, mistakes, disappointments, and failures, the Holy Spirit will always be able to counter them, always able to change disadvantages into advantage, threat into opportunity, the negative into the positive, just as he changed the Cross of Jesus into the victory of the Resurrection.[122]

In assessing their approaches, it is clear that Reid and Magee used many of the tactics common to secular peacemakers. But at all times they brought their deep religious roots to the table. Religion informed their relationships, their communications, and helped to establish their credibility. Looking back, both say that the first step to their work was establishing personal relationships characterized by genuine, caring human contact. Affiliating with known killers, of course, was not what one might ordinarily expect from religious leaders, but both men were driven by their faith and by a shared conviction that such relationships are necessary for the peace process and possible only when grounded in genuine respect.

To be effective, Reid and Magee both emphasize that one must command respect. For Father Reid, respect is "the most powerful and, at the end of the day, the only effective dynamic of peaceful and democratic conflict resolution."[123] To assure that one gains this respect, one must be fair. As Reid explains: "[T]he reason they [fighting factions] would send for you is because they believe that you will be fair to both sides, that you won't take sides."[124] From his perspective, respect is the foundation of relationships and of the ability to tackle deeply held positions. "They don't think you agree with them," Reid explains, "but they feel there is a kind of relationship that starts to develop, and they will actually tell you . . . what is going on and then . . . they will kind of listen to you because you have a relationship with them."[125]

Central to Father Reid's approach is listening through what he terms the "spirit of Christian compassion and discernment."[126] This entails being true to one's own religious calling as well as listening for the kernels of truth in the statements of those involved in the conflict. "Listening is crucial to the process of resolving a political conflict," he explains, "because it is by listening to the conflict itself that one discovers the formula for peace. In other words, the way to peace is to be *found within* the conflict itself, and, as experience has shown, can only be found there."[127] Reid's concept of listening consistently motivated his peacemaking strategies and position papers, in which he stressed that the path to peace was through exchanges and dialogue by those who preferred not to engage one another and through compromise and negotiation.

Father Reid's emphasis on fairness and openness is consistent with the inclusive approach he takes to peacemaking. Thus, he insists that it is important to obtain a "male-female consensus." That is, male and female experiences each bring to the peace process part of the solution in themselves, and each "has a natural capacity to ... [create] ... a synergetic blending of the spiritual, intellectual, and emotional characteristics of both."[128] Men often sideline women in the peacemaking process, but to create sustainable peace, women must be included.

In his search for answers to the Troubles, the Rev. Roy Magee also took an inclusive approach. He reached out to different constituencies from his parishioners to the paramilitaries, and he talked with the media when he felt it was strategically helpful. Ready to reach beyond his own congregation to identify allies, Magee believes that religious leaders have a responsibility to stress that one will not lose their faith by interacting with people from other religious communities. He believes that it is important for people of different religions to work together. As a religious leader, he believes it is his responsibility to reach out, just as he and Reid did when they brought their respective nationalist and unionist parties together for meetings. Magee explains:

> [C]hurches have got to interrelate ... so that people see churches can work together within the community, without there being any threat on the faith and belief of individuals. ... Once this comfort sets in, it will create a new climate.
>
> That is already happening in Northern Ireland, though it didn't happen for many years, since there was such a wide division between the people of the various religious bodies who were practicing their faith. But once the churches began to get involved, they [the people of his community] saw that they [the people of other religious communities] were human,

they were ordinary people. They were like themselves, and then many of the fears were dispelled.[129]

But before this type of exchange can happen, Magee emphasizes that one must know his or her own community. "The church has got to be with the people. Because if the people don't know you when the sun's shining, they're not going to send for you or listen to you when the storm's blowing," he says.[130] Similarly, "if you go to the people who are not involved with your particular denomination, if you go to them first and neglect your own people, you're creating a conflict. You can't then bring your own people along with you."[131]

Like Father Reid, the Rev. Roy Magee's peacemaking work is also grounded in his ability to create mutually respectful relationships. Although some were suspicious of him, Magee was a strong presence in the community, often seen ministering at the funerals of innocent victims of the violence, as well as responding to those who instigated the violence. As he explains, "even though they may have been . . . vicious people and violent people, they have problems. They have difficulties which need to be addressed. And I always left myself open and said to them, 'If you have any problems, don't be afraid to come to me . . . [it will] be totally between ourselves.'"[132] His status as a loyalist minister helped Magee to establish credibility within the community and among the paramilitaries, and his lack of affiliation with a specific party enabled him to convey messages across different factions.

Even when Magee sharply disagreed with the strategy and tactics of an organization or its members, he did not try to compel his views. He stresses, "to get involved with someone who does not think theologically as you think, or politically as you think, does not necessarily weaken your own particular thinking. If you're open enough, it should strengthen your own faith."[133] Accordingly, Magee's approach was to be direct about his own beliefs, while nonetheless assuring the paramilitary leaders throughout negotiations that he was not trying to coerce them:

> My method was to work with the military leadership of the Paramilitary Organisations on the basis that when convinced, they could take decisions. When road-blocks were erected (and there were many), I refused to be distracted from what I saw as my main aim, namely the bringing about of a Cease Fire. As we progressed from stage to stage, I always ensured that the decision to move was THEIRS.[134]

It is admirable to consider what it must have been like to work directly with people who saw violence as a necessary tool toward an end, when both Reid and Magee had great clarity that such violence was the antithesis of the reconciliation they struggled to achieve. It is interesting to compare their reflections and how they approached this dichotomy. From Father Alex Reid:

> I would be inclined to dwell primarily on the difficulty, as I see it, of uniting people by force. I feel there is a contradiction in that you can unite people by showing your interest in them, by caring for them, by loving them. But you can't unite them by using violence on them. Therefore I would argue … that, in fact, instead of bringing people together, violence is widening the gap between them.[135]

From the Rev. Dr. Roy Magee:

> I think one of the most important things is force begets force and violence begets violence. Instead of bringing a man to a problem, it will exasperate the problem and create more violence and more killing. So the principle is that however you seek to bring a man to violence, violence is not the way to end it. And that the only way to end it is by means of dialogue and by means of making room for people with whatever religious or political views they may have. … [136]

Both men thus condemned the violence, yet both successfully engaged with those responsible for it by relying on their strengths as religious leaders, reinforced by their unique personalities. Magee did this by being directive but not coercive, and by bringing his witty yet fair and open approach to relationships with people from all walks of life. His style was evident during a recent interview when he was asked about when to compromise and when to stand firm in one's views. He responded playfully to his questioner, with a joke about his relationship with his wife. "I often say that Maurine and I – my wife and I – we don't agree on everything. But I'm big enough to tell her, if she wants to be wrong, that's her responsibility," he laughs, and continues:

> I think we have got to get to that place where we acknowledge that people have a right, and we should be defending their right to take any stance they want politically and theologically. So long as they allow other people to hold their particular religious and political views. This should not be a problem. And we make room for each other. I think we're getting there very, very soon.[137]

Reid also worked through his relationships, while using his great intellect to develop documented strategies for peace. Reid's numerous letters, position papers, summaries of meetings, and proposals helped define solutions to the Northern Ireland conflict and created a roadmap that later helped to define the conditions of the cease-fire and the framework for peace.

In one position paper, Reid used his critical skills to detail his religious approach to peacemaking and to promote "a Christian presence in the midst of the conflict which could light and lead the way to peace by the power and after the example of the Good Shepherd who is always among us...."[138] In "A Pastoral Response to the Conflict in Northern Ireland," Father Reid outlined a four-step methodology for religious leaders and ministries to use in reaching out to parties in conflict and identifying common ground through which the conflicts can be resolved.

Basing his approach on Jesus's example, Reid's suggested steps include:

1. Meet with "authoritative representatives of the party group in question with a view to hearing an explanation of their political principles. To listen in a spirit of Christian compassion and discernment is, therefore, the first pastoral activity of this ministry."

2. In writing, identify from within the party position "the elements of democratic truth and justice" and that "which would not be compatible with the principles of democratic truth and justice...." After, give the party the written response "with a view to developing the dialogue with them."

3. Communicate the pastoral ministry's views on the elements of democratic truth and justice to all the main parties to the conflict. This would, "Promote the whole dialogue of peace" by helping "to uncover and identify the common 'democratic' ground between the main parties, the only ground where agreement and reconciliation can be established."

4. Engage the greater religious community by keeping them updated on the dialogue between the pastoral ministry and the parties to the conflict. This will "Gain their spiritual and moral support.... Promote the dialogue of peace among them...[and] Preach the message of Christian hope in a conflict where they are often tempted to despair."[139]

Reid's four steps clearly draw on his own experiences and the methods he used so successfully (in hindsight) in the peace process. He encourages a relationship based on respectful listening and dialogue focused on shared democratic values among the religious leadership, religious community, and the key parties to the conflict. Rather than focusing on what divides, his pastoral response concentrates on finding the common ground for "democratic truth and justice," – just as Reid believes Jesus, the Good Shepherd, would have done.

Similarly, the Rev. Magee strongly believes that the peacemaking role of religious leaders must gain more attention, instruction, and support. "I think that in the seminaries . . . there should be a place for the teaching of conflict resolution, and an analysis of conflict resolution and conflict prevention. Training for the various ministries . . . is totally ignored here [in Northern Ireland]."[140] Based on the crucial role each has played in halting the violence in their own community, Father Reid and the Rev. Magee understand the impact that religious leaders can have – if given the chance – in resolving conflict and finding a way to transform it into peace.

The striking similarities in Father Reid's and the Rev. Magee's commitments to peace ultimately speak to the shared fundamental passions of the nationalist and unionist communities. Father Reid explains this by telling the story of a leisurely walk he took through Belfast, the city that both groups call home:

> One afternoon last April, I went for a walk through the woods that climb the steep sides of Cavehill, one of Belfast's beauty spots. The promise of Spring was everywhere. Daffodils lined the wood-land paths, the trees were bursting into leaf, the music of a cascading stream blended with the singing of the birds. Through the trees, I could see the great expanse of Belfast Lough shimmering in the April sun. As I came down one of the little paths, a man of thirty or so came towards me. I bade him good-day but he didn't seem to hear or even to notice me. Then I saw that his eyes were totally absorbed in the peaceful beauty all around us. They had, indeed, an enchanted look and, when he spoke, it was more to himself than to me. "This," he said, "is the greatest place on earth."
>
> I don't know whether he was a Unionist or a Nationalist because his sentiments, with their echoes of "this is my own, my native land," would have suited a Belfast person of either persuasion. They certainly suited me; which is probably why I thought, on that enchanted evening, that wherever I am on this green isle, whether I am on this side of "the peace-line" with "our 'uns'" or on the other side with "them 'uns,'" I am still (pardon just that little bit of native prejudice) among the greatest people on earth.[141]

Moving Forward: The Future of Northern Ireland

The Rev. Magee joined the faculty in the Conflict Resolution Department at the University of Ulster in 1995, a position that he held until 2000. Today he continues to serve on the Parades Commission, a committee that authorizes and sets conditions for marches in Northern Ireland.

He also has been active in calming continuing tensions among loyalist paramilitary factions, and persuading them to remove threats that they had placed on people and institutions they perceived to be hostile. Both the Rev. Roy Magee and Father Alex Reid also remain active in negotiating internal disputes within their respective religious traditions. Furthermore, Father Reid has become active beyond his beloved island of Ireland. Since early 2000, he has been in the Basque region of Spain. The same skills, intelligence, and devotion that helped him transform his own country through a peace process has helped him here. In fact, Father Reid was instrumental in bringing about the Basque separatist group ETA's cease-fire of 2006. Although modest about his role, those involved in the cease-fire point to Father Reid as the key behind-the-scenes player.

In the last two decades, many days have been hailed as the moment peace finally arrived in Northern Ireland – after the Anglo-Irish Agreement, when the IRA called its first cease-fire, when the Good Friday Agreement was announced – yet all of those days have been followed by violence. Peace may not come swiftly and decisively. In the words of Magee, "we're staggering backwards into the future, so we're just moving very slowly."[142] Still, through the efforts of peacemakers like Father Alex Reid and the Rev. Roy Magee, peace now has the chance to permeate and transform the culture gradually, outside of traditional diplomatic channels, entering and changing the hearts of people.

Father Reid drew on the never-dying strengths and hopes of the people of Northern Ireland when concluding one of his papers on the conflict:

> My own conviction, based on daily experience of the faith-inspired goodness of the ordinary men and women of Belfast, is that, because of that goodness, peace will come sooner rather than later; a peace that will be inspired by the spirit of justice and compassion which, in spite of the crippling effects of historical myth and distortions, in spite even of all the terrible tragedies and violent confrontations, still beats in the hearts of ordinary people of both traditions as a common heritage. Deep down, behind the facades of inherited fears and prejudices, that spirit, in hearts of gold, is the real spirit of Belfast and indeed of Northern Ireland as a whole. Once it has been released by the right kind of leadership, it will, I believe, amaze the world.[143]

He wrote that paper in 1989, seventeen years before the writing of this case study and over eight hundred years after the conflict began. Today, "the priest and the reverend" both hold onto hope for peace in Northern Ireland, as their land struggles to assert itself as a democracy based on equality of its citizenry and peaceful coexistence for all.

The island of Rockall is not shown.

Geography

Location:	Western Europe, occupying one-sixth of the island of Ireland in the North Atlantic Ocean.
Area:	*Total:* 14,160 sq km
Area comparative:	About the size of the U.S. state of Connecticut.

Climate: Temperate maritime; modified by North Atlantic Current; mild winters, cool summers; consistently humid; overcast about half the time.

Population

Population: 1,685,267 (April 2001)[145]

Ethnic groups: Celtic, English

Religions:

Roman Catholic:	40.3%
Presbyterian:	20.6%
Church of Ireland:	15.3%
Methodist:	3.5%
other:	6.3%

Languages: English, Irish (Gaelic).

Government

Government type: United Kingdom: Constitutional Monarchy

Capital: Local: Belfast; National: London

Legal system: United Kingdom: Common law tradition with early Roman and modern continental influences; no judicial review of Acts of Parliament; accepts compulsory International Court of Justice jurisdiction, with reservations; British courts and legislation are increasingly subject to review by European Union courts.

Conflict Background[146] and the Parties Involved

Northern Ireland is located on the northern part of the island of Ireland, on the land historically known as Ulster. During the Reformation of the sixteenth century, Henry VIII founded the Church of England and declared that all the citizens of the British Isles – including the island of Ireland – were to become members of the new church. Many Irish Catholics resisted conversion and remained loyal to the Pope. Ulster in particular was a center of Catholicism until the early seventeenth century, when the British established a colony there. Protestants then settled in the area and, during the next century, came to politically and economically dominate the community. As a result, many of the local Catholics were reduced to lives of servility.

In 1801, Ireland was formally brought into the new United Kingdom of Great Britain and Ireland, which recognized the union of the predominantly Catholic

Ireland to Protestant England, Scotland, and Wales. Ireland objected to the union and fought it from the very beginning. During the nineteenth century, Belfast, Ulster's largest city, became industrialized and drew many Catholic migrants from other parts of the island. Interreligious infighting infused community politics, reflecting tensions between Protestants and Catholics throughout Ireland.

Following the early-twentieth-century war in Ireland known as the War of Independence, the 1921 Anglo-Irish Treaty declared most of the island of Ireland independent, as the Republic of Ireland. However, the United Kingdom kept control of Ulster, which had more Protestants, under the name of Northern Ireland. Conflict thereafter focused mainly in Northern Ireland. Although sectarian violence continues to this day, progress toward peace has been achieved, particularly with the 1998 Belfast Agreement, better known as the Good Friday Agreement.

Nationalists

Nationalists are generally Catholic and seek to unify the island of Ireland (the Republic of Ireland and Northern Ireland) to make it one republic – hence, republican is often used as a synonym for nationalist. Key national groups include:

- The Social Democratic and Labour Party (SDLP), a political party that was the largest nationalist party in Northern Ireland until 2001. The SDLP was instrumental in the talks that led to the 1998 Good Friday Agreement, and its leader at the time won a Nobel Peace Prize.
- Sinn Féin, the party historically identified as the political arm of the paramilitary organization called the Irish Republican Army (IRA), an association it strongly denies today. After the IRA cease-fire, Sinn Féin was welcomed as a strong supporter of the Good Friday Agreement. It is currently the only party to have seats in both the Republic of Ireland and in Northern Ireland, where it is now the largest nationalist party.

Only a small handful of nationalist groups seek an independent Ulster or Northern Ireland.

Unionists

Unionists are generally Protestants and have historically been loyal to the British crown; hence, loyalist is often used as a synonym for unionist. Since the beginning of the Northern Ireland peace process, the term "loyalist" increasingly has been used to refer to extremists. However, for simplicity's sake in this chapter, "unionist" and "loyalist" are used interchangeably because of the breadth of history covered. When Ireland became independent in 1921, unionists settled for British-controlled Northern Ireland. The key unionist parties want the Republic of Ireland to keep out of Northern Ireland, and reject executive power sharing with nonunionist parties. In addition, they are concerned that Britain is not sufficiently committed to its union with Northern Ireland:

- The Ulster Unionist Party (UUP), which dominated the parliament of Northern Ireland from 1921 to 1972. Its leader worked with the nationalist SDLP toward the Good Friday Agreement and was also honored with the Nobel Peace Prize.
- The more recently established Democratic Unionist Party (DUP), which opposes Irish nationalism and did not support the Good Friday Agreement. The DUP is the more extreme unionist party and is also currently the largest political party in Northern Ireland.

The Paramilitary Organizations

Both sides of the conflict also have paramilitary organizations.

- The republican paramilitary organizations believe that force is necessary to remove the British from Northern Ireland. Initially, they identified as defenders of the Northern Catholic minority; later, their military activities expanded to Britain and Europe. The best known paramilitary group was the Irish Republican Army (technically the Provisional IRA but usually referred to as the IRA), which abandoned armed struggle and dismantled its arsenal in November 2005.
- Most loyalist paramilitary groups maintain that they formed in response to republican violence and to defend unionist civilians. However, not all of their activities were defensive and they were involved in proactive violence toward republicans, including civilians. Loyalist paramilitary groups include the Ulster Volunteer Force (UVF), the Ulster Defense Association (UDA), and the Loyalist Volunteer Force (LVF).

The United Kingdom

The official position of the United Kingdom is that Northern Ireland is a part of its jurisdiction.

- The 1985 Anglo-Irish Agreement acknowledged that the Republic of Ireland has the right to be consulted on Northern Irish affairs.
- The 1998 Good Friday Agreement instituted a power-sharing devolved government in Northern Ireland: the Northern Ireland Assembly was created with proportional representation of both unionists and nationalists, and legislative authority over a wide range of issues. The United Kingdom's Northern Ireland Office retained control over constitutional, security, and some financial issues.

The Republic of Ireland

Through most of the conflict, Ireland's constitution claimed the entire Island of Ireland, including the six counties of Northern Ireland. After the 1998 Good Friday Agreement, the Irish Republic's position changed: it gave up its constitutional claim to Northern Ireland and, in turn, was assured a role in its affairs. It also agreed that the Republic of Ireland and Northern Ireland would be unified only if the majority of the people in Northern Ireland chose unification.

4   "Would You Shoot Me, You Idiot?"

Friar Ivo Markovic

Bosnia and Herzegovina

The multiethnic and multireligious state of Bosnia and Herzegovina plunged into violence following the breakup of Yugoslavia in 1992. Nationalist leaders emerged and stoked ethnic tensions. Pulled by Croatia to the west and Serbia to the east and south, Bosnia and Herzegovina ultimately declared independence from Yugoslavia, triggering a bitter internal battle that lasted for three years. By the time the U.S.-brokered Dayton Peace Agreement ended hostilities in 1995, over 250,000 Bosnians were dead, thousands of women had been raped, and some two million people had been driven from their homes.

Friar Ivo Markovic, a Catholic Franciscan Bosnian Croat, was in the middle of a predominantly Orthodox Christian Serb area of Sarajevo when the hostilities erupted in the spring of 1992. Despite the anger and divisiveness of those days, he managed to maintain peaceful relations with his Orthodox neighbors until Serb paramilitary units from outside the area stormed and ransacked his seminary. He narrowly escaped death.

In the midst of this turbulence, Friar Ivo tried to prevent and resolve conflicts through interfaith work among Croats (generally Catholics), Serbs (generally Orthodox Christians), and Bosniaks (generally Muslims). These efforts often put his life at risk. Once, in the midst of a battle, Friar Ivo approached a Bosniak Muslim village by crossing the Croat forces' line of fire. Threatened with being shot if he went any further, Friar Ivo nonetheless continued on – and eventually was able to negotiate a meeting between the local commanders, who agreed that their respective armies would not fight each other.

Today, Friar Ivo continues his interfaith work with the organization he helped found, Interreligious Service Oci u Oci ("Face to Face"). Friar

Ivo's story shows that religiously motivated action aimed at promoting a shared desire for peace and stability can be more effective than the often self-serving agendas of politicians.

Background: The Era of Empires

At the close of World War I in 1918, the former Austro-Hungarian territories of the Serbs, Croats, Montenegrins, Macedonians, and Slovenes were cobbled together into one entity to function as a homeland for the region's various Slavic groups. Renamed the Kingdom of Yugoslavia in 1929, the country's tenuous existence began against the backdrop of nearly six centuries of foreign intervention and outside cultural influences.[1]

Slavs first settled the areas comprising Bosnia and Herzegovina, Serbia, and Croatia, in the sixth century. The political history of the western Balkans from the seventh to the eleventh centuries, however, was punctuated by a succession of conquests and shifting alliances.[2] During significant portions of these early centuries, the Byzantine Empire had nominal authority over the land, with little real control. The Serbian and Croatian Kingdoms exercised power at various points in the region, sometimes under the overall rule of the Byzantine Empire. Serbia's greatest influence was in the geographic area of Herzegovina, whereas Croatia's was in the area of Bosnia.[3]

During the eleventh to twelfth centuries, the Kingdom of Hungary consolidated control over Bosnia and Herzegovina. But Bosnia and Herzegovina fought for and gained its independence, thereafter existing as an independent medieval state from the late thirteenth century to the early fifteenth century. This era was marked by frequent infighting and division among local noble families. Finally, in 1463, the Ottoman Turks conquered Bosnia and Herzegovina, beginning a prolonged occupation during which large numbers of Bosnians, particularly landowners, converted to Islam and absorbed much of the Islamic/Turkish culture.[4]

Under Ottoman rule, those Bosnians who became adherents of Islam also became the privileged class, both economically and politically. In contrast, the Serbs and Croats who remained Christian were largely relegated to the peasantry. By the nineteenth century, Ottoman control in the region had all but collapsed, and a final revolt by Bosnian Christians against the Turks in 1878 ushered in yet another foreign occupation: the Austro-Hungarian Empire.[5]

The World Wars

In 1914, the assassination in Sarajevo of Archduke Franz Ferdinand, heir to the throne of Austria-Hungary, by a young Bosnian Serb nationalist became a catalyst for war between Austria-Hungary and Serbia. The dispute quickly escalated into World War I. Bosnia and Herzegovina, along with the rest of the south Slav lands, became part of the wider European conflict that brought an end to the old empires and ushered in the first Yugoslav union.[6]

Two decades later, the Balkans was again shattered by outside forces. An invasion by Germany, Italy, Hungary, and Bulgaria prompted Slovenes and Croats in the north of Yugoslavia to align with the Axis powers. To the south (including Bosnia and Herzegovina), German and Italian forces instituted control, but rival local militias constantly challenged them. Yugoslavs from all of the ethnic groups joined both the "Chetniks" (Serb nationalists) and the "Partisans" (Communists) led by strongman Josip Broz Tito, a Yugoslav of Croat and Slovene descent.[7]

These Yugoslav factions battled among themselves throughout the war, forming allegiances of convenience and switching back and forth between Axis and Allied powers. During the bloody conflict, many thousands fell victim to the same types of atrocities committed elsewhere in Nazi-occupied Europe and the Soviet Union (including the mass killing of civilians, concentration camps, and forced expulsions). Yet these atrocities were primarily committed by Yugoslavs against one another, and not by Germans or Italians. Tens of thousands of Serbs, Jews, Bosniaks, and Gypsies were put to death in Croatia and Bosnia and Herzegovina by Croatia's Nazi-inspired "Ustasha" movement. Widespread Serb retaliation against Croatian and Bosniak civilians also took place, though four times as many Serbs were killed as Bosniaks.[8]

Communist Yugoslavia

Tito led the Partisans to victory in 1945, leading to the creation of the second Yugoslav nation of the twentieth century, the Federated Socialist Republic of Yugoslavia. Tito then ruled as a dictator for thirty-five years, exercising absolute control and an unyielding resolve to maintain a unified Communist state. Comprised of six republics – Bosnia and Herzegovina, Croatia, Macedonia, Montenegro, Slovenia, and Serbia (including the two autonomous provinces of Vojvodina and Kosovo) – the new nation emerged largely independent of the Soviet Union, which expelled Yugoslavia from the Communist Soviet Bloc in 1948 as punishment for Tito's revolutionary policies.[9]

On the domestic front, Tito employed ruthless tactics and coercion to sustain his one-party control and was not above setting one group against another to retain power. For example, when the constitution was rewritten in 1974, it decentralized the regional governments, giving them greater administrative authority and raising them nearly to the level of fully independent republics. All of this was done in an attempt to balance ethnic influences by pitting different regions within Yugoslavia against one another using economic competition.[10]

Internationally, Tito maintained a policy of nonalignment with the superpowers, which proved highly successful. Simultaneously, he exploited fear of realignment with the Soviet Communist Bloc to secure large amounts of Western aid over the years. As a result, Yugoslavia ultimately achieved one of the highest standards of living among the world's communist nations, though the country encountered serious problems following Tito's death in 1980.[11]

The Disintegration of Yugoslavia

Tito neither groomed a strong successor nor planned for an alternative power structure, thus seriously undermining Yugoslavia's long-term stability. Attempts at joint presidency, with one representative from each of the republics, failed to produce a consensus. Furthermore, Yugoslavia's economic policies proved to be inadequate during the 1980s, the same time that other communist economic systems in Eastern Europe were beginning to collapse.[12] Inflation, debt crisis, and trade deficits plagued the country, lowering the standard of living. The richer republics (Slovenia and Croatia) resented that they were subsidizing the poorer ones (Macedonia, Montenegro, Serbia, and Bosnia and Herzegovina), whereas the poorer republics in turn felt exploited by the richer ones. A lack of interest during the post–Cold War period also led the international community to cease approving loans, which had previously bolstered the struggling Yugoslav economy.[13]

This economic and political stagnation led to the Yugoslav Communist Party's disintegration, just as the Soviet Union was collapsing along similar lines. Seizing the moment, former Communist Party apparatchik Slobodan Milosevic moved to fill the power vacuum that emerged. He exploited Serbian nationalism (the promise of a "Greater Serbia") to fuel ethnic tensions and consolidate his power base, and by mid-1989, controlled four out of eight votes in the Yugoslavian federal government. The four he did not control – Slovenia, Croatia, Macedonia, and Bosnia and Herzegovina – would secede from Yugoslavia by the end of 1992 to form independent countries along ethnic and religious lines.[14]

The first to leave were Slovenia and Croatia, primarily Catholic republics that declared independence in June of 1991. In the Yugoslav capital of Belgrade, Milosevic denounced the secessions. Claiming that the Serbian Orthodox Christian populations living outside the Serbian Republic in Yugoslavia were being isolated and threatened with destruction, he called for the Yugoslav federation to be preserved by force.[15]

Events moved quickly. Under orders from Belgrade, the Yugoslav People's Army (JNA) attacked Slovenia.[16] After ten days of skirmishes and an embarrassing defeat, the JNA withdrew its forces, allowing Slovenia to assert its independence. Because there were few Serbian Orthodox Christians in Slovenia, Milosevic was willing to let the country go and dropped his efforts there.[17]

However, in Croatia, which had a sizable minority population, the resolve of the JNA and Croatian Serb militias was far greater. They were determined to protect the enclaves of Orthodox Christian Serbs within Croatia, claiming that the successors to the Ustasha movement would subject them to discrimination and repression if Croatia were to gain independence from Yugoslavia.[18] The fighting in Croatia reached a stalemate with regard to the territory held by Orthodox Serbs and Catholic Croats, and the focus soon turned to its land-locked neighbor, Bosnia and Herzegovina, a mountainous republic completely surrounded by Croatia, Serbia, and Montenegro.[19]

Bosnian Independence

Bosnia and Herzegovina's leaders feared the impact of the independence declarations of Slovenia and Croatia and how they would affect ethnoreligious dynamics at home. Unlike its neighbors, Bosnia and Herzegovina had existed as a multireligious, multiethnic entity since the Middle Ages. Of its roughly four million people, the religious breakdown was 40 percent Muslim, 31 percent Orthodox Christian, and 15 percent Catholic, whereas the ethnic breakdown was 48 percent Bosniak, 37 percent Serb, and 14 percent Croat.[20]

With the breakup of Yugoslavia looming, Bosnia and Herzegovina – with its patchwork quilt of ethnic/religious populations – was vulnerable to the xenophobic motivations of its neighbors, especially Serbia and Croatia. The situation was complicated as new Bosnian political parties divided along ethnoreligious lines. Serbian Orthodox Christian and Croatian Roman Catholic nationalistic parties emerged and began to lay claim to lands historically considered part of Serbia and Croatia, respectively. In reaction, the Bosniak Muslims formed their own party.[21]

These nationalist parties participated in the 1990 elections held in Bosnia and Herzegovina. The results were predictable. People from each ethnic group voted overwhelmingly for their own ethnoreligious nationalist party out of fear that they would be at the mercy of the other parties if they did not support "their own." In the wake of the election, a coalition government was formed.[22]

This government, composed of representatives from each of the parties, proved ineffective. It was unable to pass even a single law during the eighteen months before the Serbian Party pulled out of the coalition and declared the existence of a separate Bosnian Serb government. The leaders of Bosnia and Herzegovina were left with three choices: continue as part of what remained of Yugoslavia, divide itself between Serbia and Croatia, or declare independence.[23]

Confronted with what seemed to be the inevitable – the United States and European Union had already recognized the independence of Slovenia and Croatia – Bosnia and Herzegovina's leaders held a referendum on independence from Yugoslavia early in 1992. The Serbian Ultra-Nationalist party feared that an independent, multiethnic nation no longer part of the Serbian-dominated Yugoslavia would put Bosnian Orthodox Christian Serbs at risk. Accordingly, they boycotted the vote and called for all Bosnian Serbs to do the same. With the boycott in place, the remaining voters chose independence. The results were announced in March and by late April 1992, the United States and most of the international community recognized an independent Bosnia and Herzegovina.[24]

The War over Bosnia and Herzegovina

As the events around the referendum for independence unfolded, Bosnia and Herzegovina slid into war. Serb and Croat forces took positions on opposite sides of the Neretva River, and the previously sporadic fighting between military reservists and residents became an everyday occurrence. When the war in Croatia ended in early 1992, the JNA officially withdrew and moved into Bosnia and Herzegovina with the approval of the United Nations. Once there, the JNA placed heavy artillery around the country's major cities, including Sarajevo, to prevent the country from gaining independence.[25]

Then, on March 2, 1992, the day that the referendum results were announced, members of the Serb paramilitary forces set up barricades and sniper positions in Sarajevo, ostensibly in response to the shooting of a Serb at a wedding party the day before. In response, thousands of Sarajevo citizens demonstrated in the streets, seeking to prevent a military coup. The people's will prevailed. Barricades were removed, and Sarajevans celebrated their "victory" over the paramilitary forces. It seemed that Sarajevo had been spared war.[26]

But the battle for that city was far from over. The Serbs initially took control of the surrounding areas. In the northern Posavina region of Bosnia and Herzegovina, fierce Croat/Serb fighting broke out. People from all three ethnoreligious groups became refugees. And Serbian paramilitary forces – led by General Ratko Mladic – began a campaign of ethnic cleansing of Bosniaks and Croats in northern and eastern Bosnia. The JNA laid siege to Mostar, a city south of Sarajevo, and in only six weeks, the Serb army and paramilitaries gained control of a majority of the territory of Bosnia and Herzegovina.[27]

Although the capital of Sarajevo also endured fierce fighting, its fate was not so quickly determined. On April 6, 1992, the day Bosnia and Herzegovina was recognized as independent by the European Union, Serb paramilitary forces once again set up barricades in Sarajevo. As before, thousands of Bosnians from all national groups took to the streets. But this time, the Serb forces opened fire on the civilians, with deadly results. This was the beginning of the siege of Sarajevo, a grueling three-and-a-half-year ordeal that pitted a well-armed Serb army against a relatively defenseless urban and mixed ethnoreligious (but predominantly Muslim) population.[28]

In May, Milosevic and the Montenegrin government announced the creation of a new federal state of Yugoslavia (made up of their two republics, Serbia and Montenegro). Milosevic withdrew the JNA soldiers from Bosnia and Herzeginia who were citizens of the new Yugoslav state, leaving behind eighty-thousand loyal and well-armed ethnic Bosnian Serb soldiers. Under General Mladic (personally chosen by Milosevic), this Serb army carried out a campaign of mass killings of civilians, using concentration camps, systematic rape, and the forced displacement of millions as daily tactics. Quickly, they created the largest flow of refugees in Europe since World War II.[29]

In this atmosphere of violence, hostilities were not limited to Serbian attacks against Bosniaks and Croats. Some Bosniak paramilitary units and Croat groups took the law into their own hands and began attacking innocent Serbs. Atrocities were committed on all sides, with more than two hundred thousand Bosniaks, Serbs, and Croats estimated to have been killed by the end of the war.[30]

Meanwhile, beginning with the establishment of the Croat community of Herceg-Bosna in July 1992, nationalist pressures from Zagreb (the capital of Croatia), and from Croats inside Bosnia and Herzegovina, increasingly pitted Croats and Bosniaks against each other in western and central parts of the country. Croatian President Tudjman put great pressure on the government of Bosnia and Herzegovina to enter into a confederation with Croatia.[31]

By October, Bosnian Croat leaders had given up all pretext of an alliance with the Bosnia and Herzegovina government. Instead, they began to implement a plan to divide Bosnia and Herzegovina between Croat and Serb nationalists. Large-scale fighting between Bosniaks and Croats followed in early 1993, when both ethnoreligious communities sought to solidify the territories under their control and influence the map-drawing process of the developing Vance-Owen Peace Plan, which split Bosnia and Herzegovina into autonomous provinces defined by regional ethnic labels. Bosniak/Croat fighting throughout Bosnia and Herzegovina left ethnically cleansed regions, an enormous number of refugees, and the infamous Croat concentration camps. Bosnia and Herzegovina was being pushed toward destruction.[32] It would take the intense involvement of the international community to bring about a workable plan to end the conflict.

International Actors

As the war loomed over Yugoslavia, the international community responded guardedly. One reason was a widely held perception in the West, during the summer of 1991, that conflict in the Balkans was inevitable and that nothing could be gained by becoming entangled in the region's internal affairs. The Soviet Union had collapsed in December of that year, bringing nearly a half-century Cold War to an end. Furthermore, given that Bosnia and Herzegovina was in Europe's backyard, the U.S. government believed that Europeans should handle the problem.

The actions that the international community did take were often not helpful. For example, the September 1991 decision of the UN Security Council to impose an arms embargo on Yugoslavia actually reinforced an existing military imbalance between Serb and non-Serb units in Bosnia and Herzegovina, because Serbia controlled the majority of the weaponry of the former Yugoslav Federal Army.[33] Similarly, the West's hurried decisions to extend diplomatic recognition to Slovenia (June 25, 1991) and Croatia (January 15, 1992) and then to Bosnia and Herzegovina (April 6, 1992)[34] unintentionally contributed to the destabilization of the region.

When the United Nations sent peacekeeping forces, its efforts were woefully understaffed and relegated throughout much of the war to monitoring arms supplies and troop movements, and to protecting aid convoys and international troops. As such, the UN's attempts to establish so-called safe havens in mid-1993 proved largely ineffective. The consequences were tragic. Over the ensuing years, entire communities were "cleansed" of Bosniak and Croat civilians while United Nations troops were temporarily detained by Serb forces.[35]

As the death toll mounted, calls for international military intervention became more vociferous. Graphic media coverage of mortar attacks on civilians in besieged cities, most notably Sarajevo, and Serb-run detention camps in northern Bosnia began to galvanize Western public opinion against the Serbs, but not against the Croats whose war crimes went less publicized. Although Western media coverage was decidedly anti-Serb, NATO forces did not use significant military power against the Bosnian Serbs at this time.[36]

Instead, in October 1992, the United Nations and the European Union produced the first draft of the Vance-Owen Peace Plan, a detailed proposal for a political settlement that would divide Bosnia and Herzegovina into ten cantons, nine of which were to be ethnically defined. However, the boundaries were not precisely defined, and this led to an increase of hostilities as each nationalist group attempted to increase the territory under its control. The final version of the plan, which reduced the number of cantons to three ethnically defined regions, was presented to each party in the spring of 1993. Under significant pressure, the Bosniaks and Croats signed, but the Serbs refused, believing that they could gain more territory on the battlefield.[37]

With the collapse of this initiative, international intervention floundered until December 1994, when former President Jimmy Carter successfully negotiated a cease-fire based on recognizing the perceived legitimate needs of each party. The cease-fire lasted four months.[38] Full-scale war then resumed, unhindered by international intervention until NATO forces attacked Serb emplacements around Sarajevo on August 30, 1995, in response to the fall of Srebrenica and Zepa to Serbian forces. By October, the warring parties had come to the negotiating table.[39]

The war ended on November 21, 1995, with the signing of the U.S.-brokered Dayton Peace Agreement. In 2004, the NATO-led Stabilization Force (SFOR) concluded its mission and handed over peacekeeping duties to a European force (EUFOR).[40] Bosnia and Herzegovina emerged as an independent state consisting of three entities: Republika Srpska (dominated by Bosnian Orthodox Christian Serbs); the Federation of Bosnia and Herzegovina (dominated by Bosnian Catholic Croats and Muslim Bosniaks); and the internationally supervised Brcko District (an administrative unit in the northeast, under the sovereignty of Bosnia and Herzegovina).[41]

Religious Actors

All the main religions in the region have been accused of complicity in the war in Bosnia and Herzegovina. Although each religious community officially denied culpability, each one also pointed accusing fingers at the other religious communities, the political nationalists, and the communists.

The question of complicity is complex. Typically, during the war, public statements by the various religious communities called for an end to the fighting, denounced the atrocities, and affirmed the need to maintain basic human rights standards. However, the denunciations of violence usually referred exclusively to atrocities committed by other groups – and not by their own. Statements of confession and regret regarding specific atrocities were few and far between.

At the same time, there were many "unofficial" statements and actions by religious leaders that inflamed and legitimized the violence. This was largely because religion was braided into the ethnic identity of the embattled parties. Following the fall of communism, nationalist leaders increasingly linked ethnicity and religion, thereby sanctifying national identity and the development of intolerance. As religious leaders legitimized the aspirations and underlying fears of their own ethnic groups, nationalist politicians manipulated these religious sentiments to solidify control over their own people and territories.

Friar Ivo Markovic: Evolution of a Peacemaker

Both during and after the disintegration of Yugoslavia, Friar Ivo Markovic, one of Bosnia and Herzegovina's most devout peacemakers, worked with determination to bring stability and healing to the region.

The second of seven children in a Bosnian Croat family, Friar Ivo Markovic was born in 1950 in the central Bosnian town of Susanj. Spiritual at an early age, Friar Ivo was educated by Franciscans, who had a profound impact on his life.

After three years of mandatory service in the Yugoslav Army, Friar Ivo attended the Theological School in Sarajevo, where he nurtured a strong interest in music and its spiritual dimensions. Ordained in 1976, he became the parish priest of Guca Gora near Travnik. He completed his theological studies through Catholic Seminary in Zagreb, Croatia in 1978 and immediately began postgraduate work.

The following year, Friar Ivo joined the Franciscan Seminary in Sarajevo, where he taught religion and music and served as a religious educator for students. He was awarded a Master's degree in 1984 from the Zagreb Catholic Faculty for his study of "Faith and Religion in Schools during Yugoslav Marxism." A scholar, he continued to teach pastoral theology in Sarajevo while pursuing a Ph.D.[42]

As Friar Ivo began to take up his monastic calling, he focused on the subject of religious communication. He discovered that however important religious symbols are for believers, they do not fully capture the deeper message of scripture. Consequently, he found it important to try to make the message behind the symbols broadly accessible by employing simpler, more direct language:

> In my devotional life, I like to read the Bible, coupled with exegetical literature. I attempt to write the Word in my own language and out of my own experience, and then tell it to people I meet. Symbols do not play an important role in my faith. As I see it, symbols very easily become the objects of worship. The only symbols I find meaningful are the words, which are fresh and, in a new way, express my relationship to God.[43]

From the beginning, Friar Ivo devoted himself to making faith more available to the people he encountered.

Peacemaking during the Bosnian War

In the late 1980s and early 1990s, the relatively peaceful world in which Friar Ivo lived began to crumble. With Tito gone from power and the wars beginning, he observed how the new political leaders, with support from religious figures, increasingly misused and manipulated religion to support nationalist aspirations on all three sides – Orthodox, Catholic, and Muslim. According to Friar Ivo, religious leaders at the local level were instrumental in mobilizing for war. Many imams were military leaders, while a number of priests in the Catholic and Orthodox churches blessed weapons. Moreover, religious figures were "there to give strength to the armies, moral strength for soldiers to be strong enough to kill." In Friar Ivo's view, the "religious leaders compromised their own activities by coordinating too much with national interests." What was lacking at the time was a "clear differentiation between religion and national identity in order to avoid the degeneration of religion into magic or paganism."[44]

Friar Ivo could not stand by idly. As political and religious leaders blessed war, he resolved to try to halt the "political instrumentalization" of religion by the nationalists. His goal was to "revive positive relationships among religious communities that we had before the war, to use the power of religion to stop the war and move toward reconciliation."[45] Friar Ivo's approach was grounded in his belief in the power of religion for "purification, healing, awareness, reconciliation and peace," and he readily assumed responsibility for exercising this power. Reflecting upon that approach, Friar Ivo believes that his actions helped to "expose the awful manipulation of religion, to open the eyes of some religious workers and leaders . . . and to establish communication as an important part of the process."[46]

Considering himself a "practical theologian," Friar Ivo began his peace-making work within the Bosnian Franciscan community – a community that often was distrusted by the mainstream Catholic Church due to its former communist affiliations.[47] In 1991, after seeing how the national-ists were manipulating the people for their own ends, he felt compelled to act.[48] First, he encouraged lay people to become involved in politics, lecturing his fellow Franciscans and calling on others to support protests for democracy. Recognizing that he was "privileged to be in a position to stimulate people of influence to act,"[49] his activism and peacemaking began to evolve. As he explains:

> The shift in my attitudes was somewhat gradual, although the experiences of war taught me a lot about conflict and the nature of conflict resolution. The suffering of others motivated me to act without compromise. I was deeply, personally involved in the happenings of war and, of course, that experience changed me spiritually, psychologically and physically.[50]

Thus motivated, he took action.

At the onset of hostilities in the spring of 1992, Friar Ivo and his Francis-can colleagues, although living in a predominantly Serb area of Sarajevo, were able to maintain peaceful relations with their Serbian Orthodox

Christian neighbors. In June of that year, however, Serb paramilitary units from outside the area stormed the seminary, which housed one of the most valued theological libraries in the Balkans, and threatened to execute the staff.

Friar Ivo narrowly escaped capture, imprisonment, and possibly even death, yet he remained in central Bosnia during the ensuing months to try to prevent conflicts between Croats and Bosniaks and organize humanitarian activities. Perhaps his single most remarkable act during this time was successfully mediating between Bosniak and Croat commanders near Travnik in July 1992 to prevent their troops from joining in the local battle. When fighting first erupted between Bosniak Muslims and Croats, he and a number of Franciscans appealed to the politicians to quell the conflict, but still it spiraled out of control. Over one million bullets were discharged toward Muslim villages on the holy holiday of St. John the Baptist. Friar Ivo recalls the dramatic events that unfolded next as he and another friar tried to intervene:

> The Croat and Muslim armies were already facing each other across a field when we decided to walk through their lines and go from a Croat village, Guca Gora, to a Muslim one, Maljina in order to ask the imam to help us. Soldiers on both sides challenged us. When approaching the Muslim side, dressed in Franciscan habit, I was told to stop or they would shoot. I became angry and ran toward them saying, "What, shoot? Would you shoot me, you idiot?" It seemed that the soldiers, though, were actually afraid of us Franciscans. Some of them followed us into the village where we found everyone in a panic. Bullets were falling on the roofs of houses and we had to go inside to escape. Some of them were threatening to return the fire. However, we found the imam and proposed that we bring together the two local commanders to see if they could prevent the violence from escalating among their troops. One of us Franciscans volunteered to remain in the Muslim village as a guarantee of good will. However, the imam insisted that there would be no hostages. We then met with both the Croat and Muslim commanders in a local café where we negotiated an agreement that the two armies would not fight. Although the region was later overrun by other troops, these commanders and their soldiers did not take part in the hostilities.[51]

Through sheer commitment, Friar Ivo created an oasis of peace. Although he avoided death, others dear to him were not so fortunate. He remembers June 8, 1993, "The Bosniaks Army (who were Muslims) occupied my native place.... There was killed also my father, nine of my relatives, more [than] 55 neighbors and parishioners."[52] Anyone in the region who managed to survive the attack was summarily expelled from their homes. Friar Ivo describes this as a test of faith:

> It was a very deep, personal, painful experience. My father and I had cooperated in attempts to stop the growth of mistrust and enmity. He was well respected by people from all ethnic groups. In my pain I understood that he was killed because of the strong movement of evil that he tried to stop.[53]
>
> When I [first] heard what happened to my dearest and to my native place, I had in my sorrow and pain also the idea to go to Bosnia, to protect these unprotected people, if it were needed, also to be included in the fighting.[54]
>
> [But then,] I asked myself what my father would expect of me. I realized that I would betray him if I did not keep working in the way he had worked. I tried to transform my pain through acting. From my personal experience, I know that it is very difficult to escape the sense of victimization. Victims are easily caught in a cycle of pain and revenge. I realized that I had to do something, to try and change some of the circumstances that had led to the killing of my loved one. It was difficult to make that first step. Yet, very soon I realized that the killers, our enemies, are also victims. Then, I found new energy to work for peace.[55]

From his father's death, Friar Ivo drew strength.

At the time of the attack, Friar Ivo was living as a refugee in Zagreb, Croatia, where he assisted in the peace efforts of the Christian Ecumenical Service.[56] At the invitation of the Presbyterian Church and Central Mennonite Council of Canada, he traveled to Europe, the United States, and Canada to spread the word about Bosnia's plight. Using Zagreb, Croatia as his base, Friar Ivo also focused on becoming more effective, diligently helping refugees by distributing humanitarian aid and acting as a liaison between the warring religious communities. He worked with the Christian Information Service, an ecumenical organization that helped coordinate humanitarian aide workers, journalists, and others. In 1993 he began working with David Steele of the Center for Strategic and International Studies, who along with Gerald Shenk of the Mennonite Central Committee assisted Friar Ivo in his peacemaking efforts.[57] By 1994, Friar Ivo had "succeeded to visit this region together with Muslims; bringing to all [the] people food, other necessities, and the hope for peace."[58]

Postwar Reconciliation Work

After the Bosnian War, Friar Ivo returned to the wartorn city of Sarajevo, where he joined Saint Anthony's Monastery in 1996 and continued his efforts to end hostilities, bring about reconciliation, and promote refugee return. Stressing the importance of individual action by religious leaders, Friar Ivo was the first Bosnian Franciscan to initiate reconciliation activities between the communities, including simple visits, finding ways to open the channels of communication, establishing mutual help, and connecting individuals with one another. Moreover, Friar Ivo was among the first to visit leaders in the hard-line Serb stronghold of Pale near Sarajevo.[59] He recalls being initially questioned by the police and the gradual transformation that took place in the months that followed:

> Early in 1996, when no one dared to go to the Bosnian Serb Republic, I decided to go to Pale. When I arrived, policemen took me to the prison to interrogate me. They wanted to know what I was doing and who sent me. I asked to call some Serbian friends who could answer these questions for them. My friends came and the police let me go. I visited with a Serbian Orthodox priest and discussed with him the need for our people to live together again.
>
> After this, I continued to go to Pale two or three times a week. I met with new people all the time, visiting with whole neighborhoods in people's homes. Slowly, I became Ivo to them and they asked about their acquaintances in Sarajevo and sent them letters and messages. I also took some of the Serb young people to Sarajevo.
>
> Even the Serb policeman who I hired to protect me gradually began to share with me his struggle to overcome the terrible pattern of violent behavior that had consumed him during the war. I was able to direct him to turn to God and encouraged him to help other people. Months later, I saw that this man had begun to slowly find his way again.
>
> Gradually, I began to see the whole situation change. The brainwashing performed by the media could be countered by meaningful personal interaction. In less than four months, I felt my presence in Pale had begun to change people's mentalities.[60]

Friar Ivo demonstrates the power of just one person in countering messages of hatred. Since the end of the war, and with support from the Franciscan community, the Mennonite Central Committee, and the Archdiocese of Canterbury, Friar Ivo continues his work today as head of the Sarajevo-based Oci u Oci ("Face to Face") Interreligious Service, which seeks to sustain a pluralistic Bosnia.[61] Among the most successful undertakings by Friar Ivo and the Interreligious Service is the formation in 1996 of the multiethnic interfaith Pontanima Choir and Chamber Orchestra, which performs a combination of Western Christian, Orthodox, Christian Muslim, Jewish, and Far Eastern religious music. It began first when Friar Ivo met with some musicians and a conductor. There, he proposed extending invitations to other musicians from across all religions in the region to sing songs together from each of their respective traditions. In this way, they could help facilitate healing through music and spirituality in postwar Bosnia. As he explains, however, there were some difficulties at first with this ambitious undertaking:

> When we started to sing it was not easy. There were some objections by people who did not want to sing the music of the enemy. But we helped one another through jokes. The first benefit was the healing experienced by members of our choir. Now they enjoy singing together. There were also protests by other groups that could not accept what we were doing. Yet, we have received even a standing ovation in Livno, one of the strong centers of Croatian nationalism.[62]

Formed initially as a means of opening lines of spiritual communication in the region, the group has also toured Bosnia and Herzegovina, Europe, and the United States performing and promoting their message of interreligious healing and understanding.[63]

In addition to his work at Oci u Oci, Friar Ivo is involved with several other organizations. Following his return to Sarajevo in 1997, he became a member of the Franciscan Commission for Justice, Peace, and the Integrity of Creation. In 1998, he and Thomas Anthony, an Anglican Franciscan, established the Interreligious Service for Advancing Interreligious Understanding in Bosnia. He also became a member of the Commission for Interreligious Dialogue of the Franciscan Order in Rome. But when speaking of his many accomplishments as a peacemaker, Friar Ivo notes, "I did not seek these positions for the status, but rather for the function they provided."[64]

Friar Ivo has also been busy providing resources for international actors eager to help in the region. Sometimes, foreign-based NGOs have money and resources to assist in the region, but their efforts are not as effective as they could be because the NGOs lack sufficient knowledge of the diverse cultures in the area. In Friar Ivo's words, "Often, the outsiders who come do not understand our situation. They start something only to discover in one year that they were wrong."[65] In 1999, the Interreligious Service sponsored an ambitious peacemaking initiative with the Alternative Peace Initiative (API) to discover ways that foreign-based NGOs can be more effective. Friar Ivo is a member of the coordinating team, and is consulted personally by foreign-based NGOs like Women for Women International and the International Bureau for Humanitarian Issues, among others.

When not working with these organizations, Friar Ivo contributes regularly to theological texts and newspaper columns. His writings cover numerous topics such as youth under communism, the role of women in the church vis-à-vis the legacy of the Virgin Mary, the Bosnian people's image of God, the church in a computerized society, and the changing face of the priesthood. He also has written on the role of the church in war, including motivations for the wartime destruction of religious buildings, the treatment of war trauma through religion, and the cultural underpinnings of reconciliation, ecumenism, and dialogue.[66]

Reflections of a Peacemaker: The Role of the Media

In addition to the support that Friar Ivo has received from other organizations for his reconciliation work, he speaks to the powerful role that the media can play. It became clear to him by 1992 that the media would be "the main tool of those seeking war" through propaganda produced in an attempt to divide people. Although there were a number of independent periodicals and some radio stations that he says "played a salient role in rejecting the typical manipulation and brainwashing so prevalent during the Balkan wars of 1991–1995," with few exceptions, nationalists controlled nearly all of the television stations.[67]

Although less in number than the nationalist-controlled media, peace-seeking individual journalists, in Friar Ivo's words, "prepared the climate for peaceful social and political change." He notes that in times of war, "peacemaking can be done only on a humanitarian and informational level."[68] Central to defusing the violence and leading to postwar reconciliation is the process of getting past the differences between one group and the "other" in order to see each other's common humanity. Friar Ivo believes that it is in this arena that the media played "perhaps the most salient role."[69]

Accordingly, Friar Ivo coordinated with many media organizations and institutions. Because he recognized "the power of reading as the basis for a spiritual life," he decided to effect change through writing and speaking.[70] He began by contributing to magazines and newspapers, large and small, because he saw the role that journalism could play in promoting reconciliation. But some magazines would not publish his work, and others attempted to censor his writings in an effort to protect the strength of Catholicism. Friar Ivo describes how one newspaper "rejected all peace, ecumenical and interreligious endeavors and, along with them, the prefixes 'multi,' 'inter' and 'co' because they were perceived to be weakening our own national, Catholic community."[71]

In addition to his own writing, Friar Ivo served as a spiritual advisor for the Croatian Association of Catholic Journalists in Zagreb, helping with seminars, counseling, and journalist round-table discussions. But his efforts to promote peace were not universally embraced. As he explains:

> Such work had an effect, but it also brought me some problems. I was attacked and accused of being a spy and a traitor to the Croatian nation and Catholic faith. My journalistic involvement helped feed an environment of conspiracy against me.[72]

For Friar Ivo like so many religious peacemakers, being a voice for peace had consequences.

Reflections of a Peacemaker: Inner Resources and Outer Obstacles

Nonetheless, Friar Ivo pushed forward with his peacemaking work. He describes how the nationalistic governments attempted to silence the voice of the peacemakers either through punishment or by trying to redirect some of them to the nationalist cause. But in Friar Ivo's view, it was difficult for the nationalist governments to succeed because the peacemakers were so passionate, radical, and committed. As he explains, peacemakers must claim these traits to be effective. Peacemaking in war and postwar situations must be radical, provocative, eye-opening, and without fear. Peacemakers must destroy the status quo and break open closed social groups that are filled with fear, hate, and egoism.[73]

Friar Ivo's fearlessness was needed not only to face the government and the media. He was equally fearless when he confronted obstacles within the Catholic Church. At times, he was actually close to receiving harsh punishment; he particularly recalls a point in 1998 when he boldly wrote that "[O]ur traditional religions can't reconcile people in the Balkans because they are too nationalistic and they coordinate their actions according to national interests." This was not an easy position to take, and Friar Ivo recognized that he was risking harsh reactions. But he was "not afraid of public opinion."[74]

Unlike the many local clergy who were, in Friar Ivo's words, "identified with their own ethnic group and systematically used by the politicians," Friar Ivo stood apart, ready to place his life in danger and to risk being branded a traitor. Through and following the war, his voice, along with the voices of likeminded clergy, grew stronger, though as he puts it, the "nationalist manipulation of religion [also] became more clever and skillful."[75]

Reflections of a Peacemaker: On a Peacemaking Methodology

The core of Friar Ivo Markovic's work has been collaborating with other religiously motivated people from across religious traditions to collectively promote peace and spiritual healing. When he describes his approach to conflict resolution, Friar Ivo suggests that strength lies in following one's own personal path while reaching out to people of different beliefs:

> I always tried to cooperate with people and bring in religious inspiration to our cooperation. I find that it is my mission to help people not to forget God. Never have I suggested to people to change their religious community. It is important to obey God, but I find that it is God who gives different roads to people, and he decides who will go on what road. People have to be free to choose the path. I cooperated with Christians, Muslims, and Vaishnavists without any problems. We prayed together and confessed our faith. In the presence of agnostics, I gave witness to my faith in a friendly way.
>
> During the war, believers from different religions organized actions inspired with faith and always it was excellent. At the beginning of 1994, for example, Christians and Muslims organized to open roads for humanitarian help. Catholics led convoys through Croat roadblocks and Muslims did the same at Muslim roadblocks. One time, when British soldiers stopped us and took us away in a tank, my friend Sevko Omerbasic, president of Muslim Meshihat in Zagreb, and I prayed together several times, each in his own tradition.[76]

Friar Ivo has also found it valuable to incorporate some Western ideas into his peacemaking work. For example, he purchased forty kilograms of books on conflict resolution when he visited the United States in 1994 at the invitation of the Presbyterian Church. He then translated numerous articles from them into Croatian. Concepts of pacifism were unknown and had been rejected under the communist educational system, and Friar Ivo therefore attempted to introduce new concepts of reconciliation and conflict resolution to his community.[77] By combining these ideas with his religious beliefs, Friar Ivo succeeded in promoting interfaith peacebuilding work, both during and after the war. In so doing, he worked with people of different faiths and ethnic traditions to reach a shared goal.

Religiously Motivated Peacemaking

Friar Ivo elaborates on his evolution as a peacemaker by describing the motivation for and religious significance of his actions. He starts by differentiating between personal faith and the sense of group belonging:

> My actions are a sign of the experience of grace. Faith is a personal experience, and not the passion that comes from belonging to a group. In the experience of my faith, I stress that life, activity, truth and spirituality are to be lived. In my opinion, the tragedy of the Balkans stemmed from replacement of personal faith with the passions of belonging to the group. That is the fundamental question for the traditional Balkan religions of Catholicism, Orthodoxy and Islam.[78]

Friar Ivo also makes clear that his commitment to peace and reconciliation comes from within and from God. Living a devout, spiritual life and following one's religious faith – however one defines it – is for Father Ivo a method for promoting peace. This is because reconciliation with God facilitates reconciliation among human beings:

> I have no special religious principle, other than my personal faith. Yet I like to be open-minded when it comes to faith. My prayer life is focused on searching, before God, for solutions to challenges I face. I find reading and writing to be the best for spiritual conditioning.
>
> The experiences of conversion and the grace of God are forgotten potentials for peace.... Religious reconciliation needs to use more of the language and methods of modern conflict resolution. I always stress to people the importance of faith, of conversion, and of meeting God. I use very simple language acceptable for all religions.
>
> - There is one God.
> - God came in human life in different ways.
> - The experiences of God's coming are written in the holy books.
> - God is not far.
> - We can all meet God.
> - We simply need to turn onto the road on which God is coming.
>
> Conversion involves changing the direction of the world, turning onto the road of a God who calls all humanity to follow the way of love, peace, forgiveness, goodness and good deeds. There, through grace, we become new human beings with an experience of eternity already here.[79]

For Friar Ivo, personal faith motivates him to peace activism. Because he believes that all people can experience the ultimate teachings of God, Friar Ivo works to translate religious principles into simple language so that they will be readily accessible to everyone. In this way, God's messages can reach the people directly, unadulterated by group interpretation.

There have been times, however, when Friar Ivo's religious principles have not led to the results one would expect. From 1991 to 1993, when the war first began in Croatia and Bosnia, he recognized the need for the international community to intervene to stop the war by force. He saw that it was necessary for someone to say, "If you try to solve this conflict by war, you will be punished." He made what he considers an important distinction in advocating the "destruction of weapons, but not the killing of people."[80] In so doing, he rejects absolute pacifism. In his view, the unilateral opposition to all forms of violence by some peace groups helped set the stage for some of the terrible killings that would occur:

> Many peace movements were against the use of any force, and so they enabled the violence that was planned by the Yugoslav-Serbian generals. In my opinion, these peacemakers – among them many believers – took the position of God and [thereby] sentenced tens of thousands of people in Bosnia to execution.[81]

Friar Ivo thus believes that absolute nonviolence contributed to what he later would call "genocide."

Friar Ivo again emphasizes that it is a personal decision to choose between violence and nonviolence:

> To choose a path of nonviolence is an individual decision, but we must not impose this view on others who are suffering. It is their choice and their right to [self] defense. Radical nonviolence is a personal decision motivated through the experience of transcendence, of God's grace, of eternity, and the acceptance of suffering and death. Such a decision can be the design for building a community, but in a situation of violence it is necessary to respect the right of the people to defense. Peacemaking based on disarmament must be balanced on all sides to escape the devaluation of peace that we experienced in the Balkans.
>
> Personally, I think that before the war I had more violence in me. I was more aggressive, more revolutionary, and more critical. Many times, I took up guns for target practice. But when the violence began in 1991, I could not imagine using a weapon. While traveling through Bosnia during the war, it was recommended that I carry a gun. I shuddered at the thought. I also recommended to my companions that they not carry guns. On all sides of the Balkan conflicts, I have seen more and more people shudder at the extent of violence and weapons.[82]

Friar Ivo also faced opposition to his peacemaking efforts from his Franciscan colleagues and others within the Catholic Church hierarchy. In response, Friar Ivo had to adapt his approaches.

> In addition to the differences within the Franciscan Order, there has also been tension between our order and the Church Government. Bishops try to control the orders, especially during the reign of the current Pope. Yet the orders also enjoy a high degree of freedom. Franciscans have traditionally been able to act on their own. It depends on the situation in the world and in the Church. My orientation is to be in accord with my Church in fundamental unity and mission, but I think creativity is important. It is also very important to be faithful to the true mission of the Church and resist any attempts on the part of the Church government to place nationalist ideology ahead of the Gospel of Christ.[83]

For Friar Ivo, peacemaking and reconciliation through conflict resolution align with what he sees as the true mission of the church: to live the Gospel of Christ. Friar Ivo's deep understanding of the core of his faith thus sustained him and helped him to transcend the opposition to persevere as an advocate for peacemaking.

Working toward Reconciliation

Friar Ivo Markovic is a powerful example of how one person can facilitate communication and reconciliation among people in conflict. During the Bosnian War, he assumed various roles. Sometimes, he was an advocate, encouraging Franciscans and others to appeal to local politicians not to inflame the conflict. At other times, he was an educator, using the written word to argue against the conflict and to educate the outside world of the plight in the Balkans. And often, he was a force for peace, successfully serving as a mediator and conciliator, bringing together disparate groups during and after the Bosnian War.

As of 2006, there is still much need for Friar Ivo's reconciliation and rehabilitation work. As one Bosnian notes, "We're definitely moving forward, but the progress is too slow.... The problem is that we're all still not pulling in the same direction.... I don't think that everybody has given up on the idea of splitting Bosnia into two or three parts."[84] Nationalistic tendencies still pervade the region, making for a shaky peace.

Yet, thanks in part to Friar Ivo's efforts to reconcile communities, people's perspectives have begun to change. His ability to listen closely to all people, to communicate compassion, and to maintain a sense of humor while standing firm in his convictions, has enabled him to address the unresolved issues still threatening the stability of the country. Even when faced with opposition from those within his own faith, Friar Ivo remains committed to focusing his efforts on relationship building and helping people constructively handle their fears. Having set this foundation in place, Friar Ivo has made Bosnia and Herzegovina a place where reconciliation and healing are more likely to succeed and someday thrive.

BOSNIA AND HERZEGOVINA FACT SHEET[85]

Geography

Location:
Southeastern Europe, bordering the Adriatic Sea, Croatia, and Serbia and Montenegro.

Area:
Total: 51,129 sq km
Land: 51,129 sq km
Water: 0 sq km

Area comparative:
Slightly smaller than West Virginia.

Climate:
Hot summers and cold winters; areas of high elevation have short, cool summers and long, severe winters; mild, rainy winters along coast.

Geography note:
Within Bosnia and Herzegovina's recognized borders, the country is divided into a joint Bosniak/Croat Federation (about 51 percent of the territory) and the Bosnian Serb-led Republika Srpska [RS] (about 49 percent of the territory); the region called Herzegovina is contiguous to Croatia and Serbia and Montenegro, and traditionally has been settled by an

ethnic Croat majority in the west and an ethnic Serb majority in the east.

Population

Population:	4,025,476 (July 2005 est.)
Ethnic groups:	Serb: 37.1%
	Bosniak: 48%
	Croat: 14.3% (2000)

Note: Bosniak has replaced Muslim as an ethnic term in order to avoid confusion with the religious term Muslim, which identifies an adherent of Islam.

Religions:	Muslim:	40%
	Orthodox Christian:	31%
	Roman Catholic:	15%
	Protestant:	4%
	other:	10%

Languages: Croatian, Serbian, and Bosnian.

Government

Government type:	Emerging Federal Democratic Republic.
Capital:	Sarajevo
Legal system:	Based on civil law system.

Recent Background

Bosnia and Herzegovina declared independence from Yugoslavia on March 3, 1992, after ethnic Serbs boycotted a referendum. In response, the Bosnian Serbs – with the support of neighboring Serbia and Montenegro – initiated an armed confrontation with the goal of partitioning the Republic along ethnic lines and merging with other Serb-held areas to form a "Greater Serbia."

In March 1994, Bosniaks and Croats signed an agreement creating the joint Bosniak/Croat Federation of Bosnia and Herzegovina, thus reducing the number of warring factions from three to two.

In the Dayton Accords of November 21, 1995, the warring parties entered into a peace agreement that effectively ended three years of interethnic civil conflict (the final draft of the agreement was signed in Paris on December 14, 1995). The Agreement maintained Bosnia and Herzegovina's international borders and created a multiethnic, democratic government, which was given responsibility for conducting foreign, economic, and fiscal policy. The Agreement also created a second level of government comprised of two entities of approximately equal size: the Bosniak/Croat Federation of Bosnia and Herzegovina and the Bosnian Serb-led Republika Srpska (RS). Each Federation's government was charged with overseeing their respective internal functions.

In 1995–1996, the NATO-led Implementation Force (IFOR) of some sixty thousand troops served in Bosnia to oversee the military aspects of the Agreement. IFOR was succeeded by the smaller, NATO-led Stabilization Force (SFOR), whose task was limited to preventing renewed hostilities. SFOR was replaced in December 2004 by European Union peacekeepers (EUFOR), who work to maintain internal peace and stability.

Economic Overview

Bosnia and Herzegovina is the second poorest of the former Yugoslav republics after Macedonia. Although agriculture is widely privatized, farms are undersized and inefficient, and the Republic is a net importer of food. The interethnic warfare in Bosnia and Herzegovina caused manufacturing output to plunge by 80 percent from 1990 to 1995, and unemployment to climb. With peace, there was some recovery of output from 1996 to 1999, followed by three years of stagnation and then a gradual turnaround until 2005. The shutdown of the communist-era state-owned banks (known as "payment bureaus") in 2001 helped speed up banking reform. Additionally, the international community provides the country with sizable amounts of reconstruction support and humanitarian assistance.

5 The Cybermonk

Father Sava Janjic

Kosovo

Both Albanians (nearly 95 percent of whom are Sunni Muslim) and Serbs (who are ethnic Slavs and primarily adhere to the Serbian Orthodox Christian religion) have long-standing ties to the land known as Kosovo, where they have shared a relatively peaceful coexistence for centuries. Though conflicts between the two groups erupted from time to time during their long and shared history, they became particularly exacerbated during the last century.

The story of Kosovo in the twentieth century is one of growing nationalism, fueled by the reemergence of latent ethnic hatred that led to violence among neighbors. Embedded within this story is one of the area's most committed peacemakers: Father Sava Janjic. His story is remarkable. By day, he was on the ground helping Serbian members of his church and their Albanian neighbors (all too often perceived to be their enemies). By night, he sought to even-handedly publicize the story of the Kosovo war. And whenever the opportunity arose, he sought to energize the international community for the cause of peace.

Father Sava's commitment was unwavering and his pace brutal. Over the course of several years, he pushed himself to the point of emotional and physical exhaustion, requiring hospitalization in 2000 after collapsing from the build-up of fatigue.

Early History of Kosovo

Located in southeastern Europe in the Balkans, the Autonomous Province of Kosovo lies nestled in Serbia and borders Montenegro, Albania, and Macedonia. A relatively flat plateau, Kosovo is surrounded by mountains on all sides, which serve as natural boundaries. At twelve thousand feet above sea level, Kosovo contains substantial mineral deposits that make it home to the richest concentration of natural resources in southeastern Europe. Indeed, its unique geography and natural resources have made it a desirable prize to the various empires that have vied for power in the Balkans throughout history.[1]

Slavs, of which the Serbs were one tribe, started conducting raids from Central Europe, across the Danube River, and into the Balkans during the sixth century. At the time, the land was administered by the Byzantine Empire. But as the raids became more frequent, Slavs began to settle down, ultimately diminishing Byzantine influence. By the twelfth century, the Serbs had begun moving into Kosovo in large numbers.[2]

Regional historians still debate whether the first settlers in the Kosovo region were ancestors of Serbs or Albanians and, consequently, disagree on who can lay claim to being the first inhabitants of the land. Regardless, by the twelfth century, Serbs controlled the area that is modern-day Northern Albania and Kosovo. Subsequently, Kosovo became the center of a thriving medieval Serbian state. But Serbian sovereignty ended in June 1389 with the invasion of the Ottoman Turks and the Battle of Kosovo Polje. Historians vary on what actually happened, but it is clear that the fighting was fierce, the leaders of both sides died in battle, and ultimately, the Ottomans won. Although Kosovo was quickly incorporated into the Ottoman Empire, the battle achieved legendary status in Serbian history as a glorious Christian sacrifice (in fact, the bones of the fallen soldiers are housed in Decani Monastery, the home of Father Sava). Interestingly, Albanians and Serbs joined in resisting their common occupier throughout the ensuing Ottoman occupation.[3]

Islamization of Kosovo

Although few Turks actually settled in Kosovo during Ottoman rule, many Albanians converted from Christianity to Islam. Such conversions were technically voluntary, but strong economic incentives existed, as Muslims were given greater trading rights than their non-Muslim neighbors. In contrast, most Serbs remained faithful to the Serbian Orthodox Church, which had many monasteries and churches throughout Kosovo.

The Ottomans viewed those who remained Christians and Jews as "people of the book," and offered them *dhimma* (protection) under the Ottoman Empire. The practice of dhimmitude dates back to the seventh century when prophet Muhammad and the Jews entered into a treaty in which the Jews forfeited their lands and agreed to defer to Muslims in business, in exchange for being allowed to continue practicing their faith in peace.[4]

Christians and Jews remained dhimmis in Kosovo until the mid-nineteenth century, when the Ottoman Sultan succumbed to European pressures and made them legal equals to Muslim citizens.[5]

The Late Nineteenth and Early Twentieth Centuries

In 1871, Serbs began to reassert their presence in Kosovo and established a Serbian seminary in Prizren. Shortly thereafter, in 1878, the Ottomans met defeat in the Russo-Ottoman war. The terms of the ensuing "Peace Accord" repartitioned the land in the region, giving Serbs control of Mitrovica and Pristina in Kosovo, with the balance remaining under Ottoman control.

Albanian nationalists actively protested the settlement. Backed by the Ottoman Sultan, they advocated for Kosovo to remain under Ottoman rule. In time, the Albanian nationalists became more overtly anti-Christian, eventually advocating what today would be called "ethnic cleansing," an alarming movement that encouraged many Serbs to leave Kosovo.[6]

In 1912, Montenegro, Serbia, Bulgaria, and Greece attacked Albania in the first Balkan War. Serbian nationalists encouraged multitudes to enlist, purportedly to avenge their defeat in the Battle of Kosovo Polje and to reestablish the great Serbian Christian kingdom defeated by the Ottomans centuries earlier. Framing that defeat as a great Christian sacrifice and a defining national moment,[7] Serbian nationalists emphasized ethnic differences to make their case.

When Serb forces entered Kosovo, they targeted the Albanians, killing many and destroying their villages. Within a year, Serbia had gained sovereignty over Kosovo. Many Serbian peasants settled in the region, even though the population remained predominantly pro-Albanian and anti-Serbian.[8] The tradition of coexistence among Albanians and Serbs became blurred, replaced by a historical fiction that the two groups had been in violent conflict for centuries.[9]

World War I and World War II

In Sarajevo in June 1914, a Serb nationalist assassinated Archduke Franz Ferdinand, heir to the throne of Austria-Hungary, setting in motion events that quickly escalated into World War I. Austria-Hungary and Germany declared war on Serbia, while Russia, France, and Britain sided with Serbia. Tensions heightened rapidly between Albanians and Serbs. Guerrilla warfare broke out in Kosovo, and atrocities were committed by both sides.[10]

Taking advantage of local infighting, Austro-Hungarian and Bulgarian troops entered Kosovo, defeating the Serb armies. Together with Serb civilians, the Serbian armies fled through the jagged Albanian mountains under the harshest of weather conditions. The resulting death toll was staggering. An estimated 150,000 died.[11]

Many Kosovar Albanians enlisted in the Austro-Hungarian and Bulgarian armies during the occupation. But when the war turned against Austria-Hungary in 1918, the Serbs regained Kosovo and took revenge, indiscriminately killing their Albanian neighbors – including women and children – and destroying their homes.[12]

The 1918–1920 peace treaties ending World War I established The Kingdom of Slovenes, Croats, and Serbs (later renamed Yugoslavia), again unifying Kosovo and Serbia. Although 64 percent of Kosovo's population was Albanian, the regional administration was overwhelmingly Serb and centered in Belgrade. Tensions fomented. When a group of armed Albanians sought Kosovo's annexation by Albania, many Serbs concluded that all Albanians were subversive nationalists who could potentially undermine their Serbian state.[13]

With the onset of World War II nearly twenty years later, Italy occupied Albania. Subsequently, in March 1941, the Yugoslav government entered into a pact with the Axis powers of Germany, Italy, and Japan. An anti-Axis coup two days later led to Yugoslavia's withdrawal from this pact, and then to Hitler's invasion of Yugoslavia in early April. Albania sided with Germany and, under the command of Nazi SS officers, Albanian soldiers brutalized the Serb population.

The combined Albanian and German armies were met with fierce resistance, led by Communist Party Leader Josip Broz "Marshall" Tito. With British support, Tito defeated the Germans and consolidated communist control of Yugoslavia. Yugoslavia would remain under Tito's leadership until his death in 1980.[14]

Kosovo under Tito

In the early years, Tito was suspicious of the Kosovar Albanians. As he solidified his control, he arrested many of them as "fascists" and waged a house-to-house campaign to disarm the community. When the Albanians resisted, Tito brutally suppressed them and an estimated forty-eight thousand soon perished. Then, in 1948, Tito broke with Stalin, but Albania remained loyal to Russia. As a result, Tito again targeted the Kosovar Albanians, characterizing many of them as "Stalinists" and arresting thousands more. By redrafting the constitution a few years later in 1953, Tito institutionalized his control by reducing Kosovo's autonomy. Tito's policies of Albanian oppression had an impact, including inadvertently encouraging Albanian nationalism.

However, by the late 1960s, Tito's position softened. He began making concessions to the ethnic Albanians and, in 1974, recognized Kosovo as an autonomous province. Albanians were given greater opportunities to participate in local government and a one-eighth share of constitutional power, making Kosovo equal to Serbia and other Yugoslav federal units. Considerable migration followed. Many Serbs left Kosovo, while many Albanians migrated to the province.[15]

Kosovo Post-Tito: 1981–1996

On May 4, 1980, Tito died, ushering in an era of political unrest, made worse by a crumbling regional economy. Nationalist groups that had been suppressed under Tito now vied for power throughout the Republic.[16]

In Kosovo, tensions heightened between Albanians and Serbs. Then, in March 1981, a seemingly innocuous protest by Albanian students at Kosovo's Pristina University over poor food spiraled into a full-fledged riot. Serbian and Montenegrin citizens were beaten, and the university came to be seen as a haven for Albanian nationalism. Massive popular demonstrations followed, taking on the character of an Albanian uprising. In turn, this led to the rise of Serbian, Montenegrin, and Macedonian nationalism, further dividing the region along sectarian lines.

By the mid-1980s, extremist Albanians were talking about the ethnic cleansing of Kosovo and unification with Albania. Droves of Serbs emigrated. Among those who stayed were a group of intellectuals who called for the de-Albanization of Kosovo. The verbal violence of these mutually exclusive calls for a region "cleansed" of the other eerily portended the physical violence that would follow.

As tensions mounted, Slobodan Milosevic began his rapid rise to power. In 1987, he seized the national spotlight during a visit to Kosovo. Speaking to a riotous crowd of Serbs demanding that the Serbian military take action against Albanian extremists, Milosevic proclaimed, "no one should dare to beat you!" – a reference hearkening back to the 1389 defeat of the

Serbs at the hands of the Islamic Ottoman Empire.[17] His words made national headlines. Seemingly overnight, Milosevic assumed the mantle of "the champion of the Serbs." With his newfound popularity and using jingoistic rhetoric, he assumed the Presidency of Yugoslavia, edging out his longtime mentor, Ivan Stambolic.

But Kosovo's Albanian-dominated local government remained an obstacle to Milosevic's quest to consolidate power in Yugoslavia. Although it was the poorest of the country's eight republics, Kosovo retained an equal vote in the national government. Accordingly, after assuming the presidency, Milosevic began a calculated campaign against Albanian nationalists, whom he accused of conspiring against Serbia and Serbian Orthodox Christians.

By July 1990, the constitution was again altered, this time putting Kosovo under Serbian (rather than Federal Yugoslav) control and officially dissolving Kosovo's government. Assuming executive control, Milosevic set up what was essentially a police state. He stripped Albanians of managerial positions and replaced them with his loyalists. He dismissed Albanian police officers and created a new force. And at Pristina University, many lecturers were fired and numerous students expelled.

Meanwhile, communism was collapsing in the Soviet Union and throughout Eastern Europe. In turn, the Federal Units of Yugoslavia began demanding independence. On December 26, 1990, Slovenia's inhabitants overwhelmingly voted for independence. By April 1992, Croatia and Bosnia and Herzegovina had gained their independence as well.

In Kosovo, both Albanians and Serbs began forming militias, stockpiling weapons and launching attacks on their neighbors. In addition, when the 1995 series of U.S.-brokered agreements known as the Dayton Accords were completed, Kosovo was not addressed, leaving the tensions between Albanians and Serbs to percolate.

It was in the midst of this growing conflict that Father Sava Janjic emerged from his monastic duties to struggle for peace.

Father Sava Janjic: Evolution of a Peacemaker

Most biographical accounts of Father Sava Janjic begin with something like the following: he lived a quiet and orderly existence until the Kosovo War. Although perhaps slightly over simplified, such a narrative nonetheless captures the basic plot of the beginning of his personal story. For years, Father Sava lived peacefully with twenty-two fellow monks in the Decani Monastery, located near the Albanian border.[18] Adorned with thousands of ornate images commissioned more than six hundred years ago, many depicting the life of Christ before his crucifixion, the monastery – the largest in Kosovo – is a spiritual oasis and a centuries-old treasure of the Serbian Orthodox Church.[19]

There, Father Sava served as secretary to Bishop Artemije – head of the Serbian Orthodox Church for the diocese encompassing Kosovo – for whom he translated and prepared all documents requiring the bishop's signature. Fluent in English and technologically savvy, Father Sava designed and updated the church's Web site, the first of its kind in the Balkans, thereby placing the monks of Decani on the Internet years before many of their Western counterparts. Had it not been for the war, Father Sava would have lived out his days much like the monks who had come before him, enjoying the quiet, cloistered life of the monastery.

The Cybermonk: Peacemaking during the Kosovo War

Throughout the war in Kosovo, Father Sava defied the stereotype of a cloistered monk. Armed with two computers, an Internet connection, a short-wave radio, and a mastery of English, he sent out a daily stream of e-mails, supplying journalists and diplomats with their only reliable on-the-ground perspective of the conflict. Father Sava answered their questions and supplied them with local news sources, which he often translated into English. In short order, his fluency in English and his position as secretary to Bishop Artemije effectively made him the unofficial media spokesperson of the Serbian Orthodox Church. As such, he was often in the public eye as the conflict escalated around him.

To many, Father Sava was known simply as "the Cybermonk." A master of modern technology, he was an invaluable resource who cut through the rhetoric of nationalist news sources and told the "real" story of the conflict on the ground.[20] The international media particularly loved him. As one journalist explains:

> Reporters, especially foreign ones, simply adored Father Sava for speaking perfect English, for being exceptionally well-educated, for being one of those who agreed to make a guest appearance on TV Kosovo, to give interviews and statements to the Albanian media when it was necessary and because, from the very beginning, Father Sava Janjic always fought against violence and vandalism with courage that many others lacked.[21]

Particularly helpful to the outside world, Father Sava understood how the media was being misused and therefore focused on correcting the various inaccuracies that distorted the reality on the ground.

Father Sava recounts how in the early stages of the war, the violence took on the form of an Albanian rebellion. On April 22, 1996, four nearly simultaneous attacks on Serbian targets occurred in Kosovo. A previously unknown group, calling itself the "Kosovo Liberation Army" (KLA), claimed responsibility. Milosevic met the KLA's armed resistance with brute force. The Serbian media downplayed the attacks, characterizing them as isolated terrorist attacks carried out by rogue combatants. In reality, it was the onset of a full-fledged rebellion. As the violence escalated, it quickly became apparent to Father Sava that "the Albanians had begun creating some sort of breakaway republic of their own...which would establish ties with Albania and enable the further expansion of the rebellion."[22]

Milosevic responded by again trying to manipulate the media, though in a different manner. No longer able to downplay the insurgency, he sought to use the media to intimidate his opponents. He therefore allowed journalists to photograph masses of unburied bodies, believing that the horrific images of the dead – once widely circulated – would induce terror and fear in the Albanian population. Father Sava described what happened:

> Disproportionately great force was used and many people were killed who could not be called terrorists: women, children and elderly persons. After this, a horrible situation ensued: the bodies were kept in a sort of improvised garage, burial was not allowed, autopsies were not even conducted. The bloody corpses were displayed to reporters and those pictures were seen around the world.[23]

However, Milosevic's perverse strategy backfired. Rather than cowering, the horror strengthened the Albanian population's resolve and further fanned the flames of violence:

> The Albanians reacted in a manner that might have been expected: with complete decisiveness to continue the rebellion. They were not frightened, quite the contrary. And so the number of rebels quickly rose to approximately two thousand, and shortly afterward, during the summer months, there were twenty thousand of them. The terrorist attacks on the police quickly became acts of armed rebellion, which continued to be called terrorism by our official media even though they had taken on far wider dimensions.[24]

In Father Sava's opinion, this was just what the KLA had hoped for: "Members of the KLA very clearly foresaw and anticipated what

Milosevic's reactions would be. Their goal was to provoke the regime as much as possible."[25]

As the violence intensified, Father Sava worked tirelessly within his local community and with the selfless monks of the Decani Monastery, who did everything in their power to care for those in need. But Father Sava was called to do more.

Concerned that the world was not paying attention to the conflict as it was growing into full-fledged war, Father Sava became involved in diplomatic efforts designed to encourage powerful nations to become involved. Aware as early as 1996 that large quantities of arms were trickling into Kosovo relatively unhindered by the police,[26] and concerned about the increasing violence, Bishop Artemije, Morricilo Trajkovic (the most prominent political opponent of Milosevic in the region), and Father Sava developed a grassroots peace proposal and went to the United States seeking support. The three men believed that they had the authority to act on behalf of all Kosovo Serbs. But despite meeting with key diplomats, the international community ultimately passed them by, pursuing negotiations with Milosevic. Their pleas had fallen on deaf ears. The international community failed to intervene during that narrow window and did nothing to prevent the conflict from escalating into full-fledged war.

Undeterred, Father Sava persevered. During the ensuing months, he redoubled his diplomatic efforts, traveling with Bishop Artemije to the United States, where he testified before Congress and met with key figures, including U.S. Secretary of State Madeleine Albright. Simultaneously, Father Sava became a prominent voice for peace: he represented the Serbian Orthodox Church on numerous television and radio programs; he maintained the Decani Web site; and his correspondence with journalists became an everyday occurrence. Father Sava became one of the most visible Serbian opponents of Milosevic's Belgrade regime – thereby placing his life at risk.

Father Sava's diplomatic work with his bishop was difficult, and their successes were often hard to measure. During one visit to the United States, U.S. Ambassador Robert S. Gelbard stopped referring to the Albanians as "terrorists." To Father Sava, this was a significant change in diplomatic language; the international community was learning that the KLA were not just a handful of violent malcontents, but that the conflict in Kosovo went deeper and was far more pervasive.[27]

Indeed, by the end of March 1998, the fighting encompassed nearly all of Kosovo. Refugees poured through the doors of the monastery in flight from the KLA's encroaching campaign. Father Sava describes how he and his brothers tried to help:

> In the region of Decani, it came down to only a few Serbs remaining in their houses; then we heard that they had been killed or were missing. Nothing was known for certain, it was not possible to go to this region. The police did not go there any more. By then, in the region between Decani and Radonjic Lake [Radonjicko jezero], with Glodjane at its center, an ethnically "clean" territory had already been created.... We took in Serbian refugees from the surrounding villages and provided them with food. They were situated on a hill above the monastery and would observe their houses in the distance, hoping to return one day. I remember once, during the summer, we went to visit them and saw villages in the distance burning, much smoke, the thud of cannon, spurts of machine-gun fire.
>
> An old woman, Milka Stojanovic, said to me: "Look, my house is over there somewhere. These young people are happy, thinking that this will end well, but I think that I will never return to that region again." And she was right, the Serbs never returned to that region again. All the Serbian houses were set on fire and destroyed. The bodies of seven or eight elderly people who stayed in their homes were later found in a grave near Radonjic Lake.[28]

The Serbian military countered by systematically decimating entire Albanian villages in a manner reminiscent of the years of ethnic cleansing in Bosnia:

> This was supposed to be a campaign against an armed rebellion, however, what happened was the systematic destruction of one part of town in which the majority of [Albanian] houses was destroyed without any fighting....
>
> It was explained to us that had this campaign not taken place, the KLA would have entered Decani very quickly and completely liquidated the Serbs and that this was prevented literally hours before it was due to occur. Many [Albanian] houses, including those which were undamaged by grenades, were subsequently looted and set on fire, as were the shops. It was the same model, which we saw earlier in Bosnia.[29]

As the conflict unfolded and brutalities were perpetrated upon all groups, Father Sava welcomed refugees to his monastery without regard to their ethnicity or religion. Father Makarije, who worked with Father Sava, describes this turbulent time:

> This was before the [NATO] bombing when all sorts of paramilitary formations were running wild throughout Metohija. If we had not hidden them, they would have been killed. There were women and children among them....

They also threatened to slaughter all the monks in the monastery if we did not turn over the Albanians. Prior Teodosije would not give in for days and Father Sava ensured safe passage for all of them.[30]

On that occasion, alone, Father Sava helped more than seventy Albanians escape death.[31] Sadly, his efforts to save all refugees were met with suspicion. Both Albanians and Serbs questioned why the Serbian Orthodox Church took Albanian refugees into its monastery. Some Serbian extremists believed that helping Albanians was tantamount to treason, and many Albanians questioned the church's motives for helping them.

Feeling the need to respond, Father Sava issued a press release explaining that it was his moral and spiritual imperative to help all of the "greatest victims" who "suffer immensely because of aggressive political ambitions." He explained that, even though the church was attached "both spiritually and historically to the Serbian people," its "spiritual obligation . . . [included all] who live in the region, especially . . . the needful and unprotected."[32] Father Sava made clear that his moral obligation to protect all people at risk superseded all nationalist politics.

For Father Sava, it was his religious duty to speak out and condemn the perpetrators of the violence. As he explains:

> Hence, if in this tragedy we have to take someone under our protection, we do not have [the] moral right to do this either on [an] ethnic or [a] religious base, but we bravely dare express our sympathy first with all innocent victims, the hungry and displaced people no matter which ethnic group they belong to. Therefore we firmly condemn any criminal act, inhuman conduct and injustice no matter by whom or where it was done. No one has [the] moral right to build his happiness on the misfortune of his neighbor.[33]

Father Sava was not religiously conflicted about these beliefs. Indeed, he sees them as being consistent with Orthodox Church teachings, including its history of advocating for nonviolence and tolerance.

> This is what our Faith is teaching us, our Saints and the holy tradition of the Orthodox Church. This is what we have preached to all who come to our monastery. From the very beginning of the conflict in this area, Decani Monastery opened its gates and brotherly helped the refugees from the neighboring villages. And now we are trying to provide enough food supplies to be able to help anyone who asks for our help and assistance. In this we are ready to cooperate with the international humanitarian organizations if necessary.[34]

In addition to publicly explaining his motivations, Father Sava began writing position papers (discussed in the section on peacemaking methods later in this chapter) on ways religious communities could become actively involved in conflict resolution and quelling the violence. These papers would later become a basis for interreligious dialogues in the region.

In response to the escalating conflict, in May 1998, NATO focused on seeking a peaceful resolution to the crisis. But when the situation continued to deteriorate, NATO turned to threats, warning that it would use air-strikes in support of its diplomatic initiatives. For a short time, it appeared that its tactic had worked. Milosevic agreed to a cease-fire, and the Organization for Security and Cooperation in Europe (OSCE) sent a verification mission to the region.[35] Father Sava was optimistic, believing that OSCE "would succeed . . . and that negotiations would be opened between the Albanian political representatives and the regime."[36] In the end, however, the real result of its efforts was that the situation in Kosovo received increased international media attention – coverage that Father Sava saw as one-sided because the conflict was framed "exclusively as organized repression and terror against the Albanian population."[37] Thus, to Father Sava, the media was oversimplifying the story, blaming the Milosevic regime for the violence and portraying the Albanians as helpless victims, rather than portraying the violence and the suffering of victims of both sides.

To Father Sava's consternation and dread, all parties involved – the Albanians, the Belgrade regime, and the international community – remained entrenched and intent on resorting to force. Violence again flared in early 1999. When efforts to reestablish the cease-fire proved ineffective, NATO convened multiparty negotiations in February and March 1999.[38]

Barred from the talks, the Serbian Orthodox Church and Father Sava could do little but wait. The talks failed to reach a consensus (the resulting peace agreement was signed only by the American, British, and Albanian delegations with the Serbian delegation refusing to sign). Almost immediately afterward, the Serbs reinitiated military operations against the Albanian population of Kosovo, and OSCE left. Anticipating NATO air-strikes, Milosevic nonetheless refused to call off the attacks, and the air-strikes began on March 23, 1999. They would last for seventy days.[39]

As Father Sava had predicted, the situation in Kosovo quickly deteriorated. Violence took a brutal toll on the entire population. Father Sava stepped up his efforts to respond to the escalating humanitarian crisis. In a widely circulated story, written two months into the NATO campaign, one journalist described Father Sava's heroic efforts to help save local Albanians from the hands of his fellow Serbs:

> The Kosovo war was ending, but Serbian police and paramilitaries were still torching buildings. Afraid of being burnt alive, ethnic Albanians fled their homes, cowering in the woods and countryside for a rainy, seemingly endless night. Then, winding down a wooded lane, came two monks in a white van from the nearby cloistered and ancient Serbian Orthodox monastery of Visoki Decani, Western Kosovo. "Come with us," they told the Albanians. "We will keep you safe...." "Without [the Decani monks]" said one Albanian, "my whole family would be dead."[40]

Sleeping an average of four hours a night throughout the nearly three months of NATO bombings, Father Sava would climb nightly into the same rickety white van and navigate through the war torn region under the cover of darkness. Often, when it became too dangerous for him to drive farther or to return, he would sleep in the van or hide until it was again safe for him to proceed. These risks would not deter him. Father Sava was committed to keeping communication open and therefore embarked each night to respond to hundreds of e-mails from correspondents eager for news and information. Father Sava used the Internet to provide daily on-the-ground perspectives of the effects of the NATO campaign.

During the war, the Serbian military systematically attacked Albanians, seeking to drive them out of Kosovo. Entire villages were destroyed and burned, civilians massacred, and in some instances, such as in Pristina, tens of thousands of Albanians were carted onto trains and dropped at the Macedonian border. The UN estimates eight hundred thousand persons – mostly Albanians – were displaced.[41]

As the NATO bombings came to an end, Father Sava was saddened by the visceral hatred and divisiveness that infected Kosovo's population – Albanians and Serbs alike. But he understood it. At the time, he explained that the "hatred is the result of both sides' inability to distinguish individuals within a collective and their insistence, instead, of viewing everything...collectively."[42]

Peacemaking after NATO's Bombing

In postwar Kosovo, the Albanian majority viewed local Serbs as indistinguishable from the Belgrade regime and its efforts to exclude Albanians from the region. Even one member of an Albanian family saved by Father

Sava could not let go of his intense hatred. When asked about the Decani monks' intervention, this man replied: "But this action [saving his family] by a few Serbs does not change how we think about most Serbs.... They have done terrible things here, and we know most of them are that way."[43]

Following the war and the reinstatement of Kosovo's autonomy under the UN Interim Administration Mission in Kosovo (UNMIK) – created by UN Security Council Resolution 1244[44] – Albanians regained control of the local government. As KLA leaders assumed power, some sought revenge and the de facto establishment of an Albanian state. This objective was supported when a majority of Albanian refugees returned (in contrast to the many Serbian refugees who stayed away out of fear for their lives). It was a difficult time. In Father Sava's opinion, the Serbs who remained in Kosovo endured living conditions far worse than the conditions faced by the Albanians years earlier: "the naked hatred of the Albanians [is] now ... approaching madness. Everything which is Serb – or to be even more precise, everything that is not controlled by the KLA – is exposed to some degree of repression and persecution."[45]

Indeed, as a member of the church, Father Sava experienced the repression firsthand. That the Serbian Orthodox Church was one of the only vocal opponents of Milosevic made no difference. Albanian extremists vandalized church buildings, cemeteries, and other sacred sites throughout Kosovo. After the bombings, local Albanian extremists also harassed Serbs. International peacekeeping forces failed to provide protection. Even though he had opposed the bombing campaign, Father Sava believed that such international involvement was necessary and looked to NATO to protect Serbs from Albanian extremists.[46] Hundreds of thousands of Serbs left Kosovo during these difficult days, whereas those who remained lived in what were effectively isolated ghettoes, scared to leave their homes out of fear of being harassed or killed.

Further fueling the tensions, regional history was being revisited with Albanians claiming that the Serbian Orthodox Church stole most of its monasteries in Kosovo during medieval times from Roman Catholics. (At that time, most Albanians were Roman Catholic and had not yet converted to Islam.)

For Father Sava, the worst injustices involved "the opening of graves, the destruction of coffins and the scattering of bones." He saw these horrific acts as analogous to the plight of the Serbs: "If the deceased are treated in this manner, one can only imagine how the living [Serb people] are treated.... The war against the dead especially represents the most morbid dimension of hate which reigns in this region."[47] Father Sava saw these efforts as part of a KLA campaign to erase Serbian and Christian culture from the region.

Following the NATO bombings, Father Sava turned openly to politics, lobbying to remove Milosevic from office and becoming involved with prodemocracy student groups. He was instrumental in writing and circulating a "Declaration on [the] Future of Serbia," which warned that "the survival of our state is seriously threatened, as well as the survival of all the citizens and above all, our common future." It then issued a call to resist the regime, remove Slobodan Milosevic and hold him and his regime accountable for their detrimental policies, and to seek "Free and fair general elections by rules overseen by the OSCE (Organization for Security and Co-operation in Europe)."[48]

Even though it was not always popular to do so, Father Sava also met with NATO officials and U.S. diplomats, seeking help in moving his country to democracy. In July 1999, U.S. Secretary of State Madeleine Albright met with Bishop Artemije and Father Sava at the Gracanica Monastery, where Father Sava had recently moved because Decani had become unsafe. Many Serbs in the region objected to Albright's presence; a boisterous mob gathered outside the monastery, filling the air with rhythmic chants of support for Milosevic. *The Washington Times* recounted what happened next:

> Serbian extremists...then stormed the gates of a monastery [Albright] had visited, forcing their own church leaders to flee.
>
> British troops ran to protect Serbian Orthodox priests...as they fled to a second-floor balcony.
>
> The Rev. Sava Janjic yelled to the soldiers: "Hold them back."
>
> But by the time the soldiers reacted, the mob already was barging through. Several dozen British soldiers held the throng of Milosevic supporters at bay. The extremists threatened Bishop Artemije and several priests with a "proper beating" for meeting Mrs. Albright....
>
> "How can [the bishop] talk to her?" shouted someone in the crowd. "Americans bombed us!"
>
> "That priest met Albright. She is Hitler!" yelled another man in the crowd, which chanted "Serbia" and "Slobo" in support of Mr. Milosevic as Mrs. Albright's motorcade left.[49]

United Press International, also covering the story, quoted Father Sava and described his concerns about NATO's effectiveness:

> The idea of the KLA or at least its extreme wing is to destroy Serbian homes and church property to create a de facto kind of independence that the world will be forced to recognize....NATO has the intelligence and force

to identify the perpetrators but so far they have failed. The worst thing they have done is leave the Albanian border open and allow all criminal gangs to enter.[50]

In February 2000, with Bishop Artemije, Father Sava continued his diplomatic efforts, again visiting the United States. This time they came with support from diverse religious leaders. Although some religious leaders made scattered appeals for tolerance as early as 1998, the faith communities joined together in the healing process on February 8, 2000, when they issued a Shared Moral Commitment.[51] In a historic event, Muslim, Serbian Orthodox, and Roman Catholic leaders jointly condemned violence and appealed to their shared moral values to "serve as an authentic basis for mutual esteem, co-operation and free common living in the entire territory of Kosovo...." They further stated, "We call on all people of good will to take responsibility for their own acts."[52] Although Father Sava was enthusiastic about the renewed contact among religious leaders and was empowered in his diplomatic work by their public collaboration, his enthusiasm was restrained because the Shared Moral Commitment did not ask forgiveness for past wrongs and for reconciliation – steps that he considered to be critically important.

To achieve real peace, both Bishop Artimije and Father Sava Janjic believed that it was necessary to provide for the safe return of Serbs to Kosovo. Accordingly, while in the United States, they sought help in arranging for the return of displaced Serbs, stopping KLA violence, and rebuilding Kosovo politically and economically.[53] To this end, they again met with Madeleine Albright. After they finished, the U.S. Department of State issued a press statement announcing their support for an initiative to safely return Serb refugees. As of 2004, however, the Serb refugees had not returned.

Father Sava's diplomatic efforts were complicated by the manner in which the Kosovo conflict was understood abroad. In the United States, many viewed the conflict as a simple tale of good versus evil; Milosevic oppressed Albanians, who with the help of NATO, resisted their unjust oppressor and regained their freedom after the war. Father Sava found that most people did not see the situation in the same way that he did. For him, the conflict in Kosovo was not a religious war; instead, it resulted from ethnic leaders using religious differences for their own ends, and from religious leaders being slow to act. Few accepted Father Sava's explanation that extremists who did not represent the majority of the population had perpetrated the conflict. Father Sava's isolation was further compounded by the poor reception his calls for peace received from fellow Serbs.[54]

On his return to Kosovo, the once-energetic monk was dismayed that his tireless efforts were bearing few or no visible results. Stress from years of campaigning in the cause of peace began to take its toll as the world he fought so hard to protect continued in turmoil: Serbian Orthodox sites were being destroyed, and even some of his fellow Serbs accused him of treason. Journalists were following war stories in other parts of the world, NATO considered the bombing campaign a success, and, gradually, the e-mails and queries from around the globe – once three hundred per day – stopped coming.

Father Sava considered withdrawing from political life but resisted the urge. After returning from his U.S. visit, he and Bishop Artemije met with a delegation of anti-Milosevic leaders in Belgrade. They urged them to sign a joint statement declaring that it was not an act of treason for Kosovo's Serbs to work with the United Nations and to acknowledge how the atrocities done in their name contributed to the hatred in Kosovo. But the delegation's leaders were not prepared to admit publicly that injustices had in fact been inflicted on Albanians.[55] Notwithstanding the efforts of the bishop and Father Sava, the delegation ultimately refused to sign a joint statement or to make a public admission of wrongdoing.

Feeling the weight of this failed attempt – his voice again falling on deaf ears – Father Sava became melancholic. He could push himself no more, and shortly thereafter, he completely collapsed. That summer, he was transferred from Gracanica to Paris, where doctors determined that he suffered from complete physical and psychological exhaustion.[56]

Father Sava withdrew from public life, returning to the Decani Monastery under the utmost secrecy in late 2000. Father Vasilije Dejic, the archdeacon who shared a room with Father Sava for more than a year at the monastery in Gracanica, explained the decision: "Father Sava returned to Decani for the salvation of his soul. He left everything: his computer, his cell phone.... His current assignment is to serve as the librarian."[57]

Father Sava has slowly made a return to public life, though the intensity of his involvement by no means matches its level prior to his collapse in 2000. This reflects his and his fellow monks' current isolation. They drive fifty miles under military escort to Montenegro for food and supplies because it is unsafe to leave their cars in the nearby town. Albanians there also refuse to sell to them. Still, Father Sava and his fellow monks have found inner peace in their solitude. To one journalist in 2003, Father

Sava commented philosophically: "The outer situation has not affected the inner, spiritual life at all.... I can say it's even become more intense." Always thinking about the big picture, he added: "In the history of Christianity, spiritual life increases under repression."[58]

Recently, position papers and statements have again started to flow out of Decani, and Father Sava's voice and image have begun to reappear in international news stories, often on behalf of Bishop Artemije. "The monastic way is no longer seen as some kind of time machine, going into the past," he shared in 2003. "It's not a petrified form of spirituality. We wear strange clothes and follow strange rules, but Orthodox Christianity is able to give something spiritually to these people today."[59] Father Sava continues to pursue peace, although only time will tell whether he will again immerse himself in full-time peacemaking work on the ground.

Father Sava's Perspective: The Conflict and Its Causes

Father Sava points to destructive nationalism and manipulation of the public through effective but divisive communications by Milosevic and others as causes of the war. Additionally, he sees the effective effort to sever the people from the church as another contributing factor.

Essentially, Father Sava sees the conflict as a byproduct of irreconcilable, mutually exclusive nationalist ideologies that began to emerge in the nineteenth century and ultimately poisoned his homeland. He explains that this was new to the region, noting that for centuries, the community had shared a more "religious self-consciousness than the present secular one [and]... Serbs and Albanians did not have global national conflicts. Of course, there were individual cases of revenges and quarrels, but they nevertheless kept living together sharing both good and evil together."[60] Though notions of a Serbian state have roots dating back to the twelfth century, Father Sava believes that "modern national consciousness" is something that emerged in recent history[61] and was manipulated by Milosevic. Thus, Father Sava believes that many – including most Western diplomats – incorrectly viewed Milosevic as a leader acting on behalf of Kosovo's Serbs, when in actuality he represented only his own interests and the interests of his regime in Belgrade. "Milosevic comes and does what he does, and then the Kosovo Serbs have to pay the bills," he observed sadly just after the Kosovo War.[62]

Nationalists such as Milosevic played on religious differences between Albanians and Serbs to leverage support for their political agendas. Religion thus became a tool to further reify the "otherness" of the

Albanians, while consolidating power. Father Sava believes that "the Belgrade regime ghettoized the country in order to preserve its political power," thus making "the situation in Kosovo unbearable with . . . [Albanian and Serb] parallel states."[63] Speaking of the Serbs, he described them as "hostages of the Serbian regime, squeezed between Milosevic – who presented himself to them as their only savior all these years – and on the other side, the Albanian nationalist idea [with no place for Serbs within it]."[64]

In stark juxtaposition to Milosevic, the Serbian Orthodox Church remained one of the few moderate voices promoting peaceful coexistence in the region. As a church spokesperson, Father Sava urged the people "not [to] forget that [Kosovo] is also important for the Albanian people and that we are both living in this land. We must face the reality."[65] But religious voices of moderation like those of Father Sava were sidelined as nationalists on both sides called for ethnic cleansing in the region.

Indeed, as the recipient of harsh criticism from Father Sava and Bishop Artemije, Milosevic's strategy was to marginalize them. He barred the Serbian Orthodox Church from all diplomatic decisions affecting Kosovo, and refused to participate in the 1999 NATO peace talks if the church was present. Milosevic thus sought to separate the people from their church, presumably because he also recognized the church as a center of regional values. Father Sava believes that "the monasteries and churches . . . helped the Serbian people to preserve their identity, their language, and their customs."[66] As people were swept up by nationalist fervor and divisions became more pronounced, they were increasingly cut off from these resources. Indeed, Father Sava laments that "many Serbs have left [Kosovo] during this century and . . . [have now become] a minority in their ancestral land."[67]

Reflections on Peacemaking Methods

What marks Father Sava most clearly as a religiously motivated peacemaker is his appreciation of the power of communication and the religious voice in protecting people in conflict and promoting peace. His commitment to truth, to presenting balanced perspectives, and to using modern technology are among his most powerful peacemaking legacies. His use of language is noteworthy. Throughout all of his writings, Father Sava consciously avoids language that enflames. For this reason, journalist Andrew Wasley, who was nominated for the Martha Gelhorn Prize for Journalism for his coverage of the Kosovo war, describes Father Sava as the conflict's "premier peace journalist."[68]

"Peace journalism," Wasley asserts, "attempts to alert audiences to the myriad of perspectives present in conflict, highlighting the agendas, mindsets and reasoning of all sides." In so doing, it "enables the audience to gain a fuller understanding which empowers them, and allows them to think about alternative courses of action, stretching beyond the typical string of unconnected facts and pictures of missiles hurtling off into the sky." Father Sava "attempted to do just this," Wasley says, by seeking "to alert his global audience to the shortcomings on all sides which had led to the crisis." Peace journalism also "attempts to address . . . distortions by applying appropriate coverage to every source, a principle vigorously adhered to by Father Sava in his reporting." As an example, Wasley points to the language used on the Decani website, which he describes as "clearly designed to avoid offence."[69]

> Whereas sections of the western media had few qualms about branding Serbian militiamen "fanatics" or "crazed murderers," Father Sava restrained himself in adopting such bloodletting descriptions to describe Serbian combatants – even when recounting in detail how the KLA had reportedly gunned down innocent Serbian boys fleeing the violence.[70]

Wasley notes that reliance by outside journalists on Father Sava's reporting diminished as news crews accompanied the NATO campaign into regions that previously had been inaccessible. However, given the criticism that Western media received for biased coverage of the conflict, Wasley suggests that Father Sava would be a good model for journalists. "The example set by the cybermonk Father Sava should be taken seriously. . . . Those eager to report in a humane and responsible manner, which considers the needs of those caught up in the violence, would do well to listen."[71]

Consistently, Father Sava was careful in his use of language as he spoke out. In a widely circulated commentary on a paper by Mr. Qemajl Morina, a lecturer at the Islamic Faculty of Pristina and a senior representative of the Albanian Muslim community, Father Sava refuted Morina's claims that the Serbian Orthodox Church perpetrated propaganda to cleanse the land of Muslims.[72] Father Sava's response emphasized that the "Kosovo conflict is not a religious war but a conflict between two extremist nationalist ideologies." In his critique of Morina's perspective, Father Sava used a personal voice and characteristically neutral language: "I must admit that I personally regret that Mr. Morina in his essay is going more and more to the past instead of looking to our common future."[73]

Although there is no direct proof that Father Sava was the cause, Mr. Morina's views changed over the eighteen months after the publication of Father Sava's piece and following their joint participation in interfaith dialogues. Within eighteen months, the World Council of Churches (WCC) reported on a meeting it had held with Morina and Xhabir Hamiti in which they no longer blamed the Serbian Orthodox Church for instigating a crusade against Muslims. "The new millennium must be marked by an interreligious approach to conflict resolution," said Hamiti.[74]

For Father Sava, the way one communicates is critical. He believes that religious communities must communicate their values. However, he believes it is even more important for religious communities to *act*. Throughout the war, Father Sava put these values into practice. Working with his religious community, he repeatedly put his own life at risk to save people on all sides of the conflict. He communicated openly regardless of the consequences, condemning Milosevic and the horror. He tried to support peace and reconciliation through diplomatic initiatives.

Beyond the war itself, Father Sava believes that religious communities have responsibility for creating the conditions for true reconciliation. Thus, he suggests that they actively encourage the acceptance of responsibility for past atrocities so that the communities they serve can move toward a better future. "[All religious communities in Kosovo] can cooperate if we all agree to condemn the violence on all sides," Father Sava argues. "Emotional gestures of friendship are vain if we do not begin to make a difference among the people on the moral level."[75]

To Father Sava, failure to admit responsibility and to ask for forgiveness is a stumbling block to peace. "Forgiveness," according to Father Sava, is "the first and [most] necessary step for reconciliation." He explained to PBS for its cover story on Kosovo in 2000:

> As a Christian . . . we all . . . say hundreds of times a day, "God, forgive. God, forgive." And why shouldn't we say this in front of other people if we say that in front of God so many times? Why should it be so difficult? That's something which we all have to learn. It's so simple, but it's so strong.[76]

As a contemplative communicator, Father Sava identified a strategy for peacemaking, which is premised on contact, dialogue, and truth. In a paper he published called "Religion in Kosovo," he laid out nine points that detail a comprehensive methodology for religious communities to become actively involved in Track Two diplomacy and conflict resolution. This pioneering work has since served as a model for interreligious dialogue and peacemaking efforts in the region. Below are his nine points:

1. Despite all their religious differences, religious communities ought to clearly demonstrate readiness to pursue a lasting peace based on truth, justice, and respect of human rights. This goal can be achieved only by developing cooperation, personal contacts, and organizing symposiums and debates in the spirit of tolerance and mutual respect for tradition and customs. Religious communities could make an active and sincere contribution to building trust and furthering coexistence.

2. Parallel with the official negotiating process, members of religious communities, academics, scientists, humanitarian activists, crisis-solving experts, could, by way of unofficial meetings, assist the negotiating process by proposing solutions as well as contribute to the implementation of the agreements reached. Religious communities should distance themselves from all forms of ethnic extremism and religious intolerance, which requires refraining from unbalanced statements, unfounded charges and referring to members of other ethnic groups in a derogatory manner, as well as reducing ethnic animosities by promoting peace and respect for one's fellow men.

3. It is essential to establish cooperation in the area of humanitarian work, especially by creating conditions for the return of refugees and other displaced people. The work of humanitarian organizations and their free access to endangered areas should be openly supported and direct cooperation with them established.

4. In no way should religious communities directly or indirectly incite or justify any use of violence against innocent people, and they should condemn every abuse or violation of basic human rights. In doing so, appeals, official announcements of certain events and active efforts within their respective communities in fighting violence would be of great assistance. It should be particularly stressed that human life is the greatest gift of God, and that human beings and their dignity should be respected as required by both earthly and divine laws.

5. There should be intense activity against discrimination along ethnic or religious lines. This could be achieved by increasing humanitarian activities and making aid available to all in need of it, regardless of

nationality or faith, as well as by protecting ethnic groups which are minorities in certain areas or are otherwise endangered.

6. Special, strong appeals should be made against the destruction and desecration of sacred places (mosques, churches and cemeteries) and cultural monuments. To destroy that which has been preserved for centuries is an act of ultimate barbarism. On the other hand, such places should under no circumstances be used for military purposes.

7. In the area of humanitarian activities, acts of personal vengeance and retaliation, together with the abduction of people and other forms of illegal detention, should be particularly condemned. Strong appeals should be launched against the unnecessary and deliberate destruction of private property: the torching of houses and crops, and slaughter of livestock, and at the same time all assistance available should be offered for the renewal of areas ravaged by the clashes.

8. Religious communities should appeal to news media to prevent provocative and biased reporting on the activities of religious communities, as such reporting often fans the flames of inter-ethnic hate and intolerance. Educational programs on electronic media should not promote quasi-historic theories denying religious and cultural identity to any ethnic group. Abusing and forging history for the sake of political objectives is an injustice which seriously undermines inter-ethnic and inter-religious relations.

9. Religious communities should demand normal contact with their congregations. All attempts to jeopardize religious freedom should be openly condemned and unobstructed activity of spiritual leaders and institutions secured, as well as free access for believers to their places of worship.[77]

Lastly, Father Sava recognizes that peacemaking takes time. Violence exacerbated tensions greatly between Albanians and Serbs, and he acknowledges that it will take much effort to overcome the mutual distrust between the two communities. But time can bring peace, and he remains hopeful that they will someday coexist peacefully.[78]

Religious Motivation for Peacemaking

Father Sava admits that he would have preferred to live the life of a simple monk, praying seven hours a day and subsisting on a meager vegetarian diet. And yet, as conflict burgeoned around him, he responded to a moral and religious imperative to become involved. In his own words:

> I would rather devote myself to monastic life, silence and prayer. But I simply cannot close my eyes in front of what is going on before us. Our brotherhood is helping all the people in need here as much as we can. I know that we cannot stop the war and make all the evils in the world disappear. But it is our Christian duty to help all in need when the situation requires.[79]

As a monk, Father Sava locates himself firmly within the spiritual lineage of the Serbian Orthodox Church, viewing his words and deeds as part of a tradition dating back hundreds of years. The numerous official position papers and public statements he made on behalf of the church, some of which have been cited earlier, consistently reaffirmed its institutional opposition to violence and its commitment to help all those in need irrespective of their nationality. "Our Orthodox faith has always encouraged peace and forgiveness," he told one interviewer. "The Church teaches us that the greatest patriot is the one who can show human love not only towards his neighbor but also towards his enemy, especially when he is disabled and unarmed."[80]

These tenets of the Serbian Orthodox Church rest on a biblical foundation. "The Holy Scripture teaches us that one cannot love God without first loving one's neighbor," Father Sava explains. "This is the way of Christ, the way of our holy forefathers but also the way leading us into the future and eternity."[81] Father Sava's words also point to the timeless and eternal truths that he believes are embodied in the Serbian Orthodox Church and the role he feels the church can play in shaping the future of his country.

Father Sava firmly believes that a happier future for Kosovo and Serbia lies in its further incorporation into Europe as a multiethnic and multireligious society. "In twenty-first-century Europe there is no place for ethnically 'cleansed territories,' terror or crimes,"[82] he explains. "Kosovo Albanians might attempt to continue systematic destruction of the Christian Orthodox heritage in Kosovo, but they must be aware that in the flames and ashes of our churches, holy icons, frescoes and relics, their chances of joining the cultured and civilized democratic world will burn out, too."[83] The choice for him is clear. Move to the future together or live together amidst destruction.

The story of Father Sava, the Albanians and the Serbs is not yet over. For his selfless efforts, the head of the UN mission in Kosovo and

Metohija – Bernard Kouchner – nominated Father Sava for the Nobel Peace Prize.

Sadly, the tensions between Albanians and Serbs turned violent once again in March 2004, when Albanians burned Serbian Orthodox shrines and torched entire Serbian villages. Speaking by phone to the *New York Times*, Father Sava commented: "There is a pattern emerging. The U.N. evacuates Serbs, and immediately afterwards Albanians come in and burn [houses and religious sites]."[84]

Weeks later, Father Sava met with the NATO commander for Southern Europe, Admiral Gregory G. Johnson, and later described the meeting on a local radio program:

> While the cultural community of the United States admires the art of Byzantium and some of the most beautiful works of Serbian medieval art in an exhibition at New York's Metropolitan Museum, the greatest holy shrines of Orthodox art are perishing here. That is why I gave Admiral Johnson a piece of the burned engraved crucifix from the destroyed church in Pristina. It is a burned angel to remind him of what transpired here.[85]

Recounting their conversation, Father Sava stated that the admiral shared his hope that evil and destruction would not be allowed to prevail.

Father Sava concluded with a gentle nudge toward peace, "I am certain that burned angel will be a meaningful token that will remind Admiral Johnson [that] everything we discussed needs to be implemented as soon as possible."[86]

SERBIA AND MONTENEGRO (& KOSOVO) FACT SHEET*,[87]

Geography

Location: Southeastern Europe, bordering the Adriatic Sea, between Albania and Bosnia and Herzegovina. Kosovo is in the southernmost part of the country.

Area: Total: 102,350 sq km
                   Land: 214 sq km
                   Water: 102,136 sq km

Area comparative: Slightly smaller than Kentucky.

Climate: In the north, cold winters and hot humid summers with rainfall; central portion continental and Mediterranean climate; in south Adriatic climate, hot and dry in summer and autumn and cold winters with snowfall.

---

* This information was compiled before Montenegro's May 2006 vote for independence from the State Union of Serbia and Montenegro, and the official proclamations of independence by both Montenegro and Serbia in June 2006. At the time of writing, new statistics had not yet been released.

Population

Population:	10,832,545 (July 2006 est.)	
Ethnic groups:	Serb:	62.6%
	Albanian:	16.5%
	Montenegrin:	5%
	Hungarian:	3.3%
	other:	12.6% (1991)
Religions:	Orthodox:	65%
	Muslim:	19%
	Roman Catholic:	4%
	Protestant:	1%
	other:	11%
Languages:	Serbian:	95%
	Albanian:	5%

Government

Government Type:	Republic
Capital:	Belgrade
	Note: Podgorica is the judicial capital.
Legal system:	Based on civil law system.

Recent Background

The Kingdom of Serbs, Croats, and Slovenes was formed in 1918 and its name was changed to Yugoslavia in 1929. Nazi Germany occupied Yugoslavia in 1941, thereby prompting the rise of various paramilitary bands that fought the Nazis and one another. The group led by Josip Tito assumed full control after the expulsion of the Germans in 1945. Although communist, Tito's new government was able to navigate its own course among the Warsaw Pact nations and the West for nearly forty-five years. During the middle of Tito's reign, in 1974, the Yugoslav constitution recognized the autonomous status of Kosovo.

After Tito's reign, Yugoslavia began to unravel along ethnic lines. In 1991 and 1992, the former Yugoslav Republics of Slovenia, Croatia, Bosnia and Herzegovina, and Macedonia all declared their independence.

The remaining republics of Serbia and Montenegro became a new "Federal Republic of Yugoslavia" (the "Federal Republic") in 1992 and, under President Slobodan Milosevic, Serbia initiated various military campaigns with the aim of uniting Serbia and its neighboring republics – such as Kosovo – into a "Greater Serbia." These efforts led to Yugoslavia being suspended from the United Nations in 1992 and the imposition of economic sanctions by the international community. With the signing of the Dayton Peace Accords in 1995, Serbia temporarily gave up its ambitions to expand its territory.

In 1999, Federal Republic forces and Serb paramilitaries moved into Kosovo and committed massive expulsions of ethnic Albanians, which included the looting of villages and the rape and murder of dozens of their residents.[88] This provoked an international response, culminating in NATO's bombing of Serbia and the introduction of Russian, NATO, and other peacekeepers in Kosovo. Federal elections in the fall of 2000 ousted Milosevic, and Vojislav Kostunica became president. Milosevic was arrested in 2001 and subsequently transferred to the International Criminal Tribunal for the Former Yugoslavia in The Hague to be tried for crimes against humanity. In 2001, the country was once more accepted into U.N. organizations (under the name of Yugoslavia); its suspension was lifted and sanctions were dropped.

U.N. Security Council Resolution 1244 installed the UN Interim Administration Mission in Kosovo (UNMIK), which has been governing Kosovo since June 1999.

In 2002, Serbian and Montenegrin interests within Yugoslavia began talks aimed at forming a looser relationship between them. As a result, lawmakers restructured the country in February 2003 into a loose federation of two republics, Serbia and Montenegro. Referenda on full independence for each republic took place in 2006, and they both proclaimed independence in June 2006. Kosovo, meanwhile, is still technically part of Serbia, but is moving toward local autonomy under the UNMIK.

President Slobodan Milosevic died of a heart attack in March of 2006 in his cell at The Hague before his trial was completed. There was mixed public reaction during his funeral in Belgrade later that month.

Economic Overview

Mismanagement of the economy, the legacy of economic sanctions, and the damage to Yugoslavia's infrastructure and industry resulting from the war have left Kosovo with an economy of half its 1990 size.

The ousting of former Federal Yugoslav President Milosevic in October 2000 led to the instillation of the Democratic Opposition of Serbia (DOS) coalition government. This new government has implemented various measures aimed at restabilizing the economy, including an aggressive market reform program.

Kosovo is reliant on the international community for financial and technical assistance. The euro and the Yugoslav dinar are its official currencies, and UNMIK collects taxes and manages the budget.

The complex nature of Serbia and Montenegro's political relationships, slow movement toward privatization, and stagnation in the European economy are holding back the economy. Arrangements with the IMF requiring fiscal discipline play a key role in policy formation. Severe unemployment remains a serious political and economic difficulty.

6 The Elder

Ephraim Isaac

Eritrea/Ethiopia

For centuries, Ethiopia was governed by a monarchy that traced its roots back to Solomon and the Queen of Sheba. Although the nation periodically suffered from conflicts – including scrambles over the monarchy, power struggles between Ethiopia and neighboring Muslim countries, and armed defense against the long imperialistic arm of Europe – these battles were infrequent and occurred during years that were otherwise marked by peace. In the latter half of the twentieth century, however, a socialist regime displaced the monarchy and the pace of violence in Ethiopia accelerated. For many Ethiopians, war became part of their daily lives.

Just before World War II broke out, Italy invaded Ethiopia from its military bases in Eritrea. In the midst of the ensuing war between Italy and Ethiopia, one of the country's most committed peacemakers was born: Ephraim Isaac. Despite early childhood memories of war and his adult experiences with the conflicts that subsequently plagued Ethiopia, Ephraim Isaac still views Ethiopians as one of the world's most peaceful, patient, and polite peoples. His peacemaking method – which include reinstating the ancient social system of elders as mediators – suggest that he sees peacefulness as an extension of the wisdom imbedded within Ethiopia's culture. In Ephraim's reconciliation efforts, therefore, he strives to tap into this collective wisdom to create a sustainable peace, such as Ethiopia previously enjoyed.

An Overview of Ethiopia

Ethiopia bears the proud distinction of being the oldest independent African country, one that staunchly retained its sovereignty despite colonial powers' occasional stabs at conquest. Most of its neighbors were not

151

so fortunate. To the west, Sudan was colonized by Britain and Egypt; to the north, Eritrea was colonized by Italy; to the south, Kenya was colonized by Britain; and to the east, Djibouti and Somalia were part of Italy's colonial territory. Fallout from the colonial era in East Africa has contributed to instability in this area and, in particular, to Ethiopia's current problems with Eritrea.

Although Ethiopia is landlocked by its neighbors, it has important access to the Blue Nile, which flows northward into the Nile River that sustains Egypt. Eighty-five percent of the water in Egypt's Nile River comes from the Blue Nile, and current treaties give Egypt (and, to a much lesser extent, Sudan) almost exclusive control over the Nile and its headwaters, including the Blue Nile. Some believe that Egypt historically fomented unrest in East Africa as a means of preserving control over the river. Today the challenges of the region's water sources and the treaties are under discussion.

Within Ethiopia, the nation's many ethnic groups coexisted for years, generally in peace, although they have at various times in the country's long history tried to form independent states. Especially during the years of turmoil in the twentieth century, ethnically identified political movements became more influential.

The Beginnings of Nationhood

Ethiopia is the home of the famous hominid fossil Lucy (dated 3.1 million years old), and is today viewed by some as the site of the origin of human evolution, including the development of Homo sapiens and early humans.[1] Little is known about the first inhabitants of the region that became Ethiopia and Eritrea. They were probably hunters and gatherers who were just beginning to develop agriculture, when in the late first millennium BCE, the peoples of northern Ethiopia unified and developed into what is now known as the Aksumite Empire.[2]

Around 325 CE, the Aksumite Empire adopted Christianity as its state religion. The empire peaked during the fourth through sixth centuries when it ruled over a large part of the Horn of Africa and present-day Yemen, spreading its religion that is today known as Ethiopian Orthodox Christianity.[3]

Central to the Aksumite Empire was the Solomonid dynasty, so-called because it derived legitimacy by claiming Solomon and Sheba as its ancestors. When the Solomonids lost the throne to another dynasty called Zagwe during the ninth century, the Aksumite Empire began to wane.[4] It was during this same period that Islam was becoming popular in Egypt and other regions in East Africa, and Muslim influence began spilling over into coastal regions in Ethiopia. Although the Christian Solomonids regained control of Ethiopia in 1270, Islam remained strong in the east and along the Red Sea coast.[5]

International Interest

In 1527, under Ottoman influence, Muslim leaders from the walled city of Harar in eastern Ethiopia infiltrated and overran much of the rest of the country. Disturbed by this sign of Muslim ascendancy, Emperor Lebna Dengel (1508–1540) of Ethiopia entered into an alliance with Portugal, which sent troops to battle the Muslims during the final years of his reign. His son and successor Galawdewos (1540–1559) conquered the Muslims and revived a Christian Ethiopia. Though the Portuguese sent in Jesuit missionaries to solidify Catholic-Christian hegemony, the emperors of the following decades were not successful in foisting Roman Catholicism on their unwilling subjects, who rebelled in fury. Eventually, emperor Fasilides put an end to the effort by exiling the Catholic priests and expelling all foreign missionaries from Ethiopia during his rule from 1632 to 1667. Ethiopian Orthodoxy prevailed, remaining distinct from Catholicism.[*,6]

The Ethiopian Orthodox Church grew stronger as the monarchy weakened between the seventeenth and the nineteenth centuries, and foreign countries – including the Ottoman Empire, Egypt, and Italy – vied for control of the country. Although this destabilized the government and divided the people, Ethiopia nevertheless survived this difficult period intact.

The Roots of an Eritrean Identity

By the seventeenth century, highland Ethiopia was predominantly Christian. It remained culturally and politically integrated with Eritrea until the eighteenth century, when their identities began to diverge. For one thing, Islam gained a stronghold in the coastal and eastern regions of Eritrea, strengthening the sense of a distinct national identity. Perhaps

---

* The Ethiopian Orthdox Church is distinct primarily in its Judeo-Hebraic character, which is similar to the early Christian community of Jerusalem; in its calendar, which begins seven years and eight months later than the Gregorian calendar; and in its belief in the single – not dual – natures of Christ.

more importantly, Italy infiltrated Eritrea in 1882, just thirteen years after France completed the Suez Canal.

With the opening of the Canal, European powers flooded into East Africa, eager to seize new ports and trading opportunities. Britain collaborated with Egypt to conquer the Sudan. France, whose colonial strongholds were in West Africa, was determined to circumscribe the power of Britain in the East, and Italy aimed for Somaliland and Eritrea. After leasing the port of Assab in Eritrea, Italy conquered the country on January 1, 1890, and declared Eritrea to be both a nation-state and a colony.[7]

Under Italy's influence, Eritrea developed a market-based economy, upgraded its infrastructure, and further developed its own nationalist identity. Italy wanted to expand into the rest of Ethiopia, but Britain's presence in neighboring Sudan kept its aspirations in check. When rebel groups weakened Britain's influence in Sudan, it adopted a different strategy of "regional stability." It thereafter supported Italy's invasion of Ethiopia in 1895. But Italy's attack was poorly thought out; severely outnumbered by the Ethiopian army, the Italian army was soundly defeated.[8] Retreating back into Eritrea, Italy joined its fellow European powers in acknowledging Ethiopian sovereignty. Nonetheless, Italy retained its aspirations and, over the next forty years, periodically launched raids into Ethiopia from Eritrea – something the League of Nations tried in vain to stop. In 1936, the raids escalated, marking Ethiopia's second war with Italy.

Relations with Italy and the Reign of Haile Selassie: 1930–1974

The last of Ethiopia's monarchs – Emperor Haile Selassie I – began his reign in 1930 and established Ethiopia's first constitution.[9] When the war with Italy broke out six years later, the young monarch left Ethiopia and Benito Mussolini declared Italy's King Victor Emmanuel III emperor of all "Italian East Africa," abruptly dissolving the borders separating Eritrea, Italian Somaliland, and the previously independent Ethiopia.[10]

Denied his rightful role in governing Ethiopia, Haile Selassie turned to international diplomacy. In exile, he pleaded his country's case before the League of Nations. His pleas fell on deaf ears until Great Britain came to Ethiopia's aid. In 1941, the Ethiopian patriotic forces with assistance from the Allied Forces of Great Britain defeated Italy and restored Haile Selassie to the throne.[11]

Among the many challenges after World War II was what to do with Eritrea. Although the country had been within Ethiopia's borders for

centuries, it had become a nation-state in its own right during Italy's occupation. More recently, both Ethiopia and Eritrea had been absorbed into
the wider sphere of "Italian East Africa." The Allies decided that Britain
should administer Eritrea as a protectorate until an international body
finally resolved the issue. In 1950, the United Nations General Assembly voted to federate Ethiopia and Eritrea and to allow Eritrea to hold a
referendum on independence ten years later.[12]

However, Emperor Haile Selassie I prevented the referendum from taking place. Instead, he finagled an arrangement by which Eritrea became
a province of Ethiopia. Piqued by this disregard for Eritrea's right of
self-determination, the Eritrea Liberation Front (ELF) was formed and
began a guerrilla campaign against Ethiopia.[13]

Simultaneously, dissatisfaction was growing among Ethiopians
because of the emperor's preoccupation with foreign affairs and his
neglect of urgent concerns at home. Serious problems were everywhere:
unequal distribution of land and wealth, rural underdevelopment, government corruption, rampant inflation, high unemployment, and a severe
famine. Perhaps predictably, a revolutionary socialist movement gathered momentum among Ethiopian students. As for Eritrea, the ranks of
the rebel Eritrean Liberation Front swelled, eventually splitting along
religious lines into the Muslim-based ELF and the Christian-based
Eritrean People's Liberation Front (EPLF).[14]

Socialist Ethiopia: 1974 to 1989

Inattentive though he was to many of Ethiopia's problems, Emperor
Haile Selassie I did try to modernize the country by opening the door
to Western culture and supporting study-abroad programs in the United
States. Many students who took advantage of these opportunities were
exposed to Marxism and Leninism and, as a consequence, rejected not
only Ethiopia's monarchy but also the blind acceptance of Western political ideals and values. After the 1973–1974 famine claimed the lives of
about two hundred thousand Ethiopians, many of these students and
their supporters embraced socialism as the solution to their country's
problems. Some founded socialist opposition groups to Haile Selassie's
reign, and in 1974, they successfully deposed the Emperor Haile Selassie
I in a military coup.[15]

The new regime was initially named the Derg, which in English trans-
lates to "the organization." (It was also known as the Provisional Military
Administrative Council, but regardless of how "provisional" it was originally meant to be, the regime never abandoned its military roots.) The

Derg began institutionalizing a socialist state with help from Cuba and the Soviet Union. In the process, it killed General Aman, the first chairperson of the Derg (and a friend of Ephraim Isaac), along with sixty former leaders of the imperial regime. At the time, the movement was deeply divided. The Ethiopia Socialist Party (MEISON) was aligned with the Derg, while the Ethiopian People's Revolutionary Party (EPRP) accused the Derg of having a fascist ideology and moved into the opposition. Three years later, a second chairperson of the Derg was killed, and Mengistu Haile-Mariam declared himself the new leader.[16]

The Derg regime was brutal, and tensions erupted among the various parties. By February 1977, a two-year killing spree was underway. Disgusted by the regimes policies, the opposition EPRP targeted and killed approximately eight members of the Derg party. In response, the Derg hunted down and killed thousands of EPRP supporters and others suspected of opposition – especially students – in the first of three waves of violence and bloodshed that came to be known as the Red Terror. In the second wave, the Derg turned on its former ally MEISON, fearful that its members were no longer loyal. In the end, thousands died.[17]

The EPRP and MEISON were not the Derg's only opponents. The Derg refused demands for negotiating Eritrean independence, which angered both the Eritrean Liberation Front and the Eritrean People's Liberation Front. The Derg's harsh policies fomented wide rebellion, and many new antigovernment and antisocialist factions sprang up.* From 1974 to 1990, the support for these fledgling groups grew among the public, until the vast majority opposed the Derg.

The Fight for Ethiopia and Eritrea

As Eritreans fought for independence from the Derg, various groups sought a regime change in Ethiopia. Among those frustrated by Mengistu's oppressive reign was a coalition led by the Tigrayan People's Liberation Front. Calling themselves the Ethiopian People's Revolutionary Democratic Front (EPRDF or the "Ethiopian Coalition"), the group launched an offensive in March 1988 that ultimately solidified control of Ethiopia by seizing Addis Ababa three years later. The Ethiopian Coalition's leader, Meles Zenawi, assumed the presidency of a multiparty

---

* Among these groups were the Ethiopian Democratic Union (EDU), the Tigre People's Liberations Front (TPLF), the Oromo People's Liberations Front (OLF), the Afar Liberation Front (ALF), and the Ethiopian Peoples Democratic Alliance (EPDA).

provisional government, and later became prime minister of the Federal Democratic Republic of Ethiopia.[18]

As it turned out, the Ethiopian rebels attempted to capture Addis Ababa at just the time that the Eritrean resistance was attempting to take over Asmara, the future capital of Eritrea. The Eritreans got there first by a few days. Isaias Afewerki then became head of the Eritrean government in 1991 and later became president as the result of a referendum.

Although the Eritrean People's Liberation Front and the Ethiopian Coalition were in part estranged, for years they had shared a common enemy – the Derg. Accordingly, it was not a surprise when the leaders of the two groups, the future President Isaias and Prime Minister Meles, actually celebrated together when the Derg fell. Ephraim Isaac recalls hearing that the two men "joined hands and danced at the celebration party that night."[19]

A close alliance between the two leaders continued for some time, until disputes over Ethiopia's access to the ports of Assab and Massawa and over the terms of trade between the two countries began to erode their goodwill. In 1998, with relations souring fast, a border dispute escalated into large-scale violence that lasted nearly two years. Despite a cease-fire and peace talks moderated by the United Nations, unresolved issues over the border demarcation continue to fester well into 2006.

Dr. Ephraim Isaac

When you first meet Dr. Ephraim Isaac – the depth and range of the man – his gifts and experiences are overshadowed and what you notice are his warmth and rapid-fire, enthusiastic conversation. Often wearing traditional Yemenite Jewish dress in New York City business establishments, Ephraim is a distinctive figure and a true renaissance man.

In the course of his lifetime, he has witnessed the rapid evolution of Eritrea from an Italian colony and of Ethiopia from an Italian-occupied territory into sovereign states. To understand how he has influenced this political story, we must first appreciate how the development of Ethiopia and Eritrea shaped Ephraim's own personal story.

When asked how he defines himself, Ephraim starts with an acrostic poem based on his name, clearly showing his love of ideas and language (of which he speaks seventeen). "Ephraim Isaac," he announces, and then continues as follows: "Eternity, paradise, heaven, revelation, Adam, inspire, mercy. Inspire, salvation, Adam, Adam, covenant."[20] He beams. When pressed to identify himself, Ephraim chooses the label, "Ethiopian nationalist," but adds that he is also Yemenite Jewish. He explains that Yemen and Ethiopia share a similar culture, and therefore sees alignment between his national and religious affiliations.*

Ephraim likes to talk about Yemenite Judaism and says that it denotes a specific brand of Judaism, much like Sephardic or Ashkenazi Judaism, although he is quick to point out the many ways in which it remains distinct from these groups, being "the oldest continuous surviving form of the Late Second Temple form of Judaism from about two thousand years ago."[21] Ephraim credits his father with passing the tradition on to him.

As a Jewish man, Ephraim's father memorized much of the Bible (including the Torah, Haftorah, and Psalms of David) and the Mishnah (the third-century Jewish legal text, which is the basis of the Talmud). Having learned from him, Ephraim proudly announces that he knows Hebrew and Aramaic and that he reads the five books of Moses once a year. As a Yemenite Jew, Ephraim has memorized many ritual prayers that he chants in Aramaic and Hebrew (rather than Ladino or Yiddish). This custom marks one of the ways in which the Yemenite Jewish tradition maintains distinct practices from the Sephardic Jews, with whom they are often grouped.[†] Although Yemenite Jews associate religiously with their Sephardic brothers and sisters, they maintain their own synagogues where they worship in a language that, according to Ephraim, "is closer to what the Jews spoke in Jesus' time" and "sounds like...a brother-language to Arabic, as Isaac was a brother to Ishmael."[22]

Ephraim's identity is also shaped by his ethnicity: his father was Yemenite, his mother Oromo Ethiopian. This culture-straddling permeates his peacemaking efforts and helps to explain his ability to move among cultures and peoples.

Early Influences: Encounters with Violence

When Ephraim describes how he came to peacemaking, he starts with his father and his father's story, his childhood, and the values in his family. All influenced the choices Ephraim would later make in his life's work.

---

* "Yemenite" denotes someone of a nationality of Yemen, but "Yemenite Jew" refers to a particular religious tradition.

[†] As a Yemenite Jew, Ephraim learned Hebrew and Aramaic, and has memorized many parts of the Hebrew Bible, including: the Ten Commandments and the Song of the Sea in Hebrew and Aramaic; the Haftorah readings from I Samuel, Jeremiah, Isaiah, and the Book of Jonah.

Ephraim relates how both of his parents admonished him always to seek peaceful conduct rather than violence, regardless of how he was bullied. This expectation burned itself into Ephraim's young mind because he saw his father as a *sadik* – a righteous person – who had suffered yet still believed in peace. Indeed, in Ephraim's community, the story of his father's suffering was widely known.

It begins with the migration of Ephraim's father, Yeshaq Mesha, across the Red Sea to Ethiopia. A year after he was married, Yeshaq was sent to the Ethiopian town of Dire Dawa to assist its Yemenite Jewish community in religious rituals and services during the high holidays. While there, a local jeweler named Menahem hit his wife in the head with a hammer. Believing that he had killed her, Menahem fled in fear. When his wife survived to tell her story (and then gave birth to a baby girl), the community decided that the man had to be brought to justice. As one of the seven able-bodied young men in the community, Yeshaq volunteered to pursue Menahem two hundred miles west to the capital of Ethiopia, Addis Ababa.

By the time the search party arrived in Ethiopia's capital, the guilty man had fled again. The party discovered that he had changed his name to Ibrahim and adopted a different religion (Islam) to avoid being caught. Hearing that the man had gone further west to the Ethiopian town of Nedjo, the group decided to send a party of three to find him. They charged Ephraim's father and two others with bringing the man back. No one realized that the three were about to be trapped.

The hardships came quickly. In those days, it was an arduous journey of some two weeks to reach Nedjo, and before the trio even arrived, one of the three died. By the time Yeshaq and his companion Harun finished the trek, they saw that something was amiss in Nedjo: Menahem was not living as a fugitive, but as a man of influence. An able jeweler, he had ingratiated himself with the local governor, who conducted himself like a feudal lord. Because Nedjo was far from the central administration of Ethiopia, the governor felt no accountability to Ethiopian law and used his power to indulge his whims. When Yeshaq and Harun arrived, Menahem whispered to the governor that these newcomers could be valuable as silversmiths, if the governor wished to retain them. Yeshaq and Harun were thus trapped. They attempted to flee but were caught in a small town about three hours away, where Harun got sick and died.

Yeshaq returned to Nedjo and was forced to work as an unpaid silversmith assisting Menahem. He had no way to send a message to Dire Dawa, or to his wife and son in the more distant Aden. Thoughts of suicide tempted him. Although he knew Jewish law forbade taking his own life, he decided, in desperation, to drink a bottle of strong alcohol called *arak* and locked himself in his room. To everyone's surprise, he awoke a week later. To placate him, the administration brought a woman to be his wife, but Ephraim's father did not want to marry under those circumstances, especially someone who did not share his religious convictions. Dejected, and hoping hyenas might devour him if he slept by the riverside, Ephraim's father spent every night by the river for two months, awaiting God's judgment. When it appeared that the hyenas were not going to oblige him (as hyenas do not touch living humans), Yeshaq resigned himself to the will of his Creator.

Two years of despondent prayer convinced him that it was God's judgment that he remain in Nedjo and accept marriage. Taking the advice of some local people, Yeshaq found a woman named Bushure Karayu, whom he named Ruth. Ephraim's mother-to-be studied Judaism, converted, and subsequently married Yeshaq. In the meantime, Yeshaq's relatives went to Addis Ababa and learned from a caravan group that he had not perished. Once found, he reported his story to the Ethiopian court, and British colonial officials thereupon detained the governor of Nedjo. The government awarded Yeshaq his freedom, gave him a silversmith job to support his children, some livestock, and an annual stipend on each Jewish New Year.

Ephraim's father began a new life. He determined to remain with his new family and not abandon them in a foreign land. Recognizing that the child of his first marriage would be growing up among his own people, Yeshaq sought to preserve the honor of his first wife and granted her a divorce.

Because of his experiences, Ephraim's father harbored no illusions about human nature, a perspective he passed on to his son. Ephraim smiles mischievously as he comments, "Thomas Hobbes says that *man is wolf to man*, but that is unfair to the wolves." The suffering caused by greed, hatred, and war, and the great harm human beings do to one another, convinced his father that violence and fighting are useless. He passed this conviction on to his son, who says, "We are all mortal ... why should we kill each other? Why fight with each other? Why hurt each other?"[23]

One childhood experience that was to haunt Ephraim particularly reinforced his passion for peace. It was 1941, the year the Italian occupation ended and the Italians were driven out of Ethiopia. Ephraim was very young and vividly recalls living in a bunker for two days, constantly hearing explosions, shootings, and bomb showers in Nedjo. When he emerged from the bunker, Ephraim learned that his best friend and playmate was dead. The power of this tragedy has stayed with him. Years later in 1960 during an attempted coup in Ethiopia, Ephraim's memories of his childhood playmate vividly returned. It was then that he recommitted himself to the work of peacebuilding. And the rest is his history.

Textual Influences

Ephraim interprets his father's experiences and his own experience in losing his friend to war within the framework of Scripture. Comforted that the prophets were among the first to argue against warfare, Ephraim names Isaiah and Jeremiah as his two favorite books of the Bible, and quotes and chants from Isaiah specifically when talking about his own peacemaking efforts. Two of his favorite passages offer visions of peace:

> [A]nd they shall beat their swords into plowshares, their spears into pruning hooks: nation shall not lift up sword against nation, neither shall they learn war anymore.[24]
>
>   The wolf shall reside with the lamb, and the leopard shall lie down with the kid; and the calf and the young lion and the fatling together, and a little child shall lead them. And the cow and the hyena shall feed; their young ones shall lie down together; and the lion shall eat straw like the ox. The suckling child shall play on the hole of the asp, and the weaned child shall put his hand on the cockatrice den. They shall not hurt nor destroy in all my holy mountains. For the earth shall be full of the knowledge of the Lord, as the waters cover the sea.[25]

In addition to offering visions of peace in the end times, Isaiah and Jeremiah also convey a vision for how humans ought to interact in the world. Describing how he memorized sections of the Bible as a child, Ephraim refers again to Isaiah, alluding to and chanting in a sonorous voice a passage which explains that God does not care about sacrificial offerings, but about the beneficence of his people and their readiness to feed the hungry, cloth the naked, and nurture their family.[26]

Ephraim recalls his father's strong emphasis on Judaism as a religion of love, peace, and the responsibility for building a loving community. He also recalls his father's daily chanting of the Psalms at dawn and his deep spirituality, which Ephraim compares to the beliefs of Isaiah. Whenever Ephraim's siblings fought with each other, their father would tell them a story to illustrate the meaning of Judaism:

Once, there were two rabbis. One goes to speak to God and praise the
children of Israel by saying how devout they were; how religious they
were; how much they loved God.

But God asks simply, "Do they love each other?"

When the rabbi says they do not, God replies, "then I don't care who
they are. Destroy them."

Another rabbi goes to God to report on the children of Israel and says,
"The children of Israel worship stones. They don't love you."

God asks, "Do they love each other? Is there peace among them?"

"Yes," says the rabbi.

"Then," says God, "they are my children."[27]

Ephraim follows this story by quoting the first letter of John in the
Christian testament which he notes is based on Jewish teachings. "If
anyone says he loves God, yet hates his brother, he is a liar. How can you
love God, whom you have not seen, when you don't love your brother,
whom you do see?"[28] Ephraim summarizes, "Peace and love are related.
Love and respect are related."[29]

Evolution of a Peacemaker: Establishing Respect

In describing his work, Ephraim begins by emphasizing how he earned
the respect of the people of Ethiopia, his homeland. After receiving a
scholarship to study in the United States, Ephraim traveled to Concordia
College in Minnesota, where he studied chemistry, music, and philosophy
as an undergraduate. In 1959, he organized the first Ethiopian Students
Association in North America and served as its president for three years.

When he returned to Ethiopia in 1960, he translated Handel's *Messiah* into Amharic, the official language of Ethiopia. His version of the
Messiah was performed in April 1961 in the Ethiopian National Theatre
and later in the Imperial Palace of Emperor Haile Selassie to standing
ovations. This performance was the first time people in Ethiopia began
to notice Ephraim. (Forty years later, an international choir in Ethiopia
performed the *Messiah* and invited Ephraim to be a guest conductor for
the "Hallelujah Chorus," which was once again received with a standing
ovation and much acclaim in the packed Addis Ababa City Hall.)

Ephraim then came back to the United States to study religion at
Harvard Divinity School in 1961, where he was the first Ethiopian to
receive a Bachelor of Divinity and, subsequently, also the first Ethiopian
to receive a Ph.D. from the Harvard Graduate School of Arts and Sciences.

However, as he pursued his second degree, Ephraim felt a growing sense of guilt. "How can I get so much education," he thought, "when so many people in Ethiopia are totally illiterate?"[30] The idea led to action. Ephraim became an activist in seeking to combat illiteracy. He transformed the Ethiopian Student Association, served as the Chairman of the Committee for Ethiopian Literacy, and became Executive Director of the National Literacy Campaign of Ethiopia for seven years. With his usual enthusiasm, he notes, "When you believe in goodness, you want to do something. You cannot just think, *why is this not so?* You must *move.*"[31]

The first African-led nonprofit organization in the United States, the Committee for Ethiopian Literacy also became the first African organization to raise money in the United States for educational and charitable causes. As its chairman, Ephraim organized exhibits, held fundraising dinners, and developed mentorship networks within Ethiopia. The organization enjoyed widespread support; Ethiopian women students organized fund-raising parties throughout the United States to help meet the organization's financial goals, and during the mid-1960s – thanks largely to Ephraim and the committee's efforts – an estimated 1.5 million people in Ethiopia received literacy instructions.[32] Ephraim's rare ability to tell the stories of the children whose lives were changed by the campaign helped him raise money for Ethiopian literacy, and his ability to create reform in Ethiopia was facilitated because the people already knew him as the translator of the *Messiah*.

The National Literacy Campaign won the prestigious Haile Selassie Prize Trust and a United Nations award, making Ephraim more visible and better positioned for his future work. In 1989, Ras Mengesha – the grandson of the Ethiopian Emperor Yohannes and one of the leaders of the anti-Derg political parties – invited him to a peacemaking conference in Toronto along with major Ethiopian political figures. This conference was organized after a failed attempt by President Carter to negotiate peace between the Derg and the strongest opposition party at the time, the Eritrean People's Liberation Front.

Dozens of Ethiopian leaders respected by their communities were invited to attend, but three important groups were not officially represented: the Eritrean People's Liberation Front, the Oromo Liberation Front – who refused to participate – and Tigray People's Liberation Front, who did not have an official representative. At the meeting, the participants committed themselves to peace and decided to hold future meetings and to involve all groups in the formation of a transitional government.

Because full participation was essential to their efforts, the Toronto Congress decided that the best way to further its goal of reestablishing justice and peace in Ethiopia would be to send a party of three respected elders to those who had not attended. Ephraim Isaac was one of the three. Unlike his father's mission to find the man who beat his wife, Ephraim's role went beyond seeking justice. He was also seeking peace.

Ephraim Isaac was chosen as chair of the three elders – who included Kassahun Besrat, former president of the Ethiopian Teachers Union, and Assefa Adifaris, a former high government official. Their job was to reach out to representatives of the absent parties and to bring them into the newly formed community of peacemakers.

During these initial endeavors, Ephraim began to exhibit the skills required to be a successful peacemaker. As he worked to align the nonparticipating parties with the aims of the Toronto Conference, he faced obstacles. Some people were willing to speak with Ephraim but not with his colleagues. Eventually, however, he was able to persuade them to speak with the other elders. Reflecting on this process, Ephraim observed, "To be a negotiator, you have to be known and respected, and loved as a person who serves his people without ulterior motives. People must want to listen to you."[33]

After many conversations, Ephraim and his colleague Besrat drafted a document to form a transitional government. Everyone agreed on all points except whether the Toronto Conference should be counted as the first meeting. Those present at Toronto wanted the next meeting to be deemed the second meeting, because they wanted to take credit for their work in Toronto. Those who were absent from Toronto wanted the next meeting (where everyone would be present) to be counted as the first. Despite Ephraim's tireless attempts at mediation, the groups remained at an impasse.

Accepting that there was no way out, Ephraim took the lead and dissolved the original peacemaking committee. With new people, he set up another group, the Ad Hoc Ethiopian Peace Committee (AHPC).

Ad Hoc Peace Committee for Ethiopia

Ephraim had several criteria for choosing people to serve with him on the Ad Hoc Ethiopian Peace Committee. Believing that community elders – traditional leaders – were the key, Ephraim sought to model the AHPC after the elder culture of Ethiopia. In so doing, he looked for individuals who had connections with the political parties and who were respected in their communities.[34] In addition, he searched for individuals with "good linguistic skills and experience in conflict resolution." In their diversity, the members of Ephraim's new committee represented a wide variety of ethnic, religious, and political affiliations of all ages and both sexes.[35]

A brief survey of the members shows where each member came from and indicates the level of respect they enjoyed:

Dr. Ahmed Moen, former Ethiopian Director General in the Ministry of Health and professor of public health at Howard University.

Dr. Haile Selassie Belay, former President of the Ethiopian Agricultural College and former governor of Tigray; former senior UN advisor.

Ato Kassahun Besrat, former Secretary General of Ethiopian Teachers Association.

Prof. Abaineh Workie, Norfolk University, former Dean of the School of Education at Haile Selassie University.

Ato Fisseha-sion Tekie, former Secretary General of the Ethiopian Labor Federation.

Dr. Mulugeta Eteffa, former professor and Dean of Students at Haile Selassie I University.

Dr. Tilahun Beyene, former President of the Eritrean Teacher Association and Dean at the University of Maryland.

Dr. Yacob Hailemariam, prominent lawyer of political dissidents and Lecturer at Norfolk State University.

Prof. Astair G. Mengesha, University of Iowa, currently in Women's Studies Department at the University of Arizona.

AHPC had two main offices. One was in Princeton, New Jersey, where Ephraim served as director while he taught as a visiting professor for a year at a seminary and for seven years at Princeton University. The other was in Uppsala, Sweden, where support came from the Life and Peace Institute. Locally, contacts were made with elders in Ethiopia who remained close to developing conflicts.

Together with Ephraim Isaac, AHPC's elders agreed on certain ground rules. First, they would not speak to the media. Ephraim explains: "You cannot negotiate peace while it's being published in the *New York Times*. Once the media reports what people said other people said, it sinks peace efforts."[36] Second, the elders should agree to distance themselves from the conflicting parties so that they could act strictly as mediators for peace.[37] They singled out *shimagele-jarsa* to be of great value, a traditional Ethiopian technique that "support[s] efforts to resolve conflicts. It is characterized by sympathetic listening, respect for the opponent,

patience, broadmindedness, impartiality, and advocacy for serious dialogue."[38] Third, and underlying all these techniques and methods, participants had to have a commitment to Ethiopian peace.

With these principles in place, the idea was to approach all the groups
involved in the conflict through oral and written correspondence, and to
assure that each member of AHPC would maintain contact with one of
the various political parties. With this process defined, an agreement was
reached to hold a meeting in June 1990.

The London Peace Talks

As fighting in Ethiopia intensified toward the end of 1990 and the beginning of 1991, the balance of power among the political parties began
shifting away from the government, and the need for peace talks grew
urgent. With support from funders in Sweden and the Swiss government,
the AHPC and Ephraim planned a conference for June 1991 in the neutral
setting of Caux, Switzerland. The purpose was to bring the ruling Derg
and all opposition political and military factions together to establish a
transitional government with representation from all the groups.

But as these events unfolded, the Ethiopian Coalition's army captured strategic regions in northwestern Ethiopia and pressed in on
Addis Ababa. The Derg was losing control over the country and tensions were increasing. Keen to minimize violence, the Ethiopian Coalition approached Ephraim Isaac and asked him to hold the conference in
May so that a transitional government could be put in place before they
reached the capital. Every group except the Derg agreed to send representatives to a conference on May 22–26. The Derg sent vague messages,
refusing to commit while never clearly declining to participate.

Meanwhile, the United States' interests emerged as a factor. In Addis
Ababa, over fourteen thousand Ethiopian Jews languished in camps
around the Israeli Embassy, eager to emigrate to Israel and leave wartorn
Ethiopia behind. The American Joint Distribution Committee and the
Jewish community petitioned President George H. W. Bush to help these
people in their desperate situation. President Bush sent a delegation
headed by Senator Rudy Boschwitz to Ethiopia to pressure the Derg
to allow the Jews stranded in Addis Ababa to go to Israel. Meanwhile, the
American Joint Distribution Committee and the Israeli Jewish Agency –
supported through the United States' offices of the United Jewish Appeal
and the Jewish Federation – began a quiet, unpublicized campaign to col-
lect donations from the American Jewish community to finance a rescue
mission.

With the United States urging the movement of the fourteen thousand people to safety, President Mengistu decided to seize this opportunity to reverse the fortunes of the Derg regime. Rather than attend peace talks as the leader of a declining government, he decided to acquire American and Israeli assistance for his cause by using the fourteen thousand Jews as a bargaining chip. In exchange for agreeing to protect the Jews, Mengistu demanded weapons, 60 percent of the seats in a new transitional government for the Derg, and a promise that Eritrea would not secede from Ethiopia.

Fully appreciating that the Ethiopian government lacked control of the country and that a power vacuum existed, a U.S. official – the late Robert Frazier of the National Security Council – nonetheless decided to placate the Derg government because he believed its army might still do harm. He led the Derg to believe that the U.S. government would meet its demands and set up a meeting on May 20 in London to discuss them.

During this time, Ephraim was speaking with all of the party leaders. The opponents to the Derg were firm. They preferred to go to Caux, Switzerland, where all could be equal partners, rather than to London, where the United States was preparing to negotiate with the Derg. However, Ephraim realized the talks in Switzerland would not be meaningful if the current Ethiopian government was not involved. Meanwhile, the London talks were pushed back to May 27 and, as the parties waited for them to commence, an article appeared in the *Washington Post* crediting the Ethiopian government with agreeing to the United States' suggestion for peace, and stating that it was the opposition groups – rather than the Derg – that were unwilling to meet to resolve the situation.

Stunned, Ephraim decided to violate his own policy of not speaking to the press in order to correct what he considered an egregious misrepresentation of the peace process. He threatened to go to the *Post* with the truth and a demand to print a revised story revealing that it was the Derg who was refusing to meet. Mengistu's chief advisor called Ephraim and promised a letter of commitment to meeting with the opposition parties and to finding a peaceful solution. Ephraim says of his decision to go to the press, "There is no peace without truth."[39] In the end, when a letter came from the Derg and an explanation from the Embassy, Ephraim did not submit his information to the press.

As all of this was transpiring in London and Washington, United Jewish Appeal–sponsored Israeli planes were arriving unannounced in Addis. On Friday, May 24, in the dead of night, the planes landed, collected the Ethiopian Jews and transported all fourteen thousand of them out of

Addis Ababa, in a rescue today known as Operation Solomon. Although several women gave birth on the flight, there were, miraculously, no accidents.

On Sunday, the rescue was made public and all the Jews were declared safe in Israel, protected from continuing conflict in their native land. And, shortly thereafter, the Eritrean People's Liberation Front successfully captured the capital of Asmara. Frazier announced that the London meeting between the United States and the Derg would still begin on Monday the 27th without further postponement. Wanting to see what would happen, the AHPC again readjusted its plan and decided to meet in Switzerland on June 5.

Unaware they had lost their bargaining power, the Derg leaders arrived in London hopeful that the United States would meet their demands. Ephraim and Dr. Haile Selassie Belay, his fellow AHPC member, flew to London to observe but not participate in the talks. The meeting presented an opportunity for them to meet representatives from most of the opposition parties, who were to be in or around London at that time. Ephraim explains why he decided not to participate, "If people in Ethiopia thought the Ad Hoc Peace Committee were bed fellows with the United States, that would hurt the organization's credibility in Ethiopia."[40]

On the morning of Monday, May 27, Herman Cohen of the State Department made clear that the United States was not going to assure the Derg the 60 percent of the transitional government seats it desired. The United States was not keen to support a dictatorial, socialist, and failing regime. Now that the Ethiopian Jews were safe, it no longer needed the consent of the Derg. The Ethiopian government representative walked out of the meeting, angry that he had been misled. The following day, the Ethiopian People's Revolutionary Party forces entered Addis Ababa and met minimal resistance. To their credit, the remnants of the Derg army chose to minimize bloodshed by not fighting inside the city, a battle it would certainly have lost. At last the Derg fell, and the leaders of the various political parties were able to return home safely from places of exile around the world.

When the London meeting ended, Ephraim and Dr. Haile Selassie Belay had extensive private discussions with the three top leaders of the opposition parties (the present Prime Minister of Ethiopia, President of Eritrea, and the chairman of Oromo Liberation Front) regarding how to establish a lasting peace in the Horn of Africa. Holding the planned conference in Switzerland now seemed unnecessary because they could all meet in the city where the transitional government would actually function. They therefore met in Addis Ababa, and the 1991 Peace and Democracy Conference opened in June.

1991 Addis Ababa Peace and Democracy Conference

Rather than running the meeting, AHPC chose to be an observer when the political parties met in Addis Ababa. With Ephraim's guidance, the AHPC transferred the funds it had raised to support the meeting in Addis Abbba. For a week, Ephraim watched negotiations, and when asked to speak at the conclusion of the meeting, he spoke to inspire rather than to admonish or direct, saying:

> It is the beginning of the fulfillment of [our] hopes.... Peace is not just a passive state of mind or existence, my dear friends. Indeed, if so, it will not be meaningful or lasting. Peace must be an active and dynamic human experience.... There is now hope for us, and for the future generation. Our country Ethiopia, a land of great history – a long history, a short history – can truly become an example for all of Africa and the world.[41]

The leader of the Ethiopian Coalition, Ato Meles Zenawi, chaired the conference. Most of the important parties participated, with the exception of two socialist groups (the Ethiopian People's Revolutionary Party and MEISON) who had joined forces a year earlier to form the Coalition of Ethiopian Democratic Forces (COEDF). Despite pleas from Ephraim and the AHPC, this group hesitated to sign onto the unequivocal commitment to peace, as representatives from all the other parties had done. Ephraim was troubled by their nonparticipation and predicted that if they did not join, true reconciliation in Ethiopia would be impossible. Today, many years later, Ephraim's concerns have proved prophetic. Allies of the now defunct COEDF continue to agitate against the government.

Despite the absence of these groups, however, two important decisions emerged from the Addis Ababa Conference. First, the Eritrean people would remain part of Ethiopia for two years, after which they would determine their fate in a 1993 referendum. Second, the transitional government would be determined by a system of proportional representation, which would include all the major opposition groups. Meles Zenawi, the current prime minister of Ethiopia, became president of the new transitional government of Ethiopia.

Although members of the AHPC approached the political parties to bid them farewell at the end of the conference, it became clear that although a type of peace had come, reconciliation had not yet been achieved. Hence, instead of disbanding the AHPC, the members met and decided to continue under a new name – the Peace and Development Committee (PDC).

Staying Involved: Peacemaking as a Way of Life

As Ethiopia was moving toward a period of greater stability, Ephraim found a new context in which to continue work, namely, within the Ethiopian Orthodox Church, an institution that had served as Ethiopia's cultural backbone for years. As a student of the history of Ethiopia's religions, Ephraim had a deep respect for and interest in the Ethiopian Orthodox Church – the oldest, largest, and most powerful institution in the country. Even though he is Jewish, he specialized in the study of Geez (the language of the church), published many articles on the church, and wrote a small book on it. As a result, Ephraim had been invited in the early 1970s by His Grace Archbishop Tewoflos to lecture to the church's bishops on the history of writing and literature in that venerable institution.

As often happens when people meet Ephraim, he established strong relationships and credibility with the church leaders. And when he later heard of a conflict developing within the church in the early 1990s, he felt comfortable offering his assistance. The distinguished Archbishop Melchizidek, as it turned out, was leading a group of bishops in what threatened to become a schism. Ephraim called him from the United States and pointed out how a division could destroy a critically important Ethiopian institution. The archbishop agreed with him and committed himself to working out his differences with the other archbishops.

In response, Ephraim organized a teleconference with several Ethiopian archbishops, including Archbishop Atenatewos of Jerusalem and Archbishop Yishaq of the Western Hemisphere; priests from New York, Toronto, and California; and two of his own Ad Hoc Peace Committee Board members from Maryland, Dr. Haile Selassie Belay and Dr. Tinahoun. From rural Ethiopia to New Jersey, New York, California, Canada, and Jerusalem, all these church leaders were connected via modern technology on April 19, 1992, in what seemed like a miracle.

Ephraim organized the teleconference as an exercise in peacemaking. He began the call with a prayer from the Archbishop Atenatewos in the sacred city of Jerusalem, which inspired humility and respect in the participants. Sustaining this spirit, one of the priests who happened to have a beautiful voice, Gezahagne Qes, chanted for all present. By means of this shared experience, the participants found something in common greater than their various views on the immediate conflict. Bound together in good spirits and goodwill, they turned their attention to the issue dividing them.

One by one, each archbishop voiced his opinion and recounted his perspective of the conflict. As they spoke, Ephraim recognized that the archbishops were beginning to see that they each shared the same objective, the same purpose. They reached an agreement and the problem was resolved. To confirm the teleconference agreement, Ephraim asked Dr. Haile Selassie Belay to travel to Addis Ababa and join local elders at the Synodic meeting (a special meeting of church leaders to which even lay Christian outsiders are usually not invited). Notwithstanding that he is Jewish, the Archbishops also invited Ephraim to address the Synodic meeting as a way of expressing their gratitude to and respect for him. In his speech, Ephraim referred to the difficulties of reaching the agreement, but also spoke of the process as "one of the most personally and spiritually satisfying efforts I have ever played a role in." He then went on to talk about how to build understanding in other contexts by reflecting on the connection of the Church to Judaisim.[42]

PDC Conference at Addis Ababa Red Cross Center

When AHPC closed its operation and created the Peace and Development Committee (PDC), it opened an office in Addis Ababa and became the first local NGO in Ethiopia. Its mission reflected Ephraim's priorities – to enable peace to take root and flourish across Ethiopia and Eritrea. Ephraim commends Dr. Haile Selassie Belay, the first Director General of PDC, for successfully establishing the organization so that it has received international support and continues its work. Today Ephraim serves as the Chair of its International Board and Ambassador Bekle Endeshaw as its Executive Director.

But when PDC first began operating in 1992, it had to establish itself. Quickly, it held a follow-up conference (organized by Dr. Haile Selassie Belay and Ephraim, and sponsored by the new PDC with the assistance of the Swedish Life and Peace Institute and the German Evangelical Church). Church leaders, Muslims, Christians, and Jews came together at the Addis Ababa Red Cross Center to talk about reconciliation among all Ethiopian political, ethnic, and religious groups. Participants came from every walk of life: elders, civil servants, religious leaders, businesspeople, government officials, women leaders, the youth, and representatives of various organizations. Ephraim gave the opening address and succeeded in inspiring the attendees to establish three Ethiopian NGOs for the purpose of strengthening the ongoing peace and reconciliation process.

Interfaith Prayer Day

With nearly superhuman energy, Ephraim concurrently continued other activities to help build sustainable peace in Ethiopia. Although the political parties had agreed to a transitional government, he understood that there was still deep-seated resentment emanating from the years under the Derg regime and that continuing interethnic and interreligious tension and violence made for an uneasy peace. To help the people of Ethiopia begin to overcome these problems, Ephraim decided to organize an interfaith prayer day in Addis Ababa. Ephraim prepared for the event by holding a religious service for the major religions in Ethiopia on the Ethiopian New Year, according to the Julian calendar, on September 11, 1992. The service was open to everyone in Ethiopia and was well attended, with political leaders from all the major groups participating.

Because it was the oldest religious organization in the country, the Ethiopian Orthodox Church opened the meeting with a prayer by the head of the church. Next came a prayer and sermon by the Muslim society, followed by a Catholic Cardinal and the head of the Protestant churches in Ethiopia. Finally, Ephraim spoke to the gathering, as a representative of the Jewish community. The focus of the entire service was on the future of Ethiopia and the need for peace, reconciliation, and courage to overcome a difficult past. Ephraim notes:

> Religious peace comes through respecting both self and tradition....A prayer meeting where a Christian does not say the name of Jesus is not honest; it is a show. To live together, we must remain honest and true to our respective faiths and respect one another.[43]

Expanding on this idea, Ephraim suggests that he might not hold an interfaith prayer day again. While the day had its intended effect, Ephraim's thinking has evolved. Today, he sees more value in going to church and listening to a Christian prayer, or to a mosque and listening to a Muslim congregational prayer. He believes such actions show more respect for the various traditions than trying to bring them all together as though there were no differences among them.

Peace and Development Organization: Engaging Ethiopian Traditions for Peace

When the time came to discuss the constitution for a new Ethiopia in the early 1990s, Ephraim was invited as one of the keynote speakers at a national symposium on the subject, organized by Professor Andreas Eshete, now president of Addis Abba University. He addressed the question of the relationship between church and state, calling for their separation, while at the same time suggesting the importance of close collaboration between them.

The constitution was accepted later that year, and included a provision requiring the separation of church and state. There was strong public approval for all but one article in the constitution, namely, the right of every Ethiopian ethnic group to secede if it so desired. That right was slipped into the constitution without full deliberation, and it remains a thorny issue.

With the new government in place, there was a widespread belief that peace in Ethiopia needed to be nurtured. Through the Peace and Development Committee, Ephraim, as usual, became proactive. He wrote to the Prime Minister of Ethiopia and the President of Eritrea and proposed that they establish a Ministry of Peace and Reconciliation to parallel the Ministry of Defense. If a country intends to wage war, Ephraim argued, it requires an army sustained by training, planning, and financial support. Waging peace, he contended, depends on no less. He envisioned an "army" of young people supported and trained for the purpose of resolving conflict. They would use neither guns nor force, but would work instead by means of persuasion and dialogue. Whenever a conflict began to develop, they would be dispatched. Though intrigued by the idea, the prime minister and president lamented that the war had drained their resources, leaving no money to carry out this suggestion.

Undaunted, Ephraim decided to create a new Peace and Development Organization with an established network of peacemaker elders. Although he could not provide the resources to train armies of young people, he could call on the country's traditional resources by reviving and strengthening the tradition of eldership in Ethiopia. His idea was to go to every village in Ethiopia and ask the people to identify the elders of their community – those people known for their kindness, wisdom, and love of peace. As the leaders respected by their communities, these elders would have the authority to make peace. They would be given offices and some money to ensure their readiness to intervene and reconcile conflicting parties, as well as to enhance relations. As the network developed, the elders could be convened for discussion and training.

Since its inception, this network has been growing, despite limited funding. It includes respected elders living both inside and outside of Ethiopia. Ephraim points out that the elders who are chosen are often former soldiers – the very people who have suffered some of the worst tragedies and seen the bloodiness of war firsthand. The experience of being so close to violence, he says, caused them to ask the same questions that he had asked as a child after he witnessed violence: "Who am I? I am just like the people who were killed. We are all mortals."[44] It is Ephraim's observation that the people most intimately aware of the horror of violence are often the first to try to put an end to it.

Referendum for Eritrean Independence

In 1993, when the Peace and Development Organization was in its first year, it was time for a referendum on the status of Eritrea. Invited as an observer, Ephraim watched as the Eritreans overwhelmingly voted for autonomy. Ethiopian Prime Minister Meles Zenawi helped celebrate the event by joining Eritrean President Isaias Afewerki at a party for Eritrea. Many years of war had produced a strong desire for peace in both Ethiopia and Eritrea, and to sustain the peace, Ephraim urged the leaders to build grassroots collaboration across borders. Although they endorsed the idea, many people felt that the Ethiopian-Eritrean conflict was "finished business" and that this type of effort wasn't necessary. Unfortunately, time and history proved them wrong.

Further Fighting and Reconciliation Efforts: 1998–2000

In the years immediately following Eritrea's independence, the new country maintained a close alliance with Ethiopia. By 1998, however, tensions erupted and violence again broke out. Widely described as a border dispute, Ephraim says that the war started with a dispute over currency. At the beginning of independence, Eritrea used Ethiopia's currency, the *birr*, although it later minted its own currency, called *nakfa*, which was marked with a camel. Ephraim was told that when the staunchly Christian people in the region of Tigray in Ethiopia saw the nakfa, they identified it as "Muslim money" because they associated the camel with Islam. For that reason, the Tigrayans, who as Christians contributed tithes to the church, refused to accept the nakfa because they saw it as an unfit offering.

In the meantime, in the village of Badme that straddled the border between Ethiopia and Eritrea, a fistfight broke out in the marketplace over the nakfa and quickly escalated. Several people were killed, and the leaders of Ethiopia and Eritrea – once close friends who had fought together against the Derg's socialist regime – became enemies. Both countries called the vague border between Ethiopia and Eritrea into question. Each laid claim to some of the same towns, including Badme, and another war began.

When Ephraim heard rumors of this conflict in December 1997, he offered help but was told not to worry, that it would soon be resolved. Only five months later, one of his Peace and Development Organization board members called to tell him that the small dispute had escalated into open warfare, and a U.S. effort to stop it had failed.

Many of the Peace and Development elders were in the United States at the time, though the office in Addis Ababa had continued its work since its founding in 1992. As soon as Ephraim grasped the gravity of the situation, he met with his elders in the United States, called the office in Addis Ababa, and coordinated with the offices of Prime Minister Meles and President Isaias Afewerki to arrange a meeting with the elders and each side, respectively. The idea was welcomed by all, and the first meeting in Addis Ababa went smoothly.

However, when it came time to travel to Asmara, Ephraim and the elders could not go by land because of wartime dangers. They took a small plane, but the flight was interrupted when the plane had some equipment problems. The emergency landing put all the elders at risk of attack from soldiers fighting in the region. Ultimately, they were rescued by the UN, which provided its own small plane from Somaliland. They held their meeting with President Afewerki and also met with refugees exiled from Ethiopia. When they finally returned to Addis Ababa, it was to develop proposals to resolve the conflict.

As things proceeded, Ephraim came to realize that, sometimes, his work could be accomplished more easily if the negotiations involved only a few people. Although he remains committed to the model of eldership, he recognizes that when groups negotiate, internal arguments often slow the process. People on the same side may disagree on method or timing, and expenses for group travel can mount.

Over the next two years, Ephraim therefore had to work alone in his capacity as an Ethiopian elder. He continued to make unpublicized flights to Addis Ababa and Asmara, meeting privately with Prime Minister Meles and President Isaias, respectively, as both leaders also preferred this to negotiating with a larger group. Ephraim credits his fellow elders for their support and encouragement, which provided the guidance to move things forward. Because he could not fly directly from Ethiopia to Eritrea during the war, Ephraim flew through Yemen. And when he could not make personal visits, he mediated using modern technology. By means of faxes, Ephraim helped the two leaders discuss the fourteen border towns in dispute.

Initially, Ephraim and the elders received the cooperation of the United States, Germany, Norway, the United Nations, and the Organization of African Unity (OAU). Yet he does not shy away from complaining that "the UN, U.S., and OAU mess[ed] up" because "their professionals lacked real understanding of the issue," and because they gave "false promises."[45] In this situation, Ephraim believes that the use of multiple levels of peacemaking (i.e., Track One diplomacy as well as his Track Two diplomatic efforts) was not the most effective methodology. The war ended with The Algiers Peace Agreement negotiated through UN, U.S., and OAU arbitration. But the large number of casualties and the continuing refusal of Ethiopians to accept the borders decided by the Permanent Court of Arbitration in The Hague have continued to fuel mutual suspicion between the parties. To the time of this writing, there has been neither final action on the borders nor a total peace.

Religious Peacemaking Methods

Ephraim's peacemaking is a complex blend of strong values and everyday pragmatism. When asked about his work, Ephraim starts by discussing the values that he believes should drive any peacemaker. Without hesitation, he states: "to be honest and love the people you work with, to know the truth, and to be respectful and respected."[46] Ephraim emphasizes the importance of honesty. He believes that conducting oneself honestly can actually be a valuable asset to achieving peace and, simultaneously, that honest relations are a characteristic of individuals and societies who are genuinely peaceful.

As he has often said in his public remarks, peace is more than the absence of conflict; it is something greater – a state of reconciliation. In his attention to reconciling political groups after a conflict has ended, in his wariness of the current calm between Ethiopia and Eritrea, and in his effort to create a Ministry of Peace and Reconciliation, Ephraim views peace as something that is dynamic and requires positive human interaction.

Ephraim also recognizes that his vision can be accomplished only if actors at all levels of society are involved. A pragmatist, he recognizes that each individual brings something valuable to the table. When asked to comment on diplomat Herman Cohen and Robert Frazier's effective yet less-than-forthright dealings with the Derg during Operation Solomon, Ephraim talks about the different roles and values that come into play:

> A judge makes a determination about who is wrong, who is at fault, but elders do not make these determinations. Unlike judges, elders might tell both parties that they are at fault and need to apologize, because the duty of an elder is not to determine fault or figure out who started the war. I do not know, for example, who started the Ethiopian-Eritrean War. The job of the elder is to bring people together, to make peace. The duty of the elder is to say: how can I fix this situation? They use psychological clout – respectability, knowability, character – which is often more powerful in de-trenching entrenched ideas. The diplomat works in a totally different way. The diplomat works using military and political clout to try to bring peace, and diplomats therefore do not value truthfulness as highly.[47]

As he speaks, the way that Ephraim views each of the players becomes clear: a judge works for justice; a diplomat for resolution; and an elder for reconciliation. The three work in different ways and bring different strengths and weaknesses to the process. It is understandable why Ephraim prefers to work through the ancient Ethiopian tradition of eldership. Although he sees diplomacy as necessary in today's world, he also perceives (and dislikes) what he views as the ulterior motives and self-interest that can come into play. Ephraim believes that diplomats frequently seek publicity and credit for themselves and compete with each other to do so. Furthermore, he notes that they rely on power – direct and sometimes indirect – to pressure people. And, finally, he views them as being concerned with financial compensation, yet another thing that can get in the way.

Ephraim has a vision of what can happen if the methods and values of the elders prevail. "In the future, in the best of all worlds, we would use gentle persuasion, high ethical standards and a spiritual approach to resolving inter-people and international conflicts."[48] Elders do not invoke power, nor do they trumpet their achievements; in fact, they eschew the media and publicity. Neither does their approach get bogged down by the desire for money and compensation, prestige, and power.

How the elders traditionally conduct themselves, therefore, is more consonant with healing. In Ephraim's words, elders are more "salubrious, more effective."[49] As such, the peace they achieve is likely to be more stable because it is embraced for its own sake. Most important, by encouraging people to work through their grievances together, the elders' approach presses toward reconciliation.

Again, it is the lived experience of reconciliation more than an attempt to achieve quick peace that is the focus of Ephraim's work. He explains:

> Reconciliation means being close again. In ancient times, peace did not come without reconciliation. If the Israelis and the Palestinians make peace, it will not come for some time. They will not eat together immediately. I am more interested in reconciliation than peace. I see demarcation on the ground as obviously important. However, more important for reconciliation is demarcation in the core of the human heart.[50]

Working for reconciliation is also core to the Peace and Development Organization. Ephraim explains that, without it, "Peace is always in danger and democracy and representative discussion of diverse positions is impossible."[51]

For Ephraim, the interdependence of these concepts grows out of a larger vision that also associates peace with other values. In a lecture entitled "Religion and World Peace in the Twentieth Century" at Kent State University, Ephraim described a world that is in need of a range of positive values in order to achieve his vision of a comprehensive peace:

> What we see today is not a happy world, a world of justice, peace, tolerance, and truth. Even right in our own backyard, we see a dark, cold, insensitive, and corrupt world – a world which has lost a sense of justice, the spirit of equity and responsibility; a world where the worship of pleasure is central, fast food, fast values, fast friendships; a world in which the suffering of the human soul fetches a large sum of money, a world in which people are more at peace with their dogs and cats than with their fellow human beings.[52]

He then indicated how the wisdom of a religious tradition can help us to reach his goal:

> Understanding spiritual and cultural matters in perspective, we can acquire wisdom which helps us to live with our fellow human beings in peace – knowing our limitations, respecting others, appreciating non-material things.[53]

The implication is clear: because full peace cannot thrive in a vacuum, it is vain to pursue it in isolation from other values. To pursue peace requires an entire orientation of self toward others and away from materiality. On the basis of a lifetime of experience, Ephraim has developed a way of understanding peace that makes an idea that is otherwise quite abstract both vivid and concrete.

As to the other characteristics of a true peacemaker, Ephraim emphasizes how important it is to have relationships of respect. And his life is a testament to that conviction. With one foot in academia and another in international diplomatic and religious circles, with one day in Ethiopia or Eritrea and the next at Harvard or Princeton University in the United States, Ephraim has had a lifetime of opportunity to meet and influence a number of significant figures.*

In addition, given his personal effervescence and enthusiasm for ideas and action, Ephraim easily establishes rapport with different individuals while commanding respect for his many accomplishments from music (translating Handel's *Messiah*), to academia (founder and first professor of the Afro-American Studies program at Harvard University in 1969), to his years as an activist for Ethiopian literacy and peace.

It is the community's relationships with and regard for its elders, and not bureaucratic mandates, that gives them authority. To determine whether a person has such stature in the community, Ephraim suggests that one must "go to the village where they were born; then you can know who that person really is. Then you go to the next place, then the next. . . . A person's connection with people where he or she lived tells much about them."[54]

Ephraim suggests that it was a lack of respect that turned out to be a key obstacle for the EU, U.S., and UN representatives when they attempted to negotiate peace between Ethiopia and Eritrea. Local communities did not hold the diplomatic negotiators in high regard, nor did they feel respected because the negotiators were not sufficiently familiar with their culture. Ephraim notes:

> Those who do not understand the cultural nuances of our rich traditions will only muddy up the conflict. The solutions could have come from us tapping into our traditions of age-old conflict resolution mechanisms,

---

* For example, the former Prime Minister of Pakistan was his student at Harvard, and earlier – during his doctoral studies in graduate school – his path crossed with the future prime minister of Mexico. Ephraim speaks fondly of the 1960s at Harvard, during which he and Osama Elbaz, the vice president of Egypt, danced together at the International House in Cambridge. On the basis of another close friendship with Ambassador Abu Odeh – the former Defense Minister of Jordan – he had the opportunity to meet King Hussein. Many of Ephraim's students from Harvard in the late 1960s and 1970s are today leaders in America and the world in law, religion, politics, business, education, medicine, and civic society.

using the services of our elders for their wisdom, neutrality, and impartiality. Yet out of respect for the professional foreign negotiators, the elders stepped back time and again, many times. So we had a huge tragic Horn of Africa War!

In other words, respect is a communal value, and is as important to receive from impartial negotiators and enemies as from friends:

Even if you don't agree with someone, you still have to respect your enemies and the people you deal with. And also, there is an old saying that you must not judge anyone until you have put yourself in their position. Think: what would I have done if I were in their position? You must have a very, very high ethical standard.[55]

For Ephraim, making peace therefore requires respect with empathy, and appreciation of difference. It also requires commitment to peace above all other things: above fame, above personal interest, and above past hurts. A peacemaker must be flexible, willing to adjust his or her approach to reach the goal and willing to consider anyone as a possible partner. Indeed, Ephraim believes it is important for community members, elders, and diplomats to work together, even though – and maybe especially because – their approaches may differ. In fact, Ephraim jokes that if Satan called asking for negotiations, he would agree to help if he thought that it might bring greater peace to the world.

This commitment demands more than a willingness to talk. In Ephraim's view, waging peace requires as much energy and ingenuity as waging war. And this is a concept he is always pursuing. Thus, in 1993, at the Council of the World Parliament of Religions, he called for a UR (United Religions) – analogous to the United Nations in form and structure – in the hope that it might marshal the resources of religious traditions to create world peace.[56]

Religious Motivation

In addition to the words of the prophet Isaiah and his personal and spiritual understanding of peace as reconciliation, Ephraim is motivated by an interreligious call to peace – a call that he believes is within us all. He notes that all religions teach the same core values of justice and human value. "Whether it comes from Hillel, Jesus, or Confucius, most of the great religions have some form of the Golden Rule."[57] For Ephraim, the fact that this prescription is found in the full range of religions and cultures shows a deep human yearning for peace.

However, he also believes that people respond best when they hear a call to peace in the words of their own cultural and religious traditions. In part, this is why elders and religious leaders can become such powerful advocates for peace. But people also respond to the call when they hear it articulated in everyday experiences in the world. Peacemaking is not just a diplomatic exercise, but a way to live and a motivation in itself, as Ephraim illustrates in his usual way – by telling a story.

Ephraim was at a train station in Princeton, New Jersey and was having trouble finding a parking space. He circled around in his car for thirty minutes, missed a train, and just as he caught sight of another train approaching, he saw a car pulling out. Ephraim waited, but before he could park his car, another man came from behind and grabbed the spot. Ephraim called out, "I was waiting for that space! The man parked there just told me he was leaving."

"Yes, well I was waiting for a long time," the gentleman replied dismissively. Ephraim envisioned three responses: he could fight over the space; he could be angry; or he could talk to the man and seek a bond through their common frustration. Ephraim chose the third response, explaining, "Fighting is hard on the physiology and anger is hard on the psyche, so I chose to relax both and make peace. It is always like this in a conflict."[58]

Having found another spot, Ephraim approached the man as they boarded the train, "Sir, I'm glad you found a parking space, but it really wasn't fair what you did." They talked, the man apologized, and they had a pleasant train ride to New York together.

Ephraim explains that creating a peaceful response did not mean avoiding the issue. That would have led Ephraim to repress his anger rather than express it constructively. By dealing with the conflict, he was able to establish a relationship with a stranger, who may think twice next time and act more courteously. Peacemaking thus involves facing issues truthfully, regarding the other party respectfully, and working from a disposition of empathy.

The decision to resolve the conflict with the man on the train seems logical to Ephraim, though he acknowledges that it also requires an attitude of courage, much more courage than to fling one's arms in the air and react in anger or to simply avoid the situation. Ephraim knows that it takes spiritual and psychological energy to bring about reconciliation, even in such everyday situations. But, in the end, such work contributes to one's own spiritual and psychological health. Ephraim believes that ethnic and religious groups need to have the same courage and to come together for the sake of reconciliation.

From Ephraim's perspective, individuals and groups – in short, all of humanity – yearn for peace. To be a peacemaker is to strive to be an honest and respectful human being, to embody and live by the values embraced by all.

The Power of Eldership for a Peaceful Future

At the time of this writing, the relationship between Ethiopia and Eritrea is formally peaceful, but there has been no true reconciliation between the nations. The state of peace remains fragile, and it would not take much to rekindle a war.

Ephraim reflects on the past conflict in Ethiopia and Eritrea and how the peace process might be moved forward:

> Conventional mediation failed here because the people themselves could and indeed must have played a significant role in the peacemaking. International professional peacemakers address the political parties only, not knowing any way to reach the peoples. They falsely believed that the proud Ethiopians and Eritreans would capitulate to international pressure, but they did not. Had they supported the national elders' efforts, they would have gotten a real result and reaped a venerable credit; unfortunately, their ulterior motives – political or financial – stood in the way.
>
> Councils of trusted native elders, ignored by foreign professionals, constitute an ancient local agency for peacemaking. Some ancient modes of human mediation remain superior modes, wherever they are extant. Elders profoundly understand the psychology and history, not just the ideology, of the combatants, and that peace and reconciliation is not only between political parties, but also between the populations, even if they are two states. Elders feel the blood of their own kind on both sides that will flow if they fail.[59]

The Peace and Democracy Organization continues to work to revitalize the power of eldership. With its expanding human network and deepening cultural resources, Ephraim's organization may well represent Ethiopia's best hope for a future of peace built on reconciliation.

ETHOPIA FACT SHEET[60]

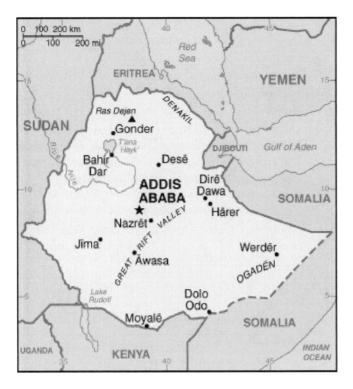

Geography

Location:	Eastern Africa, west of Somalia.
Area:	*Total:* 1,127,127 sq km *Land:* 1,119,683 sq km *Water:* 7,444 sq km.
Area comparative:	Slightly less than twice the size of Texas.
Climate:	Tropical monsoon with wide topographic-induced variation.

Population

Population:	73,053,286 (July 2005 est.)	
Ethnic groups:	Oromo:	40%
	Amhara and Tigre:	32%
	Sidamo:	9%
	Shankella:	6%
	Somali:	6%
	Afar:	4%

	Gurage:	2%
	other:	1%
Religions:	Muslim:	38%–50%
	Ethiopian Orthodox:	35%–50%
	Indigenous African:	12%
	other:	3%–8%

Note: Accurate statistics for religious affiliation are difficult to determine, in part because, for political reasons, both Muslims and Christians claim that their respective groups constitute a majority of the population. The percentages above take into account the variety of claims made by both religious groups.

Languages:	Amharic, Afaan Oromo, Tigrinya, Guaragigna, Somali, Arabic, English (major foreign language taught in schools).

Government

Government type:	Federal Republic
Capital:	Addis Ababa
Legal system:	Currently a transitional mix of national and regional courts.

Recent Background

With the exception of an Italian occupation from 1936 to 1941, Ethiopia has been unique among African countries, retaining its freedom from colonial rule and for most of the twentieth century maintaining its ancient Ethiopian monarchy. In 1974, Emperor Haile Selassie (who had ruled for nearly forty-five years) was deposed by a military junta – the Derg – which established a socialist state. Fifteen years later, the Derg regime was overthrown by a combination of rebel forces known as the Ethiopian People's Revolutionary Democratic Front (EPRDF). Later, in 1994, a constitution was adopted, leading to Ethiopia's first multiparty elections in 1995. Within a few years, however, Ethiopia became embroiled in a two-and-a-half year border war with neighboring Eritrea. Although the war officially ended with the signing of a peace treaty on December 12, 2000, a final demarcation of the boundary is on hold because Ethiopia objects to the findings of the Permanent Court of Arbitration that would require it to surrender sensitive territory.

Economic Overview

Agricultural production accounts for half of the GDP, 60 percent of exports, and 80 percent of total employment in Ethiopia. Historically, coffee has been the county's main export. However, recent historical lows in prices have led many farmers to switch their crops to qat, a natural stimulant derived from the Catha Edulis plant, and flowers as a means for supplementing their income. The two-and-a-half-year war with Eritrea, frequent drought, and poor cultivation practices have plagued the agricultural sector. Ethiopia's land tenure system provides for government ownership of all land and long-term leases to the tenants. The result is that the industrial sector's growth has been stifled because entrepreneurs lack the ability to use land as collateral for loans. In November 2001, Ethiopia qualified for and began to receive debt relief from the Highly Indebted Poor Countries (HIPC) initiative. Although its GDP recovered in 2003 and 2004, the government estimates that greater annual growth is needed to reduce poverty.

7 The Power of Ritual

The Rev. Dr. William O. Lowrey

Sudan

Facing the mountain of shoes confiscated during the Holocaust, the Sudanese refugees were moved. It was their first visit to a Holocaust Museum, their first knowledge of Hitler, in fact, their first confrontation with the Holocaust at all. Filled by a feeling of solidarity with the Holocaust victims, one Sudanese commented, "The only difference in Sudan is we don't have shoes and no one knows our names."[1]

This Sudanese refugee identified with victims of the Holocaust, recognizing the shared experience of pain in the two communities. He saw a parallel between the path of anguish traced in the Holocaust Museum of Washington, D.C., and the underreported suffering he had lived out in his home country. For over the last twenty years, Sudan has been ravaged by a war that has left two million people dead and over four million displaced. And, when hope for the resolution of this conflict seemed greatest, a rebellion in February 2003 triggered a government-sponsored campaign of violent oppression in the Darfur region of western Sudan that the U.S. State Department has labeled genocide, resulting in additional death and displacement. War-induced famine has impoverished formerly rich tribes, and security – when it exists – occurs only in pockets. As tragedy has been compounded by further tragedy, Sudan arguably constitutes one of the world's worst humanitarian crises facing the twenty-first century.

The conflict in Sudan is often characterized as a civil war, but the modern Western notion of civil war fails to convey the reality of overlapping tensions in Sudan. In the modern Western context, a civil war generally connotes two poles of power – two factions vying for control of a unified entity, or one faction fighting to secede from a state. Although this understanding of a civil war does describe a major axis of conflict in Sudan, namely, the battle between the government in the north and the rebels in the south, it is misleading to speak as if there were one unified rebellion and one unified progovernment movement.*

Within the south, there is also much inter- and intratribal fighting, particularly between the Nuer (pronounced *noo-AIR*) and the Dinka, as well as within the Nuer themselves. These tribal conflicts play out in national politics. A tribe or tribal subsection's allegiance to progovernment or antigovernment militias grows out of real grievances against the government or against the rebels, although such grievances tend to change as tribal politics change. Some progovernment militias have ended up fighting the government, while still other militias cannot be categorized as either pro- or antigovernment, but simply as opposing another militia. During the years of conflict, the Khartoum government played on the divisions among tribes, the agriculturalists and pastoralists, and the southern political factions, favoring one or the other in order to exacerbate tensions to Khartoum's benefit. While the Comprehensive Peace Agreement, signed by the government and southern rebels in 2005, gives hope that the ongoing conflict between the north and south is ending, the conditions in Darfur and continuing tribal fighting throughout the country still pose considerable obstacles for the Sudanese.

In seeking to reduce the conflicts in Sudan, the Reverend Dr. William Lowrey has worked at the tribal level to establish reconciliation that could enable peace for all in the country. Through the New Sudan Council of Churches (NSCC), Lowrey developed a People-to-People Peace Process among the Nuer and Dinka, and his work produced some of the earliest signs of encouragement for Sudan's future. To understand that work and the reasons for its success, one must first be familiar with Sudan, its history, and the story of its tribal relations.

The Geography and People of Sudan

Sudan is the largest country in Africa, covering one million square miles and encompassing a richly diverse populace. Its thirty-seven million people include more than fifty ethnic groups, which in turn divide themselves into 570 distinct peoples. Observers who try to explain how this diversity defines the region rarely do it in the same way.

For example, in *Sudan: Contested National Identities*, Ann Lesch classifies the population as 34 percent southerners, 40 percent Arabized people

---

* When "civil war" is used in this case study, it will refer to the North-South (or progovernment and antigovernment) axis of the conflict.

of northern Sudan, and 26 percent non-Arabized peoples of northern Sudan.[2] From a different perspective, Francis Deng, a Dinka from an area claimed by both the north and the south and an official with the United Nations, sees northern Sudanese identifying as Islamic and Arab, whereas southerners see themselves as black, non-Arab Africans.[3]

For Deng, this particular division helps to explain years of conflict. He believes that northern Sudanese Muslims have a need to "prove" their Arabness. This is in contrast to lighter-skinned Arabs, who claim to be directly descended from Muhammad the Prophet and, thus, practitioners of a more "authentic" form of Islam. Deng argues that this could have resulted in a "deep-seated inferiority complex," in which northern Sudanese find need to "exaggerate" their Arab character by asserting a strongly ethnic version of nationalism, and acting aggressively toward the mostly non-Muslim, non-Arab south.[4]

This analysis suggests the influence and power of religion in Sudan. But precisely defining the role of religion is difficult. The *CIA World Factbook 2005* described religious allegiances in Sudan as 70 percent Muslim, 5 percent Christian, and 25 percent indigenous religions.[5] Christian leaders, however, put their numbers much higher. And religious loyalties sometimes shift. Individuals frequently identify with the religion of the nearest militia or army unit, while privately practicing a mix of Christianity, Islam, and the religion of their ancestors. To some extent, therefore, religious identities align with political and military factions, in addition to being a source of practice and belief.

Although categorizing the diversity of the people of Sudan is not simple, one thing quickly becomes clear: both religion and ethnic identities play an important role in the conflicts that have persisted over the last several decades.

Sudan before Independence

Long before Islam became a major influence in North Africa, the land today known as Sudan was inhabited predominantly by Nubian civilizations in the north, and diverse ethnic tribes in the south. It is well documented that the Egyptian pharaohs heavily influenced the northern Nubian kingdoms economically, culturally, and politically. However, less is known of the ancient southern tribes, where knowledge was passed down through oral history and the Egyptian influence was negligible. What we do know is that among the innumerable southern tribes, there were wide varieties of ethnicities, languages, politics, and cultural practices.

Beginning in the seventh century, the Muslim-Arab conquest of Egypt began to significantly impact the neighboring Nubian kingdoms, even though the inhabitants and ruling families had previously been converted to Christianity by missionaries.[6] Arab influence was felt in many ways but especially economically, given Egypt's numerous contracts with Nubian kingdoms for the exchange of Nubian slaves, as well as other goods.[7]

Over the ensuing centuries, Islamic influence gradually increased and, by the sixteenth century, intermarriage between Arabs and the natives changed the cultural and religious make-up of the northern Sudanese population.[8] Both immigrant and indigenous "holy families" emerged and began shaping the Sudanese spiritual understanding and practice of Islam. These families were believed to possess a spiritual power inherited by the descendants of Prophet Muhammad. Although they were imbued with the responsibility to serve as religious and political teachers, this did not result in a cohesive society, and northern Sudan's tribes and political life were far from homogenous.[9]

Like most African states, Sudan became a political entity as a consequence of imperialism. After Napoleon's French expedition displaced the ruling class of Egypt but failed to retain French occupation of the land, the Ottoman Empire appointed Albanian soldier Muhammad Ali to rule Egypt in 1805. He rapidly assumed control and extended his power throughout the country. Less than twenty-five years later, in 1821, with the help of Great Britain, his son Ismail invaded Sudan and quickly secured control of northern and central Sudan.

Unlike Ottoman conquests that focused on adding territory, Muhammad Ali and his son also were interested in exploiting Sudan's people and resources, specifically, to use the slave trade to supply his Egyptian army.[10] Ismail used heavy taxation in this effort. Native Sudanese who could not afford to pay his burdensome taxes in cash were forced to pay in slaves, who were then trained as soldiers. The Sudanese were enraged, as almost all but the poorest were dependent on slaves for their households and fields. Late in 1822, their anger erupted into a series of revolts in which Ismail was killed.[11] The revolts did not unseat the Egyptian-Ottoman reign or put a stop to the slave trade, which continued to grow and supply large profits to the Arab elite.[12] Once considered too far for Egyptian reach, the slave trade reached south Sudan, where many were captured during brutal raids and sold into slavery.

Other influences were also shaping Sudan during the nineteenth century. Shari'a courts and religious schools espousing Ottoman Orthodox Islam were introduced into the country, bringing a new perspective to the natives' traditional reverence for mysticism and those who possessed spiritual power. In addition, European colonial influence, primarily British, was increasing both in Egypt and Sudan, perhaps most visibly in the British-built splendor of Khartoum in northern Sudan.[13]

Not surprisingly, tensions brewed and, within decades, southern Sudan exploded in rebellion under the seemingly unlikely leadership of a "soft-spoken mystic" and "religious recluse,"[14] Muhammad Ahmad. Proclaiming himself as the awaited Mahdi (in Arabic meaning one who is divinely guided), Muhammad Ahmad drew on the people's beliefs in spiritual power. In 1881, he united his followers in a holy war against what he perceived as the ruling infidels – the Ottoman-Egyptian rulers – and their foreign rule and imposition of Orthodox Islam. The Mahdists soon secured southern Sudan, and in 1884, Muhammad Ahmad won a monumental victory by overtaking Khartoum: his troops defeated the British garrison and killed famed General Charles Gordon. Egypt and Britain were expelled from Sudan.[15]

Victorious, Muhammad Ahmad ruled a united Sudan through a self-serving version of Shari'a law designed to strengthen his own power,[16] before he died of typhus after only five months. His successor, Khalifa Abdallah, was unable to sustain unity. Having fought the Ottoman-Egyptians and their Arab elite to rid themselves of brutality, southern Sudanese soon saw the Mahdiyya (Mahdist rule) as just another force seeking to control and suppress their indigenous tribal practices. Within just a few years, Sudan was again plagued by war, rendering it vulnerable to reconquest.[17] Taking advantage of this weakness, Britain and Egypt again joined forces and in 1898 invaded, quickly defeating the Mahdiyya's forces. Anglo-Egyptian joint rule commenced a year later and was to last for twenty-five years.[18]

It was during the early decades of the twentieth century that Britain decided to rule the north and south Sudan separately. Fearing that fervent Islam could again destabilize the south, the British decision was formalized in the Closed District Ordinance in the mid-1920s, which attempted to revive southern Sudan's indigenous roots by preventing northern Sudanese from working in the south and eliminating other Arab and Islamic sources of influence. In fact, only Christian missionaries were allowed to operate in south Sudan, where they ran a few schools and social services. These policies had long-term consequences. The south's agricultural development suffered due to its isolation and the abolition of slave labor,[19] and economic, educational, and religious divides were exacerbated between the two regions.

Meanwhile, Egypt gained independence from Britain, and a dispute between the two countries resulted in Egypt's expulsion from Sudan in 1924.[20] The ensuing decades saw rapid change. First Britain dominated, then Egypt returned with Britain's permission twelve years later. However, Egypt was not universally welcomed and its return inspired a wave of Sudanese nationalism dominated by Islamic political and religious leaders.

In the meantime, north and south Sudan were reunited under colonial rule in 1947. Although this did not significantly change the underdeveloped status of the south, the union laid the foundation for an independent Sudan that would include both regions.[21] These were tense years, as local factions continued to play the British and Egyptian powers against one another, and objections to the Anglo-Egyptian rule grew. Finally, in 1953, both Britain and Egypt signed an agreement to move Sudan toward self-government.

Although south Sudanese were concerned that the unequal material and educational conditions existing between the north and south would lead to political domination by the north after colonial withdrawal, northern politicians assuaged them with vague promises of equitable representation. On January 1, 1956, Sudan finally gained international recognition as a modern, independent state.[22] Britain's hurried change of policy in support of independence and north-south integration – in large part motivated by a fear of growing Egyptian influence in the region, especially among Sudanese Muslim groups – left south Sudan a poor sibling with untapped natural resources ripe for exploitation by its richer, better educated, politically more sophisticated countrymen from northern Sudan.

From Independence to 1998

By the time Sudan became independent, racial, political, religious, and economic tensions dominated the nation, and it soon erupted into civil war between the northern Arab–controlled government and the southern rebels who demanded greater autonomy. Hundreds of thousands of Sudanese were killed, and the economy of the south was nearly destroyed. The war continued until 1972 when the parties entered into a peace agreement called the Addis Ababa Accord, which recognized and affirmed the ethnic, linguistic, and religious diversity of the country. In brief, it granted greater economic, political, and cultural autonomy to southerners, who had felt suppressed by the north.[23]

Despite economic problems and some political instability, the peace survived for over ten years until September 8, 1983. On that critical day, President Jafaar Nimeiry, who had taken power in a 1969 coup, imposed Shari'a on Sudan's Muslims and non-Muslims alike.[24] His politically Islamic leaning was a major shift from the secular nationalism and leftist ideologies that dominated the start of his regime. But over those years, alliances had shifted: Muslim states in the region gained power, nearby Arab countries rich with oil offered much-needed aid, and Nimeiry's own Islamic beliefs strengthened.[25] President Nimeiry thus divided the south into three provinces to be governed from Khartoum, further polarizing the north-south divide and destabilizing the south. The civil war restarted. Over one million people died while hundreds of thousands were displaced. Rebellion broke out in the south, and not even President Nimeiry's overthrow in 1985 could mollify the southerners, who now demanded larger systematic change.[26]

Chief among the southern rebel groups was the Sudanese People's Liberation Movement/Army (SPLM/A), which was strongly aided by the then-Communist Ethiopian government. The assistance lasted until 1991, when a revolution in Ethiopia displaced Ethiopian President General Mengistu, and the new democratic government withdrew support from the SPLM/A.[27] That same year, SPLM/A leader Dr. John Garang quarreled with onetime friend Dr. Riek Machar over the goals of the SPLM/A. Whereas Garang wanted a united Sudan under a secular government, Machar favored an independent southern Sudan. When Machar's effort to seize control of the group failed, he and his supporters split off to form the South Sudan Independence Movement/Army (SSIM/A) in 1994.[28]

Further complicating the split of the SPLM/A was the tribal element involved. Garang and the people who stayed with the SPLM/A were mostly Dinka;[29] Machar and those who broke off to form the SSIM/A were largely Nuer. The split had ramifications at the tribal level, setting off a series of disputes and battles that continued for years, creating in effect a civil war within a civil war.[30]

In April 1997, one year after signing a political charter of principles with the government, Riek Machar and Sudan's government reached an accord and both signed the Khartoum Peace Agreement. This agreement officially brought Machar into the government of Sudan, together with SSIM/A, which was thereafter known as South Sudan Defense Force

(SSDF). As their collaboration grew closer, the government increased Machar's power by making him chairman of the South Sudan Coordinating Council, a body established to govern the government-controlled areas of the south.[31] Around that same time, another militia began gaining prominence and governmental favor: the South Sudan Unity Movement/Army (SSUM/A), created by Paulini Matiep, a Nuer and long-time warlord who split from the SSDF in 1998 after a disagreement with Riek Machar. In 2000, Machar resigned from his position when the government failed to fulfill its responsibilities within the 1997 Peace Agreement.

In addition to these tribal, ideological, and religious divisions, the country's internal disputes were further complicated by another factor – oil. In Sudan, most disputed territories are either believed to have oil or are already producing it. The SPLM/A often attacked oil sites it believed the government was wrongfully controlling, claiming that the government was using oil in an attempt to tighten its grip on the southern Sudanese people.

As the war continued with little respite, the situation in Sudan grew more desperate. Conflicts between tribes and militias were exploited and intensified by the government, making for a war with multiple layers.

Intra-Nuer and Nuer-Dinka Conflict

The Rev. Lowrey describes the southern tribes as historically acephalous, meaning there were no paramount chiefs or kings. Instead, the tribes were governed by several custodians or elders with different responsibilities. One custodian, for example, might mediate water conflicts, whereas another would oversee cattle rights and disputes. When the British came, they did not know how to manage (or exploit) such a decentralized structure, so they tried to impose chiefs on the tribes, thus centralizing power and authority.

The situation in southern Sudan today reflects a blurring of these cultural patterns. Some people are commonly called chiefs but function like traditional custodians. At other times, individuals assume the role of paramount chief with responsibility over the custodians, who in that case become sub- or vice chiefs.

War also has changed the culture by militarizing it. Power and authority now depend more on possessing guns than honoring custom. In many cases, the people who became chiefs or custodians through traditional means have been marginalized by militia leaders. As a result, it is more difficult for chiefs/custodians to resolve tribal disputes than in the past, and the participation of whole communities is often required when conflicts need to be addressed.

The Dinka and the Nuer, 1.35 million and 750,000 people, respectively, are the largest tribes in southern Sudan, and, after decades of civil war with the north, their conflict represents the greatest threat to peace in their region. Both tribes are Nilotic peoples who speak a similar language, but it is the very similarity of their lifestyles and mutual proximity that has often caused problems.

Primarily located in the Nile basin's Savanna lands in the southwestern region of Bahr El Ghazal, the Dinka are traditionally cattle herders. Located just to the north and east of the Dinka in the Upper Nile region, the Nuer are also cattle herders. Since cattle is central to the economy of both the Dinka and Nuer, cattle-stealing between them is a long-standing problem. For centuries, these two tribes have clashed over grazing land, as well as fishing pond rights and other related issues. The current famine, caused by the civil war and the extended dry season, has exacerbated these tensions. The tactics and technology of modern warfare have made their relations even more dangerous.

Until the civil war, feuds were fought with spears, and when a conflict escalated, it was conventionally resolved by a meeting of chiefs, sacrificing of bulls, and assignment of compensation and penalties, based on agreement and application of customary law. Today, things have changed. The Dinka and Nuer have begun to acquire advanced weapons, radically altering traditional patterns of warfare and conflict resolution. Initially, these new weapons were used only against the northerners in the fight for independence, but when the split between the Dinka-based SPLM/A and the Nuer-based SSIM/A occurred in August 1991, ethnic tensions heated up and the militias used modern weapons against one another.

Because of the war environment, the Nuer had not been able to conduct intratribal meetings since 1972, resulting in much estrangement. Then, in 1993–1994, two Nuer subtribes or clans, the Lou and Jikany, used their modern weapons against one another when a conflict erupted over fishing rights, leaving some dead. Traditionally, the Nuer custodian/chiefs would have congregated to arbitrate the dispute and any changes in customary law. The chiefs of the Jikany would have separated the killers from their families and initiated a conflict resolution process to negotiate proper compensation for the loss of life. But war had eroded traditional relationships and remedies. The Jikany refused to allow the Lou access to the bodies of their dead but, instead, left the bodies exposed to the elements. The Lou retaliated by attacking the Jikany, and the conflict escalated. The Dinka-based SPLM/A's efforts to curb the violence only aggravated the conflict. The Khartoum government, eager to keep the southerners from becoming a unified force against the north, began shipping arms to both sides.

Long-standing values pertaining to the spiritual pollution and individual responsibility associated with killing, values that in many ways defined the warriors within the Nuer culture, were not applied to killings accomplished with firearms. For example, the Nuer held a belief that someone who kills another retains that person's blood, which a priest must bleed out of the warrior's upper arm. To eat or drink before reaching the priest was to die. A rifle exempted the warrior from the risk of being haunted by the deceased, depersonalizing the violence by removing tribal rituals that historically made warriors accountable for their actions. Unintended consequences of modernity (and its accompanying military technology) are intimately bound up with southern Sudan's regional crisis.

The last decade of conflict between the Nuer and Dinka, touched off by SSIM/A's split from the SPLM/A, has cost thousands of human lives and hundreds of thousands of cattle that both tribes depend on for sustenance. On the west side of the Nile, a large stretch of land along the border between the two groups is now deserted. Although it is abundantly rich in grazing pastures and fishing lakes, no one will venture into it for fear of being killed.

This tribal warfare has intensified the impact of the current famine and also made it difficult to provide relief. As a result of the fighting, the UN and NGOs often cannot attend to basic needs such as food, medical care, and clean drinking water. Four hundred seventeen Nuer and Dinka villages have been destroyed by the fighting, and both Nuer and Dinka cultures steadily erode. Women, children, and the elderly, once protected from the effects of war, are now involved in the common suffering.

Furthermore a conflict (described by the U.S. State Department as genocide) that developed in the western region of Darfur in 2003 has led to hundreds of thousands of deaths and added over one million refugees and internally displaced people to the millions displaced by the years of civil war. In response, the Holocaust Memorial Museum in Washington, D.C. has issued a genocide warning, advising the world that it cannot afford to wait until it unequivocally proves genocide. The tragedy triggered by the Darfur conflict continues today.

The Reverend Dr. William O. Lowrey

The Reverend Dr. William O. Lowrey first became involved with the Nuer and Dinka in 1991, but his interest in cross-cultural reconciliation far predates his coming to Sudan. Attending the University of Southern Mississippi during the 1960s, Lowrey began by working for racial reconciliation within Christianity. As a first-year student, he cofounded the first multiracial Christian organization at the school. His interest in racial reconciliation began to take shape when the first two black students were admitted to the University of Southern Mississippi. At the time, he was the president of the freshman class, and his brother was president of the student body. Lowrey and his brother escorted the students around during their first day, and over the next year, Lowrey became friends with the black students and invited them to join his Christian fellowship on campus. When he tried to take them to his church, however, the church leaders refused to allow them to come. Lowrey remained determined. Although his home congregation never relented, he eventually found one church that would admit his friends.

The Rev. Lowrey attributes his ability to challenge existing mores to his family upbringing, his understanding of faith, and particularly to his belief in the central importance of people. His mother, a Sunday School teacher, used the Epistle of James to teach him that distinctions between rich and poor do not matter in regard to the character of people or how they are viewed by God.

Still, Lowrey's parents did not immediately embrace their son's ideals of racial reconciliation. In fact, his mother was shocked by them. Troubled, she decided to reexamine the Bible and the Epistle of James, and there she saw the evil of partiality in a new way. Even though the words referred specifically to socioeconomic differences, Lowrey's mother saw the connection to race.

Lowrey's experience at the University of Southern Mississippi solidified his commitment to building bridges between people and effecting racial and socioeconomic reconciliation. After graduating with a Bachelor's degree in computer science, he joined the staff of a Christian campus ministry called InterVarsity, where he continued his involvement with racial issues. Thereafter, he entered a seminary in Jackson, Mississippi and pursued his Master's of Divinity and ordination in the Presbyterian Church (U.S.A.). At the same time, Lowrey helped to start a new church. Intending to bring people from different backgrounds together, the Rev. Lowrey contacted members of various segments of the community – including the poor, middle class, black, and white – in order to attract them to his church, which focused strongly on issues of economic justice.

While he was at the church, Lowrey helped organize a statewide campaign to regulate the pulpwood industry. Pulpwood cutters, who included people from both the black and the white communities, were being abused by international paper companies. By fighting for fair treatment, Lowrey moved from engaging in purely interpersonal reconciliation to tackling unjust institutions. He also joined the Presbyterian Hunger Program Committee, which was part of a national program to dispense funds for hunger relief projects around the world. During these years, he also traveled abroad, expanding his awareness of global affairs.

Lowrey's work with the Presbyterian Hunger Program Committee continued when he moved to Cincinnati, Ohio and joined the pastoral staff of a large church there. As Minister of Missions, Lowrey became involved in inner-city Cincinnati. His economic and racial reconciliation work continued, and Lowrey was introduced both to missions projects around the world and to Appalachian communities of poor people. As he did this work, the Rev. Lowrey was accomplishing two things. He was actively following his ministry, and he was honing cross-cultural skills that would later serve him in his work in Sudan.

The Rev. Lowrey's desire to become more intimately involved in issues abroad peaked when he traveled to El Salvador with the last living member of the Human Rights Commission. She had been an assistant to Archbishop Oscar Romero – an outspoken human rights activist – when he was assassinated. She introduced Lowrey to the underground church in El Salvador and to some of the suffering that was taking place during the country's civil war. Lowrey reports that after this experience, he decided to become involved in international relief and development. He says, "I had strong interests in working in another country, and when my family seemed ready to relocate at the end of 1990, the church thought my gifts would fit best with southern Sudan. It seemed like the right match, although I did not know anything about Sudan before the move."[32]

The Rev. Lowrey has been described by *Washington Post* journalist Karl Vick as "A compact figure who seems to make himself smaller by some calculation that he will be more useful the less he is noticed."[33] Devoted to his wife Linda and their three children, Lowrey is quick to note their involvement in his peace work. He remembers how his wife and second daughter, Lela, survived a Sudanese government air bombing when helping to organize and train a women's tailoring cooperative. "All of our family members have experienced the pain, risk, and difficulty of work in southern Sudan," Lowrey states. "They embrace the same sense of call that I have and therefore we take the risks as a reasonable sacrifice in a high calling to stand with the people who someday will make a full and complete peace in Sudan."[34]

The family first went to Sudan in 1991, where Lowrey served as a mission worker among the Nuer. Officially, he first worked as a projects director for an ecumenical organization based in Nairobi, Kenya doing cross-border relief, rehabilitation, and church ministry in rebel zones. But he was also drawn into other work including the Lou-Jikany conflict of 1993–1994, where he sought to repair broken relationships among the Nuer. Lowrey describes this work as "seeking to stand in solidarity with those enduring great suffering, providing relief through church mission and nongovernmental organizations, and facilitat[ing] grass-roots peace processes."[35]

As he became more involved in Nuer peacemaking, Lowrey reports that he discovered rich wisdom in their traditional methodologies of making peace. He dedicated much time and energy to observing these methodologies among Nuer groups across Sudan and identified ways to draw from existing Nuer practices. Capitalizing on the role of leaders in the traditional Nuer religion as well as the Christian churches, Lowrey's strategy was to integrate indigenous peacemaking methods with modern theories of conflict resolution.

In 1994, he moved on to facilitate advocacy and peace research on Sudan as the Sudan desk associate in the Presbyterian Washington Office. During that time he also worked as the Sudan partnership facilitator, based in Washington, D.C., and collaborated with mission workers, various councils of churches, and partner agencies providing assistance in Sudanese government and rebel controlled areas.

While he was in Washington, D.C., the Rev. Lowrey completed a Ph.D. in Intercultural Organizational Behavior and Development. He titled his dissertation "Passing the Peace From People to People: The Role of Religion in an Indigenous Peace Process Among the Nuer People of Sudan." Written in 1996, his dissertation both came out of and shaped his later work as, in his words, a participant-observer of the Nuer-Dinka peace process.

In 1998, Lowrey returned to Sudan as the peace consultant for the New Sudan Council of Churches (NSCC), which includes the African Inland Church, the Presbyterian Church, the Church of Christ, the Roman Catholic Church, and the Episcopal Church, all of which are active in Sudan. Among the Dinka, the strongest churches are the Episcopal and Catholic, whereas the Presbyterians are dominant among the Nuer.

Working through the NSCC, Lowrey engaged global resources and mobilized cultural traditions to facilitate peace.

Lowrey focused on the Nuer during his first stay in Sudan, but his later sojourn centered on Nuer-Dinka relations. He quickly initiated a series of conferences and meetings between the Dinka and Nuer. Lowrey himself participated in these as an independent consultant rather than an agent of any particular organization, a decision he made because individuals operating on their own are more flexible than institutions. From Lowrey's perspective, individuals can make decisions more quickly and move back and forth across lines of conflict more easily than institutional representatives.[36] Although he maintained links with the Presbyterian Church, therefore, he did not go as the church's representative.

The Conferences of the People-to-People Peace Process

In June 1998, the Rev. Lowrey convened the Nuer-Dinka Chiefs and Church Leaders Reconciliation Conference in Loki, Kenya. With a $35,000 grant from the Presbyterian Church, the NSCC gathered twenty key chiefs and church leaders from the Dinka and Nuer border areas in the conflict zones. Because everything had to be translated into Dinka, Nuer, and English, Lowrey used powerful visuals with minimal writing. An interesting example of how he married indigenous culture with modern strategy was a diagram he designed. It was in the shape of a Nuer house, or *toukel*, and he used the diagram to demonstrate how conflict can threaten an entire structure, namely, the whole community, including, most important, its various levels of leadership.

At the end of this nine-day conference, the leaders signed the Loki Accord, committing themselves to a peace process and, ultimately, to ending the Dinka-Nuer war. They demanded that commanders of both sides refrain from hostile acts, local agreements be respected and honored, cattle-raiding stop, killing and abduction of women and children cease, abducted women and children be returned, homesteads no longer be burned, and freedom of movement be protected. Lowrey describes one chief's reaction after signing the Accord:

> [H]e was shuffling and dancing and shouting, "Praise God! Let the nation be in peace; let the peace continue!" over and over and over. After signing the Accord, he went around shaking hands and embracing both Dinka and Nuer. Then he began to dance in the middle of the group. The old man at times can hardly walk. His feet look like clubs. But it looked like joy and hope had captured his heart.[37]

Several months later, the support was in place for an even more substantial initiative, the Wunlit Dinka-Nuer West Bank Peace and Reconciliation Conference. Wunlit was the largest and most groundbreaking of Lowrey's People-to-People Peace conferences. Lowrey understood that the decentralized nature of leadership among the Nuer and Dinka meant that peace could come about only by broad consensus. The entire community needed to be involved in making peace. At Wunlit, therefore, he brought over three hundred delegates to a village constructed exclusively for hosting the conference. Three hundred youth worked for over three months to make the 150 houses and large meeting hall of mud and grass. To attend, the Nuer had to trust the Dinka enough to travel into Dinkaland.

At the end of ten days of storytelling, problem-solving meetings, consensus decision making, singing, dancing, and sharing rituals, the Wunlit Covenant was signed and thumb-printed by all the delegates on March 8, 1999, to end the tribal war. The participants sealed the covenant by sacrificing a bull, an act echoed at holy sites all over Nuer and Dinka lands across southern Sudan. The following September, the Dinka-Nuer West Bank Peace Council met to implement peace and discuss the success of the decisions made at Wunlit.

The Rev. Lowrey knew that he had to continue his work among the Nuer, who were still fragmented. Different Nuer had allied themselves with different rebel factions, and one of those factions (SSIM/A) was part of the government. To convene the Nuer, Lowrey concluded that he had to bring them to a common location. Drawing on his understanding of U.S. history and the particular realities during the U.S. Civil War, when many slaves traveled secretly in order to reach freedom, Lowrey created an underground railway. This became a vehicle through which displaced Nuer leaders, who had taken refuge in the north, could return home to the south and help with the reconciliation process. Lowrey wanted them to be part of the process and to be home to provide leadership after peace was reached. Thus, he found funding for them to travel by bus, barge, and foot.

As Nuer from the north rejoined their fellow tribespeople in the south, Lowrey conducted the Waat Lou Nuer Peace and Governance Conference in November 1999. Notwithstanding the Wunlit peace between the Nuer and Dinka, there were still problems to be addressed. The government had responded to the Wunlit peace by actively fostering conflict among the Nuer. Most injured among these groups were the Lou Nuer, who were thrown into near anarchy by five Lou youth militias allied with different armies. After groundwork mediation by Lowrey, the Waat Peace Covenant united military forces in the area and established a Peace and Governance Council to rebuild a community-based system of civil governance.

The Format of the Conferences

The Rev. Lowrey describes the logic behind his conference format by summarizing his aims for the earlier conference at Loki:

> As we gathered, there were three primary objectives. The first was to help Dinka and Nuer chiefs and church leaders reconcile with one another and rebuild or establish new relationships across their differences. Secondly, they needed to reflect upon their traditional patterns of peacemaking from Dinka and Nuer customary law and practice and gain new understanding of conflict management and reconciliation in the modern context. Finally, it was hoped that Dinka-Nuer teams would form and develop strategies for building peace at the grass-roots and middle levels of society.[38]

With these meetings, Lowrey encouraged the Dinka and Nuer to plum their rich heritage for practices that could lead to reconciliation, and to consider those methods in light of modern conflict resolution theory. Within this framework grievances were discussed and addressed.

The Loki conference began by allowing the participants to experience their relative proximity to one another. With a rope on the floor to represent the Nile, each person situated his or her chair where s/he lived. They established who neighbors were and how many hours it would take to walk to each place. They then prioritized the neighboring relationships as they moved toward the first of the conflict resolution goals.

The next phase of the Loki conference was what opened every other conference: storytelling. Encouraging the Nuer and Dinka "to show wounds to one another and speak openly of the pain and suffering that they had caused one another,"[39] Lowrey protected each person's opportunity to speak. First, he gave one group time to tell their stories completely. Then, the next group told its stories and responded to the first group's stories. This was followed by dialogue, rebuttal, and comments from key border chiefs and observers. (At Wunlit, three-and-a-half days of the ten-day conference were spent in storytelling.)

Years of pain and suffering were unleashed as people relived the slaughter of their families, the abduction of children, and the destruction of homes. Instead of affirming old bitterness and hatred, however, the storytelling and listening bonded them together in their shared suffering. Those present became more committed to the peace process.

After the stories of pain at Loki, Lowrey asked the Nuer and Dinka, whose traditions strongly connect them to previous and future generations, to draw on the wisdom of their father's fathers and their mother's mothers. He told them, "Tell your stories of how you have resolved conflicts in the past. Draw on the wisdom of your ancestors and reflect on what gifts you want to give your grandchildren who want to be born in peace."[40] From each story, they summarized principles of conflict resolution derived from their traditions and began to build a repertoire of Dinka and Nuer resources for making peace.

As they talked, the participants agreed to refrain from placing all the blame on the militia leaders. Instead, they accepted responsibility for their own destructive cycles of behavior. At Loki, Nuer Chief Nyuong Danhier from Nyal noted, "We are capable of making reconciliation and peace even if Garang and Riek are not present. Don't blame them – we are capable to make peace.... We are responsible."[41]

The next conference, held at Wunlit, expanded the breadth of the process within the Dinka-Nuer communities. There, an elected committee identified six categories of ongoing concerns that needed to be addressed in order to move forward with peacemaking: missing persons and marriages to abductees; reclaiming the land and rebuilding relationships; institutional arrangements for conflict resolution; border control; the problems posed by people outside the peace process; and extending the peace to the east bank of the Nile and province of Equatoria. Each concern was discussed in turn by a working group that proposed solutions to be voted on by the larger group. Discussion did not end until consensus was achieved.

At the conclusion of the conferences, the Dinka and Nuer were firmly committed to living with greater stability and peace. Lowrey describes the excitement at the conference, "One morning Chief William Ruaei, the oldest of the Nuer chiefs, a man with 30+ wives, his own army of soldiers, rugged and yet sweet, said, 'I did not sleep at all last night. My body was so happy because my mind could only think about peace.'"[42]

The Rituals of the Conferences

Tribal rituals and shared symbolism helped to structure and enrich all of Lowrey's conferences. Proceedings began and ended with the sacrifice of a bull, an animal that signifies wealth for both the Nuer and Dinka. In preparation for the opening feast, a white bull was tethered outside.

Men danced around the bull, pointing their spears at it and confessing their sins – as a weight to be laid upon the bull for him to take to the spirit world. Finally, using their bare hands, they struggled with the bull and wrestled him to the ground, forcing his open neck to face the sun in preparation for death. Once the bull was dead, all participants stepped over it, thereby indicating their desire to withdraw from conflict and allow peace to begin. After the ritual, the elders warned that anyone violating the covenant would wind up like the white bull. All participants then partook of the bull together.

The libation rituals were introduced by the women. A calabash of water with a sesame seed representing new life was passed around, and all present took turns spitting into the bowl, mingling their life fluids with those of everyone else. The cool, fine spray spittle flying off the hot tongue recalled that words can be a source of consolation and peace, as well as the source of conflict and violence. All participants came forward to wash their hands in the calabash, and to sprinkle its water all over themselves, cleansing themselves of past sins and conflict. In another libation ritual, a chief walked around the circle of participants sprinkling water on everyone's feet to symbolize cooling down from the heat of conflict, and preparing for the journey toward peace.

Dinka Bishop Nathaniel Garang dramatized his presentation by acting out a message about the perils of leadership under conditions of conflict. Despite his age and advanced arthritis, he lifted a large wooden chair above his head, and proceeded to walk and sometimes stagger around the room, crying that the weight was too heavy. "Who will help me with this burden? Who will lift this load from me?"

Suddenly, the oldest Nuer chief shouted the name of his favorite bull and responded, "I will help you with your burden!" He helped Bishop Garang take the load from above his head and slowly put it down on the floor. Lowrey describes that moment:

> The whole community of Nuer and Dinka were on their feet, shouting for these elderly leaders as they removed the load together. The symbolic imagery was dramatic and moving, causing the group to burst into clapping and joyful shouts.

Participants understood the symbolism: if the Dinka and Nuer worked together, they could remove the burden of war that was crushing them.[43]

The Rev. Lowrey's conferences often ended with a time of shared singing and worship dedicated to peace. At Wunlit, for example, participants concluded by composing a peace song in both the Nuer and Dinka languages. Later, in Nuerland, during an impromptu ritual occasioned by the visiting Dinka presence, a chief and twenty women engaged in traditional dancing that simulated fighting that first escalated and then diminished.

In these cultures, as in Western ones, symbolic acts have a powerful resonance. When some Dinka heard that Chief Isaac Magok, a Nuer warrior with a fearful reputation, would be crossing the border into Dinkaland for the Wunlit conference, they declared over and over, "If Chief Isaac is in Dinkaland there will be no more fighting."[44] The chief's crossing into Dinkaland carried a symbolic significance even greater than his attendance of the peace conference. Moreover, because the Nuer went to Dinkaland for the conference, the Dinka understood that they must reciprocate by visiting Nuerland, whatever the security situation. For their part, the Nuer were ready to leave some of their chiefs behind after the Wunlit conference as a pledge of the Dinka's protection. If the Dinka chiefs were killed in Nuerland, the Dinka could reciprocate and kill the Nuer chiefs.[45]

These frequent and elaborate forms of ritual performance were largely inspired by the related though distinct, spiritual heritages of the Nuer and Dinka. They practice different traditional religions and different versions of Christianity, but both groups deeply respect rituals and symbolic acts as valuable tools for peacemaking.

Because the groups do not separate religion from government (nor for that matter do they very clearly define what constitutes a religious act), sensibilities about religious differences were not that strong. Conversely, the ability to use ritual that resonated was important. Whether one was an indigenous religious practitioner or Christian, therefore, their church leaders and chiefs engaged in ritual acts, some of which were for the traditional people and others of which were uniquely Christian. Both practitioners of traditional religions and converts to Christianity were able to join in the rituals of their own religious tradition while showing the utmost respect to each other.

Connecting the Fair Fighters

According to the Rev. Lowrey, peacemaking begins with deep respect for other peoples and cultures, respect, in Lowrey's case, that springs from his theology. He views people as having great potential because there is "wisdom resident in them." He refers to a passage in Genesis saying that all people, male and female, are made in the image of God. Stressing that this idea is endemic to all the Abrahamic traditions, Lowrey finds in

Christianity the additional belief that humanity is so close to God that God became human in Christ. "Even though sin and rebellion has marred humanity," Lowrey says, "all was not lost. People carry potentialities for both good and evil within them, and there is frequently a battle between these potentialities."[46]

The fundamental idea of peacebuilding, Lowrey believes, is to find a way to connect the fair fighter in each person, or that part of every person that "fights for what is good rather than for personal desire." Drawing out the fair fighter requires calling on every individual's deep personal resources. The first question Lowrey asks is, "What is the wisdom that's already there in people?" He explains, "No matter how poor, how uneducated people are, there is a rich knowledge base in them, and you can only tap into it by listening to them." Before he helped orchestrate the peace process for the Nuer and Dinka, he spent hours listening to their stories told around the fires.[47]

Lowrey remains humble about his contributions to the process. "What I brought to it," he says, "was some ability to organize, to bridge the tribal world with the modern world in terms of logistics, which in one sense is fairly easy to do compared to knowing how people organize and understand themselves. I was just adding a little bit to what they already had."[48]

Achieving Peace Group by Group

In his doctoral dissertation "Passing the Peace From People to People," Lowrey approaches peacebuilding not just as a process of one person mediating between representatives of opposing sides, but as developing the capacity of groups to solve their disputes themselves by drawing on their own cultural resources. Lowrey says, "Relatively seldom do I end up in a mediator role – though there is always some mediation that takes place peripherally. I help design a process and support structure to bring people together in an environment that is safe enough for them to engage with one another and find their own solutions."[49]

Lowrey acknowledges that when relationships are bitterly impaired, or sectarian political interests intervene, much preparatory work is sometimes necessary through a neutral intermediary. More important to the ultimate success of the peace process, however, is the capacity of local actors to generate their own solutions, incorporating their own cultural practice and experiences into their own decisions. The neutral intermediary acts most effectively when facilitating this free and open dialogue.

Spheres of Brokenness and Spheres of Peacebuilding

Part of peacemaking for Lowrey, therefore, is reconciling relationships torn apart by conflict. In this regard, Lowrey employs a diagram that pictures human relationships as a set of circles that exist either in conflict, "spheres of brokenness," or in harmony, "spheres of peacebuilding." One circle stands for our relationship with ourselves; another with our friends, family, and affinity groups; another with the others who are different from us (ethnic, religious, national, etc.); another with the environment; and another with wider social and political institutions.

Reconciliation, Lowrey explains, is easiest to effect with those people who are most like us and speak our language. To begin the process of reconciling, therefore, it is effective to start by repairing relationships with people culturally closest to us: our friends, families, and near neighbors. At the next level, we must link the affinity groups to which we belong to the other groups with whom we may have both significant similarities and differences. The farther away from our immediate circle we move, the greater the challenge. The demands are particularly daunting at the institutional level, where we confront entrenched oppression and structural injustice. Lowrey's people-to-people peace begins the process of peacebuilding, but unless institutional deformities are overcome, there is no chance for a truly secure and sustained peace.

Understanding conflict and reconciliation in terms of a series of interlocking circles sheds light on Lowrey's own peacemaking efforts, which began with Nuer subtribes, and then expanded to include the broader Nuer-Dinka conflict. For Lowrey, all the parts are deeply interdependent. Conflict at any level spreads through the interlocking circles to infect the whole system, and when reconciliation begins, all the circles can experience substantial healing.

An Insider-Partial

John Paul Lederach, the noted Mennonite peace theorist and practitioner, coined the term "insider-partial" to describe people who were somehow part of a culture but also able to gain critical distance from it. Lederach believes that these people are best positioned to serve as peacemakers. When the Rev. Lowrey is asked whether he views himself in this way, he responds that he sees himself as an outsider who is nevertheless linked with the insiders. He agrees with Lederach that peace cannot be imposed on a people from the outside, but that it must in some sense be self-initiated.

Although he resolutely avoids the terminology of victimization, Lowrey advocates showing partiality toward those who are suffering, something he maintains is quite different from having a particular agenda or solution. Where power and pain are distributed unequally, neutrality simply strengthens the hand of the oppressor.

"There are times," he says, "when there is a rough equilibrium of power. In those cases, which in the circles I work in, tend to be a minority of the time, you must be neutral. But when there is a clear difference between the oppressor and the oppressed, though the oppressed can be just as dirty and unfair as the oppressor, their resources are quite different."[50] In the interests of peace, one must sympathize with the suffering on both sides.

Lowrey gives the Middle East as an example. A peacemaker must be sensitive to Israelis who have suffered from the acts of suicide bombers and to Palestinians who have been abused by the Israeli military. However, to take political sides (justifying everything Israel does), "is [a] political and philosophical commitment rather than [a] careful judgment of who is suffering." Lowrey believes that a person who holds such a view has opted out of the peace process. The same is true of the person who excuses everything Palestinians do; such opinions only perpetuate the cycle of conflict. Lowrey concludes, "If you are an engaged peacemaker, then you engage with those who are suffering in order to relieve the suffering. At the same time, you look for solutions at the institutional and systemic level and advocate for a sustainable peace."[51]

Lowrey adds that when there is a power imbalance, conflicts tend to persist for a long time because there are fewer incentives for peace. "That is part of what we're seeing in Iraq," Lowrey says, "and part of what has happened in the Middle East. In cases of asymmetrical power the less powerful side will find it extremely difficult to initiate the peace process, and the more powerful side has little reason for doing so. In these cases, the less powerful side often turns to unorthodox and frequently injurious ways to claim power. One reason Sudan is now able to negotiate peace is because the rebels and the government have gained relatively equal footing."[52]

Scripture in Lowrey's Work

In addition to the Epistle of James, which initially inspired Lowrey to peacemaking, and the book of Genesis, which laid the basis for his peacemaking strategy, Lowrey explicitly cites two passages that inform his peacemaking work. One is Micah 6:8, a verse from the Hebrew Bible that reads: "What does the Lord require of you but to do justice and to love mercy and to walk humbly with your God?" The link between justice, mercy, and humility before God has been important to Lowrey's understanding of himself and his mission.

Chapter 5 of Paul's second letter to the Corinthians in the Christian Testament contains Lowrey's second guiding passage. In this chapter, Jesus's mission in this world is described as the work of reconciliation, and it claims that those who follow him are entrusted with the same sacred work. As a Christian, the Rev. Lowrey felt called to be an ambassador of Jesus and a minister of reconciliation. "That has helped me to see that this is the heart of the mission of God in the world: to reconcile all things to himself. God's doing the work, and we're the instruments that he uses."[53]

Scripture takes on an instrumental value within the Rev. Lowrey's work as well. For example, to explain the value of storytelling in peacemaking among the Dinka and Nuer, Lowrey says:

> I told the story of the Apostle Thomas who had to see, reach out, and touch the wounds of Jesus before he could be reconciled (John 20:24–29). The Christian understanding is that Thomas, along with all humanity had caused the wounds of Jesus. Therefore, I invited the Dinka and Nuer to tell their stories, to show their wounds to one another and speak openly of the pain and suffering they had caused one another over the past seven years.[54]

In this way, scripture served both to elucidate and validate the importance of telling stories as a means of resolving conflict.

Lowrey speaks of the earlier-cited libation ritual, "I was reminded of the words of the prophet Isaiah: 'How beautiful on the mountains are the feet of those who bring peace and good news.'"[55] Here, Lowrey was not invoking Christian scripture as a teaching tool. Scriptural language and imagery simply infuse all of his reflections on peace and reconciliation.

In Psalm 46:9, God is depicted as breaking the bow and shattering the spear. Lowrey relates the use of this passage in a south Sudan peace conference. During the accompanying service, all the Nuer and Dinka present passionately echoed the refrain, regardless of their ethnic or religious identity. Voices rose and enthusiasm increased as they repeated the words pointing to a force for peace greater than themselves.

Since the 1998 Peace Conferences

Conditions in southern Sudan have improved since the peace conferences Lowrey facilitated. Communication between the Nuer and Dinka has resumed, and grazing lands and fishing lakes have opened for shared use. Such cooperation helps to provide food for all during the onset of famine, and has permitted the UN and NGOs to return to offer what assistance they can.

At the national level, political liberalization and reconciliation often took a backseat to the central government's interests. In 1999, President Omar Hassan al-Bashir declared a state of emergency, disbanded parliament, and instituted martial law. The government continued to foster rivalry between southern factions by supplying arms to Paulino Matiep's SSUM/A and granting its members high-ranking positions within the Sudanese army.

Wary of the growing power of SSDF and the support of its leadership (Machar) for the Nuer Dinka Peace and Reconciliation Conference at Wunlit (which concluded in March 1999), the government moved to counterbalance SSDF by supporting its rival SSUM/A. Machar responded by dissolving his relationship with the government. When fighting between SSDF and SSUM/A intensified in 1999, thousands of displaced Nuer sought refuge in Dinka areas administered by chiefs who had signed the Nuer and Dinka Peace and Reconciliation Agreement. They were welcomed.

On October 23, 2002, the long-estranged John Garang of the SPLM/A and Riek Machar (then associated with the Sudan People's Democratic Front, which was the most recent incarnation of the SSDF) signed a joint statement to integrate their two groups. Concurrently the SPLM/A took steps to improve its relationship with the Khartoum government. Talks brokered by the Intergovernmental Authority on Development (IGAD) resulted in the 2005 Comprehensive Peace Agreement, which authorizes south Sudan to attempt self-rule for six years before holding a referendum on independence. Currently, there is a cease-fire between the government and the SPLM/A. New discussions are now being brokered by Kenya on topics that are outside of IGAD's jurisdiction. Focus has narrowed to three disputed territories for which the SPLM/A seeks self-rule and waiver of Islamic law.

With the conclusion of the Comprehensive Peace Agreement, official peace was reached between north and south Sudan. John Garang was named vice president of the autonomous government of south Sudan, but held this position for only three weeks before dying in a helicopter crash. Taking his place, Riek Machar became the region's vice president and vowed to keep Garang's promises and the peace agreement alive. But for peace to be a lasting reality for all Sudanese, all of the institutional and material imbalances existing in the country must be addressed, foremost among them the horror in Darfur.

Spreading the People-to-People Peace Process

Since leaving the Sudan in 2000, the Rev. Lowrey has become the Director of Peacebuilding and Reconciliation at World Vision International, a Christian relief, development, and advocacy organization serving eighty-five countries around the world. Although he has taken a step back from the frontline, he continues to build on his work in Sudan, now addressing peacemaking at the global level. Lowrey has helped to build, and is currently overseeing, regional networks of peace in more than thirty-five countries and links the peace programming with global advocacy in a World Vision network called PAXnet, standing for Peacebuilding and Advocacy Network. Through World Vision, Lowrey has integrated peacebuilding with emergency relief and development work, and linked them all with advocacy.

Despite the violence in Darfur, southern Sudan inches closer to peace and Lowrey's legacy remains evident. At the end of the Loki conference Dinka Chief Kakeny Kamic spoke of how the process had affected him. "What is good is for people to face each other. After this, I will allow the Nuer to come to my grazing area and water points starting in January so they will know we are serious about his peace." Another leader, Chief Makeny, spoke of an expanded vision of peace that Lowrey had introduced. "You have brought us here successful for this reconciliation. Why don't you go to the Arab chiefs and bring them here for reconciliation?"[56] He punctuated his statement with a song and a dance of victory; everyone present cheered and clapped as he moved to the rhythm of his own joy. Amid the hope and optimism, Telar Dang, the ceremonial chair, concluded the conference by calling attention to the new opportunities for peace, at the same time warning of the challenges and obstacles that lay ahead:

> It has been a great achievement. Since 1991 we have never had a time to come together. As we say in Dinka, 'What destroys a home is not death –

it is hatred. Death cannot kill all of us, but hatred will disperse us and destroy us. When we leave, let us go home and unite our communities and face the difficult road ahead of peace, reconciliation, and unity. We must know it is not easy. If you have the willpower, it doesn't matter who stands in front of you. I know after this, the practicality on the ground, death will still be there, attacks will still be there. Don't be discouraged – pursue peace and reconciliation – don't give up![57]

Whether the People-to-People Peace Process will work on a larger scale and whether the local peace agreements it helped to produce will last are questions for another day. Regardless, the process gives people a chance to make their own peace rather than having it imposed on them. At its best, the process illuminates the humanity of its participants, and elevates their aspirations for their community's future.

Unquestionably, the Rev. Lowrey helped the people of southern Sudan create a beacon of hope in the midst of a bleak and bloody conflict. In light of the violence today wracking western Sudan, William Lowrey's legacy becomes all the more important. It is a reminder that hope is not a naïve virtue, and that, even in the midst of horror, passionate commitment and wisdom have a say in the course of world events.

SUDAN FACT SHEET[58]

Geography

Location:	Northern Africa, bordering the Red Sea between Egypt and Eritrea.
Area:	*Total:* 2,505,810 sq km *Water:* 129,810 sq km *Land:* 2.376 million sq km
Area comparative:	Slightly more than one-quarter the size of the United States.
Climate:	Tropical in South; arid desert in North; rainy season April to October.

Population

Population:	40,187,486 (July 2005 est.)	
Racial/ethnic groups:	Black:	52%
	Arab:	39%
	Beja:	6%
	other:	3%

Religions:	Sunni Muslim:	70%
	Indigenous beliefs:	25%
	Christian:	5%
Languages:	Arabic (official), Nubian, Ta Bedawie, diverse dialects of Nilotic, Nilo-Hamitic, Sudanic languages, English.	

Government

Government type:	The nation is transitioning from an authoritarian regime that was established when a military junta took power in 1989, leaving the government to be run by an alliance of the military and the National Congress Party (NCP), which espouses an Islamist platform. In 2005, after the Comprehensive Peace Agreement (CPA) was signed, a unity government was formed that includes people from the previous government as well as from the Sudan People's Liberation Movement (SPLM), the political wing of the largely southern rebel groups.
Capital:	Khartoum

Background

Since achieving independence from the United Kingdom in 1956, Sudanese national politics have been characterized by military dictatorships that historically favored Islamic-oriented government. And for all but ten years (1972–1982) until 2005, Sudan was entangled in civil war. Since 1983, the war has resulted in two million deaths and over four million people have been displaced. The war has generally divided the Arab/Muslim majority in the North against the mostly non-Arab, Christian, and indigenous African populations in the South, although alliances shift often.

In 2005, a peace was achieved when the Comprehensive Peace Agreement was signed to stop the civil war and give tentative autonomy to the southern rebels, which is to be followed by a vote on independence in 2011. However, a separate conflict in the western region of Darfur, which broke out in 2003 and continues to the time of this writing, has resulted in hundreds of thousands of deaths as well as the displacement of over one million more of Sudan's citizens. Tensions with the neighboring country of Chad are also adding destabilizing elements to the situation, so that the future following the Comprehensive Peace Agreement is uncertain.

Economic Overview

Sudan's economy corresponds to its reality; decades of war and instability have left it with one of the highest debts and the poorest people in the world. A country still dependent on its agricultural sector (80 percent of its workforce and 43 percent of its GDP come from agricultural production), the Sudanese remain highly susceptible to drought and weak world agricultural prices.

The World Bank classifies Sudan as a Heavily Indebted Poor Country (HIPC). Continued international humanitarian and development aid is imperative for the survival of millions of Sudanese, who are at risk of famine and disease.

However, in recent years the economy has begun to improve. Starting in 1997, Sudan began implementing IMF macroeconomic reforms to stabilize inflation. Two years later, it began exporting crude oil and saw its first trade surplus during the last quarter of 1999. An increase in oil exports, favorable weather for agriculture, and the government's economic reform policies have resulted in a steady increase in GDP.

Organizations and Their Abbreviations

NSCC
New Sudan Council of Churches
Organization out of which the Reverend William Lowrey functioned.

IGAD
Intergovernmental Authority on Development
Mediates many of the disputes in Sudan.

SPLM/A
Sudanese People's Liberation Movement/Army
John Garang; first southern resistance militia and best funded; goal is a secular Sudan; primarily a Dinka organization.

SSIM/A
South Sudan Independence Movement/Army.
Led by Riek Machar; formed after Machar split from Garang in 1991; goal is an independent southern Sudan; primarily a Nuer organization.

SSDF
South Sudan Defense Force
Led by Riek Machar; new name of the SSIM/A military after the Khartoum Peace Agreement of 1997.

SPDF
Sudan People's Democratic Front
Led by Riek Machar; political wing of Machar's move-ment after he became disillusioned with the govern-ment; Machar united the SPDF with the SPLM/A in 2002.

SSUM/A
South Sudan Unity Movement/Army
Led by Paulino Matiep; pro-government; formed as a rival to SSDF.

8 The Nonviolent Deputy Minister of Defense

Nozizwe Madlala-Routledge

South Africa

The story of South Africa's struggle to end apartheid and create a constitutional democracy dedicated to equal freedom for all is closely intertwined with the personal story of one of South Africa's most committed peacemakers: Nozizwe Madlala-Routledge.

As a Quaker, Nozizwe Madlala-Routledge has long been a leader on issues of women's rights, development, peace, and security. Active in the underground African National Congress (ANC) during the antiapartheid years, Nozizwe was in and out of detention, the last time spending a year in solitary confinement without trial. A committed activist, Nozizwe was sustained by her beliefs and her commitment to pacifism, even when she served as Deputy Defense Minister in the government following the death of apartheid. Today, Nozizwe continues to address issues of human security now that she is the country's Deputy Health Minister. To understand her story, it is useful to examine South Africa within a historical context.

The Context: An Overview of South Africa

When thinking about South Africa's history, people often focus on the racial divisiveness that resulted from colonialism and tend to neglect the rich diversity that characterized the region throughout most of its history. Fossil records indicate that the area has been populated for over one hundred thousand years. The earliest inhabitants were a hunter-gatherer people, ancestors of the Khoisan people, Khoikhoi and San who later came to be known as "Hottentots" and "Bushmen." These hunter-gatherers lived harmoniously for centuries and had viable systems for resolving disputes. Today, the Khoikhoi are no longer an identifiable group, having effectively disappeared from exposure to smallpox brought by Europeans, assimilation, and extermination.[1]

As the society progressed, mixed farming communities emerged in the eastern part of southern Africa, eventually replacing hunter-gatherers as the dominant lifestyle in the eastern region. Some of these early farmers evolved into the modern day Xhosa and Sotho people in the south, the Zulu in the north, the Pedi in the east, and the Tswana in the west. Autonomous farming societies continued to grow until the late 1700s, when the Europeans began to arrive in large numbers.[2]

First Colonial Contact

The traditional diversity of the region was of little concern to Jan van Riebeeck and his crew on April 6, 1652, when they anchored at the Cape of Good Hope under the flag of the Dutch East India Company.[3] Their original intention was to create a small supply station for the fleets that roamed the seas during this period of remarkable Dutch economic expansion, but within ten years, a dynamic, autonomous colony had developed. Complex and racially stratified, the Dutch colony foreshadowed the system of apartheid that was destined to plague South Africa centuries later.[4]

The colony's racial stratification reflected the rapid growth of the European community, their presence among the original residents of the land, and the emergence of a slave economy. The Dutch East India Company increased the numbers of Europeans by releasing some of its employees from its service and granting them land. In addition, the primarily Dutch population (later called "Boers" and, even later, called "Afrikaners") swelled by Huguenot settlers from the Netherlands (who were originally refugees from France) and German settlers. Finally, the Company imported slaves from Ceylon, India, Indonesia, Madagascar, and Mozambique. Not only did this create a slave class, but the slaves also contributed to the racial and cultural diversity by introducing their faith, Islam, to the South African region.[5]

Throughout the 1700s, governors encouraged immigration. Those who pushed into the northeast came to be known as "trekboers." The Khoisan, who inhabited that region, resisted unsuccessfully, but the Xhosa, who lived in what is now called the Eastern Cape, took up arms in a series of wars.[6] Later, a group known as "colored" emerged as descendents of these groups and slaves imported from other regions of Africa mixed together. By 1806, the British had captured the Cape. Although the white population was diverse, the colonists identified as part of a singular, white Christian community whose shared identity was primarily defined by their race. Indeed, the government's appointed Calvinist ministers reinforced this perspective, by defining society as a racial hierarchy with white Christians at the top and indigenous African populations below. The Christians were further unified by the evolution of a common language – Afrikaans, a modified version of Dutch.[7]

The British saw the Cape as a stepping stone to Asia and set out to solidify their control over all of southern Africa.[8] Seeking to establish the rule of law over what they perceived to be an anarchic eastern frontier zone, the British engaged in a series of violent confrontations with the indigenous peoples, most notably the Xhosa and the Zulu.[9] They also transported settlers to the region in an effort to permanently change the landscape and create a buffer between the indigenous people and the permanent Cape settlement. Not realizing that the land was claimed by the Xhosa people, these British immigrants and those who followed became embroiled in a decades-long struggle with the Xhosa. Their battles ended tragically in 1857, when the Xhosa acted upon a prophecy that foretold the whites would return to the sea if the Xhosa slaughtered their own cattle and destroyed their crops. The Xhosa followed the prophecy, ultimately suffering mass starvation. This effectively ended their resistance against the colonialists.[10]

During this same period, the great Zulu warrior Shaka assumed the Zulu chieftaincy. As he ascended to power, Shaka conquered much of the territory in eastern southern Africa, from the Pongola River form the Tugela River from the mountains to the sea, creating a period of chaos that became known as the *mfecane*.[11]

Dutch trekkers, called "Boers" by the British settlers, moved east, unaware of the Zulu's control of the land. Their leader, Piet Retief, planned to meet with the Zulu to negotiate for the land but Shaka's successor, Dingane, murdered him. In the Battle of Blood River that ensued, the Boers were victorious, paving the way for Boer settlements in Natal. Subsequently, the British annexed the region, reasoning that it was necessary to protect the Cape Colony. The Boers formed two republics, the Transvaal and the Orange Free State to its south.[12]

The indigenous populations resisted the British and Boer efforts to colonize them. Some, like the Xhosa and the Zulu, held onto their independence longer than others. But in the end, almost all lost their fight to halt colonial expansion, which eventually encompassed nearly all of what is now called South Africa. One exception is the mountainous region where King Moshoeshoe gathered the deluge of tribes seeking refuge from the mfecane and formed the Basotho nation. In 1868, the British annexed the land then called Basotholand, which has retained its independence to the present. Today, it is the separate country of Lesotho, surrounded on all borders by the nation of South Africa.[13]

Gold, Diamonds, and the Unequal Distribution of Resources

During the later nineteenth century, the Cape Colony evolved politically and economically. In 1853, the British granted the Cape Colony a representative legislature, and in 1872, the Colony obtained the right to self-government. The discovery of precious minerals during this period – diamonds in 1867 and gold in 1886 – led to a new economy buoyed by mining. But even as the Colony was changing, the racial/social structure of pre-industrial colonial South Africa persisted.[14] The labor force in the mines was split along racial lines, with white workers experiencing substantially better conditions than the coloreds and blacks.[15]

In contrast, the Colony of Natal, which earlier had broken off from the Cape Colony, was ideal for sugar cane. Although it subsequently developed along different economic lines, it was also a very racially stratified society – in keeping with the practices in the rest of South Africa. In Natal, large numbers of Indians accepted contracts of indentured servitude and chose to remain when their contracts expired, despite great discrimination. As a group, they became the forbearers of South Africa's influential Indian population and from 1892 to 1914, began a strong tradition of resistance that was to continue through the twentieth century.[16]

As the nineteenth century came to a close, Britain solidified its stronghold on southern Africa. By 1902, the British had conquered the remaining Afrikaner republics.[17] Many blacks hoped for better treatment and equal rights under British rule but their hopes proved to be empty when, in 1906, Britain recognized parliamentary government in those former republics and enfranchised only the whites. In 1909, a delegation of the South African Native Convention, including colored and Indian representatives, went to London and unsuccessfully pled for black enfranchisement. The Cape became the only province with a nonracial franchise; but even there, blacks were not permitted to participate in parliament.[18]

On May 31, 1910, the Cape Colony and Natal, and the independent Boer Republics (the Transvaal and the Orange Free State) joined to form the Union of South Africa with Louis Botha as Prime Minister. The new Union of South Africa had four million Africans, 500,000 coloreds, 150,000 Indians, and 1,275,000 whites.[19]

The Segregation Era

Between 1910 and 1948, the white government introduced a legal policy of racial segregation to the Union of South Africa, through laws that limited black workers to menial work, restricted African landownership to reservations and specified areas, formalized segregation, and deprived Africans of the right to vote or strike. As the Union of South Africa moved toward self-sufficiency, the white population slowly eliminated the British government's legal power to intervene in South African affairs.[20] As one example, the Union of South Africa adopted Afrikaans together with English as official languages of the land in 1925.[21]

Following the establishment of the Union, Christian missionary efforts heightened among the African and colored populations. By 1951, 59 percent of the Africans and 91 percent of the coloreds had converted to Christianity, a faith that would later become a major source of strength for many of them during their resistance to white oppression.[22]

To counter white hegemony, in 1912 Africans founded the South African Native National Congress (SANNC), which later became the African National Congress (ANC). The ANC was founded by mission-educated Christians who had received law degrees in England, and remained under the control of lawyers, clergy, and journalists who attempted to gain white support to effect change via constitutional means.[23]

The country of South Africa supported the British in World War I. Believing that negotiations with Britain would help further racial equality, the ANC also backed South African involvement in the war, even though it meant that numerous black soldiers would meet their deaths. The war led South Africa to view itself within a global context. Similarly, the ANC came to see itself as a Pan African Association fighting against colonialism in Africa. It attended a congress of the International Pan African Movement in 1921, and three years earlier adopted a constitution in which it referred to itself as a "Pan African Association."[24]

The ANC's battle against colonialism found inspiration in the Russian Revolution, as numerous strikes mounted throughout South Africa against the white elite. Seeking better pay, numerous black workers joined in strikes in 1918 and 1920, when they finally were able to win higher wages. During these years, the South African Indian Congress also convened and the Industrial and Commercial Workers' Union of South Africa was formed.[25]

The Great Depression in the 1930s brought a decline in popularity for the government, ultimately contributing to a viable two-party system – the more liberal United Party and the Nationalist Party, which had Afrikaner nationalism at its center. The United Party took control in the 1930s, and although left-leaning, it passed policies that further reinforced racial stratification. For example, in 1936, it removed blacks from the Cape common roll, effectively barring them from the political process. And in 1937, it passed laws prohibiting blacks from acquiring land from nonblacks in urban areas.[26]

In the meantime, Afrikaners strongly opposed World War II and bolstered support for the Nationalist Party, which gained control of the government in 1948 – beginning nearly half a century of political dominance. With strong public backing, the government moved quickly to Afrikanerize every state institution.[27] The Nationalist Party also implemented its policy of apartheid and banned any form of black participation in the political system.[28]

Simultaneously, black resistance was increasing in the ANC. In 1943, young professional Africans founded a youth league in the ANC – a league that included many of the movement's future leaders, including Nelson Mandela, Oliver Tambo, and Walter Sisulu.[29]

Apartheid, Resistance, and Struggle

Hendrik Frensch Verwoerd, prime minister of South Africa from 1958 to 1966, was the man primarily behind the National Party's policy of apartheid. Four premises underpinned apartheid: first, South Africa had four "racial" groups – white, colored, Indian, and African; second, whites should control the state; third, white interests were paramount to those of all other races, who were deemed unequal; and fourth, the whites represented a unified nation while Africans comprised ten distinct nations.[30]

From ideology to reality, these ideas translated into a society in which segregation of the races was not limited to the economic and political domains as it had been in earlier centuries. Privately, marriage was prohibited between the races. Publicly, racial groups were segregated in all public institutions, offices, modes of transportation, restrooms, and educational institutions.[31]

Among these new apartheid laws, the government passed the Population Registration Act in 1950, classifying people by race: white, black (African), or colored (people of mixed decent).[32] That same year the government passed the Group Areas Act, forcing people to reside in racially zoned areas. In many circumstances, places once occupied by blacks were zoned for whites. According to the Surplus People Project, between 1960 and 1983, approximately 3,548,900 blacks were uprooted and placed in areas called "homelands," which quickly became overcrowded. Statutes known as Pass Laws restricted the movement of blacks and the government assumed control of African education.[33]

Support of segregationist policies was not always unanimous, but the Nationalist Party government was willing to go to great lengths to maintain apartheid. For example, when they fell short of the two-thirds majority vote required to allow them to take coloreds off of the common voters' roll in 1958, the Nationalist Party government took administrative action to expand the size of the Senate and, hence, provide the Nationalist party with a majority vote.[34]

Confronted with a worsening situation for the black and colored populations, the ANC and its allies began a campaign of passive resistance to apartheid. In 1955, the ANC met with its allies in a Congress of the People and signed the Freedom Charter, making a commitment to freedom: "South Africa belongs to all who live in it, black and white, and . . . no government can justly claim authority unless it is based on the will of the people."[35]

The government responded with further repression, charging 156 members of the ANC and its allies with high treason. What followed was the longest trial in South African history – one that eventually ended with acquittals of all in 1961.[36] But the violence was not limited to government repression. Under apartheid, blacks were divided into groups called "nations," with each nation granted its own "homeland." Years later, these divisions contributed to intraethnic, or what some call "black-on-black," violence. Many view this phenomenon as yet another terrible byproduct of the apartheid system.

Violence under apartheid was escalating, and blacks were divided over how best to fight for racial equality. A group led by Robert Sobukwe broke from the ANC to found the Pan-Africanist Congress (PAC) in 1959 and began campaigning against segregation.[37]

The next year, police killed sixty-nine unarmed protesters engaged in civil disobedience and chaos ensued throughout the country. In response, the government declared a state of emergency and outlawed all African political organizations, including the ANC and PAC. The police also began taking control by detaining without trial those it suspected of involvement with the protests and the outlawed organizations.[38]

In 1961, South Africa became an independent republic and left the British Commonwealth, but the change had no impact on the country's apartheid policy. Blacks organized a general strike on the day South

Africa became a republic. And calls for economic sanctions came from the UN General Assembly, as it put international pressure on the new republic to end apartheid.[39]

Meanwhile, Nelson Mandela desired international help to oppose apartheid, and in 1962, he went abroad seeking support for the decision to take up armed struggle in that effort. Following his return, Mandela was arrested and sentenced to three years in prison for incitement. Following a questionable legal process, his term of imprisonment was subsequently extended. When Walter Sisulu and other ANC leaders were arrested in a raid two years later, Mandela was required to stand trial with them. All were convicted of sabotage and sentenced to life imprisonment on Robben Island, four miles from Cape Town.[40]

The next decade was characterized by heightened repression, strikes, and increasing militancy by the resistance movements. Tensions that had been mounting for years culminated on June 16, 1976, when the police fired on Soweto youth marching to protest the government requirement that they be taught in Afrikaans. Violence erupted throughout the country. And a year later, Steve Biko, a charismatic leader of the influential new Black Consciousness movement who had shaped Nozizwe's early activism, died in the hands of the police.[41]

Apartheid Crisis

By 1978, South Africa was in a state of crisis. The National Party had been tainted by scandal for misappropriation of funds used for propaganda. To bring order to the party, Pieter Willem Botha was elected prime minister on September 28, 1978, a position he continued to hold until 1989.[42] Botha's government set about to change apartheid society while maintaining Afrikaner supremacy.

In 1979, parliament passed legislation granting twenty-seven democratically organized African trade unions legitimacy, including access to the industrial court and the right to strike, thereby giving the workers a democratic means to voice opposition to government policies. Four years later in 1983, delegates of all races from over 575 organizations founded the United Democratic Front (UDF) to promote internal opposition to apartheid.

The Botha government also developed a new constitution that replaced the parliamentary system with a presidential one. But this constitution was inadequate; South Africans continued to be grouped along racial lines. Whites still dominated and Africans had little say in how the new governmental policies would be implemented. It gave Asians and colored – but not Africans – limited participation in the central government.[43] As a result, black South African townships widely resisted the government and the unilateral constitutional reforms. Progressive whites, Indians, and colored in the UDF and allied organizations rallied behind them.

As issues of political power were playing out, economic and land use pressures also became more pressing. The African homelands could no longer support their growing populations. In response, the government repealed the Pass Laws, which had prevented Africans from moving to urban areas, in the hope that it could introduce a policy of orderly urbanization. By June of that year, the government also repealed the bans on multiracial political parties and interracial marriage.[44]

This was a time of great tension in South Africa. The UDF continued to oppose apartheid but some black South Africans opposed its inclusive policy, not trusting whites to cooperate with them. Foremost among the African opposition groups was Inkatha, which appeared to be a national liberation movement, but was also an ethnic movement, deriving most of its support from rural Zulu. Violent conflict between the Zulu supporters of Inkatha and the UDF followers of the ANC policies complicated the struggle against apartheid and continued for the next decade.[45]

Growing governmental opposition, internal violence, increasing international pressure, disinvestments and sanctions, and rising political uncertainty contributed to a deteriorating economic situation in South Africa. Feeling the international pressure, President Botha came to accept that the outside world would never invest in South Africa unless he enfranchised the Africans. But his National Party remained divided over how to address the country's unrest. In 1986, the government proclaimed a nationwide state of emergency and detained thousands of people while prohibiting the press, radio, and television from reporting the unrest.[46]

With most secular antiapartheid leaders in exile or jailed in places such as Robben Island, South Africa's clergy took on the fight against apartheid. Best known among these clergy is Desmond Tutu, the Anglican archbishop of Cape Town, who would later be awarded the Nobel Peace Prize. In June 1988, Tutu joined clergy from sixteen denominations in a call to Christians to boycott elections that would segregate municipal councils and to refuse to legitimate an unjust system that would result only in the further oppression of others.[47]

By 1989, it had become clear that Botha's government could no longer effectively lead South Africa.

Political Transition

Between 1990 and 1994, black and white South African politicians brought apartheid to an end and effectively transferred power from the white minority to the black majority through nonviolent means.

In 1989, Frederik Willem de Klerk of the National Party succeeded Botha as president. On February 2, 1990, de Klerk lifted the ban on the ANC, PAC, and SACP (South African Communist Party) and released many of the political prisoners, including Nelson Mandela, who had become their leader and a strong advocate of reconciliation between whites and blacks in a postapartheid South Africa.[48] The state of emergency was revoked, the apartheid laws were repealed, and exiles were also allowed to return.

Determined to work collaboratively, de Klerk and Mandela brought together a group of twenty organizations that established ground rules for negotiation talks. A Convention for a Democratic South Africa (CODESA) wrote an interim constitution under which elections would be held to form a Constituent Assembly, which ultimately was to be charged with writing a final constitution. By 1993, CODESA endorsed a liberal democratic interim constitution based on universal suffrage, a bill of rights, an independent judiciary, elimination of the African homelands, and the incorporation of their lands into nine new provinces with eleven official languages.[49]

New Era for South Africa – Postapartheid

During three days in April 1994, South Africa's first nonracial elections were held for the new legislature. The ANC won the majority of seats in the National Assembly, and Mandela was elected president with Thabo Mbeki as first deputy president and de Klerk as second deputy president. On May 10, 1994, history was made when Nelson Mandela was sworn in as president and formed a Government of National Unity. Reconciliation became the dominant theme of his presidency. Foreign governments lifted economic sanctions, and South Africa rejoined the British Commonwealth.[50]

Despite minor setbacks, the country has been moving toward reconciliation. In February 1995, the Constitutional Court was inaugurated, and in May of that year, the Commission for the Restitution of Land Rights was inaugurated. The Truth and Reconciliation Commission also built bridges to a new South Africa. Vested with the power to grant amnesty, provided that the people who appeared before the Commission truthfully admitted their actions during the prior regime and proved that their actions were politically motivated, the Truth and Reconciliation Commission published a report of its findings in 1998, including defining apartheid as a crime against humanity.[51]

In 1999, South Africa again held general elections, and the ANC won 66 percent of the vote, whereas the Democratic Party replaced the National Party as the opposition party. Perhaps most notable, Mandela retired and was peacefully succeeded by Thabo Mbeki.

Over the next five years, South Africa struggled to revive its economy. Governmental employees went on strike in 1999, followed by large-scale industrial strikes in 2000. To remedy past wrongs, South Africa instituted affirmative action, especially for Africans. The AIDS crisis has also emerged as a major issue demanding attention in the country.

New elections were set for April 14, 2004, and the ANC won almost 70 percent of the vote, securing control of all nine provinces.[52] Thabo Mbeki was sworn into his second term as president on April 27, 2004, ten years after the first postapartheid elections. In another symbolic event, in August 2004, the successor party to the apartheid National Party officially disbanded and merged with the ANC to work as one in building a nonracial South Africa. Much has been done, and there is reason to believe that the country will continue along its path toward reconciliation.

Nozizwe Madlala-Routledge

Amidst the backdrop of South Africa's struggles and triumphs, Nozizwe Madlala-Routledge serves as a quiet yet powerful advocate for peace. Nozizwe is a South African of Zulu descent and a member of the Religious Society of Friends (Quakers). Her maiden name, "Madlala," is Zulu. Routledge is the name of her husband, Jeremy, who says that Nozizwe was born a peacemaker, because her mother used to call her "Nokuthula," which means peace. When asked how she identifies herself, Nozizwe replies, "I am Zulu by birth, and I identify myself as a South African."[53]

On June 29, 1952, Nozizwe Madlala was born in the southern region of the KwaZulu-Natal province, located in the eastern part of the country.[54] KwaZulu-Natal, formerly the Zulu kingdom, includes Durban, the Drakensberg, Pietermaritzburg and Midlands, Zululand, South Coast, Dolphin or North Coast, Battlefields and East Griqualand regions.

Geographically picturesque, KwaZulu-Natal has not always been a place of congenial social relations. Nozizwe recalls what it was like growing up there, in a mud-baked hut where her single mother worked as a schoolteacher:[55]

> We suffered from discrimination under apartheid but had very little con-
> tact with whites. Coming from the south of the province, we also were
> subject to prejudice by Zulus from the centre of the Zulu kingdom in the
> north.
>   As a Zulu, we have a line that divides the so-called "genuine" Zulus from
> the "not so genuine" Zulus, and I fell below the line. This division was
> subtle and not as strong as apartheid, but apartheid bred discrimination,
> because if you have a dominant system that looks at color and allocates
> resources on what you consider to be a discriminatory basis...this men-
> tality extends to all parts of life because everyone wants and tries to identify
> with the majority. It created a system of exclusion and domination.[56]

Nozizwe experienced prejudice from an early age. And as she grew, Nozizwe came to understand that these experiences mirrored the larger issue of racial relations in apartheid South Africa.

In Durban, Nozizwe received her primary and secondary education respectively from Magog and Fairview Schools and Inanda Seminary (an American Board Mission girl's high school). She then attended her first year of medical school at the University of Natal before transferring to Fort Hare, where she enrolled for a Bachelor of Science degree. Fol-lowing student protests, however, she was excluded from further study.[57] To complete her studies, she enrolled for a diploma in Medical Labo-ratory Technology and completed two diplomas in Clinical Pathology and Microbiology at Edendale. Following graduation, she worked for twelve years as a medical technologist at Edendale, King Edward VIII and Katlehong hospitals.

During these years of schooling, Nozizwe became an activist. While in Durban and Fort Hare, Nozizwe met Steve Biko, a young black-consciousness leader who increased her awareness of the evils of apartheid in her personal experience and in her society.[58] As she began to focus on police tactics – using guns and tear gas to stop student protests – her resentment toward the government grew. As the years passed, she became more involved in the antiapartheid struggle and, ultimately, resigned from her position as a technician in a medical laboratory to devote herself fully to the cause.

Throughout this period, she also became disenchanted with many of the traditional Christian churches because of how they interpreted the Scriptures and steered clear of politics: "I was very angry...I had a prob-lem with this God who was presented to us as white. How could God look like these people who were humiliating us, oppressing us through apartheid?"[59]

Nozizwe was convinced that the South African government was using religion in support of the apartheid regime. But she did not let this undermine her beliefs, and she identified religious groups who were uniting to oppose suppression based on race:

> Religion was used to justify apartheid and to justify dividing the people of South Africa on racial lines. But religion was also used in opposition to apartheid. The faith communities formed opposition groups to apartheid. For example, the struggle to end apartheid was supported by the World Council of Churches . . . it became an international struggle by churches in support of the liberation of South Africa.
>
> The basis for this opposition to apartheid is that all people are created equal and in the image of God.[60]

Through her own spiritual journey, Nozizwe would subsequently embrace the idea that religion is a positive source for resolving conflict and a sustaining resource through difficult times of struggle and oppression.

Evolution of a Peacemaker

Nozizwe's transition from casual bystander to activist peacemaker occurred gradually as a response to the oppressive conditions of living under the apartheid regime. As she explains, "I became involved in politics in the liberation movement . . . in the 70s, it was a normal thing to do because there was so much oppression that made it impossible to ignore the struggle for economic and political justice." At the time, a number of people influenced Nozizwe, including Archibald Gumede, who became president of the UDF. He opposed violence and the armed struggle the ANC adopted in the 1960s. As the antiapartheid movement grew, she recalls the many "vibrant debates on the use of violence in fighting apartheid . . . and among the issues we discussed were whether the means justify the ends, and whether you could talk of a 'just' war."[61]

During these years, Nozizwe first began her work for peace and justice by joining the ANC underground movement in 1979, though she held dear the principle that she would not hold a gun.[62] But this did not protect her from threats to her life and freedom. Throughout the 1980s, Nozizwe was in and out of detention three times under the government's Internal Security Act, the last time spending one year in solitary confinement without a trial.[63] In 1983, she helped form the Natal Organization of Women, becoming its chairperson and chief organizer. And a year later, she joined the South African Communist Party (SACP), where she served first as regional chairperson and later as a member of its Central Committee.[64]

As Nozizwe found her stride, she turned to Christianity. In the early 1980s, Nozizwe's pacifist ethics led her to work with activists in the End Conscription Campaign, where she met her future husband, Jeremy Routledge, a Quaker: "We met in Durban when we were both active in the liberation movement. He was in the teacher's union and we met at a meeting in support of detainees and their families."[65] Jeremy took her to Quaker meetings in Durban in the early 1980s, and after attending regularly, Nozizwe became a committed member of the Religious Society of Friends.[66] In 1989, Nozizwe married Jeremy; later they had two sons, Martin and Simon.

The Religious Society of Friends, like the Mennonites and the Brethren, is historically a peace-oriented church committed to the belief that war is against the will of God.[67] Quakers uphold five basic tenets: truth, equality, peace, simplicity, and community. Quakerism originally arose in Britain in the 1640s, and Quakers have historically been strong advocates for peace, social service, and nonviolence. Although Quakers represent a small sliver of South Africa, their voices have been heard and they have been active in resolving its conflicts.[68]

Being a member of the Society of Friends quickly became a core part of Nozizwe's identity. She describes South Africa's Quaker community:

> Quakers are a small group of less than a hundred in South Africa, but we are very active in social and economic justice issues . . . and the equality of individuals.
>
> One of our Quakers was a professor at the University of Cape Town – Professor H.W. van der Merwe, an Afrikaner who became a Quaker. He played a crucial role in bringing together the African National Congress (ANC) with some of the leaders in the apartheid government. . . .
>
> When I became active with the Quakers, I learned to understand that God is in everyone. It was not easy for me to realize that God was in my oppressor. This was an important transformation for me, to embrace it, to realize that even my enemy has God in him.[69]

From Quaker role models, Nozizwe would come to solidify her opposition to violence as a means to effect change.

Intragroup Peacemaking

Inspired by Gandhi, Nozizwe focused her peacemaking work in Bambayi, near Durban; originally called the Phoenix Settlement, this was where

Gandhi had lived from 1893 to 1914 before returning to India. Nozizwe recalls being inspired to do her peacemaking work where Gandhi started his:

> I was able to live where Mahatma Gandhi did. Gandhi lived in South Africa and developed his philosophy in Durban where I went to school and where I lived. So his philosophy became part of my life and as a student, I went to where Gandhi had lived.... From him I also understood that the struggle for peace means actively getting involved in fighting for social and economic justice.[70]

Despite the success of the Phoenix Settlement, riots damaged the area in 1985 when African squatters occupied the settlement and renamed it Bambayi.[71] At the time of these riots, Nozizwe was in Durban. There, she saw black-on-black violence firsthand:

> In the late 1980s, the violence intensified in South Africa and turned into what became known as black on black violence. It was state sponsored so it infiltrated into the community. Where I worked in Durban, a lot of people killed each other, and I was part of a group to try to stop this war. I was involved in bringing the two groups together and persuading them to put their arms down. Bambayi was where the fighting was.[72]

Bambayi declined severely. Residents lacked basic needs, and the absence of street lighting and electricity exacerbated threats in the area.[73] But Nozizwe believed that things could change, and she set about to reconstruct and reconcile the community:

> I became known by both groups. Each group needed to acknowledge to the other that they had been hurt. This is what I tried to do, to help them see how the violence had affected them all personally. Then, I tried to help them to see how they could work together to repair their homes that had been burned down and how to rebuild community. There was much fighting because there was no electricity, etc.... I helped them see how they could work together to redevelop the community. I tried to remind them what had united them as a community before the violence. I reminded them what they had in common.
>
> But this process took many meetings and took time to build trust, a genuine process of negotiating where we tried to listen to both sides without taking sides. The fighting was across two different organizations, the Inkatha Freedom Party and the ANC (which I was identified with), but I worked hard to be seen as neutral. In the process, because the men were predominantly fighting, I tried to bring women in to see what their viewpoint was. Adding women to the negotiations changed the dynamic because the women found it easier to reach out to the other women.[74]

Key to Nozizwe's work was that she took the time to rebuild communal relations. By conducting herself as a neutral party, she created an environment of trust in which the parties could truly listen to each other.

Elevating Women's Voices in Peacemaking

Through her work during the Bambayi riots, Nozizwe recognized how powerful women could be as a resource in resolving conflicts. Involving women in reconciliation work remains an important part of her approach to peacemaking to this day. She elaborates on the challenges of trying to integrate issues of gender and justice as she worked to further South Africa's women's movement:

> Gender and justice. They are both central to my work because I was part of the women's movement and one of the things that we did was to reinterpret for the movement the importance of integrating gender issues. This was a struggle because we had to try and convince the men that this was an important issue. The movement had not taken women's issues into account. In this regard, I learned about women leaders both in South Africa and in the world and learned a lot.[75]

In 1989, coming off the heels of her successful reconciliation efforts in Bambayi, Nozizwe worked with the Natal Organization of Women (NOW) to help organize a forum in which black-on-black violence could be mitigated:

> We dealt with black on black violence, mainly between the ANC and Inkatha Freedom Party (but the ANC was banned, so when I refer to the ANC, I mean the organizations supporting the ANC).
> We organized a meeting and we were assisted by Women for Peaceful Change Now (WPCN) [which] worked as [the] facilitators. I approached WPCN, and they acted as an intermediary between the Inkatha Freedom party and the ANC allied organizations.[76]

Meetings designed to reconcile intrablack violence, although not common, increasingly became recognized as necessary for creating a unified front against the policy of apartheid. Frederik Willem de Klerk had just been elected president of South Africa, and both internal and outside pressures were forcing the government to reevaluate its policies. The year 1989 thus marked a new beginning.

In 1991, when President de Klerk and Nelson Mandela formed the Convention for a Democratic South Africa (CODESA) to create a new constitution for South Africa, Nozizwe was invited to participate as a delegate. She later worked as a Managing Secretary for the transitional government Sub-Council on the Status of Women. She also served on the Reconstruction and Development Program (RDP) Task Team to draft policy on the empowerment of women.[77]

Nozizwe used her position as a CODESA delegate to help ensure that women's issues would be addressed in South Africa's new constitution. But it was not easy: "[w]e had to struggle for women to be fully represented as equals in the process. The women were not in equal numbers at first, but eventually we got a requirement for 50 percent women in each team in the negotiations."[78] Led by Nozizwe, diverse women from the Women's National Coalition campaigned to assure that women's issues, particularly issues involving women from poor and rural areas, be addressed in the new constitution. Nozizwe helped assure that women would play a prominent role in the new South Africa.

When she completed her service on CODESA, Nozizwe continued to voice women's interests as she transitioned from a leader in the ANC resistance movement to a leader in South Africa's new democratic government. In the 1994 elections, she was elected as a member of parliament. She moved to Cape Town, where she remained as a member of parliament through 1999. During these five years, she wore many hats but actively continued her fight for women's rights and peace. Among other positions, she served as member of parliament for the ANC, activist for Women's Rights and Peace, member on the Parliamentary Committee on the Improvement of Quality of Life and Status of Women, Chairperson of the multiparty Parliamentary Women's Group, Chairperson of the ANC Parliamentary Women's Caucus, and a member of a number of women's organizations.[79] Additionally, she coauthored a chapter for a book, which became the report of South Africa for the UN Conference of Women, held in Beijing in 1995. Nozizwe used her positions to raise issues that affect women such as domestic violence, and she pushed for full rights and active participation by women in all stages of the political decision-making process.[80]

Ministry of Defense

Nozizwe remained in parliament advocating for women until 1999, when she received an unexpected announcement: President Thabo Mbeki had appointed her to serve as Deputy Minister of Defense. She accepted her position in the Ministry of Defense as an opportunity to offer a pacifist perspective in national decision making on security. She did this as a black woman in a largely white male security system.

A fellow Quaker remembers her reaction when she heard of Nozizwe's appointment:

> As I poured my morning cup of Rooibos tea, I heard the distant voice of President Mbeki announcing the new Ministry appointments from the radio in the resource room. "Defense: Patrick 'Terror' Lekota, Minister. Nozizwe Madlala-Routledge, Deputy Minister. . . . " I paused, sugar poised above my cup. Nozizwe Madlala-Routledge? Deputy Minister of Defense? I wiggled a finger in my ear and looked around the [Quaker] Peace Center to see if anyone else's jaw was on the floor. Surely, the President of South Africa could not have just appointed a Quaker woman as second in command of the national military.[81]

Admittedly, Nozizwe was surprised by the announcement: "I had not put it in my mind that I would be appointed as a deputy minister let alone the [D]eputy [M]inister of [D]efense! When I got the phone call, I said you must have made a mistake, and I gave the name of the person I thought (the President's office) was trying to reach." Figures in high places, however, assured her, "[T]he President wants you to be there."[82]

During apartheid, South Africa's military had developed a negative image, one of secretiveness and racial and gender inequality. According to Nozizwe, President Mbeki wanted to change this image and identified Nozizwe as the woman to accomplish this task. He saw her appointment as a message that there was political will to create change and that women were expected to fully participate in the new South Africa.[83]

Nozizwe saw her new position as an opportunity to offer a pacifist perspective in decision making on national security, and she did so as a black woman in a largely white male security system.[84]

One observer commented that her appointment, particularly as a Quaker and as a woman, was "either a stroke of genius or a monumental gaff,"[85] whereas another said, "It is like appointing a vegetarian to be deputy head of a butcher shop."[86] But Nozizwe maintains that her commitment to pacifism as a Quaker posed no conflict to her work on behalf of the country's defense. She explains that Gandhi and Martin Luther King Jr. both led by example.[87] Viewing them as role models, Nozizwe reconciled any concerns she may have had as a Quaker before entering the Ministry of Defense:

> I have reconciled both positions in my life. I feel that there has been support for me to do my work, but also it is an important area to be involved in

because my experience is that if you want to change things, you have to get involved and are supported by those who are like you. It's possible at this time to be involved for change from within the government, but sometimes this is impossible. From within, it is not always possible to make change. So now it's possible for me to work from the inside, but it's important for me to continue to be in contact with those who are on the outside, who have the same beliefs. This link is very important.[88]

Her husband Jeremy likened his wife's situation to that of William Penn, the Quaker who founded Pennsylvania. At the beginning of the Quaker movement, Penn asked his followers if he could continue to carry his nobleman's sword. They told him to do so for as long as he could, but eventually he found that he could carry it no more. Jeremy explains his support for his wife in this manner: "Nozizwe is carrying the sword right now.... And I support her all the way. But ... the day may come when she can carry it no more."[89]

Nozizwe would, in fact, carry the sword as the Deputy Minister of Defense for five years. She believed that the position was an extension of the commitment to social justice that has been an inherent part of Quakerism for hundreds of years, as she explains:

> Quakerism is about recognizing and upholding life, and being a Quaker helps me to center myself and to think deeply about issues, and I believe we need that to achieve peace....
>   The Religious Society of Friends is a pacifist organization, but like Gandhi who believed in non-violence, many Quakers are very active in bringing about social justice and have been (doing it) throughout history. I have never met a Quaker who thought that sitting and meditating would solve the world's problems.[90]

After Nozizwe accepted her appointment, she received mixed reactions from her fellow Quakers. They challenged her at the annual gathering of Quakers, a meeting similar to a church diocese where members gather once a year to worship together and discuss business and issues of direct relevance to being a Quaker. The gathering, including Nozizwe, eventually reached consensus through a comprehensive statement on their beliefs and their role in working for peace in Africa. In it, they outlined an agenda for the future of South Africa and also a commitment to a nonviolent foreign policy to guide Nozizwe in her new role (See Appendix at the end of this chapter for a reprint of the full statement).

Having gained the support of her fellow Quakers, Nozizwe still had the difficult task of being the first woman ever to serve as Deputy Minister of

Defense. She began by trying to understand the South African National Defense Force (SANDF) of previous administrations. In particular, she consulted with senior officials, notably past generals, because of the significant roles they still occupied in different institutional structures. Nozizwe found that "they were more worried about the fact that I am a woman, rather than that I am a pacifist." By consulting the old guard, she gained their acceptance and mitigated harsh feelings that conceivably could have plagued the ministry after the political transition. She learned through experience that "it is okay to plead ignorance, to say I don't know everything, but to assert that I have a right to be here." Nozizwe found that as she settled into her role, others were receptive and welcoming. In her words, "There is this message coming through that says having a woman means that if there is something to get done it will get done. They find I am more accessible."[91]

During her five years in the Ministry of Defense, Nozizwe transformed the new government in numerous ways – all reflecting her holistic approach to peacemaking. Following the death of apartheid, civil-military relations were a central concern and it was imperative to ensure that the military did not overstep its role. Nozizwe helped design a system that allowed parliament and the broader civil society a voice in the role of the military.[92]

Nozizwe used her position to reform the SANDF. She made the defense forces more conducive to the participation of women and blacks. For example, she helped formulate a policy on sexual harassment and another on pregnancy issues, which clarified when it is safe for a pregnant woman to be in the frontline, or when she should stop participating in parades. One of her foremost concerns throughout her tenure was equal benefits for blacks and women.[93]

Nozizwe notes that her attentiveness to gender and racial equality quickly became institutionalized: "When people come and brief us, they already prepare points on issues they know I would ask. If they do make mistakes and fail to mention them, they know I will raise them."[94] Her decisions were all guided by principles of nonviolence. She explains:

> We try to limit the use of violence and to say as much as possible that all conflicts should be resolved through negotiation and through diplomacy. Even though we have adopted a doctrine of using violence as a last resource, we have made a strong commitment to prevent a case from arising where violence would be used.[95]

Nozizwe also utilized the resources of the Defense Department for community development. In 2000, she helped to found the African Women's Peace Table, which gathers women from the SANDF once a year to meet with women peace activists and South African NGOs to discuss practical solutions to issues relevant to defense and civil society. Among many other initiatives, she has helped to launch the Multi-Skilled Development Program aimed at teaching youth job skills for the type of jobs that the country needs.[96]

Nozizwe's approach to security and peace preservation engaged the African continent. She helped to establish the New Partnership for Africa's Development (NEPAD), which functions within the framework of the African Union. NEPAD plans to establish a Peace and Security Council to deploy peacekeeping troops when necessary to intervene and prevent conflicts. Nozizwe notes that NEPAD is, "the program for Africa's renewal." Leaders throughout Africa are involved in this effort, which is particularly important because "when people from inside are not part of the decision making, this causes resentment."[97] Nozizwe believes that peacebuilding requires a focus on development because she views most African conflicts as resource based.

As part of her development-focused approach to peacemaking, Nozizwe also addressed difficult social issues such as the alarming growing rates of HIV and AIDS in South Africa. Many experts have viewed Africa's wars and rebellions as a major factor in the spread of the AIDS virus across the African continent. Anticipating the potentially demobilizing effect that the epidemic could have on South Africa's military, Nozizwe – along with Defense Minister Mosiuoa Lekota – moved to make HIV/AIDS testing available to the SANDF. Reports in 2004 verified earlier projections by showing that 20–22 percent of South Africa's national defense force was HIV-positive. To prevent this number from increasing, and to assist those who have AIDS, Nozizwe officially opened a clinical research project on January 20, 2004 in Pretoria focused on the treatment and management of HIV infections among uniformed SANDF members and their dependents.[98] Her ability to identify and address social issues that were once seen to be of no concern to the Ministry of Defense only served to strengthen peace in the country.

Just as Nozizwe has been a strong advocate for women's rights throughout her peacemaking career, as a political leader, she still continually emphasizes UN Security Council Resolution 1325, calling for more women to be engaged at all levels of peacemaking, particularly at the negotiation tables. On April 27–28, 2001, at a seminar conducted by the Washington D.C.–based organization Women In International Security (WIIS), Nozizwe articulated a vision for how women can contribute to a comprehensive peacemaking process throughout the globe:

> The horrifying statistics illustrating war's catastrophic destruction confirm the urgency with which we must find a lasting solution to the scourge it brings. We need new visions of peace: women's voices could contribute that missing piece of the peace puzzle. Women must challenge the male-dominated security paradigm, which emphasizes the military dimension, rather than the totality of the dimensions encompassed by the human security paradigm. Human security brings into the peace equation issues of economic, social, ecological, political and gender justice. It incorporates collective security and challenges the narrow, male-dominated understanding of power. It offers a new vision of peace, based on an inclusive, rather than exclusive exercise of power.
>
> This comprehensive approach to security is beginning to emerge and gain ground in the world. . . .
>
> Throughout the world women are largely missing from the negotiations that attempt to bring peace. From Dayton to Rambouillet, Arusha to Burundi to Colombia, it is predominantly male leaders who are negotiating an end to war. At the Dayton Peace Talks there were no women present in the regional delegations. At Rambouillet there was not even one Kosovar woman. At Arusha, the women's delegation had only observer status. There is a serious discontinuity here, as women are very active in grassroots peacebuilding organizations.
>
> The absence of women means that a crucial perspective is missing from the negotiations to end wars and other armed conflict. Peace making cannot be left to the male elite. Women bring a crucial perspective that is focused, not on absolute power for a few, but rather on shared power. Women bring focus on meeting basic human needs as part of the peace process.[99]

According to Nozizwe, women are an untapped resource for the betterment of humanity. At the end of the conference, she called on women to make the twenty-first century a century for women, a century for the abolition of wars, and a century for Africa's renewal.

Nozizwe was an opponent of the war in Iraq that began in 2003. She participated in many marches, both in South Africa and in the United States, and wrote an article protesting the war for the Quaker Network for the Prevention of Violent Conflict. At the end of that year, she reaffirmed her commitment to peace by sending out a Christmas card with a message advocating nonviolent opposition to the war. To her delight, those who received her card shared her views on war and peace:

> What has been fantastic is that people have been coming up to me to say that I've freed them to think differently about war and peace. People are celebrating. Human beings would rather have peace. So leaders, such as myself must see that this is the right thing to do, to orient ourselves toward peace so that the people below will respond positively to this concept. In my opinion, leaders who send youth to war must be prepared to go as well. We as leaders shouldn't put our youth where they have no alternative, where they must fight for their country. Rather, I think we should be working together to fight for a world where we can all agree that war is bad. War destroys life and there are alternatives; peace is possible.[100]

Reflections on Peacemaking Methods

For Nozizwe, nonviolence and peacemaking go hand in hand. When asked about her work, she begins by stressing the importance of finding shared values and ideals akin to the Golden Rule:

> I think that it is important to start with some basic values that we all cherish, because I think different societies, different communities, have a set of values that they hold dear which have been a part of their societies and their lives forever, if you can look at it that way. Then say, "What is it that is common among us with regard to this value?" and you will find there is quite a lot that is common.[101]

Unfortunately, those who are embroiled in conflict often emphasize differences – racial, ethnic, and religious – rather than similarities. This, in turn, becomes a way for the dominant group to divide and justify subjugation of others. In South Africa, rulers not only divided the nation by race but also constructed categories of ethnicity within the indigenous population and then distributed resources disproportionately among the various ethnic groups. The result was what Nozizwe terms a "stigmatization" of some of the groups. In some cases, there were incidents of intraethnic conflict. But in Nozizwe's eyes, "the actual situation . . . that . . . was called 'black-on-black-violence' was actually the racial and political violence taking a different form."[102]

Indeed, Nozizwe even views cases of extreme brutality in some regions of Africa (such as the cutting off of limbs) as a continuation of the violence that began with colonialism. Such violence results from the loss of the basic values and rights that individuals must have, if there is to be peace. Nozizwe explains:

> When I look at the present form of violence, it is just a continuation of [the fact] that ... people were rendered powerless through a system that really took away from their security – something that all of us hold dear. Each and every person values security – whether it is about where your next meal will come from; or that your children can grow up in a safe environment; that you will not be exposed to harm; and that you'll also be able to participate in the democratic process, in the decisions that are made about your life and government. All of those issues – these are the basic values that all of us share.
>
> And when this is taken away from you – human dignity and human security – when these are taken away from you, you are left in a situation where it is quite easy for you to be mobilized into a violent force.... [103]

When people are dehumanized and lose their security, violence is a predictable outcome.

Similarly, Nozizwe believes that violence can become entrenched. When violence pervades all aspects of a given culture, people learn to resolve conflicts through violent means. Because of this, Nozizwe emphasizes the importance of optimism and hope.

> We need to start believing that a peaceful world is possible. Even though where you start may be extremely violent – and you cannot believe when you look at it [that] a different situation would be possible – it is best to start by believing that it is possible, because I think that is what then would lead you to overcome whatever is in your way to try to reach that goal that you are striving towards.[104]

Nozizwe understands her approach to peacemaking to be similar to that of Gandhi. She believes that one should not prepare for peace by preparing for war, for in her words, "[what you] want to achieve must be reflected in the way you work toward it."[105] And the way you work toward it is through nonviolence.

Religious Motivation for Peacemaking

When asked what motivates her peacemaking, Nozizwe emphasizes her Quaker faith. A document drafted and accepted in 2000 by Quakers throughout Africa well reflects Nozizwe's own philosophy toward peacemaking in her own country, including recognition of the role of development, equality, gender, and democracy (see Appendix at the end of this chapter). Historically a nonviolent tradition, Quakerism provides Nozizwe with guidance on how to mentally prepare to resolve conflicts:

> In the Quaker faith, we belong to a tradition steeped in meditation, so I am aware of the importance to appeal to the inner spirit and to appeal for guidance. So I ask for guidance. There is an awareness that brings you closer with the people you're trying to reach out to.[106]

Once Nozizwe reaches this state of self-awareness, she tries to become as deeply in-tune with those with whom she is negotiating. She does this by "putting myself in the [parties'] shoes" in order to "think how they could be supported." By taking into consideration the position of the other, she becomes able to assess how to "take that step to move closer." The process starts with oneself and one's own faith: "My experience has been that it's important to start with yourself, and to work to strengthen those aspects which are positive that would link to the next person's religion, which would then bring those values together in a positive way."[107]

Nozizwe's strong personal faith in turn helps her to respect those who are different from her. Differences are not viewed negatively, but rather she views them as innate indicators of the fact that we are all diverse human beings sharing the same world:

> Prayer is important in whatever form it takes. Respecting other faiths is also very important because if you want to go into a situation believing in only your own, you are not recognizing all people as having God within them. God is the one who supports and gives you power ... but you must also be aware that the person with whom you interact may be of a different faith. The link that you are both human beings is from where you must build.[108]

Although she was not born into the Quaker faith, the religion's universal calls for love and community even in the face of conflict have always spoken to her. She says that because we are all created in the image of God, religion "even addresses the issue of gender equality and whatever physical differences we have." Nozizwe explains that God has touched her in many ways. She finds solace and inspiration during difficult times in reading the Bible, particularly passages such as Psalm 23. In her words, the image of God as a shepherd "emphasizes that I'm not alone. I have God guiding and supporting me and shining his light on me, and leading me."[109]

Even when she has been alone, Nozizwe has never succumbed to fear. Her faith strengthens her resolve. In Nozizwe's view, the feminist voice of

Audre Lorde best defines her relationship and trust in God that enables her to work tirelessly for the betterment of humanity:

> When I dare to be powerful, to use my strength in the service of my vision,then it becomes less and less important whether I am afraid.[110]

Serving South Africa

Nozizwe Madlala-Routledge's willingness to stand in a difficult place and maintain her witness to peace is inspiring. She has committed – and risked – her life to serving all South Africans and to transforming the society around her.

Nozizwe's contribution to South Africa's national reconciliation is both personal and public. In April 2004, Nozizwe faced reelection and, after a sweeping victory by the ANC, was named Deputy Minister of Health on April 29, 2004. By continuing her public service, she persists in seeking positive changes for the people of South Africa. Once a land divided, thanks to Nozizwe's peacemaking efforts and those of the men and women with whom she has worked, South Africa is one step closer to attaining lasting unity.

APPENDIX

Below is a document accepted at the Central and Southern Africa yearly meeting of the Religious Society of Friends (Quakers) in December 2000 at Modderpoort, South Africa, representing Friends from Malawi, Madagascar, Namibia, South Africa, Swaziland, Zambia, and Zimbabwe. The document was offered as a point of departure to all who may consider it useful for their own deliberations and decisions about peacemaking in Africa.

> **Quakers have a long tradition in working for peace. We believe that war and the preparation for war are inconsistent with the gospel of Christ.**
>
> 1. The governments of the world at the United Nations General Assembly have declared the years 2001–2010 a "Decade for a Culture of Peace and Non-violence for the Children of the World."
>   *We commit ourselves, and call on all citizens and governments to initiate programmes that will bring this culture into being.*
> 2. There are more wars in Africa than in any other part of the world.
>   *We commit ourselves, and call on all citizens and governments to:*
>   • *work towards the abolition of war in Africa,*
>   • *build peace by non military means,*

- *demilitarise and reduce expenditure on arms,*
- *convert arms industries to socially useful production and in the interim to ensure transparent and accurate reporting of all subsidies, direct and indirect, to the arms industry and related activities.*
- *consider voluntary or national youth non-military service as a means of building peace and development.*
- *consider state funded 'Institutes for Peace' to research non-military means to ensure the security of the state against the strategic threats as well as research the experience in peacemaking that has been developed on the African continent.*

3. Nobel laureates have proposed a code of conduct for the transfer of small arms. Africa is awash with arms, particularly small arms, which have not contributed to stability and have diverted scarce resources away from peace and development.

   We commit ourselves, and call on all citizens and governments, to:
   - *Work towards a moratorium on the import to and manufacture of arms in Africa and in the interim legislate and implement rigorous controls on arms transfers.*
   - *Ensure effective gun control legislation as well as its effective implementation.*
   - *Recover and destroy*
     - *illegal arms,*
     - *arms left over after cessation of hostilities,*
     - *arms surpluses to police and military requirements.*

4. Peace is not brought about by preparation for war. Peace is achieved by ensuring democracy, good governance and justice and upholding the rule of law and human rights. It is achieved by addressing the basic needs of people such as provision of adequate health care, fighting the scourge of HIV/AIDS, eliminating inequality and poverty and providing education, including early childhood education, adult literacy and peace education.

   We commit ourselves, and call on all citizens and governments to work towards democracy, good governance, human rights, equality and meeting the basic needs of all people in the region.

5. Economic inequality is a major cause of war, instability and lack of security. Our security is not ensured by arming ourselves, employing armed response and building high walls with razor wire, but by economic justice and building strong communities.

   We commit ourselves and call on all people to contribute by way of wealth, talent or effort to the promotion of peace, reconciliation and economic justice. We call on governments to ensure that their policies create a more equitable distribution of wealth.

6. Leaders of government have committed their armed forces to war in foreign countries as well as invited foreign armies to their territories

without informing their citizens or getting a mandate from their citizens by a decision of parliament.

We commit ourselves and call on all citizens and governments of the region to work for the abolition of armed forces and in the interim, to ensure transparency and accountability when military decisions are made.

7. Women are major victims of war and potentially major contributors to peace, but are seldom consulted when decisions are made which result in war or when peace treaties are negotiated.

    We commit ourselves, and call on all citizens and governments to ensure that peace and peacemaking are enhanced by equal participation of women and men.

8. Conflicts in the region are fuelled by the exploitation of natural resources from which only a few individuals benefit. The majority of citizens suffer the effects of war and are not organised so as to be able to bring an end to the conflict.

    We commit ourselves, and call on all people and governments to
    - *Identify and expose those who benefit from conflicts in the region.*
    - *Support civil society movements working for peace.*

9. South Africa destroyed the nuclear weapons that had been built by the apartheid regime without the knowledge of its citizens.

    We commit ourselves, and call on all citizens and governments, to
    - *Ensure that never again are nuclear weapons manufactured in Africa.*
    - *Ensure that nuclear weapons are never transferred to any African country.*
    - *Ensure that nuclear weapons never enter the territorial waters of any African country on a foreign naval vessel nor that they ever be flown over any African air space.*
    - *Ensure that nuclear weapons are never targeted at any African country.*
    - *Ensure that Africa remains a nuclear weapon free zone.*

10. We would like to draw attention to the fact that The Coalition Against Military Spending (CAMS) in South Africa has called on organisations and individuals in South Africa to sign their Charter:
    - Declaring their opposition to the recent and the prospective increases in military spending.
    - Demanding a substantially increased allocation of resources to poverty eradication and development.
    - Demanding transparency and honesty of the government on defence spending and its economic implications.
    - Committing them to building real security in the Southern African region.

We commend this charter to all people and governments in the region. We call on people in South Africa and its government to support this charter. We call on citizens and government of the other countries in the region to work towards initiating similar charters and coalitions within their own countries.

SOUTH AFRICA FACT SHEET[111]

Geography

Location:	Southern Africa, at the southern tip of the continent of Africa.
Area:	*Total:* 1,219,912 sq km *Land:* 1,219,912 sq km *Water:* 0 sq km *Note:* Land includes Prince Edward Islands (Marion Island and Prince Edward Island)
Area comparative:	Slightly less than twice the size of the U.S. state of Texas.
Climate:	Mostly semiarid; subtropical along east coast; sunny days, cool nights.
Geography Note:	South Africa borders Namibia, Botswana, Zimbabwe, Mozambique, and completely surrounds Lesotho and most of Swaziland.

Population

Population:	44,344,136 (July 2005 est.)	
Ethnic Groups:	Black:	75.8%
	White:	13.6%
	Colored:	8.6%
	Indian:	2.6%
Religions:	Christian:	68%
	Muslim:	2%
	Hindu:	1.5%
	Indigenous and animist beliefs:	28.5%
Languages:	Eleven official languages, including Afrikaans, English, Ndebele, Pedi, Sotho, Swazi, Tsonga, Tswana, Venda, Xhosa, Zulu.	

Government

Government type:	Republic
Capital:	Pretoria
	Note: Cape Town is the legislative center and Bloemfontein is the judicial center.
Legal System:	Based on Roman-Dutch law and English common law; accepts compulsory International Court of Justice jurisdiction, with reservations.

Recent Background

In 1806, the British seized the Cape of Good Hope area from the Dutch. The majority of the Dutch settlers (the Boers) fled north to establish their own republics. In 1867, diamonds were discovered in the region, followed by gold in 1886. Immigrants followed the discoveries and the Dutch grew wealthy, while suppressing the native inhabitants.

The Boers resisted the British advance, but were beaten in the Boer War (1899–1902). The result was the establishment of the Union of South Africa, which operated under a policy of apartheid – institutionalized segregation of the races. In the 1990s, the apartheid system was replaced by constitutional democracy and black majority rule.

Economic Overview

South Africa is a middle-income, budding market rich in natural resources. It possesses well-developed financial, legal, communications, energy, and transport sectors; one of the world's ten largest stock exchanges; and a modern infrastructure that supports a well-organized supply of goods to major metropolitan areas throughout the region. Nevertheless, economic growth has not been able to lower South Africa's high unemployment rate; and poverty and lack of economic opportunity among the historically disadvantaged groups from the apartheid era continue to present daunting economic problems. South African economic policy is fiscally conservative but pragmatic, attempting to increase job growth and household income through targeting inflation and liberalizing trade.

9 Warriors and Brothers

Imam Muhammad Ashafa and Pastor James Wuye

Nigeria

Throughout most of its forty-plus years as an independent state, Nigeria, the most populous country in Africa, has been plagued by civil strife. In fact, ethnic and religious divisions fostered by British colonial policies became even more politicized and inflamed in this postindependence period, as relations between many Nigerian communities became tense and, too often, violent.

As youths, Imam Muhammad Ashafa (a scholarly Muslim) and Pastor James Wuye (a charismatic Penticostal Christian) were caught in the maelstrom of Nigeria's interreligious violence. Both were active leaders in militant youth organizations of their respective religions. And both took an active part in the riots that shook their home state of Kaduna in the early 1990s.

But later, both men had profound religious experiences that transformed them and ultimately brought them to a new understanding. From within their different traditions, each discovered a belief in tolerance that replaced his earlier attachment to religiously justified violence and bloodshed. In particular, they came to the common conclusion that they needed to work together by preaching this new message to their communities and putting it into action. Together, they founded the Interfaith Mediation Centre (known at its founding as the Muslim-Christian Dialogue Forum [MCDF]), a religious grassroots organization that has been active in mediation and reconciliation efforts between Muslim and Christian communities in Nigeria since 1995.

Despite the many challenges it has had to face, the Interfaith Mediation Centre has made significant contributions toward easing local religious tensions and reconciling warring communities. Together, Imam Ashafa and Pastor James daily show extraordinary courage and dedication. On the basis of their joint commitment to a theology of inclusion, they have

together accepted the difficult and dangerous task of leading their fellow
Nigerians toward peace and stable lives of coexistence.

The Context: An Overview of Nigeria

Nigeria is one of West Africa's largest countries, extending from the Gulf
of Guinea in the south toward the Sahara Desert in the north, and from
Cameroon and Lake Chad in the east to Benin in the west. It is also
Africa's most populous state and has over 250 different ethnic groups.
Among these, the Hausa and Fulani are concentrated in the north of the
country, whereas Ibo dominate the southeast and Yoruba the southwest.
Despite these concentrations, however, no region in Nigeria could be
described as ethnically homogenous.

The dominant religions are Islam and Christianity, though a significant
minority adhere to traditional African religions. Most figures suggest that
Nigeria has about 10 percent more Muslims than Christians, yet some
observers (especially Christians) tend to insist that the gap between the
two religious groups is even narrower. Both ethnic and religious differences have fueled tension throughout Nigeria's turbulent postindependence history, which has been marked by decades of military rule. In
1999, the country instituted a new democratic regime, which has been
faced with the challenge of ending Nigeria's long history of ethnic and
religious violence. This task is all the more difficult because of the country's history of corruption and financial mismanagement; its continued
dependence on its abundant petroleum and natural gas reserves, which
generate over half of the country's GDP[1] and make it Africa's leading
oil producer; and the government's failure (to date) to foster substantive
social and economic development for the entire population.

Background: Evolution of Islamic Rule in Northern Nigeria

The history of religion and religious conflict in Nigeria predates the modern Nigerian state. Traditional religions in West Africa were animist. In
the eighth and ninth centuries, Muslim merchants spread Islam through
the north of the country, settling in the kingdom of Borno in northeast-
ern Nigeria. By the tenth century, Islam penetrated the ruling classes,
whereas the general population largely continued to follow their indigenous African religious practices.

Further west, the independent city-states of Hausaland retained their
traditional religions until the fourteenth and fifteenth centuries, when
Muslim merchants of the Fulani ethnic group gained influence in the

courts of the Hausa kings. Many of the Hausa rulers and political elites converted to Islam and began incorporating the new religion into their culture and political administration. However, compromises between Islamic and the traditional religious practices emerged, so that Islam's influence was contained. Meanwhile, political and economic instability were increasing. Combined with the emergence of a radical Muslim intellectual elite that would not tolerate the discrepancy between their Islamic ideal and the current reality, the Hausa rulers began to loose influence.[2]

These trends culminated in the Fulani *jihad* declared by Usman dan Fodio in 1804. The jihad's stated aim was to establish a purer form of Islamic rule in the area. Some observers have also interpreted it as an ethnic war between Fulani and Hausa, because the uprising was led, primarily, by Fulani residing in Hausaland. It was remarkably successful: the Muslim Sokoto Caliphate was established, and by 1830 Muslim Fulani ruled most of northern Nigeria.[3] Many areas that had not been under Hausa rule were conquered as well.

Throughout these conquered territories, the Fulani established a system of emirates that centered on the caliph's city of Sokoto. Islam became the dominant religion, but even this emirate system failed to completely Islamicize the population.

Colonial Occupation and the Separate Administration of Northern and Southern Nigeria

The next defining episode in Nigerian history was the British colonial conquest.[4] It began in 1860 from the south, and by the early 1900s both northern and southern Nigeria were declared separate British protectorates. The last military resistance to colonization in northern Nigeria was carried out at Sokoto in March 1903. The defeat of the emirates, however, did not bring an end to their political system.

Rather, northern Nigeria became a showcase example of the British colonial policy of Indirect Rule, which sought to compensate for weak British colonial presence on the ground by administering conquered territories through existing indigenous authorities and state structures. Indirect Rule was effective because it successfully coopted existing authority structures. It also was inexpensive because it required only a few strategically placed individuals to be effective. Because it was in the interest of the colonial power to strengthen the conquered state and avoid resistance by the colonized people, many traditional practices were allowed to continue, even those that were contrary to the laws, values, and motivations of the conquerers.[5]

More specifically, Indirect Rule favored the ruling Muslim establishment of the Fulani and Hausa (whose populations – although distinct – had become quite integrated by this time, especially within Hausaland) over other ethnic and religious minorities. The British declared that the whole of the protectorate of northern Nigeria was to be governed by the Fulani emirs, who would apply Shari'a (Islamic) law under the supervision of the colonial authorities, who were instructed to interfere as little as possible. This decree assumed a greater degree of religious homogeneity within the protectorate than in fact existed, and it had catastrophic consequences for the status of religious and ethnic minorities, who became subject to the Islamic emirs and Shari'a law.[6] Christianity's influence was minor and rarely stemmed beyond the non-Muslim indigenous minorities of the north, because missionary activity was allowed only outside the central Muslim areas.[7]

Unlike in the north, the British found no equivalent of the Fulani state structures in the protectorate of southern Nigeria. Southern societies generally were more decentralized and less suitable for Indirect Rule. Although the British did try to institute suitable structures,[8] their attempts lacked the cohesion and legitimacy of the northern Fulani State. Consequently, the British resorted to a more sustained administrative and military presence. Between 1902 and 1914, there were twenty-one British military expeditions into the Igbo territories.[9] In addition, the colonial administration allowed, and even encouraged, missionary activity in southern Nigeria. Missionaries symbolized the colonial presence, provided some administrative structures, and promoted Western education alongside their religious messages.

These disparate approaches resulted in two distinct models of colonial rule: a relatively Western-educated and Christian south, and a more traditional north in which ethnic and religious minorities were subject to Islamic rule. Nonetheless, in 1914, the two regions were consolidated into a single administrative unit under British colonial hegemony, largely for administrative convenience. Named the Colony and Protectorate of Nigeria, it was as this single unit that Nigeria attained its independence in 1960.

Postindependence Tensions

Following World War II and a growing Nigerian nationalism, preparations for Nigerian independence began in the 1950s. The colonial administration envisioned a federal Nigeria composed of three regions. The Southern Protectorate would be split into an Eastern and a Western

Region, while the Northern Region would remain united. In each region, political parties were allowed to develop, and their membership came to reflect the main ethnic divisions in the country: the Northern People's Congress (NPC) represented Hausa and Fulani northerners, the Action Group (AG) represented the Yoruba of the Western Region, and the National Council of Nigeria and the Cameroons (NCNC) represented the Ibo of the Eastern Region. (Several smaller parties, including notably the Northern Elements Progressive Union [NEPU], represented minorities in the regions, but early postindependence politics were mostly played out among the three dominant ethnicities with little recognition or power going to minorities.)

Because of the numerical preponderance in the Northern Region, the Northern People's Congress won Nigeria's first general election in 1959 and formed a coalition government with the Eastern Region's National Council of Nigeria and the Cameroons. It was this government that began to administer the three regions of Nigeria, which officially gained independence on October 1, 1960. Immediately, the government faced the difficult task of uniting a country whose religious and ethnic groups had little affinity for one another.

The geographic size and demographic composition of the north made the Eastern and Western Regions hesitant to unify as one nation, whereas the educational advantage of those in the south was troubling to the north. At the same time, the competition between the southern Ibo and Yoruba for the opportunities opening up to educated Nigerians in the new postcolonial state led to bitter confrontations.[10] Instead of seeking to unite these groups, corrupt politicians played on these tensions to consolidate their electoral bases and increase their power. The politicians thus increased the stakes of the political game by tying economic gain to politics.

Violence soon followed. The state censuses of 1962 and 1963 generated suspicions and rioting, as the census results provided the data on which the makeup of the seats in the House of Representatives was to be determined. A leadership challenge in the Yoruba's Action Group led to intense political turmoil in the Western Region. With the Yoruba in disarray, the Northern People's Congress and the National Council of Nigeria and the Cameroons came to see each other as rivals for power. Meanwhile, widespread political abuses, corruption, intimidation, and violence severely damaged the people's confidence in the politicians and the judicial system. Riots in Tiv were quelled by the intervention of the Nigerian army, and a massive general strike paralyzed the country.

Despite these challenges, in late 1963 Nigeria declared itself a Federal Republic, and Dr. Benjamin Nnamdi Azikiwe became its first president. New federal parliamentary elections followed in 1964, feeding existing tensions. Campaigning was violent and a failed election boycott by the opposition parties allowed the Northern People's Congress to exaggerate its political dominance. Regional elections in the Western Region in 1965 were openly rigged, resulting in a further explosion of rioting that lasted from October 1965 to January 1966 and killed an estimated two thousand people. Reacting to the turmoil throughout the country, a group of Ibo army officers from the Eastern Region launched a coup attempt in January 1966, killing the prime minister.[11] Although their attempt was foiled, it nevertheless ended civilian rule in Nigeria. Frightened, the government had abdicated power to the highest-ranking loyal officer who had survived the coup attempt – Major-General Aguyi Ironsi – and he quickly instituted military rule. Because Major-General Ironsi also was Ibo, however, suspicions arose in the north that the whole episode represented an Ibo power play.[12]

Violence against Ibo residents living in the north exploded in May 1966, and a coup by Northern Region officers later that summer overthrew Major-General Ironsi and brought General Yakubu Gowon to power. Tragically, the massacre of Ibos in the north continued, killing thousands and forcing hundreds of thousands to migrate to the Ibo-majority Eastern Region, which became further alienated from the new nation. In May 1967, the Eastern Region announced its secession from federal Nigeria and announced the formation of the independent Republic of Biafra. Nigerian federal troops promptly invaded the territory.

The ensuing Nigerian Civil War lasted almost three years, causing tens of thousands of more deaths before Biafra's bid for independence was defeated. This was partly due to a political masterstroke by General Gowon, who created twelve federal states out of Nigeria's three regions, thus giving minorities a stake in the federal republic. Because eastern minorities preferred to preserve their power by having their own federal state within the Nigerian Republic rather than submit to domination by the Ibo majority in a unitary independent Biafra, an internally fissured Biafra faced a relatively unified Nigerian Republic during the war.[13]

After the war, General Gowon recognized the importance of reconciliation with the east and rejected calls for retribution against the secessionists. He thus presided over the reunification and strengthening of the Nigerian Federation. However, the corruption of his regime over five years and his refusal to allow a return to civilian rule doomed him, and he was overthrown in July 1975. Brigadier Murtala Ramat Mohammed took power, and announced plans to bring democratic civilian rule to Nigeria in four years with the inauguration of the Second Republic.

During the 1975–1979 transition to the Second Republic, new tensions emerged. In 1976, Brigadier Mohammed was assasinated and replaced by Lieutenant-General Olusegun Obasanjo. The next year, the Constitutional Assembly sought to craft an administrative structure for the Second Republic but was paralyzed by religious clashes between the predominantly Christian south and the Muslim north, and by members of the different religions within each region. The tension was particularly acute in the north, where religious and ethnic divisions overlapped because Christian missionary activity had occurred only among people from oppressed minority ethnicities.

The most heated debate among those working to establish the Second Republic was the status that Islamic law – the Shari'a – would have, and whether there would be a federal Shari'a court with the power to rule on appeals from the state Shari'a courts.[14] The First Republic had instituted a dual legal system in which a secular federal judicial structure was supplemented in the Northern Region by a system of Islamic courts that functioned only at the state level.[15] In planning for the Second Republic, the issue deadlocked the Constitutional Assembly, prompting bloody riots, especially in northern Nigeria.

The crisis was overcome only when General Obasanjo decreed that instead of a separate Federal Shari'a Court of Appeals, there would be a panel of three judges within the Federal Supreme Court who would be versed in Islamic law and could hear appeals from state Shari'a court decisions.[16] This compromise seemed to settle the issue for a time,[17] but the overthrow of the Second Republic just four years later in 1983 (because of corruption, political rivarly, and economic strains after a drop in oil prices) effectively put an end to the debate at the political level.

The issue resurfaced in the late 1980s, when military ruler General Babangida called yet another Constitutional Assembly to consider judiciary arrangements for a Third Republic. Time had not calmed the opposing positions. Christian delegates now demanded that all references to Shari'a courts be struck from the constitution, whereas Muslims insisted on a federal Shari'a court and, moreover on making the establishment of Shari'a courts obligatory for the entire country.[18]

The deadlock was once again ended by an administrative decree, and General Babangida ordered that the compromise of 1979 be retained, with the important exception that the jurisdiction of Shari'a courts was extended from "Islamic personal law" to "questions of Islamic law where all the parties are Muslims."[19] There was little opportunity to test this compromise, however. General Babangida used a series of excuses to delay the transition to democracy and never instituted this judicial system of review. Preliminary results of the 1993 presidential elections showed that Chief Moshood Abiola would win, but Babangida annulled the election. The resulting protests reached such a high pitch that Babangida resigned, transferring power to an interim government led by Ernest Shonekan and reinvigorating the hope for democratic rule. Within months, however, General Sani Abacha overthrew the Shonekan government, returning the country to military rule.

The Abacha era, arguably the most oppressive in Nigerian history, ended with General Abacha's death in 1998. During his rule, political parties were banned, the press muzzled, and opposition members arbitrarily arrested. The trial and execution in 1995 of Ken Saro-Wiwa and his fellow Ogoni activists protesting the exploitation of oil in their region came to epitomize this repression and brought to Nigeria a virtual pariah status in international relations.

Domestic and international pressure for democratization was intense, and the transitional government that succeeded the Abacha regime duly held elections in March 1999. Retired General Obasanjo, the military ruler who had presided over the transition to democracy in 1979, won the elections. Unfortunately, despite the hopes raised by his victory, tensions persisted and, indeed, still simmer in Nigeria. Ethnic divisions remain profound, the dispute over Shari'a persists, control of the country's oil continues to fuel violence in the south, and religious tensions both between the northern and the southern states and among different ethnic groups have resurfaced, leading to several bloody riots.

The Conflicts of Kaduna State[20]

It is against this backdrop of violence and instability that Imam Muhammad Ashafa and Pastor James Wuye currently work.

Of particular importance to their story is the situation in Kaduna State in northern Nigeria. It is often said that when Kaduna sneezes, the rest of the country catches a cold. The capital of the state is also called Kaduna, a city of well over 1.5 million people, some 200 km north of the Nigerian capital of Abuja. The city was once merely a fief in the Zaria emirate, but was declared the capital of the Protectorate of Northern Nigeria during the colonial period. As the colonial capital, Kaduna attracted people from all over the protectorate, giving the city a cosmopolitan character and enhancing its already impressive ethnic and religious diversity.[21]

The city of Kaduna is home to Hausa, Fulani, Gwari, Kataf, and Yoruba families, among others. Christians tend to live in the south of the city, whereas the north is largely Muslim. Numerically, the two religions have roughly achieved parity there. Both Imam Ashafa and Pastor James are native to Kaduna, but although Pastor James is a Gwari Penticostal Christian, Imam Ashafa is a Yoruba Muslim.

Kaduna State has been subject to repeated bouts of ethnic and religious violence, mirroring the tension in postcolonial Nigeria. Some clashes were born out of local disputes among the area's religious groups, while others were reactions to national debates. Among these debates, the Shari'a issue and the perception that Muslims sought hegemony over other religious groups clearly are the most inflammatory, as evidenced by violent disputes that originated from the town of Zangon Kataf, also in Kaduna State, in 1992.

Zangon Kataf, like the city of Kaduna, was originally part of the Zaria emirate. "Zangon" is a Hausa word meaning "temporary resting place." Zangon Kataf was the Hausa name for the town, which was inhabited by the Kataf people and was used as a resting place for northern trading caravans on their journey to the south. It grew into a full-fledged Hausa-Fulani settlement in the seventeenth century, but the area around the town remained in the hands of local Kataf, who never ceased to view the Hausa-Fulani as mere newcomers to the area.[22]

Pastor James identifies the British colonial policy of Indirect Rule, which extended and strengthened the power of the Hausa-Fulani in the area, as "the remote cause" of Zangon Kataf's problems because it stimulated interethnic and interreligious tensions:

> On arrival in the North, the British met a government structure established there before their advent: an Islamic system of government, based on emirs, district heads, ward heads, and hamlet heads.... They felt the structure was good and used it to govern the people – even in areas in the North that had not been conquered. Britain was the colonial master. They penetrated society first through the power of superior weapons, then by Indirect Rule through the emirs. And under Indirect Rule the influence of these emirs expanded into areas beyond the Islamic tradition of governance.[23]

Zangon Kataf was ruled politically and economically through Muslim Hausa-Fulani district heads dispatched from Zaria. The Kataf people were treated as second-class citizens and subjected to heavy taxation. Adding to the ethnic divisions, Hausa-Fulani traders controlled Zangon Kataf's market in the center of the town, to which the Kataf had to transport their wares from their homes outside the city center. The Hausa-Fulani also owned most of the market's stores, leaving little space for the Kataf to display their goods. Predictably, this caused economic and ethnic tensions that were further exacerbated by religious differences that emerged when many of the Kataf began converting to Christianity.

Until the early 1990s, political power in Zangon Kataf remained firmly in Hausa-Fulani hands. But the situation prepared to shift as several trends converged to encourage the Kataf people to become politically engaged. First, native Kataf who had made their careers in the postindependence Nigerian army returned home in the 1980s, bringing with them military know-how and a determination to end their people's oppression.[24] Additionally, after over a decade of northern rule the perceived need for northern solidarity against the south (especially the Ibo) had abated.

Under the growing influence of more radical evangelical churches,[25] and as a reaction to a perceived increase in Muslim fundamentalism,[26] Nigeria's Christian churches also broke with their tradition of apolitical devotion and embraced political activism. And, finally, the first Shari'a debate in the Constitutional Assembly for the Second Republic stirred the people. Pastor James explains: "From the Christian point of view, non-participation in politics would allow laws alien to Christianity to be imposed. So Christians started using the Scriptures to convince other Christians to enter politics – 'David was a politician,' they said. It is the Christian duty to become politically active."[27]

In 1992, a breakthrough in local politics occurred. Partly because of the growing politicization among the Kataf people, and partly because of a redrawing of local government boundaries that left them with an absolute majority in their local government area, an "indigenous" Christian won the local elections. Among the first acts of his government was the transfer of the market from the center of town to its outskirts. The relocation created more space, but local Hausa-Fulani saw it as an attack on their control of the market, especially as oversight was given to an indigenous Christian who, as Pastor James explains, "was not even a trader."[28] Pastor James describes the ensuing crisis:

> When the order for the relocation of the market was issued, the Muslims went to court to stop the order, and the court stopped it, pending

investigation. But there was a breakdown of communication: the local government was not informed of the court's order . . . and tried to implement the council's order. . . . When tension rose, some indigenous groups started destroying some Hausa-Fulani farms, destroying crops. There were stories of letters by Muslim groups saying that they would fight if the market was relocated. These were small groups – but the word *jihad* was used by those boys, and this increased the tensions. In the meantime, there were announcements and counter-announcements about what was going to happen to the market.

Eventually, some indigenous women took their wares to the relocated market. Some Hausa youths overturned their wares and they were beaten and chased out – at least that's one of the stories about how exactly the crisis was triggered. Their men then came to retaliate by destroying crops and attacking Muslims – and they killed some Muslims.[29]

The crisis did not remain localized but spilled over into the city of Kaduna. Imam Ashafa explains:

> The Muslims [in Zangon Kataf] were in a minority, and so for the first days, the indigenous population could walk over them. It was like an ethnic cleansing of a local minority. And so Hausa-Fulani started coming back to [the city of] Kaduna with the coffins of their loved ones – and some did not go to the hospital, but to the mosques. This created the awareness that Muslims were being killed in Zangon [Kataf] – and the youth reacted, felt the need to fight back. [The city of] Kaduna is a mixed town, and we know where the indigenous people live – so it was easy to take revenge. At this stage, it became a matter of religion: all Muslims, even if they were not Hausa, but Yoruba, for example, formed a bloc and all Christians, even if they were Ibo rather than Kataf, formed a bloc. The conflict was not intraethnic – Yoruba Christian fought against Yoruba Muslims.[30]

The Shari'a in Kaduna

The violence stemming from Zangon Kataf was soon followed by more fighting when the state of Kaduna was thrust into the center of the national debate on the Shari'a issue. Just months after the establishment of the Third Republic, the governor of the state of Zamfara declared that it would henceforth use and enforce Shari'a law as both its personal and criminal law.[31] Repercussions of this decision were felt far beyond Zamfara. Muslims in other states began demanding that their governments follow its lead. Consequently, Niger State enacted Shari'a in December 1999, with Sokoto and Kano following suit in January and February 2000, respectively. Unlike Zamfara, these states (especially Kano) had significant non-Muslim minorities. Observers expected resistance. But perhaps because most of the indigenous population in Kano is Muslim, with Christianity concentrated among more recent settlers and migrants, large-scale clashes did not occur there. Indeed, there were no major clashes about Shari'a law in Nigeria – until the issue reached the state of Kaduna.

There, it was not only migrant and recent settlers but also indigenous peoples who objected to statewide imposition of Islamic law. Christians made up a far larger proportion of the Kaduna population than in other states. Moreover, Kaduna's religious groups had a history of violent clashes. In fact, both Christian and Muslim militant youths had already organized vigilante groups, which were poised to act at the first sign of a crisis.

Proposals to institute Shari'a law in the state of Kaduna primed Kaduna city for violence. Tensions were already high after evidence of the Zangon Kataf market riots reached Kaduna city. It was as if a spark had been thrown onto a powder keg, provoking a series of protests that began intensively in January 2000. Attacks and retaliation between Christians and Muslims raged for three days, claiming over two thousand lives and destroying property worth hundreds of millions of naira. Families were dislocated, children were orphaned, and women became widows. The state's economy became a mere shadow of itself by February 22, 2000.[32]

Kaduna's struggle over Shari'a received national attention. As one government official put it, "The resolution of the issue in Kaduna is a test case for religion in Nigeria."[33] Accusations flew, with some believing that groups promoting a larger national agenda had actually incited the clashes in Kaduna. Colonel Madaki, a former military governor in the Babangida administration, accused the "Kaduna Mafia" of northern notables of manipulating people in Kaduna to prolong the riots and create a crisis that might lead to the downfall of the Obasanjo regime.[34] Others, however, accused the Southern Kaduna People Union (SOKAPU), a political wing of an ethnic minority group of southern Kaduna, for instigating the conflict.

Eventually, the militants became locked in a stalemate, and the violence began to diminish. By September 2000, locals were commenting on how quickly the city was recovering from the violence and beginning to rebuild. Optimists hoped that the issue would die down. But levels of distrust and hatred have not yet fully dissipated, and violence remains poised to erupt again.

Imam Muhammad Ashafa, Pastor James Wuye: Warriors First

Like the militant vigilante youth in Zangon Kataf, Imam Ashafa and Pastor James were religious militants in Kaduna during their early years. But that is not their whole story.

Imam Ashafa came from a religiously educated family. His father was a spiritual leader. The family was proud of its traditions and of being learned in Arabic, the language of the Prophet. From an early age, Muhammad showed skill as a teacher of the Qu'ran to younger children, predicting his path to becoming an Imam. As he recalls his path, he also talks about how his family shunned Western education from the colonial powers and their disrespect for his community's historic language and traditions.

In contrast, Pastor James was not always religious. He remembers going to church, but only to wink at the choir girls. Then, he would rush out and spend his time drinking all his friends under the table. When he thinks about those days, he now laughs, and says that they used to call him coach because he was such a good drinker. However, one day while in church, James heard the preacher in a different way – as if he was talking right at him. Moved, he was inspired to follow the path of Jesus. Yet, this did not mean that he rejected all violence. Even as a pastor, he became a leader of militant youth.

Pastor James describes how he saw the world during this period: "We [didn't] want anything to do with Muslims. If one sits next to me, I [would] change seats. This was justified by Scripture – 'Do not get unequally yoked together with unbelievers, for what fellowship has righteousness and lawlessness...' II Corinthians 6:14."[35]

Imam Ashafa had a similar negative perspective about his Christian neighbors. "I was a Muslim youth activist... seeking to Islamize the country, to bring back the Islam of Usman dan Fodio days. I felt that our tradition had been submerged by Western tradition, that our core values had been marginalized. And I could not and did not separate Western culture from Christian culture."[36]

Both men were deeply moved by hatred of the other's group. And both were ready to put their hatred into practice. It was not a surprise, therefore, when they joined militant youth groups, quickly rising to leadership positions within them. Imam Ashafa joined the Jama'atu Nasril Islam (JNI), which brought together Muslims from the northern Nigerian establishment (with its traditional interpretation of Islam), from the

Tijaniyya and the Qadiriyya brotherhoods (with their own understandings of Islam), and from other Islamic groups as well. Ultimately, Ashafa became the Secretary-General of the National Council of Muslim Youth Organizations (NACOMYO), the second highest official in the organization after the chairman in the state.

Pastor James occupied a similar position in the Youth Wing of the Christian Association of Nigeria (Youth CAN), the principal ecumenical organization uniting Nigerian Catholics and Protestants of diverse denominations. He also was an active trainer for the Christian vigilante group:

> I became a militant Christian because initially Christians in Kaduna and northern Nigeria generally felt that Muslim youths were destroying religious places of worship and attacking pastors – that this had been the trend for several years. I see now that this was usually provoked [sic] by Christians who did not understand Islam – but at the time I felt that Christians were allowed to do whatever they wanted. For example, Christians are said to quote the Qu'ran out of context, which according to Muslims is sacrilegious for them, but I felt it was OK for Christians to do it. This led to killings and maimings. That was the trend until 1987. Then, in Kafanchan, the most developed town in South Kaduna State, a Christian preacher quoted from the Qu'ran, the Muslims felt it was a sacrilege, and attacked him – and the conflict spread through Kaduna and Katsina State. The attackers were not responsible people, but hoodlums; we didn't distinguish between them [or] the other Muslims. It became imperative for us to establish a militant group of Christian youth to checkmate them. At the time, I was the secretary of Youth CAN. . . . We started training ourselves in self-defence and martial arts. Everybody had to make a vow: not to attack first, but you can defend yourself.
>
> We did not see anything good about Islam and Muslims nor our [own] scripture about loving your neighbour. We believed that if you kill a Muslim, you are doing something good.[37]

Given their backgrounds, it was perhaps inevitable that both men were drawn into the thick of Zangon Kataf's 1992 market riots. Imam Ashafa recounts simply: "I was involved in the hospitals, so I saw the wounded come in [i.e., the Muslim corpses from Zangon Kataf]. And [when Kaduna Muslims joined the fight] I was happy that we were taking our revenge."[38] Pastor James recalls:

> In 1992, the riots in Zangon town spread to Kaduna. Initially they [Muslims] were selective, they looked for Kataf [people]. I'm Gwari. But I went in to see what could be done to save these people – I went with bodyguards, which I had because of my position in CAN.

[It was there, during the fighting, that] I lost my hand in defensing [*sic*] the church and a youth working with me died in this operation.[39]

The riots also cost Imam Ashafa dearly: "[O]nly at the end did I discover my losses: two brothers and my teacher – Sheikh Ahmad Tijani. He was living in the Christian part of town. He was my mentor, and he was murdered."[40]

Both men paid a heavy price for their involvement in the riots. And though both cite these as life-changing experiences on their path to becoming peace activists, neither became a pacifist directly because of them. Imam Ashafa recollects how he learned that his enemy, Pastor James, had lived, and how unjust that seemed.

Only later did it slowly dawn on me that we can't take this any more, that the cost of vengeance was too high – after this traumatic experience – but only in 1995. Before then, I knew that James Wuye was a member of a militant Christian group [the Youth CAN]. I expected to hear at least that James also is gone.

But only his hand was gone – they called him the Gold Hand. I had lost two brothers and my teacher – why should he still be alive? So I carried vengeance within me. I felt that vengeance was necessary.[41]

Pastor James had a similar reaction. He was bitter at the loss of his hand and anxious for revenge. He remembers: "I thought: if I ever find those boys [who fought us in the riots], I must kill them. The training of the boys [in the Christian self-defence groups] became more aggressive – we wanted vengeance."[42]

Becoming Brothers

Nevertheless, when Pastor James Wuye and Imam Muhammad Ashafa later encountered one another, the exchange – although not quite cordial – remained nonviolent. Imam Ashafa describes that moment:

The state government was holding a meeting on immunization [in 1995] as part of a program run by UNICEF. But people feared that the injections were actually meant to sterilize the women. Muslims feared this, so the state government called a meeting to get the Mosques and Churches involved. Both James and I were sent as representatives of our religions to this meeting.

So we met at the State House. But we couldn't fight there. During the break, we had tea. And during this break, a mutual friend, an engineer with the local radio station, took both of us by the hand and said: "The two of you can pull this nation together, or you can destroy it. Do something."

He left me at the table with my worst enemy. We [shook] hands. And we [decided] to hold a debate – each with the intention of exposing the other's fallacies.[43]

We agreed to meet, but where? Our mutual friend Idris Musa offered his office for the first formal meeting, where members of our associations came together at the Kaduna State Media Corporation.[44]

At this point both men still believed that their respective religions needed to rely on violence. Yet their meetings to plan the debate unexpectedly helped build an element of trust between them. Imam Ashafa explains, "It took one year to organize it, because [at first] we had no trust or confidence in each other, and no clear focus or direction. But during these discussions, we started building some trust, our perceptions changed from our passions to our reality."[45] Both men insist, however, that the true breakthrough in their relationship came because of personal religious experiences rather than these encounters.

Imam Ashafa had his epiphany first, shortly after the encounter with Pastor James at the State House. It all started with the words of a spiritual Imam, who noted that while there is religious justification for retaliation, to really embody the Prophet Muhammad, one had to forgive just as the Prophet forgave those who stoned him. Imam Ashafa recalls:

> I went to prayer, and the Imam there – it was as if he had been sent just for me. The sermon was on forgiveness, and the need to forgive our enemies. He was quoting from the Qu'ran, how Muhammad forgave the pagans at Mecca. And I was thinking: How can I forgive these enemies? They have killed so many – I can't forgive. But deep inside me, there was the re-awakening of the thought that Islam says I must forgive my enemies, if they no longer persecute me. The prayer finished, but I still wept internally. I [decided to] build my trust in James, and teach him that Islam never taught any Muslim to be a terrorist.
>
> I went to his office, at CAN. I was the first Muslim there, and they were shocked. But he received me fine. And after persistent meetings, James came to my office, too. I was told: why do you let him come here? But we continued having meetings. This is how we started building some trust. Then I went to his house for the first time: his mother was sick, so I went to greet the mother. Later, his mother [passed] away. I [felt] that he [was] still not trusting me, so I went with a group of others to deliver a condolence message. This create[d] the opening. After that, he start[ed] coming to my house, too.[46]

From Wuye's perspective, Ashafa's change of behavior posed a challenge, but it was not until he too underwent a religious experience that he could truly reciprocate. But that did not mean that Pastor Wuye was not affected by the persistent, and genuine, kindness that Ashafa showed him.

> When he visited me with a group of Muslims when my mother...died, I was broken. Can there be sincere Muslims? His persuasion and persistence, and the love he showed – I didn't know he had had a spiritual awakening. I worked with him until 1997, when I [had] to go to Abuja for a meeting of the 700 Club [a Christian organization] about the evangelization of the Hausa-Fulani in the North and the Kanuri Muslims.
>
> And they said to us: How can you preach to somebody you can't love? We have all sinned. I should see a Muslim, as God would want to see a Muslim, not as I would want to see a Muslim. God has spared my life to bring peace – and this incapacitation [loss of hand] is not a curse: if I can give my hand to make peace, it is well given.[47]

Their respective religious transformations prepared the two men to develop a profound level of trust. The days when they were anxious to take the other's life slowly became a thing of the past. In fact, Pastor James concedes that it took him three years to overcome a deep-seated impulse to take revenge and take his new friend's life. He explains:

> All the years before, I was not fully committed. Now, I trust Ashafa. He can make a decision on my behalf, and I will accept it. Before, there were temptations: we were working together, and there were opportunities to kill him – on a project, far from Kaduna, I could have suffocated him when he was asleep. But there was this force in me that stopped me.[48]

Finally, Pastor James received clarity – that Christ's message is love and that he had to learn to forgive because one cannot preach the message of Jesus Christ with hate in one's heart.

Despite their growing friendship, however, obstacles remained. The rapprochement did not automatically bring the other members of Youth CAN and NACOMYO closer together. Both Ashafa and Wuye were aware of the difficulties they would face in reconciling their followers. "We were talking at the leadership level only," notes Ashafa. "I had not informed the Muslim youth. [Among them,] many were still skeptical."[49] They still considered the Youth CAN a militant group, and refused to meet with them.

In May 1995, despite having no formal training in conflict management, the former warriors founded the Muslim-Christian Youth Dialogue Forum (MCYDF) in Kaduna to further their commitment to bringing reconciliation to their communities. To overcome their lack of experience, and with funding from the British Council, they attended a 1996 work-shop organized by the Academic Associate Peace Work (AAPW) and the Strategic Empowerment and Mediation Agency (SEMA), a con-flict management NGO founded in 1990 by Sam Ihejirika and based in Kaduna.

Ihejirika had met Wuye shortly after the Zangon Kataf riots at a meet-ing in which SEMA attempted to mediate that conflict. Wuye was at the meeting as secretary of Youth CAN, his missing hand still a fresh wound.[50] Based on this encounter, Ihejirika invited Wuye to the 1996 workshop and asked him to invite a counterpart from the Muslim community. Ashafa was originally reluctant to accept the invitation – "I trusted James, but not the other Christians. I asked myself, 'Who is organizing this confer-ence? What is it meant for?' I had no idea what conflict management or resolution was back then."[51] Nonetheless, he eventually agreed.

After the workshop, participants were encouraged to develop their own mediation projects and submit them to the British Council for funding. Ihejirika collaborated with the nascent MCYDF, helping them to orga-nize a prospective debate on salvation in the two religions and point them to further training opportunities in Nigeria and elsewhere. With his assistance, in 1997 Ashafa and Wuye were able to attend a three-month course, "Responding to Conflict," at the Federation of Selly Oak Colleges, Birmingham, U.K.[52]

Thanks to this training and to the recruitment work done by Pas-tor James and Imam Ashafa within their respective communities, the MCYDF began to grow in its capacity as a nongovernmental, grassroots, and interreligious conflict-resolution organization. But the Forum's com-ing of age was in 1999 – when they eliminated the word "Youth" from MCYDF's name. As Ashafa explains somewhat ruefully, "We changed to the Muslim-Christian Dialogue Forum, with a special department for youth . . . when we all turned 40 . . . and thus we were not youths anymore ourselves."[53]

The Mission of the Muslim–Christian Dialogue Forum (MCDF)

As MCDF's cofounders, Imam Ashafa and Pastor James serve as the orga-nization's National Coordinators and oversee a core staff consisting of an equal number of Christians and Muslims. MCDF's key philosophical tenet is that religion can and should make a positive contribution to peace and reconciliation within a society. They often call on religious doctrines, par-ticularly doctrines of forgiveness, in their work. "There are deep-rooted misconceptions across class divides and between ethnic groups," Ashafa explains. "Only religion can unite them, because it changed the psyche of the youths who were used as soldiers of destruction."[54] Personal experience has been a powerful teacher. Both men have learned the many ways in which religion can be manipulated into a destructive force. According to Pastor James:

> Nigeria is a very religious country. Disrespect for religion more than anything else tears this country apart. Religion is [also] used as a smokescreen for political things, because there is lots of sympathy for it.[55]

The MCDF founders appreciate that it is primarily among the youth that religion is used to incite violence. Consequently, the MCDF targets and seeks to transform militant youth groups. James reflects on the time-honored process of making and fighting wars:

> Usually, the elders make the policy, and the youth execute it. If there is a war, the youth fight it. By reconciling the youth, we make sure that there is nobody to go and fight. That's what happened to us. But we were healed from the virus of aggression.... Now we say: 'no more.' We are reprogramming the youth, [but] still using religion.[56]

Together, they work to break the link between the foot soldiers who carry out much of the violence and the people in power who manipulate them.

Imam Ashafa and Pastor James began their reconciliation efforts in a conflict area they both knew well: Zangon Kataf. They partly relied on their status as religious leaders for influence. Says Pastor James, "that's why we get attention – because we are first and foremost religious people. With our status as religious leaders, we can go knock on any door. Our peers who are not religious leaders cannot go there."[57] But they relied even more on their insider status as prior leaders of militant youth groups. This strategy, however, was not without risks. According to James:

> Reconciling the people in Zangon Kataf is a Herculean task. It is high risk: I may lose my relevance in church circles, Ashafa in Muslim circles. But I was a militant church leader and could kill for the church. I had that credibility, so I could get away with going into areas of fanatics – and we each guarantee the other's life in areas where one religion is in dominance. We could have been killed – they knew who we were. But I am preaching a new gospel to the youth I used to train to fight. And we go to the leaders and say that we cannot be used again for violence.[58]

Ashafa and Wuye believe that after two years of work, their efforts in Zangon Kataf showed success. Pastor James continues:

> By the grace of God we have successfully de-escalated [the] crisis in this area. We have transformed the youth there and made them... agents for peace.... Together we went to the old religious groups in Zangon Kataf – and now there is a new structure in place. MCDF had developed a process for keeping tense situations from escalating:
>   When a crisis begins, the Muslim youth leader goes to the Christian, and they can discuss it. When a Muslim is attacked by a Christian, the Muslim leader goes to the Christian leader who will in turn punish the offender, and then informs the Muslim leader of his action, who then reports to his constituency.
>   These youth leaders are identified and trained by our organization, and given basic skills in conflict management and trauma counseling. We are using the Bible and the Qu'ran as a base for this advocacy. Our targets are the militant youth groups – and now the transformed ones are in the majority and they now control the few deviants. We are happy the government of the area is supporting them and listening to them now.[59]

Since this initial success, the MCDF has expanded its work to other areas. Regular meetings have been held in Kano to foster dialogue between local youth and religious and community leaders. Pastor James expands on these initiatives:

> We are the catalyst for these dialogues to continue. We break down stereotypes, de-program people, create platforms for dialogue. We invite grassroots religious leaders and seek the active consultation of all those involved in the conflict. And we use religion to make them remorseful of their [previous violent] conduct.[60]

Similar efforts are carried out at Bauchi State for Sayawa and Fulani of Tafawa Balewa, and Bogoro local government areas, all in northern Nigeria. The MCDF identifies areas to target for intervention by assessing the risk of conflict within them.

Today, their most extensive initiatives continue to be in Kaduna, their home state. Imam Ashafa describes how they are trying to find ways to sustain peace, by rebuilding lives and houses of worship:

> After the Shari'a riots, we are doing workshops with youth, women, tribal and religious leaders for reconciliation and trauma counseling. We are also working on the reconstruction of mosques and churches, using the youth from the affected areas who played a role in their destruction.[61]

Within days of the riots, the MCDF launched into action, visiting ravaged areas, beginning reconstruction efforts, consulting with religious leaders, and mounting a publicity campaign for peace on both television and radio, as well as through "Peace is Divine" posters. Even in the face of personal risk and organizational challenges, the MCDF had an impact. It is their efforts in Kaduna that brought the MCDF increased praise and respect.

In addition to direct intervention in conflict-prone areas, Imam Ashafa and Pastor James are heavily involved in teaching and training a new generation of Nigerian peacemakers. In 1999, their insights on the ways in which the Bible and the Qu'ran enjoin believers to manage their conflicts peacefully were published in a book entitled *The Pastor and the Imam – Responding to Conflict*.[62] In addition, the MCDF holds workshops to train "peace agents." The organization has at least two youth leaders in each of the thirty-six states of the country who are trained for conflict resolution. It also has trained almost ten thousand people in interfaith mediation and conflict management, and it maintains a membership of over ten thousand youths and members of the clergy.[63]

MCDF Outreach: Partnering for a Sustainable Peace

The MCDF does not, of course, operate completely alone. Imam Ashafa and Pastor Wuye understand that it takes a variety of actors from all levels of society to address religious violence in Nigeria and Kaduna. The *Peacemakers* therefore make sure to work with and involve many others, including, these days, Nigerian government officials. Relations with state and federal government officials were less productive under the military regime. Today, Ashafa and Wuye stress the generally cordial relations MCDF enjoys with many local governments.

In Zangon Kataf, for example, they partnered with SEMA and AAPW to work with the local government toward ending the conflict.[64] "First, if [local government officials] had a problem, they would come to us, and we would get moral support from the government at the state level," Imam Ashafa explains. "Now they also approve some projects – they help finance them and get participants on board. And we feel comfortable moving closer to the government now through the State Bureau for Religious Affairs."[65]

The Nigerian media has also begun to serve as an ally in this work, at least sometimes. Over the years, many observers have criticized the often inflammatory behavior of Nigerian journalists,[66] and Imam Ashafa and

Pastor James have echoed this criticism. Pastor James notes that for most of its history, the MCDF avoided contact with the press in order to avoid politicization. As Ashafa further explains, as a religious organization, it faces an additional challenge when dealing with the media:

> We avoided them initially, because they were very far from the ethics of journalism.... They believed religion should be out of politics and government. They wanted secularism, and didn't like NGOs with religious base activities. We realized that they might divert our ... efforts, give a negative interpretation of them to the people, and undermine our efforts to mediate at a grassroots level.[67]

More recently, however, MCDF's relations with the media have improved somewhat; in fact, they have written editorials and worked on television programs on interreligious dialogue. Yet, despite their improving relations with the media, Imam Ashafa and Pastor James remain wary, faulting the Nigerian press for its sensationalism and commercialism. Imam Ashafa complains of the commercial focus on bad news:

> A lot of the press is interested in negative news – war, violence, 'breaking news' – because violence will sell. The press guy is not interested in reporting positive news at the grassroots level.... The press has to change, has to develop a greater spirituality.... Until then ... it is better to work without it.[68]

The MCDF also interacts with Nigeria's principal religious organizations, including those still instigating the violence. Both Imam Ashafa and Pastor James have retained their contact with the religious militant organizations of their youth. These associations do not conflict with their mediation work but are part of it. Thus, the MCDF is supporting and strengthening the federal government's efforts to mediate the conflict between the Christian Association of Nigeria (CAN) and the Jama'atu Nasril Islam (JNI). Ashafa clarifies:

> We are in the middle, trying to bring the two together at the grassroots level. The Government has created NAIREC – the Nigerian Interreligious Council – with twenty-five Muslim and twenty-five Christian senior religious leaders, but nothing for the youth or other groups. So we complement, supplement their effort. But we get no funding, we have no grant, support from or direct link with the federal government for now.[69]

Their personal experiences with militant religious activism give Imam Ashafa and Pastor James unusual insight and connections. As former militant youth leaders, they have unparalleled access to those most directly involved in violence and local fighting. They know the structure of their former organizations, have strong reputations within them, and have personally helped train some of the fighters.

It is also well known that both have suffered great loss in the face of violence and hatred. This gives them increased legitimacy among the militant youth, and they consequently enjoy a tremendous advantage in approaching and seeking to influence them. For the youth, the example of their former leaders turning to nonviolence sends a powerful signal throughout the community.

Their greatest strength, however, is how they talk with the youthful fighters. They know what it is like to be angry, and describe how they found another way to achieve justice. They point to themselves as living proof that giving up militancy can work. And even though they do not always agree, they have developed ways to overcome their differences. (In fact, they say that they have no choice. Their relationship is an irrevocable commitment, because the work is simply too important.)

Despite their efforts, however, the militant youth groups CAN and JNI continue to resist establishing an official relationship. Each seems reluctant to engage the other in dialogue, partly because the leaders of the organizations fear their hardliners, but also because of the overall level of mistrust that persists between the religious organizations.

In fact, Nigerian religious organizations have adopted increasingly uncompromising stances. This is most obvious with regard to the Shari'a issue; as scholar Klaus Hock explains, "the decision to do without nuanced and complex perspectives has finally blinded both opponents to both the complexities of the problems of the Nigerian judicial system and the perceived interests of the opposing religious community. Thus, the Shari'a debate has . . . ceased: there is no more debate, only eloquent mistrust."[70] As Imam Ashafa puts it, "there is a lot of mistrust – the phobia is always there against the other religion – Islamophobia or phobia of Western culture and therefore Christianity."[71]

Nevertheless, he insists that there is reason to hope. Increasingly, leaders of the two organizations are willing to try something new. "They think: We have failed, maybe you can do something better. The personal relations between the leaders are improving, though community-based distrust still exists. But something is happening positively – there is a willingness to start trying to understand."[72]

In addition to working with the government, media, and the religious militants, the *Peacemakers* and MCDF are in a key position as religious leaders to reach Nigeria's expansive religious communities. Imam Ashafa and Pastor James see the religious foundation of MCDF's work as giving it a comparative advantage, placing it at the forefront of reconciliation efforts. The average Nigerian is strongly attached to his or her religious beliefs. Notes Pastor James: "Through the Church and the Mosque, we can reach across class lines and professions. The vast majority of Nigeria's population – about 90 percent – is either Muslim or Christian."[73]

Accordingly, the *Peacemakers* are called in even when the conflicts they seek to mediate are really motivated by political and economic factors and overlain with ethnic differences. This is because the conflicts are still cast in religious terms and viewed in this light by most of Nigeria's religiously affiliated population. Religious leaders, especially in a country such as Nigeria where religion historically has played a significant role, have an opportunity to loom large in reconciliation efforts. For Imam Ashafa and Pastor James, their religious status affords them a position of authority within Nigerian society, which they have recognized and used to preach their nonviolent interpretations of their religions. Given the level of distrust among local religious communities, that this message is sent by two leaders of different religions who are working together – without either renouncing his own religious beliefs – is invaluable.

Although he asserts that they rely on international standards for conflict resolution, Pastor James believes that the concepts of "mediation and conciliation are found in the Bible." MCDF was the first transparent and true interfaith organization in Nigeria, and the value of its approach was quickly apparent. As James observed some years ago:

> The issue of rivalry does not arise. . . . I am a Christian. My fellow Christians will not stone me. Ashafa is a Muslim, and his Muslim brothers will not stone him. So this is unique. If there is a land dispute, we can mediate it to stop the situation from escalation into violent conflict. No other NGO has this ability to address both communities, to the best of our knowledge, in Nigeria.[74]

Today, the country does have a few other effective interfaith organizations. They often work together, but also have to compete for funding and outside support, much of which comes from foreign government and charitable donors.

Threats to Religiously Motivated Peacemaking

Many factors give Imam Ashafa and Pastor James unique access to local communities and enable them to speak and act powerfully for peace and reconciliation. But even their status does not always guarantee access or protect them from danger. The MCDF works in a very tense and volatile environment. Members from their own religious communities who view the organization's peacemaking efforts as treasonous have made threats to both men.

MCDF, like too many other grassroots organizations, also suffers from a lack of sufficient resources. Even by Nigerian standards, its offices are very basic, and such circumstances do not facilitate the MCDF's task. Imam Ashafa and Pastor James both stress the difficulties they face because of inadequate funding, unreliable systems of communication with members of the MCDF in the field, and lack of enough training opportunities in conflict management for staff and volunteers. This has been attenuated to some extent by cooperation with other local NGOs, and even closer ties with these organizations may ultimately strengthen the MCDF's reach. But this cooperation is only part of the solution as MCDF expands its work.

As MCDF initially began to extend its influence beyond Kaduna State, it became evident that what may be one of the organization's greatest strengths in Kaduna did not readily translate to other regions. In Kaduna, Imam Ashafa and Pastor James are insiders. Outside that area, however, they no longer benefit from their personal relations and local reputations, and as such have been more likely to confront resistance as outsiders. Their status as religious leaders remains useful in these instances, however, and has helped Imam Ashafa and Pastor James access religious communities in other Nigerian states. As such, MCDF has been able to begin building a national network of members and trained conflict mediators.

While the MCDF could not prevent the tragic 2000 riots in Kaduna over Shari'a law, during which numerous mosques and churches were destroyed and an estimated two hundred thousand people were displaced, it strongly advocated for nonviolence and dialogue throughout that traumatic period. Today, it remains a voice for the possibility of peaceful compromise (even their vehicle wears a sticker proclaiming "Peace is Divine"). And it makes a real contribution to the healing process in conflict-torn communities through its workshops on trauma and reconciliation, its work with widows and orphans of the violence, and its efforts to facilitate the rebuilding of destroyed churches and mosques. Pastor James and Imam Ashafa speak with one voice when they maintain: "We believe that a compromise is possible [only] if we understand each other's needs. We need dialogue. We have to create an enabling atmosphere in which each can feel secure with his own religion."[75]

MCDF and its *Peacemaker* leaders prove that grassroots leaders and NGOs can play key roles in armed conflicts. With their members, Ashafa and Wuye have courageously dedicated themselves to ameliorating religious tensions and to spreading nonviolent teachings from their respective religious traditions. And they have persisted notwithstanding threats, disappointments, recurring violence, and lack of resources. Ultimately, their perseverence may be their greatest strength.

Moving Forward: The Interfaith Mediation Centre and the Future of Nigeria

The tensions in Nigeria remain today, and the country continues to suffer outbreaks of violence conducted in the name of religion. Pastor James sadly explains, "Kaduna is like dynamite, and everybody is treading carefully, because conflict of any form can have a devastating effect on both [the Christian and Muslim] communities."[76] In the years since the Kaduna riots, Imam Ashafa and Pastor James have waded through a tenuous peace marked by moments of real progress. They also renamed their organization the Interfaith Mediation Centre to better reflect the active mediating work beyond just dialogue.

One highlight was on August 22, 2002. The two men convinced twenty senior religious leaders, ten from each faith, to sign the Kaduna Peace Declaration. The governor also signed the Declaration and unveiled a plaque of it for all the public to see. The Declaration calls upon the community to oppose incitement, hatred, and misrepresentation of one another (see Appendix at the end of this chapter).[77] According to some observers, the November 2002 protests over a newspaper article connecting the Prophet Muhammad to the Miss World beauty pageant did not escalate into more violence in Nigeria only because this declaration had real influence in the community and bound it to peace.[78]

Shortly thereafter, Imam Ashafa and Pastor James also succeeded in bringing together the two warring communities of Plateau State, the nomadic Fulani cattle rearers and the native Beroms. First, they arranged to hold talks in the neutral location of Lokoja in Kogi State. This served to break sustained hostilities, and Imam Ashafa and Pastor James actively facilitated the mediation process between the Fulani and Beroms. By February 2003, both parties had started a healing process, and progress toward creating a pragmatic solution to their conflict was reported.

More recently, in 2006, after a number of European newspapers printed cartoons that negatively portrayed the Prophet Muhammad, the men were instrumental in keeping the peace in Kaduna even as the cartoons triggered extremely violent outrage elsewhere throughout Nigeria. Through a press release by the Interfaith Mediation Centre and joint statements with the local government, the *Peacemakers* made it clear that inciting violence is not only against the law but also against religion. Today, Pastor James and Imam Ashafa are traveling throughout the country and working within the Interfaith Mediation Centre's national network of trained conflict management practitioners to help ensure peace amid the tensions surrounding upcoming elections in 2007.

At the time of this writing, these two tireless peace activists have begun to expand their work even beyond the borders of Nigeria. In Burundi, they helped an interfaith group develop a faith-based approach to peacebuilding. They are also working to forge a pan-African network of religiously motivated peacemakers designed as a regional model of the Tanenbaum Center's *Peacemakers in Action* initiative. Their vision is clear: it is to be a regional collaboration that will involve trained activists who can be mobilized and will support each other's efforts throughout Africa.

Nigeria has been plagued by ethnic and religious tensions for as long as it has existed as an independent state. As it struggles to evolve as a democracy, to establish itself economically, and to fight corruption, the country faces a serious threat of increased interreligious violence. For the "Pastor and the Imam," religion was once an excuse for violence. Today as brothers, religion is their answer to peace. Through fearlessness, sacrifice, and remarkable perseverance, these Nigerian *Peacemakers* are forging their own path by creating possibilities for peace grounded through putting into practice interreligious respect for our differences, and our commonalities.

APPENDIX: Kaduna Peace Declaration of Religious Leaders, August 22, 2002[79]

Kaduna, Nigeria

In the name of God, who is Almighty, Merciful and Compassionate, we who have gathered as Muslim and Christian religious leaders from Kaduna State pray for peace in our state and declare our commitment to ending the violence and bloodshed, which has marred our recent history.

According to our faith, killing innocent lives in the names of God is a desecration of His Holy Name, and defames religions in the World. The violence that has occurred in Kaduna State is an evil that must be opposed by all people of good faith. We seek to live together as neighbours, respecting the integrity of each other's historical and religious heritage. We call upon all to oppose incitement, hatred, and the misrepresentation of one another.

1) Muslim and Christians of all tribes must respect the divinely ordained purposes of the Creator by whose grace we live together in Kaduna State, such ordained purposes include freedom of worship, access to and sanctity of places of worship and justice among others.

2) As religious leaders, we seek to work with all sections of the community for a lasting and just peace according to the teachings of our religions.

3) We condemn all forms of violence and seek to create an atmosphere where present and future generations will co-exist with mutual respect and trust in one another. We call upon all to refrain from incitement and demonization, and pledge to educate our young people accordingly.

4) Through the creation of a peaceful state we seek to explore how together we can aid spiritual regeneration, economic development and inward investment.

5) We acknowledge the efforts that have been made within this State for a judicial reform and pledge to do all in our power to promote greater understanding of the reform, so that it can provide a true and respected justice in each of our communities.

6) We pledge to work with the security forces in peace keeping and implementation of this Declaration in the State.

7) We announce the establishment of a permanent joint committee to implement the recommendations of this declaration and encourage dialogue between the two faiths for we believe that dialogue will result in the restoration of the image of each in the eyes of the other.

This declaration is binding on all people in the State from this day of 22nd August 2002 and [it is] agree[d that] any individual or group found breaching the peace must be punished in accordance to the due process of the law.

NIGERIA FACT SHEET[80]

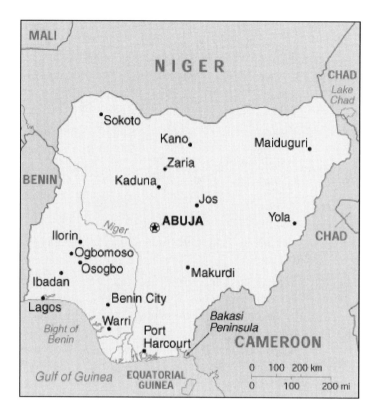

Geography

Location:	Western Africa, bordering the Gulf of Guinea, between Benin and Cameroon.
Area:	*Total:* 923,768 sq km *Land:* 910,768 sq km *Water:* 13,000 sq km
Area comparative:	Slightly more than twice the size of the U.S. state of California.
Climate:	Equatorial in south, tropical in center, arid in north.

Population

Population:	128,771,988 (July 2005 est.)

Ethnic groups:	Hausa and Fulani:	29%
	Yoruba:	21%
	Igbo (Ibo):	18%
	Ijaw:	10%
	Kanuri:	4%
	Ibibio:	3.5%
	Tiv:	2.5%
Religions:	Muslim:	50%
	Christian:	40%
	Indigenous beliefs:	10%
Languages:	English (official), Hausa, Yoruba, Igbo, Fulani.	

Government

Government type:	Republic transitioning from military to civilian rule.
Capital:	Abuja
	Note: In December 1991, the capital was officially moved from Lagos to Abuja. Many government offices remain in Lagos pending completion of facilities in Abuja.
Legal system:	Based on English common law, Islamic law, and tribal law.

Recent Background

Nigeria achieved its independence from the British in 1960. But political instability, a result of long-standing ethnic and religious tensions, characterized life in Nigeria for nearly forty years, until 1998. That year, sixteen years of military rule came to an end, and a process of peaceful transition to civilian government began. In 1999, Nigeria adopted a new constitution and elected former General Olusegun Obasanjo to the presidency. And in April 2003, President Obasanjo was reelected in Nigeria's first civilian-administered election in two decades. The president continues to face the daunting task of institutionalizing democracy and battling corruption and mismanagement.

Economic Overview

The failure of Nigeria's former military rulers to expand the economy beyond a focus on the oil sector has left oil accounting for 20 percent of the Gross Domestic Product (GDP), 95 percent of foreign exchange earnings, and about 65 percent of budgetary revenues. The agricultural sector, largely subsistence-based, has been unsuccessful in keeping up with rapid population growth. As a result, Nigeria, once a large net exporter of food, must now import to meet its needs. By signing an IMF agreement in August 2000, Nigeria received a

$1 billion credit, conditional on economic reforms. In 2003, a new economic policy was initiated that included the privatization of the country's oil refineries, deregulation of fuel prices, and the implementation of the National Economic Empowerment Strategy for fiscal and monetary management. In October 2005, Nigeria reached an agreement with its Paris Club creditors that reduced its debt by 60 percent, with the other 40 percent to be paid gradually through oil windfalls. This frees up at least $1 billion each year for poverty reduction programs.

10 The Power of Organization

Alimamy Koroma

Sierra Leone

Throughout the 1990s and into the first years of the twenty-first century, Sierra Leone was plagued by a bitter and gruesome civil war that disrupted the country's diamond industry and further increased poverty and violence throughout the country. Tens of thousands of rapes, amputations, and murders turned this West African nation into the site of some of the world's most unspeakable brutality.

The Sierra Leone conflict can be traced to the nation's history of economic inequality, greed, and corruption. It can be traced also to tribal and ethnic power struggles that emerged when European colonization began and continue today. Interestingly, the conflict was not driven by the religious differences of its people. Sierra Leone has a limited history of interreligious hostility, and its tolerance for different religions actually permeates much of the country's culture. Interreligious respect is the frequent experience of people at all levels, including in villages and within families, who often have extended relatives of differing religious beliefs.[1] Perhaps as a result, it was natural for *Peacemaker* Alimamy P. Koroma to draw on religion as a tool for establishing peace for the people of his country.

Indeed, with the aid of religious peacemakers such as Koroma, Sierra Leone is slowly emerging from an era of violence. As someone born into a Muslim family who later converted to Christianity, Koroma is uniquely positioned to tap into the good relations that have existed between Christians and Muslims and to inspire them to collaborate and address conflicts in his wartorn region.

Although Koroma's peacemaking work is personal, his efforts are largely visible through the organizations with which he works. It all began when the Christian Council of Churches Sierra Leone provided him with the legitimacy and wherewithal to establish the Inter-Religious Council of Sierra Leone. During the dark days when it seemed nearly impossible for the government and guerrilla groups to communicate effectively to end the civil war, it was Koroma and his Inter-Religious Council that were largely responsible for keeping the conversations going, while representing the voice of the common people.

When Koroma describes his work, it becomes clear that he positioned the Inter-Religious Council as a bridge between the government and the guerrilla groups. In his words: "at the Council, we came together as religious leaders of both [Christian and Muslim traditions] and agreed to work on issues that unite us, namely: no violence, peace, reconciliation . . . we engaged ourselves . . . [this is] not an easy exercise."[2] But even though it was not easy, Koroma persisted and the work of the Inter-Religious Council became a striking example of the power of grassroots peacemaking as a form of Track Two diplomacy.

In the current post–civil war years, Alimamy P. Koroma has moved beyond his days of bringing different groups together to mediate the resolution of seemingly intractable conflicts. Today, his passion is building community life beyond war through a range of creative strategies. His story is one of vision, perseverance, and action.

Sierra Leone at the Time of European Contact

When the Portuguese first came to Sierra Leone in 1460, they found at least seventeen ethnic groups, with the Temne, Mende, and Limba in the majority[3] (today the Temne and Mende together comprise about 60 percent of the population whereas 10 percent of the population is Creole and the balance comes from different native tribes).[4] Politics and culture in those precolonial days were dominated by kings working in close consultation with various chiefs, subchiefs, councils of elders, and members of royal families.[5] They presided over various ethnic tribes, which had migrated to the area over time due to wars, displacement, or a search for more fertile land.[6]

When the Portuguese arrived, change was inevitable. These foreigners came to trade in African products and slaves, and the slave trade proved disruptive. Ethnic and class-based hostilities were exacerbated as groups sought to consolidate power by forcing others into slavery. The Portuguese did not leave a strong cultural imprint on the area, but they did leave behind a name for the land: *Serra Lyoa*, or

Lion Mountains, after the striking range that dominates the country's peninsula.[7]

By the early sixteenth century, Portugal lost its monopoly on trade with Sierra Leone, as wider European involvement in the area grew. The post–Portuguese period saw the expansion of international trade, with commerce in slaves becoming an ever increasing element of regional economic activity. Tribal migrations (not uncommon in the region) continued during this period, highlighted by a mass migration of Mande-speaking people into Sierra Leone from Liberia in the south.[8]

Over the next two hundred years, other Mande-speaking people joined with Fulani-speaking people from the Fouta Djallon region of modern day Guinea and moved into the northern part of Sierra Leone, converting many local Temne to Islam.[9] By the late eighteenth century, when the British began to arrive in large numbers, most of the country's people were practicing Islam or traditional African religions. The influx of the British put new pressures on these realities, religiously, ethnically, and culturally.[10]

The Creoles Arrive

In the 1780s during the British abolitionist movement, English philanthropists bought land from the Temne in Sierra Leone and began using it as a home for liberated slaves (the first Creoles), many of whom had been granted freedom after fighting in the British Army during the American Revolutionary War. From the perspective of the Temnes, however, the land was not really sold. Rather, they were only giving the newcomers permission to stay on the land because, within their culture, land cannot be "owned."[11] Naturally, this led to tensions.

There are conflicting views as to why the liberated slaves were brought to Sierra Leone. Some scholars credit the British with an altruistic desire to provide former slaves with their own home, whereas others see a racist effort to locate former slaves far from England (and also from the United States – for Americans later joined the English in these efforts). Another explanation lies in the religious zeal among British Christians who – as described by Sierra Leone historians Earl Conteh-Morgan and Mac Dixon-Fyle – saw the placement of a community of Christian freed-slaves as a means to "bring light to what was generally considered a benighted continent."[12]

Regardless of the true motivation, the first community of Creoles in the newly established Freetown, or "Province of Freedom," was doomed by unaccustomed diseases, poor crop performance, and hostility from tribes whose cultures they did not understand. In fact, the original settlement was completely destroyed after being caught in the middle of a dispute between a local tribal king and slave traders. The settlers were forced to take shelter among those whom they saw as inferior people: the local indigenous residents.[13] Over time, however, the Creoles adjusted to life in the new land, which was heavily influenced by the British-controlled Sierra Leone Company. From 1808 to 1864, when they were joined by liberated slaves from Nova Scotia, the United States, Jamaica, and England, the Creole community grew both in population and economic strength.[14]

In 1808, Freetown became an official British Crown Colony from which the Gold Coast (now Ghana) was governed. The Temne had officially lost their land to the Sierra Leone Company, which had quelled their attempted attacks on Freetown and quashed their demands to resume control of the land.[15] As a result, Sierra Leone's political identity evolved, though its sense of national identity was far from cohesive. Western influences, promoted by the British and the Creoles, mixed uneasily with local culture.

Although Creoles could trace their roots to all parts of Africa, they had been cut off from African life, sometimes for centuries. When they came to Sierra Leone, they brought knowledge and experiences of Western life and culture, including Christianity and a Creole language (the African-American English of the time period). For the Creoles, success would not involve living as their indigenous neighbors lived. Rather, it came to be measured by differentiation from the poor and indigenous groups, and by preferences for two-story homes and Western-style dress.[16] When the first Western-style university in sub-Saharan Africa, Fourah Bay College, was founded in 1827, members of the Creole community made up most of the students in attendance.

The community endeavored to maintain its cohesiveness in the face of its tribal neighbors. Nonetheless, divisions among the Creoles formed. An elite class emerged, and lower-class Creoles living in the villages outside of Freetown were often regarded with disdain by their urban Creole neighbors. Ultimately, the community divided according to their differing religious beliefs and practices, education, and culture.[17]

Even though they were a small minority in Sierra Leone, the British and Creoles held almost all the power and continued to extend their influence. During the nineteenth century, they captured indigenous African territory in the country's interior. Sometimes using violence to establish control, they expanded trade and sought the conversion of the predominantly Islamic and indigenous peoples to Christianity. Ultimately, the British successfully coerced many African kings and their people to become "protected persons," whose territories would be governed under an official British protectorate established in August 1896. But what followed was not exactly what the people had expected. Former African kings had to take lower level positions in the government, and the protectorate imposed taxes. The resulting furor exploded into the Hut Tax War of 1898. Many homes and crops were destroyed, but British power remained entrenched.[18]

By the beginning of the 1900s, the Creole community began losing some of its power and status, as others in the protectorate became more educated and took on new political and societal roles. Overall, however, many in the country remained laborers. By the late 1930s, almost seventeen thousand African laborers were working in European-owned – and often very dangerous – mines. They were paid little for their efforts, yet the fruits of their labor contributed to over half of the country's exports by the 1940s.[19]

During the first half of the twentieth century, there were several attempts to organize a revolt against the British and Creole elite, but each was unsuccessful. This movement had an impact, however, and following World War II, a constitution was adopted in 1951 that granted majority-rule rights to the people of the protectorate and provided greater representation to the African chiefs.[20] Following the adoption of the constitution, the country (still a protectorate) held its first elections that same year. Dr. Milton Margai of the largely Mende-based Sierra Leone People's Party (SLPP) claimed victory.

It was to take another ten years, but in 1961 the movement for self-rule finally reached its true goal, and Sierra Leone celebrated complete independence.[21] This was not achieved without a price. The years leading to independence were marked with rioting and attacks protesting low pay, unfair taxation, political corruption, and the lack of opportunity for indigenous entrepreneurship – issues that would continue to influence the political climate for years to come.[22]

Sierra Leone Becomes a Nation-State

When Milton Margai died in 1964, his brother Albert Margai succeeded him. Three years later, Margai lost power in the general elections of 1967 and was replaced by Siaka P. Stevens of the Temne-based All People's Congress party (APC).[23] However, a coup ousted Stevens minutes after he took office, and the next year was punctuated by coups backed by different parties grasping at power. In 1968, Stevens regained his position and became prime minister. After changing the parliamentary system of Sierra Leone to a republic in 1971, Stevens was appointed president.[24]

Stevens quickly seized the lumber trade and most of the mining industry, which dealt primarily in diamonds. The APC's sweep of the 1973 elections created a *de facto* one-party state – a situation that Stevens formalized through a referendum in 1978. Appeased by government positions that Stevens had created for them, the opposition did not respond with widespread protest.[25]

Despite Stevens's attempts to solidify power and squelch opposition, his popularity declined as living conditions worsened. In 1981, a national strike expressed the depth of the public's discontent. And several years later, in 1985, Stevens submitted to public pressure and bequeathed his position to General Joseph Saidu Momoh, whom he had groomed to take power.[26]

Civil War

Soon after taking office, President Momoh declared an economic state of emergency, levied a surcharge on imports, and reduced government salaries. However, living conditions continued to plummet, unrest grew, and rebel groups gathered strength on Sierra Leone's borders. By 1991, what was to become a particularly notorious rebel group known as the Revolutionary United Front (RUF), based in neighboring Liberia, occupied two eastern border towns.[27] It quickly took control of the diamond mines in the Kono District and received substantial support from disaffected Sierra Leoneans from within and outside of the country. This event marked the beginning of serious guerrilla activity and an almost eleven-year civil war.[28]

Shortly after the insurgency began, the International Monetary Fund (IMF) sought to reform Sierra Leone's foundering economy, in which the vast majority of its citizens lived below the poverty line and income distribution was one of the most unequal in the world.[29] As President Momoh faced the IMF-imposed fiscal management procedures, he and those in the All People's Congress reverted back to a multiparty system in 1992, but quickly found that the people no longer trusted them or their intentions. Seven months later, a coup rocked the country and Captain Valentine Strasser and the National Provisional Ruling Council (NPRC) seized power on the premise that they would end the war and foster democratization and economic expansion.[30] The Strasser regime started with vast infrastructure improvements, but the pace of these early successes quickly slowed, as the situation in Sierra Leone continued to deteriorate.[31]

Violence was everywhere. The Revolutionary United Front (RUF) led by Foday Sankoh, caused much of the conflict and was charged with unprecedented human rights violations. As journalist David Johnson describes:

> The RUF quickly earned a savage reputation, as they amputated limbs of civilians, routinely raped women and girls and abducted boys to join their army. Young recruits were often forced to rape or kill a family member, thus preventing a return to their previous lives. RUF young soldiers were often forcibly injected with cocaine before going into battle.[32]

By 1995, Sierra Leone was engulfed by a horrific civil war.

An Interlude: Foday Sankoh, Leader of the Rebels

Foday Sankoh died of a stroke on June 30, 2003, while awaiting trial in a UN court for crimes against humanity. Many Sierra Leoneans regretted his merciful death, as he was intensely hated by the population at large for having created and commanded their country's most powerful – and most sinister – rebel group. Although many of his followers referred to him as "Papa," Sankoh's capture on May 17, 2000 triggered an outburst of cheering and dancing throughout Freetown,[33] whereas his burial a few years later brought out much anger, including one woman who was heard to shout, "Take his body to hell or give it to us, the crowd, to burn . . . to ashes."[34]

Sankoh had started out as an outspoken critic of the corruption plaguing Sierra Leone in the 1970s. A former Army Corporal, photographer, and TV cameraman, Sankoh attacked the military and political elite for plundering the nation's wealth and driving the people into poverty. His antigovernment views and alleged role in a 1971 coup attempt lost him his job as a cameraman and led to a brief stint in prison.[35]

Soon after, Sankoh joined a group of exiles in Libya and met Muammar al-Qaddafi, who was recruiting West African dissidents to his revolutionary ideology. Sankoh also met the future president of Liberia, Charles Taylor, whose later financial support enabled him to launch his insurrectionist campaign from Liberia. With two other comrades, Sankoh founded the RUF with the goal of ending the corrupt, military-run political system in Sierra Leone.[36] With Taylor's support, he attacked in 1991, marking the beginning of the civil war. As reported by Derek Brown in *The Guardian*, it was shortly thereafter that "the RUF imposed its will in the interior of the impoverished country with systematic barbarity. Its ragtag forces, including a high proportion of press-ganged and brutalized children, became notorious for abduction, gang rape and summary execution."[37]

The RUF had quickly degenerated into a multiethnic, multireligious band of poor, young men who sustained themselves by looting the countryside.[38] As noted, Sankoh and the RUF resorted to inhuman tactics, especially including sexual violence targeting women and girls. *Human Rights Watch* observes:

> These crimes of sexual violence were generally characterized by extraordinary brutality and frequently preceded or followed by other egregious human rights abuses against the victim, her family and her community. The rebels abducted many women and girls, who were subjected to sexual violence as well as being forced to perform housework, farm work and serve as military porters. The rebels sought to dominate women and their communities by deliberately undermining cultural values and community relationships, destroying the ties that hold society together. Child combatants raped women who were old enough to be their grandmothers, rebels raped pregnant and breastfeeding mothers, and fathers were forced to watch their daughters being raped.[39]

At least fifty thousand died (with some reports claiming two hundred thousand). Approximately 250,000 fled into exile during RUF's campaign of violence. Meanwhile, Taylor's faction in Liberia supported RUF's efforts and, unhampered by competition from Sierra Leone, Liberia's diamond revenues steadily mounted.[40]

The International Community Intervenes

There was a moment of hope in the midst of all this bloodshed – a fleeting promise of redemption after a coup that began, unexpectedly, to restore order. In 1996, Brigadier-General Julius Maada Bio assumed power in a bloodless coup and surprised the world three months later by peacefully handing the reins over to an elected civilian government headed by Ahmad Tejan Kabbah.[41] In November of that year, Kabbah signed the Abidjan Peace Accord with the RUF, but the rebels soon failed to abide by the agreement. Government soldiers led by Lt. Col. Johnny Paul Koroma (the Armed Forces Revolution Council [AFRC]) then aligned with the RUF in 1997 in an effort to take power. Kabbah, unable to control the military, was overthrown.[42]

The year 1998 proved to be a turning point. The Military Observer Group of the Economic Community of West African States (ECOMOG) restored order under the banner of the UN, as Charles Taylor ascended to the presidency in Liberia. Foday Sankoh was arrested and sentenced to death, and President Kabbah was reinstated. Kabbah continued to pursue an end to the violence and negotiated the Lomé Peace Accords in 1999. As a peace overture, he pardoned Sankoh and offered to give him the position of vice president in the government with control over the diamond mines, despite a UN resolution prohibiting Sankoh from traveling without its permission.

Once again, the peace did not last long. The RUF violated the Lomé Accords shortly after signing them. Ramping up guerrilla warfare, the RUF took hostages, and attempted a costly, although unsuccessful, coup. The RUF captured several hundred ECOMOG soldiers, and fighting erupted in the interior. Meanwhile, ECOMOG and the UN, with strong British support, continued interventions into 2000. That same year, Sankoh was arrested again in Freetown after his soldiers gunned down a crowd that was protesting the RUF; soon after, he was put on trial for crimes against humanity.

The fighting continued as the government and rebels entered into peace talks, and the UN called for disarmament.[43] Finally, after signing two agreements in Abuja, Nigeria that detailed a program for disarmament, demobilization, and reintegration (DDR), President Kabbah announced the end of the civil war in January 2002. The DDR program helped to maintain security in the country and better reintegrate ex-combatants into their communities.

Alimamy P. Koroma and the Inter-Religious Council of Sierra Leone

In 1997, after Kabbah had been deposed as president and while Lt. Col. Johnny Paul Koroma was ruling the country, another (unrelated) Koroma was helping to found a nongovernmental initiative called the Inter-Religious Council of Sierra Leone. Often referred to as the Inter-Religious Council, Alimamy Koroma's group is a national chapter of the World Conference on Religion and Peace (WCRP).

Koroma was born in July 1959 in the Kambia District of Northern Sierra Leone. Growing up as a child who was one of the only Muslims in a Baptist school, Koroma knew what it felt like to be from a religious minority. As an adult, this experience continued to affect his thinking, even as his religious beliefs evolved. In pursuing his studies, first in agricultural education and later in development planning, Koroma attended universities in Japan, Germany, Ghana, as well as Sierra Leone. However, it was while teaching at a secondary school in the northern province of his country that Koroma had a life-defining moment, when he met a Baptist minister and the minister's daughter, Linda. Koroma, although "com[ing] from a Muslim background," was converted to Christianity in 1985 by Linda and "with [the] support of [my] family." Soon after, Alimamy married Linda and they established their own family. Today, they proudly boast of their three children. In describing his wife, Koroma says: "Linda was my transformation."[44]

Soon after marriage, Koroma became a Baptist worker himself and in the year of his conversion joined the Christian Council of Churches in Sierra Leone. There, he immediately established himself, initially serving in the development section before quickly moving up the ranks and becoming its secretary general ten years later. It was during those ten years that war broke out in neighboring Liberia. Refugees poured into Sierra Leone, often stopping for help at the churches. Alongside of his duties in the development section, therefore, Koroma started the Council of Church's Relief and Rehabilitation Department (today, its biggest department) in order to provide assistance to refugees and internally displaced people.

It is perhaps this background – as first a Muslim, then a Christian, and very quickly immersed in helping those afflicted by conflict – that uniquely suited him for leadership of the Inter-Religious Council. While still serving as the Council of Church's Secretary General in 1996, he leveraged the respect he had earned among the civilian population, the government, and the rebels – as well as the resources he had acquired from the WCRP – to start the Inter-Religious Council. Koroma was no longer satisfied with simply reacting to the war. He was ready to proactively address the violence at its core.

When the Inter-Religious Council of Sierra Leone officially launched on April 1, 1997, Koroma served as its secretary general with no pay, while maintaining his position at the Council of Churches. But with determination, he led the Inter-Religious Council as an informally structured organization that aids and supports the independent projects of its members. Its members include both Christian and Muslim individuals and institutions, who collaborate as partners in one another's endeavors and draw on the Council's religious resources to strengthen their work.

Koroma reflects that he had "worked in humanitarian assistance" before becoming involved in the Inter-Religious Council. Despite recognizing that his work with the refugees and internally displaced persons was critically important, he says that he "realized it wasn't changing the situation, but rather sustaining it."[45] It was this understanding that formed Koroma's thinking and defined his leadership of the Inter-Religious Council, which has adopted a broad vision and commitment to changing daily life by resolving conflicts and building a society in which peace can thrive. He notes that when the organization was created, "the leadership of the Council [of Churches] decided to tackle the war itself, not just the casualties of war."[46]

The Inter-Religious Council has been able to wield remarkable influence in a relatively short time and to emerge unscathed from some quite dangerous situations. The reason, Koroma suggests, is that the organization and its work are protected by divine intervention. It has also benefited from considerable human energy.

Soon after its founding, Koroma and the Inter-Religious Council launched campaigns to sensitize the civilian population, members of parliament, tribal chiefs, students, journalists, and youth organizations to the real consequences of war on people's lives. As Koroma wisely states, "when everyone is sensitized, our governments begin to sit up straight."[47] Through these campaigns, the organization gained a reputation for being neutral and for effecting collaboration among Christian and Muslim communities so that they would both work toward a just peace in Sierra Leone.

A Policy of Neutrality and a Focus on the Average Citizen

Koroma understands the importance of being known as effective and fair. To protect that reputation, therefore, members of the Inter-Religious Council consciously committed themselves to pursuing peace in a spirit of neutrality. This turned out to be a very challenging undertaking. Koroma points this out by posing questions: "Where there is conflict or war, the level of mistrust is so high. How do you build confidence?" And, "How do we be nonpartisan but at the same time NOT be truthful to the issues? It is very difficult to balance the two."[48] He recounts an incident that illustrates the difficulty of negotiating these challenges each day in Sierra Leone:

> Just before the January 6th, 1998 [coup that restored Kabbah to the presidency], there were demonstrations against RUF as a number of expatriates were being evacuated. Though [members of the Inter-Religious Council] agreed the evacuation was wrong and agreed with demonstrators on their content, we did not agree on their execution, their methodology. There was supposed to be a peaceful demonstration, but we tested the temperature and [so] we knew [what] a demonstration at this time would lead to.
>
> So we asked, "Is it wise to have a demonstration at this time?" This is what happened: People took advantage of the situation, and two innocent people were burnt alive by the demonstrators. They were accused of being RUF supporters and were burnt alive, just as a result...and at least one of them was discovered to not be an RUF supporter.[49]

If he or the Inter-Religious Council had supported such a demonstration, Koroma maintains, they could have lost their credibility. And that would have prevented them from accomplishing their peacemaking goals during the years that followed.

In his work, Koroma is "influenced by [his] confidence and hope in ordinary people."[50] He therefore focuses his work at both the Inter-Religious Council and the Christian Council of Churches on the effect that war has had on the average citizen of Sierra Leone. He believes that a sustainable peace can be created only by taking account of the damage and injury average citizens have endured and then by building upon the people's own resources. Koroma explains:

> Over the years I came to learn and realize that human resource is the greatest asset in any community. When properly developed and motivated, the human resource can bring about the other components for sustainability of activities. From our experience of war in Sierra Leone, I see that developing local manpower needs emphasis, especially when, during heightened moments of problems, expatriate personnel are evacuated, leaving behind nationals. There should therefore [be] an investment in developing the potential of local manpower.[51]

Among the most valuable of the local people's own resources is their attitude toward one another's religion (the country is primarily Muslim [60 percent]; about 10 percent, mostly Creoles, are Christian; and the balance follow traditional religions). Koroma says of his achievements during the peace process, "[w]e have been able to do what we have done because of religious tolerance."[52] He continues, "In Sierra Leone, religion is very central. People may not appear too religious but they respect religion and religious leaders. A combination of these virtues coupled with the high level of religious tolerance creates a solid platform for common action by religious leaders. [Our work] has been possible because we accept and respect each other."[53]

Others would agree that interreligious cooperation has been a core theme in Sierra Leone's journey to peace. According to Thomas Mark Turay, a leader in community-based development in Sierra Leone, it was the voices of local religious leaders that moved the country away from the spiraling violence:

> Ordinary Muslims and Christians began to urge their religious leaders to act to end the violence and they in turn condemned the war and urged the RUF to lay down its arms. Churches and mosques around the country preached against the barbaric nature of the violence, prompting rebel forces to target religious leaders and institutions.... As the attacks intensified, it became evident that Muslims and Christians needed to cooperate to a greater extent and use their religious influence and mandate to prevail on both the rebels and the government to find peaceful resolution.[54]

Having established a reputation for inspiring greater cooperation among people from different religious traditions, the Inter-Religious Council was able to initiate communication with both rebel and government leaders. In late May 1997, less than two months after starting the Inter-Religious Council, Koroma became aware of growing tensions in the north. In an attempt to avert a surge in violence, he alerted President Kabbah. "We wanted to ensure he [had] the information. I advised him about the position in the upsurge of tensions and fighting in the north. [Our] intensions were to increase his awareness."[55] But this information did not stop the violence. Only two days later, the coup that was to overthrow Kabbah achieved its objectives.

"The religious community did not support...[the coup, and] religious leaders stayed home in protest and looked to each other for our strength."[56] These were tense times. But because Koroma and the Inter-Religious Council had access to the highest levels of government, they were able to conduct dialogues with government and rebel leaders. Listening carefully to both sides, Koroma and the Inter-Religious Council also made clear that they condemned human rights abuses on all sides. Turay notes that during 1997, "there is little doubt that the Council's high visibility and engagement...prevented greater abuses against civilians."[57]

Religion had neither caused nor nurtured the conflict in Sierra Leone, but the people had trust and confidence in their religious leaders. As embodied in the Inter-Religious Council, Koroma and other grassroots religious figures became a powerful force in resolving disputes. In other conflicts around the world, religious leaders often seek peace by urging their people to repent for wrongs they have committed against one another. In Sierra Leone, religious practitioners began by assuming the burden of rectifying wrongs in which they had never participated and staying with the people, throughout the process on the ground.

Koroma notes that religious leaders are positioned to play a unique role, different from other types of peacemakers. "The United Nations, etc., disappoint people, they do not deliver." In contrast, he observes that "Religious leaders/Churches/Mosques did not flee in Sierra Leone during the war." Rather, "They remained behind to inspire us that all was not lost. We still work with people to say that all is not lost."[58] In addition to having credibility because their commitment had staying power, religious leaders had something else. They were close to the conflict and able to understand its impact directly.

Mediating Peace Talks

The Inter-Religious Council's high visibility came with a cost. Some Sierra Leoneans saw revenge as the only way to stop the RUF, and they were enraged by the Inter-Religious Council's policies of nonviolence and reconciliation. In January 1999, several members of the Inter-Religious Council were attacked. Although they subsequently recovered, this incident reminded Koroma and the other members of the Council that when they spoke for peace, they risked their lives.

Not surprisingly, risk was a daily reality that haunted their families, and Koroma recognized how trying this was for them. "I also sacrificed my family because everybody was so concerned," Koroma reflects, "there was a time, I remember when I got arrested. . . . I was interviewed by BBC, [but my family hadn't been notified yet] and I could just imagine when they found out, how broken down they must have been."[59] Yet Koroma is quick to point out that, not only does his family support him, but their willingness to do so – notwithstanding the danger – provided incentive for others to do the same. "Because I didn't flee, that provide a lot of courage and moral guidance to the people who I see around. People would say, 'Is Alimamy around?' [My family] would say, 'yes, he's around,' and they'd say 'Ok, I guess I'll stay.' I risked, but my family also contributed . . ."[60]

Despite the dangers, Koroma did not waver. When the RUF invaded and overtook Freetown in January 1999, Koroma and the Inter-Religious Council intensified their campaign for dialogue between the government and rebels. By February, UN Special Envoy Francis Okelo was encouraging Koroma and the organization to begin that conversation between the reinstated President Kabbah and Foday Sankoh. Both the rebels and the government trusted the Inter-Religious Council, believing that Koroma and his organization would ensure fair negotiations.

Koroma responded to Okelo's request in the affirmative and attended the resulting dialogues with other members of the Inter-Religious Council, where he acted as a consultant to both sides and as a procedural guarantor. Throughout this effort, Koroma and his colleagues made sure to inform both sides of all meetings with the other, while declaring their own neutrality and maintaining a commitment to addressing all of the issues, regardless of how difficult they might be. As Koroma notes, Sankoh "listened to us and the population had confidence [in us] because I believe we were transparent about our activities."[61] Kadi Sassey, head of the Human Rights Commission in Sierra Leone, praised their involvement, saying, "The Inter-Religious Council made it possible for the rebels to talk with the government."[62] Utilizing its position to influence the course of the dialogue, by the end of February, the Inter-Religious Council found it necessary to warn the government to talk less and listen more. They also urged the parties to let the people of Sierra Leone hear the positions of the RUF and its allies.

During these difficult times, it was the children who were frequently pawns in the conflict. Many, including some as young as four, were being abducted from their villages and taken to the bush to join the RUF. Fully understanding the challenges of getting caught in the middle, the Council nonetheless began to seek the children's release. They started by using radios and were soon directly contacting the combatants hidden in the bush. Koroma concedes that this involved "... a lot of effort." But his efforts paid off. The combatants became convinced that the Council was sincere and neutral. Soon thereafter, they released 33 children "as a token to show commitment to continue working with the Inter-Religious Council."[63]

Perhaps to test their trustworthiness, the combatants invited members of the Inter-Religious Council to a face-to-face meeting in the bush. Koroma agreed. In keeping with his usual practices, he informed the government and, in early March, led a delegation from the Inter-Religious Council to meet with Sankoh and the RUF. Traveling by road and then by foot through dangerous territory, Koroma's delegation arrived at the agreed upon site. Gifts were exchanged and then the meeting began. The location was risky for everyone – for Koroma and the Inter-Religious Council, because they were traveling into the heart of land controlled by the RUF; for the RUF, which was risking the exposure of its military operations and secrets; and for the government, which was allowing the negotiations to occur in a location where it had no power. In fact, Koroma soon realized that the "security" he observed when he arrived in the bush was not there for their own protection but, rather, to take action against Koroma and his delegation, if it turned out to be necessary. Everyone had to invest some measure of trust even before the talks could begin. That the RUF called for the meeting and the government agreed to it happening, is a testament to the Inter-Religious Council's ability to function with neutrality and to the respect it was accorded by both sides.

The results validated the risks. During the meeting, Sankoh announced to Koroma and the delegation that he was willing to negotiate peace, and he explained how he thought negotiations should take place. The delegation, in turn, asked for Sankoh to demonstrate his commitment to peace by authorizing the release of some abducted children and child soldiers. Before agreeing to this gesture of good faith, Sankoh made a final request that the Inter-Religious Council provide food, medicine, and other humanitarian assistance to the rebels. The delegation agreed and arranged for the delivery of clothing, blankets, and sanitary kits to surrendered rebel soldiers, as well as food to civilians. Koroma recalls what happened next:

> These activities helped to consolidate real confidence and thus marked the beginning of actual dialogue between the RUF and the government of Sierra Leone through the facilitation of the Inter-Religious Council.[64]

Susbsequently, Koroma brokered a radio conversation between Sankoh and his field commanders, which ended with the rebel commanders releasing an additional twenty-one of the abducted children.

Koroma's impact reaches beyond Sierra Leone, just as the conflict in his country has had implications for a much wider region. Koroma led a delegation of the Inter-Religious Council to neighboring Guinea and Liberia to meet with their counterparts, as well as the countries' political leaders. By the time he did this, it was already well known that Liberia's President Charles Taylor had been supporting the rebels in Sierra Leone, even though Taylor was denying those allegations. In an effort to stop him, the Inter-Religious Council met with Taylor. They presented an objective analysis of the conflict and emphasized how it related to the entire African subregion. Koroma stressed that a collective effort of Sierra

Leone, Liberia, and Guinea was required to effectively end the conflict and its reach throughout the region.

Perhaps unsurprisingly, the meeting inflamed civil society groups and ordinary Sierra Leoneans, many of whom felt strongly that negotiations with the enemies should not take place.[65] Yet, the Inter-Religious Council had a strong impact on Taylor. For the first time, he openly acknowledged his relationship with Foday Sankoh and the RUF. And from then on, Taylor's actions shifted "as if to clear his already dented message."[66] He agreed to participate in the peace process.

The Inter-Religious Council's Role in the Lomé Peace Accords

These events positioned Koroma and the Inter-Religious Council to serve as an important force in negotiations that took place in Lomé, Togo (held under the auspices of the UN and the Organization of African Unity), during which it continued to maintain a neutral posture. In fact, in addition to his role as secretary general, Koroma also served as coordinator and spokesperson on the peace process for the Inter-Religious Council. Here again, the Council members functioned as facilitators between the government and rebels whenever the parties encountered an impasse. When representatives of opposing sides appeared hopelessly obstinate, the Inter-Religious Council delegation kept their patience and worked overtime to bring together the most resistant parties.

Watching their work, U.S. Ambassador Joseph Melrose observed, "The Inter-Religious Council raised the concerns of the average Sierra Leonean. When things looked bad in the negotiations, they kept the dialogue going."[67] The Inter-Religious Council's activity was noticed by journalists as well. Turay described their work in the *Accord:*

> Among the numerous players involved in shaping the Lomé Peace Agreement, the Inter-religious Council of Sierra Leone stands out as the most highly visible and effective non-governmental bridge builder between the warring factions and a population devastated and divided by more than eight years of violence.[68]

The Inter-Religious Council remained active in the peace process until the Lomé Peace Accords were signed on July 7, 1999. Immediately after, they distributed thousands of free copies of the agreement to local civil society groups and international NGOs.

In many ways, this was the beginning of the next stage of Koroma's work. Through the Council, he continued working with ordinary Sierra Leoneans, holding "experience-sharing" sessions every two weeks, in which the people focused on how to move forward from the agreement. Those who attended the sessions came from different experiences and included RUF members, combatants, government officials, the media, NGOs, and, of course, everyday people.[69] Although the peace process suffered setbacks after Lomé, neither Koroma nor the Inter-Religious Council have slowed their efforts.

Reflections on Religiously Motivated Peacemaking: A Policy of Nonviolence, Forgiveness, and Reconciliation

Koroma founded the Inter-Religious Council to empower his people, who are threatened daily by violence. By developing a philosophy of resistance to violence, he helped to advance a vision of peace for Sierra Leoneans surrounded by hostility and destruction. In these efforts, Koroma drew on religious notions of forgiveness, urging parties to overcome their injury and resentment by means of reconciliation. At the same time, he realized his approach was not universally appreciated, even by those who shared his long-term vision:

> [P]erhaps as religious leaders, we are too bold for our civil society activists, in terms of our method, we are too compassionate, we are too endearing, or we are too tolerant with ex-combatants. . . . We tried to let [other activists] understand that our leaders, our style of work cannot be the same as others on the right, and [on the left], others who have been incited and who called for demonstrations. We will say that we are working toward the same goal, but our strategy is not to go in this way or in that way, but to behave as mature and legitimate leaders. So we have this sort of difficulty in that we are all headed towards the same goal. One is going by train and another one is going by bus, but we are all going to the same destination.[70]

Despite these criticisms, Koroma and the Inter-Religious Council remain committed to their core principles of forgiveness and reconciliation. It is this commitment, together with their steadfast nonpartisanship, that has gained them such high respect from the key leaders of the conflict. For Koroma, one of the most important lessons from the peace process was recognizing the value of his particular role, while also respecting the specific roles that everyone else played:

> We never claimed to have all the answers and to know it all. So we called upon the traditional leaders and parliamentarians, and we said to them, "you are the natural rulers." . . . If we went to them with our encyclopedia and we came to them as solicitors, perhaps we would not succeed in accomplishing [everything we did] . . . so this is our own way of getting

them on our side. We are also very open to sharing that and to sharing this, not for our own accomplishments. We are committed to soliciting permission from them and then keeping our mouth shut."[71]

Koroma's effectiveness thus came from functioning as a facilitator and convener, looking to participants to evolve solutions, and doing all this while giving – and not taking – the credit.

Koroma approached the conflict by first trying to stop the immediate harm. Thus, he has always insisted that the first priority must be to end the killing because only then can hope and reconstruction begin. Once the peace treaty was in place, and after many of the relief workers and international agencies had moved on, he threw himself into recreating a stable society. He is wise enough to note that, in many ways, this work requires even greater stamina than the work of bringing daily violence to an end. Speaking in 2005, he noted that there had been continuing changes in his country, "in particular, crisis and peace. My experience is that many times we're active, when there is conflict. When conflict is not active, we go home and relax and prepare for the second cycle of violence. In Sierra Leone, though the crisis has ended, we are involved and engaged in reconciliation, building new lives, reconciliation at both the top – politicians – and grassroots."[72]

To this end, Koroma is leading a series of innovative programs at the Christian Council of Churches in Sierra Leone to target some of the greatest threats to the postconflict climate. For example, in one initiative, Koroma addresses the problem that too many children have access to small arms:

> As part of our campaign against small arms, we're asking children with toy guns at school to disarm. The idea is to catch them young. We ask them to bring their toy weapons to the Council of Churches and we replace them with other toys and educational tools like crayons, footballs, etc. A lot of children have seen what arms can do. They see amputees and other maimed people all around them. They are getting the idea. They are beginning to say "I don't want a gun." The Council has also set up the Sierra Leone Action Network on Small Arms and brought other NGO's on board.[73]

But this is only one way in which Koroma and the Christian Council of Churches focus on young people. In a second program, the issue is sexual abuse:

> We run a human rights program for sexually abused children, to help them gain access to legal representation, and to help them return to normal life by linking them to agencies that provide support. We pursue the

perpetrators through the courts. We also provide support for the reintegration of young ex-combatants and girls displaced or otherwise affected
by the war.[74]

Since the end of the civil war, Koroma has also taken the lead to
address the needs of other vulnerable populations, for example HIV/AIDS
patients. Specifically, "we're sensitizing religious communities. At the
government hospital in Kenema District, we support a consulting unit
for people that have tested positive and need treatment. We also train
volunteer educators."[75]

And Koroma still remembers and works to address the needs of those
with whom he first worked when he established the Christian Council
of Churches' Relief and Rehabilitation Department. With the Council of
Churches, today he focuses on "the rights of Liberian refugee women and
supports their efforts to maintain their livelihoods in the camps in the
south and east."[76]

In addition to these varied programs for targeted populations, Koroma
is also working to address the destruction of the past. He therefore focuses
on preparing people who lived through war to live in peace. Koroma concentrates a great deal of energy on trauma and conflict transformation.
"There is a need for justice in our region now," Koroma says, "but when
some talk of justice, they're [often] really talking of revenge. What we
need is a restorative justice that will open up additional avenues ... the
kind of restorative justice that permits true reconciliation and supports
sustainable peace."[77]

Koroma uses resources wherever he finds them. During a trip to the
United States, he attended a program offered by the Church World Service called the Seminar on Trauma Awareness and Recovery (STAR).
Developed after the September 11 attacks on the World Trade Center,
STAR training is now conducted around the world to help people understand that the healing of trauma is a process and that it takes time to
achieve.[78] Koroma recognized that the program could be valuable for his
people and took it upon himself to bring STAR training to Sierra Leone,
the first country outside the United States to hold a training. With the
Council of Churches in Sierra Leone, Koroma first offered the trauma
counseling training in 2004 to men and women from Angola, Ghana,
Guinea, and Liberia, as well as Sierra Leone.

Koroma explains why this training is so important: "After the atrocities and destruction of civil society the Mano River Region has suffered,
people are crying out for a plan that goes beyond UN Peacekeeping
and the foundational work of Sierra Leone's Peace and Reconciliation

Commission." Koroma continues, "We intend to train ourselves and our fellow caregivers so they can go on and provide trauma healing in a way that encourages the kind of restorative justice that permits true reconciliation and supports sustainable peace."[79] Tirelessly, and through every avenue possible, Koroma continues his work today so that a lasting peace can be more than just a dream for his fellow Sierra Leoneans.

Moving Forward: The Future of Sierra Leone

Despite RUF's blatant violations of the Lomé Accords, the accords had a lasting impact on the country. Most notably, they led to the establishment of a Truth and Reconciliation Commission and set the stage for the later Abuja Agreements, which spelled out the "DDR process" for disarmament, demobilization, and reintegration. That same month, the UN imposed sanctions on Liberia for supporting Sierra Leone's war.

Several months after the government and rebels signed a declaration formally ending the war in January 2002, elections were held. Kabbah was reelected to serve another five-year term as president. Lamenting Sierra Leone's violence and suffering, President Kabbah declared that his country had endured "the most brutal warfare in the modern world."[80] In 2004, a UN War Crimes Tribunal was inaugurated in Sierra Leone and charged with bringing justice to victims of the brutal war and holding trials of some of the conflict's worst instigators.

After a difficult period of civil war and the departure of the last of the UN peacekeepers in 2005, the country's leaders, ever mindful of the perceived triumph in 1998, have tentatively declared that a chapter of peace may have truly begun for Sierra Leone. The ability of the government to reach stability (evidenced by the successful local elections held in 2004) and of its economy to recover depend largely on estranged groups reconciling and continuing to confront their grievances collaboratively and through dialogue rather than through violence. During this tender time in Sierra Leone's recovery, organizations such as the Truth and Reconciliation Commission and Alimamy Koroma's Inter-Religious Council will be critical to maintaining the commitment to peace, dialogue, and reconciliation. For Koroma and Sierra Leone there is only one true goal: "to write our history and say 'never again,' concerning the atrocities that occurred during the conflict."[81]

SIERRA LEONE FACT SHEET[82]

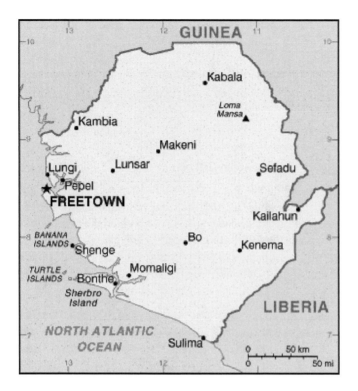

Geography

Location:	Western Africa, bordering the North Atlantic Ocean, between Guinea and Liberia.
Area:	*Total:* 71,740 sq km *Water:* 120 sq km *Land:* 71,620 sq km
Area comparative:	Slightly smaller than the U.S. state of South Carolina.
Climate:	Tropical; hot, humid; summer rainy season (May to December); winter dry season (December to April).

Population

Population:	6,017,643 (July 2005 est.)	
Ethnic Groups:	Temne:	30%
	Mende:	30%
	Other African Tribes:	30%
	Creole (Krio):	10%

Religions:	Muslim:	60%
	Indigenous beliefs:	30%
	Christian:	10%

| Languages: | English (official language), Mende (principal vernacular in the south), Temne (principal vernacular in the north), Krio. |

Government

Government Type:	Constitutional Democracy
Capital:	Freetown
Legal System:	Based on English law and customary laws indigenous to local tribes; has not accepted the jurisdiction of the International Court of Justice.

Background

Sierra Leone, meaning "Lion Mountains" in Portuguese, was founded by freed slaves in the late eighteenth century. The country was a British Protectorate from 1896 to 1961, when it gained independence. In 1991, a civil war was started between the government and the Revolutionary United Front (RUF), which led to tens of thousands of deaths and the creation of more than two million refugees and displaced people (roughly one-third of the population). The involvement of UN peacekeeping forces led to the disarmament of the RUF and government forces in 2002. Since then, the government has gradually been reestablishing its authority. However, the withdrawal of UN peacekeeping forces in Sierra Leone in 2005, along with the challenges of reconstruction, deteriorating conditions in neighboring Guinea, the shaky state of security in bordering Liberia, and mounting tensions related to planned 2007 elections, threaten to lead Sierra Leone to more instability.

Economic Overview

Sierra Leone has considerable agricultural, fish, and mineral resources – particularly diamonds. However, extreme poverty and inequality in income distribution continue to dominate the country. Following years of civil war, the country's economic and social infrastructure are poorly developed and serious social disorders persist. About two-thirds of the working-age population engages in subsistence agriculture. Manufacturing consists chiefly of the processing of raw materials and the production of light goods for the domestic market. The major source of hard currency consists of the mining of diamonds, whereas bauxite and rutile mines are opening again after a hiatus during the war. Still, the economy's development suffers severely from official corruption. The country's economic future is likely to depend on the maintenance of a stable peace, government competence and transparency, and continued foreign aid.

11 Israel and Palestine: A History

Located in the Middle East, modern-day Israel occupies land considered holy by several religious traditions. It borders the Mediterranean Sea to the west, Jordan to the east, lies between Lebanon and Syria in the north and Egypt in the south, and borders the Sinai Desert in the southwest and the Red Sea in the south.

For centuries, modern day Israel has been home to Jews, Christians, and Muslims – people who regard themselves as descendants of the biblical figure Abraham. A review of the history of these people reveals that their relations have evolved over time, responding to internal changes and changes on the world scene. Moreover, although faith is individually important to many Israeli Jews and Muslims, the present conflict is hardly reducible to religion alone. Political, economic, and cultural factors are also of the greatest importance.

No matter how discouraging the present situation, peace efforts continue. The U.S. government claims not to have given up on the Road Map to Peace, unveiled in April 2003. In addition, nongovernmental representatives from both sides worked out what are now known as the Geneva Accords in December 2003.[*][1]

To better understand both the promise and difficulty of finding peace, it is necessary to review briefly the history of relations between Jews and Arabs in the region.

---

[*] Within Israel, the Geneva Accords are viewed from a range of perspectives. Some view this as a political move by politicians who were out of power, thus placing doubt on their motivation as peacemakers.

Early History of Israel and Palestine

Over thousands of years, both the population and ownership of the area that today encompasses Israel and the Palestinian Territories have evolved. In 2000 BCE, Amorites, Canaanites, and other Semitic peoples mixed with the indigenous population of the area that came to be known as the Land of Canaan. Sometime between 1800 and 1500 BCE, a Semitic people called the Hebrews emigrated from Mesopotamia. The modern-day Jewish people trace their common lineage to the biblical patriarch Abraham and his descendants who, according to biblical traditions, were later enslaved in Egypt until they escaped and conquered Canaan. By 1000 BCE, the figure known as King David incorporated Jerusalem as the capital of an expanded Israelite kingdom that covered Canaan and the Transjordan area. His son Solomon consolidated the kingdom, and devoted himself to the construction of a temple in Jerusalem. But after Solomon's death, the kingdom split. The southern part became known as Judah and the northern part became Israel. Jerusalem, located in Judah, remained the center of Jewish worship.

Around 722 BCE, the Assyrians conquered Israel and in approximately 587 BCE, Judah came under Babylonian rule. In 586 BCE the Babylonians destroyed Solomon's Temple and exiled many of the Jews during the decades that followed. When the Persian King Cyrus conquered Babylonia, he permitted Jews to return to Jerusalem, but some chose to remain in Babylonia. Not long after, the temple (known as the "Second Temple") was rebuilt in Jerusalem.

The Persians continued to rule the land until 331 BCE, when Alexander the Great conquered the Persian Empire. Following Alexander's death two years later, one of his generals, Seleucus, founded a dynasty in 200 BCE that controlled the area. At first, the Jews were permitted to practice their religion freely in this land, but later, King Antiochus IV banned Judaism. Led by the Maccabeans, the Jews revolted, drove the Seleucids out of the region and by 165 BCE, had formed a kingdom with Jerusalem as the capital.

Roman to Ottoman Rule

In 63 BCE, Roman troops invaded Judah and sacked Jerusalem. Called Judea, the area fell under Roman control. During early Roman rule, Jesus of Nazareth, a Jew known by his followers as "the Christ" (or Messiah) and as the founding figure of what became Christianity, was believed to have been born in Bethlehem. In 66 CE, the Jews again revolted, this time against the Romans. In retaliation, the Romans destroyed the Second Temple in 70 CE, leaving only the remnants of the Western retaining wall of the Temple complex. Known today as the *Kotel* (or the "Western" Wall), this site is located below the temple mount, which was the actual location of the Temple. The Kotel is a place of prayer more holy than any other to Jews worldwide.[2]

Once again, in 132 CE, the Jews revolted against Roman oppression, leading to the complete expulsion of the Jewish community from Jerusalem in 135 CE. Around this time, the Romans renamed the area Palaestina and, eventually, Palestine. With most Jews now dispersed throughout the Roman Empire in what is today described as the Jewish Diaspora, the Roman Empire continued to rule Palestine until the fourth century CE when the Byzantine Empire took control. Throughout this period, Christianity expanded its influence.

Around 570 CE, Muhammad ibn Abdullah, an Arab born in Mecca, came to be regarded by his followers as the last of the great prophets of Judaism and Christianity, and as the founding figure of Islam. This new religion began to spread during Muhammad's lifetime and thereafter throughout the seventh century, when Muslim Arab armies conquered much of the Middle East, including Palestine. For the greater part of the ensuing centuries until the early 1900s, different Muslim rulers controlled the area. They permitted Christians and Jews to practice their faiths to varying degrees, but also encouraged the adoption of Islam and of Arab-Islamic culture. For Muslims, Jerusalem became a holy site where, according to Muslim tradition, Muhammad ascended to heaven on his horse. Today, the Dome of the Rock and al-Aqsa Mosque stand on the site of his ascension, the former location of the Jewish Temple, above the Western Wall.

Over the years, the city of Jerusalem has been the object of significant political and religious contention. In 1071 CE, the Seljuk Turks briefly gained control. But by 1099, European Christian crusaders had captured the city, where they ruled for nearly one hundred years until a Muslim leader, Saladin, regained control in 1187.

In the mid-thirteenth century, the Mamelukes of Egypt established an empire that came to include Palestine and the mostly Arabic-speaking Muslims who lived there. Meanwhile, in the late 1300s, Jews who had relocated to Spain and elsewhere in the Mediterranean returned and began settling in and around Jerusalem. In 1517, Palestine became part of the Ottoman Empire after the Ottomans defeated the Mamelukes. The

Turkish Sultan invited Jews fleeing from the Catholic Inquisition to settle in Palestine and other parts of the Ottoman Empire, whose capital was Constantinople.[3]

Rise of Zionism

The Jewish community of Palestine in the early nineteenth century was comprised mostly of small Ultra-Orthodox communities located around holy locations such as Jerusalem, Hebron, and Safed. At the time, Jews made up a very small number of the overall population.

In the 1840s, Rabbi Yehuda Alcalay published some of the first Zionist writings urging Jews to return to Palestine and cultivate the land in preparation for the return of the Messiah.[4] Coinciding with the end of Egyptian rule, the reestablishment of Ottoman control, and the greater security this provided the existing Jewish population, his ideas took hold among some European Jews. By 1880, according to scholar Ami Isseroff, there were approximately twenty-four thousand Jews living in Palestine out of a total population of about four hundred thousand.[5] By the end of the century, more Jews suffering from oppression in Eastern Europe were leaving their homes and emigrating to Palestine.[6]

In 1897, Zionist ideology became the basis of an official movement. Although some prominent Zionists continued to believe in a biblical right to the land, Theodore Herzl organized the first Zionist Congress in Basle, Switzerland, envisioning modern Zionism as "a political movement for a Jewish national state in Palestine."[7] Herzl was convinced that Jews would remain a beleaguered minority so long as they lacked a homeland. Notably, his vision was not a religious one, and he did not premise his thesis on the belief that God had designated the land comprising historic Palestine as the ultimate home of the Jews.[8]

During that same period, the combination of Jewish immigration and Ottoman land reform was changing the relationship of the Palestinian Arab* community to its land. Although historically cultivation was enough to ensure possession of land, the Ottoman Land Law of 1858 required that land had to be registered with the state to establish ownership rights. Local leaders and Palestinian notables began to buy up land, using it to build farms to raise their own cash crops or selling large tracts to Zionists for sizeable profits. Left out of this scenario were the peasant farmers, or *fellaheen*, who found themselves on the outside of a steadily

---

* Majority Muslim with minorities of Druze and various Christian denominations.

growing economy that was centered around the farms created on land being purchased by Jews and Arab-Palestinian notables, each of whom would exclude them from the labor market.[9]

Zionists hoped that persecuted European Jews would be attracted to Palestine and eventually constitute a majority of the population there. Accordingly, Jewish farm communities and cities were formed, and by 1914, about 615,000 Arabs and between 85,000 and 100,000 Jews inhabited Palestine.[10]

World War I

During World War I, the Ottoman military ruled Palestine, and for part of the time, the Turkish military governor ordered the internment and deportation of many foreign nationals. Then in 1916, Britain and France signed the Sykes-Picot Agreement and secretly agreed to divide the Middle East so that after the war, France would rule Syria and Lebanon, whereas Britain (or possibly a joint Allied government) would rule Palestine.

At the same time that this agreement was being made, Britain also was promising the Arabs that it would support their demands for independence from the Ottomans. As a result, the Arabs aligned with the British. Led by T. E. Lawrence and backed by Sharif Hussein, the Arabs revolted against the Ottomans, believing that they would receive independence. However, the vision for Arab independence was less than uniform. Various ways to implement it included Pan-Arabism (one large, inclusive Arab state), a confederation of Arab states, or a set of independent Arab states based on national identity. Later, however, the British denied Palestinian national self-determination and statehood.

The British Mandate

In 1917, Britain issued the Balfour Declaration, which stated Britain's support for the "establishment in Palestine of a national home for the Jewish people ... being clearly understood that nothing shall be done which may prejudice the civil and religious rights of existing non-Jewish communities in Palestine."[11] Many Arabs living in the British-occupied territories objected to Britain's support for a Jewish state. And in the decades that followed, Arab rebellion and pressure led the British government effectively to repudiate the Balfour Declaration and, ultimately, to adopt an anti-Zionist policy by the outbreak of World War II.[12]

In 1919, the United States – another victor of World War I – created the little known King-Crane Commission, whose stated purpose was to gain input from the inhabitants of the region regarding the borders to be established and the design of future governments. Ultimately ignored by the Allied powers, the report was later published independently. It revealed that the people of the region (with the exception of the Jews, who stated their preference for the establishment of a Homeland for the Jews to be located in Palestine) overwhelmingly supported the establishment of one Greater-Syria Mandate (comprised of Syria, Lebanon, and Palestine). According to the report (which was drafted by Americans), the stated preference was for this mandate to be administered under American authority with an ultimate goal of complete autonomy. The report further noted the opposition of the people of the region "to a Zionist state and Jewish immigration."[13]

Meanwhile, the Zionist Organization (renamed the World Zionist Organization in 1960) lobbied for a Jewish homeland in Palestine at the post-World War I Paris Peace Conference. This proposal was aimed at convincing the conference to create a British Mandate over Palestine, which the Zionists saw as the first step to fulfilling the Balfour Declaration and creating a Jewish Homeland in Palestine.[14]

In the end, the League of Nations adopted the British plan. In so doing, it gave greater weight to the desire of the British and French to divide the area between themselves and all but ignored the views of most inhabitants on how the region should be governed.

The British Mandate would eventually include Palestine and Transjordan, as well as Iraq, whereas France received the Mandates for Syria and Lebanon. Palestine and Transjordan were treated as a single administrative unit until 1946. However, in 1922, the Hashemi family was given control of Transjordan, which eventually become an independent Arab state (indeed, the Hashemite Kingdom of Jordan is still ruled by members of the Hashemi family).[15]

The Palestine Mandate of the League of Nations provided for the establishment of an organization that in 1929 became The Jewish Agency for Palestine. This organization represented Jewish interests in Palestine to Britain, functioned as the de facto government of the Jewish settlement community, and promoted Jewish immigration.[16] Although the British Mandate authorities also attempted to set up an Arab Agency as a counterpart to The Jewish Agency, the Arabs refused to participate, rejecting Britain's support for a future Jewish state and governance of the Palestine Mandate.

During the mandate period, Britain also attempted to establish other self-governing institutions, but institutions inclusive of both Jews and Palestinian Arabs never came to be. Continued Arab discontent with the situation led to riots and pogroms against the Jews in 1920, 1921, and 1929. Indeed, they took place throughout the mandate – in Jerusalem, Hebron, Jaffa, and Haifa. Arab nationals, refusing to relinquish their aspirations for statehood, opposed the Balfour Declaration, the British Mandate, and a Jewish national homeland in Palestine. Riots led the Jewish community of Hebron to evacuate, and about half of the residents of the Jewish quarter fled the old city of Jerusalem. Soon after, the Jews formed a militia known as the *Haganah*.

Notwithstanding this situation, Jewish immigration to Palestine increased in the 1930s, driven by persecution of Jews in Eastern Europe. Hitler's rise to power in Germany, culminating in the horrors of the Holocaust, also contributed to increased Jewish immigration to Palestine. This mass migration by Jews occurred despite the fact "that in the 1930s, the British government drew back from the pro-Zionist commitment of the Balfour Declaration and in 1939 even barred Palestine as a place of refuge for Jews fleeing the Nazis."[17]

In 1936, riots (later referred to as the "Arab Revolt") broke out among nearly all strata of Palestinian society, at least partly in response to the transformation of Palestinian society resulting from the influx of Jews and the rule of the British.[18] The Husseini family led the revolt, which resulted in hundreds of Arabs and Jews (including many civilians) being killed.

Around the same time as the Arab Revolt, a Jewish underground paramilitary group was formed known as the *Irgun*, which used violence as its tactic for bringing about the creation of a Jewish state. Although mostly targeting British troops and interests (they are most well known for bombing the King David Hotel in Jerusalem in 1946), this group also attacked Arab civilians. Initially unprepared for the outbreak of violence, the British authorities eventually restored some semblance of calm, exiling those Arab leaders deemed responsible for fomenting the violence.

The British proceeded to place restrictions on Arab political activity and refused to permit exiled Arab leaders (including those who had encouraged the strike and subsequent riots) to return to Palestine. In an attempt to further limit agitation between the Arabs and Jews, Britain decreed in a 1939 White Paper that fifteen thousand Jews a year would be permitted into Palestine over the next five years, after which time Jewish immigration would be subject to Arab approval.

Despite the White Paper, secret Jewish immigration continued. Given rising anti-Semitism and the Nazi threat, many European Jews saw little hope for their survival. Barred from refuge by most of the world's nations, European Jews viewed the creation of a Jewish state in Palestine as their only hope of survival.[19]

During the World War II years of 1939 to 1945, the future of the Palestine Mandate was foremost on the minds of Jews and Palestinian Arabs alike. Those Jews who chose to fight in the war fought for the Allied powers against the Nazi led Axis, whereas most Arabs called for neutrality, siding neither with the British nor with the Axis powers.[20] Following the war, the Jews in Palestine were desperate to bring about 250,000 Jewish Holocaust survivors and displaced people to Palestine. In the meantime, Britain relinquished control of the Palestine Mandate and returned it to the United Nations to govern.

During that period, over six million European and North African Jews were killed by the Nazis. The Holocaust and the world's response had a significant effect on the situation in Palestine. It came to inform the Jewish identity from then on, and led to sufficient international support for providing Jews with a homeland of their own.

Transition from Mandate to the State of Israel

In the region, the two years following the end of World War II were rife with violence, committed by the British, Jews, and Arabs. On November 29, 1947, in anticipation of the British relinquishment of the mandate it had held since the end of World War I, the UN General Assembly adopted Resolution 181 and announced the partition of Palestine into a Jewish state and an Arab state.[21] Before the resolution, there were about 600,000 Jews and 1.2 million Arabs in Palestine.[22] Under the partition plan, the Jewish State was to receive 15,850 km^2, or almost 60 percent of the 27,000 km^2 in Palestine.

All too soon, it became apparent that neither all Jews nor all Arabs would accept the resolution. Some Jews rejected a partition plan of what they perceived to be the legitimate Jewish homeland. Likewise, many Arabs perceived the land to be their homeland and did not want it to be divided. The Arab League (whose members included Syria, Transjordan, Iraq, Saudi Arabia, Lebanon, and Yemen) declared war, and two armies of Arab militia volunteers fought against the Haganah, the Zionist underground army. The Arabs also fought against other Jewish paramilitary factions: the *Irgun, Palmah,* and *Lehi.*

Although present, the British did little to quell the violence. They refused to implement the UN partition plan because it was not acceptable to most Arabs and some Jews. Riots resulted and, eventually, the Arab militia laid siege to Jewish Jerusalem, cutting off food, water, and fuel. Then on April 9, 1948, the Irgun killed over 120 men, women, and children at Deir Yassin, an Arab-Palestinian village.[23] The Irgun also attacked the Arab town of Jaffa, forcing many residents from their homes. Also in April, "an Arab group ambushed a bus going to the Hadassah Medical Center on Mount Scopus, killing 75 Jewish professors, doctors, and nurses. The British . . . did little to stop the escalating violence, as they were preparing to withdraw from Palestine altogether."[24]

By April 1948, the war turned in favor of the Jewish forces. The Haganah attacked the hilltop village of Qastel, the last remaining Palestinian military stronghold overlooking the road to Jerusalem, thereby temporarily breaking the siege on the city.[25] The battle for Qastel was one of great significance for the Arab-Palestinians as well, as their most loved and respected military leader, Abd el-Kader el-Husseini, fell in battle that day.[26] On May 14, 1948, the Jews declared the independent State of Israel based on the boundaries that the UN had designated for a Jewish state, and the British withdrew from their Palestine Mandate.[27]

1948 War

On May 15, 1948, the day after Israel declared independence, Egypt, Jordan, Iraq, and Syria attacked Israel, leading to a regional war that ultimately led to the collapse of the UN's partition plan. During this time, the Jewish underground armies of the Haganah, Palmah, Irgun, and Lehi combined into a single entity called the Israel Defense Forces (IDF), as the army of the new state of Israel.

During the first phase of this war, the troops fought each other for about a month, followed by a truce. During the second phase, from July 8 to July 18, 1948, the Israeli forces took over part of the Galilee and the Tel Aviv–Jerusalem corridor that had been allotted to the Palestinian Arabs under the UN proposal. At the same time, the Egyptian army took control of part of the Negev region originally intended in the UN proposal as part of the land that was to become Israel. The last phase of this war occurred from October 1948 through January 1949, when the Jews expelled Egypt from the Negev region and simultaneously gained control of Palestinian areas up to the border of the Sinai.

By the time the fighting ended in 1949, Israel held territories beyond the original UN outline in Resolution 181 and occupied 78 percent of the area between the West Bank and the Mediterranean. Jerusalem was divided between Israel and Jordan; Jordan occupied the territory known as the West Bank; and Egypt occupied the Gaza Strip. Palestinian statehood remained unrealized. Israel, Egypt, Lebanon, Jordan, Iraq, and Syria signed the July 1949 armistice, effectively ending the violence. Scholars differ as to whether the 1949 armistice lines created a clearly defined border for the State of Israel or whether it merely created a cease-fire line, still subject to interpretation.

During the 1948 War and in its aftermath, thousands of Palestinians either fled – based partly on the advice of *mujtars* of individual villages – or were forced out of their homes. By 1949, the majority of the one million Palestinians (both Muslim and Christian) who had lived in what became Israel were refugees in countries such as Jordan, Lebanon, Egypt, and Syria, and were barred from returning to Israel.[28] About 150,000 to 170,000 of the Palestinians remained and eventually became legal Israeli citizens.[29]

Sinai Campaign

Suspicious of Israel's intentions and cognizant of Cold War politics between the United States and the U.S.S.R., in the years following the 1948 War, Egypt began to secure arms from Czechoslovakia – a state aligned with the U.S.S.R. Similarly, Israel was wary of its neighbors and began to arm with help from France. Then, in the early 1950s Egyptian President Gamal Abdel Nasser closed the Straits of Tiran and the Suez Canal to Israeli shipping.[30]

In further defiance of the United States and Britain, Nasser nationalized the Suez Canal on July 26, 1956. Objecting to the nationalization of and the restricted access to the Suez Canal, Israel, France, and Britain met in the summer of 1956 and developed a plan to reverse the nationalization of the Suez Canal. On October 29, 1956, their plan was implemented, and Israel invaded Sinai. Two days later, Britain began bombing raids near Cairo. And on November 5, Britain and France began to advance on Suez City. By the following day, however, the United Nations called for a cease-fire, and Britain and France complied. The United States condemned the actions of Israel, France, and Britain and supported UN General Assembly Resolution 997, which called for immediate withdrawal of the countries from the Sinai. Under great pressure,

Israel withdrew on March 16, 1957. In return for the withdrawal of its troops, Israel insisted that the United States and United Nations commit to maintaining freedom of navigation in the Straits of Tiran. In response, a UN Emergency Force was created to supervise the territories vacated by Israeli forces.

1967 Six-Day War/June War

Following the wars of 1948 and 1956, tensions remained unabated between the Arab states and Israel. Palestinian refugees now lived in each of the Arab states surrounding Israel. Having lost their property and livelihoods, they became "utterly destitute... in miserable [refugee] camps."[31] Egypt, Syria, and Jordan were still smarting from their recent defeats and publicly continued to call for the destruction of the Israeli state. In light of the hostilities with its neighbors, Israel, for its part, continued to successfully build up its military strength.

During the interwar period between 1948 and 1967, Egyptian President Gamel Nasser stoked pan-Arab pride and brought Arabs together to fight for the liberation of Palestine and the destruction of Israel. The Egyptian Voice of the Arabs radio broadcast continually preached total war and annihilation of Israel. Such rhetoric was not lost on the Israeli public (a public that included many Holocaust survivors), and many became fearful that their destruction was imminent. However, most of the Israeli military leadership knew of their military superiority and thus did not share this pessimistic view (however, military censorship then barred them from sharing such information with the people).[32]

In May 1967, Nasser requested that the UN troops withdraw from the Sinai and they did so on May 18. He then reoccupied the area with Egyptian troops and tanks and declared a blockade on Israeli shipping and passage through the Straits of Tiran. Egypt, Jordan, and Iraq soon signed a mutual defense pact.[33]

Although there was some military intelligence that an attack was likely at some point, the combination of the blockade on Israeli shipping and the rise of Arab solidarity under Nasser's leadership provided enough of an impetus for Israel to launch an attack. On June 5, 1967, Israeli Prime Minister Levi Eshkol ordered the Israeli Air Force to attack air bases in Egypt, Syria, and Jordan. Israel destroyed most of their planes while they were still on the ground.[34]

With control over the air, Israel moved its campaign to the ground. That same day on June 5, based on a pact between Jordan and Egypt, the Jordanian army attacked Jewish parts of Jerusalem. Countering the Jordanian attack, Israel pushed Jordan out of East Jerusalem and the West Bank.

Israel also defeated the Egyptian army in the Sinai and advanced to the Suez Canal, where it stopped another attempted blockade by Nasser. On June 9, 1967, Egypt and Israel signed a cease-fire. The Israeli Army then turned to Syria and wrested the Golan Heights (militarily strategic to each side), from where Syrians had been frequently firing on Jewish civilian settlements below, from its control by June 11, 1967. In total, Israel gained control of the territories of the Gaza Strip, the Golan Heights, the Sinai, and the West Bank, including East Jerusalem.[35]

A second wave of Palestinians became refugees in the wake of the 1967 war.[36] By 1968, approximately 1.3 million Palestinian refugees from the 1948 and 1967 Wars constituted the Palestinian Diaspora. They experienced varying degrees of receptivity from the surrounding Arab host countries. Israel, for its part, continued to hold onto the territories captured in the 1967 War. Those Palestinians who remained in the West Bank and Gaza Strip came to live under Israeli occupation without Israeli citizenship.

From 1967 to 1977, Israel launched a settlement movement of Israeli Jews in those occupied territories. For secular Israelis, the settlements served strategic and tactical importance as they were built to serve as a buffer between Israel and her neighbors. Religious Zionists too were in favor of settlements, as they saw the settlement of the biblical land of Israel by Jews as a religious duty. After 1977, Israel, led by Prime Minister Menachem Begin and a religious settlers' movement, became committed to a policy of establishing a Jewish presence in the West Bank and the Gaza Strip. Thereafter, Israel acquired settlement land for Jewish Israeli citizens by seizing private Arab land and by classifying unregistered and uncultivated land as state land.[37]

Jerusalem

Before 1948, Jerusalem had been a tense, but not physically divided, city. Access to the holy sites in the Old City by adherents of their respective faiths was reasonably unfettered. From the 1948 war onward, however access to and within Jerusalem became more of an issue.

From 1948 to 1967 the eastern part of Jerusalem, including the entire Old City, was under Jordanian control. The armistice line in Jerusalem separating the Israeli side from the Jordanian side was heavily fortified and very hot. During this period, the community of the Jewish Quarter of the Old City was forced out, synagogues were destroyed and Jewish access to the Western Wall (the last remaining portion of the Second Temple and considered by many to be Judaism's holiest site) was denied. Jordanians and Palestinians desecrated Jewish cemeteries, monuments, and holy sites throughout the West Bank.[38]

In 1967, East Jerusalem came under Israeli control and the situation changed. While Jews now regained the ability to visit the Western Wall, the ability of Palestinian Muslims and Christians from the West Bank and Gaza to enter Jerusalem was severely disadvantaged. The Old City of Jerusalem is also home to the al-Haram al-Sharif, or Noble Sanctuary (the location of the Dome of the Rock and al-Aqsa Mosque and considered one of the holiest places in Islam), and the Church of the Holy Sepulchre (shared by the Greek Orthodox, Catholic, Armenian, Syrian, Coptic, and Ethiopian Churches and said to be located on the hill of Jesus' crucifixion as well as the location of the tomb of Christ's burial). Presently, Israeli law guarantees the rights of all to worship in Jerusalem. However, entrance into Jerusalem by residents of the occupied territories is subject to the discretion of the Israeli security services. As a result, getting permission for Palestinian worshippers to travel from West Bank towns and cities to the Old City is extremely difficult, and from Gaza, the trip is nearly impossible.

War of Attrition

In the three years following the 1967 War, Egyptian president Nasser broke the cease-fire and launched a prolonged, low-intensity war with Israel across the Suez Canal. By this time, Golda Meir had become the Israeli prime minister. Through pressure from the United States, however, the two countries eventually established another cease-fire in 1970.

Both countries officially accepted UN Resolution 242, which emphasized the "inadmissibility of the acquisition of territory by war and the need to work for a just and lasting peace in which every State in the area can live in security"[39] and called for the withdrawal of Israeli troops from territories occupied in the 1967 War. The resolution also called for "achieving a just settlement of the refugee problem."[40] Even today, the divisive issues reflected in Resolution 242 are yet to be resolved.

In 1970, shortly after the cease-fire, President Nasser died, and Anwar Sadat replaced him. President Sadat attempted to make peace with Israeli

Prime Minister Meir, offering partial peace for partial Israeli withdrawal from Sinai. Prime Minister Meir doubted the sincerity of Sadat's intentions and refused, stating that Israeli troops would not move until a peace agreement was in place.

The October War/Yom Kippur War

Tensions persisted, and in October 1973, Egypt, led by President Sadat, along with Syria, launched another war against Israel. On October 6, Yom Kippur – the holiest day in the Jewish religious calendar – Egypt crossed the Suez Canal. Israel purportedly had received intelligence reports of possible attack and President Sadat had announced his intentions to declare war many times, but Prime Minister Meir and Defense Minister Moshe Dayan believed that Israel's military power would deter Egypt from making such a move.

Israel was caught almost completely by surprise when the Egyptians attacked. Fighting between the sides continued for several days in the Sinai. Eight miles east of the Suez Canal, Egyptian forces consolidated. Simultaneously, Syrian forces began to cross into the Golan Heights, which were now less heavily armed by Israeli forces. Despite many setbacks, Israel held onto the Golan Heights. Having regrouped, Israel then crossed the west bank of the Suez Canal, closing in on Cairo. At this point, a cease-fire was finally established after approximately twenty-seven hundred Israeli and eighty-five hundred Arab soldiers had died.[41]

With the help of the United States, Egypt and Israel eventually reached a peace agreement via a negotiation process now known as shuttle diplomacy. On November 19, 1977, President Sadat became the first Arab head of state to visit Israel. By 1978, President Sadat and Prime Minister Menachem Begin, then the leader of Israel, signed the Camp David framework agreements, which led to the 1979 peace treaty between the two countries. Three years later, in 1982, Israel withdrew from Sinai.[42]

1982 War in Lebanon

That same year, under orders from Defense Minister Ariel Sharon, Israel invaded Lebanon to rid that country of the Palestinian Liberation Organization (PLO) fighters, who had made Lebanon their home base and were using it to attack Israel. Founded in 1964 under the auspices of the Arab League, the PLO had come to represent the wandering leadership of the Palestinian people. Originally housed in Egypt, the PLO moved several times before it settled in Lebanon. Once there, the PLO began to orchestrate attacks on Israeli targets. The Israeli invasion of Lebanon resulted in the expulsion of the PLO leadership to Tunisia.

Following the expulsion, Defense Minister Sharon exceeded his mandate by allowing the right-wing Lebanese Phalangist militia to commit massacres in the Sabra and Shatilla Palestinian refugee camps. Over one thousand Palestinian civilians were killed.[43] This event raised grave concerns within Israel and the international community. Both condemned the deaths and Defense Minister Sharon. As a result, he was formally reprimanded, and Israel subsequently slowly removed itself from Lebanon – but not before the Shiite anti-Israel militant group, Hezbollah, had been created.

First Intifada/Oslo Process

Palestinians of the West Bank and Gaza grew increasingly discouraged by the bleak nature of life under military occupation. Prospects for economic prosperity and a Palestinian state were seemingly nonexistent. Experiences of harassment and humiliation at the hands of the Israeli security forces added to the tensions and growing frustration within the Palestinian population.

After twenty years of a stateless existence, this situation came to a head in 1987 with the onset of what became known as the first Intifada (or uprising). Palestinians staged mass protests calling for an end to the occupation and the establishment of a state of their own, in accordance with UN resolutions. Following the Gulf War and the breakup of the U.S.S.R. in the early 1990s, the international community turned its attention toward resolving the issue of the Palestinian refugees.

Then, in 1993, Israel and the PLO shocked the world by signing the Oslo Declaration of Principles, known as Oslo I. At a series of clandestine meetings in Oslo, Norway, Israeli and PLO officials met outside the normal diplomatic channels. For the first time, the PLO and Israel mutually recognized one another.[44] The agreements also detailed a five-year interim plan for the foundation of Palestinian autonomy in the West Bank and the Gaza Strip.[45] Notably, this agreement was an interim one, designed to lead to a final settlement. But the possibilities embodied in these agreements were recognized around the world when, on September 13, 1993, PLO leader Yasser Arafat and Israeli Prime Minister Yitzhak Rabin shook hands on the lawn of the White House in a ceremony hosted by President Bill Clinton. A year later, Jordan and Israel signed a peace treaty between their two countries.

In 1995, the leaders again met and developed the Interim Agreement, known as Oslo II. In much detail, Oslo II outlined steps for transition of power to a Palestinian civil authority (known as the Palestinian Authority or PA). Among several items, the West Bank was to be divided into different zones, and the Israeli Army was to be redeployed from significant portions of the West Bank and Gaza Strip to allow for free elections.[46]

On the evening of November 4, 1995, Prime Minister Rabin was assassinated by an extremist Israeli-Jewish student opposed to his peacemaking efforts. Nonetheless, as prescribed in the peace process, Israeli troops withdrew from the Gaza Strip and many areas of the West Bank in 1996, and the Palestinians gained control of these areas. Although 97 percent of the Palestinians in these areas were then nominally under Palestinian rule, the PA controlled only 8 percent of the land of the West Bank and Gaza. To formalize their governing structure, in January 1996, the Palestinians in the West Bank and Gaza elected a legislature controlled by the PLO's Fatah faction. The Palestinian territories did not become an independent state, but Yasser Arafat, as Chairman of the Palestinian Authority, administered the areas Israel ceded to Palestinian control.[47]

Second Intifada

Throughout the 1990s, the Oslo agreements created considerable excitement. Some Palestinians and Israelis worked together to fulfill the incremental trust-building steps of the agreement spelled out in more than 350 pages of the Oslo II Interim Agreement.[48] However, at the same time, Israeli settlement expansion continued in the West Bank, and Palestinian lands were taken by the settlers in order to build new outposts. These actions increased the sense among Palestinians that Israel was not committed to transferring the West Bank to them for the creation of a Palestinian state.[49] Additionally, in large part because of the denial of promised economic aid from the global community, limitations on freedom of movement by the Israeli security forces, and corruption and financial mismanagement within the Palestinian Authority, the economic conditions of the Palestinians deteriorated, with per capita income declining every year following the Oslo agreement.[50]

The stagnating peace process brought with it the introduction of Palestinian suicide bombers on Israeli soil. As such attacks on Israeli civilians grew in number and severity throughout this period, the level of mistrust toward Palestinians grew among the Israeli population. Israelis began living with the daily threat of suicide bombing and the reality of submitting to safety measures designed to deter such attacks (such as having bags checked upon entry into restaurants or shopping malls). Indeed, 689 Israeli civilians have lost their lives in suicide bombings and other violence, including 119 children, whereas several thousand have been injured.[51]

Rising tensions on the other side of the border have ushered in an increase in Palestinian civilian deaths and injuries as well. According to the Israeli human rights group, B'Tselem, 1,722 Palestinians have been killed by the Israel Defense Forces and one third of them were children; thousands more have been injured.[52] Casualties on both sides have exacerbated tensions on the ground, adversely affecting the willingness of both Israelis and Palestinians to negotiate and wearing their patience with the peace process thin.

At the negotiating table, contested issues such as the "return" of Palestinian refugees from the 1948 and 1967 Wars to what is now Israel proper remain unresolved. Those refugees and their descendants continue to see this "return" as a basic right, citing UN General Assembly Resolution 194 and the Geneva Conventions as evidence of the legality of their claim.[53] To Jewish Israelis, this demand is "nothing less than a blueprint for the destruction of their state."[54] Additionally, from the Israeli perspective, Resolution 194 does not demand the return of the refugees if compensation is given, and, based on political analyses beyond the scope of this brief recitation, some believe that the Geneva Convention does not apply. The inability of both sides to resolve this issue contributed to the failure of the Oslo process.

In July 2000, American President Bill Clinton (at the request of Israeli Prime Minister Ehud Barak) invited Barak and Chairman Arafat to negotiations at Camp David. At this summit, issues that had heretofore never been significantly discussed (Jerusalem, final borders, Palestinian statehood, and refugees) were put on the table. At the conference, Barak made an offer for the creation of a Palestinian state made up of all of Gaza and over 90 percent of the West Bank and further offered to recognize East Jerusalem (not including the Jewish holy sites in the Old City) as its capital. For many Israelis, this plan was perceived as compromising Israel and the Jewish people's very identity and vital interests, representing sweeping concessions to the Palestinians. To Arafat and most Palestinians, however, such an offer was not a concession at all. It would have left them a state that did not include all of the pre-1967 West Bank and thus would compromise less than 35 percent of historical Palestine. It was also devoid of significant water resources and air rights, and was nearly cut in half by territory that was to remain part of Israel. Such sentiments ultimately led to Arafat being the first to leave the table. Nonetheless, secret negotiations between the Israelis and Palestinians would continue.[55]

Tensions erupted on September 28, 2000, when Ariel Sharon (who in Palestinian consciousness was firmly associated with the massacres of Sabra and Shatilla) visited the Muslim holy sites at the Temple Mount in Jerusalem. Although Sharon claimed that his visit was without political motivation, Palestinians perceived Sharon's move as staking a claim on the holy site for Israel. Violence erupted almost immediately.

In response to the intractable violence, President Clinton moved to preserve the Oslo Accords by bringing the Palestinians and Israelis together at Taba, Egypt, but nothing came of his efforts, given the short time left for the Barak and Clinton governments, other issues absorbing the American administration, and the continuing violence. Not long after, Israeli Prime Minister Ehud Barak was voted out of office by Israelis disillusioned with the peace process, and Ariel Sharon was elected to serve as prime minister.

Israel in the Twenty-First Century

In 2002, Saudi Crown Prince Abdullah attempted to rekindle the peace process by floating a proposal, modified and adopted later by the Arab League. Under Abdullah's plan, Israel, in return for a full withdrawal from all territories occupied since 1967 (including East Jerusalem) and an agreed upon solution to the Palestinian refugee issue, would receive full diplomatic and peaceful relations with the whole of the Arab world. On March 12, 2002, the UN Security Council passed Resolution 1397, which welcomed the contribution of Prince Abdullah's proposal. The resolution also marked the first official call since 1947 for the creation of a Palestinian State alongside Israel.

Since Prince Abdullah's proposal, a number of other peace plans have been suggested, all with the intention of bringing peace to the Middle East. On April 30, 2003, American President George W. Bush announced a revised version of his Road Map to Peace for the Israel-Palestine conflict. In December 2003, Israeli opposition political leaders led by Yossi Beilin and Palestinians led by Yasser Abd-Rabbo announced the nonofficial Geneva Accords. These Geneva Accords proposed historic concessions by both sides, with Palestinians renouncing the right of return to Israel and Israel giving up sovereignty over Arab portions of Jerusalem. Although these accords occurred at the Track Two diplomatic level, the agreement was praised by former U.S. Secretary of State Colin L. Powell and Palestinian National Authority Chairman Yasser Arafat. Thus far, these agreements have had little to no tangible effect on the situation.

Progress made through political channels toward peace is moving slowly. UN Security Council Resolution 1515 endorsed the Road Map to Peace plan that was introduced by President Bush and called upon both sides to uphold their obligations in the Road Map. In recent years, the peace talks have been further complicated.

Between 2003 and 2005, the Sharon government initiated two plans that were controversial both inside and outside of Israel. The first is to build what the Israeli government calls a "Security Fence" between Israel proper and the majority of the West Bank. To many Israelis, "the Fence" (sometimes called "the Wall") was built to keep suicide bombers from entering Israel from the West Bank (and for that purpose, it has been successful). To many Palestinians, the "Security Fence" (which they refer to as the "Apartheid Wall" or "Separation Barrier") has divided some villages and boxed in others, separated families from their lands and livelihood, and is a vehicle for creating a de facto border and claiming Palestinian land. Not surprisingly, this barrier has caused considerable contention, both locally and internationally.

The second is Sharon's "Disengagement Plan." By September 2005, Israel's military and civilian presence had completely withdrawn its troops and citizens from the Gaza Strip. Even though the Palestinian Egyptian border is no longer under Israeli control, Israel still controls the Gaza waterfront. Although settlement expansion has continued in the West Bank, the withdrawal from Gaza caused great discord among the Israeli population as they watched scenes of Israeli soldiers physically forcing Jews out of their homes.

On November 11, 2004, Palestinian Authority Chairman Yasser Arafat died. With the prospect of new leadership for Palestinians, many now saw a new possibility for creating peace and a Palestinian state alongside Israel. In January 2005, Mahmud Abbas (abu Mazen) was elected to succeed Arafat as president of the Palestinian National Authority, and new outreach between the communities began. Legislative elections held in the West Bank and Gaza in January 2006 resulted in the transfer of control of the PA to Hamas (labeled a terrorist organization by the United States and the European Union, Hamas has claimed credit for and supported suicide bombings that have killed hundreds of Israeli civilians). Because of its history and its refusal to recognize the right of the state of Israel to exist, international reaction to the election of Hamas has been mixed. The United States, the European Union, and Japan have all with-held nonhumanitarian aid from the PA, and Israel has refused to turn over several million dollars in taxes it has collected on the Palestinians' behalf. The lack of financial aid has resulted in increased poverty among Palestinians and has created barriers to building a critically needed infrastructure.

On November 24, 2005 Prime Minister Sharon announced that he would lead a new party – to be known as Kadima – that would follow up the withdrawal from Gaza with further unilateral withdrawals from the West Bank. On January 4, 2006, Sharon suffered a major stroke that has left him in a coma. His successor to the leadership of Kadima, Ehud Olmert, led the party to victory in the Israeli parliamentary elections held on March 28, 2006. Olmert's campaign centered on his plan to define Israel's borders by 2008, with or without negotiations with the Palestinians. This policy of unilaterally defining Israel's borders has caused great dismay among the Palestinian population, who expect to be a party to negotiations defining borders between Israel and a future Palestinian state.

At the time of this writing, the conflict and many of its issues remain intractable, frustrating both Israelis and Palestinians. The end result of Track One diplomatic efforts ultimately remains to be seen. However, many ordinary Israelis and Palestinians are still working daily to build a sustainable peace. In the absence of much official progress, grassroots efforts within Israel and the Occupied Territories are keeping hope alive.

"I Am Palestinian, Arab, Christian, and Israeli"

Abuna Elias Chacour

The distressed village of Ibillin in Galilee is where Abuna Chacour began his peacemaking work, drawing on his heritage as a native of the region and his stature as an ordained Melkite Catholic priest. Abuna, which means "Our Father" in Arabic, considers himself a person of many iden-tities: Palestinian, Arab, Christian, and an Israeli citizen. Above all, how-ever, he defines himself as a human being made in the likeness of God:

> There are four components to my identity. These components are in his-torical order rather than in order of significance to me. First, I am a

Palestinian. Second, I am Arab. I am from an Arab family, and we speak Arabic. Third, I am Christian. I live within a Christian society. Fourth, I am Israeli. From the time I was eight or nine years old, I became an Israeli citizen.

There is a problem now in how one considers identity. These multiple identities can be viewed either as contradictory or as a new challenge. I have chosen to view the multiple identities as a new challenge. This new reality means accepting plurality to create unity. . . . It is important not to condemn these identities. We can feel privileged to have these many identities.[56]

This appreciation of plural identities pervades Abuna Chacour's life and work. As his story illustrates, Abuna Chacour came to engage people of different faiths and ethnicities both by choice and out of necessity.

Abuna Elias Chacour

The youngest of six children, Elias Chacour was born into a Melkite Catholic family in 1939 in the village of Biram, which was located in the Upper Galilee region of Palestine. Although all the inhabitants of Biram were Christian Maronites and Melkites, Jews also resided nearby and often came to the village to barter.

The Maronite Catholic Church, which traces its origins to the fourth century, was central to the life of Biram and quite influential throughout the Palestine region.[57] Abuna Chacour, who belongs to the more scattered Melkite Catholic Church, explained why his religious community is less concentrated:*

The Melkite Church is from the time of the Apostles. The Melkites were the first Christian community, and these Christians were a mixture of many different communities. They were originally Jewish, Greek, Roman, and Arab. The Middle East was "Arabized" and so Arab traditions were incorporated.

There are Melkite Catholics all over the Middle East and in every Arab community. In fact, there are communities in the United States and in

---

* The distinction between the Melkite and Maronite Christian faiths is made easiest by a reflection on their origins. In the fifth century, the Council of Chalcedon affirmed that Christ had two natures: one divine, the other human. The Christians in the region stretching from Syria to Egypt who accepted this ruling came to be called Melkites (from the Syriac for "king," a reference to a Byzantine emperor who also affirmed the doctrine). The Maronite community traces its origins to St. Marun, a Syrian hermit of the late fourth and early fifth centuries. Although the Melkites are a small, trans-Middle Eastern faith community, the Maronites are a larger more concentrated one. In fact, the Maronites have long been one of the dominant actors in Lebanese politics.

Canada. The Melkites were scattered into a Diaspora under the Ottomans and especially since 1947.[58]

Both Abuna Chacour's mother and father were instrumental in his early religious education. To instill a religious identity within him from birth, Abuna Chacour's mother gave him the name Elias, a variation of Elijah, the prophet. Although his mother could not read or write, she knew the biblical stories by heart, and regularly told them to her children in vivid detail. Abuna Chacour recalls his childhood daydreams, imagining Jesus roaming throughout Biram, and wondering whether the Chacours who had lived during biblical times were personally touched by Jesus. His mother's stories brought the Bible alive, and Jesus became a childhood hero to the young Elias.[59]

His parents also taught him that above all else, upholding the values of his heritage, culture, and religion were most important. "We do not use violence ever, [even] if someone hurts us," Abuna Chacour's father would tell him. "The Jews and the Palestinians are brothers – blood brothers. We share the same father, Abraham, and the same God. We must never forget that."[60]

During the difficult period from 1947 to 1948, when part of the Palestine Mandate became the State of Israel, Abuna learned from his father that the Jews had endured great suffering. He remembers how his father prayed in anticipation of the arrival of Jewish soldiers: "Father in heaven help us to show love to our Jewish brothers. Help us to show them peace to quiet their troubled hearts."[61] And when they came, his family welcomed the Jews into their home, even buying a lamb and preparing a feast:

> I still remember my father saying that the Jewish soldiers were coming to our village and that we were going to prepare a banquet for them. My father told me that we must show these Jews that somewhere they were welcome – especially [because of] what they had gone through earlier because of an evil man, Hitler. Later we were ordered to leave our village for ten days, after which time, they told us we would be able to return home. This promise was not fulfilled.[62]

When trying to comprehend why his childhood home was taken away, Abuna Chacour turned to his Christian faith. As he tells it, he found guidance by exploring two questions asked by God. First, after Adam and Eve ate the forbidden fruit and hid themselves, God called to man, asking, "Where are you?" (Genesis 3:9). In the second, God asked of Cain, "'Where is Abel your brother?' And [Cain] said, 'I do not know. Am I my brother's keeper?'" (Genesis 4:9). After reflecting on these passages,

Abuna Chacour concluded, "Yes, I am my brother's custodian. [He] is my responsibility. Depending on what I do, I can encourage sharing and reconciliation."[63] This conclusion left Abuna Chacour with little choice. He became an activist.

Similarly, the opening passages of Jesus's Sermon on the Mount – known as The Beatitudes (Matthew 5) – further inspired Abuna Chacour to act:

> Blessed are the poor in spirit, for theirs is the kingdom of heaven.
> Blessed are those who mourn, for they will be comforted.
> Blessed are the meek, for they will inherit the earth.
> Blessed are those who hunger and thirst for righteousness, for they will be filled.
> Blessed are the merciful, for they will receive mercy.
> Blessed are the pure in heart, for they will see God.
> Blessed are the peacemakers, for they will be called children of God.
> Blessed are those who are persecuted for righteousness' sake, for theirs is the kingdom of heaven.
> Blessed are you when people revile you and persecute you and utter all kinds of evil against you falsely on my account.
> Rejoice and be glad, for your reward is great in heaven, for in the same way they persecuted the prophets who were before you.[64]

In his mother's opinion, the Beatitudes were at the heart of Christianity. Yet as a youth, Abuna Chacour read their message as a passive one, and he had a hard time reconciling this with the active, lively Jesus he found in the New Testament:

> *What did He mean?* I puzzled. *How can you be blessed – or happy – if you are poor or in mourning – if someone insults or persecutes you? How can you be hungry and thirsty for righteousness? What is a peacemaker?*
>
> These things were a mystery to me. What I understood about Jesus, what attracted me, was His strong, sometimes fiery nature: the way He erupted in the temple courts, driving out the greedy merchants and scattering the coins of the moneychangers; His habit of helping the crippled and the blind, even if He broke the laws and offended the overly-pious religious leaders. Sometimes I thought He was the only one who could understand a small boy who also threw himself into situations – somewhat blindly – a boy whose tongue sometimes got him into trouble, too.[65]

Gradually, as Abuna Chacour grew, he found ways to reconcile these tensions, to retain his fiery nature, to stand up for what he believed and always to remain faithful to the message of the Beatitudes. Abuna

Chacour toiled with the question, "What is a peacemaker?" Understanding came as he matured, and he concluded that if he were truly to be a servant of God, his calling would be to peacemaking.[66]

Evolution of a Peacemaker

As Abuna Chacour began to recognize his calling, the Arab-Israeli conflict burgeoned around him. Even though religion played an increasing and positive role in Abuna's development, its role in the conflict was markedly less positive. Abuna asserts that at the local level, religion's negative role was minor, but when the Arab-Israeli conflict is looked at comprehensively, he believes that religion has been a divisive factor and has failed to fulfill its potential for good:

> Widely, religion has not played a unifying role when dealing with religious extremists such as: Christian fundamentalists in the United States; Muslim fundamentalists in Israel; and Jewish fundamentalists in Israel.
>
> The conflict is not caused by religion, but religion has been distorted to negatively convert religious principles. Muslims, Christians and Jews who believe in killing are saying that God is wrong. But God cannot be wrong and those who kill are acting against God's will. God is the first victim and is insulted by the extremist groups.[67]

He emphasizes that religion is distorted when it is used to incite violence between Arabs and Israelis. For Abuna Chacour, it is clear that God does not intend the faithful to invoke religion to justify killing.

To understand how he might make a positive difference in his community, Abuna Chacour turned to the Melkite Catholic Church. From the age of twelve, he moved to Haifa to study the Bible under the direct supervision of the Bishop of the Galilee, where he lived away from his family in the church's orphanage. Nightly, he wrote in his journal, recording his journey to peacemaking. One entry from 1951 reflects his searching:

> Mother says you have a purpose in everything.... But I don't understand what you want from us. Is it your plan that Mother and Father suffer as you suffered? Father will not fight to get his land back as others are willing to do. Is this the kind of 'peace' you want to show the world? Will anyone hear our cry and help us?[68]

Clearly, as he studied, he continued to be haunted by the loss of his family's home and the pain of his Palestinian neighbors.

In 1954, Abuna Chacour transferred to St. Joseph's Minor Seminary in Nazareth, and from there was sent by his church in 1958 to study theology and Bible studies at Saint Sulpice and the Sorbonne in France.

When Abuna first arrived in France, he discovered that most people in the West viewed the Palestinians as (in his words) "ignorant, hostile, and violent."[69] He recalls one incident in particular when he realized just how challenging these biases could be. An affluent and prominent man in the local church invited Abuna Chacour to Christmas Eve dinner with his family and friends in their country home and asked to introduce him as a "special guest."[70] A couple arrived and Abuna Chacour began to introduce himself:

> "Pleased to meet you, I am from the village of Bi – "
>
> "From Bethlehem!" my host interrupted, clapping me on the back. "Elias is a Jewish student at our seminary. Can you imagine? I thought it would be a lovely surprise to have a Jewish believer from the Holy Land to celebrate Christmas with us," he finished with a jaunty smile.
>
> The visitors were delighted. I stared at him in disbelief. Why was he lying about me? At my first opportunity, before any more guests arrived, I pulled him aside to ask if he had made some mistake.
>
> "Tonight you are Jewish – from Bethlehem," he said with a cool smile. "That's not such a big favor to ask, is it? You'll get along much better if you stop announcing to the world that you are Palestinian."[71]

Notwithstanding the sense of being an outsider at the seminary, Abuna Chacour did well, receiving good grades. Still, he felt that something was missing. For him, the seminary's teachings differed from the true essence of Christianity that he had learned at home from his parents and his church. He recounts a conversation with his old friend Faraj, who was the only other Palestinian student at the seminary, in which they discussed Christianity in the West:

> "The real problem," Faraj said, "is that Western theology starts with man as the center of all things and tries to force God into some scheme that we can understand. Then He can be regulated. Elias, we've grown up believing that God is the beginning and the end of all things. He is central, not an afterthought. He's alive and has His own ways. Here, they want to tame God with their philosophy."
>
> "Worse than that," I countered, "I'm afraid the Western philosophies have *killed* God. If there's no respect for Him, what value do men have? Without God there is no compassion, no humanity."[72]

In addition to his concerns about Western perspectives, Abuna Chacour's stay in Europe was also a time in which he came to have greater understanding and compassion toward the Jewish people. While taking a trip to Germany, he experienced a moment of terror and insight. As if transported back to 1937, he imagined "men in dark green helmets and high black boots . . . with machine guns . . . [and visible] swastikas of the Third Reich." He saw them asking for papers, imagined Jewish people showing their papers and being taken: "Men and women . . . hugging small children, huddling together miserably. They would be taken to other destinations – never to be seen again." Abuna Chacour experienced "the ache of compassion." And he devoted himself to understanding more about Zionism, political influences, and how his people had come to be oppressed.[73]

His searching moved Abuna Chacour toward action. But it was the message of one of his most influential mentors at St. Sulpice – Father Longère – that sealed Abuna Chacour's fate. He still remembers Father Longère's words:

> If there is a problem somewhere . . . this is what happens. Three people will try to do something concrete to settle the issue. Ten people will give a lecture analyzing what the three are doing. One hundred people will commend or condemn the ten for their lecture. One thousand people will argue about the problem. And *one person* – only one – will involve himself so deeply in the true solution that he is too busy to listen to any of it. Now . . . which person are you?[74]

Abuna Chacour listened and acknowledged his path. He committed himself to a lifetime of actively searching for peace. Again, the message of the Beatitudes emerged to guide him, and Abuna felt certainty: "Suddenly I knew that the first step toward reconciling Jews and Palestinians was the restoration of human dignity. . . . If I was to go out as a true servant of God and man, my first calling was to be a peacemaker."[75]

Ministering in Galilee

With his calling clarified, Abuna Chacour turned to the ministry in the Melkite Catholic Church when he graduated from the seminary in 1965. But his return home – and the path that lay ahead – was not going to be easy.

In Paris, he had sometimes felt like an outcast because of his Palestinian identity, but was always able to go where he pleased without harassment. All that changed the moment Abuna Chacour returned to start his ministry. After landing, an Israeli customs officer interviewed Abuna and then told him to strip for a body cavity search:

> "Take off all of your clothes. You must be searched."
> That was my limit. "No," I said firmly. "I do not strip."
> "You will strip or you will not get back into the country."
> Moistness soaked my shirt. It was entirely likely that he could carry out his threat and not admit me. With all the calmness I could muster, I dug through my bag.
> He looked at me wearily. "What are you doing?"
> "You are not going to admit me. And I am not going to strip for you," I replied. "And so I am going to sit here and read a book."[76]

Eight hours later the stalemate ended, and Abuna was admitted back into his country.

Such brazen determination and his refusal to compromise his principles typify his steadfast, unique approach to peacemaking. It also helps to explain his deep commitment to his church:

> I was born into the Melkite Catholic Church. I wanted to find ways to minister to my community and the best way for me I found was within the Church. Since 1965 I have been ministering in the Galilee region. I minister to Christians, Muslims, Jews, and Druze and try to help "others" come closer. I do this by trying not to change their identities, but rather their minds and outlooks.[77]

Abuna Chacour thus challenges the members of his community to reflect on how they may relate to others without surrendering their religious, ethnic, and cultural identities.

He began his work in the troubled village of Ibillin in the Galilee. Ibillin's social fabric was torn apart after the 1948 War, and Melkite Christians, Muslims, and Greek Orthodox Christians vied for power. These divisions resulted in community problems including hatred of the "other," alcoholism, and bitter rivalry over the distribution of scarce resources such as water. Most distressing to Abuna Chacour was the hatred that grew among Christians. They came to despise the church, themselves, and their neighbors.[78]

Abuna Chacour began his ministry by committing himself to healing the community. He started by working to mend relations among the Christians themselves. When his initial approaches did not bear fruit, Abuna Chacour took more drastic action. On his first Palm Sunday in

Ibillin, he padlocked the church with the congregation inside and spoke from the heart:

> You are a people divided. You argue and hate each other – gossip and spread malicious lies. What do the Muslims and the unbelievers think when they see you? Surely, that your religion is false. If you can't love your brother that you see, how can you say you love God who is invisible? You have allowed the body of Christ to be disgraced....
>
> For many months, I've tried to unite you. I've failed because I am only a man. But there is someone else who can bring you together in true unity. His name is Jesus Christ. He is the one who gives you power to forgive. So now I will be quiet and allow Him to give you that power. If you will not forgive, we will stay locked in here. You can kill each other and I'll provide your funerals gratis.[79]

Stunned by his words, the congregation sat silent. Abuna recounts how he waited, fearing that his words had sowed greater separation of the people from the message of the Church. Then, slowly, one by one they began embracing one another and asking for forgiveness.[80]

From that day on, Abuna Chacour continued to preach about love and reconciliation, expanding his efforts beyond the Christian community. He enticed a few members of a community of Christian Sisters headed by his friend, Mother Josephate, to come to live and work in Ibillin. With their help, Abuna started building bridges among the Christians and Muslims. The sisters started by providing nursing care for local children. And soon, the love for children that both Christians and Muslims share became the connecting point for people from both traditions. After teaching Muslim women sewing, tailoring, baking, and engaging in joint Bible study, the sisters worked with all of the people in the city to open a school.[81]

Through actions and words, Abuna was helping Ibillin to heal. He repeatedly emphasized the importance of mutual respect based on a commitment to pluralism:

> I focus my work within the Arab, Palestinian, Christian and Muslim communities. I try to encourage them to believe in nonviolence and the importance of a pluralistic society. It is important that we recognize that we can be different from each other but still be complementary.
>
> My main job first is to help these Christian and Muslim communities open up to the outside Jewish community. I try to help them discover what is human versus what is [artificial]. I encourage them to open themselves to others.[82]

In 1967, Abuna's church sent him to Hebrew University to further provide him with enhanced tools to understand and teach about pluralism and the "other." He was the first Arab student to ever study Bible and Talmudic studies there, a great honor. Shortly after his arrival, however, the 1967 War erupted. Abuna gave blood for fallen Israelis. But then, two days before classes started, he witnessed hundreds of religious men and women – Christians – parading and celebrating the decisive victory of the Israeli army. For Abuna Chacour, these men and women were celebrating destructive might. He wept as he witnessed Christian ministers, priests, and nuns waving banners and messages including, "Prophecy is fulfilled." Profoundly disturbed, he instinctively navigated his way through the crowded streets to find his way into the Holy Sepulcher:

> I felt betrayed. Alone. My difficult work at reconciling Christians of Ibillin seemed so puny, so worthless in light of what I had just seen. I could understand the love of Christians for Jews – as my brothers I loved them too. But instead of demanding a true reconciliation to our conflict, my Christian brothers and sisters were applauding destructive might. And if Israel was so squarely in the center of prophecy and God's will, why was the nation coming unglued from within? The question of the suffering refugees was forgotten totally.[83]

He felt defeated, fearing that he would be unwelcome and isolated when he began his studies days later. Fortunately, his fears were groundless. Abuna Chacour was "continually amazed"[84] by his professors and fellow students, whom he found to be respectful intellectuals. In fact, Abuna represented a new voice in the university as its only Palestinian Bible and Talmudic scholar and therefore received invitations to receptions and events that brought him into contact with some of the most elite religious and government leaders from around the world. His introduction to such highly influential ambassadors, diplomats, ministers, priests, and rabbis would prove to be invaluable to his peacemaking efforts in years to come. On his graduation, the university issued an international press release that introduced Abuna Chacour to the world. Invitations for speaking engagements followed, as well as the opportunity to move to Geneva, where he taught for a year before returning to his peacemaking work in Ibillin.[85]

Abuna Chacour returned to Ibillin in 1970, where he remains today. There, he met his new bishop, a Christian leader and friend to Martin Luther King Jr. named Joseph Raya. He would become an inspiration and a colleague of Abuna's in nonviolent protest of Israel's treatment of the Palestinians. Together, in Abuna Chacour's childhood home of Biram, they organized a six-month camp-in of fifteen hundred people. The number fifteen hundred had particular meaning: it was exactly the size that the population of the village had been at the time of its destruction two decades earlier. Abuna Chacour explains why he organized the camp-in: "Our goal was simply to show the government of Israel that Palestinians wanted only to return to their homes to live in peace."[86]

This peaceful but dramatic protest was only a beginning. After the sit-in, he collaborated with Bishop Raya to organize a peaceful march to the Knesset in Jerusalem, calling on friends from Hebrew University and others to participate. On August 13, 1972, it was Abuna Chacour – as a Palestinian Christian – who led professors from Hebrew University and eight thousand Muslims, Druze, Jews, and Christians in a march designed to show the world that Jews and Palestinians alike oppose violence and affirm human dignity. In this, he succeeded, but the doors of the Knesset remained closed to the marchers.[87] Abuna Chacour returned to Galilee, his hopes unrealized. Again, it was Bishop Raya who provided inspiration, calling on him to move further – beyond protest and dialogue to action:

> You once told me that Palestinians need hope. You've seen how many Jews are for you. There's hope in that. But you've got to continue to build up the Palestinians.... When you build dignity, you begin to destroy prejudice.... [S]ometimes you must work and sweat if you are going to be a peacemaker: Not just talk about it. *You* build the communities. *You* build the schools.[88]

And within a few years, Abuna Chacour was doing just that – constructing community centers and promoting education.

Abuna Chacour is both a spiritual leader and a realistic man. Looking around him, he saw the lack of quality education for disadvantaged Palestinian students. Not surprisingly, he turned his focus to educating the next generation of Israeli Palestinians and Jews. To this end, he has helped found a library, summer camp, and community centers, and he has helped build numerous schools throughout the region. Simultaneously, he pioneered efforts to bring students of diverse backgrounds together to coexist peacefully. However, his efforts were not always welcome. Vandals more than once disrupted the construction of the community centers and schools – even sabotaging one site so seriously that Abuna was badly injured by falling bricks when he came to inspect it.[89]

But risk was not limited to the construction sites. Indeed, risk often seemed to follow Abuna Chacour. In the mid-1970s, Abuna was called to Beruit, Lebanon. En route, he was kidnapped by men in fatigues carrying rifles and taken to a barren room lit by just one light bulb. Abuna Chacour was then interrogated by a man whose identity he could not ascertain: "Was he Lebanese? Palestinian? Syrian? Or perhaps Jewish Israeli dressed as an Arab? It was impossible to tell." As it turned out, the kidnappers – members of the PLO – could not tell who Abuna Chacour was either. All they knew was that foreigners were entering Lebanon (including a Jewish man masquerading as a priest) to destroy Christian and Islamic houses of worship. Abuna Chacour, in a new cassock, was suspect, and his captors threatened him. But when he began talking about coming from Biram and about the nonviolent protests he had led, Abuna's captors realized that he was not an infiltrator. Once recognized as a fellow Palestinian, Abuna Chacour was freed. He soon returned to his work in building coexistence and providing education for the children.[90]

Mar Elias Educational Institutions (MEEI)

The perhaps most notable of his many educational initiatives started in 1982, when he founded the Prophet Elias High School on the Mount of Light in Ibillin. The school began with eighty students, but has since developed into a larger center known as Mar Elias Educational Institutions (MEEI). By 2003, the school had grown to more than four thousand students from kindergarten to the university level. The university is the first Arab-Israeli Christian University in Israel. The legacy of reconciliation that Abuna Chacour initiated in Ibillin many years ago now thrives at MEEI.

MEEI is a place where students of all backgrounds live, learn, and are given the opportunity to establish a common future together. Both Christian and Muslim students from Ibillin attend the schools, although there are more Christian than Muslim students. And despite the fact that there are no Jews and Druze living in Ibillin, students from both groups also attend MEEI.

Founding such a groundbreaking school was not easy. Abuna Chacour received considerable resistance from the government and went to court thirty-seven times to obtain building permits. When he was repeatedly thwarted, he took matters into his own hands and began building at night, despite receiving orders from the Israeli military to stop. When the police asked him how he could build without a permit, he responded: "I don't build with permits. I build with sand, cement, with cinder blocks, steel, and wood, not with permits."[91]

His stubborn resolve proved useful. On September 1, 1982, the Prophet Elias High School opened its doors, still without a permit. It was not until over one year later that Abuna was finally able to secure a building permit for the high school. But as the school grew, it became clear that it also needed a gym, which required a second permit. This time Abuna faced opposition not just from the standard biases of the Israeli bureaucracy, but from those within his own church who opposed his work. It took Abuna several more years to obtain this second permit and then only after U.S. Secretary of State James Baker advocated on Abuna's behalf to the Israeli government.

Notwithstanding these difficulties, MEEI has thrived. The Israeli Ministry of Education rated it as one of the best schools in all of Israel based on student test scores and the variety of technological courses it offered. Its groundbreaking emphasis on pluralism and inclusion has brought it worldwide recognition. Not surprisingly, MEEI attracts students from all over Israel, from as far as the Negev to the Lebanon border. However, students from certain areas are notably absent: "We do not have any students from Gaza and West Bank. They cannot come because of the current political situation. Palestinians in those areas are not permitted to visit Israel. But if they could, we would welcome them."[92]

One way Abuna Chacour encourages respect among his students is by celebrating the traditions of all the religions represented at the school:

> For holidays, I give my students two weeks off, but this is not a Christmas break. I tell my students that this is a holiday for Hanukah, Ramadan, and Christmas. I give the holidays to all the students so they can celebrate all of them. And for example, at New Years, for all the students we have banquets, eat, drink, and dance. [We] get to know each other as human beings.[93]

By celebrating their traditions together, the students learn about one another.

Abuna Chacour also integrates the teaching of interreligious understanding into the daily curricula:

> At MEEI we look at the positive values common to all religions. We do not propagandize for any of the religions. We teach the students to respect each other. We teach the students to look at each other as brothers and sisters. We live peacefully together. We do not simply talk, but we are actively living respectfully.

> For example, Jewish students come to MEEI for day exchanges. We have many student exchanges. We have also traveled with Jews to Jewish places. When there was a suicide bombing in Haifa, we donated blood [regardless of the religion or ethnicity of the recipients of the blood]. We do simple acts. We are not making miracles, we are not trying to bring Sharon and Arafat together because that would be impossible. But we can bring together the common Jewish, Christian, and Muslim man.[94]

Through small acts, Abuna Chacour teaches his students that each of them, working together, has the power to have a positive impact on their community.

MEEI also strives to promote a model of diversity through daily dialogue. By example, Abuna Chacour illustrates the value of dialogue to his students:

> Every day, I meet all the students and talk this same language, whether it is with the high school or university students of the community. Every day at MEEI, I ask everyone when they meet me anywhere on campus to look at me and give me a smile of hope.[95]

In response, the students eagerly smile back and shake his hand. Dialogue, it appears, need not always be verbal.

After learning about dialogue from Abuna Chacour and their teachers, the students at MEEI practice the technique in their daily interactions. Abuna recalls one situation in which he used his position to encourage Christian and Muslim students to use these skills to put new Jewish students at ease:

> I remember the first time we brought to MEEI a whole group of Jewish students to the 12th grade. During the first week, the Jewish students would not leave their classroom because they were suspicious of the other students and afraid of them. So, I sent to the Jewish students a few girls and boys, Christian and Muslim Arabs, and they tried to talk together. At the end, I could see that they tamed each other, and after three weeks you could hardly find them in the classroom anymore. They were all out in the basketball field or in the gym.
>
> They [Jewish, Muslim, and Christian students] discussed very simple things when they went to talk to each other. For example, "Who are you?" "I'm from here ... this town, that village." "We're happy to have you here." The Christian and Muslim Arab students introduced themselves, and they were prepared to meet the Jewish students. . . .
>
> They are prepared to meet students from different backgrounds. We at MEEI try to explain to the students about the human parts of the Jewish students. We teach that they are the same and have ambitions like the

Muslim and Christian students, but they come from different societies. The Jewish students do not need to be a copy of our society... they can remain themselves, they are different but complementary.[96]

Simply by introducing themselves and seeking to learn more about the backgrounds of their new classmates, the Christian and Muslim students were able to establish friendships with the Jewish students. Abuna explains that similar dialogue techniques are used every year by the staff at MEEI to welcome the new ninth grade students:

> Every year new ninth graders who come from far away villages are reluctant. Some of them are even afraid because they will be mixed with almost fifteen hundred other students. Those from purely Muslim villages are afraid of Christians and some students from purely Christian villages are afraid of the Muslim students. They often do not gladly agree to establish spontaneous friendships with each other. They needed to use tutors [each class has professionally-trained tutors] to convince them of the beauty of being different and that the challenge is to get to know each other, and that they can be enriched by each other.... These tutors are skilled professionals... and they teach this same ideology, but with their own language. They do not use the same words because they aren't copies of each other, but they use the same ideology. "[97]

Once again, dialogue succeeds in bringing together the students at MEEI. With the help of trained tutors, the students learn how to transcend differences in order to form friendships.

Abuna Chacour makes sure that MEEI actively keeps the parents informed of the students' progress in their studies and relationships at the school, thereby expanding the message of coexistence:

> We have a parents meeting twice a year. Out of sixteen hundred parents, we have at least fourteen hundred parents who come. The mother and father usually come together. You know, the best ambassadors for a school are its own students and the students act as good ambassadors. And the students go to their parents and join them in spreading the news about the children at MEEI.
>
> At the meetings we talk about the students, about their relations, about updates on different institutions and programs at MEEI. The parents get to be informed about the campus as well.[98]

At these meetings, Abuna Chacour receives positive feedback from the parents. But the best feedback is the fact that the parents continue to bring their children and their friends' children to MEEI. The parents approve of the relationships that their sons and daughters form while at

MEEI and reinforce their support of the school by participating in a parents' network. They give their time and money to help organize activities
such as fund-raisers for the school. MEEI has thus become the focal
point around which both the students and parents of the community
come together. Through their commitment, MEEI's positive reputation
now extends beyond the Galilee region.

Just as he preached to his congregation in his early days in Ibillin,
Abuna now uses his position as president of MEEI to expound on the
theme of pluralism in Israeli society:

> We educate our students at MEEI about the fact that we are living together
> in Israel and we come from different religions and ethnic backgrounds.
> We are a pluralistic society and we pride ourselves on belonging to the one
> God ... the descendants of Abraham from Mesopotamia.
>
> The question is, whether we will be able to create a certain unity of
> destiny together through a very strict respect of the differences and of the
> personalities and of the ethics and traditions – in other terms, will it be
> possible to create a concrete human community within this big diversity
> of options and venues? This could be a role model for Israeli citizens, both
> Arab and Jew, and for all of the Middle East, and in particular, for the
> international community.[99]

Especially after the terrorist attacks of September 11, 2001, Abuna
believes it is of utmost importance that people work together to build
a community model that values diversity. As a result of the attacks, he
has found heightened suspicion and divisiveness, particularly at U.S. air-
ports. To counterbalance this suspicion, Abuna Chacour believes that
schools must take action:

> Much depends on the education of the individual to promote the good
> or evil that is inherent in human nature. I do believe that the goodness
> that is in every human being is as contagious as the evil, if not much
> more, provided we do it with conviction, with determination, and with
> perseverance. This is exactly what MEEI campus aims at doing, at living
> and at sharing inside worldly and outside worldly.[100]

Blood Brothers and International Peacemaking

In 1984, two years after the founding of MEEI, Abuna Chacour published *Blood Brothers,* an autobiography telling of his experiences as
a Palestinian Christian growing up in Israel and his struggle to overcome the conflict in his homeland. The book has since been translated into twenty-eight languages and has been read by thousands,

including numerous prominent religious leaders, kings, and heads of state.

The book's publication increased Abuna's visibility, allowing him greater access to influential people such as those he met during his studies at Hebrew University. He uses these connections to lobby on behalf of his fellow Palestinians and to further his educational work with children. Over the years, he has received recognition for his efforts – including several honorary doctorate degrees and awards – and in 2001, he was given the prestigious Niwano Prize and named Man of the Year in Israel. In addition, Abuna Chacour received the *Peacemaker in Action* award from the Tanenbaum Center and was nominated for the Nobel Peace Prize three times (1986, 1989, and 1994). And in 2006, Abuna was named the archbishop of the Galilee by the Vatican and the Synod of the Greek Catholic Patriarchate of Antioch. This appointment makes him the most senior cleric of the Greek Catholic Church in the Holy Land, with a congregation of about fifty-five thousand, the single largest Christian community in Israel.

On behalf of his fellow Palestinians, Abuna travels widely and receives hundreds of Christian pilgrims who visit him in the remote town of Ibillin. He is a vocal proponent of interaction across differences, starting with the "living stones" (the indigenous Christians in the Holy Land who are descendants of the first Christian communities in Galilee). "Living stones are more important than holy shrines," he once said.[101] "Travelers visit the sand and stones, but don't want to share the faith with their brothers and sisters."[102]

Both theologically and philosophically, Abuna Chacour focuses on differences and how to achieve reconciliation. Theologically, he is quick to assert that God is accessible to all: "God is not a tribal God.... Not being tribal, God can no more be the God of Israel or [of] the church or even [of] Christianity.... We do not have a monopoly over God or the Holy Spirit."[103] Philosophically, Abuna starts with our commonalities while recognizing differences and different identities. "I wasn't born an Arab, or an Israeli, or a Christian. I was just born a baby in the likeness of God, not more, not less either," he said.[104] Such characteristically simple language allows Abuna to cut across complex divides, including religion, race, and nationality to emphasize each person's common humanity and their shared relationship with God.

Abuna's approach to reconciliation in Israel involves these beliefs. For him, differences are to be understood merely as "different"; they do not involve one side always being right and the other always being wrong.

This is the premise from which Abuna Chacour begins his work of reconciliation. But this is just the beginning of his analysis:

> [Conflict resolution] is a matter of building bridges among members of
> the same family. Always there is the temptation of violence and might, but
> the ones who build bridges acknowledge, "My friend is also right, and I
> am also wrong."
>
> This is to become Godlike. God cares for the oppressed and feels their
> torment and suffering. In these struggles, God always takes the side of
> liberation, not the side of particular people or nations as favorites. God also
> calls to the oppressor to be liberated from fear, anger, and lust for power.
>
> This land, this Palestine, this Israel, does not belong to either Jews or
> Palestinians. Rather, we are compatriots who belong to the land and to
> each other. If we cannot live together, surely we will be buried here together.
> We must choose life.[105]

Thousands have heard Abuna Chacour's words and have listened to his
message – through his books, his talks, his meetings with visitors, and
his schools. And his message is one of action: "Peace needs no contem-
plators, it needs actors, people who are willing to get their hands dirty,
to get up and do something. The same is true for justice."[106] As his life
demonstrates, these are principles that guide Abuna Chacour.

Reflections on Peacemaking Methods

When asked if he has any specific methods that he employs as a peacemaker, not surprisingly, Abuna refers to the Bible. After pondering for a
moment, he offers insight into the role of dialogue in his peacemaking
work:

> It is extremely moving to see that the first crime in human history is
> described as the absence of dialogue and the giving in to one's own emo-
> tions and hatred, and by an evasive answer to the Creator, which in itself
> was a lie. When Abel answered God and said, "Am I my brother's custo-
> dian," he was lying because he pretended not to know where his brother
> was and he wanted to hide the fact that he murdered his brother. Dialogue
> is the contrast of confrontation, the dismissal of confrontation. Dialogue
> in itself is a denial of rejection and the acceptance of a potential break-
> through through the heart and mind of the other.[107]

Abuna Chacour elaborates on the intricacies of dialogue with references
to the Talmud:

> It is what we read in the Talmud – who is the hero? It is the man who can
> control his own emotions. The hero of heroes is the man who can turn his

enemy into friend or . . . a brother or sister. This is the meaning of dialogue, the ultimate goal of dialogue unless a person is so paranoid that he enters into dialogue with hidden agenda and he starts by suspecting the others and looking for their failures. If you look for failure, you will always find failures. This is an inclination toward evil.[108]

For Abuna, these passages in the Bible and Talmud establish dialogue as a critical means of reaching out to the "other." Through dialogue based on calm, controlled interaction, people are able to see one another, not as their greatest enemies, but as family members.

By resisting the emotions of hatred and engaging one another in honest discussion of underlying problems, Abuna believes that enemies can resolve even the most sensitive and complex issues, including the current Arab-Israeli conflict. He contends that it is time to address the real obstacles that impede the peace process: "I believe that we need to speak less about peace and more about justice and integrity. We need justice and integrity for security."[109] If Israelis and Palestinians would truly listen to one another – as is essential in genuine dialogue – it is Abuna's conviction that progress toward an acceptable resolution could be made:

> The ongoing violence here in Israel, whether against the Jews or Palestinians, is a very big factor that has convinced me to shout out loudly and clearly "Stop the bloodshed!" All those who are killed are beloved by their own people. On one side they are seen as martyrs and on the other as terrorists. We need to listen to the victims on both sides who say "no more martyrs."[110]

Since suicide bombings and missile strikes have done so little to resolve the Arab-Israeli conflict, it may be time to heed Abuna's call to listen to the victims of both sides who demand that there be no more martyrs.

Religiously Motivated Peacemaking

What drives people such as Abuna Chacour to become professional peacemakers? As we have seen, one passage in the New Testament continually speaks to him, motivates him, and sustains him – the Beatitudes. Abuna Chacour explains why he still finds this scripture so compelling:

> The Sermon on the Mount has been most influential on my peacemaking. The Beatitudes is three chapters of the Gospel of Matthew within the Sermon on the Mount. The Sermon summarizes all of the teachings of the

New Testament. Following these teachings helps us become God like, and we can become his people.[111]

By following these teachings, Abuna Chacour believes he moves closer to God and all that God represents. "The only definition that we have of God has moved me deeply – God is love."[112]

Abuna Chacour's understanding of the Beatitudes has also deepened since the time his mother first recited them to him when he was a child. During the course of his graduate studies, he gained a mastery of the biblical languages – New Testament Greek and biblical Hebrew as well as Aramaic, the language Jesus used to preach when he was alive. This allowed Abuna to read original texts rather than simply relying on translations. In so doing, he has reconciled the discrepant views of Jesus that plagued him as a child. The key lay in a mistranslation of the word "Blessed." As he explains:

> "Blessed " is the translation of the word *makarioi,* used in the Greek New Testament. . . . However, when I look further back to Jesus's Aramaic, I find that the original word was *ashray,* from the verb *yashar. Ashray* does not have this passive quality to it at all. Instead, it means, "to set yourself on the right way for the right goal, to turn around, repent; to become straight or righteous."[113]

Abuna Chacour asks rhetorically: "How could I go to a persecuted young man in a Palestinian refugee camp, for instance, and say: 'Blessed are those who are persecuted for the sake of justice, for theirs is the kingdom of heaven'? That man would revile me, saying neither I nor my God understood his plight, and he would be right."[114] When Abuna Chacour reads the Beatitudes in the original Aramaic, the message of Jesus becomes active, visceral, and powerful. Perhaps predictably, Abuna Chacour prefers his own translation:

> Get up, go ahead, do something, move, you who are hungry and thirsty for justice, for you shall be satisfied.
> Get up, go ahead, move, you peacemakers, for you shall be called children of God.[115]

In Abuna Chacour's words, the essence of Jesus's message can really be summarized as follows: "Get your hands dirty to build a human society for human beings; otherwise, others will torture and murder the poor, the voiceless and the powerless."[116] Be active, be God-like.

Moving Forward: The Future of the Mar Elias Institutions

As of 2006, Abuna Elias Chacour continues to serve as president of the Mar Elias Educational Institutions. In 2004, MEEI celebrated its twentieth anniversary and now consists of the following: Miriam Bawardi's Kindergarten; the Elementary School; the High School; the Engineering College; the Regional Teacher's Center; and the Gifted Children's School. Additionally, in October 2003, MEEI opened its Arab-Israeli Campus, a university that has been accredited in both Israel and the United States.[117]

To this day, Abuna Chacour can be found at MEEI, greeting students with open arms and a warm smile, and actively practicing dialogue.

The Settler Who Spoke with Arafat

Rabbi Menachem Froman

At the edge of the Judean desert resides Orthodox Rabbi Menachem Froman of Tekoa, the biblical home of the prophet Amos. A founder of the Gush Emunim (Bloc of the Faithful) settler movement and father of ten children, Rabbi Froman has spent the majority of his life promoting Jewish-Muslim reconciliation between Jewish settlers and Palestinian residents in the West Bank and Gaza.

With the land he loves defining his perspective, Froman describes the conflict in this region in the simplest of terms as a tragedy of "two peoples loving the same land." Nonetheless, he remains optimistic that peace is possible:

> Perhaps for most basic problems of human existence there are no solutions, but in this situation – where two peoples love the same land – I see a solution: we can't think it will happen in one day (when you hear Arabs, youngsters and adults, speaking with hatred about the Jews and Jews speaking with hatred about Arabs), but gradually, I hope that this land – one of its names in Arabic is The Land of Peace or The Land of God – will be large enough, generous enough to give love to those two peoples living here.[118]

Froman's hope derives from the religious mandate to "'Love your neighbor" (the Golden Rule), which he believes is the core value that unites all the Abrahamic faiths. Supported by this core belief, Froman works for the peaceful coexistence of Israelis and Palestinians within what he envisions as a "humane state." This vision has inspired him to make a revolutionary call to declare Jerusalem an ex-territorial, shared "City of God," which has helped him bridge the gap between the diverse peoples who share his beloved land.

Froman's religious sensibility and commitment to peace have given him a unique perspective that consequently has provided him with unusual access to a variety of influential political and religious figures. He has been able to work with Israeli and Palestinian leaders to help lay a foundation of peace, and has helped bring adversaries together. Far more than a mere network organizer, Froman has been a key mediator in conflicts, serving as a respected advisor to groups from diverse backgrounds and opposing political affiliations. In turn, he has received the friendship and respect of individuals from a range of traditions. Yasser Arafat called Froman "Wise One" and Sheikh Talal Sider, a former Hamas sympathizer, fondly refers to him as an "Israeli Hero."

Rabbi Menachem Froman

Menachem Froman was born into a Polish family in the mid-1940s and later attended the Reali High School in Haifa.[119] The school's goal is to produce well-rounded Jewish students who value tolerance and humanism and are well prepared to contribute to Israeli society.[120] Rabbi Froman is a model product of this education, becoming a fully engaged Israeli citizen.

When the 1967 Six-Day War erupted, Froman fought as a paratrooper in the *Nahal* unit of the Israel Defense Forces. He recalls the experience: "For my generation, the Six-Day War was *the* war. It was the first war in which I fought [as a *Nahal* paratrooper]."[121] "*Nahal*," which stands for "*Noar Halutzi Lohem*" (Fighting Pioneer Youth), is a unit that combines military service in a combat unit with civilian service in a newly founded *kibbutz* or *moshav* (collective and semicollective villages).[122]

A few years later, Froman moved to Jerusalem and enrolled in *Mercaz HaRav* Yeshiva, one of the largest Talmudical colleges in Israel. The college was founded in 1924 by the first Ashkenazi Chief Rabbi of *Eretz Yisrael*, HaRav Avraham Yitzchak HaCohen Kook (often referred to as Rav Kook the Elder), who taught "that the inner spark of divine light shines in all the different religions."[123] The school was established to "raise up and educate scholars and leaders in Israel, filled with a deep love for their fellow Jew, and imbued with the love of the Torah and the love of the Land of Israel."[124] During Froman's years as a student at Mercaz HaRav, the college was under the leadership of Rav Kook the Elder's son, Tzvi Yehuda Kook, who took on a more messianic and nationalist tone, encouraging the students to settle the biblical Land of Israel; to oversimplify, the younger Kook focused on redemption for Jews and saw settlement of all of the biblical land of Israel as the first step in achieving full redemption.

Froman, however, "was the ultimate student of Rav Kook [the Elder], and one of the few who took all of [his teachings] ... seriously, including the universally redemptive, the care expressed for all humanity that became overshadowed by ultra-nationalism at the hands of Rabbi Kook's successor."[125] As such, his worldview went beyond issues of Jewish nationalism and valued Jews and non-Jews alike.

Rabbi Froman fondly remembers Mercaz HaRav Yeshiva, where he was ordained as rabbi by the Chief Rabbinate of Israel. He laughingly recalls how the walls of Mercaz HaRav were filled with numerous pictures of bearded rabbis, side by side with "pictures of [Theodor] Herzl with a top hat; but in ... [one] photograph, he was bare-headed."[126] For Mercaz HaRav, the pictures are symbolic, showing that even secular Zionists were welcomed when seeking to achieve redemption.[127] This belief that even the secular can have a religious impact can be viewed in any number of ways, but with regard to Froman, it sheds light on his belief that people of all religions must be taken into account if peace in the holy land is to be achieved.

Evolution of a Peacemaker

After the October 1973 Yom Kippur War, the Israeli Likud party, then in power, supported the establishment of Jewish settlements beyond the Green Line. That same year, Froman completed his studies and made his home in the West Bank settlement of Tekoa, where he later was to become cief rabbi. A founding member of the settler movement Gush Emunim, Froman actively sought to bring his knowledge from Mercaz HaRav into his new community.

Tekoa is a small town; in 2003 it had a population of about 1250. The community is diverse, consisting of native-born Israelis and Jewish immigrants from the United States, Russia, France, Britain, Argentina, Chile, South Africa, India, Burma, and Mexico, among others. The diversity is also reflected in the distinct traditions of its Jewish citizens – Sephardic, Ashkenazi, Yemenite, and others – and in the languages they speak: English, Hebrew, French, Spanish, Russian, and Yiddish. Professionally, they are farmers, urban professionals, artists, musicians, craftspeople, doctors, lawyers, and nurses.[128]

Tekoa is located at the geographical center of the conflict between the Palestinians and Israelis over land in the West Bank.[129] But when Rabbi Froman and his fellow settlers first came to the area, this conflict was not what they expected:

> I am ... one of the first people to come to what was called the "English Territories," and what we now call "Judea and Samaria." You have to believe me; we thought that the Arabs – the Palestinians – would be glad that we were coming. I remember many years before. I was with a friend who is now the editor of "Necouda," the settlers' newspaper. His wife had just given birth and I asked him what he wanted me to buy as a gift. He replied, "Buy me an Arabic grammar book, because if we are going to settle here, we have to know Arabic." Gradually, of course, we understood that the Palestinians were not so happy that the Jews are coming back to Judea.[130]

In short, Rabbi Froman and his fellow settlers did not appreciate the extent to which their presence would affect Palestinians already in the area.

Although Froman and some of his friends anticipated that they would be neighborly to the nearby Palestinians and become well versed in their language and customs, as time passed, close relations failed to develop. Settlers barely interacted with the Palestinians, and it became apparent to Rabbi Froman that the Palestinians found their presence in the West Bank disturbing. Ultimately, the rise of the First Intifada in 1987 brought the point home unmistakably:

> The very concrete expression of Palestinian unhappiness was the [first] *Intifada*. For all of us, the *Intifada* was the beginning of a mental process to understand what was happening. My wife says that the Palestinians stoned us because they want a human touch with us. [For] many years we passed through this road and we didn't speak to them. They wanted a human exchange so they throw stones.
>
> My first contact with the *Intifada* was immediately after I had an interview published in a famous Palestinian newspaper. In Jerusalem, they gave me a copy of the newspaper in which I was interviewed. On my way back to Tekoa where I live, I was in a car with a friend and was reading what I had said about peace and good intentions. While I was reading, I was hit

by a stone, which wounded me. There was the blood on the page where I was talking about peace and hope for the future.

Most of my friends in the settlements speak about the *Intifada* as the story of disappointment because, believe it or not, most of them have not come to live in these territories to rule the Arabs. Most of them aren't politicians, and they hope that there will be a way for the two populations to live together in those territories.[131]

The Intifada was a wake-up call. Through it, Rabbi Froman came to better understand the impact of the Jewish settlements. As a consequence, he began to move away ideologically from some of the early settlers. They continued to believe that it was imperative for Israel to maintain sovereignty over the biblical land of Israel, which they viewed as part of their Jewish birthright. However, although still attached to Tekoa – the community that had become his home – Rabbi Froman started to espouse a different concept. He envisioned an arrangement in which Israel and Palestine might, as two states, rule simultaneously over the Holy Land. Later, he would expand on that concept with the idea that Jerusalem should become ex-territorial, a city for all religions and all people.[132] Convinced that the Jews and Palestinians are destined to live together, Rabbi Froman took it on himself in 1989 to help create a network of life for both groups, what he calls a "humane state" – *medina enoshit*. In this way, he has become an activist working to forge peaceful coexistence among the Muslims, Jews, and Christians in the Holy Land. Froman explains:

> Every effort for peace is important. God has his treasure to pay everyone who makes any effort for peace, be it a politician, a farmer or a journalist. In Hebrew and in Arabic, to say you are acting for peace is to say you are acting for God.[133]

Acting for God, Rabbi Froman thus embarked on his campaign for inter-religious peace.

Grassroots Peacemaking

To the surprise of many, the Oslo Accords of 1993 created considerable excitement and brought hope to Israelis and Palestinians that the Arab-Israeli conflict might at last be resolved. When asked what effect he believed the accords could have on his country, Rabbi Froman said the pressing goals of the present were to "refine the military foundations of our nationality" and to work to make provisions for a system to be developed in cooperation with the Palestinians where both groups could live together. Froman envisions in the future the creation of a "humane state," consisting of two states in one territory. In such a state, Froman imagines that Palestinians and settlers each enjoy full independence while living on the same land, conducting business together, and not giving way to violence. He also hopes that the citizens of Israel can live in Judea and Samaria and stresses the political significance of peaceful coexistence between the Palestinians and the settlers:

> I would not want to see after the Berlin Wall already fallen that we put up a Hebron Wall, certainly not in Jerusalem. From this perspective, the settlements serve an important purpose since they, like the Arab communities in Israel, force politicians to think of models of living together and not to coalesce behind their walls.[134]

Rabbi Froman notes that "If you want to make peace in Washington or Oslo, or on the moon, you can ignore the settlements, but not here." He envisions a system built on cooperation and reciprocation to reflect and accommodate the two populations. Even though he admits that such a vision does not appear realistic at the moment, he stresses the importance of holding on to the ideal, because he firmly believes that such a vision is possible. He also believes that, at least to a certain degree, the "humane state" that he supports already exists.[135]

Although the people living in the region often see themselves as belonging to one nation or the other with mutually exclusive claims to the land, Rabbi Froman thinks otherwise. He makes reference to Behar in the Torah, which explains that the land belongs to God (Leviticus 25:23): "And the land shall not be sold in perpetuity; for the land is Mine; for you are strangers and settlers with Me."[136] As such, Froman finds biblical justification for his vision of a shared land.

Shortly after the signing of the Oslo Accords, Rabbi Froman determined to promote peace practically by working at the grassroots level. During one of his early attempts at reconciliation, he introduced himself to General Nasser Yussef, who would later become the interior minister of the Palestinian government formed by Ahmed Qureia in 2003.

Yussef, a refugee from the small village near Beit She'an and a military man, had just arrived in the Gaza Strip from Tunis. To Rabbi Froman's surprise, Yussef eagerly expressed an interest in partnering with Froman to promote religious reconciliation between Muslims and Jews. Since then, Rabbi Froman and Yussef – along with their families – have been inseparable. They pray together and recite each other's prayers. At one point, Yussef served as a link to arrange meetings between Rabbi Froman and Dr. Mahmoud a-Zahar, a Hamas leader in Gaza, which led to a peace agreement that set in place the first *hudna*, or cease-fire.[137] On January 21, 1997, Rabbi Froman met with the Arab Mayor of Hebron, Mustafa Natshe, to improve settler-Palestinian relations. Froman initiated the meeting to improve cooperation between the two groups: "My premise is that for Jews to live in all of *Eretz Yisrael*, they have to create a network of life with the Arabs."[138] To move forward, Rabbi Froman says, "You have to recognize the new reality. Neither Natshe nor I prayed for this agreement, but it's what we have." He also explains that good relations between the Palestinians and settlers were necessary so that "every time a mobile home is put up somewhere, there will not be an international uproar."[139]

Overall, the meeting went well. According to Rabbi Froman, Mayor Natshe told him "that he invites Jews to live in Hebron, that he has no problem with this, and that all the problems are only from troublemakers." After the meeting, Mayor Natshe also remarked that "We welcome any Jew or Israeli who wishes to recognize the Palestinian Authority in Hebron, and to say we wish to live in peace."[140]

Rabbi Froman believes that regular meetings with the "other" can help build trust. In early fall 1997, he met with the spiritual leader of Hamas – Sheikh Ahmad Yassin – at his home in Gaza in an effort to bring an end to attacks on Israelis. The two had met previously over the years, and Rabbi Froman had actually visited the sheikh in Israeli jails several times. He recalls the 1997 encounter:

> It is not easy to confront a person who openly calls for murder. I went to see him because I thought my visits might result in less killing. I prayed and continue to pray for this. I didn't go to Sheikh Yassin as a sign of forgiveness.[141]

By emphasizing what Islam and Judaism share in common, the two men – it was hoped – might begin to build community and thereby reduce violence.[142]

As the end of the century neared, progress toward peaceful interreligious reconciliation seemed possible. To celebrate this possibility, Rabbi Froman joined Buddhist, Christian, Jewish, and Muslim spiritual leaders for common prayers on November 23, 1999, on the shores of the Sea of Galilee in Israel. The shared prayer was part of an interreligious conference organized by the Interreligious Coordinating Council in Israel and by Jubillenium, a commercial company dealing with millennium-related activities. Linking hands, Rabbi Froman along with His Holiness

the Dalai Lama, Sheikh Ali Abu-Salach of Ramallah, Franciscan Father
Maximillian Mizzi from Assisi, Canon Andrew P. B. White of Coventry
Cathedral,* and Rabbi Avraham Soetendorp – a Liberal rabbi from The
Hague – all came together and stood silently in prayer. Rabbi Froman
gently turned HH the Dalai Lama toward the south, explaining that "this
is the way we pray, in the direction of Jerusalem. It is also the direction
of Mecca."[143] The symbolism of these spiritual leaders standing together
was lost on no one.

Advocating for the "Other"

Rabbi Froman's work focuses on creating positive one-to-one interactions with spiritual men and women of other religious traditions. In
July 1999, he met with the Palestinian Sufi Sheikh Abu Salih of Deir
Qaddis in Ashkelon. They immediately found a common spiritual language, and decided to reconvene again on May 14, 2000, to hold a "Holy
Land" seminar at Yakar Center. There, the two of them spoke to an audience of one hundred about the challenges of spiritual freedom and about
the dangers of not taking responsibility for achieving it. They stressed
that hatred and fear are the result of exaggerated attachments to one's
ego. All present attested to the moving intellectual, mystical, and emotional exchange between the two men. Since then, just as with General
Yussef, Rabbi Froman and Sheikh Abu Salih have maintained their deep
friendship.

In late September 2000, negotiations that seemed to be making
progress throughout the year came to a crashing halt. The second Intifada
broke out following a visit by Ariel Sharon to the Temple Mount/al-Haram
al-Sharif area, a site of great religious significance to both Jews and
Muslims. The progress toward peace and reconciliation that Rabbi Froman had been working toward seemed to be derailed almost overnight.
Despite attempts by the Israeli government to quell the ensuing violence,
the Intifada continued.

On October 16, 2000, the eve of the Sharm-el-Sheikh Summit (which
was called to quell the violence), Rabbi Froman delivered an impas-
sioned call to the Israeli government and the international community, warning that there would never be peace in Israel and Palestine

---

* Canon Andrew P. B. White was named the Tanenbaum Center's 2004 Peacemaker in
  Action. His case study – including his tireless work to resolve the Israeli-Palestinian
  conflict, mediate in Nigeria, and bring peace to Iraq – will be featured in an upcoming
  Tanenbaum Center publication.

until the negotiators understand the power and importance of religious dialogue.[144] Rabbi Froman pointed to the violence of the Second Intifada and predicted that any peace initiative that did not take Muslim sensitivities into account would ultimately fail.

He characterized the Israeli governments of the past, particularly those on the left, as routinely attending to other issues under the false assumption that issues stemming from religious difference would resolve themselves. While recognizing that economic factors are important, Rabbi Froman maintains that economics did not trigger the riots after Ariel Sharon visited the Temple Mount/al-Haram al-Sharif area: "It is true that the Israeli Arabs face economic frustration, but it was not over this that they burned the post office in Jaffa and blocked the highway in Wadi Ara."[145] Rather, Muslim sensitivity over the Temple Mount/al-Haram al-Sharif has been a source of unrest since the 1929 revolts during the mandate period. Rabbi Froman therefore urges that: "In the Holy Land, you can't make peace without attending to the issue of holiness."[146] Certainly many factors are at play, but religion cannot be ignored.

Several months later in early April 2001, Yasser Arafat invited Rabbi Froman to his presidential palace in Ramallah. Arafat, who refers to Rabbi Froman as *Alhakeem,* or "Wise One," wanted to know his Orthodox Jewish perspective on the rising Intifada. Rabbi Froman eagerly shared his perspective and argued for the establishment of a joint committee of sheikhs and rabbis:

> I urged Arafat to give his blessing to the formation of a joint committee of sheikhs and rabbis to discuss religious aspects of the Israeli-Palestinian conflict. Religious problems must be separated from political ones. I want Arafat to draw up a letter addressed to the two chief rabbis of Israel, stating his approval for such a committee. He said he would seriously consider it.[147]

Rabbi Froman envisioned a council of sheikhs and rabbis devoted to creating a "joint solution of all problems existing between Israelis and Palestinians and the creation of a peaceful atmosphere between all believers."[148] In addition to the joint committee, Rabbi Froman also requested that Sheikh Talal Sider – a former Hamas sympathizer with whom he had been meeting for over a decade and the only Muslim cleric in Arafat's cabinet – meet with Israeli Chief Rabbi Eliyahu Bakshi-Doron. Chairman Arafat did not respond immediately to Rabbi Froman's suggestion, but later said that it was an "excellent idea."[149] Several days after this meeting, Sheikh Sider called Rabbi Froman to tell him that Arafat had approved of the meeting. Prime Minister Ariel Sharon also gave his approval.

Accordingly, on April 11, 2001, Rabbi Froman convened Sheikh Talal Sider and Sephardic Chief Rabbi Eliyahu Bakshi-Doron at Bakshi-Doron's home in Jerusalem. Israeli Deputy Foreign Minister Michael Melchior also was in attendance. Sheikh Sider conveyed his best wishes for the Israeli people for the Passover holiday on Arafat's behalf, and the entire meeting was used to begin building relationships. When their time together was over, Deputy Foreign Minister Melchior said he expected a joint call for ending violence on both sides to be issued shortly by the religious officials. Of the meeting, Sheikh Sider commented that it was the Palestinian Authority's opportunity to declare that "we are saying to the people in Israel that we are interested in the path of peace, not war."[150] In addition to shared sentiments and joint statements, the meeting also produced a concrete outcome. After working hard to promote the idea, Rabbi Froman and Sheikh Sider established a joint council of Jewish and Muslim clerics to work for peace.[151] His vision was becoming a reality.

Coming off the heels of this successful meeting, on April 12, 2001, Rabbi Froman published his views on the status of Jerusalem, long a controversial point in the Arab-Israeli conflict. Drawing on biblical teachings, he articulated his vision of Jerusalem as a city for all of humanity, regardless of faith or nationality:

> In framing a view of Jerusalem's future, we would do well to draw upon our divine heritage. Isaiah's famed vision of Jerusalem at the End of Days, for example, was that "instruction shall come forth from Zion, and the word of the Lord from Jerusalem . . . nation shall not take up sword against nation; they shall never again know war."
>
> Why not bring that prophecy to fruition by turning Jerusalem into a place worthy of her name: a city of peace?[152]

Following its victories in the War of Independence and the Six-Day War, Rabbi Froman hopes that Israel will use its sovereignty over the region to declare the Old City of Jerusalem what he terms "ex-territorial." Similar to his vision of the "humane state," discussed earlier, he envisions Jerusalem as being a shared, sacred city, one that transcends the national power games that have troubled the region for years. Israel, he asserts, is now at a unique moment in history where it has the opportunity to help establish peace, a move that as a rabbi he believes is in line with the Jewish tradition:

Jewish tradition contains many expressions of the idea that Jerusalem is not confined by the bounds of common territoriality. The *Midrash,* for example, cites it as the place from which Jacob's Ladder connected earth with heaven. And the *Gemarah* (Baba Batra 75) tells us that Jerusalem is named after God and is the place where the commemoration of God's name, His essence and intent must be expressed throughout history.

If the purpose of Zionism is to transform the sublime visions of our heritage into reality here on earth, wouldn't its true fulfillment be the realization of Isaiah's vision here in this temporal city. . .

Isn't it only proper that Jerusalem be the place where members of all faiths convene to renounce their breeding of prejudice, hostility and war and work to fashion world peace? We do Jerusalem no honor if we insist that it be to us what Belgrade is to Yugoslavia. Jerusalem deserves to be more: a realization of our potential to rise above the narrow sense of nationalism.[153]

Just as Rabbi Froman believes that the Israeli government has a unique opportunity to promote peace in the region, he also recognizes the significance of Jerusalem to all members of the Abrahamic faiths throughout the world. Thus, if Israel were to act in such a way with international support, an ex-territorial Jerusalem could help to promote peace throughout the world, acting as

a bridge between the Muslim world and the West to help defuse tensions that spread well beyond the Middle East. Both the United States and Europe can make meaningful contributions in this sphere. The Pope has repeatedly expressed his desire to have the start of the new millennium mark the end of the historical conflict between Christianity, Judaism and Islam, and other Christian denominations will be able to endorse the plan on similar grounds.

. . . We must work to ensure that Jerusalem's future is built in the spirit of "yeru-shalom," a legacy of peace.[154]

Rabbi Froman's focus on shoring up goodwill in the midst of the Intifada was tested a month later when two fourteen-year-old Israeli boys from Tekoa were found murdered in a cave near Bethlehem on May 9, 2001.[155] The boys had been beaten to death with stones. Despite the outrage in his community, Rabbi Froman was determined to turn the dark energy into something positive. He reminded his fellow settlers of the Jews who had come before them in that part of the Judean desert, including King Jehoshaphat who had praised God in the face of his enemies and prevailed, and the prophet Amos who lived in Tekoa. "All of them are looking over us to see how we bear our responsibility in the current situation,"

Rabbi Froman explained to the Tekoa settlers. Comforting them, he said that they would work together to ensure that the Jews would remain and prosper in the lands of their ancestors. To help the families of the murdered children during their time of grief, Rabbi Froman introduced them to his good friend, Sheikh Abu Salih. In particular, one of the mothers, Rina, felt a connection with Sheikh Salih. Although he was Sufi and Palestinian and she was Jewish and Israeli, he reached out across the divide and consoled her with the depth of his spiritual nature.[156]

Peacemaking via Interreligious Conferences

On September 11, 2001, al-Qaeda operatives attacked the World Trade Center in New York. Shocked, religious leaders from around the world convened under the auspices of the World Conference on Religions for Peace to condemn the attacks in October 2001. This conference would be only one of many in which Rabbi Froman would participate to promote his vision of interreligious reconciliation.

At the symposium titled "Rejecting Terror, Promoting Peace with Justice: Religions Respond," religious leaders addressed root causes of terrorism and proposed solutions to the Israeli-Palestinian conflict. Rabbi Froman served as chief rabbi of Eliyahu Bakshi-Doron's envoy for interreligious affairs. As part of a panel discussion called "Conversation for Peace in the Middle East," Froman took the opportunity to share his vision of an ex-territorial Jerusalem and for it to become the capital of the world to be overseen by a committee of all religious traditions: "It is possible to galvanize the political leaders and to declare Jerusalem the city of God."[157] Speaking for his friend Sheikh Sider, who was unable to attend the conference because of visa difficulties, Rabbi Froman floated the idea of establishing a hudna, or cease-fire, as described by Shari'a (Islamic law). Years before, in the 1990s, Rabbi Froman had helped to establish a hudna, and he saw no reason why Israel's chief rabbinate and the Palestinian Authority's Islamic leadership could not attempt this once again to help resolve the conflict. Religious leaders in attendance at the symposium greeted these proposals with enthusiasm.[158]

From January 21 to January 22, 2002, Rabbi Froman participated in "The First Middle East Interfaith Summit with the Leaders of the Three Monotheistic Faiths in Alexandria," which came to be known simply as the "Alexandria Summit."[159] Prominent Jewish, Muslim, and Christian clerics came together to call for an end to violence in the Holy Land.

Rabbi Froman's friend, Sheikh Sider, who by this time had come to see religion as a positive resource for peacemaking, was also present. Sheikh Sider partially credits Rabbi Froman with the success of the Alexandria Summit:

> In my eyes, [Rabbi Froman] is an Israeli hero. He has been coming to my home to talk with me for eleven years. At the beginning, when I was a Hamas leader, he still visited me. I think such meetings are more important than declarations by politicians. Froman told me I had to meet the Israel chief rabbi in his home, so I did [in April 2001]. Eventually these private meetings bore fruit in the Alexandria Summit and Declaration [January 21–22, 2002]. This was the first time in history that an interreligious document was produced by the regional leaders of the three monotheistic faiths. Despite the difficulties, these meetings must continue, alongside the official political discussions.[160]

From the summit, seventeen religious dignitaries produced a seven-point statement entitled the "First Alexandria Declaration of the Religious Leaders of the Holy Land." According to the statement, they declared:

> In the name of God who is Almighty, Merciful and Compassionate, we, who have gathered as religious leaders from the Muslim, Christian, and Jewish communities, pray for true peace in Jerusalem and the Holy Land, and declare our commitment to ending the violence and bloodshed that denies the right of life and dignity.
>
> According to our faith traditions, killing innocents in the name of God is a desecration of His Holy Name, and defames religion in the world. The violence in the Holy Land is an evil, which must be opposed by all people of good faith. We seek to live together as neighbors respecting the integrity of each other's historical and religious inheritance. We call upon all to oppose incitement, hatred and misrepresentation of the other.[161]

After the summit, the religious leaders established a Permanent Committee for the Implementation of the Alexandria Declaration. Since early 2002, the committee has worked to limit violence and incitement and has attempted to convince militant religious leaders to end the bloodshed.[162]

In early January 2004, Rabbi Froman and the group of religious leaders reconvened, this time with some thirty Palestinian Islamic clerics from the West Bank and Gaza Strip. All involved recommitted themselves to working for a just and durable peace.[163]

Reflections on Religious Peacemaking Methods

Rabbi Froman's faith has profoundly influenced his life's work. When helping to resolve conflicts, he constantly reminds himself that human beings have strong moral feelings.

> Hatred is the other side of love. You can't imagine human beings without human feelings. I hope this energy will be a victory. Baruch Goldstein [a Brooklyn-born Jewish fundamentalist who killed 29 Muslims at Sabbath prayer on Friday, February 25, 1994 at a Hebron site holy to both Muslims and Jews] and Yigal Amir [a Jewish fundamentalist who shot and killed Israeli Prime Minister Yitzhak Rabin at a peace rally in Tel Aviv on November 4, 1995] are murderers: they aimed their energy to the side of hatred. I pray that the victory will be to the aim of love between Arabs and Jews in this Holyland.[164]

This view – that hatred is the other side of love – allows Rabbi Froman the optimism to believe that the right kind of energy can convert hatred into love. In his peace work, therefore, he takes on the challenge of transforming the sentiments of Arabs and Jews, an immense task that he nonetheless has the faith to believe is possible.

To meet this challenge, Rabbi Froman recommends involving religion in the peace process. Although he admires what the government can accomplish, Froman notes that officials "are now a little confused" by their inability to reduce violence. Slowly, their failures are causing them to see what he has asserted all along, namely, that "They have a little bit to learn [from religious leaders]."[165] Of Western leaders, Rabbi Froman hopes that the inefficacy of their past efforts to promote peace will lead them to pursue Track Two alternatives that utilize religious leaders. To date, however, this is not the case: "President Bush is too busy. Blair might be more available to help. George Carey, still a member of the House of Lords, remains active in this process."[166]

Rabbi Froman does not view his work as becoming directly involved in the resolution of conflict. Instead, he defines his actions as assisting in the creation of an environment conducive to cooperation and reconciliation:

> I don't solve problems, but I try to improve the basis upon which issues may be settled. I'm not a political person nor am I a subcontractor of politicians. I have pure religious interests in learning together with Muslims. This is the whole secret of religion – to meet the other side. "Love your neighbor" is the key to religion.[167]

The first step to resolving conflicts is to prepare one's mind by accentuating, where possible, the enemy's positive attributes:

> It is easy to be influenced by the media. First step to peace: throw away your television. We are not only a picture on the television. Of course, television prefers to photograph the stoning, the clashes, the hatred; but as a man who is living in the land, I am sure that you will find much more than that. It is hard to photograph gentle feelings, men praying, relations between a man and his neighbors, but I pray that those feelings will dominate this land of peace and that this land will be a place where those journalists who like to photograph hatred will have nothing to do and those interested in gentle feelings will have a lot to do.[168]

To avoid yielding to such one-sided images, Rabbi Froman recommends a religious solution, which means "to be open [to God], and not to think you are managing the world."[169] Praying to God together for several hours is one way that he believes people of different religions can reach a state of mind conducive to peacemaking. Also important is listening to the other and engaging in religious dialogue: "I am a Jew who is commanded to hear, not only to see."[170] Because what is seen is not always reliable, it is also necessary to listen intently to the other side. Doing so paves the way for productive religious dialogue, which includes regular meetings between all parties.[171] Such meetings advance the peace process by helping the participants to understand that religion, although often portrayed as a negative force, can be harnessed for good:

> Religious energy is like nuclear energy. It can either destroy the world or build it. Politics and religion is like gunpowder and matches. In the Middle East, the energy and the motivation come from religion, on both sides. If politics and religion can be separated, religion can fulfill a positive role.[172]

Negotiators seeking to resolve the Arab-Israeli conflict have often avoided addressing religious issues. Rabbi Froman insists that "Jerusalem is the easiest problem to tackle. Material issues such as water and land are much more difficult. I have always said that peace cannot be achieved in the Holy Land without taking religion into account first."[173] Now may be the time to do so.

Religiously Motivated Peacemaking

When asked how religion motivates his peacemaking work, Rabbi Froman invokes the teachings of Rav Kook the Elder. According to Rabbi

Froman's interpretation of Rav Kook's teachings, the existential problems of the Jews have been God's way of pushing them to behave as they "ought" to, thus prodding them to engage with people who observe other religions.

> The present political conflict challenges us to make peace with Islam. Along with the rest of humanity, we are moving toward peace, an end to hatred and bloodshed, and greater democracy. This is not a utopian vision. It is based on a real, tragic situation. We are challenged to find a higher level of religiosity that will enable dialogue with Islam.[174]

Rabbi Froman has taken the teachings of Rav Kook the Elder to heart. Each day, he recommits himself to strengthening Jewish-Muslim dialogue.

Moving Forward: The Future of Israeli-Palestinian Reconciliation

Rabbi Menachem Froman is still working to promote Jewish-Muslim reconciliation between Israelis and Palestinians. For the first time, he has opened up channels of communication between Jewish settlers and Palestinians living side by side on the West Bank.

Over the years, relations between the groups have ranged from suspicion to outright violence. Yet, Rabbi Froman remains committed to a new era of mutual recognition, respect, and cooperation. In January 2004, he again met with Chairman Arafat to ensure that his joint committee of rabbis and sheikhs becomes a strong force for reconciliation. Considering the remarkable friendships Rabbi Froman has built with the likes of Sheikh Sider, Sheikh Abu Salih, and General Nasser Yussef, there is a glimmer of hope that one day, many more Israelis and Palestinians will enjoy such relationships themselves.

An Open House

Yehezkel Landau

Behind the backdrop of the Arab-Israeli conflict labors Yehezkel Landau, a Jewish dual citizen of the United States and Israel. Growing up in Rockland County, New York, Yehezkel came of age during the Cold War. Two weeks after celebrating his Bar Mitzvah in the fall of 1962, the Cuban

Missile Crisis erupted. President John F. Kennedy announced that Soviet missiles had been deployed in Cuba, aimed at the United States. He responded by declaring a quarantine of Cuba to block further Soviet arms from entering, and demanded that all missiles be removed.

Amidst the threat of a nuclear strike on the United States, Yehezkel came to question the efficacy of war as a means to achieve peace. He recalls thinking, "Well, I've just been initiated into adulthood, and the adults in this world can't even guarantee me a future. I remember the drills [in the event of nuclear attack] in junior high school, as if those were going to keep us alive."[175] As the crisis came to a peaceful resolution, the words of President Kennedy became imprinted in Yehezkel's consciousness: "If mankind does not put an end to war, then war will put an end to mankind." From that point on, Yehezkel believed that if humanity were to have a future, young people would have to forge a new path toward peace.

As the Vietnam War followed the Cuban Missile Crisis, Yehezkel came to believe that the leaders of the day were pursuing a troubling course of action that could lead only to disaster. Reacting to the Vietnam War, he came to consciously reject modern warfare and "all wars which kill innocent people." In Yehezkel's eyes, "the means corrupt the ends."[176] Throughout the war, he was active in antiwar demonstrations.

As he went through these experiences, Yehezkel became determined to find a way to resolve conflict that would promote healing and true reconciliation for all of those affected: from the politicians, military, and upper echelons of society, to innocent women and children. This search for a method of reconciliation to facilitate healing that is truly inclusive of all members of society – a search for what he terms a more "holistic" approach – would become the goal of his life's work.

For Yehezkel, the Bible and the Jewish tradition offered instruction on achieving peace. He found the stories of reconciliation in Genesis particularly inspirational, because they showed how to resolve conflicts of the family, from the sibling rivalry of Cain and Abel to Joseph and his brothers. To Yehezkel, these seem to be "relevant for all humanity, especially for men, whether they are fighting it out on the battlefield or the football field."[177] The themes of peace and reconciliation in many of the Torah's rabbinic teachings also spoke powerfully to Yehezkel. Outside his tradition, he discovered further inspiration in the teachings and examples of His Holiness the Dalai Lama, Thich Nhat Hanh, Mohandas Gandhi, and the Rev. Martin Luther King Jr., as well as other Christian and Muslim activists.[178]

As Yehezkel pondered how to apply these teachings, he continued his formal education. In 1971, Yehezkel received his A.B. in social relations from Harvard University after pursuing a program combining psychology, religion, and education. Five years later, he received his M.A. in theological studies from Harvard Divinity School, specializing in psychology, theology, and Jewish-Christian relations. With his formal education complete, Yehezkel prepared to enter a new chapter of his life in Israel.

Evolution of a Peacemaker

On April 5, 1978, Yehezkel Landau left the familiarity of the United States and arrived in Israel. Of his journey, Yehezkel recalls, "I came on an El Al plane from New York, courtesy of a rabbi who had bought me a one-way ticket so that I could work and study at his academy in Jerusalem."[179] Yehezkel never bought the other half of his ticket.

Instead, he remained in Israel and became a dual citizen, all the while maintaining his strong convictions. As a result, when the Israeli army wanted to conscript him, he was able to negotiate a civil defense position in the military. In this way, Yehezkel says that he "serve[d] my conscience and my country." Yehezkel explains his position on war. "I'm not a pacifist, but I am a selective conscientious objector." Yehezkel married Dalia Ashkenazi, a native Israeli, and together they built a home in the southwest corner of Jerusalem where they lived with their son Raphael and three "endearingly neurotic" dogs.[180]

Viewed from the United States, Yehezkel could see that both sides of the Arab-Israeli conflict were suffering. The time had come, he concluded, to fulfill his earlier impulse to pursue peace work and to put into practice the peace and reconciliation lessons he had been studying. Importantly, he decided to do this in Israel:

> I was the last member of my immediate family to visit Israel and the only one who stayed. This is because I did not go as a tourist or as a pilgrim, but as a prospective resident and citizen. The Jewish yearnings in my soul had intensified to the point where I needed to experience life in Israel first-hand. While still in the U.S., it pained me deeply to watch the evening news and vicariously suffer the indignities of Palestinians and the existential dread of Israeli Jews. I felt that, as a Jew who identified with the Zionist homecoming, as an interfaith educator, and as someone committed to seeking inclusive justice and the reconciliation of wounded, angry, embittered hearts, I might be able to contribute something to the alleviation of people's suffering.[181]

During the time he was enrolled at the Jerusalem Academy of Jewish Studies from 1978 to 1980, he looked carefully at the Arab-Israeli conflict that was gathering momentum around him. He observed that although religion was not a primary cause, it was nonetheless important as a means of legitimating partisan claims.

> Fortunately, it's not a religious war between Jews and Arabs. It's a political war between Arabs and Israelis. That's good news, because if it were a religious war, it would be much more difficult to compromise....
>
> The problem is, people invoke religious arguments to justify their territorial claims, and that face of religion grabs all the headlines and adds fuel to the fire.[182]

Yehezkel found that the extremists who promote violence capture the spotlight in the media and occlude from public view religious moderates or pluralists interested in building bridges and promoting peace. The media in turn, by only covering such distorted forms of religion, perpetuates a view that religion is only a source of conflict rather than a source of conflict resolution.

Yehezkel was gravely concerned by the degree to which relations between the inhabitants of Israel and Palestine were deteriorating. In Yehezkel's words:

> It is only in the past one hundred years that the conflict over the Holy Land, whether called Israel or Palestine, has engendered competing nationalisms and the violation of basic human rights affirmed as sacred by all three faith traditions. The conflict has also undermined the historic cross-fertilization of these traditions.
>
> The mixture of religion and nationalism is dangerously combustible. On a human, pragmatic level, two nations in a dispute over a land claimed by both should be able to compromise and share the territory. But when God's will is invoked to absolutize one or the other claim, then compromise becomes sacrilege, and religious extremism generates grotesque ideologies of domination, death, and destruction.[183]

Competing nationalisms, violations of human rights, and the self-serving use of faith traditions all exacerbated the Arab-Israeli conflict.

Beneath the noisy claims of "divine right" in support of various positions in the conflict, Yehezkel sensed a deeper issue. People were suffering human rights violations and indignities, and religion was used to justify violence rather than as a resource to meet their spiritual needs. This has gone on for a long time: from notable events like the dispossession of Palestinians in 1948 and the series of Arab-Israeli wars; from the occupation of the Palestinian territory beginning in 1967 to the status of what Jews call the Temple Mount and Muslims call the al-Haram al-Sharif. Yehezkel says that these and other conflicts have left "festering wounds that require spiritual, not only political, remedies." But, furthermore, the use and misuse of religion to justify partisan claims has contributed to and helped to sustain what Yehezkel terms a "chronic religious pathology."[184]

Sensitive to these underlying matters, Yehezkel embarked on his first attempt to address the Arab-Israeli conflict. In 1980, he accepted the position of program coordinator at the Israel Interfaith Association in Jerusalem, with responsibility for designing programs to bring Israelis of all religious backgrounds together to learn about each other.[185] After two years, Yehezkel concluded that "my work was more intercultural than truly interfaith, and [therefore] it did not address sufficiently the suffering of people in this land."[186] At some financial risk, he left the Israel Interfaith Association in 1982.

Oz veShalom–Netivot Shalom

Determined to make a meaningful contribution to peace in Israel, Yehezkel turned to intrafaith work in 1982 and became the information director, and then executive director, of the religious Zionist peace movement, Oz veShalom. In 1985, this small movement merged with another religious Zionist group that had emerged during the Lebanon War, Netivot Shalom. Oz veShalom's goal was to be a bridge between all Jews – observant and nonobservant, Israelis and those in the Diaspora – who each had their own views of what might constitute an authentic Jewish state.

The movement aimed to accomplish this by finding "a common and moral political agenda through the lens of our Torah tradition" in order to forge what he terms a "sacred synthesis."[187] Speaking of the importance of such peacemaking work and his involvement in the organization, Yehezkel says, "It is my personal conviction that, unless Jews in Israel can articulate a shared vision of what a Jewish state means, and what values it should uphold, it will be difficult to reconcile with our Arab neighbors."[188] As such, the movement had a dual mission of bringing both a "vision and commitment toward peacemaking to the religious community" as well as offering "a religious foundation for justice and peace to the largely secular peace camp in Israel."[189]

For the next ten years, Yehezkel directed the movement's staff and attempted to achieve the goals of Oz veShalom–Netivot Shalom, summarized as "Strength and Peace – Paths of Peace" (from two verses in Psalms and Proverbs). "I helped design and carry out programs that would get our educational message out to the larger public. We did a booklet in Arabic, translated so that Palestinians could see Torah Judaism and religious Zionism were not the monopoly of the . . . settler movement."[190]

One of Yehezkel's key roles was to convey the message of the religious Zionist peace movement to the outside world. He explains why it was critical to distinguish Oz veShalom–Netivot Shalom from Gush Emunim, the better-known representative of religious Zionism:

> To some, the notion of a "religious Zionist peace movement" may sound like an oxymoron. For decades, the chauvinistic spokespeople among the Jewish settlers in the West Bank and Gaza, using the media very effectively, have offered their own version of religious Zionism. Their movement, *Gush Emunim* (Bloc of the Faithful), espouses a pseudo-messianic ideology rooted in "territoriolatry" and historical determinism. They see the covenant linking God, the People of Israel, and the Land of Israel as a "no-fault insurance plan" from heaven, promising the Jews political victory and spiritual blessing so long as they control the whole land from the Mediterranean Sea to the Jordan River. In this worldview, the human and political rights of the other nation in the land are dismissed as irrelevant or nonexistent.
>
> Those of us who are the "minority within a minority," religious Zionists who advocate territorial and political compromise (now represented in the Knesset by the dovish Meimad Party), have received scant media coverage. As a result, secular left-wing groups like Shalom Akhshav (Peace Now) or Gush Shalom or Women in Black tend to see the cause of peace as incompatible with Jewish religious tradition and practice. This mutual alienation, between the secular left and the religious right, has created a seismic fault line that threatens to tear Israeli society apart. Shalom, one of God's Holy Names, is ironically perceived as the monopoly of secular leftists and is therefore deemed an anathema by religiously committed Jews.[191]

Yehezkel believes that other religious Zionist groups have neglected the human and political rights of Palestinians, while Oz veShalom–Netivot Shalom has given full attention to these issues in the context of territorial and political compromise. "For us, human life, justice and peace were holier than territory. It was a Jewish imperative to sacrifice territory in

Judea, Samaria, and Gaza . . . for a Palestinian state so that Israel would remain Jewish, ethnically and religiously."[192]

Since its founding in 1975, Oz veShalom–Netivot Shalom has achieved limited success in making peace between the secular left and the religious right. It has sponsored many seminars and retreats, disseminated published materials, participated in public protests and demonstrations, made media pronouncements, and directed appeals to both political and rabbinic leaders. Yehezkel admits that reaching out to the settlers has not been easy. Nevertheless, Oz veShalom–Netivot Shalom continues to put ads in papers and uses the media to disseminate its message.[193]

Oz veShalom–Netivot Shalom's primary achievement, according to Yehezkel, has been its ability to "demonstrate that there is an alternative interpretation of religious Zionism, grounded in Torah Judaism, which challenges the ideology of the Gush Emunim settlers."[194] He continues, "My work has been largely aimed, in a sense, at breaking the monopoly on the public face of religion held by zealots, extremists, intolerant people, who basically create the God they worship in their own image, rather than humbly acknowledging that we are all in God's image, with all our diversity."[195]

Open House: Activist Interfaith Peace Work

In 1991, the Gulf War erupted, and Yehezkel served as a civil defense soldier. Similar to his experience at thirteen with the Cuban Missile Crisis, he recalls feeling that "the threat of chemical warfare, with people donning gas masks whenever the sirens sounded, was an ominous sign of the horrors that a future war could bring."[196] But the anxiety of these circumstances was also accompanied by the pressing need that he should find a more practical way to apply his religious convictions.

After almost ten years at Oz veShalom–Netivot Shalom, Yehezkel Landau left the stability of a secure position in order to focus on concrete interfaith (as opposed to intrafaith) work. Together with his wife Dalia and their Arab partners, he cofounded the Open House coexistence center. The center is located in Ramle, a working-class, religiously mixed city outside Tel Aviv, consisting of about sixty-six thousand Jews and Arabs. Yehezkel became its administrative director and Michail Fanous, a Palestinian Israeli partner, served as executive director.[197] For Yehezkel, the Gulf War had made it clear that dormant grievances needed attention. Founding Open House was his way of confronting those destructive forces. The dramatic story that lies behind the selection of the specific house in Ramle as the location for the Open House, however, is a personal one:

Dalia was born in Sofia, Bulgaria, and came to Israel with her family when she was a year old, at the end of 1948. Like many other immigrant families at that time, hers was placed in an "Arab house" in Ramle, between Tel Aviv and Jerusalem. The Israeli government considered the confiscated homes of Palestinian refugees as "abandoned property." After the Six-Day War in 1967, the original Palestinian owners of her family home came to visit. They were living in the West Bank city of El-Bireh, next to Ramallah. The Al-Khayri family paid several visits to the house in Ramle, and Dalia also visited them. Over time, a special bond developed between the two families, brought together by a house and garden that each called "home."

Dalia came to learn that the Al-Khayris did not leave the Ramle house voluntarily. They had been forcibly evacuated by the Israeli army in July of 1948, along with most of the residents of Ramle and nearby Lydda/Lod. These expulsions were deemed necessary at the time, as Israel was waging a war of survival following the Arab world's rejection of the 1947 U.N. partition plan.

After her father died in 1985 and she inherited the house, Dalia and I sought out the Al-Khayri family to consult with them about what to do with the property. The resulting discussions led to the creation of Open House, a peace education center based in that Ramle house. The house remains the home of two families, symbolizing Israel/Palestine as the homeland of two nations.[198]

By creating the Open House, Yehezkel and Dalia put their commitment to action into practice. They turned a property taken from a displaced Arab family and given to a Jewish family into something jointly owned and shared. In doing so, they sought to "transform [Dalia's] childhood home into a laboratory for reconciliation."[199] Today, Open House stands as a striking metaphor for peacemaking in the Middle East.

Since its founding, Open House has touched the lives of thousands of Jews and Arabs. Focused mostly on the Arab and Jewish youth, it has used "affirmative action" programs for Arab children and their families, as well as joint programs for Jewish and Arab Israelis.

Recalling the two Divine attributes that are the criteria for consecrated living in God's Holy Land (Genesis 18:19), I would say that the first program area, which addresses the discrimination experienced by the local Arab community, reflects our commitment to *mishpat*, justice; while our mixed activities are meant to keep hearts open and caring, as a practical model of *tzedakah*, compassion.[200]

Open House transforms relationships among Jews and Arabs from estrangement to trust in practical ways. In October 1991, Open House established the first Arabic-speaking nursery school in Ramle, a city that includes about twelve thousand Palestinian Christians and Muslims in its locale. In four years, the facility expanded from four to thirty-five Arab children, ages two and three.

Since 1992, Open House has also launched a number of coexistence initiatives: two annual summer peace camps for one hundred youths; professional coexistence training for educators; a Jewish-Arab parents network; after-school and evening classes in computer skills and English; young leadership training for teenagers; youth delegations to Europe and the United States; and an Anne Frank Library and Resource Center with educational materials and multilingual resources.[201] Taken together, these Open House programs foster relationships based on equality and solidarity.[202]

With the outbreak of the Second Intifada, Open House faced new problems. Everyone was traumatized, but to face the challenges posed by the violence, the Open House organized healing sessions, bringing together activists who were all under severe strain to allow them to share their feelings of anger, fear, and hope. Years of working to develop what Yehezkel terms "organic relationships of trust within the civic environment" were key to the continuing success of the Open House. The mayor of Ramle, for example, had been their strongest ally since 1993, and that relationship would ensure that they were able to continue their important work in the most difficult of times. Still, the Intifada had a significant impact on activities promoting Jewish-Arab coexistence, and Yehezkel says, "[e]ncounters, especially among young adults...have been more intense, painful, honest, and cathartic."[203]

Ongoing violence presents at once a danger and an opportunity. It can trigger a downward spiral of fear and hostility in Israel, or it can inspire an effort to integrate Arab citizens more fully and equitably into Israeli society:

The mutual demonization is rampant (exacerbated by the media on both sides) and people are succumbing to either despair or rage; that is, the liberal humanists are immobilized by the scale of violence and what it signifies, while those who were already angry (on either side) are energized to add their venom to an already pathological situation....

Part of our problem is that we Israelis elect former generals as our leaders, at the national and municipal levels, and their mindset is conditioned by the professional assignment of thwarting the worst-case scenario rather than imagining and bringing about the best-case alternative. And so we are in a "pre-emptive strike" mentality, which distorts the Golden Rule: "Do unto others before they get a chance to do it worse unto you."[204]

Yehezkel worried about his country and the impact of violence on all of them. The Open House held fast to its positive vision through this agonizing period. Currently, trust remains strong among its participants and clients. Yehezkel attributes the organization's strength not only to its programs but, more important, to the story behind the house:

> I believe in the power of stories, much more than in declarations, documents, even peace plans. Inspiring stories that touch people's hearts are much more effective in transforming conflicts to peaceful coexistence than rational plans for changing the political situation.
>
> All of the well-intentioned peace plans have not worked because the emotional environment is not conducive to their acceptance. They work just on the head, not the heart, and that's what has to be changed. Feelings and self-images have to be transformed.
>
> One of the primary media for religion is sacred stories (I use "sacred stories" rather than narratives or myths), and that's the transformative power of a story, like ... the Open House Story. It gets through people's mental filters. People are jaded; they know it all already. They know why they're fighting, who's to blame for what. A story like the Open House story breaks through the dualism, the "us versus them." And it's usually the case that most people on either side are waiting for the other side to make a magnanimous gesture, to which they can reciprocate. But they aren't going to risk their political careers or social status by making the first move.
>
> You cannot argue with a story. You can argue with a political claim, but when someone tells his or her life story, you can't say, "No, you didn't live that." We are very good, we human beings, at developing all kinds of rationales for why we shouldn't do anything to change the situation, for why we can blame anybody but ourselves. And here's a woman who recognizes the suffering and dehumanization the other side has faced. Israel is certainly no worse than any other nation fighting for its life. It's probably better than most, on the whole. But that doesn't give me much satisfaction, especially after a thirty-seven-year occupation.[205]

When Yehezkel shares the story behind Open House, its positive message of mutuality, reconciliation, and peaceful coexistence resonates with people worldwide.

Peace Work in the United States

In 2002, after spending nearly twenty-five years in Israel, Yehezkel Landau returned to the United States to pursue his peacemaking efforts

from abroad. His reasons were personal but also reflected his commitment to peacemaking and the terrible toll that the increasing toxicity of
the Second Intifada was taking on him:

> I was walking around with hives on my hands every day for two years, as
> an allergic response to the political pollution.
>   This war of terror and reprisals and targeted assassinations, this is a
> qualitatively different war from all the ones Israel has fought up until
> now. Two people have been sucked into this vortex of violence, bloodshed,
> and despair. Despair is a crippling thing.[206]

Yehezkel concluded that the matrix of violence in the Middle East could
finally be changed only with help from the outside, and especially from
the United States: "It's the United States government that really calls
the shots and [it] can be an active peacebuilder if it chooses to do
that [but]...the United States has not chosen to do that. It's fighting
a war on terrorism. So it's easy to lump Palestinians with Osama bin
Laden."[207]

Convinced that Washington, D.C. and New York City had become focal
points for transforming the Arab-Israeli conflict, Yehezkel resolved to
concentrate his peacemaking efforts in these cities. Although the decision
to move was difficult, Yehezkel returned to the United States:

> In leaving Israel, my heart is in Jerusalem, and my body is in Hartford
> [where Yehezkel teaches]. Partly, I think, because the leverage points
> for transforming the conflict in Israel-Palestine are outside. It's not in
> Jerusalem and Ramallah that the conflict will be transformed but in New
> York and Washington. I go to Washington [D.C.] as often as I can to meet
> people there. New York is also important because the UN is here and
> because of the Jewish community.[208]

Since returning to the United States, Yehezkel has cultivated a number
of relationships with individuals and organizations in Washington, D.C.
who influence American foreign policy. The United States Institute of
Peace (USIP) commissioned him to write a report for them, called *Healing
the Holy Land: Interreligious Peacebuilding in Israel/Palestine.* He also has
met with members of Congress, religious leaders, and has established
contacts in the State Department.[209] In addition, he helped establish the
Friends of Open House USA to support the work in Ramle, where he now
serves on the Board.

Part of his impetus for returning to the United States was to try to
influence American foreign policy, particularly to make policy makers
factor in the religious dimension of conflict and resolution. His work,

however, has been difficult, and he admits being frustrated because of what he views as a fundamental misunderstanding on the part of most American policy makers of the inhabitants of the Middle East:

> There seems to be an inability to grasp what really motivates people in the Middle East. American foreign policy people seem to think Jews and Arabs want to be just like Americans – that is, individualists and materialists. They don't fit most of the world, and they certainly don't fit the Middle East.
>
>   So the kinds of incentives to change their attitudes and behaviors are not there. Diplomats and politicians tend to have a rationalist, utilitarian, usually incrementalist approach to conflict resolution, and so they fail to address some of the emotional and spiritual aspects of the conflict. They focus on security, not dignity, freedom, honor, spiritual yearnings, identity needs, educational reform, textbooks, television. They don't value the work of grassroots peace builders. They work with governments mostly, and that's a missed opportunity.[210]

Although Yehezkel does not yet appear to have converted the Washington establishment to his ideas for peace in the Middle East, he has had much success in disseminating his views through universities, seminaries, and congregations. When he is not lobbying in Washington, D.C. or New York, Yehezkel has served, since 2002, as a Faculty Associate in Interfaith Relations at Hartford Seminary. There, he has taught courses on religious peacemaking and helped develop interfaith training programs. One such program, titled "Building Abrahamic Partnerships," was launched in 2004 as an initiative for clergy, religious educators, and seminarians from the three Abrahamic faiths. Joined by two of his fellow Tanenbaum Center *Peacemakers* from Nigeria, his course content included: historical overviews; shared text study of primary sources and prayers; demographic and sociological data on Jews, Christians, and Muslims in North America; descriptions of obstacles to interfaith partnership; strategies for countering negative media portrayals; proposals of joint interfaith projects in local communities; and Web links and e-mail exchanges to foster communication among the graduates of the program.[211]

Today, Yehezkel continues to divide his time between Israel and the United States. His marriage to Dalia has ended, but they continue to share a commitment to peacebuilding, especially through the Open House in Ramle, and to their son Raphael, who will soon enter the army to fulfill his commitment as an Israeli citizen.

A Holistic Approach to Peacemaking

Yehezkel's religious knowledge and his inclusive understanding of its dictates influenced his approach to peacemaking, which he defines as holistic in the sense that it addresses the needs and perspectives of all involved. His academic and theological training, as well as his extensive, on-the-ground experience in conflict resolution, have taught him that different people in different environments understand conflicts in different ways. Similarly, the root causes of particular conflicts vary. This is why the first step he takes in conflict resolution work is to assess his audience to determine whether to take a more theoretical and theological, or a more pragmatic, approach.

Yehezkel described how this assessment process works when he discussed his experiences in "two peacemaking laboratories" in Jerusalem and Ramle. In Jerusalem, he worked as a regular faculty member at the Tantur Ecumenical Institute, St. George's (Anglican) College, and the international program at the Ecce Homo convent of the Sisters of Sion. In what he describes as the "Holy City atop the Judean Hills, with its messianic symbolism and destiny," Yehezkel taught Christians about biblical resources for peacemakers and Jewish tradition and spirituality, while at the same time engaging in interfaith dialogues that covered the theological with visitors from around the world.[212]

By contrast, Yehezkel notes that Ramle turned out to be "not a locale for theological conferences and courses...[but] a working-class city whose demography parallels that of Israel as a whole: 82 percent Jews and 18 percent Arab Muslims and Christians." These diverse peoples essentially lived separate lives, and even their children attended separate schools. Yehezkel understood that the different people of Ramle would not be brought together through theoretical conversations but, rather, required "private initiatives like Open House...[which could] bridge the experiential gap and overcome the fears and suspicions on both sides."[213] By assessing each environment and the needs of its communities, Yehezkel was able to tailor his approach to his audience and increase his impact.

At Open House, Yehezkel takes what he terms a direct approach. It involves dialogue, yet is designed to be face-to-face, human-to-human. As previously noted, Yehezkel believes that calls to violence in the name of God frequently mask underlying, deeply felt religious and spiritual conflicts. At the Open House, he encourages reconciliation between both Jewish and Arab Israelis by letting them work through these deep seated crises together, thereby creating a microcosm for the type of change he envisions throughout Israel:

> We address those factors explicitly; we put them on the table. We get Jews and Arabs to outgrow their victim scripts and see the greater emotional complexity. Fear has to be transformed to trust, anger to acceptance and forgiveness; and grief has to be transformed into compassion for the sufferings of other people. We help people find an outlet for their anger, to find some transcendent comfort for pain ... reconciliation, not victory or vindication, is what is required.
>
> The most emotional meetings are those that follow atrocities and/or military reprisals. Teenagers have cried together as they share their raw pain, fear, and doubts about the future.
>
> There's kind of a zero-sum equation that people in conflict generally adopt. We need win-win rather than win-lose. That means stretching people's hearts and imaginations to experience an alternative to the us-versus-them typology, to make equality and peaceful relations something they can experience.
>
> We create microcosmic vessels for equality, justice, and peace within a war zone. We need to multiply that a thousandfold. Peace is possible – "I just had an amazing experience with my enemies. I didn't have to threaten them; they didn't have to threaten me." That's what we try to do. That's what has to happen. If it happens in a thousand places, things will change. Just as Israel was built one kibbutz at a time, peace will be forged one peace center at a time. That's not just talking about peace, that's building peace.[214]

By crying, sharing, and debating together, the participants at the Open House come to recognize each other's common humanity. In doing so, these people who at one time shared only their citizenship in Israel – living out their lives independently of one another and attending separate schools – have begun to move beyond mere dialogue to establish relationships.

Years of work have honed a three-step philosophy and method to facilitate conflict resolution at the Open House. Developed by Dalia, this methodology can be summarized by what she calls the "Three A's": *acknowledge, apologize,* and make *amends.* According to this approach, both parties in the conflict must take three steps: (1) *acknowledge* the harm done by one's own side to the other side; (2) *apologize* for the hurt and injustice inflicted; and (3) make *amends* for past actions by acts of repentance and rectification, now and into the future.[215]

Throughout his professional life, Yehezkel has had one foot in the "real world" of active peacemaking and another in academia and the world of theological scholarship. Just as his training at Harvard Divinity School informed his approach for on-the-ground solutions to conflict resolution, so have his experiences in "practical" conflict resolution provided him with an inclusive, theological perspective that he communicates through his writing:

> I am convinced that there will be no genuine peace between the two peoples fighting over God's Holy Land until there is a shared commitment to consecrate life and land. Hebrew Scripture, in Exodus 19:5–6, teaches us that the land belongs to God, and that, by the grace of God, we Jews belong to the land.
>
> In our time, the challenge is to share the land equitably with another people that has its own sense of belonging. This theological re-visioning, with a willingness to sacrifice territory in both directions to safeguard human life and welfare, is essential for a political transformation. At present, what is professed to be holy by Jews, Christians, or Muslims is being desecrated by horrific violence and by the trampling of basic human rights in the name of "security" or "freedom" or "liberation."[216]

In Jerusalem and at universities, churches, synagogues, and mosques, Yehezkel engages audiences who are open to, or at least intrigued by, the idea of hermeneutically transforming the Arab-Israeli conflict. His experiences and successes in such diverse communities as Jerusalem and Ramle are a testament that such a transformation is possible.

Just as Yehezkel has helped to facilitate interreligious dialogue, he has also helped promote intrareligious dialogue among Jews who have contested visions over what might constitute an "authentic" Jewish state. In such instances, he turns to the rabbinic tradition, and points to the wisdom found in the *Pirkei Avot*, particularly in the sage Hillel, whom he often cites: "Be of the disciples of Aaron, loving peace and pursuing peace, loving humankind, and drawing them closer to the Torah." Through such "a holy common denominator rooted in its wisdom," Jews are able to find a "healing approach" that helps to build a "community on this sacred foundation."[217] Thus, again, in a situation of conflicting viewpoints, Yehezkel points to a shared tradition – that of engaging the Torah – to facilitate understanding and reconciliation.

In order to assess the particular needs of one's audience in what he has described to be a "holistic" approach to reconciliation, Yehezkel believes that it is necessary to assess what he views as the four levels to conflict – political, cognitive, emotional, and spiritual. These four levels are not necessarily mutually exclusive of one another, but some will be more prevalent than others depending on the particularities of a given situation.

By identifying how a conflict is operative at each of these various levels, it becomes possible to approach resolution holistically by treating each dimension involved.

At the political level, there is a need to recognize the ways in which tangible compromises might be negotiated over issues in dispute. For example, in Yehezkel's work at Oz veShalom–Netivot Shalom, Yehezkel identified a need for Jews and Palestinians to come to a point of agreement on issues such as sovereignty in Jerusalem, water resources, arsenals of weapons, and repatriation of refugees.[218]

At the cognitive level, Yehezkel stresses the need to develop new understandings of identity – understandings that are integrally connected to the third level of the "emotions." For too long, Israelis and Palestinians have been locked in dualistic worldviews pitting "us" against "them" – categories that emphasize difference and distance. But emotions connect: they are shared and are also felt by all. Yehezkel urges professional educators to address emotions (especially fear, anger, and grief) in order to develop a humanistic vision of inclusion that transcends exclusionary constructions of identity. Teens who share and cry together at the Open House are another striking example of how addressing emotion can help move beyond the politics of identity.[219]

Perhaps most important, Yehezkel advises that it is necessary to address the spiritual dimension of a conflict in order for complete transformation to take place. Healing becomes possible through looking for "an inclusive understanding of holiness,"[220] without which peace efforts are doomed to fail. As Yehezkel explains, "many of us need the conflict, at least unconsciously, for our own sense of who we are in the world."[221] Conflict, in other words, becomes a vehicle for self-identification that runs deep within each individual. He continues, "in order to redefine ourselves, not as victims or warriors but as partners in consecrating the Holy Land, we need visionary spiritual leadership."[222]

Yehezkel proposes that "Jews, Christians, and Muslims need to develop, together . . . an inclusive understanding of holiness that applies not only to Jerusalem, Hebron, and Nazareth, but also to Sarajevo, New York, Johannesburg, and Melbourne."[223] Religious leaders, in other words, can promote an approach to holiness that makes spirituality a point of connection among religions rather than a catalyst for division.

Although Yehezkel believes that religious leaders should be involved in Track Two diplomacy to help facilitate political change, he also suggests that such interreligious discussions should parallel Track One diplomacy between governments to help bring an end to religious extremism. He feels that religious leaders need to be more proactive and utilize outlets such as the media, which are often exploited by groups that promote division and exacerbate religious tensions. As he says:

> Inclusive "Abrahamic" approaches to transcendent questions of meaning, value, and national purpose need to be articulated through the mass media by credible religious authorities. Only then can we move on to negotiating practical compromises that accommodate the conflicting claims over Jerusalem/Al-Quds, Hebron/Al-Halil, the Temple Mount/Haram al-Sharif and other holy sites. And only then can our souls be liberated from the dread, the anguish and the hatred which contaminates our spiritualities and constricts our human potential as children of the one God, each reflecting the Divine image in a unique way.[224]

Religious leaders must be willing to take a stand and to say that violence in the name of religion must be stopped. They must reclaim their traditions from those who have attempted to hijack religion to perpetuate a cycle of violence that is antithetical to the central core of all the Abrahamic faiths.

The task of addressing very powerful emotions – anger, sadness, resentment, frustration – is essential to a truly holistic reconciliation process, but Yehezkel cautions that it is necessary not to let these feelings hinder the peacemaking process itself. The transformation of what he terms an "emotional matrix" is a delicate and sensitive issue that requires the efforts of people throughout all levels of society. The emotional matrix is the dense, overwhelming feelings of fear, anger, resentment, grief, and at times hatred and despair – feelings that provide militants with "the emotional 'justification' for their destructive agendas." To promote lasting peace, Yehezkel stresses the need to change this "emotional matrix" – an enormous task that requires participation of a range of people, from political and religious leaders and grassroots activists, to representatives of the media.[225]

Despite the difficulty of confronting and addressing emotional issues, Yehezkel believes that they must be faced directly. In the Arab-Israeli conflict, the people of Israel and Palestine need to mentally prepare and be patient in order to effectively bring about the type of holistic transformation necessary to productively work toward peace.

Resolving conflicts need not involve only active parties to the conflict. In addition to working with foreign governments (especially the U.S. government), Yehezkel believes that Western Christians can contribute positively to resolving the Arab-Israeli conflict. As members of another Abrahamic faith with a different perspective on the conflict, Christians can help identify common ground between Jews and Muslims, who are often polarized by their opposing viewpoints. But Yehezkel also hopes that the involvement of Western Christians will inspire them to "make amends for their own bloody history toward the other two Abrahamic communities." Involvement of Western Christians also would help the minority of Palestinian Christians who have been in the area for centuries, for whom reconciliation between Muslims and Israeli Jews would further their own spiritual and economic interests.[226]

Ultimately, Yehezkel anticipates that the main burden for resolving the Arab-Israeli conflict will fall on those most intimately involved. By working to encourage what he terms a holistic approach to peacemaking – following the three A's (acknowledge, apologize, and make ammends) and by addressing political, cognitive, emotional, and spiritual issues – Yehezkel maintains hope that the men and women, boys and girls directly involved in the conflict will overcome their respective prejudices and resentments.

Religiously Motivated Peacemaking

Yehezkel Landau additionally recommends turning to the sacred teachings of the Abrahamic traditions and finding within them the tools for making peace. Since his childhood, he has been motivated by biblical passages to pursue a career in peacebuilding. By enlisting these writings to build bridges of respect, reconciliation, and cooperation, progress toward a just peace may be achieved.

Yehezkel firmly believes that the Holy Land is "God's laboratory on earth." He roots his opposition to the violence stemming from the Arab-Israeli conflict in his religious beliefs, stating that "Jews and Palestinians are called to sanctify the land together by ending the bloodshed, the injustice, the suffering of both peoples."[227] He finds great inspiration in the book of Genesis, which is the story of the origins of life shared by all of the Abrahamic people. He explains:

> A . . . biblical paradigm for the Israeli-Palestinian situation is found in Genesis, in the motif of two brothers fighting over the birthright and the blessing. . . . One may gain the upper hand at one moment, but both are weak and sinful and neither can be readily labeled the oppressor.
>
>   The sibling-struggle motif runs throughout Genesis, from Cain and Abel to Joseph and his brothers, from the second to the 23rd generation of humanity. Only when Jacob, on his deathbed, is called upon to bless his grandsons Ephraim and Menasheh in the 24th generation is this rivalry

stopped: he gives the two boys a joint blessing. He asks God to "bless the lads; and in them let my name be recalled and the name of my fathers Abraham and Isaac; and let them grow into a multitude in the midst of the earth" (48:16). Jacob does this while crossing his arms, symbolizing an equal portion of the blessing to the first- and second-born. Joseph protests, trying to correct what he considers his father's mistake. The patriarch persists, because he knows (through prophetic insight, as well as the painful lessons of his own life) what he must do. He can see into the future and knows what will become of both tribes, but that is a matter separate from the blessing.

Moreover, he goes on to say, "by thee shall Israel bless, saying, 'God make thee as Ephraim and Menasheh.'" And that is precisely how Jewish fathers like myself bless their sons at the Sabbath table every Friday night, invoking as role models these two relatively minor biblical figures rather than heroic personalities like Moses, David, Solomon or Samson.[228]

These passages in Genesis send the message that everyone is equally deserving in God's eyes. The blessing should be shared and not fought over, lest everyone suffer.

Future Religious Peacemaking

Today, Yehezkel Landau continues to teach at Hartford Seminary and to lobby decision-makers in Washington, D.C. and New York. Now based in the United States, Yehezkel still actively supports Open House as a member of the Friends of Open House/USA Board. He raises funds and organizes local activities among Jews, Christians, and Muslims to promote the message of Open House in the United States. For example, Friends of Open House has organized an interfaith Seder in Boston and hosted youth from Ramle, who visited Cincinnati, New York, and Massachusetts for twenty-five days in August 2002.[229] Yehezkel Landau continues to bring together Jews, Muslims, and Christians from the United States, Israel/Palestine, and other countries to promote the idea that they do not have to choose sides in the Arab-Israeli conflict and that true reconciliation is possible. Yehezkel's effectiveness as a *Peacemaker* can perhaps best be summarized by Yossi Klein Halevi, acclaimed author and chair of the Open House Board: "Yehezkel has the rare capacity to enter into the most painful conflicts – including those in which he has a direct stake – without giving in to anger or hatred. He can stand at the center point of bitter dispute and – with an open heart and generous spirit – transform enemies into friends."[230]

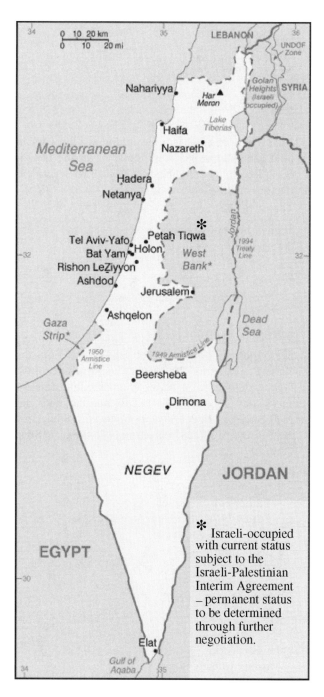

* Israeli-occupied
with current status
subject to the
Israeli-Palestinian
Interim Agreement
– permanent status
to be determined
through further
negotiation.

Geography

Location:	Middle East, bordering the Mediterranean Sea, between Egypt, Jordan, Syria, and Lebanon.
Area:	*Total:* 20,770 sq km *Water:* 440 sq km *Land:* 20,330 sq km *Note:* There are 242 Israeli settlements and civilian land use sites in the West Bank, 42 in the Israeli-occupied Golan Heights, and 29 in East Jerusalem (October 2005 est.)
Area comparative:	Slightly smaller than the U.S. state of New Jersey.
Climate:	Temperate; hot and dry in southern and eastern desert areas.

Population

Population:	6,276,883 (July 2005 est.)	
	Note: Includes about 187,000 Israeli settlers in the West Bank, about 20,000 in the Israeli-occupied Golan Heights, and fewer than 177,000 in East Jerusalem (July 2004 est.). This number does not include 2,385,615 Palestinians in the West Bank (July 2005 est.) or 1,376,289 Palestinians in the Gaza Strip (July 2005 est.).[232]	
Ethnic/religious groups	Jewish population:	
	Israel-born:	67.6%
	Father born in Israel:	33.4%
	Father born in Europe-Americas:	14.6%
	Father born in Africa:	10.4%
	Father born in Asia:	9.2%
	Africa-born:	5.9%
	Asia-born:	4.1%
	Europe-Americas-born:	22.4%
	Arab:	18.8%
	other:	5.4%[233]
Religions:	Jewish:	75.6%
	Muslim: (mostly Sunni Muslim)	16.8%
	Christian:	2%
	Druze:	1.6%
	other:	3.8%

| Languages: | Hebrew (official), Arabic, English. |

Government

Government type:	Parliamentary democracy.
Capital:	Israel proclaimed West Jerusalem as its capital in 1950 and annexed East Jerusalem in 1967. The international community has not recognized the annexation. The United States, like nearly all other countries, maintains its embassy in Tel Aviv, which is the internationally recognized capital of Israel until the issue of Jerusalem is resolved.
Legal system:	Mixture of English common law, British Mandate regulations, and, in personal matters, Jewish, Christian, and Muslim legal systems; in December 1985, Israel informed the UN Secretariat that it would no longer accept compulsory International Court of Justice jurisdiction.

Economic Overview

Israel has developed a technologically advanced market economy with substantial yet declining government participation. It relies on imports of crude oil, grains, raw materials, and military equipment. Despite limited natural resources, Israel has intensively developed its agricultural and industrial sectors over the past decades and is largely self-sufficient in food production except for grains. Cut diamonds, high-technology equipment, and agricultural products (fruits and vegetables) are the leading exports.

Israel usually posts sizable current deficits, which are covered by large transfer payments from abroad and by foreign loans. Roughly half of the government's external debt is owed to the United States, which is Israel's major source of economic and military aid.

The influx of Jewish immigrants from the former U.S.S.R. during the period of 1989–1999, coupled with the opening of new markets at the end of the Cold War, energized Israel's economy, which grew rapidly in the early 1990s. But growth began moderating in 1996, when the government imposed tighter fiscal and monetary policies and the immigration bonus petered out. Growth was 6.4 percent in 2000. But the bitter Israeli-Palestinian conflict as well as a global recession contributed to declines in Israel's high-technology and tourist sectors, and fiscal austerity measures in the face of growing inflation led to declines in GDP in 2001 and 2002. Improvements in tourism and direct foreign investment have led to rising business and consumer confidence, boosting GDP in 2003 and 2004.

GAZA STRIP FACT SHEET[234]

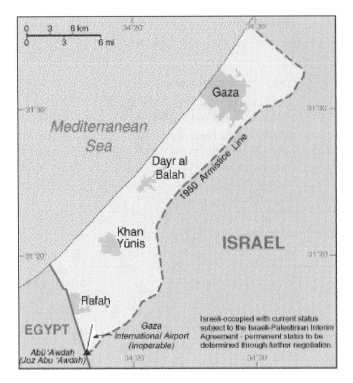

Geography

Location:	Middle East, bordering the Mediterranean Sea, between Egypt and Israel.
Area:	*Total:* 360 sq km *Water:* 0 sq km *Land:* 360 sq km
Area comparative:	Twice the size of Washington, D.C.
Climate:	Temperate winters; hot and dry summers.

Population

Population:	1,376,289 (July 2005 est.)	
Ethnic/religious groups	Palestinian Arab and other:	100%
Religions:	Muslim:	99.3%
	Christian:	0.7%
Languages:	Arabic, English.	

WEST BANK FACT SHEET[235]

West Bank is Israeli-occupied with current status subject to the Israeli-Palestinian Interim Agreement - permanent status to be determined through further negotiation.

Med. Sea

Janïn

Ţūlkarm

Qalqīlyah

Nāblus

Jordan River

1994 Treaty Line

JOR.

▲ Tall 'Āşūr

Ramallah

Latrun Salient

Jericho

Mount Scopus

No Man's Land

Jerusalem

ISRAEL

Bethlehem

Hebron

Dead Sea

1949 Armistice Line (Green Line)

0 5 10 km
0 5 10 mi

Geography

Location:	Middle East, west of Jordan.
Area:	*Total:* 5,860 sq km
	Water: 220 sq km
	Land: 5,640 sq km
	Note: Includes West Bank, Latrun Salient, and the northwest quarter of the Dead Sea, but excludes Mt. Scopus; East Jerusalem and Jerusalem No Man's Land are also included only as a means of depicting the entire area occupied by Israel in 1967.
Area comparative:	Slightly smaller than the U.S. state of Delaware.
Climate:	Temperate; warm to hot summers, cool to mild winters.

Population

Population:	2,385,615 (July 2005 est.)	
	Note: In addition, there are more than 187,000 Israeli settlers in the West Bank and fewer than 177,000 in East Jerusalem (July 2004 est.)	
Ethnic/religious groups	Palestinian Arab and other:	83%
	Jewish:	17%
Religions:	Muslim:	75%
	Jewish:	17%
	Christian and other:	8%
Languages:	Arabic, Hebrew, English.	

Economic Overview of the Gaza Strip and the West Bank

The Gaza Strip is one of the most densely populated places on earth. Both its northern and eastern borders and coastline are controlled by Israel. Its southern border with Egypt is monitored by observers from the European Union but remains fully under Palestinian control. The West Bank remains under Israeli security control, has slightly better conditions, but still over a third of its population lives in poverty. The second Palestinian uprising (intifadah) that started in September of 2000 has led to a worsening of the economic situation in both territories as a result of Israel's increased security policies, which prevented many residents from trading and working in Israel. From 2001 to 2003, Israeli military operations created chaos for businesses in the Palestinian territories. It is estimated that more than 80 percent of Palestinians who used to work in Israel lost their jobs during this period. Two billion dollars of international aid to the West Bank and Gaza in 2004 helped to keep the economy afloat and allowed for some of the government's financial operations to be improved. Israeli with-drawal from the Gaza Strip in September of 2005 allows for the potential of economic growth because of the removal of restrictions on internal movement. However, the difficulties in conducting trade resulting from having control over only one border crossing has left 80 percent of the population living below the poverty line.

12 Underground Woman

Sakena Yacoobi and the Afghan Institute of Learning

Afghanistan

Afghanistan came under international scrutiny after the terrorist attacks of September 11, 2001. The ruling Taliban militia refused to hand over ringleader Osama bin Laden, and the United States intervened. Bombing Afghanistan in October 2001, the United States displaced the Taliban and installed the anti-Taliban Northern Alliance as the new government. Today, infighting and a weak infrastructure plague the country, and, notwithstanding the aid it receives from the United States and the world community, Afghanistan continues to struggle with its post-Taliban legacies.

In the midst of Afghanistan's upheaval, the Afghan Institute of Learning (AIL) stands equipped to serve as one of the nation's architects. Since 1995, AIL has been filling the education gap the Taliban created. Led by Sakena Yacoobi, AIL trains women and girls in leadership, literacy, and marketable skills. Equally significant, it empowers women by teaching them about human rights, religion and how to negotiate constructive relationships in a patriarchal society. In these efforts, Sakena Yacoobi and AIL are helping to prepare Afghanistan to become a more peaceful and just society. Through an array of programs, AIL now reaches 350,000 people per year. The story of Sakena Yacoobi and the AIL are that of a woman with faith, an organization with vision, and the nation they are working to transform.

The Context: An Overview of Afghanistan

Afghanistan is a land of severe terrain, divided northeast to southwest by the craggy cliffs of the Hindu Kush Mountains. The country is land-locked and bordered by Turkmenistan, Uzbekistan, Tajikistan, with a tiny finger of land in the northeast jutting into China. But it is the nations that meet Afghanistan toward the west and south, Iran and Pakistan, respectively, that have figured most prominently in the country's history.[1]

In part, Afghanistan's social structures and politics have been molded by its geography – with tribes isolated from one another, and each maintaining relative local independence in the face of repeated attempts to unify them. Over time, the harsh and imposing Hindu Kush Mountains have thwarted the ambitions of those who would build enduring empires, making it difficult to maintain centralized power over the region.

And yet, Afghanistan has a vibrant history, with three of the world's major religions flourishing in the land at various points in its history. Around 2000 BCE, the Rig Veda (the Hindu book of mantras) is thought to have been created in Afghanistan; Zoroaster introduced his new religion in the seventh century BCE; and Buddhism flourished in the third and second centuries BCE.

Muslim monarchs later wiped those religions from the land, and modern Afghani society bears little evidence of its multitextured religious heritage.[2] Today, the country's population is predominantly Muslim: 84 percent of Afghans are Sunni and 15 percent are Shia. Islam thus serves as both the national religion and the backbone of Afghan culture and values. Its citizens, however, remain divided by their rival interpretations and understandings of Islam.[3]

For centuries, outside conquerors and historians took note of Afghanistan primarily as a crossroads among important regions of the world. To them, the country was significant because it bridged the west with the east, as the Silk Route to Central Asia and China and as a "highway of conquest" linking western, central, and southern Asia. Charles H. Norchi, scholar of international security studies at Yale University, describes Afghanistan as historically "a land on everyone's way to someplace else," a "buffer state," and "a pawn in the games of others."[4] Renowned British historian Alfred Toynbee calls it "the roundabout of the ancient world."[5] The story of Afghanistan reflects both internal and external perspectives. It is a story of a tribal federation whose struggle to unite is punctuated by partial takeovers from different empires. Each empire left a mark on the land, but the absence of a strong, centralized government in Afghanistan ultimately left regional identities and cultures to prevail.

Empires, Rulers, and War: The Fifth Century BCE through the Late Nineteenth Century

One of the first recorded conquests of Afghanistan occurred from the early sixth to the late fifth centuries BCE, when Darius the Great expanded the Persian Empire to include much of Afghanistan. His reign was marked by constant rebellion from the Afghan tribes. Later, in the fourth century BCE, Alexander the Great conquered Persia and then Afghanistan, but again, the Afghan people continually revolted, finally ending Persian rule. The Kushans ruled for a longer period, beginning in 50 CE and lasting until the fifth century, when the White Huns invaded, destroying Afghanistan's then-thriving Buddhist culture and leaving the country in ruins.[6]

Afghanistan's modern cultural landscape began to take shape when the Arabs introduced Islam in the mid- to late seventh century. Under Arab influence, Afghanistan overcame internal dissension, expanded its borders, and expelled the Hindus, who had lived on the land for years. The Arabs (and later the Persians, who again conquered the land in 998 CE) solidified and centralized power in Afghanistan. Notably, by the tenth century, Afghanistan was ruled by the Ghaznavids, a Sunni dynasty, which prevented the spread of Shiism eastward from Iran. Their legacy remains, and even today, the majority of Muslims in Afghanistan and the rest of South Asia are Sunnis.[7]

Under Arab and then Persian rule, the infrastructure of Afghanistan grew stronger and more intricate, until Genghis Khan invaded in 1219 CE. He destroyed Afghanistan's irrigation systems, leaving fertile soil to desiccate until it became permanent desert. Following his death in 1227 CE, a succession of chiefs and princes struggled for supremacy. But by the end of the next century, Genghis Khan's descendant Tamerlane had again overtaken Afghanistan, incorporating it into his own vast Asian empire. Babur, a descendant of Tamerlane and the founder of India's Moghul Empire at the beginning of the sixteenth century, later made Kabul the capital of an Afghan principality.[8]

But it was not until the rule of Ahmad Shah in 1747 CE that the borders of present-day Afghanistan acquired greater definition. An Afghan tribal leader, Ahmad united the tribes of Afghanistan under a loose confederacy whose borders stretched across Central Asia from Kashmir (in present day Pakistan) to parts of Iran. He established a tribal dynasty, known as Durrani, a name that has come to be used by nearly half of the tribes of Afghanistan. Ahmad's powerful legacy is evident in how he is remembered – as "the Father of the Nation."[9]

Less than one hundred years later, in 1826, another Durrani ruler named Dost Mohammad Khan emerged as a powerful leader, becoming emir after an eight-year skirmish for power. His reign marked a time of cultural exchange and openness. Charles Masson, a British citizen visiting Afghanistan and other Central Asian countries during that period, gave the following account:

> It is a matter of agreeable surprise to any one acquainted with Mahommedans in India, Persia, and Turkey, and with their religious prejudices and antipathies, to find that the people of Kabul are entirely [devoid of] them. In most countries few Mahommedans will eat with a Christian; to salute him, even in error, is deemed unfortunate, and he is looked upon as unclean. Here none of these difficulties or feelings exist. The Christian is respectfully called a "Kitab," or "one of the Book."[10]

But this openness was not destined to last. Britain was vying with Russia for control over Central Asia in what came to be known as "The Great Game." Seeking to solidify control of its Indian Empire, Britain began pressing into Afghanistan. The first Anglo-Afghan War (1839–1842) ensued, and Britain replaced Dost Mohammad Khan with Shah Shuja, an Afghan king who answered to the British. It took only three years before the Afghans killed Shah Shuja, and the Afghan hero Akbar Khan led Afghanistan to victory against the British. Dost Mohammad Khan again assumed power. He reigned until his death in 1863.[11]

This struggle changed Afghan culture forever. Afghans came to memorialize the victory as a defeat of Western imperialism. And they also came to view foreigners as people to be "distrusted as potential aggressors and despised as infidel and immoral people."[12] Xenophobia began to infiltrate the culture.

Britain, the Soviet Union, and the Rise of the Taliban: Late 1800s to 1998

Nonetheless, relations with Britain were civil immediately following the First Anglo-Afghan War, deteriorating again in the 1870s. In 1878, the Second Anglo-Afghan War broke out. It ended two years later with the Treaty of Gandamak, which effectively made Afghanistan a protectorate of Britain. Britain agreed to provide Afghanistan with an annual subsidy as well as military protection in case of foreign invasion. The Treaty placed Abdur Rahman Kahn in power, and in exchange for its protection, Britain took control of the country's foreign affairs and placed British representatives in Kabul and other parts of Afghanistan. During the next twenty years, Abdur Kahn centralized control over the majority of the people of Afghanistan.[13]

Not long after, tensions between Afghanistan and Russia increased along Afghanistan's northern border. After a series of Russian incursions, Russian and Afghan forces confronted one another at Panjdeh. The British saw these incursions as a Russian affront to its Asian territory. Although the Russians eventually secured Panjdeh as their own, in 1895 Britain negotiated for Afghanistan to retain its northern border, which thereafter served as a buffer between Britain and Russia.[14]

Another event that defined Afghanistan's modern borders occurred in 1893 with the official demarcation of the Durand Line, named after Sir Mortimer Durand, the Indian government's foreign secretary.[15] Drawn to settle disputes with British-controlled India, the line, according to Ewans, "took little note of ethnographic, and sometimes not even topographical, factors. Tribes, sometimes even villages, were divided."[16] The Peshawar region became part of India, and years later when Pakistan gained its independence, the line served as the border between Afghanistan and Pakistan.[17]

Although Afghanistan closed its borders during these years, in 1919, King Amanullah Kahn attacked British troops in India, launching yet another Anglo-Afghan War. This month-long conflict ended on August 19, 1919, with the Treaty of Rawalpindi, in which the British agreed to relinquish control over all Afghani foreign affairs. Later that same year, the 1919 Paris Peace Conference recognized Afghanistan as an independent state. In the decade that followed, Amanullah attempted to modernize the country, establishing coeducational schools and abolishing the traditional Muslim veil for women. His efforts were met with great opposition, and within ten years he was forced to abdicate the throne.[18]

The three Anglo-Afghan Wars reframed Afghani attitudes and culture. Isolationism gained hold. In contrast with the "cross-roads identity" of its earlier history, it was this isolationist spirit that helped keep Afghanistan out of two world wars in the twentieth century.

But those wars nonetheless had an impact on Afghanistan. When British rule in India ended in 1947 and India and Pakistan were created, Pakistan caused an international dispute by claiming some Pashtun tribal lands that also were claimed by Afghanistan. Additionally, Britain's departure left room for the Soviet Union to begin exerting influence on Afghanistan's government, relatively unhindered by other foreign powers.[19]

Indeed, Soviet policy from the end of World War II through the late 1970s was designed to bring Afghanistan under Soviet hegemony. Welcomed by Mohammed Daoud during his first period of leadership (1953–1963), the Soviets built roads, tunnels, and initiated other infrastructure projects in northern Afghanistan. However, when Daoud distanced the nation from the Soviets during his second period of rule (1973–1978), the path to war became inevitable.[20]

In April 1978, Daoud ordered the arrest of several leaders of the Afghan Communist Party (PDPA). The Communist Party, although small and split into competing factions, had Soviet-trained officers in positions of leadership in the military. With these key individuals under their control, the PDPA orchestrated a coup, removing Daoud from power.[21]

The new PDPA government quickly implemented a variety of Communist reforms (including some affecting marriage and coeducation.) The response was swift and violent. Fighting flared in nearly every region. Units of the Afghan army mutinied and joined the *mujahedin*. In response, the Soviets invaded and by early 1980 had nearly one hundred thousand troops in the country,[22] thus beginning what some have called "Russia's Vietnam."

Afghanistan became a nation divided, with the pro-Soviet socialists based in Kabul and mujahedin forces based in Pakistan, Iran, and different regions within Afghanistan. In an effort to gain the upper hand in the Cold War, the United States provided financial support and military training to the mujahedin, again transforming Afghanistan into a buffer state, this time between the Soviets and the United States and its regional allies.[23]

By the time the Soviets finally withdrew in 1989, rival factions of mujahedin were fighting for control of the country, and local warlords ruled through rapidly changing, violent, and repressive regional coalitions. Simultaneously, the superpowers lost focus, if not interest, in Afghanistan.[24] Not surprisingly, Afghanistan deteriorated. During the 1990s, poverty was rampant, the number of refugees increased exponentially, and the infrastructure of the country collapsed, leaving a serious power vacuum.[25]

The moment was ripe for the Taliban, a group of teachers and students committed to a fundamentalist interpretation of Islam, which they had been cultivating in private, rural-based schools called *madrasas* (the only schools before 1978 to educate school-aged Pashtun boys). Seizing on the anarchic conditions in the country, the Tailban called for national unity under strict Islamic law. Some Afghanis were receptive, and with aid from Pakistan and Saudi Arabia, the Taliban took control of 90 percent of Afghanistan by 1998. The remaining 10 percent – opposed to the Taliban's rule – organized under the name of the Northern Alliance.[26]

The Taliban up to the Present Day

In 1996, during the Taliban's rise to power, Charles H. Norchi authored an article suggesting three reasons why the United States should become reengaged in Afghanistan: the "horrific human rights abuses" there; the two million Afghan lives spent helping the United States win the Cold War (by pushing the Soviet Union out of Afghanistan); and the potential for "blowback," a term initially used by the CIA and increasingly employed by international relations scholars to refer to the unintended consequences of U.S. intervention in foreign countries. With uncanny prescience, Norchi predicted subsequent events: "Absent a well-devised U.S. Afghan policy buttressed by regional authority and power, Afghanistan will become a springboard for the projection of ideological violence cloaked in religious symbolism."[27]

Norchi anticipated the 2001 terrorist attacks against New York City by tracing the 1994 World Trade Center bombing back to clues in Afghanistan. His concern about the potential for "blowback" rested on his observation that certain elements in Afghanistan were spawning the "operationalization" of anti-U.S. sentiment, especially by sheltering Osama bin Laden.[28]

It was less than two years later that American embassies in Kenya and Tanzania were simultaneously bombed on August 7, 1998, allegedly by al-Qaeda. In retaliation, the United States struck al-Qaeda's Afghan bases with cruise missiles. And with these events, the media turned attention to Afghanistan and the Taliban.[29]

Among other things, news stories began to focus the public on the Taliban's gender policies: how Afghan women no longer had access to healthcare; how they had minimal access to employment; how girls could not be educated at all;[30] and how boys were also being affected, because many of their teachers were women. The Taliban was unflinching and took the position that its policies revitalized the family and protected both the honor and dignity of Afghan women.

And this was the situation when terrorists attacked the United States on September 11, 2001. As the reality of that event began to be understood, international attention again turned to Afghanistan. When the United States subsequently invaded the country months later in search of Osama bin Ladin, over 50 percent of the country's population already had personally suffered death, injury, or displacement.[31] The U.S. military soon overthrew the Taliban, and a new government was installed. But the country has still not been fully rebuilt, in part due to insufficient international assistance.

As of 2005, there are still over 150,000 internally displaced persons in Afghanistan, with little support to rebuild their lives for those who do return home.

Sakena Yacoobi

Intensely interested in religion from childhood, Sakena Yacoobi reaffirmed her Muslim faith when she left her home in Afghanistan to attend college and then graduate school in the United States. There, she studied side-by-side with devout Christians who "made faith the center of their lives." As she witnessed their faithfulness, Sakena was moved, beginning a process of transformation in which her own life and beliefs as an observant Muslim became totally aligned.[32] Throughout her education in the United States, she observed how faith could inspire people to serve. It was this realization that would later come to motivate Sakena to pursue a life's work devoted to serving the needy.

As she experienced the power of religion, Sakena also developed a new and more academic understanding of her faith. She studied Islam and found that this religion – her religion, which extremists had used to terrorize the people of her country – also provided immense resources for understanding peace, justice, and equality. Indeed, these are its central values. This understanding deepened Sakena's faith and led her to more intently seek out knowledge of Islam. Over time, both the academic and experiential dimensions of her religious beliefs coalesced with an intense focus on social justice. Sakena found herself growing closer to Allah.

Born in Herat in northwestern Afghanistan, Sakena traveled to the United States in 1973 to earn her Bachelor of Science in biological sciences from the University of the Pacific in Stockton, California. Four years later, she began her studies for a Master's in Public Health from

Loma Linda University, a Christian university also in California. After earning these degrees, she stayed in academia, teaching physiology, psychology, and mathematics at D'Etre University in Grosse Pointe, Michigan.

Throughout these years, Sakena carried a dream that she would return to Afghanistan one day to help the women of her native country, a goal she harbored from the time of her youth when she dreamed of being a doctor. But serving as a doctor was not to be her destiny. She gradually concluded that she could be of most help by preparing herself in the field of public health. Sakena could not forget how much her mother had suffered as the result of annual pregnancies and numerous miscarriages, a common situation that caused suffering for many Afghan women. What was most needed, she concluded, was a campaign to educate women and empower them to begin to take control over their bodies and their lives.

The political climate of Afghanistan radically changed during the course of her studies in the United States. After the Soviet Union invaded her country in 1979 and initiated its era of violence, Sakena became determined to bring her family to the United States. It was only when her efforts ultimately succeeded that she was free to turn her focus elsewhere. In 1992, Sakena flew to Peshawar, Pakistan to work in an Afghan refugee camp. Serving with the International Rescue Committee (IRC), first as a manager and then as the coordinator for their Female Education Teacher Training Program, Sakena supported girls' schools, developing new teacher training manuals.

It was during these years that Sakena saw firsthand the overwhelming poverty, the destruction of the educational system, and the security problems (including threats from militias and ongoing fighting) that plagued the desperate women living in the refugee camps. Some had to leave Afghanistan because their families had died. Others suffered and struggled to support their families while living in tents, usually unable to develop the skills or incapable of utilizing opportunities to earn money.

Sakena witnessed suffering from the trauma of war, and in particular how the cycles of violence entrapped whole families in patterns of mutual abuse. Despite the risks involved, Sakena decided to stay in the camps and help Afghan women; but her goal was to do more than meet their immediate needs. Sakena recognized the need to implement long-term change among the refugee community. Disregarding danger and the controversy about educating women and girls, Sakena focused on education. And during her one-year tenure with the International Rescue Committee, she increased the number of students from three thousand to fifteen thousand.

The Afghan Institute of Learning

In 1995, the same year the Taliban came to power, Sakena founded the Afghan Institute of Learning (AIL). AIL grew out of Sakena's commitment to Afghan women and her experiences with the International Rescue Committee. Using a manual written by Mahnaz Afkhami of the Women's Learning Partnership and incorporating an understanding of human rights and leadership derived from the Qu'ran, she conducted workshops that showed women that everyone can be a leader. She taught that leadership is evident among women and that even housewives can lead by guiding their family and instructing their children. Sakena's students also learned that women can – and indeed, must – contribute in fundamental ways to establishing a peaceful society.

Most of the women who participated in Sakena's classes considered discussion of personal problems with nonfamily members taboo. Not surprisingly, many were reserved and hesitated to speak in the workshops. Their reluctance was no match for Sakena; she broached the difficult subjects, including incest, rape, and spousal abuse. By reading case studies, she showed the women that others, just like them, shared similar life circumstances. This helped the participants to open up. Consider the following example of a case study used by Sakena to encourage the women to think about issues of gender equity, from Afkhami's *Safe and Secure: Eliminating Violence Against Women and Girls in Muslim Society:*

> Maliika is 40 years old and has worked on a construction site just outside of Dhaka since before she married Saiful 20 years ago. Her hands and feet are raw and covered with cuts and blisters from breaking stones. Yet Maliika has never seen her earnings in full; her husband takes the pay envelop from her as soon as she receives it. Is Saiful violating Maliika's human rights? If so, which rights is he violating?[33]

Case studies helped women to recognize the concept that they also had rights. This, in turn, allowed them to turn to practical questions, such as how they were to defend themselves in a society where their rights are often violated. The resulting discussions served as stepping-stones for women to reach out from their isolation to support each other and to collaborate to solve common problems. Sakena's initial workshops were inspirational and her impact evident in the work that participants subsequently undertook, including opening hospitals for women, running literacy classes, and establishing poorhouses to assist widows and their children.[34]

Just as her own education had helped Sakena develop a view of how Islam is a source for promoting peace and resolving conflict, so, too, did the curriculum she developed for AIL. As she explains:

> Peaceful education was incorporated into the curriculum. People here have become suspicious of one another and have so much revenge to take out on one another, and we used sensitivity to culture, tradition, and religion to introduce them to our curriculum of peace.[35]

By teaching women to read and especially to read the Qu'ran, Sakena successfully equipped her students with knowledge of their faith and society. In Afghanistan, religious teachings were often passed on orally, as a result women had little opportunity to assess or challenge the teachings. As Sakena taught them to read, however, they were able to claim the Qu'ran as their own, empowered with the capacity to identify verses that asserted the equality of women and men. They studied how the Qu'ran provided important protections and guidance for women. Daughters must not be forced to marry, but should be consulted, and men must not abuse women, but should be kind and fair toward them.

Learning to read the Qu'ran and its powerful message was only the first step. To bring these ideas to their families and communities, the women also had to learn how to negotiate on the basis of shared values: diversity, equality, fairness, justice, and inclusiveness. Sakena taught this by emphasizing the overlap between the principles found in the Qu'ran and numerous international human rights doctrines. Accordingly, when the women with whom she worked spoke with their brothers or fathers, they were ready and had learned ways to say "You are a good Muslim, aren't you? Then look: the Qu'ran says that husbands must be fair with their wives."[36]

Many fathers and brothers were shocked. Because they wanted to be faithful Muslims, some even changed their behavior toward their wives, and even their daughters. Remarkably, rather than resenting this new source of female empowerment, many men became excited about it. "Traditionally," Sakena reports, "men did not want their wives to learn, but now all men want their wife and daughter to learn. They can see the result of the workshops, and they say, 'Islam has taught you this.'"[37]

AIL's popularity resulted in organizational growth. Sakena has directed the training of over 8,500 female Afghan teachers, and AIL now serves 350,000 women and children annually in the Afghan cities of Kabul, Herat, Mir Bacha Kaot, and Jalalabad, in addition to the Pakistani city of Peshawar. Besides literacy classes, which are particularly aimed at older girls who lost five years of education under the Taliban, AIL also offers an array of practical training in such subjects as sewing, embroidery, rug weaving, health education, counseling, English, computers, leadership, and human rights.

To enable women to attend, AIL also provides childcare and preschool education. Under Sakena's supervision, AIL has grown substantially over the last few years. During 2003 alone, AIL built a health clinic in the rural area of Mir Bacha Kot, opened two new computer labs in Kabul and Herat, began training midwives and female nurse/health educators, launched the publication of a health and education magazine, and started to support smaller Afghan NGOs in need of funding and training.

The story of Pari Gul, a widow with four children, exemplifies how Sakena and the Afghan Institute of Learning change women's lives, and by extension, Afghan society. The only work Pari Gul could find to do – washing clothes, sweeping, and cleaning for other people – took her away from her children, who were left to fend for themselves. One day, on the advice of a family for whom she worked, Gul contacted the AIL office for help. AIL accepted her as a student in its carpet-weaving center, and after several months of training, Gul was able to purchase a carpet-weaving frame. Now she is able to work at home weaving and selling carpets, and simultaneously be near her children. Of her experience, Pari Gul says: "I am very happy [because of the] AIL office. I always pray for AIL staff to be successful and help with all our poor homeland people."[38] Because she had such a positive experience with AIL, she sent her children to be educated by AIL in English and carpet weaving.

Sakena's teaching methods diverge from the traditional educational methods used in Afghanistan. Skeptical of the conventional technique of rote memorization, she designed a curriculum that is interactive and student centered, as well as focused on the values of inclusivity and cultural sensitivity. Because human-rights education is new in Afghanistan and also touches on subjects sometimes considered controversial, Sakena developed for her teachers what she termed a "Guide to Teaching Human

Rights in the Afghan Classroom." Consider, for example, the following list of "Do" and "Do Not" guidelines:

Do	Do Not
Teach negotiation skills and effective communication.	Teach "no war" or passiveness. Afghans have been fighting for a quarter century to protect their homes, families, religious beliefs, livelihoods and country. Instead, recognize and respect Afghan history and the threats facing Afghans.
Teach people to respect each other.	
Teach strategies for solving problems peacefully.	
Teach alternatives to war.	
Use interactive teaching techniques such as role-play and group work to engage students in learning.	
	Teach in a way that is not interactive and that does not value student's perspectives.
Model the human rights principles that your organization is advocating when making decisions and managing a classroom.	Treat students disrespectfully or use violence or intimidation to force students to attend to their studies.
Teach self-advocacy and assertiveness.	Teach submissiveness. (In Afghan culture, a principle such as "turn the other cheek" is considered weakness and letting others use you.)
Teach communication skills that help solve rather than exacerbate problems.	
Consult religious law as well as human rights principles.	Try to impose values that are foreign to Afghan culture or Islam.
When describing human rights problems, use examples that are relevant to Afghans, their lives, their country, and their daily experiences.	Tell people to behave peacefully and respectfully toward each other because it is good for them. (Be able to give logical reasons.)[39]
Teach people to use logic and reason to solve problems. Explain human rights by giving examples and basing your argument on logic and legal arguments. Say that "resorting to violence begins an endless cycle of violence" and is one example of a logical reason for not using violence.	

AIL's work is premised on two core beliefs: grassroots movements that involve the entire community are critical, and education is necessary for building a just, peaceful, and equitable society. Sakena and her educators also know that long-term changes will take time. To these ends, AIL has developed the following strategy to guide its work:

- Begin at the grassroots level with locally identified needs.
- Start with the least controversial service in the least conservative area.
- Do not impose services on a community.
- Offer high-quality, culturally sensitive programs, incorporating feed-back from participants.
- Act at the request of the community when expanding services.
- Require that the community help develop the program.
- Recognize that in Afghan culture, trust and relationships are personal, not organizational.
- Set flexible rules.
- Hold high standards, have high expectations, and model them.
- Offer more controversial programs in a voluntary, culturally sensitive way after trust has been established.

Guided by these principles, under Sakena's leadership AIL has been instrumental in shaping the future of Afghanistan. Change has been gradual but progressive, building up one program at a time. Community involvement has been essential to the success of AIL, and communities now contribute 30 percent of all project resources.[40]

Although its focus is on women and girls, AIL recently realized that it also had to educate boys. Sakena describes the moment in 2002 when she decided to include boys among her students:

> One time, [some AIL staff were] driving through the country, and boys, aged sixteen to eighteen stopped us and said, "You're providing education to girls, but what about us? We only have these guns. We just kill, but we can't do anything." They asked me if they could learn. I told them to come to the Center, even though it was dangerous, and . . . we gave them our literacy program and peace training.
>
> Two years later, the boys behave and dress well. . . . If you live what you believe, other people will come to you. . . . I believe in the power of inner peace.[41]

Sakena believes peace has the power to influence all aspects of human experience: individual, relational, communal, national, and international life. The desire of the boys to find alternatives to fighting testifies to that power, and educating them helps in their transformation.

Regarding the Afghan Institute of Learning's overall contribution toward peacemaking, Sakena says, "If people are educated, they will be able to stand on their own feet and be good citizens. If they don't have education, they don't even know what their religion says to them."[42] Certainly, Sakena's belief is reflected in the reality of the women whose lives she has touched – women who have strengthened their social roles after learning how the Qu'ran empowers them – and in the lives of young boys, who are learning and becoming responsible, peaceful citizens.

Motivation for Peacemaking: Faith, Love, and Responsibility

Afghanistan is still not completely secure, but when AIL began its work in 1995, the risks were terrifying. Sakena discusses the danger: "Sometimes people ask, 'How come you're not scared?' or 'How come a busy schedule runs your life?' But when I see the children and the women, they really want to learn. They always light up when they come into the classroom. It's hard not to be excited by my work. I get a lot of satisfaction from it."[43]

Sakena cannot speak of danger and fear for long without speaking of her faith. Over and over again, she attributes her courage and success to God. "There have been times when it has been dangerous," she concedes, "but I always feel that God is over me, so I don't really have anything to be scared of." Speaking of the specific terrors under the Taliban, she comments, "If the Taliban caught someone, they didn't have any mercy. I really believe that God has been watching over us and enabled us to keep doing our work continuously."[44]

Sakena's faith provides her with the confidence that God will not only protect her, but also will watch over her organization. In discussions of her faith and her God, she refers to Islam and speaks of God in personal language. She says that "with my heart, I know I am going to do this work and that I will be successful. Now, for example, even though the economy is not good and there is little funding, I know I will get it somehow."[45]

Both before and during Sakena's involvement with AIL, she repeatedly risked her life to do her work. She explains:

> There was always endangerment in the refugee camp. We were dealing with Pakistani, government soldiers, and people from different [militant] groups in Afghanistan. Under the Taliban, I knew I could be trapped, kidnapped, and killed. The Taliban lashed people, hung people. Those were things we feared. Now Afghanistan is quite different, but there is still not

much security in Afghanistan. People throw bombs, rockets, kill people. There are still people who are against women's programs, and we are the largest women's program....

I believe strongly that God is protecting us. We have no protection other than God, and somehow we have managed to get out of potentially danger- ous situations.... One time, for example, some children told the Taliban, "A woman was in our class today." But we have taught our teachers how to be resourceful, and the teacher said, "Oh, we didn't have any school; we just had some religious teachings, and someone from the hospital came to give vaccinations." If someone had caught the class, every one of them in it would have been killed or jailed.[46]

Despite the dangers, Sakena is quick to point out that there have never been any casualties among AIL leadership, staff, or students. For her, it is those she works with and teaches who make the work worthwhile:

I am often asked why I do the kind of work I do with the Afghan Institute of Learning. Each time the question is posed, I am reminded of the children in Peshawar when they first come to school. In their eyes, I see fear, sadness and hopelessness. But in just a few weeks, the same children are standing taller, laughing, and playing with smiles across their faces. And I answer the question with this: When you make education available to the Afghan children, it is like giving them new life and hope for the future.

The women served by AIL experience similar transformations. They come into our programs with nothing and they leave with, not only an education and income-generating skills to help provide for their families, they leave with hope in their hearts and a healing in their souls. And that is more than enough reason for me to continue on in my quest to see quality educational opportunities and basic health services offered to the women and children of Afghanistan. I count it a privilege to be helping the Afghan people reach beyond their circumstances to forge a new Afghanistan in the days to come.[47]

Along with Sakena's personal faith, she harbors a deep respect for all religions, a respect fostered in part by the Christians who inspired her to be a better Muslim. She points to commonalities in all religions and is hopeful about the possible ways in which religion can be a resource for promoting peace:

In all religions, we have things in common; we have things we share. I am open to all kinds of religion because I feel that every religion has very good things to offer people. If you can learn to be just and to share, that is all God wants you to do. I have very close friends from all religions, wonderful friends from all around the world.[48]

By embracing this perspective of God, Sakena is better able to carry out her work toward justice and generosity.

Moving Forward: Sakena's Vision for the Future of Afghanistan

As she looks toward the future of the country, Sakena readily shares her vision. "I pray in the future that Afghanistan will be a safe and secure place for children. As a believer in education, I think education is the key to civilization, health, and escaping poverty. I would like Afghanistan to completely successfully master its attitude toward education and for all to be healthy."[49]

Turning to her own future, Sakena says, "For me personally, I am a very simple person. I don't care about material things or being jobless. I want to learn more in religion, to be wiser, to have a better understanding of God and religion."[50] It is a simple wish, but it also is one that has been powerful enough to help guide a nation in its long road toward recovery.

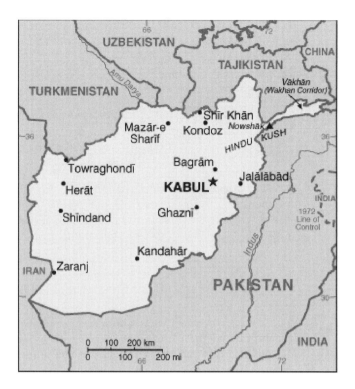

Geography

Location: Southern Asia, north and west of Pakistan, east of Iran.

Area: *Total:* 647,500 sq km
                     Water: 0 km
                     Land: 647,500 sq km

Area comparative: Slightly smaller than the U.S. state of Texas.

Climate: Arid to semiarid; cold winters and hot summers.

Population

Population: 29,928,987 (July 2005 est.)

Ethnic groups: Pashtun: 42%
                     Tajik: 27%
                     Hazara: 9%

Uzbek:	9%	
Aimak:	4%	
Turkmen:	3%	
Baloch:	2%	
other:	4%	

Religions:	Sunni Muslim:	80%
	Shi'a Muslim:	19%
	other:	1%

Languages:	Afghan Persian or Dari (official): 50%
	Pashtu (official): 35%
	Turkic languages (primarily Uzbek and Turkmen): 11%
	other: 4%

Government

Government type:	Islamic Republic
Capital:	Kabul
Legal System:	According to the new constitution: no law should be "contrary to Islam"; the state is obliged to create a prosperous and progressive society based on social justice, protection of human dignity, protection of human rights, realization of democracy, and to ensure national unity and equality among all ethnic groups and tribes; and the state shall abide by the UN charter, international treaties, international conventions that Afghanistan signed, and the Universal Declaration of Human Rights.

Background

The recent history of Afghanistan has been characterized by war and civil unrest. In 1979, the Soviet Union invaded to bolster the failing Afghan Communist government but withdrew after ten years of fighting anticommunist rebels. The communist regime fell in 1992, followed by a civil war between various anticommunist factions. The fundamentalist Muslim movement known as the Taliban rose to power during the mid-1990s and ruled most of Afghanistan from 1996 to 2001. The Taliban instituted a strict form of Shari'a Islamic law, requiring men to grow beards of a specified length and women to wear the burqa in public as well as instituting such punishments as hand amputation for theft and stoning for adultery. After the terrorist attacks of September 11, 2001, and because the Taliban provided Osama bin Laden with a safe haven, the United States and allied forces invaded and toppled the Taliban. In the period since the Taliban's ouster, Afghanistan has adopted a constitution, held presidential and parliamentary elections, shown greater economic stability, and instituted the rule of law. Hamid Karzai became the first democratically elected president of Afghanistan in 2004, and the National Assembly was inaugurated in 2005. The new government has little authority beyond Kabul, however, because of an insurgency led by the Taliban, which continues to create havoc in the country.

Economic Overview

The economic situation is mixed. The infusion of more than $2 billion worth of international aid, rebuilding of the agricultural sector, and strengthening of market institutions have helped Afghanistan's economic outlook improve since 2001. Today, continued support by some international donors provides some hope for the future. However, drought conditions have kept the agricultural sector unstable, and much of the country remains extremely poor. Conditions are difficult; much of the population struggles with a lack of clean water, medical care, education, electricity, developed housing, and jobs. The cultivation of poppy (used to produce opium) has increased, and the opium trade now accounts for an estimated one-third of the GDP, presenting one of the greatest policy challenges to the government in Kabul.

13 Toward a Zone of Peace

The Rev. Dr. Benny Giay

West, Papua, Indonesia

In 2002, East Timor won its independence from Indonesia after years of mutual hostility, mistrust, and conflict. Today, two other parts of Indonesia are engaged in similar struggles: Aceh and West Papua. Once a Dutch colony, West Papua was slated to gain its independence in 1969, but Indonesia seized control of the region. Conflict ensued, and the military has since violently suppressed all efforts to move toward independence.

What began as a conflict between the Papuans and the government now has a horizontal dimension as well, with conflicts between indigenous Papuans and Indonesian migrants to West Papua. Tens of thousands of indigenous Papuans have lost their lives or been forced from their homes with no place to go.

In a land where the indigenous inhabitants feel betrayed and the government remains suspicious of activists, the Rev. Dr. Benny Giay has managed to gain credibility with all parties and become a force for hope and peace. His efforts began when he served in the Protestant Evangelical Church of Indonesia and as a lecturer on church and society at the S.T.T. Walter Post Theological Seminary, the school he founded in June of 1986. As a religious leader, innocent members of his congregation sought him out and shared personal stories of their suffering at the hands of the military.

Deeply moved, Benny became involved in humanitarian work through grassroots activism and by working through NGOs. By 1999, he had taken this on full-time, working night and day to alleviate the suffering of his fellow Papuans. Benny became director of the Papua Peace Commission and worked to establish a "zone of peace" – a vision yet to be realized. The year 1999 also marks the point at which the risks of Papuan peacemaking became a stark reality for Benny. He began receiving death threats. Secret police started following him. And he ceased traveling at night, unless in the company of others.

The Rev. Benny Giay's life is a remarkable and courageous one, filled with obstacles, optimism, and a yearning for peace, independence, and the establishment of what he calls in books and articles a "New Papua."

West Papua: From the Beginnings to the 1980s

The Papuan people thrived for thousands of years before the first colonial powers arrived and changed the course of their history. Although the origins of the Papuans remain uncertain, evidence shows that the island of New Guinea was inhabited anywhere from thirty thousand to sixty thousand years ago. The two main ethnicities were of those who migrated from nearby islands – the Melanesians – and those who likely migrated from East Africa.[1] Today, over 250 different tribes live on the island, which boasts hundreds of distinct languages – totaling 15 percent of the world's known languages.[2]

Spain was the first European country to advance into the island in the early 1500s, naming the land "Nueva Guinea" because it seemed to resemble Guinea in Africa. But Spain never actually colonized New Guinea, and after Napoleon conquered the Iberian Peninsula in 1808, Spanish influence disappeared from the region.

The Dutch came next, moving into New Guinea in the early nineteenth century (two hundred years after colonizing the western islands of today's Indonesia). Because the people of New Guinea had different racial and other indigenous characteristics, the Dutch governed the region separately from their other territories.

By 1883, other European powers were asserting their interests, as Germany and the British Empire also staked claims to New Guinea. The three European countries partitioned the island into three sections: the eastern half was claimed by the Germans in the north and the British in the south, while the western half was claimed by the Dutch. This arrangement persisted for some time. However, many of the native tribes resisted the European presence and attempted to fight the colonials (who were armed with rifles and explosives) with their own weapons (which included spears, stone axes, and bows and arrows). The unequal weaponry, coupled with the introduction of foreign illness, ensured the rapid decimation of entire Papuan communities.[3] In addition, hundreds of tribal men were coerced or forcefully recruited to work in the colonials' plantations.[4]

New Guinea's native inhabitants were also devastatingly affected by World War II. From 1942 to 1944, the Japanese occupied parts of New Guinea and nearby lands, thus bringing the war to the island. The United States also established a headquarters in today's Jayapura to support General Douglas MacArthur's activities in the Philippines. During these years of the war, more than one million troops from Japan, the United States, Australia, and the Netherlands occupied New Guinea. Tens of thousands of indigenous people supported them by providing food and labor. In the process, however, more than 140,000 people were displaced, thousands were killed, and towns were destroyed.[5]

By the mid-twentieth century, the Netherlands began to relinquish some of its colonial claims. Following World War II, in 1949, it granted independence to the colonized people of the former Dutch East Indies, and the Republic of Indonesia was created out of its postcolonial territories.[6] Notwithstanding this decision, the Netherlands opted to retain West New Guinea, which it had always deemed to be culturally distinct. Within just a few years, however, the Dutch government began preparing West New Guinea for independence, even though the eastern half of the island, today's Papua New Guinea, did not receive full independence from its colonizers until 1975. Anticipating autonomy, in December 1961, West Papuans elected their own New Guinea Council and raised their own flag, called the Morning Star flag. Instead of flying over an independent region, however, the flag today serves as a symbol of resistance to Indonesian rule.[7]

Only three weeks after the Papuans raised their flag, President Sukarno of Indonesia laid claim to West Papua and announced plans to invade and take over the area. Despite the Netherlands' original declaration that West Papua would be an independent state, the Dutch responded to Sukarno's aggression by handing control over to the United Nations Temporary Executive Authority (UNTEA). In a U.S.-brokered transfer, it was stipulated that Indonesia would administer West Papua and that, within six years, the Papuans would hold a referendum to decide whether they wanted independence or integration with Indonesia.

Indonesia quickly made clear that it had no intention of allowing a free referendum and suppressed all things associated with West Papuan independence. In 1963, it disbanded the elected council, banned and burned the West Papuan flag, and forbade the singing of the Papuan national anthem. Papuans who protested were imprisoned, tortured, and murdered. In response, some West Papuans formed the Free Papua Movement (OPM, after the name of the mother tongue, Organisasi Papua

Merdeka), which began as a low-grade militant, pro-independence group, and subsequently developed into a secessionist movement that continues its struggle into the twenty-first century. This conflict, together with persistent Indonesian repression, destabilized the region and triggered a steady flow of refugees into Papua New Guinea.[8]

The referendum was held six years later, but the voting process was not democratic. In what scholars and activists have referred to as a "sham," Indonesia handpicked 1,025 electors and reportedly coerced them into choosing union with Indonesia. Notwithstanding the way the result was achieved, subsequent to the election, the Netherlands formally transferred the administration of West Papua to Indonesia, thereby making it the twenty-sixth province of that country. This process was called the "Act of Free Choice" – a term the Papuans use with biting irony.[9]

Recently declassified documents show that the international community fully understood what was happening yet sat back as West Papua was handed over to the Indonesian government. According to reports, they knew the transfer of control to Indonesia was against the will of the majority of the Papuan population. One British official explained the choice as a matter of self-interest: "I cannot imagine the U.S., Japanese, Dutch, or Australian governments putting at risk their economic and political relations with Indonesia on a matter of principle involving a relatively small number of primitive peoples."[10]

President Sukarno was succeeded by Indonesia's infamous President General Mohammad Suharto, who renamed West Papua as Irian Jaya ("Victorious Irian") in 1973. The indigenous movement rejected the new name and to this day identify themselves as West Papuans. Under Suharto's leadership, both Indonesian oppression and Papuan discontent persisted, triggering a mass exodus of native West Papuans. In 1984, over thirteen thousand people, many of them members of the Free Papua Movement, fled to neighboring Papua New Guinea to seek asylum from political persecution. An article from the Australia West Papua Association described the situation:

> The [Indonesian] army also conducted operations to undermine support for the resistance by persecuting the families of people believed to be fighting in the bush. The wives of guerrillas were assaulted, their parents arrested. Villages suspected of supporting the OPM were destroyed, people chased from their homes, livestock killed and property looted. It is difficult to put an exact figure on the number of West Papuans killed since Indonesia took control in 1963, but estimates vary from between 70,000 to 200,000.[11]

Throughout its rule, the Indonesian military has suppressed any move toward West Papuan independence, and has even targeted peacemakers and human rights activists in recent years.

Economic realities have also served to destabilize the region. West Papua is home to the largest gold mine and third largest copper mine in the world, run by the U.S.- and British-owned Freeport Mining Company (Freeport). Lucrative security contracts to guard the mines have been given to the Indonesian military, and the company conducts business virtually unhindered by government interference. In effect, this has given Freeport the power to push thousands of West Papuans off of their land without compensation. And despite local and worldwide protests condemning human rights violations and environmental damage done at the hands of the company, Freeport remains a powerful economic force. The situation in West Papua remains precarious, with frequent violent outbreaks and the emergence of radical groups.

The Reverend Dr. Benny Giay

In the 1990s, the story of West Papua became inextricably connected to the peacemaking efforts of one of Papua's greatest moral and intellectual voices, the Rev. Dr. Benny Giay. Born into a family from the Melanesian Me tribe, Benny is the oldest of six children. Although the family's roots were indigenous, Benny's parents converted to Christianity in the 1950s. And when Benny married, he and his wife practiced Christianity, raising their two daughters in the church, where the family is still very active.[12]

Although the Rev. Giay's evangelical Christian roots run deep, his story reveals a search to reconcile both lines of his family traditions. Over the years, therefore, Benny has evidenced passions for Christianity, the indigenous people, and their traditions, all of which have resulted in his sometimes ambivalent relationship with the Evangelical Church. Over time, his solution and the direction of his work has focused on reconciling indigenous practices with his Christian beliefs and eloquently imparting his vision to the public.

Looking back, Benny concedes that he did not truly understand the meaning of evangelical Christianity until he was a college student. Then, one day in 1974, he attended a sermon on reconciliation. The pastor to whom he was listening described human beings as always living in a state against God, so that there was a need for reconciliation with God that comes to people through Jesus. After the sermon, the listeners reflected on how Christianity might fit with their own tribal backgrounds, which calls on them to restore their relationship with the spirit world while at the same time building harmonious relations with neighbors and the environment.

For Benny, this was a formative experience. To be a Christian, Benny ultimately concluded, is more than pursuing an interior spiritual life; one must also work actively in the world to help restore relationships with one's neighbors and the environment.[13] It is this integrated understanding that has become, for Benny, a calling.

Benny briefly served as a minister, became a member of the Protestant Evangelical Church of Indonesia, and to this day identifies as an evangelical Christian. Yet the Rev. Giay has often been critical of the Evangelical Christian Church in Papua. He describes the church as "concerned with the work of saving souls and build[ing] new churches – which are sometimes [done] in cooperation with oppressive government officials in Papua."[14] Benny believes that the church should instead be addressing important social concerns in practical and meaningful ways.

When describing how he reached these conclusions, Benny gives some examples of the church's failures. He starts by talking about CAMA (Compassion and Missionary Associates), an American mission body that founded the Alliance Papuan Church with which Benny is affiliated. As Benny tells it, students at a Bible school run by CAMA in the coastal town of Nabire in the early 1970s needlessly died:

> Within a month or so, almost thirty students died of malaria. The missionaries and the Church believed at that time that it was God who was taking their lives. The only solution they sought was prayer because they believed that there was nothing they could do. I felt this was a problem. This death could have been prevented if students had been given some basic instruction on malaria and other tropical disease as part of their Church leadership training.[15]

Unfortunately, this was not the only experience of its kind.

During the 1980s, CAMA, in cooperation with Alliance Papuan Church, sent ten couples to the Papuan coast to work as pastors. Thoroughly trained to do their pastoral work, they did not receive even basic education in health care and nutrition. In just months, all but one of the couples died "and the mission and the church did nothing except pray for them."[16] Benny ruefully recalls:

> Only two people survived. One of these survivors came to Jayapura (the capital city) to take his wife to the hospital. As he had no money, he went to find some work, and yet he, too, was crushed by a big truck and died right

away, on his way home from work. This experience struck me. These pastors were not informed about tropical or food differences between Highlands and the coast or even about cultural problems. They were just sent to the coast to be pastors.[17]

The church's failure to prepare its missionaries to be safe – as well as effective in promoting its teachings – troubled Benny. If basic education in health and nutrition had been part of missionary leadership training, these deaths likely would have been prevented.

Benny was equally disturbed by the church's failure to address violations of the human rights of its own Papuan constituency, especially during the 1970s and 1980s. He notes that the evangelical mission "knew very well the killings of innocent West Papuans, particularly in Eastern Central Highlands in 1977 by the Indonesian military, but it was not addressed."[18] Some of the evangelical missionaries even cooperated with the military and government. Benny explains what occurred when the Freeport Mining Company invited CAMA missionaries to conduct Bible studies:

> During the 1980s, CAMA missionaries were invited by Freeport to conduct Bible studies. In response to that CAMA received funding to build churches and do the work of evangelism, even while we all knew very well that Freeport was working with [the] military to drive out our Amungme Church members (from this mining area). I regret that our Papuan Church leaders joined the missionary to cooperate with Freeport, which has been exploiting and killing our Amungme tribes.[19]

Despite these serious frustrations, Benny's work is conducted within the religion of his upbringing. He has spent his life introducing new ideas through his role as a religious leader and teacher and new practices that speak to the reality of his Papuan community. In so doing, he is tackling one of the community's highest priorities: education. Until the 1980s, West Papuans had to leave the country to receive theological training. This was very expensive, and many of the students were badly mistreated while studying abroad. Benny quickly concluded that West Papua needed its own theological school.

At first, the Evangelical Church rebuffed his efforts. But Benny worked tirelessly to gather a core group of potential students until the church agreed to back him. On June 8, 1986, he proudly founded the S.T.T. Walter Post Theological Seminary and became the first head of the school. Over the years, the school has grown. Today, the seminary has accreditation from the Indonesian Department of Religion and boasts hundreds of students and some of West Papua's leading intellectuals as professors.[20]

Benny was evolving during these years, and so was the church. In 1992, in a departure from its former indifference, the Evangelical Church of West Papua published a comprehensive report on the treatment of Papuans by the Indonesian government (i.e., "atrocities, torture and killing"[21]). Benny read the report and, even though he had known much about the violence, he was still struck by the magnitude of the government's horrific acts – including the killing of Papuans in the 1970s and 1980s in the name of development. This proved to be a pivotal moment:

> This report changed me in the sense that there was awareness that these forms of human rights violation have been done by the military throughout West Papua, and to stop this or deal with culture of terror and violence requires a cooperative and communal effort. That means we have to work together with other religious and Church groups.[22]

Only two years later, the atrocities directly touched the church. While delivering his Christmas sermon on December 25, 1994, a Christian pastor was shot by the military. The killing provoked outrage among the Christian community and eventually led to the formation of a new human rights organization, ELSHAM (Institute for Human Rights Studies and Advocacy), which has since become the leading human rights organization in West Papua and Indonesia. As one of its foremost proponents, the Rev. Giay serves on its board.[23]

It was shortly after the pastor's murder that Benny found himself again challenged to integrate his religious beliefs with the traditions of his indigenous community. Benny was attending a meeting in which church synods were trying to convert local residents to Christianity. There, he observed John Rumbiak, a West Papuan human rights activist now living in New York and affiliated with Columbia University's Center for the Study of Human Rights.

Showing no fear of the church or the military, John openly challenged the church leaders: "Do these people need your religion?" he demanded. "If you claim to give them Christianity, and now you use them after they become part of your church, you are bringing suffering on these people." Moved by Rumbiak's bold exhortation, Benny again considered what he could do for the people given that he was part of a church community and a college professor. As his later work demonstrates, there was much he could do.

Both in private conversations and in his published writings, Benny speaks plainly about the military and the way it has been killing Papuan pastors for years. The pastors are often the only people in rural areas with education and knowledge of the outside world. As a result, they are frequently suspected of being advocates for independence and human rights. By threatening, torturing, and sometimes killing these religious leaders, the military sends a message – that no one who threatens (or is perceived to threaten) the sovereignty of Indonesia is safe. That has not stopped Benny. In fact, he decided to draw attention to these martyrs by writing a book to tell their stories, even though he realistically expected the government to ban it from publication.[24] A prolific writer, in the coming years Benny's books and articles on the West Papuan experience – a subject that has received far too little international attention – would become one of his greatest peacemaking achievements.

When asked about danger or whether his work puts him at risk, Benny laughs softly and demurs, "I don't think so, not really."[25] He then talks about those who, he believes, have suffered – losing land, livelihoods, homes, and lives. (Military operations and violence by migrants have resulted in over one million West Papuan deaths.) But notwithstanding his denials, the reality is that Benny is not safe. And when pressed, he reluctantly admits that on several occasions, he has been blacklisted and even barred from leaving the country. His car is routinely trailed by military or secret police. And, at the insistence of family and friends, he now travels at night only when two or three people are available to accompany him.[26]

Evolution of a Peacemaker

Just as the attitude of the Evangelical Church changed slowly throughout the 1980s and 1990s, so too did the Rev. Giay evolve as a peacemaker. During these years, Benny pursued his lifelong dream of obtaining a Ph.D. from a European university, focusing his studies on a subject that would ultimately influence and strengthen his peacemaking. In 1995, after many years of hard work, he obtained his doctorate from the Department of Cultural Anthropology and Sociology of Development at the Free University in the Netherlands. Pursuing a formal, high-level education was not an easy feat, and occurred only because of the support Benny received from his family and community. Indeed, he and his family made great sacrifices; as he says in the preface to his dissertation: "No word could express my gratitude to both my mother and father, who often had to rush to the government post or missionary station to sell their garden products in order to support me at school." Benny's wife and children also came with him while he studied abroad, and numerous CAMA missionaries made personal contributions to help finance his studies.[27]

In his dissertation, which he says marks "the last phase of my formal training," Benny articulated his conclusions about what it means to be both a West Papuan and a Christian. Titled "Zakheus Pakage and His Communities: Indigenous Religious Discourse, Socio-political Resistance, and an Ethnohistory of the Me of Irian Jaya," the dissertation focused on Zakheus Pakage, a West Papuan convert to Christianity who became an itinerant preacher during the 1950s. A deeply personal dissertation topic, Pakage was responsible for converting Benny's entire village, including his parents, to Christianity. However, Pakage's version of Christianity differed from the one taught by Benny's Evangelical Church, because it was built on and included indigenous symbols and beliefs.[28]

Benny acknowledges that he took a "sympathetic" approach toward Pakage and his activities because, from Benny's perspective, they represented an attempt "to formulate their own version of Christianity from the standpoint of their own cultural background." He explains why this is important:

> all human beings see . . . reality from the cultural views of the group in which they have been brought up. . . . As a church worker, I want to see the development of an indigenous church: a church which is in the hands of indigenous leadership, which takes up the task to spread Christianity by its own means, which bears its own financial responsibility.[29]

Benny's thesis presented an intellectual analysis of how one religious leader integrated Christianity with indigenous practices. As a religious leader himself, Benny put this into practice and taught his church to treat indigenous people and their traditions respectfully. Not everyone agreed with Benny's approach. In fact, many in the evangelical tradition were shocked, including his "own mother [who] thinks that the kind of . . . [approach] adopted in this study [i.e., the dissertation] is heretical. She was upset when she finally realized that the information she had given was used to establish a dialogue with men who had been teaching a different gospel, which was in her eyes not a gospel at all."[30]

During the course of writing his dissertation, Benny came to understand what it means to be "an Evangelical and an ecumenical pastor at the same time."[31] He came to see that many of the basic values found in traditional West Papuan culture are also in Christianity. This realization enabled him to reconcile some of his questions about his own identity. Accordingly, Benny developed a perspective of tolerance and inclusiveness that would prove to be critically important.

Shortly after receiving his Ph.D., Benny demonstrated his commitment to education and its power for his community when he reclaimed the Educational Foundation for the Indonesian Evangelical Church in 1997. The organization had been established in the 1960s but nearly ruined by corrupt leaders who sold off much of its property and then pocketed the profits. As its unanimously elected chairman, Benny successfully recovered some of the lost property and then raised funds to provide back wages for teachers who had not been paid in years.[32] At present, the Educational Foundation successfully administers about one hundred elementary schools, fifteen high schools, and two junior colleges.

The next year, the Rev. Giay joined with other church leaders, traditional councils, Papuan NGOs, and student and women's groups to create the Forum for Reconciliation of Irian Society (FORERI).* Responding to the bitter divisions both between ethnic Papuans and Indonesian migrants, and between the government and the inhabitants of West Papua, FORERI's intention was to serve as an independent and impartial body capable of initiating a dialogue and mediating between the government and Papuan representatives. In February 1999, such a dialogue took place, but with unhappy results. Benny sadly reports that participants were "terrorized by the military. The houses of the Papuans who participated ... were destroyed in the night by unknown people.... So, people did not want to support FORERI out of fear that they would be killed."[33] Benny's house was spared, but only because students from a local university guarded it. The Indonesian government labeled FORERI a pro-independence group, and it is now blacklisted.

Indonesia's leadership also changed in 1999. After decades of rule by Suharto, Abdurrahman Wahid was elected as the new Indonesian president. Early in his presidency, he publicly announced that the government should accept partial blame for West Papua's difficulties, and he declared that reforms would be instituted promptly. As part of his reforms, Wahid's government sought a team of West Papuan intellectuals to mediate between separatists and the Indonesian government and draft the Special Autonomy Law for Papua. Benny was selected as a member of the team and was the only Melanesian scholar and expert of West Papua's indigenous roots among the group. The law permitted

* As previously mentioned, Irian Jaya is the name the Indonesian government imposed on West Papua in 1969.

greater self-governance by Papuans and more local ownership of natural resources, while still respecting the territorial integrity of Indonesia. In another promising turn, Wahid, who had spent New Year's Day 2000 in West Papua, announced that the region would be allowed to give up the Indonesian-imposed name of Irian Jaya and could again be known as West Papua (although "West Papua" was never formally readopted).

Wahid did not favor independence for West Papua, but he did allow the Papuans to raise the Morning Star flag and prepare for a Papuan People's Congress, an entity intended to serve as a clearing-house for Papuan concerns, grievances, and proposals. During a preparatory meeting for the upcoming Congress, twenty-five thousand ethnic Papuans from all of the 253 indigenous tribes elected the Papuan Presidium Council (the "Council") to represent them and their nonviolent aspirations for liberation. Deemed the administrative head of the Papuan independence movement, the Council was a peaceful, inclusive, pro-independence political body. The Rev. Giay was elected as a member, and Theys Eluay was named its chairman. To preserve the Council's strong commitment to peace, it excluded from participation the more violently inclined Free Papua Movement. The Council also unanimously denounced the "Act of Free Choice," because the hand-picked electors had not voted freely on the future of West Papua. In its public condemnation, the Council made a point of condemning the events as part of a conspiracy among the Netherlands, the United States, and the UN to integrate West Papua into Indonesia.

Only a few months later, in October 2000, controversy erupted in the Council. Before becoming a Papuan leader that espoused nonviolent activism, Eluay was one of the hand-picked electors who had voted against West Papuan independence in the "Act of Free Choice," an action he later said he was forced to take. Having also served in Suharto's ruling party, he made an unpopular decision to honor a departing Indonesian army commander by elevating him to the rank of "Great Warrior of the Papuans." The Papuans from the highlands, Benny's home, were dismayed. They refused to supply the funds and celebratory pigs required to honor the commander, declaring that they would not make such sacrifices for someone who had ordered the killing of Papuans. As a form of nonviolent support for their protest, Benny left the Council.

Over the next few months, Wahid's administration changed course, in part because his political adversaries in Jakarta were characterizing his administration and the Papuan People's Congress as anti-Indonesian. In response, Wahid reversed his government's position on West Papua and aligned it with the more conservative stance of Suharto's administration.

However, the Special Autonomy Law, which Benny had worked so hard to help mediate, was passed in late 2001.

By 2001, the violence in Papua started attracting more attention worldwide. That year, Belgian filmmakers Philippe Simon and Johan van den Eynde were abducted by the Free Papua Movement. To negotiate their release, the National Liberation Army of Papua sought to find representatives that were agreeable to both sides. It called upon the churches, who selected the Rev. Giay and Father Theo Van den Broek of the Peace and Justice Secretariat of the Jayapura Diocese, a man whom Benny credits – along with human rights activist John Rumbiak – with first showing him that it is possible to represent the people by standing up for both human rights and the church. Together, Benny and Father Van den Broek met with the hostage-takers and hostages, confirming through photos that the Belgian men were doing relatively well. From their meeting, they also carried back a letter that asked CNN to report on the conflict and the plight of the Papuans, and the Belgian government to internationally defend the Papuans. Within a few weeks, Benny and Van den Broek had created enough momentum to successfully begin negotiations for the release of the hostages. On August 16, 2001, the hostages were released unconditionally and in good condition. Despite the Indonesian government's desperate attempts to suppress any contact between the hostage-takers and the Belgian diplomats and the press, the movement's cause still received significant media attention.

But that did not mean an end to the violence. Only a few months later, the Council's leader, Theus Eluay, was kidnapped. Just when Eluay was expected to return from an event celebrating Indonesian Heroes Day, his family received a frantic call from his driver reporting that Eluay and his car had been abducted by non-Papuans. The driver had been left on the side of the road, severely beaten. The following day, Eluay was found dead in his car, his body showing clear signs of torture. Almost immediately, human rights groups claimed that the military was to blame. According to Human Rights Watch's Asia Director, Sidney Jones, "this was clearly a well-planned assassination of one of Papua's best-known leaders."[34] Later reports supported that conclusion. It turned out that high military officials had held a secret meeting and developed a strategy for the systematic oppression of the independence movement. Several key people were specifically named as targets of suspicion, among them, Theys Eluay – and Benny Giay.

Eventually, seven members of the military's elite special forces were tried, found guilty, and sentenced to three to three-and-half years' imprisonment. At their trials, the soldiers admitted that Eluay's death was a deliberate murder and testified that he was killed to prevent him from declaring independence in West Papua. No high-level officials were ever prosecuted in connection with Theus's death, and the investigation was not treated as a political crime. However, General Ryamizard Ryacudu, Indonesian Army Chief of Staff, referred to those found guilty as "heroes" who had justly defended Indonesian sovereignty. Over twenty thousand Papuans traveled by foot to gather for Eluay's burial.[35]

Notwithstanding the apparent cover up and the clear risks, Benny decided that the circumstances surrounding the murder of Theus Eluay had to be publicized. He wanted to ensure that Eluay's legacy would not only be remembered but that it would live on through the peace movement he had led. Using his great communication skills, Benny wrote a book on Theus Eluay in which he showed that although Eluay's career had begun with his support of a unified Indonesia, he ultimately came to believe in the importance of Papuan liberty. As such, Eluay became a hero to the Papuan people and then died at the hands of the Indonesian military. Benny's book also included concrete ideas on how West Papuans can continue the movement for peace through nonviolent actions.

The Indonesian government quickly banned the book, never giving a reason why. It was nevertheless published and sold secretly by people involved in the independence movement, gaining wide readership among Papuans. Today, the anniversary of Eluay's death is widely recognized as a holiday among Papuans, especially near Jayapura where Eluay's tribe resides.

Since September 11, 2001, the conflict between West Papua and Indonesia – traditionally defined along ethnic and cultural lines – has been viewed increasingly through a religious lens as well. West Papuans are majority Christian, but overall, Indonesia is majority Muslim. In the tense post-9/11 climate, the Islamic fundamentalist group, Laskar Jihad, has established a foothold in West Papua, publishing and disseminating literature that opposes West Papuan independence efforts as part of an anti-Indonesian, Christian, separatist, and fringe religious movement. This has exacerbated cultural differences in the region and incited greater opposition to West Papuan independence throughout Indonesia. Today, as numerous countries, particularly the United States, engage in waging a "war against terror," many human rights groups express concern that the need for stronger diplomatic ties with Indonesia will lead the international community – once again – to overlook abuses against West Papuans in an effort to ensure cooperation from the Indonesian military.

Toward a Zone of Peace: A Peacemaking Strategy

In 2002, the Rev. Giay had became involved in what appeared to be a new peacemaking strategy for West Papua, although he maintains that West Papuans had been thinking about it since President Suharto's resignation four years earlier. The idea emerged when a tribal chief suggested to human rights activist John Rumbiak that a West Papuan "zone of peace" be established. This concept, which emerged from the thinking of an indigenous leader, is also a recognized approach in the world community. In 1971, the UN started to declare particular regions of the Indian Ocean and the Caribbean as zones of peace. In 2002, in an effort to say "no" to violence, the Provincial Parliament of Papua established its own "zone of peace" in West Papua, within which no acts of violence would be permitted.

To put the vision into practice, a Papua Peace Commission was created, and Benny was named its director. The commission's aim is to build a coalition of all segments of the Papuan community (including nongovernmental, religious, women's, and student organizations) in support of a zone of peace. As director, Benny works with these diverse groups through peace seminars that he conducts in five different districts each year.[36]

Using the zone of peace as a point of departure, the Papua Peace Commission sought to enter into a comprehensive national dialogue about peace and justice with the central government in Jakarta, similar to what FORERI was intending to do before it was outlawed by the government in 1998. Muhammad Thaha Al-Hamid, secretary general of the Papuan Presidium Council in 2002, described the zone of peace as a place where Papuans "say NO to violence, military operations, and the use of guns as solutions." Instead, "they say YES to the respect for the human dignity and human rights and choose dialogue as the only peaceful way to solve communal and political problems." Referring to the leadership of the Rev. Giay and his colleagues, he added, "The Papuans need some guidance from some experienced figures and institutions in order to create and maintain West Papua as a zone of peace."[37]

As of 2004, however, Benny looks back on the efforts of the Papuan Presidium Council and concedes that he is discouraged:

> Our peacemaking attempt to create a Peace Zone in West Papua can be described as an attempt to boil a stone which will never cook. In other words, our attempt to change the conflict-ridden Province of Papua to

a Peace Zone has not made any progress so far because the Indonesian military as an institution has not been willing to support the idea.[38]

For starters, the military refuses to acknowledge the legitimacy of the West Papuan viewpoint. Even more distressing, as Benny points out with great sadness, the government secretly supplies guns to rebels fighting for independence, and then uses the resulting violence to justify military intervention. He is also troubled by the "provocateurs" – people who come into an area to provoke intratribal fighting as additional justification for the use of force against West Papuans. According to Benny, the military's unwillingness to cooperate rests on its belief that any movement toward peace and stability would bring West Papua one step closer to independence.[39]

Despite the disappointments, however, Benny remains committed to the idea of a zone of peace. As someone with numerous roles and identities – a native Papuan and religious leader, an activist and peacemaker, an author and risk-taker, and an anthropologist and lecturer on church and society at the S.T.T. Walter Post Theological Seminary – the Rev. Giay is well positioned to impart his message to many audiences, including the general public, churches, academic institutions, and within his own community.

He is a strong believer in the power of educational communication, and in fact has been called "the leading public intellectual of Papua."[40] Accordingly, when Benny works with a group, he first reaches his audience by focusing on their interests and predispositions, and only after establishing credibility, introduces his message of peace. In reaching out to the academic community, for example, he draws on his widely translated papers and books (with titles such as "West Papuan Peace Zone: A Possible Dream" and "Towards a New Papua") to set the stage. Conversely, when he engages with churches, he changes hats to lead Bible studies and discussion groups.

Additional Peacemaking Strategies

Above all, the Rev. Benny Giay believes that knowledge is power. Explaining his commitment to education and its role in promoting peace, he says:

> I believe in education as an institution for healing, for human education, so in all those educational projects I am involved, I encourage all the future pastors, church and community leaders to study and learn human rights issues, so when they become leaders they will become an instrument to

bring peace, to help those Papuans who have been traumatized for years, who have no one to assuage their hurts, their feelings.[41]

This strategy derives, at least in part, from Benny's unusually strong empathetic skills. Not only does he understand the struggles of others but he also recognizes the power of people who can inspire others to action. Indeed, when talking to Benny, it becomes clear that he rarely takes credit himself but, instead, tends to describe the men and women who inspired him. Benny calls them heroes, and they include human rights activist John Rumbiak and Father Theo Van den Broek. They also include Papuan women. He talks about Yosepha Alomang, a woman who dedicated her life to struggling against the Indonesian army and Freeport for the Papuan cause. Likewise, he has been inspired by Priscilla Jacadewa, who joined five other Papuan women to raise the West Papuan flag as a gesture of protest against Indonesian justices in Papua – an act for which the women were imprisoned for over four years. From Priscilla and her cohorts, Benny says he learned about the importance of peaceful resistance.[42]

Because he recognizes the power of such heroes and because he sees parallels between the struggles of his own people and those of oppressed peoples around the world, Benny believes it is important to educate his people about human rights heroes from diverse settings. In a book he wrote in 2000, *Towards a New Papua,* he discusses the struggles of African Americans and South Africans, as well as the work of significant peacemakers like Gandhi and Martin Luther King, Jr.[43]

Believing that their stories can educate and inspire others to action, Benny encourages his people to read and then works to make inspirational stories accessible. He does this by renting houses and creating makeshift libraries so that entire West Papuan communities can learn about other peoples who have suffered and overcome circumstances similar to those that Papuans suffer at the hands of the Indonesian government.

Benny can best be understood as an activist educator. In June 2002, years after he founded the S.T.T. Walter Post Theological Seminary, he founded yet a second theological school in the interior of West Papua, called the Institute for Social and Pastoral Studies. "This school," he says, "is specifically dedicated to train local pastors how to deal with the past trauma, because in the 1980s up until the year 2000, the area was declared a military operation zone. There's a lot of trauma, where people lost many lives."[44] The school's purpose is to prepare future leaders to help heal the community. Today, it is also multidenominational and hosts both foreign and local missionaries. The school is training the next generation of West Papuans to continue the work of promoting peace, reconciliation, and healing.

Reflections on Religiously Motivated Peacemaking

The Rev. Giay has a complex and inclusive religious identity. At one with evangelical Christians, he nevertheless criticizes them for having over-looked social concerns. Appreciative of the contributions of Western missionaries, he objects to their emphasis on divine-human reconciliation to the neglect of social concerns and the human relationship with the environment.

Benny's Christian beliefs inspire him to embrace peacemaking and nonviolence, but he also recognizes that Christianity, as preached by missionaries, has served to distort West Papuan culture. In particular, it has failed to emphasize the West Papuan tradition of personal community among neighbors, which includes the environment and their spiritual life. Benny reflects:

> I think Christianity as it has been preached by Western missionaries in West Papua for years has destroyed some of the essential elements of Christian values [already] found in Papuan culture. Christianity as Western missionaries have presented to Papuans overemphasized one element – restoring man's relationship to God – while neglecting [the] social and ecological dimensions.
>
> From the West Papuans' cultural viewpoint, man is in trouble and going through crises because man's relationships with his neighbor, the natural environment, and spirit forces have been broken. Man's task, if he is to be whole, is to renew and maintain harmonious relationships with (a) spiritual beings, (b) the natural environment, and (c) neighbors. I think [these views are] more biblical than those of [the] missionaries.[45]

The Rev. Giay notes that many West Papuan Christians identify with the Exodus narrative. They believe that God, as the Great Liberator, is leading the Papuan people to their Promised Land. They see the Indonesians as modern Pharaohs who are holding Papuans in bondage. As they await liberation, they believe that God is using the Indonesians to teach the Papuans what it is like to live under oppression so that, in the future, they will not treat others as they have been treated.[46]

For Benny, this message of redemption and liberation is repeated in the Gospel. Through his Christian and West Papuan beliefs, he offers three core principles of peacemaking:

1. Christ came to establish a "shalom society," and Christians are called to be part of this mission.
2. Violence to the Christian community is violence against life and the "shalom society" as it was commissioned by Christ.
3. Violence in West Papua during the last four decades has only perpetuated a new series of violence. Therefore, this type of violence can only be stopped when victims of violence face violence by a true commitment to the Zone of Peace and other nonviolent means.[47]

Essentially, Benny believes that true Christianity requires the renunciation of violence. From the Bible, Benny has developed an understanding that there can be a new society where "peace reigns" – what he terms a "shalom society." His belief is grounded in reality. He does not envision this as the "kind of peace ... [that] ... come[s] down from the sky instantly. The Bible tells us that we have to work on it, and we have to create that new society. The Bible functions in this context as a guide and source of inspiration." Thus, for Benny, the Bible leads us to understand God as a source of peace, which "will be with his people as they seek to bring this new society."[48] He turns to specific texts in support of his vision, in particular passages from the Psalms:

> For God will deliver the needy who cry out,
> the afflicted who have no one to help.
> He will take pity on the weak and the needy
> and save the needy from death.
> He will rescue them from oppression and violence
> for precious is their blood in his sight.[49]

In his article "Towards a New Papua," Benny looks to yet another Psalm:

> For the needy will not always be forgotten, nor the hope of
>   the afflicted perish forever;
> O Lord, you have heard the desire of the humble;
> You will strengthen their heart, You will incline your ear
> To vindicate the orphan and the oppressed,
> That man who is of the earth may cause terror no more.

"Because of the devastation of the afflicted, because of the
   groaning of the needy, Now I will arise," says the Lord,
   "I will set him for the safety for which he longs."[50]

Benny encourages his fellow West Papuans to turn to the Bible for solace,
inspiration, a vision of a new world, and to verses that restore their dignity and identity. The Bible, he says, "portrays a new world, free from
manipulation, intimidation, and trauma. It lifts up the eyes of those who
are oppressed to a new world."[51] And for the Rev. Giay, that new world
is a peaceful New Papua.

Toward the Future

In "Towards a New Papua," Benny refers to the belief, widespread among
Papuans, that they are a unique people created by God. To explain what
he means, Benny points to an incident in August 1998, when the Indonesian Parliament sent a delegation to Papua led by Abdul Gabur to better
understand why people want independence:

> Mrs. Agu Iwanngin, Deputy Synod Secretary of the Papuan Protestant
> Church, explained it to him. At the bottom there is God, because God gave
> Papua to Papuans as a home, so they could eat sago and sweet potatoes
> there. God gave them a penis gourd *(koteka)* and loincloth *(cawat)* for
> clothes. God gave them curly hair and black skin.
>
> Papuans are Papuans. They can never be turned into Javanese or Suma-
> trans, nor vice versa. The Javanese were given Java. Tahu and tempe is
> their food. Their skin is light and their hair straight.
>
> The real problem is that those in power in this republic have tried as best
> they could to make Papuans talk, think, look, and behave like Javanese (or
> Sumatrans), and that goes against the order of God's creation. That is
> where the conflict comes from.
>
> How to end it? Let the Papuans and the Javanese each develop according
> to their own tastes and rhythms, each according in their own land.[52]

Today, West Papua continues to fight for freedom and for the full implementation of the Special Autonomy Law. They also face the continuing
negative economic, environmental, and social effects on their local communities by foreign-controlled mines. For Benny, however, West Papua's
urgent challenge is how such a unique people can live together with others. As they confront the realities of transmigration, Papuans are in a
position where they have to find ways to accommodate Javanese (who
have a different religion and culture) within their territory, and create a

land where no one is a second-class citizen – where peace, rather than violence, reigns.

This challenge is central to Benny's work. In talking about what others can learn from his experience, he says, "Peace is costly and you have to wait for it. You have to fight." Benny's perception of peace is that it involves a way of living (rather than the absence of war), and he calls on people whose countries are peaceful to be grateful and to celebrate what they have. Sadly, he notes that in Papua, "even celebrating peace has been for us a threat to the state." Despite the pressing problem of continuing violence from the Indonesian military, his faith and his love for his fellow West Papuans sustain him in his struggle.

On receiving the Tanenbaum Center's *Peacemaker in Action* Award, Benny characteristically called attention to the contributions of others: "I feel like I'm doing what West Papuans have been doing for years. This is a recognition of other people's dreams." He emphasizes the tendency of the groups in the area to focus on their differences rather than their similarities, a practice that he traces to colonialism. Historically, hundreds of tribes in West Papua were able to live peacefully together in a harmonious relationship with one another and the environment. Benny longs for the day when they can do so again.

WEST PAPUA, INDONESIA FACT SHEET[53]

Geography

Location:
West Papua is the western half of the island of New Guinea and borders the country of Papua New Guinea, located on the eastern half of the island. New Guinea is the easternmost island in which Indonesia has territory and is the second largest island in the world, next to Greenland. Indonesia is in southeastern Asia and is an archipelago between the Indian Ocean and the Pacific Ocean.

Area:
West Papua: 421,918 sq km
Indonesia *Total:* 1,919,440 sq km
Indonesia *Land:* 1,826,440 sq km
Indonesia *Water:* 93,000 sq km

Area comparative:
Indonesia is slightly less than three times the size of Texas.

Climate:
West Papua is generally tropical, but it has mountain ranges, where the climate is much colder.

Population

Population:
West Papua: 2,300,000
Indonesia: 241,973,879 (July 2005 est.)

Ethnic groups:

West Papua:

Melanesians (indigenous Papuans):	60%
Migrants/Transmigrants (mostly Javanese):	30%
other:	10%

Indonesia:

Javanese:	45%
Sundanese:	14%
Madurese:	7.5%
Coastal Malays:	7.5%
other:	26%

Religions:

West Papua:

Protestant:	50%
Roman Catholic:	20%
Muslim:	20%
Traditional indigenous religions (often practiced alongside these major religions):	10%

Indonesia:

Muslim:	88%
Protestant:	5%
Roman Catholic:	3%
Hindu:	2%

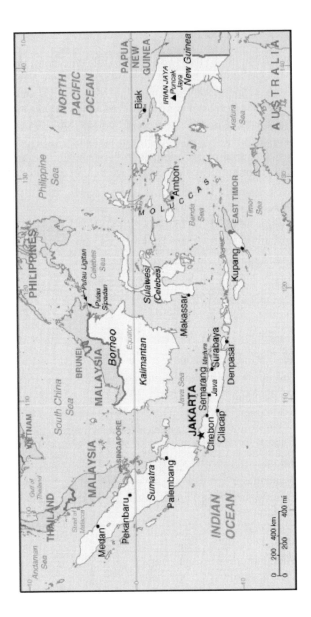

424

Buddhist:	1%
other:	1%
	(1998)

Languages:	West Papua: Bahasa Indonesia (official, modified form of Malay), 254 indigenous languages are spoken.
	Indonesia: Bahasa Indonesia, English, Dutch, local dialects (the most widely spoken of which is Javanese).

Government

Government type:	Indonesia: Republic
Capital:	West Papua: Jayapura National: Jakarta
Legal system:	Indonesia: based on Roman-Dutch law, substantially modified by indigenous concepts and by new criminal procedures and election codes; has not accepted compulsory International Court of Justice jurisdiction.

Recent Background of West Papua

West Papua is a territory of Indonesia and is located on the western side of the island of New Guinea. Indonesia, the world's largest archipelagic state, was colonized by the Dutch in the early seventeenth century. West Papua was colonized in the nineteenth century but was held separately from the rest of the Netherland's holdings in Indonesia because the Dutch asserted that West Papuans represented a different race and had a distinct culture. On gaining independence in 1945, Indonesia resisted the Dutch claim of West Papua's distinctness and officially incorporated West Papua as part of Indonesia in 1969 under a name imposed by the government, Irian Jaya. Today, Indonesia and West Papua face a myriad of social, economic, and political problems that serve to hamper their development.

The indigenous population in West Papua is predominantly Christian, a result of missionary activities carried out during the nineteenth century. Recent Indonesian migration to West Papua has led to a stronger Islamic presence and has increased the political and ethnic influence of the Javanese people, who are the largest ethnic group in Indonesia. West Papua's basic ethnic/religious divide is between Melanesian Christians, who are descendants of native Papuans, and Javanese and Sumatran Muslims, whose families migrated to West Papua from the other Indonesian provinces.[54]

The overwhelming majority of indigenous West Papuans favor independence from Indonesia. According to many Papuans, they have been reduced to second-class citizens in their own homeland. They contend that they have been unjustly forced to give up their land by the Indonesian government and prevented from reaping the benefits of West Papua's rich natural resources.[55]

The Indonesian government, however, has a significant stake in retaining the territory and has made it clear that it will not willingly relinquish control. Since the secession of East Timor from Indonesia in 2002, the government has been even more opposed to West Papuan independence, fearing it could spark the Balkanization of Indonesia.[56]

Economic Overview of West Papua

West Papua has abundant natural resources: gold, silver, copper, oil, gas, marine deposits, and timber. However, most West Papuans are not involved in the mining of these resources, and West Papua benefits little from its own assets. Only 20 percent or so of the resources go toward local consumption.

Under Indonesian control, West Papua is directly affected by Indonesia's economic status. Despite recent economic growth, Indonesia faces economic development problems stemming from endemic corruption, weaknesses in the banking system, unequal resource distribution among its regions, and a poor rate of foreign investment. After graduating from its IMF program at the end of 2003, Indonesia issued a "White Paper" that committed the government to maintaining the fundamentally sound macroeconomic policies previously established under IMF guidelines. Investors, however, continue to face a host of on-the-ground microeconomic problems and an inadequate judicial system. The tsunami of late 2004 took more than 130,000 lives and caused approximately $4.5 billion in damages. Future growth requires internal reform and increased confidence on the part of international and domestic investors.

PART III

CONCLUSION

14 Religion, Violent Conflict, and Peacemaking

David Little

Correcting Misimpressions

The testimony and accomplishments of the sixteen remarkable individuals represented in this volume help to correct and refine two common oversimplifications regarding the connections among religion, violent conflict, and "peacemaking," a term used in these pages to comprehend the wide variety of ways there are to achieve peace. In the process of appraisal, several general lessons emerge, and a promising way of better understanding the theory and practice of religious peacemaking begins to take shape.

One oversimplification is that religion is at bottom about nothing but violent conflict, about generating "clashes of civilization" and "bloody borders." Therefore, it is easy to conclude, the less religion the better. The second oversimplification is in sharp contrast to the first: "real" or "authentic" religion, it holds, never contributes to violence, only "flawed" or "distorted" religion does that. "Good religion" always brings peace. There is of course some truth to both claims, and it is important to disentangle what is true from what is false about each of them. Fortunately, the *Peacemakers* included in this book are of great help here.

"Religion and Violence Are Inseparable"

As to the first oversimplification, several of our *Peacemakers* provide eloquent testimony regarding what is and is not true about it. Whereas Yehezkel Landau, a Jew who practiced peace work in Israel for twenty-five years, rejects the idea that the conflict between the Jews and Arabs is "really" a religious war – rather than one that is fundamentally political – he emphasizes that religion is used to feed the conflict. He notes that participants on both sides do indeed "invoke religious arguments to justify their territorial claims," and religion dominates the headlines and elevates extremism to fuel violence. Moreover, by identifying with exclusionary nationalism, religion on either side contributes to "grotesque ideologies of domination, death, and destruction" that are "dangerously combustible."

Speaking from a Palestinian Christian perspective, Abuna Elias Chacour comes to similar conclusions. The conflict is not, he agrees, caused by religion, but it is certainly manipulated in a violent direction by extremist groups. One of the most negative influences, he believes, is the disposition of religious groups to intensify the divisions between the Palestinians and Israelis, thus making the achievement of peace all the harder.

As to the former Yugoslavia, neither Friar Ivo Markovic, the Franciscan monk from Bosnia, nor Father Sava Janjic, the Serbian Orthodox priest from Kosovo, is willing to reduce the war in the former Yugoslavia to a battle over religion. In their view, it was a much more complicated affair than that. Still, they both report disturbing levels of complicity with chauvinism and violence, especially on the part of local Catholic, Orthodox, and Muslim clergy. For Friar Markovic, many clergy were guilty of serious sins of commission. Some actively participated in the bloodletting, while others went out of their way to bless weapons and give spiritual encouragement to the militias, and to reinforce the confusion of authentic religious commitment with the special interests of ethnonational leaders. In Kosovo, Father Sava emphasized what the clergy didn't do, rather than what they did. They either failed altogether to mount significant resistance to the ultranationalism around them, or they were unpardonably slow in doing so.

There is also compelling evidence in the testimony of Pastor James Wuye and Imam Muhammad Ashafa, the Christian-Muslim peacemaking team in Nigeria, that religion is – under some circumstances – capable of contributing to violence. Each recalls finding himself a member of rival religious youth groups that took an active part in the Kaduna riots of the early 1990s. Although each man eventually turned his back on such activity, groups of that kind have apparently not disappeared from the Nigerian scene. According to Pastor Wuye and Imam Ashafa, most people in the areas of conflict are very religious, as are most people in Nigeria. Although religion undoubtedly serves "as a smokescreen for political things," they also believe that lack of respect for religious difference is of great consequence in dividing the country.

In sum, if evidence like this confirms the proposition that religion contains a propensity for violence under some conditions, it also underlines the fact that the connection between religion and violence is very complicated. The idea that lethal conflict in places like Israel and Palestine, the former Yugoslavia, or Nigeria is somehow a simple function of religion (or of any other one thing, for that matter) is highly suspect. As our witnesses attest, we shall need to resist easy answers, and instead look with great sensitivity at the complex causes of violence, while not ignoring, of course, the role of religion. Nor, by the way, should we fail to recognize the strong ring of plausibility that sounds from the conclusions of these religiously motivated peacemakers. They constitute "insider testimony" in the fullest sense. They are not second-hand or the result of cost-free observation but are born instead of a readiness on the part of our informants to "stay close to the action" by running risks and bearing burdens that most students of violence are not willing or able to accept.

Moreover, the suggestion that religion serves only to foment hatred and destruction in such places is definitively disproved by the life and work of our witnesses, Landau, Chacour, Markovic, Janjic, Wuye, and Ashafa, not to mention the other *Peacemakers* in this book. What comes clear is this: if religion sometimes makes war, it also sometimes makes peace.

Consider the efforts of these six men: in the face of less-than-hopeful prospects for peace between Israel and the Palestinians, Yehezkel Landau remained in Israel for around twenty-five years endeavoring to alter Jewish and Palestinian attitudes toward each other – first, by means of the Oz veShalom–Netivot Shalom experiment, and later by means of the Open House project he founded with his former wife. Facing similar realities on the Palestinian side, Abuna Chacour has labored for over thirty years to spread the spirit of interethnic and interreligious love and reconciliation, particularly among Muslim and Christian Palestinians. Toward that end, he has managed to expand the enrollment of the Mar Elias Educational Institutions he created from eighty students in 1980 to four thousand in 2003, and to found the first accredited Arab university in Israel.

Against severe threats to personal safety in Bosnia and Kosovo, Friar Ivo Markovic and Father Sava Janjic have displayed an almost superhuman degree of dedication to the ideals of cooperation and peace, something reminiscent of others in this book. During the war, Friar Markovic braved the danger of being shot in order to work out local cease-fires, and throughout the conflict he persisted against stern opposition from fellow Catholics, church authorities, and others to establish the interreligious organization Face to Face and the multiethnic Pontanima Choir and Chamber Orchestra, organizations dedicated to cultivating reconciliation and mutuality in postconflict Bosnia. Father Sava's indefatigable internet efforts to inform the outside world of the situation in wartorn Kosovo, the risks he ran by opening his monastery to both Serb and Kosovar refugees, and the unrelenting series of death threats he received from Serb extremists eventually brought on a condition of complete nervous exhaustion from which he has not yet fully recovered.

The inspiring story of Pastor James Wuye and Imam Muhammad Ashafa, the Nigerian Christian-Muslim team, further underscores the conspicuous peacemaking potential of religion. A product of their own personal efforts to overcome Christian-Muslim hostility in Nigeria, the Muslim-Christian Dialogue Forum (now known as the Interfaith Mediation Centre) quickly developed into an extraordinary vehicle for training youths and others in the techniques of mediation and conflict reduction, and in the practice of reconciliation. By now the Interfaith Mediation Centre has worked with nearly seven thousand youths, has a membership of ten thousand people, and has located at least two youth leaders trained in conflict-resolution in every one of Nigeria's thirty-six states. What gives this group its distinctiveness is precisely its religious – and especially its interreligious – character. Pastor Wuye and Imam Ashafa report that most other nongovernmental organizations are not capable of bridging the acute religious divide that exists in the country at present.

Because Nigeria is a place where religious identity is of special importance, religious leaders can be enormously influential, for good or ill. Pastor Wuye and Imam Ashafa believe that their status affords them rare authority in Nigerian society, something on which they can capitalize in advancing the cause of interfaith harmony and nonviolence. Because of the deep distrust among local religious communities, the impact of a Christian and a Muslim openly cooperating – without either one renouncing his own faith – represents a powerful witness to the country at large.

One other important example of the constructive contribution of religion to peace, drawn from the experience of our *Peacemakers,* is the critical emphasis on mobilizing and empowering women as agents of peace. This point is highlighted with particular force by the two women represented here, Sakena Yacoobi and Nozizwe Madlala-Routledge. Both were provoked to action by the radical discrepancy they perceived between their religious ideals of gender equality and mutuality – grounded in Islam for Sakena and in Quakerism for Nozizwe – and the reality of severe discrimination and inequity toward women in their own countries, Afghanistan and South Africa, respectively. They concluded that the objective of equipping and enabling women to address and rectify long-standing and deep-seated gender injustice by methods of assertive nonviolence could itself become a metaphor for the wider role in peacemaking that women could and should play.

Sakena Yacoobi's decision to found the Afghan Institute for Learning – dedicated to the education of women – and to develop it on the basis of an Islamically oriented "curriculum of peace" is a striking example. Among other things, the aim of the institute is to make women into leaders who might negotiate new, fairer relationships with their male counterparts, and then go on to expand their activities toward confronting and resolving other forms of social conflict. The chapter concerning her work details what remarkable success the institute, along with Sakena's other efforts, have had.

The activities of Nozizwe Madlala-Routledge are similarly impressive. In 1983, she built upon her commitment to "gender and justice" and established the Natal Organization of Women. In the face of destructive government-instigated violence in her local area, Noziwe engaged women in resolving differences between Inkatha and the ANC. She found that women could be very effective in reaching out to other women across political divisions, thereby activating previously disregarded methods of peacemaking. Appreciating the unique power of women for inspiring peace and justice, she pledged thereafter to accentuate and make room for the exercise of that power. In 1989, she organized against violence and apartheid with Women for Peaceful Change Now, and she carried this commitment with her, first as a member of parliament, and then as a member of the government of Nelson Mandela.

"Good Religion Always Brings Peace"

The second of the oversimplifications our *Peacemakers* help rectify is the claim that any connection between religion and violence is the result of corrupted or debased religion. Individuals and groups that rigorously follow the bona fide and pristine teachings of Judaism, Islam, Christianity, or of other traditions will – it is supposed – invariably become instruments of peace and harmony, rather than of chaos and destruction. Not surprisingly, this view is particularly popular among religious representatives in conflict zones. The idea seems to be that admitting any association between "correct" religion and violence gives religion a bad name, and therefore all such admissions should be resolutely denied.

We have already seen that this claim is not altogether mistaken. It is certainly the belief of the *Peacemakers* we have just cited (and of others we might mention) that what is typically called "extremist religion" – religion that readily demonizes whole groups of people, whether on ethnic, national, or religious grounds, and advocates abuse and violence against them – is both an important source of lethal conflict and a debasement of religion. Friar Markovic makes the point when he declares that local clergy during the Bosnian War "compromised their own activities by coordinating too much with national interests." What was needed, in his words, was "a clear differentiation between religion and national identity in order to avoid the degeneration of religion into magic or paganism." The same idea is expanded on by Abuna Elias Chacour. Not only the basic principles of Christianity, he says, but also those of Judaism and Islam are severely distorted by groups who take up a life of animosity and violence in the name of God. Whether Muslims, Christians, or Jews, such people oppose the divine purpose; to them, "God is the first victim and is insulted by the extremist groups."

By contrast, the experience of most of the *Peacemakers* in this volume, and of many others besides, proves that even those figures most consistently devoted to the principles of conciliation and amity are not in fact strangers to conflict and violence. Those who seek peace by peaceful means are, despite their intentions, often the objects of hatred and retaliation; they predictably heighten tension rather than relax it, because they denounce what they believe is injustice and abuse. The American pacifist and civil rights leader Martin Luther King, Jr. used to tell those who blamed him and his movement for "disturbing the peace" that true peace is more than the absence of violence. It is based, he said, on justice and mutual respect, and these ideals are seldom achieved without arousing the violent hostility of the profiteers of oppression. Nor should it be forgotten that not only King but other famous proponents of this vision of peace and nonviolence, such as Jesus and Gandhi, met with violent deaths.

Of the *Peacemakers* in our volume, we think of course of the perilous experiences of Friar Markovic and Father Sava during the various phases of the war in former Yugoslavia. Although their honorable actions were hardly connected in any way to the basic causes of overall violence during that time, their specific efforts on behalf of peace and justice did excite life-threatening animosity on the part of their enemies.

Two other dramatic examples of the same phenomenon are manifest in the lives of José Alas, the former Salvadoran Catholic priest and longtime Central American antipoverty and peace worker, and of the Rev. Dr. Benny

Giay, the evangelical peace activist and proponent of independence for West Papua. First as a priest and even now as a deeply religious layman, Alas has organized rural peasants and trained them in biblically based, nonviolent techniques of land and educational reform, thereby inciting the wrath of landowners and others in power. Notwithstanding his status as a priest, these activities led to his being abducted, tortured, and eventually abandoned and hospitalized. Undaunted, he and his associates continued to expand their efforts, and in the late 1970s and early 1980s, were continually subjected to increasing harassment and persecution, and – in some cases – assassination. Consequently, he was driven from the country for fifteen years, but not away from his commitment to peace and justice.

As for the Rev. Giay, the work he and his associates conduct on behalf of human rights, improving relations between Papuans and Javanese immigrants, and for a peaceful transition to West Papuan independence, has aroused a relentless pattern of abuse, blacklisting, and death threats at the hands of the Indonesian military and secret police. But in a way characteristic of peacemakers, the Rev. Giay transmuted vice into virtue. By publicizing the atrocities, he rallied public sentiment to the cause of peace.

As yet one more example of the antagonism and repression peacemaking can generate, we should not overlook the impressive record of Nozizwe Madlala-Routledge, the South African Quaker. Her work in the ANC and later in the training of women and in other forms of development and reconstruction led to positions in parliament and government after the overthrow of the apartheid regime. Because of her political activities against the South African government in the 1980s, she was repeatedly detained without trial, at one point being held in solitary confinement for one year.

It can, of course, be claimed that there is a deeper sense in which the oversimplification "good religion brings peace" is true. This deeper claim rests on a two-part conviction shared to a large extent by all the religious peacemakers in this book. The first part is connected to heartfelt beliefs that "true religion" entails a strong preference for nonviolent over violent means. The idea is that although promoting peace and justice by peaceful means may provoke hostility and violence in the short run, it is nevertheless the best way, if not the only way, to subdue hostility and violence *in the long run.*

The second part of the conviction is that although peacemakers, like those in this book, may frequently find themselves in the position of aggravating resentment and retaliation from their enemies, they do not – from a moral point of view – bear the major responsibility for whatever bloodletting and mistreatment may occur as the result of their actions. On the contrary, it is the opponents of justice, "the profiteers of oppression," who are truly at fault. By resorting to violence to protect their wrongful interests, they prove themselves to be the real enemies of peace.

It should be added within this preference for nonviolence over violence that there is the hint of an interesting discrepancy in the differing testimony of several of our *Peacemakers*. As a Quaker influenced by Gandhi and Martin Luther King, Jr., Nozizwe Madlala-Routledge seems to hold – on religious grounds – a position of steadfast pacifism. She consistently opposed the use of force in the liberation struggle in South Africa and, after the change in government there, went on – very creatively – to represent a pacifist perspective in, of all places, the office of deputy Minister of Defense.

Although Friar Markovic, in contrast, eventually came close to a similar position because of his growing revulsion against violence in the Bosnian war, he is nevertheless more permissive in regard to the use of force. Choosing the path of steadfast nonviolence is a personal decision that, he implies, ought to be made in the face of the genuine moral perplexity that touches all people confronted with the prospect of imminent suffering and death at the hands of others. That some people might honorably elect to exercise their right of self-defense ought to be respected, even if not embraced for oneself. "Radical nonviolence," says Markovic, "is a personal decision motivated through the experience of transcendence, of God's grace, of eternity, and the acceptance of suffering and death. Such a decision can be the design for building a community, but in a situation of violence, it is necessary to respect the right of the people to [self] defense."

The Rev. Dr. Roy Magee, the Presbyterian clergyman from Northern Ireland committed to reducing the violence of the Protestant militias, displays a similar ambivalence. As the result of the killing he witnessed, he came to believe that "revenge is not the solution and . . . I should do all in my power to help end the bloodshed." At the same time, he is not, he says, a pacifist, recognizing that were he ever forced to defend family, fatherland, or faith, as the "very last resort . . . I may be compelled to take up arms."

This difference of perspective raises an acute and unavoidable issue, namely, the place of force in peacemaking. The issue lurks in the background of all attempts at religious peacemaking and remains unresolved among our subjects. Even if force is never the preferred means for achieving peace – as all the representatives in this book undoubtedly hold – is it ever morally permissible, or at least excusable on occasion? If so, under what conditions is that the case? Father Sava questions the particular ends and means of NATO's use of force in Kosovo, but he does not give his views as to whether or not force is ever morally acceptable. In their ambivalence, Friar Markovic and the Rev. Magee call attention to the larger problem, leaving the question of the use of force hanging as a continuing challenge for all religious peacemakers.

General Lessons

In the process of correcting and refining two familiar oversimplications concerning the connections among religion, violent conflict, and peacemaking, several general lessons have suggested themselves. They both enrich and complicate our understanding:

- Religion neither causes violence by itself, nor, by contrast, is it without influence, particularly in its extremist form, on the course and character of violence.
- Religion is not just a source of violent conflict but also a source of peace.
- Proper religion exhibits a preference for pursuing peace by peaceful means (nonviolence over violence) and for combining the promotion of peace with the promotion of justice.
- Religion dedicated to promoting justice and peace by peaceful means often prompts a hostile and violent response, at least in the short run.
- Hostility and violence are best overcome, morally and most likely practically, by favoring the promotion of justice and peace by peaceful means and by willingly bearing the risks and costs associated with such activity.
- Because of their innovative efforts in places such as Afghanistan and South Africa to overcome gender-based, political injustice and conflict by assertive nonviolence, women represent a particularly important resource for peace.
- The question of the use of force in the proper pursuit of peace is unresolved (as far as the testimony in this book goes) and remains a moral dilemma to be considered.

Toward clarifying the theory and practice of religious peacemaking, it will be useful to reflect further on these general lessons – on what lies behind them, and on what is implied by them – in the light of the experience and testimony of our *Peacemakers*.

The Theory and Practice of Religious Peacemaking

What Difference Does Religion Make?

At least three answers to this fundamental question emerge from the case studies in this book.

1. *The hermeneutics of peace.* Manifest in all of our examples is the pertinence of religion to the self-understanding of peacemakers. Religious belief provides a critical basis for the vision, motivation, and perseverance required for the chosen task. In various ways, all our figures affirm the centrality of a theological tradition from which to draw strength and insight. But they also share something more specific that is of enormous significance. It is what might be called a *hermeneutics of peace*, namely, an interpretive framework that begins with the conviction that the pursuit of justice and peace by peaceful means is a sacred priority in each of the traditions represented. Then, within this framework, particular texts, doctrines, and practices contained in one's own tradition – and often in the traditions of others – are examined for guidance in the process of elaborating and implementing the fundamental commitment to peace and justice. The Rev. Roy Magee and Father Alex Reid, the clergy team from Northern Ireland who acted as peace intermediaries to warring Protestant and Catholic militias, respectively, provide one good example. They share a common theological orientation – namely, the image of Jesus Christ as "the friend and companion of sinners," as one who takes part in and identifies with the "fallen condition" of all human beings – in order to exemplify mercy and reconciliation as the means of overcoming hatred and violence.

A second example is the approach of Afghani Muslim Sakena Yacoobi, the educator and public health worker, dedicated with special passion to the cause of empowering women. She affirms that her own religious understanding has been enriched by studying together with devout Christians while attending college and graduate school in the United States and by intimate and sustained cooperation with people of other faiths. After witnessing what she regards as the debasement of Islam by the Taliban, she used her deepened understanding of her own religion as a means to promote peace, justice, and equality. This was a discovery, she reports, that brought her closer to God.

Dr. Ephraim Isaac, the Ethiopian Jew and multitalented mediator and humanitarian, is a third example. For him, the ultimate triumph of justice and peace as promised in Hebrew scriptures, especially by the prophets Isaiah and Jeremiah, undergirds all his activities. Additional inspiration comes from the rabbinic stories told to him by his father accentuating the expression of love and respect among humans as the fulfillment of obedience to God. Isaac's approach also illustrates a tendency among the *Peacemakers* to draw on other religious traditions. The incompatibility of loving God and hating neighbor is reinforced by a citation from the New Testament, and here and there he invokes related themes in other traditions. Moreover, his extensive cooperation with the Ethiopian Orthodox Church appears to rest on the belief that having constituted Ethiopia's backbone for years, the church is indispensable in promoting peace and reconciliation in the land.

Isaac carries the theme of interreligious and intercultural respect even further. At one point, he emphasizes the superiority of the methods and values of indigenous elders in resolving local conflicts to the techniques and practices typically employed by diplomats and government officials. The traditional elders do not advertise their achievements or seek publicity the way diplomats tend to do, nor do they try to impose a settlement by coercion and threat. Rather, they employ "gentle persuasion, high ethical standards, and a spiritual approach," which is, he believes, more "salubrious [and] more effective" because it encourages the parties to work through their grievances in their own way. This procedure is thus more conducive to stable peace and genuine reconciliation than the methods of conventional diplomacy.

Several other *Peacemakers* exemplify this theme of interreligious and intercultural respect with comparable force. The Rev. Dr. William Lowrey, the Presbyterian clergyman who facilitated an important agreement between the Dinka and Nuer tribes in southern Sudan, provides a theological basis for an intercultural peacemaking strategy. According to the Rev. Lowrey, the idea that all human beings share a sacred nature – the image of God, as represented in the book of Genesis – assures us that there is "wisdom resident" in all people. Therefore, every peacemaking effort needs to begin with a deep respect for other peoples and cultures. Christian texts, he believes, give support: despite the consequences of human failure, people everywhere continue the struggle between good and evil. What can be learned from that struggle in every culture is applicable to the worldwide campaign for peace and justice.

Such an attitude explains the Rev. Lowrey's readiness to utilize indigenous dispute-resolution procedures, and his belief that peacemaking is not primarily a matter of external mediation or determination. Rather, it involves finding a way to develop the capacities of the parties themselves for resolving their own disputes, encouraged and supplemented, to be sure, by outside advice and techniques. What the Rev. Lowrey brought to the peacemaking process in southern Sudan, he says, "was some ability to organize, to bridge the tribal world with the modern world."

The Rev. Giay of West Papua reflects a similar attitude. There is, on the one hand, the urgent relevance, he says, of the Exodus narrative – the promise to the ancient Israelites of deliverance from bondage – which gives hope to West Papuans that they will one day be freed from oppression at the hands of the Indonesians, whom they see as the modern Pharaohs. Moreover, this account is combined with New Testament ideas of mercy and reconciliation according to which West Papuans, once liberated, are urged to break the cycle of retaliation by refraining from treating others as they have been treated. According to the Rev. Giay, they ought instead to renounce violence and retaliation in favor of creating a "shalom society," a Zone of Peace, that extends equal rights and benefits to all the inhabitants living together in a common area.

But whereas admitting that these beliefs constitute a welcome inspiration, Giay also acknowledges that Christianity – at least as preached for years by Western missionaries – has had the countervailing effect of disparaging and destroying valuable traditions indigenous to Papuan culture, traditions that might profitably be marshaled in the cause of justice and peace.

2. *Empathetic detachment.* A second answer to the role of religion is more practical. In some circumstances, prominent religious identity provides a badge of trustworthiness and impartiality that can be of great benefit in either formal or informal negotiations. That was clearly the case in regard to the remarkable achievements of the Inter-Religious Council of Sierra Leone, led by Alimamy Koroma, in facilitating a peace agreement between the rebels and the government over the period from 1999 to 2003. As is reported in Koroma's story, the fact that the insurgents and the government agreed early on to participate in preliminary talks at a certain site, one proposed by the Inter-Religious Council, confirms the neutrality and the respect the council was accorded by both sides. The same remarkable contribution, made possible by the degree of trust and esteem accorded the council by all parties, is manifest throughout the subsequent, and often difficult, peace process that led up to the final

accord of January 2002. It is worth emphasizing that external observers, such as the U.S. ambassador and the local media, singled the council out "as the most highly visible and effective non-governmental bridge builder between the warring factions and a population devastated and divided by more than eight years of violence."

Father Alex Reid testifies to a similar mediating contribution he was able to make in regard to violent groups active in Northern Ireland. Members of the fighting factions sent for religious actors like himself, due to their position within the community and "because they believe that you will be fair to both sides, that you won't take sides." He adds, "they don't think you agree with them, but they feel there is a kind of relationship that starts to develop, and they will actually tell you…what is going on and then…they will kind of listen to you because you have a relationship with them." This sort of relationship, based on participation that is at once empathetic and detached or critical – after the fashion of Jesus's example – makes continuing dialogue and eventual progress toward peace possible. It is in such a relationship that a sincere "search for common truth" begins to develop. Reid implies that gradually coming to see a conflict in shared rather than simply partisan terms "identif[ies] the common 'democratic' ground between the main parties – the only ground where agreement and reconciliation can be established."

What makes people like Alimamy Koroma and Father Reid so effective is the subtle and creative combination of detachment and empathy. They are seen to transcend narrow partisanships, even though they have their own loyalties and commitments, which – in some cases – are well known. It is perhaps their reputation for empathy – based on a well-documented sense of moral engagement and passionate concern – that makes them credible mediators.

The work of Nozizwe Madlala-Routledge of South Africa is a third excellent example. The fact that she has strongly identified herself with the ANC may have eventually enhanced her efforts to make peace between the ANC and the Inkatha Freedom Party. By means of the arduous process of coming "to be seen as neutral" and "build[ing] trust," Nozizwe was able to exemplify to other participants what it meant to establish effective negotiations wherein "we tried to listen to both sides without taking sides."

3. *Persistent religious concerns and peace agreements.* A third answer concerning the salience of religion is suggested by Yehezkel Landau on the basis of his work in Israel. Landau believes that the rise of religious extremism in all faith communities should be enough

to convince anyone committed to Middle East peace that a diplomatic paradigm which is rationalist and utilitarian, addressing only military and economic issues, will never work. What is urgently needed in peace-making, he claims, is concerted understanding of and attention to the specifically religious dimensions of a conflict, something that will require, at some stage, the active participation of "credible religious authori-ties." "Only then," Landau goes on, "can we move on to negotiating practical compromises that accommodate the conflicting claims over Jerusalem/Al-Quds, Hebron/Al-Halil, the Temple Mount/Haram al-Sharif and other holy sites." Rights of access and control over holy sites, or, more broadly, of religious freedom and equal treatment, may not constitute a central part of every peace agreement. Nevertheless, as Landau sees it, they certainly are central to the Israeli-Palestinian conflict, just as they are to several of the other conflicts alluded to in this book, such as Sudan, Nigeria, Afghanistan, Northern Ireland, and Bosnia/Kosovo.

Rabbi Menachem Froman, part of the Jewish settler movement in the West Bank, stresses a comparable point in his efforts to work out improved relations between Jews and Palestinians. Like Yehezkel Landau, he recommends involving religious figures in the peace process. The Israeli government may try to find peace, but they become "a little confused" by their inability to reduce violence. Gradually, their lack of success is causing them, he hopes, to see that "they have a little bit to learn [from religious leaders]." Sooner or later, negotiators must address religious issues. "I have always said that peace cannot be achieved in the Holy Land without taking religion into account first."

The Ends and Means of Religious Peacemaking

As we are beginning to appreciate, religious peacemaking is a compli-cated matter. Once the general place and role of religion is sorted out – at least in a preliminary way – the rich variety of possible objectives and methods must still be considered. There are at least four general types of peacemaking that apply to the work of religious peacemakers, as well: *enforcement, peacekeeping, institution-and-capacity building*, and *agreement-making*.

Enforcement is the attempt to reduce violent conflict, or the imminent threat thereof, by coercive means, and to do it as a way of inducing a will-ingness to find an agreement between the warring parties. Such work is undertaken in what is known euphemistically as a "nonconsensual environment." The NATO military campaigns in Bosnia in 1995 and Kosovo in 1999 are examples, and they touched in important ways on the activities of Friar Markovic and Father Sava. The UN-sanctioned use of force in Afghanistan in 2002 for the purpose of overthrowing the Taliban government is another example, one that had a telling effect on the prospects and work of Sakena Yacoobi.

Peacekeeping is the use of third-party personnel, frequently military, who are accepted by the belligerents for the purpose of monitoring cease-fires and peace agreements and of discouraging violations. In contrast to enforcement, peacekeepers supposedly operate in a "consensual environment." The use of NATO "stabilization forces" in support of agreements in Bosnia, Kosovo, and Afghanistan, and UN operations to implement settlements in El Salvador and Sierra Leone, are examples. Both enforcement and peacekeeping typically involve the use or threat of force, and in so doing signal an issue that, as we saw, is a sensitive one for religious peacemakers. Several of our subjects, especially Friar Ivo Markovic of Bosnia and Father Sava Janjic of Kosovo, and, more indirectly, José Alas of El Salvador, Sakena Yacoobi of Afghanistan, and Alimamy Koroma of Sierra Leone, have all operated under conditions of peacekeeping.

But while enforcement and peacekeeping have had a certain impact on the work of some of the individuals in this volume, these activities are not at the center of attention for religiously motivated peacemakers such as these. Of much greater concern, it so happens, are two other types of activity: *institution-and-capacity-building* and *agreement-making*. The first is occupied with the design and creation over time of an array of institutions and practices capable of increasing and sustaining the balance of social harmony and civil unity over hostility and violence. This entails broadening and strengthening commitment to and training in multireligious and multiethnic respect and tolerance, along with the management and reduction of violence, human rights compliance, rule of law, empowerment of women and minorities, advancement of educational and vocational opportunities, expansion of health care, reduction of inequities in wealth and power, and so forth.

Agreement-making is the process of sustained interaction by which hostile parties are brought to work out and accept a peace settlement. The process consists of what is known as "Track One" diplomacy, or official diplomatic efforts to achieve agreement, and "Track Two" diplomacy, or unofficial endeavors by nongovernmental groups and individuals to assist official negotiations or to create an environment conducive to peace. It is informative and illuminating to summarize the special contributions and innovations of some of our *Peacemakers* in these two areas.

We may indicate, in passing, that examples of these two types of diplomacy drawn from the case studies in this book occasionally display a difference of emphasis as between a *religiously focused approach*, with an emphasis on working directly with religious organizations and policies, and a *publicly focused approach*, which concentrates on the policies and programs of governments, nonreligious NGOs, nonsectarian educational institutions, and so forth, whose sphere of operations and constituencies extend well beyond the work and membership of religious organizations. Nevertheless, too much should not be made of this distinction. Given their general outlook, it seems unlikely that any of our *Peacemakers* would wish to differentiate too sharply between working in the religious and public spheres. They would be more inclined, it seems, to understand their work in either sphere as supplementary to the other.

Institution-and-capacity-building. An illustration of institution-and-capacity-building that started out with a strongly religious focus, but came – as things worked out – to serve wider public objectives, are the efforts of Abuna Elias Chacour. In the 1960s, Chacour began by attempting to combat the suspicion and hostility both within the Christian churches in Galilee, as well as among the Christian, Jewish, Druze, and Muslim communities. He did this, he says, not by trying "to change their identities, but rather their minds and outlooks." Such reorientation involved learning to embrace shared attitudes of nonviolence and reconciliation, and of mutual religious respect and tolerance both within and outside one's group.

Gradually, Chacour worked together with Muslims and others to create an expansive school system built on the principles of interreligious and interethnic acceptance. The objective of the Mar Elias Educational Institutions was to equip students from different communities for professions of various kinds, such as teaching and engineering, but to do that in a way that would reshape occupations and professions as public agents of "peacebuilding."

The peace efforts of Friar Markovic are another example of a "bifocal" approach. Both during the war and after, Friar Markovic concentrated much of his work on transforming Bosnian religious institutions from being accomplices in war to agents of peace. He worked with the Mennonites and Anglicans, among others, to build his Face to Face Interreligious Service and the Pontanima Choir and Chamber Orchestra as a means of demonstrating the possibility of new multireligious and multiethnic institutions in postwar Bosnia. At the same time, he used Face to Face as a basis for sponsoring a center for peace research and practice, which could also assist in improving the effectiveness of international humanitarian organizations working in Bosnia.

Beyond that, Friar Markovic undertook an effort to reform the media. He understood that newspapers, radio, and television incited hatred and violence during the period leading up to the war. The whole system, he concluded, would have to be reconstructed, and he devised a series of conferences and workshops to begin to try to make that happen.

A comparable approach is exhibited in the activities of Pastor Wuye and Imam Ashafa. Their efforts are, of course, strongly focused on reforming the attitudes and practices of Christian and Muslim communities in Nigeria in the direction of interfaith cooperation and nonviolence. Still, their work rather naturally extends into the public sphere. The Interfaith Mediation Centre (formerly the Muslim-Christian Dialogue Forum) has developed mediation and peacebuilding organizations in cooperation with local governments, and collaboration with the federal government has improved with the advent of the Obasanjo administration. Like Friar Markovic, Pastor Wuye and Imam Ashafa have tried to address the connection between the media and conflict, making some progress in that area. Finally, they have endeavored to moderate the competitiveness among nongovernmental organizations working in Nigeria.

The accomplishments of Sakena Yacoobi certainly deserve attention in regard to institution-and-capacity-building. In the early 1990s, Sakena witnessed the suffering that resulted from the trauma of war, and in particular the cycle of violence that entrapped whole families in patterns of mutual abuse. In response, she worked with the International Rescue Committee, first as manager and then as coordinator for the Female Education Teacher Training Program, supporting girls' schools and developing teacher training. Based on that experience, she went on to set up the Afghan Institute of Learning (AIL), emphasizing the importance of women's rights, family training, and peace education – especially for women – in building a peaceful society. AIL's popularity has grown to the extent that Sakena now directs the training of over eighty-five hundred female Afghan teachers. It serves as many as 350,000 women and children annually in Kabul and other cities in Afghanistan and Pakistan, and works with midwives and female nurse and health educators as well. The organization also has had considerable success helping boys overcome a disposition toward violence.

Agreement-making. We have already had occasion to refer in general to the Rev. William Lowrey's creative work in helping to facilitate agreements between the Nuer and the Dinka tribes in southern Sudan. The details are also worth recalling. In June 1998, Lowrey convened a conference in Kenya bringing together Nuer and Dinka chiefs and church leaders. The conference resulted in the Loki Accord, the beginning of the end of the Dinka-Nuer conflict. That event was followed by the Wunlit conference a few months later that convened three hundred Dinka and Nuer delegates. It produced the Wunlit Covenant, which further reduced hostilities between tribes and paved the way for the resolution of differences between John Garang of the Sudanese Peoples Liberation Movement and Riek Machar of the Sudan Peoples Democratic Front, who signed a joint statement on October 23, 2002, integrating their two groups. Perhaps most significant of all, this series of agreements opened the door to eventual negotiations between the Sudanese government and the southern forces that culminated on January 9, 2005, in a peace agreement between the north and the south.

The Rev. Lowrey's accomplishments are an example of "Track Two" agreement-making. He himself did not play a direct role in working out the terms of agreement but, rather, acted as a facilitator, providing background assistance and counsel in the process of working out a series of official ("Track One") settlements by the representatives of the Nuer and the Dinka, and thereby setting the stage, ultimately, for an official agreement between the Sudanese government and the SPLM. The efforts of Ephraim Isaac in providing a setting for and helping to arrange the peace settlement after the defeat of the military government, the Derg, by the Ethiopian People's Revolutionary Democratic Front (EPRDF) in 1991, and later between the Ethiopian and Eritrean governments in December 2000, are other examples of Track Two work.

Particularly in his role in the Ethiopian-Eritrean negotiations, Isaac may be described as a "critical auxiliary participant" by offering an evaluation of Track One methods from his rather unique perspective. Based on his preference – mentioned above – for the inclusion of local, indigenous elders rather than conventional diplomats (referring in this case to official representatives of the United Nations, the European Union, the Organization of African Unity, and some individual countries), Isaac proceeds to complain that as they took over the negotiations, the latter "mess[ed] up" because they "lacked real understanding of the issue" and because they gave "false promises." It is the elders' inclination to *use persuasion and sympathetic understanding* – rather than coercion and threats – to *stress fidelity and trustworthiness* over hectoring and suspicion that Isaac believes can produce truly stable agreements and the prospect of real reconciliation between the parties. In Isaac's view, the present peace agreement between the Ethiopians and Eritreans is neither very stable nor is it aimed very effectively at reconciliation. Although professional diplomats are undoubtedly unavoidable, as Isaac himself concedes, the implication is that they could learn some very important lessons in negotiation from local leaders.

The contribution of Alimamy Koroma and the Inter-Religious Council to the peace settlement between the government and the insurgents in Sierra Leone is another example of effective Track Two agreement-making. Koroma and the members of the council are not themselves Track One negotiators, nor do they guide the negotiations in any direct way. Rather, they help create a congenial setting in which fruitful deliberations can proceed and help legitimate both the process and the outcome by effectively utilizing empathetic detachment, as we put it above. It seems unlikely that without the good offices of Koroma and the council, the talks would have had the successful outcome they did. Thus, Track One and Track Two diplomacy can work closely in tandem.

A final example of effective Track Two agreement-making is the work of Father Alex Reid, both in mitigating violent divisions within the IRA – as a preparation for peace – and then by means of his published reflections on possible terms of agreement between the Unionists and the Republicans. His position papers on the principles of self-determination and consent as a basis for negotiation are acclaimed as being "remarkably prescient." Father Reid's ideas did, as a matter of fact, turn out to influence in substantial ways the later agreements between the two sides, especially the Downing Street Declaration of 1993 and the Good Friday Agreement of 1998. In this example, the distinction between Track One and Track Two diplomacy is fairly tenuous.

Conclusion

In addition to the benefits of considering each of the compelling accounts contained in this volume on its own merits, we can profit also by examining them together, both in relation to one another and to broader questions, as well.

As we have seen, the testimony and experience of the religious peacemakers in these pages helps, in the first place, offset some widely held exaggerations about the relation of religion, violent conflict, and peacemaking. On the one side, the testimony properly cautions us against oversimplifying the causal connection between religion and violence. A growing number of studies of violence and civil war confirm the conclusion that religion is neither the only thing of importance, nor is it, in case after case, merely incidental either. This is an important conclusion. To realize that religion is one among a number of causes of violent conflict explains two things: one, why religious actors, such as the figures in this book, who work to counteract the destructive effects of religion may be able to make such a significant contribution, and, two, why most of them focus not just on religious reform, but on many broader concerns as well. Complexity of understanding leads to complexity of response.

On the other side, the proposition that religion, even in its most ennobling form, is somehow "above" or disconnected from violence is decisively disproved by the experience of our *Peacemakers*. Working for justice and peace by peaceful means can be dangerous. Such activity frequently arouses the hostility of those inconvenienced by it. It is one thing to recommend nonviolence over violence; it is another to be unprepared for the violent effects of nonviolent behavior. The figures in this volume are fully prepared and demonstrate how willing they are to take the costly consequences of their action, if necessary – in the belief that, ultimately, nonviolence trumps violence.

As to the theory and practice of peacemaking, we also have gotten some illuminating insights from the testimony and experience contained in this book. We have come to understand a bit better the connection between religion and peace – in interpreting the texts, doctrines, and practices of various religious traditions, in inspiring "empathetic detachment," and in identifying and clarifying specific religious interests and concerns that lie close to the heart of several of the conflicts mentioned in this book.

Beyond that, we have sampled something of the richness and range of activity undertaken in the name of religious peacemaking. The contributions of people in this book, particularly to institution-and-capacity building and to agreement-making, especially in the latter's "Track Two" phase, are in many ways pathbreaking and provide invaluable guidance for others who wish to follow in their footsteps.

Notes

1. The *Peacemakers* in Action

1. Peter Wallensteen and Margareta Sollenberg, "Armed Conflicts, Conflict Termination, and Peace Agreements, 1989–1996," *Journal of Peace Research* 34, no. 3 (1997), 339.

2. Kofi A. Annan, *Prevention of Armed Conflict: Report of the Secretary General* (New York: United Nations Department of Public Information), 78.

2. Peasant Power: José Inocencio Alas

1. Federal Research Division of the Library of Congress, *El Salvador: A Country Study*, Richard A. Haggarty, ed., Washington, D.C.: U.S. Government Printing Office, 1990, 4–7.

2. Ibid., *El Salvador*, 7–14.

3. Ibid., 14–15.

4. Ibid., 15.

5. Ibid., 15–16.

6. Federal Research Division of the Library of Congress, "Economic Crisis and Repression" in *El Salvador: A Country Study*, online version, http://countrystudies.us/el-salvador/7.htm.

7. Federal Research Division, *El Salvador.*, 16–17.

8. Ibid.

9. Ibid.

10. Ibid., 17–18.

11. Ibid.

12. Ibid., 24–26.

13. Ibid., 26–29.

14. Ibid., 26–29.

15. José Inocencio Alas, *Iglesia, Tierra, y Lucha Campesina: Suchitoto, El Salvador, 1968–1977* (San Salvador: Asociación de Frailes Franciscanos, 2003). For a detailed description of the history of the Catholic Church in El Salvador in the 1970s, see Phillip Berryman, "No Law Higher than God's," in *Religious Roots of Rebellion* (Maryknoll, N.Y.: Orbis Books, 1984).

16. Alas, *Iglesia*, 6–24.

17. Ibid.

18. José Inocencio Alas's Personal Statement for his Nomination for the Tanenbaum Center *Peacemaker of the Year* Award.

19. For more, see Foundation for Self-Sufficiency in Central America, "Biography: Jose Chencho Alas," http://fssca.net/fssca/bio.html.

20. José Inocencio Alas's Personal Statement.

21. Ibid.

22. Ibid.

23. Ibid.

24. Alas, *Iglesia*, 6–24, 119–124.

25. Ibid.

26. Ibid., 110–119.

27. Richard Salem's Nomination Form for the Tanenbaum Center *Peacemaker of the Year* Award.

28. José Inocencio Alas's Personal Statement.

29. Ibid.

30. Alas, *Iglesia*, 218–224.

31. José Inocencio Alas, interview by the Tanenbaum Center, July 6, 2000.

32. Ibid.

33. Ibid.

34. Ibid.

35. Alas, *Iglesia*, 224.

36. José Inocencio Alas, *Guidebook for Peacemakers: Culture, Spirituality and Theology of Peace Project* (2002), unpublished.

37. Ibid., 5.

38. Jose "Chencho" Alas, "Your New Executive Director," FSSCA Newsletter, Winter 2005, http://fssca.net/pastreports/1205/index.html.

39. Alas, *Guidebook*.

40. Alas, *Iglesia*, 224.

41. *The CIA World Factbook Online*. http://www.cia.gov/cia/publications/factbook/geos/es.html (accessed April 3, 2006).

42. Esther Cassidy, "Enemies of War – El Salvador: Civil War," PBS, http://www.pbs.org/itvs/enem'esofwar/elsalvador2.html (accessed November 7, 2002).

3. Men Who Walked the Street: Father Alex Reid and the Rev. Dr. Roy Magee

1. Mary Holland, Editorial, *The Guardian*, April 12, 1998.

2. R. Scott Appleby, *The Ambivalence of the Sacred: Religion, Violence, and Reconciliation* (New York: Rowman & Littlefield Publishers, Inc., 1999), 174.

3. Peter Fry and Fiona Somerset Fry, *A History of Ireland* (Oxford and New York: Routledge), 58–73.

4. Mike Cronin, *A History of Ireland* (London: Palgrave Press, 2001), 39–49.

5. *BBC History Online*, s.v. "Elizabethan Conquest: The Flight of the Earls 1603–7," http://www.bbc.co.uk/history/timelines/ni/flight_earls.shtml (accessed February 6, 2004).

6. Fry, *History of Ireland*, 136.

7. John Darby, "Conflict in Northern Ireland: A Background Essay," CAIN Web Service, http://cain.ulst.ac.uk/othelem/facets.htm#chap2 (accessed February 6, 2004).

8. Ibid.

9. Appleby, *Ambivalence of the Sacred*.

10. Fry, *History of Ireland*, 153–158.

11. Cronin, *History of Ireland*, 75–77.

12. Jonathan Bardon, "Orange Order," *The Encyclopedia of Ireland*, ed. Brian Lalor (New Haven: Yale University Press, 2003), 836–837.

13. Fry, *History of Ireland*, 165.

14. Cronin, *History of Ireland*, 81.

15. Ibid., 104–114.

16. For a more thorough discussion of the impact of the potato famine in Ireland, see R. F. Foster, *Modern Ireland, 1600–1972*, (London: Penguin Press, 1988), 318–344.

17. Patrick Geoghegan, "Act of Union," *The Encyclopedia of Ireland*, ed. Brian Lalor (New Haven: Yale University Press, 2003), 7.

18. Ibid.

19. Foster, *Modern Ireland*, 461–493. See also Michael A. Hopkinson, "War of Independence," *The Encyclopedia of Ireland*, ed. Brian Lalor (New Haven: Yale University Press, 2003), 1121.

20. "Northern Ireland During the 1960s," Irelandseye, www.irelandseye.com/aarticles/history/events/conflict/bttc4.shtm (accessed February 6, 2004).

21. *BBC History Online*, s.v. "Northern Ireland's Civil Rights Movement," http://www.bbc.co.uk/history/war/troubles/origins/nicivil.shtml (accessed February 6, 2004).

22. Appleby, *Ambivalence of the Sacred*, 176–177.

23. See, e.g., Margaret Lauber, "Peace Lines," in *The Encyclopedia of Ireland*, ed. Brian Lalor (New Haven: Yale University Press, 2003), 862–863. The "peace lines" were built and financed in collaboration with numerous government departments, such as the Northern Ireland Housing Executive, local police departments, and the Security Policy and Operations Division of the Northern Ireland Office. In many instances, the "peace lines" were erected to replace temporary boundaries and barricades constructed previously by the local communities.

24. For a thorough treatment of the symbols and graffiti used in Northern Ireland from the time of the Troubles to the present, see Jack Santino, *Signs of War and Peace: Social Conflict and the Use of Public Symbols in Northern Ireland* (New York: Palgrave Press, 2001).

25. Paul Bew and Gordon Gillespie, *Northern Ireland: A Chronology of the Troubles 1968–1999*, (Dublin: Gill and Macmillan, 1999), 16.

26. *BBC Online*, s.v. "Battle of the Bogside," http://www.bbc.co.uk/history/war/troubles/origins/bogside.shtml (accessed February 6, 2004).

27. Ibid., see also Bew and Gillespie, *Chronology of the Troubles*, 17–19.

28. Laura Friel, "In the Shadow of the Wall," An Phoblacht/Republican News, http://www.irlnet.com/aprn/archive/1999/August19/18bom2.html (accessed February 6, 2004).

29. Bew and Gillespie, *Chronology of the Troubles*, 19–20.

30. For a more thorough treatment, see Thomas Hennessey, *A History of Northern Ireland, 1920–1996* (Ireland: Macmillan Press, 1997), 206–213.

31. *BBC History Online,* s.v. "War and Conflict. Northern Ireland. The Troubles," http://www.bbc.co.uk/history/war/troubles/origins/bloodysun.shtml (accessed July 27, 2005); see also Keith Jeffrey, "Bloody Sunday, Derry," *The Encyclopedia of Ireland,* ed. Brian Lalor (New Haven: Yale University Press, 2003), 98.

32. Keith Jeffrey, "Bloody Friday," *The Encyclopedia of Ireland,* ed. Brian Lalor (New Haven: Yale University Press, 2003), 98.

33. "Roy and Religion," *The News Letter,* September 23, 2000.

34. Ibid.

35. Reverend Dr. Roy Magee, interview by the Tanenbaum Center, May 5, 1999, Belfast, Northern Ireland.

36. Ibid.

37. Reverend Dr. Roy Magee, fax message to the Tanenbaum Center, September 3, 2003.

38. Magee, interview.

39. Ibid.

40. Niall Stanage, "The Chutzpah of David Trimble," *The Guardian,* December 18, 2002, http://www.guardian.co.uk/Northern_Ireland/Story/0,2763,861975,00.html (accessed July 27, 2005).

41. Magee, fax.

42. Jane Bardon, "The Minister Who Offers to Mediate," *BBC News Online,* August 22, 2000, http://news.bbc.co.uk/2/hi/uk_news/northern_ireland/891412.stm (accessed April 21, 2006).

43. "Roy and Religion," *The News Letter.*

44. Bardon, "The Minister Who Offers to Mediate."

45. Magee, interview.

46. Kevin Rafter, *Martin Mansergh: A Biography* (Dublin: New Island Books, 2003), 180.

47. John Mullins, "Figure of Peace Stays in Shadows," *The Guardian,* December 9, 1998.

48. Gerry Adams, *Hope and History: Making Peace in Ireland* (Kerry: Brandon Books, 2006), 5.

49. Ibid., 8.

50. Cronin, *History of Ireland,* 239–240, see also Keith Jeffrey, "Robert (Bobby) Sands" and, Jonathan Bardon, "Hunger Strike" in *The Encyclopedia of Ireland,* ed. Brian Lalor (New Haven: Yale University Press, 2003), 961–962, 507.

51. Adams, *Hope and History,* 13.

52. Rafter, *Martin Mansergh,* 181.

53. Adams, *Hope and History,* 16.

54. Ibid., 18.

55. Jonathan Bardon, "Anglo-Irish Agreement," *The Encyclopedia of Ireland,* ed. Brian Lalor (New Haven: Yale University Press, 2003), 26.

56. Magee, fax.

57. Magee, interview.

58. Ibid.

59. Ibid.

60. Ibid.

61. Ibid.

62. Magee, fax.

63. Magee, interview.

64. Ibid.

65. Adams, *Hope and History,* 31–32.

66. Father Alex Reid, interview by the Tanenbaum Center, May 5, 1999, Belfast, Northern Ireland.

67. Ibid.

68. Gerry Adams, *A Farther Shore: Ireland's Long Road to Peace* (New York: Random House, 2003), 43.

69. Adams, *Hope and History,* 75.

70. Reid, interview.

71. Ibid.

72. Rafter, *Martin Mansergh,* 182.

73. Ibid., 183.

74. Adams, *A Farther Shore,* 45–46.

75. Ibid., 60.

76. Mullins, "Figure of Peace."

77. *BBC History Online,* s.v. "The Enniskillen Bomb," http://www.bbc.co.uk/history/war/troubles/agreement/ennibomb.shtml (accessed July 27, 2005).

78. Mansergh, "The Early Stages of the Irish Peace Process."

79. Rafter, *Martin Mansergh,* 187.

80. Ibid., 189.

81. Adams, *A Farther Shore,* 77.

82. Ibid., 78–80.

83. Brian Rowan, *Behind the Lines: The Story of the IRA and Loyalist Ceasefires* (Belfast: Blackstaff Press, 1995), 165.

84. Mary Holland, Editorial, *The Guardian,* April 12, 1998 (italics added).

85. Martin Mansergh, "The Early Stages of the Irish Peace Process," *Accord,* no. 8 (1994).

86. Adams, *A Farther Shore,* 108.

87. Sean Duignan, *One Spin on the Merry-Go-Round* (Blackwater Press, 1995), 104.

88. Rafter, *Martin Mansergh,* 184.

89. Ibid., 206.

90. Bardon, "The Minister Who Offers to Mediate."

91. Magee, interview.

92. Ibid.

93. Ibid.

94. Ibid.

95. Rafter, *Martin Mansergh*, 192–193.

96. Mullins, "Figure of Peace."

97. Magee, interview.

98. Adams, *A Farther Shore*, 164.

99. Tom Deignan, "The Craic; Giving 'Peace' a Chance," *Irish Voice*, December 30, 2003.

100. Magee, interview.

101. Reid, interview.

102. Adams, *A Farther Shore*, 173.

103. Rowan, *Behind the Lines*, 165.

104. Conor Hanna, "Minister Silenced the Guns," *The Mirror*, December 31, 1996.

105. Rowan, *Behind the Lines*, 119–121.

106. Eamon Phoenix, "Belfast Agreement/ Good Friday Agreement," in *The Encyclopedia of Ireland*, ed. Brian Lalor (New Haven: Yale University Press, 2003), 82–83.

107. Department of Foreign Affairs, *The Good Friday Accords: Declaration of Support*, http://foreignaffairs.gov.ie/angloirish/goodfriday/declarat.asp (accessed July 27, 2005).

108. Keith Jeffrey, "Omagh bombing," *The Encyclopedia of Ireland*, ed. Brian Lalor (New Haven: Yale University Press, 2003), 826–827.

109. Bardon, "The Minister Who Offers to Mediate."

110. Although official numbers remain at 38 percent for Roman Catholics, studies suggest that a figure adjusted to include those who refused to state their religious affiliation would put the percentage of Roman Catholics at 41 percent; see *MSN Encarta Online*, s.v. "Northern Ireland: Ethnicity and Religion," http://encarta.msn.com/encyclopedia_7615714 15_2/ Northern_Ireland.html#endads (accessed July 27, 2005).

111. Magee, fax.

112. Father Alex Reid, "The Conflict in Northern Ireland" (1989).

113. Ibid.

114. Father Alex Reid, lecture, Tanenbaum Center's *Peacemaker in Action* Retreat, Amman, Jordan, May 4, 2004.

115. Magee, fax.

116. Appleby, *Ambivalence of the Sacred*, 185.

117. Magee, interview.

118. Reid, "The Conflict in Northern Ireland."

119. Ibid.

120. Reid, interview.

121. Father Alex Reid, "A Pastoral Response to the Conflict in Northern Ireland" (2000).

122. Reid, "A Pastoral Response."

123. Father Alex Reid, "The Lessons of the Irish Peace Process" (2002).

124. Reid, interview.

125. Ibid.

126. Reid, "A Pastoral Response."

127. Ibid.

128. Reid, "The Lessons of the Irish Peace Process."

129. Magee, interview.

130. Ibid.

131. Ibid.

132. Ibid.

133. Ibid.

134. Magee, fax.

135. Reid, interview.

136. Magee, interview.

137. Ibid.

138. Reid, "A Pastoral Response."

139. Ibid.

140. Magee, interview.

141. Reid, "The Conflict in Northern Ireland."

142. Magee, interview.

143. Reid, "The Conflict in Northern Ireland."

144. *CIA World Factbook Online*, http://www.cia.gov/cia/publications/factbook/geos/ei.html (accessed April 5, 2006).

145. *Northern Ireland Statistics and Research Agency*, http://www.nisra.gov.uk (accessed January 14, 2003).

146. John Darby, "Conflict in Northern Ireland: A Background Essay," CAIN Web Service, http://cain.ulst.ac.uk/othelem/facets.htm#chap2 (accessed July 27, 2005).

4. "Would You Shoot Me, You Idiot?": Friar Ivo Markovic

1. Noel Malcolm, *Bosnia: A Short History* (London: Macmillan, 1994), 159–181.

2. Ibid., 6–12.

3. Ibid., 9–10.

4. For a more detailed analysis of the medieval Bosnian state, see ibid., Chapter 2.

5. For a more detailed analysis of the Ottoman conquest and its ramifications, see ibid., Chapters 4, 5, 7, 8.

6. For a more detailed analysis of World War I and the interwar period, see ibid., Chapter 12.

7. Ibid., 174.

8. For a more detailed analysis of Bosnia's experience in World War II, see ibid., Chapter 13.

9. Ibid., 193–194.

10. Ibid., 201–203.

11. For a more detailed analysis of Titoist Yugoslavia, see ibid., Chapter 14.

12. Neven Andjelic, *Bosnia-Herzegovina: The End of a Legacy* (London: Frank Cass, 2003).

13. Malcom, *Bosnia: A Short History*, 202–212.

14. For a more detailed analysis of the breakup of Communist Yugoslavia, see ibid., Chapter 15.

15. Ibid., Chapter 15.

16. Andjelic, *Bosnia-Herzegovina,* 41.

17. Malcom, *Bosnia: A Short History*, 225.

18. Ibid., 215–216.

19. Andras Riedlmayer, "A Brief History of Bosnia-Herzegovina," The Bosnian Manuscript Ingathering Project, http://www.kakarigi.net/manu/briefhis.htm (accessed August 26, 2003).

20. *CIA World Factbook Online*, http://www.cia.gov/cia/publications/factbook/geos/bk.html (accessed May 24, 2005).

21. Malcom, *Bosnia: A Short History*, 216–219.

22. Ibid., 222–223.

23. Ibid.

24. Ibid., 233–234.

25. Ibid., 236–238.

26. Ibid., 231.

27. Ibid., 237.

28. Ibid., 235–238.

29. Ibid., 239.

30. Javier Solana, "From Dayton Implementation to European Integration," NATO Review: Historic Change in the Balkans, http://www.nato.int/docu/home.htm#Reference (accessed August 2, 2005).

31. Andjelic, *Bosnia-Herzegovina,* 144–145.

32. Malcom, *Bosnia: A Short History*, 247–248.

33. Ibid., 242–243.

34. Ibid., 230, 234.

35. Ibid., 250.

36. Ibid., 246–252.

37. Ibid., 248–252.

38. "President Carter Helps Restart Peace Efforts in Bosnia-Herzegovina," The Carter Center, http://www.cartercenter.org/doc214.htm (accessed May 24, 2005).

39. Tim Ito, "Overview: Bosnia and Herzegovina," *The Washington Post,* October 1998, http://www.washingtonpost.com/wp-srv/inatl/longterm/balkans/overview/bosnia.htm (accessed May 24, 2005).

40. "NATO Ends SFOR Mission," North Atlantic Treaty Organization, http://www.nato.int/docu/update/2004/12-december/e1202a.htm (accessed May 24, 2005).

41. *CIA World Factbook Online*.

42. Friar Ivo Markovic, Curriculum Vitae, April 17, 1998.

43. Friar Ivo Markovic, interview with the Tanenbaum Center, April 1, 2000.

44. Ibid.

45. Ibid.

46. Ibid.

47. Friar Ivo Markovic, e-mail message to the Tanenbaum Center, September 2, 2005.

48. Ibid.

49. Ibid.

50. Ibid.

51. Ibid.

52. Ibid.

53. Markovic, interview.

54. Markovic, e-mail.

55. Markovic, interview.

56. Markovic, e-mail.

57. Markovic, interview.

58. Markovic, e-mail.

59. Ibid.

60. Markovic, interview.

61. Markovic, Curriculum Vitae.

62. Markovic, interview.

63. Markovic, Curriculum Vitae.

64. Markovic, interview.

65. Ibid.

66. Markovic, Curriculum Vitae.

67. Markovic, interview.

68. Ibid.

69. Ibid.

70. Ibid.

71. Ibid.

72. Ibid.

73. Ibid.

74. Ibid.

75. Ibid.

76. Ibid.

77. Ibid.

78. Ibid.

79. Ibid.

80. Ibid.

81. Ibid.

82. Ibid.

83. Ibid.

84. Colin Woodard, "In Rebuilt Bosnia, No Terror Toehold," *The Christian Science Monitor*, March 24, 2004, http://www.csmonitor.com/2004/0324/p01s01-woeu.htm (accessed August 2, 2005).

85. *The CIA World Factbook Online*, http://www.cia.gov/cia/publications/factbook/geos/bk.html (accessed April 5, 2006).

5. The Cybermonk: Father Sava Janjic

1. Noel Malcolm, *Kosovo: A Short History* (New York: Harper Perennial, 1999), 1.

2. Ibid., 22–57.

3. Ibid., 58–80.

4. Khurshid Ahmad, ed., *Islam: Its Meaning and Message* (Leicester: The Islamic Foundation, 1980).

5. Malcolm, *Kosovo: A Short History*, 213.

6. G. Richard Jansen, "Albanians and Serbs in Kosovo: An Abbreviated History," Colorado State University, Fort Collins, CO, http://lamar.colostate.edu/grjan/kosovohistory.html (accessed April 8, 2004).

7. Malcolm, *Kosovo: A Short History*.

8. Jansen, "Albanians and Serbs in Kosovo."

9. Malcolm, *Kosovo: A Short History*.

10. Ibid., 258–261.

11. Ibid., 260.

12. Ibid., 273.

13. Jansen, "Albanians and Serbs in Kosovo."

14. Ibid.

15. Ibid.

16. For a more detailed discussion of the impact of the death of Tito on the Yougoslav community, see Chapter 4, "Friar Ivo Marcovic of Bosnia and Herzegovina."

17. Malcolm, *Kosovo: A Short History*, 341.

18. Leander Kahney and James Glave, "Net Dispatches from Kosovo's War," *Wired News*, March 26, 1999, http://wired-vig.wired.com/news/politics/0,1283,18755,00.html.

19. Don Korth, "Kosovo: Website War and Cyber Warriors," *The Digital Journalist*, http://www.digitaljournalist.org/issue9903/north.htm (accessed March 22, 2002).

20. Zoran B. Nikolic, "A Witness of the Times: Father Sava," *Vreme*, 463, November 20, 1999. http://www.kosovo.com/sava_vreme.html (accessed April 7, 2004).

21. Lidija Kujundzic, "Return to the Monastery," December 14, 2000, http://www.cdsp.neu.edu/info/students/marko/nin/nin66.html (accessed March 22, 2002).

22. Nikolic, "A Witness of the Times."

23. Ibid.

24. Ibid.

25. Ibid.

26. Ibid.

27. Ibid.

28. Ibid.

29. Ibid.

30. Kujundzic, "Return to the Monastery."

31. Ibid.

32. Decani Orthodox Monastary, "The Public Statement by Decani Orthodox Monastery," news release, June 12, 1998.

33. Ibid.

34. Ibid.

35. North Atlantic Treaty Organization, *NATO's Role in Relation to the Conflict in Kosovo*, http://www.nato.int/kosovo/history.htm, July 15, 1999.

36. Nikolic, "A Witness of the Times."

37. Ibid.

38. NATO, *NATO's Role*.

39. Ibid.

40. Scott Canon, "In the Ashes of Postwar Kosovo, Monks' Story is a Rare Tale of Courage, Mercy," *Knight Ridder/Tribune News Service*, June 23, 1999.

41. CNN.com, "Number, Whereabouts of Kosovo Refugees," June 11, 1999, http://www.cnn.com/WORLD/europe/9904/27/kosovo.refugees.box (accessed August 9, 2005).

42. Nikolic, "A Witness of the Times."

43. Ibid.

44. *The CIA World Factbook Online*. http://www.cia.gov/cia/publications/factbook/geos/yi.html (accessed August 9, 2005).

45. Nikolic, "A Witness of the Times."

46. *Crucified Kosovo – Destroyed and Desecrated Serbian Orthodox Churches in Kosovo and Metohia, June–October, 1999* (Yugoslavia, 1999).

47. Father Sava Janjic, interview with the Tanenbaum Center, 2002.

48. OTPOR Youth Organization, *Declaration on Future of Serbia*, 1999.

49. Philip Smucker, "Mob Jeers Albright During Visit to Kosovo: Serbian Extremists Storm

Monastery to Threaten Hosts," *Washington Times*, July 30, 1999.

50. United Press International, "Albright Jeered by Angry Serbs," July 29, 1999.

51. J.I. Coffey, "Meeting with H.E. Dr. Artimije Radosavljevic, Father Sava Janjic/Serbian Orthodox Chruch," March 3, 2000.

52. Bjarke Larsen Gracanica, "Only Human Contact Can Ease Kosovo Tension, Says Orthodox 'Cyber-Monk.'" *Christianity Today*, March 20, 2000.

53. Coffey, "Meeting."

54. Ibid.

55. Jonathan Steele, "False encouragement for Serbs; Real Anxiety for Albanians," *The Bosnia Institute*, http://www.bosnia.org.uk/bosrep/marjune00/resolution.htm (accessed March 22, 2002, site now discontinued).

56. Kujundzic, "Return to the Monastery."

57. Ibid.

58. Richard Mertens, "A Resurgence in Life of Prayer: After Decades of Communist Rule in Former Yugoslavia, Monasteries are Enjoying a Revival," *The Christian Science Monitor*, June 19, 2003.

59. Ibid.

60. Mirjana Stefanovic, "The Interview to BLIC Daily By Hiermonk Sava From Decani Monastery," http://www.kosovo.com/interview_frsava.html (accessed June 24, 1999), Originally published as *Kosovski Srbi taoci reüima* (*Blic*, July 6, 1998).

61. Ibid.

62. Elizabeth Sullivan, "Serbs Pushing for Kosovo Peace Say Their Views are Being Ignored," *The Plain Dealer*, July 5, 1998. http://www.suc.org/politics/kosovo/html/pd070598.html (accessed on March 22, 2002, site now discontinued).

63. Stefanovic, "The Interview to BLIC Daily."

64. Sullivan, "Serbs Pushing."

65. Stefanovic, "The Interview to BLIC Daily."

66. Ibid.

67. Ibid.

68. Andrew Wasley, "Heavenly Dispatches," The Transnational Foundation for Peace and Future Research, http://www.transnational.org/features/2000/LynchPeaceJourn.html (accessed January 10, 2005).

69. Ibid.

70. Ibid.

71. Ibid.

72. Qemajl Morina, e-mail to Father Sava Janjic's mailing list, "Religion and Kosovo: A Christian and a Moslem View," October 24, 1998.

73. Father Sava Janjic e-mail to mailing list, "Response to Qemajl Morina: 'Religion and Kosovo: A Christian and a Moslem View,'" October 24, 1998.

74. World Council of Churches, "Who Will Take the First Step?," news release, March 23, 2000.

75. Jane Lampman, "Waking from the Balkan Nightmare: Religious Leaders in the Region Begin to Script New Roles in Support of Pluralism," *The Christian Science Monitor*, February 17, 2000.

76. Gracanica, "Only Human Contact."

77. Father Sava Janjic, "Religion in Kosovo," September 1998.

78. Gracanica, "Only Human Contact."

79. Stefanovic, "The Interview to BLIC Daily."

80. Ibid.

81. Korth, "Kosovo: Website War and Cyber Warriors."

82. Ibid.

83. News From Kosovo, "Fr. Sava meets with the NATO commander for Southern Europe, Admiral Gregory G. Johnson," Serbian Orthodox Diocese of Raska and Pizren, http://www.kosovo.com/news_pogrom.html (accessed on August 18, 2005).

84. Nicholas Wood, "NATO Expanding Kosovo Forces to Combat Violence," *New York Times*, March 19, 2004, http://www.nytimes.com (accessed March 19, 2004).

85. ERP KIM Info Service, "We Need Surgical Intervention: The Time of Voodoo Doctors and Deception in Kosovo is Over," Radio KIM, Granica, March 29, 2004.

86. Ibid.

87. *The CIA World Factbook Online*. http://www.cia.gov/cia/publications/factbook/geos/yi.html (accessed April 6, 2006).

88. Human Rights Watch Europe and Central Asia Overview. http://www.hrw.org/wr2k/Eca.htm (accessed April 7, 2006).

6. The Elder: Ephraim Isaac

1. Paul B Henze, *Layers of Time: A History of Ethiopia* (New York: Palgrave, 2000), 1.

2. Ibid., 10.

3. Ibid., 22–33.

4. For discussion of the factors that contributed to the decline of the Aksum Empire, see ibid., 44–49.

5. For a more extended treatment of the influence of Islam in Ethiopia during this period, see ibid., 39–43.

6. For more, see ibid., 83–118.

7. Harold G. Marcus, *A History of Ethiopia* (Berkeley: University of California Press, 1994) 212.

8. Henze, *Layers of Time: A History of Ethiopia*, 167.

9. Haile Selassie, meaning 'Power of the Trinity,' is the baptismal name of Ras Tafari, who chose to go by his baptismal name when he began his reign in 1930. For discussion of his rise to power, see Marcus, *A History of Ethiopia*, 116–129.

10. Ibid., 221.

11. Some scholars, such as Paul B. Henze, interpret the British intervention as a decisive move against Italy in the midst of World War II; see Henze, *Layers of Time*, 229–235, and Marcus, *A History of Ethiopia*, 147–153.

12. According to Ruth Iyob, the origins of the Eritrean-Ethiopian conflict lie in the British intervention in 1941 and the events that subsequently followed. For a more extended discussion, see Ruth Iyob, "Eritrean Nationalist Resistance and Ethiopian Regional Hegemony" (Ph.D. dissertation., University of California, Santa Barbara, 1991).

13. Marcus, *A History of Ethiopia*, 174–175.

14. For an extended treatment of the rise of the Eritrean People's Liberation Front, see From David Pool, *Guerillas to Government: the Eritrean People's Liberation Front* (Athens: Ohio University Press, 2001).

15. See "Prelude to Revolution" in Henze, Paul B. *Layers of Time*, 282–284.

16. For more see Henze, *Layers of Time*, 290–304.

17. Ibid., 305–306.

18. For more, see Henze, *Layers of Time*, 308–333, and Marcus, *A History of Ethiopia*, 202–220.

19. Ephraim Isaac, interview with the Tanenbaum Center, April 22, 2003, the Harvard Club of New York, New York, NY.

20. Ibid.

21. Ephraim Isaac, written correspondence to the Tanenbaum Center, May 28, 2004.

22. Isaac, written correspondence.

23. Ibid.

24. Isaiah 2:4

25. Ibid., 11:6–9.

26. Isaiah 58:3–11.

27. Isaac, interview, April 22, 2003.

28. I John 4:20.

29. Ibid.

30. Ibid.

31. Ibid.

32. Ephrem Akiliu. "Ephraim Isaac: A Man for All Seasons," *Ethiopian Review*, October 1991, 14.

33. Isaac, interview, April 22, 2003.

34. Ellen Friedland. "Ethiopian Jew tries to heal the rift between blacks, American Jews," *Metrowest Jewish News*, September 29, 1994.

35. Ephraim Isaac, "A Proposal to Strengthen Peace and Promote Reconciliation in the Horn of Africa and the Red Sea Region," (lecture).

36. Isaac, interview, April 22, 2003.

37. Akiliu. "Ephraim Isaac: A Man for All Seasons," *Ethiopian Review*, October 1991, 13.

38. Isaac, "A Proposal."

39. Ephraim Isaac, interview, May 15, 2003, the Center for Jewish History, New York, NY.

40. Ibid.

41. Ephraim Isaac, lecture, the Conference on Peaceful and Democratic Transition in Ethiopia, July 1–5, 1991.

42. Isaac, interview, April 22, 2003.

43. Ibid.

44. Ibid.

45. Ibid.

46. Ibid.

47. Ibid.

48. Ibid.

49. Ibid.

50. Ephraim Isaac, phone interview with the Tanenbaum Center, June 3, 2003.

51. Isaac, "A Proposal."

52. Ephraim Isaac, "Religion and World Peace in the Twentieth Century," lecture, Kent State University.

53. Ibid.

54. Isaac, "Religion and World Peace."

55. Isaac, phone interview.

56. Gillian Sorenson, "Restructuring the United Nations: A Turning Point for All Nations" lecture, Seminar of the Bahá'í International Community, October 18, 1995. Also, Isaac, "Religion and World Peace."

57. Deena Yellin, "Ephraim Isaac: Ethiopian Renaissance Man," *Lifestyles* 24, no. 133, (1994).

58. Isaac, interview, May 15, 2003.

59. Isaac, written correspondence.

60. CIA *World Factbook 2004*, http://www.cia.gov/cia/publications/factbook/geos/et.html (accessed on April 1, 2003.)

7. The Power of Ritual: The Rev. Dr. William O. Lowrey

1. William O. Lowrey, interview with the Tanenbaum Center, October 30, 2003.

2. Ann Lesch, *Sudan: Contested National Identities* (Bloomington: Indiana University Press, 1998), 17.

3. Francis Mading Deng, *War of Visions: Conflict of Identities in Sudan* (Washington, D.C., Brookings Institution Press, 1995).

4. Ibid., 64.

5. *The CIA World Factbook Online*, http://www.cia.gov/cia/publications/factbook/geos/su.html (accessed July 29, 2005).

6. P. M. Holt and M. W. Daly, *The History of Sudan: From the Coming of Islam to the Present Day* (London: Weidenfeld and Nicolson), 15.

7. Ibid., 16.

8. Ibid., 15–25, 31.

9. Gabriel Warburg, *Islam, Nationalism and Communism in a Traditional Society: The Case of Sudan* (London: Totowa: Frank Cass and Company Limited), 1–3.

10. Holt, *The History of Sudan: From the Coming of Islam to the Present Day*, 47–48.

11. Ibid., 54–55.

12. Gabriel Warburg, *Islam, Sectarianism and Politics in Sudan since the Mahdiyya* (Madison: University of Wisconsin Press), 14–15.

13. Lesch, *Sudan: Contested National Identities*, 26–28.

14. "Sudan: A Historical Perspective," http://sudan.net/government/history.html (accessed December 9, 2005).

15. Abdel Salam Sidahmed and Aslir Sidahmed, *Sudan, Contemporary Middle East* (London; New York: Routledge, 2005), 13–14.

16. Warburg, *Islam, Sectarianism and Politics in Sudan since the Mahdiyya*, 41.

17. Lesch, *Sudan: Contested National Identities*, 28.

18. Sidahmed, *Sudan*, 18–19.

19. Holt and Daly, *The History of Sudan: From the Coming of Islam to the Present Day*, 125–126.

20. Lesch, *Sudan: Contested National Identities*, 30–32.

21. Warburg, *Islam, Sectarianism and Politics in Sudan since the Mahdiyya*, 104.

22. Sidahmed, *Sudan*, 24–28.

23. Ibid., 40–41.

24. Ibid., 35.

25. Warburg, *Islam, Sectarianism and Politics in Sudan since the Mahdiyya*, 152–158.

26. Sidahmed, *Sudan*, 39.

27. Ibid., 42–45.

28. Lesch, *Sudan: Contested National Identities*, 163–164.

29. Ibid., 90–91.

30. Ibid., 159–163.

31. Ibid., 206.

32. Lowrey, interview.

33. Karl Vick, "Sudanese Tribes Confront Modern War," *The Washington Post*, July 7, 1999.

34. William O. Lowrey, Tanenbaum Center Peacemaker in Action Nomination Form.

35. Ibid.

36. Lowrey, interview.

37. William O. Lowrey, "A Flicker of Hope," http://members.tripod.com/~SudanInfonet/Nuer-Dinka/Flicker.html (accessed December 9, 2005).

38. Ibid.

39. Ibid.

40. Ibid.

41. Ibid.

42. Ibid.

43. Ibid.

44. New Sudan Council of Churches, "Dinka-Nuer Press Release, #2: Chiefs of Dinka and Nuer Stir Crowds, Emotions, and Perform Rituals," February 20, 1999.

45. Ibid.

46. Lowrey, interview

47. Ibid.

48. Ibid.

49. Ibid.

50. Ibid.

51. Ibid.

52. Ibid.

53. Ibid.

54. Lowrey, "A Flicker of Hope."

55. Ibid.

56. Ibid.

57. Ibid.

58. *The CIA World Factbook Online,* http://www.cia.gov/cia/publications/factbook/geos/su.html (accessed April 7, 2006).

8. The Nonviolent Deputy Minister of Defense: Nozizwe Madlala-Routledge

1. Big Media Publishers, "A Short History of South Africa," International Marketing Council of South Africa, http://www.southafrica.info/ess_info/sa_glance/history/history.htm (accessed May 10, 2004).
2. Leonard Thompson, *A History of South Africa* (New Haven: Yale University Press, 2001), 15.
3. "The Landing at the Cape," Southern Domain Online Travel Guides, http://www.southafrica-travel.net/history/eh_cala1.htm (accessed March 24, 2004).
4. Thompson, *A History of South Africa,* 33.
5. "A Short History of South Africa."
6. "The Expansion of the Trek Boers," Southern Domain Online Travel Guides, http://www.southafrica-travel.net/history/eh_trebu.htm (accessed March 24, 2004).
7. Thompson, *A History of South Africa,* 52.
8. Ibid.
9. "A Short History of South Africa."
10. Ibid.
11. Thompson, *A History of South Africa,* 83.
12. "A Short History of South Africa."
13. Ibid.
14. Thompson, *A History of South Africa,* 115, 119.
15. Ibid., 118.
16. "A Short History of South Africa."
17. Thompson, *A History of South Africa,* 142.
18. Big Media Publishers, "Union and the ANC," International Marketing Council of South Africa, http://www.southafrica.info/ess_info/sa_glance/history/history.htm (accessed May 10, 2004).
19. Thompson, *A History of South Africa,* 153.
20. "The Apartheid Era," Southern Domain Online Travel Guides, http://www.southafrica-travel.net/history/eh_apart1.htm (accessed March 24, 2004).
21. Thompson, *A History of South Africa,* 160.
22. Ibid., 156.
23. Ibid., 175.
24. "Union and the ANC."
25. "A Short History of South Africa."
26. Ibid.
27. Thompson, *A History of South Africa,* 188.

28. Ibid., 187.
29. Ibid., 182.
30. Ibid., 190.
31. "The Apartheid Era."
32. Monal Chokshi, Cale Carter, Deepak Gupta, Tove Martin, and Robert Allen, "The History of Apartheid in South Africa" (Final Project, Stanford University, 1995) http://www-cs-students.Stanford.edu/cale/cs201/apartheid.hist.html (accessed March 24, 2004).
33. Thompson, *A History of South Africa,* 196.
34. "A Short History of South Africa."
35. Thompson, *A History of South Africa,* 208.
36. Ibid., 209.
37. Ibid., 210.
38. "A Short History of South Africa."
39. Thompson, *A History of South Africa,* 209.
40. Ibid., 211.
41. "A Short History of South Africa."
42. Thompson, *A History of South Africa,* 223.
43. Ibid., 224–228.
44. Ibid., 226–227.
45. Ibid., 230.
46. Ibid., 235.
47. "A Short History of South Africa."
48. Thompson, *A History of South Africa,* 239–240.
49. Ibid., 226.
50. Ibid., 264.
51. Ibid., 275.
52. *BBC Online,* s.v. "ANC Celebrates Landslide Victory," British Broadcasting Corporation, http://news.bbc.co.uk/1/hi/world/africa/3631485.stm#top (accessed April 16, 2004).
53. Nozizwe Madlala-Routledge, interview with the Tanenbaum Center, March 2, 2004.
54. Nozizwe Madlala-Routledge, Curriculum Vitae, http://www.gov.za/gol/gcis_profile.jsp?id=1037 (accessed February 25, 2004); *Polity and Law Outline News,* "Nozizwe Madlala-Routledge," http://www.polity.org.za/people/Deputy_mins/madlala-routledge_.html (accessed on September 22, 1999).
55. Corinna Schuler, "Can a Pacifist Lead S. Africa's Defense?" *The Christian Science Monitor,* August 2, 1999, http://search.csmonitor.com/durable/1999/08/02/p1s2.htm (accessed March 30, 2004).
56. Madlala-Routledge, interview.
57. Madlala-Routledge, Curriculum Vitae.
58. Schuler, "Can a Pacifist Lead S. Africa's Defense?"
59. Ibid.

60. Madlala-Routledge, interview.
61. Ibid.
62. Schuler, "Can a Pacifist Lead S. Africa's Defense?"
63. http://www.umich.edu/urecord/9798/ Nov12 97/brief.htm (accessed March 30, 2004).
64. *Polity and Law Outline News*, "Nozizwe Madlala-Routledge."
65. Madlala-Routledge, interview.
66. Schuler, "Can a Pacifist Lead S. Africa's Defense?"
67. Melanie Gosling, "Pacifist Defense Deputy Says Quakers an Asset in Ministry," *Cape Times*, June 18, 1999.
68. Ibid.
69. Madlala-Routledge, interview.
70. Ibid.
71. Terri L. Kelly, "Towards an Understanding of the Transformational Nature of Satyagraha," (unpublished graduate paper, Portland State University, July 2000), http://web.pdx.edu/psu17799/gandhi.htm (accessed March 30, 2004).
72. Madlala-Routledge, interview.
73. "Environments Conducive to Victimization and Fear," *Monograph* 24 (1998), http://www.iss.co.za/Pubs/Monographs/N024/Environments.html (accessed March 30, 2004).
74. Madlala-Routledge, interview.
75. Ibid.
76. Ibid.
77. Madlala-Routledge, Curriculum Vitae.
78. Madlala-Routledge, interview.
79. "Nozizwe Madlala-Routledge," International Technologist and Technician Association, http://www.engologist.com/proroutledge.htm (accessed March 30, 2004).
80. Madlala-Routledge, interview.
81. Bridget Moix, "Conscientious Engagement: A Quaker Deputy Defense Minister," *Quaker Life*, December, 1999.
82. "Profile: Nozizwe Madlala-Routledge," *Gender Links*, http://www.genderlinks.org.za/page.php?p_id=200 (accessed March 30, 2004).
83. Ibid.
84. Madlala-Routledge, interview.
85. Gosling, "Pacifist Defense Deputy Says Quakers an Asset in Ministry."
86. Schuler, "Can a Pacifist Lead S. Africa's Defense?"
87. Madlala-Routledge, interview.
88. Ibid.
89. Schuler, "Can a Pacifist Lead S. Africa's Defense?"
90. Gosling, "Pacifist Defense Deputy Says Quakers an Asset in Ministry."
91. "Profile: Nozizwe Madlala-Routledge," *Gender Links*.
92. Madlala-Routledge, interview.
93. Ibid.
94. "Profile: Nozizwe Madlala-Routledge," *Gender Links*.
95. Madlala-Routledge, interview.
96. Ibid.
97. Ibid.
98. Stefan Lovegren, "African Army Hastening HIV/AIDS Spread," *Jenda: A Journal of Culture and African Women Studies* (2001), http://www.jendjournal.com/jenda/v011.2/lovgren.html (accessed March 30, 2004).
99. Nozizwe Madlala-Routledge, "New Bridges to Peace," lecture, Georgetown University, Washington, DC, April 27–28, 2001.
100. Madlala-Routledge, interview.
101. Nozizwe Madlala-Routledge, interview by David J. Passiak, *Lapis Magazine*, http://www.lapismagazine.org.
102. Nozizwe Madlala-Routledge, interview, *Lapis Magazine*.
103. Ibid.
104. Ibid.
105. Ibid.
106. Madlala-Routledge, interview.
107. Ibid.
108. Ibid.
109. Ibid.
110. Ibid.
111. *The CIA World Factbook Online*, http://www.cia.gov/cia/publications/factbook/geos/sf.html (accessed on April 1, 2006).

9. Warriors and Brothers: Imam Muhammad Ashafa and Pastor James Wuye

1. MBendi Information Services (Pty) Ltd, "Nigeria," MBendi: Information for Africa, http://mbendi.co.za/land/af/ng/p0005.htm (accessed July 28, 2005).
2. Klaus Hock, "Der Islam-Komplex, Zur christlichen Wahrnehmung des Islams und der christlich-islamischen Beziehungen in Nordnigeria während der Militärherrschaft Babangidas," *Hamburger Theologische Studien* 7 (1996), 16–17. Translated by Katia P. Coleman.

3. "Entry on Nigeria," *Africa Today*, 1996.

4. Although undertaken primarily for motives of profit, imperialist expansionism, and rivalry with France, the British colonial conquest of Nigeria was domestically and internationally legitimized as a crusade against slavery. See Lovejoy and Hogendorn, *Slow Death for Slavery*, Chapter 1.

5. Ibid.

6. Hock, "Der Islam-Komplex," 24.

7. Hock, "Der Islam-Komplex," 46.

8. In the southeast, for example, "Igbo territories were arbitrarily carved into administrative areas called native courts"; see Antoine Lema, *Africa Divided – The Creation of "Ethnic Groups"* (Lund, Sweden: Lund University Press, 1993), 130–131.

9. Ibid., 131.

10. L. Diamond, "Class, Ethnicity, and Democracy in Nigeria," *Comparative Studies in Society and History* 25 (1983), 471.

11. Major Nzeogwu identified the compelling factors justifying the coup as "nepotism, regionalism, [and] corruption." M. Akpan, "The Nigerian Military and National Integration, 1966–1979," *Journal of African Studies* 15, nos. 1–2 (1988), 40.

12. Luckham argues, however, that the prevalence of Ibo actors was more a function of recruitment patterns into the army during the colonial era. For this argument and more details of this period, see Robin Luckham, *The Nigerian Military; A Sociologican Analysis of Authority and Revolt* (Cambridge: Cambridge University Press, 1971).

13. Eghosa Osaghae, "Ethnic Minorities and Federalism in Nigeria," *African Affairs*, 90 (1991).

14. Hock, "Der Islam-Komplex," 194; see also David D. Laitin, "The Shari'a Debate and the Origins of Nigeria's Second Republic," *The Journal of Modern African Studies* 20, no. 3 (1982).

15. Shari'a courts had jurisdiction only over personal law and only in cases where both parties accepted Islamic law; however, once engaged, the decision of the State Shari'a Court of Appeal was final. Hock, "Der Islam-Komplex," 192–193.

16. Laitin, "The Sharïa Debate," 416.

17. Ibid.

18. Hock, "Der Islam-Komplex," 196–197.

19. Ibid., 198.

20. The following section relies heavily on information provided by Imam Ashafa and Pastor James, but other sources of corroboration include Sam Ihejirka at the Strategic Empowerment and Mediation Agency (SEMA) in Kaduna, Humphrey Orjiako at the Office of the Presidency in Abuja, Keith Morris at BBC World in London (who made a documentary on the MCDF), and Barnaby Phillips of BBC Nigeria.

21. Humphrey Orjiako (Deputy Director [Research and Planning], Office of Conflict Resolution, The Nigerian Presidency), Abuja, Nigeria, September 2000.

22. Pastor James Wuye, interview with the Tanenbaum Center, MCDF headquarters, Kaduna, Nigeria, September 2000.

23. Ibid.

24. Orjiako, interview.

25. "The mainstream Churches are increasingly willing to not only work together with these fundamentalist movements and groups, but also to adopt more and more of their theological and ideological thinking. If there is a significant trend in the theological development of the churches in northern Nigeria, it is precisely this imitation, acceptance, and internalisation of fundamentalist thought and action" Hock, "Der Islam-Komplex," 51.

26. Especially in the wake of the Islamic revolution in Iran in 1978. Imam Muhammad Ashafa, interview with the Tanenbaum Center, Kaduna, Nigeria, October, 2000.

27. James Wuye, interview, Kaduna, Nigeria, September, 2000.

28. Ibid.

29. Ibid.

30. Ashafa, interview.

31. Josiah Akalazu, "A Law unto Themselves," *News Africa* 17/July/2000. Zamfara is a relatively poor state, and there has been considerable speculation that the governor took this measure for political rather than religious reasons. According to one observer, "the young governor of the state felt he had little to offer the people, and he understood that in a poor state under a democracy, if you have nothing to offer your tenure is tenuous, so he panicked that he might lose power and played his trump card" by imposing Shari'a to garner support among the state's overwhelmingly Muslim population. Orjiako, The Nigerian Presidency.

32. Fabian Odum, "Kaduna: Long, Weary Search For Peace," *Nigeria Guardian,* November 12, 2000.

33. Orjiako, interview.

34. Col. Madaki, interview with Danlami Nmodu, September 25, 2000.

35. Wuye, interview.

36. Ashafa, interview.

37. Wuye, interview.

38. Ashafa, interview.

39. Wuye, interview.

40. Ashafa, interview.

41. Ibid.

42. Wuye, interview.

43. Ashafa, interview.

44. Imam Muhammad Ashafa and James Wuye, correspondence, June 11, 2003.

45. Ashafa, interview.

46. Ibid.

47. Wuye, interview.

48. Ibid.

49. Ashafa, interview.

50. Sam Ihejirika, interview with Tanenbaum Center, Kaduna, Nigeria, October 10, 2000.

51. Ashafa, interview.

52. Ihejirika, interview.

53. Ashafa, interview.

54. Ibid.

55. Wuye, interview.

56. Ibid.

57. Ibid.

58. Ibid.

59. Ibid.

60. James Wuye, telephone interview with the Tanenbaum Center, Abuja, Nigeria, October 3, 2000.

61. Ashafa, interview.

62. Imam Muhammad Ashafa and Pastor James Wuye, *The Pastor and the Imam – Responding to Conflict,* (Lagos: Ibrash Press, 1999).

63. Imam Ashafa and Pastor James Wuye, interview, Kaduna, Nigeria, September 30, 2000.

64. Ashafa, interview.

65. Ibid., Ashafa and James, correspondence.

66. These observers include S. Ihejirika and H. Orjiako, who both accuse journalists of fuelling religious tensions with inflammatory reporting. Ihejirika, interview, and Orjiako, interview.

67. Ashafa, interview.

68. Ibid.

69. Ibid.

70. Hock, "Der Islam-Komplex," 211.

71. Ashafa, interview.

72. Ibid.

73. Wuye, interview.

74. Ibid.

75. Ibid.

76. Mike Crawley, "Two Men Create Bridge Over Nigeria's Troubled Waters," *The Christian Science Monitor Online,* http://www.csmonitor.com/2003/0228/p07s01-woaf.html (accessed March 3, 2003).

77. "The Kaduna Peace Declaration of Religious Leaders," Network for Interfaith Concerns in the Anglican Communion, http://www.anglicannifcon.org/KadunaDeclaration.htm (accessed March 13, 2003).

78. Crawley, "Two Men."

79. "The Kaduna Peace Declaration of Religious Leaders."

80. *The CIA World Factbook Online,* http://www.cia.gov/cia/publications/factbook/geos/ni.html (accessed on April 7, 2006).

10. The Power of Organization: Alimamy Koroma

1. Jane Lampman, "Faith's Unbreakable Force," *Christian Science Monitor,* December 23, 1999, http://search.csmonitor.com/durable/1999/12/23/p11s1.htm (August 24, 2004).

2. Alimamy P. Koroma, at the Tanenbaum Center's *Peacemakers in Action* Retreat, New York, NY, September 27, 2005.

3. Earl Conteh-Morgan, *Sierra Leone at the End of the Twentieth Century: History, Politics and Society* (New York: P. Lang, 1999), 11.

4. Ibid.

5. Ibid., 18–19.

6. Ibid., 11.

7. Ibid., 22.

8. *The Columbia Encyclopedia Online,* s.v. "Sierra Leone," http://www.bartleby.com/65/si/SierraLe.html (accessed May 20, 2005).

9. Ibid.

10. Ibid.

11. The Guardian, *Death on the Grain Coast* [book extract of *Rough Crossings: Britain, the Slaves and the American Revolution* Simon Schama; date of release April 25, 2006], (August 31, 2005), http://books.guardian.co.uk/departments/history/story/060001559444,00.html.

12. Conteh-Morgan, *Sierra Leone,* 25.

13. J. E. Flint, ed., *The Cambridge History of Africa*, vol. 5. *c. 1790–c. 1870* (Cambridge: Cambridge University Press, 1976), 175.

14. Conteh-Morgan, *Sierra Leone*, 31.

15. Ibid., 26.

16. Ibid., 26.

17. Ibid., 31–33.

18. Ibid., 37–43.

19. Ibid., 48–49.

20. Ibid., 60.

21. For a more detailed account of the transition of Sierra-Leone from British Protectorate to autonomous state, see ibid., 31–73.

22. Conteh-Morgan, *Sierra Leone*, 64–66.

23. Abdel-Fatu Musah and J. 'Kayode Fayemi, eds., *Mercenaries: An African Security Dilemma* (London: Pluto Press, 2000), 79.

24. Ibid., 112–115.

25. For a more detailed account of Sierra-Leone's transition to a Republic, see Conteh-Morgan, *Sierra Leone*, 75–83.

26. Ibid., 85.

27. Musah and Fayemi, *Mercenaries*, 86.

28. Conteh-Morgan, *Sierra Leone*, 127.

29. World Bank, Sierra Leone Country Brief, http://web.worldbank.org/WBSITE/EXTERNAL/COUNTRIES/AFRICAEXT/SIERRALEONEEXTN/0,,menuPK:367833~pagePK:141132~piPK:141107~theSitePK:367809,00.html (accessed April 1, 2006).

30. Conteh-Morgan, *Sierra Leone*, 130.

31. Ibid., 132.

32. *Infoplease*, s.v. "Foday Sankoh: Sierra Leone's Rebel with a Cause," http://www.infoplease.com/spot/sankoh1.html (accessed May 23, 2005).

33. Ibid.

34. BBC News Online, "Sankoh's Body Handed to Family," August 2, 2003, http://news.bbc.co.uk/2/hi/africa/3119957.stm (accessed March 27, 2006).

35. Michael Jackson, *In Sierra Leone* (Durham: Duke University Press, 2004), 142.

36. David Bamford, "Foday Sankoh: Rebel Leader," *BBC News Online*, May 12, 2000, http://news.bbc.co.uk/2/hi/africa/737268.stm (accessed February 9, 2006).

37. Derek Brown, "Who is Foday Sankoh?" *The Guardian*, May 17, 2000, http://www.guardian.co.uk/sierra/article/02763221853,00.html (accessed May 20, 2005).

38. Bamford, "Rebel Leader."

39. "Sierra Leone: Sexual Violence Widespread in War," *Human Rights Watch*, http://www.hrw.org/press/2003/01/s10116.htm (accessed May 23, 2005).

40. Brown, "Foday Sankoh."

41. Musah and Fayemi, *Mercenaries*, 90–91.

42. Conteh-Morgan, *Sierra Leone*, 136–140.

43. For a more detailed discussion of the international community's involvement in Sierra-Leone, see ibid., 143–157.

44. Koroma, Retreat, New York.

45. Ibid.

46. Alimamy P. Koroma, at the Tanenbaum Center's *Peacemakers in Action* Retreat, Amman, Jordan, May 3–5, 2004.

47. Carol Fouke, "CWS, West Africa Delegation Tell U.S. State Department, Legislators: 'No Lasting Peace – No Development,'" *InterAction* (March 21, 2003), http://www.interaction.org/newswire/detail.php?id=1431 (accessed March 22, 2006).

48. Koroma, Retreat, New York.

49. Alimamy P. Koroma, interview with Dr. Kofi and Isha Dyfan, December 12, 2003.

50. Koroma, Retreat, Amman.

51. Alimamy P. Koroma, e-mail message to the Tanenbaum Center, May 21, 2000.

52. Lampman, "Faith's Unbreakable Force."

53. Koroma, e-mail message.

54. Thomas Mark Turay, "Civil Society and Peacebuilding: The Role of the Inter-Religious Council of Sierra Leone," *Accord* (2000), http://www.c-r.org/accord/s-leone/accord9/society.shtml (accessed May 23, 2005).

55. Koroma, interview.

56. Ibid.

57. Turay, "Civil Society."

58. Koroma, Retreat, Amman.

59. Koroma, interview.

60. Ibid.

61. Ibid.

62. Lampman, "Faith's Unbreakable Force."

63. Alimamy P. Koroma, Personal Statement to the Tanenbaum Center, April 20, 2000.

64. Turay, "Civil Society."

65. Ibid.

66. Koroma, Personal Statement.

67. Lampman, "Faith's Unbreakable Force."

68. Turay, "Civil Society."

69. Ibid.

70. Koroma, interview.

71. Ibid.

72. Koroma, Retreat, New York.

73. Church World Service, "I Don't Want a Gun," (November, 10, 2005), http://www.

churchworldservice.org/Educ_Advo/partners/
2005/koroma.html.

74. Ibid.

75. Ibid.

76. Ibid.

77. Church World Service, "Sierra Leone to Host Seminars on Trauma Awareness and Recovery," (January 9, 2004), http://www.churchworldservice.org/news/archives/2004/01/153.html.

78. Ibid.

79. Ibid.

80. Lampman, "Faith's Unbreakable Force."

81. Carol Fouke, "CWS, West Africa Delegation Tell U.S. State Department, Legislators: 'No Lasting Peace – No Development'," *InterAction* (March 21, 2003), http://www.interaction.org/newswire/detail.php?id=1431 (accessed March 22, 2006).

82. *The CIA World Factbook Online*, http://www.cia.gov/cia/publications/factbook/geos/sl.html (accessed on April 1, 2006).

11. Israel and Palestine: A History

1. Mark A Tessler, *A History of the Israeli-Palestinian Conflict*, (Bloomington, Indiana University Press, 1994), IN: 1.

2. Ami Isseroff, "A Brief History of Israel and Palestine and the Conflict," *Mideastweb*, http://www.mideastweb.org/briefhistory.htm (accessed May 25, 2005).

3. Ibid.

4. Tessler, *A History of the Israeli-Palestinian Conflict*, 37.

5. Isseroff, "A Brief History."

6. Baruch Kimmerling and Joel S. Migdal, *The Palestinian People: A History* (Cambridge, MA: Harvard University Press, 2003), 22.

7. Arthur Hertzberg, *The Fate of Zionism: A Secular Future for Israel & Palestine* (San Francisco: Harper San Francisco, 2003), 1.

8. Hertzberg, *The Fate of Zionism*, 2.

9. Kimmerling and Migdal, *The Palestinian People*, 17–24.

10. Isseroff, "A Brief History."

11. Tessler, *A History of the Israeli-Palestinian Conflict*, 148.

12. Mitchell Cohen, *Zion and State: Nation, Class and the Shaping of Modern Israel* (New York: Columbia University Press, 1992), 149.

13. Full text of "The King-Crane Commission Report, August 28, 1919," *Mideastweb*,

http://www.mideastweb.org/kingcrane.htm (accessed April 25, 2003).

14. Full text of "Statement of the Zionist Organization Regarding Palestine, presented to the Paris Peace Conference, Feb. 3, 1919," *Mideastweb*, http://www.mideastweb.org/zionistborders.htm (accessed April 25, 2003).

15. Michael J. Cohen, *The Origins and Evolution of the Arab-Zionist Conflict* (University of California Press, 1987), 64 and footnote.

16. Full text of "The Palestine Mandate of the Council of the League of Nations, 24 July, 1922," *Mideastweb*, http://64.233.161.104/search?q=cache:jwYybnrmy4EJ:www.mideastweb.org/mandate.htm+jewish+agency+mideastweb&hl=en (accessed April 25, 2003).

17. Rabbi Joseph Telushkin, *Jewish Literacy: The Most Important Things to Know About the Jewish Religion, Its People and Its History* (New York: William Morrow and Company, Inc., 1991), 277.

18. Kimmerling and Migdal, *The Palestinian People*, 104.

19. Isseroff, "A Brief History."

20. Basheer M. Nafi. "The Arabs and the Axis: 1933–1940," *Arab Studies Quarterly. Spring 1997.*

21. Donna E. Arzt, *Refugees Into Citizens: Palestinians and the End of the Arab-Israeli Conflict* (New York: Council on Foreign Relations, Inc., 1997), 13.

22. Isseroff, "A Brief History."

23. Sharif Kanani and Nihad Zitawi, *Dayr Yasin*, Monograph No. 4, Palestinian Destroyed Villages Series, second edition (Bir Zeit: Center of Documentation and Research, Bir Zeit University, 1987), 6.

24. Arthur Goldschmidt, Jr., *A Concise History of the Middle East* (Boulder, CO: Westview Press, 1996), 255.

25. Eyal Ben-Ari, lecture, the Tanenbaum Center for Interreligious Understanding, New York, January 22, 2003.

26. Tom Segev, *One Palestine, Complete: Jews and Arabs under the British Mandate* (New York: Henry Holt and Company, 1999), 505.

27. William K. Cleveland, *A History of the Modern Middle East* (Boulder, CO: Westview Press, 2000), 263.

28. Donna E. Arzt, *Refugees into Citizens: Palestinians and the End of the Arab-Israeli*

Conflict (New York: Council on Foreign Relations, Inc., 1997), 14.

29. Kimmerling and Migdal, *The Palestinian People*, 160.

30. Isseroff, "A Brief History."

31. Jeremy Bowen, *Six Days: How the 1967 War Shaped the Middle East* (London: Simon & Schuster, 2003), 8.

32. Ibid., 69–70.

33. Ibid., 40–47.

34. Ibid., 106–112.

35. Cleveland, *A History of the Modern Middle East,* 329m and Goldschmidt, *A Concise History of the Middle East,* 293–294.

36. Arzt, *Refugees into Citizens,* 17.

37. Cleveland, *A History of the Modern Middle East,* 354–357.

38. Bowen, *Six Days,* 36–38.

39. UN Security Council Resolution 242, www.un.org/documents/sc/res/1967/scres67.htm (accessed January 23, 2004).

40. Ibid.

41. Isseroff, "A Brief History."

42. Ibid.

43. Cleveland, *A History of the Modern Middle East,* 378.

44. Ibid., 361.

45. Ibid., 486 and 487.

46. Kimmerling and Migdal, *The Palestinian People*, 330–334.

47. Ibid.

48. Ibid., 345.

49. Cheryl A. Rubenberg, *The Palestinians: In Search of a Just Peace* (Boulder, CO: Lynne Rienner Publishers, 2003), 118.

50. Kimmerling and Migdal, *The Palestinian People*, 385.

51. "Statistics," *B'Tselem: The Israeli Information Center for Human Rights in the Occupied Territories,* http://www.btselem.org/english/statistics/Casualties.asp (accessed April 29, 2006).

52. "Israel: Military Must Account for Killings of Two Children," *Human Rights Watch* Press Release, http://hrw.org/english/docs/2006/02/08/isrlpa12646.htm (accessed April 29, 2006).

53. Kimmerling and Migdal, *The Palestinian People*, 406.

54. Ibid., 406.

55. Ibid., 407, and Frontline, "Shattered Dreams of Peace: Camp David Summit," *PBS,*

http://www.pbs.org/wgbh/pages/frontline/shows/oslo/negotiations/ (accessed May 5, 2006).

56. Elias Chacour, phone interview with the Tanenbaum Center, October 23, 2003.

57. Elias Chacour and David Hazzard, *Blood Brothers,* (Grand Rapids, MI: Chosen Books, 2003) p. 22.

58. Chacour, phone interview 2003.

59. Chacour, *Blood Brothers,* 34.

60. Ibid., 42.

61. Ibid., 29.

62. Chacour, phone interview 2003.

63. Ibid.

64. Matthew, 5:3–12, as recited by Chacour, phone interview (2003).

65. Chacour, *Blood Brothers,* 36–37.

66. Ibid., 37.

67. Chacour, phone interview 2003.

68. Chacour, *Blood Brothers,* 87.

69. Ibid., 114.

70. Ibid.

71. Ibid., 115

72. Ibid., 117

73. Ibid., 120.

74. Ibid., 137.

75. Ibid., 154.

76. Ibid., 141.

77. Chacour, phone interview 2003.

78. Chacour, *Blood Brothers,* 160.

79. Ibid., 177.

80. Ibid., 178.

81. Ibid., 182.

82. Chacour, phone interview 2003.

83. Chacour, *Blood Brothers,* 186.

84. Ibid., 187.

85. Elias Chacour and Mary E. Jensen, *We Belong to the Land: The Story of a Palestinian Israeli who Lives for Peace and Reconciliation,* (San Francisco: Harper Collins, 1990), 205, and Chacour, *Blood Brothers,* 189.

86. Chacour, *Blood Brothers,* 192.

87. Ibid., 198.

88. Ibid., 202.

89. Ibid., 210–212.

90. Chacour, *We Belong to the Land,* 99.

91. Ibid., 139.

92. Chacour, phone interview 2003.

93. Ibid.

94. Ibid.

95. Ibid.

96. Chacour, phone interview by the Tanenbaum Center, February 9, 2004.

97. Chacour, phone interview 2003.

98. Chacour, phone interview 2004.

99. Chacour, phone interview 2003.

100. Ibid.

101. Abuna Chacour, address to the World Methodist Conference, Rio de Janeiro, Brasil, 1996.

102. Abuna Chacour, cited in the article by Edmund Doogue, "Palestinian Priest Wins Niwano Peace Prize," *Christianity Today,* February 19, 2002.

103. Ibid.

104. Abuna Chacour, interviewed in "Elias Chacour: Prophet in His Own Country." Directed by Claude Roshem-Smith. 2003.

105. Chacour, *We Belong to the Land,* 205.

106. Bobby Morris, "Father Elias Chacour: A Living Stone of Israel," Person 2 Person: Christian E-zine, http://64.233.187.104/search?q=cache:07JM_Kmk8YgJ:www.p2pezine.com/REDESIGN/e-chacour.htm+%22peace+needs+no+contemplators%22&hl=en (accessed April 14, 2005).

107. Chacour, phone interview 2003.

108. Ibid.

109. Ibid.

110. Ibid.

111. Ibid.

112. Ibid.

113. Chacour, *We Belong to the Land,* 143.

114. Mike Oettle, "Get Up, Go Ahead, Do Something," Saints and Seasons, http://geocities.com/saintsseasons/Elias3E.html?200516 (accessed February 22, 2004).

115. Ibid.

116. Ibid.

117. Chacour, phone interview 2003.

118. Rabbi Menachem Froman, http://www.oneworld.org/peacequest/stories/Rabbi_Froman.html (accessed September 10, 2003; site now discontinued).

119. Akiva Eldar, "People & Politics: The General, the Rabbi and the Holy Spirit," *Haaretz,* October 1, 2003.

120. The Hebrew Reali School Haifa, "History," http://www.hareali-haivri.haifa.k12.il/newsite/template5.asp?typeid=1 (accessed May 11, 2005).

121. Haim Shapiro, "Tell It on the Mountain," *The Jerusalem Post,* June 4, 1999, http://www.jpost.com/com/Archive/04.Jun.1999/Features/Article-14.html (accessed February 17, 2004).

122. The Jewish Virtual Library, "The Nahal," The American-Israeli Cooperative Enterprise, http://www.us-israel.org/jsource/Society_&_Culture/nahal.html (accessed February 20, 2004).

123. Marc Gopin, *Holy War, Holy Peace: How Religion Can Bring Peace to the Middle East* (New York: Oxford University Press, 2002), 236n8.

124. Yeshivat Mercaz HaRav Kook, "About Mercaz HaRav," http://www.mercaz.org/about.htm (accessed February 20, 2004).

125. Gopin, *Holy War, Holy Peace,* 43.

126. Shapiro, "Tell It on the Mountain."

127. "Orthodox Zionism," http://www.ucalgary.ca/elsegal/363_Transp/Orthodoxy/Zionism.html (accessed May 12, 2005).

128. Tekoa Israel Home, "Welcome Home to Tekoa," http://tekoa.org.il (accessed February 4, 2004).

129. Ibid.

130. Rabbi Menachem Froman, http://www.oneworld.org/peacequest/stories/Rabbi_Froman.html (accessed September 10, 2003; site now discontinued).

131. Ibid.

132. Cameron W. Barr, "The Leaders Not at Peace Table," *The Christian Science Monitor,* November 8, 2000, http://www.csmonitor.com/2000/1108/p1s1.html (accessed February 19, 2004).

133. Rabbi Menachem Froman, http://www.oneworld.org/peacequest/stories/Rabbi_Froman.html (accessed September 10, 2003; site now discontinued).

134. Rubik Rosenthal, "A Humane Country of the 1949 Lines, Restrctions on Immigration or Equal Settlement: Ideas for the Permanent Settlement," *Ma'ariv,* December 10, 1996.

135. Ibid.

136. Ibid.

137. Eldar, "People & Politics."

138. Herb Keinon, "'Jews Welcome Here,' Hebron Mayor tells Tekoa Rabbi," *The Jerusalem Post,* January 22, 1997, http://www.jpost.com/com/Archive/22.Jan.1997/News/Article-1.html (accessed February 17, 2004).

139. Ibid.

140. Ibid.

141. Joanna Chen, "Middle East: Rabbi with a Cause – An Interview with Rabbi Menachem

Froman," *Newsweek International*, April 16, 2001, http://www.acj.org/april/april_12.htm (accessed February 9, 2004).

142. "Sheikh Yassin, Rabbi Menachem Froman to meet," *arabicnews.com*, October 9, 1997, http://www.arabicnews.com/ansub/daily/day/971009/1997100911.html (accessed February 17, 2004).

143. Haim Shapiro, "Dalai Lama joins interfaith prayer for rain," *The Jerusalem Post*, November 24, 1999, http://www.Tibet.ca/wtnarchive/1999/11/24_2.html (accessed February 19, 2002).

144. Haim Shapiro, "Rabbi Froman: Moslem religious sensitivities must be addressed in peace talks," *The Jerusalem Post*, October 16, 2000, http://www.jpost.com/editions/2000/10/16/news/news.13809.html (accessed February 19, 2002).

145. Ibid.

146. Ibid.

147. Chen, "Middle East."

148. Shapiro, "Tell It on the Mountain."

149. Yair Sheleg, "Chief Rabbi and PA Sheikh Hold Meeting after Approval is Given by Sharon and Arafat," *Haaretz*, April 12, 2001, http://www.kokhavivpublications.com/2001/israel/apr/13/0104130000.html (accessed February 19, 2004).

150. Ibid.

151. Melissa Radler, "World Religious Leaders' Conference Denounces Terror," *The Jerusalem Post*, October 26, 2001, http://www.jpost.com/Editions/2001/10/26/News/News.36997.html (accessed February 17, 2004).

152. Ibid.

153. Ibid.

154. Rabbi Manachem Froman, "Jerusalem: A Vision," *Issues of Our Days*, April 12, 2001, http://www.havurahshirhadash.org/issues6.html (accessed February 6, 2004).

155. Cameron W. Barr, "A West Bank Rabbi Argues for Expanding Settlements," *The Christian Science Monitor*, May 18, 2001, http://search.csmonitor.com/durable/2001/05/18/fp7s1-csm.shtml (accessed February 17, 2004; site now discontinued).

156. Rabbi Menachem Froman, interview with the Tanenbaum Center, December 10, 2003.

157. Radler, "World Religious Leaders' Conference."

158. Ibid.

159. Herb Keinon, "Unanswered Prayers," *The Jerusalem Post*, February 24, 2002, http://www.jpost.com/Editions/2002/01/27/Features/Features.42371.html (accessed February 18, 2004).

160. Yehezkel Landau, *Healing the Holy Land: Interreligious Peacebuilding in Israel/Palestine* (Washington, D.C.: United States Institute of Peace, 2003), 17.

161. Alexandria Summit Signatories: His Grace the Archbishop of Canterbury, Dr. George Carey; his Eminence Sheikh Mohammed Sayed Tantawi, head of Al-Azhar Islamic University, Cairo; Sephardi Chief Rabbi of Israel Eliyahu Bakshi-Doron; Rabbi Michael Melchoir, Deputy Foreign Minister of Israel; Rabbi Menachem Froman, Rabbi of Tekoa; Rabbi David Rosen, President of WCRP; Rabbi David Brodman, Rabbi of Savyon; Rabbi Yitzhak Ralbag, Rabbi of Ma'alot Dafna; Sheikh Taisir Tamimi, Chief Justice of the Palestinian Shari'a Courts; Sheikh Tal Sider, Minister of State for the Palestinian Authority; Sheikh Abdulsalam Abu-Shkedem, Mufti of the Palestinian Armed Forces; Sheikh Taweel, Mufti of Bethlehem; Archbishop Aristarchos, Representative of the Greek Patriarch; His Beatitude Michel Sabbah, the Latin Patriarch; Archbishop Boutros Mualem, the Melkite Archbishop; Archbishop Chinchinian, Representative of the Armenian Patriarch; and The Rt. Rev. Riah Abu El-Assal, the Anglican Bishop of Jerusalem. "The First Alexandria Declaration of the Religious Leaders of the Holy Land," Alexandria, January 21, 2002.

162. Landau, *Healing the Holy Land*, 20.

163. Julie Stahl, "Palestinian Islamic Leaders Want to Be 'Force for Peace,'" *Cybercast News Service*, January 14, 2004, http://www.cnsnews.com/ViewForeignBureaus.asp?Page=%5CforeignBureaus%5Carchiv (accessed February 17, 2004).

164. Rabbi Menachem Froman, http://www.oneworld.org/peacequest/stories/Rabbi_Froman.html (accessed September 10, 2003; site now discontinued).

165. Barr, "The Leaders Not at Peace Table."

166. Landau, *Healing the Holy Land*, 23.

167. Chen, "Middle East."

168. Rabbi Menachem Froman, http://www.oneworld.org/peacequest/stories/Rabbi_Froman.html (accessed September 10, 2003; site now discontinued).

169. Barr, "The Leaders Not at Peace Table."

170. Ibid.

171. Shapiro, "Tell It on the Mountain."

172. Chen, "Middle East."

173. Ibid.

174. Landau, *Healing the Holy Land*, 23.

175. Yehezkel Landau, interview with the Tanenbaum Center, New York, NY, December 4, 2003.

176. Ibid.

177. Ibid.

178. Ibid.

179. Yehezkel Landau, "Peacebuilding in Israel/Palestine: A 25-Year Retrospective," lecture, Washington, D.C., April 8, 2003.

180. Ibid.

181. Ibid.

182. Landau, interview.

183. Yehezkel Landau and Yahya Hendi, "Jews, Muslims and Peace," *Current Dialogue* 41 (June 2003), 12.

184. Ibid., 13.

185. Landau, interview.

186. Yehezkel Landau, "Statement for the Tanenbaum Center," May 10, 2000.

187. Ibid.

188. Ibid.

189. Ibid.

190. Landau, interview.

191. Landau, "Peacebuilding in Israel/Palestine."

192. Landau, interview.

193. Ibid.

194. Landau, "Peacebuilding in Israel/Palestine."

195. Landau, interview.

196. Ibid.

197. Landau, "Statement for the Tanenbaum Center."

198. Landau, "Peacebuilding in Israel/Palestine."

199. Ibid.

200. Ibid.

201. "Open House: A Center of Healing and Hope," *Holy Land Magazine*, Spring 1995, http://www.friendsofopenhouse.org/article7.cfm (accessed September 9, 2005).

202. Landau, "Peacebuilding in Israel/Palestine."

203. Yehezkel Landau, correspondence with the Tanenbaum Center, April 1, 2004.

204. Yehezkel Landau, "Letter from Israel," 2000, http://www.jewishpeacefellowship.org/News1.htm (accessed September 9, 2005).

205. Landau, interview.

206. Ibid.

207. Ibid.

208. Ibid.

209. Ibid.

210. Ibid.

211. Hartford Seminary, "Hartford Seminary Launches New Interfaith training Program, 'Building Abrahamic Partnerships,'" news release, September 4, 2003.

212. Landau, "Statement for the Tanenbaum Center."

213. Ibid.

214. Landau, interview.

215. Landau, "Peacebuilding in Israel/Palestine."

216. Ibid.

217. Ibid.

218. Yehezkel Landau, "A Holistic Peace Process for the Middle East," *Connections*, January 2, 2003.

219. Ibid.

220. Ibid.

221. Ibid.

222. Ibid.

223. Ibid.

224. Yehezkel Landau, "Religious Responses to Atrocity," *Tikkun* 18, no. 5 (Sept./Oct. 2003), 44.

225. Landau, "Peacebuilding in Israel/Palestine."

226. Landau and Hendi, "Jews, Muslims and Peace," 13.

227. "Open House: A Center of Healing and Hope."

228. Yehezkel Landau, "Blessing both Jew and Palestinian: A Religious Zionist View," *The Christian Century* (December 20–27, 1989), 1196, http://www.friendsofopenhouse.org/article6.cfm (accessed September 9, 2005).

229. Landau, interview.

230. Landau, "Statement for the Tanenbaum Center."

231. *CIA World Factbook Online 2006*, http://www.cia.gov/cia/publications/factbook/geos/is.html (accessed April 12, 2006).

232. *CIA World Factbook Online 2006*, http://www.cia.gov/cia/publications/factbook/geos/we.html and http://www.cia.gov/cia/publications/factbook/geos/gz.html (accessed April 12, 2006).

233. State of Israel Central Bureau of Statistics, *Statistical Abstract of Israel Population,*

2.24, http://www1.cbs.gov.il/shnaton56/st02_24.pdf (accessed March 30, 2006).

234. *CIA World Factbook Online 2003*, http://www.cia.gov/cia/publications/factbook/geos/gz.html (accessed March 26th, 2006).

235. *CIA World Factbook Online 2003*, http://www.cia.gov/cia/publications/factbook/geos/we.html (accessed March 26, 2006).

12. Underground Woman: Sakena Yacoobi and the Afghan Institute of Learning

1. *The CIA World Factbook Online*, http://www.cia.gov/cia/publications/factbook/geos/af.html (accessed May 24, 2005).

2. Martin McCauley, *Afghanistan and Central Asia: A Modern History* (London: Pearson Education, 2002), 4.

3. Martin Ewans, *Afghanistan: A Short History of Its People and Politics* (New York: Harper Collins Publishers, 2002), 6.

4. Charles H. Norchi, "Blowback From Afghanistan: The Historical Roots" (working paper, International Security Studies, Yale University, New Haven, 1996), 2.

5. *Wikipedia, s.v.* "History of Afghanistan, Islamic conquest of Afghanistan (642–1747)," http://en.wikipedia.org/wiki/History_of_Afghanistan#Islamic_conquest_of_Afghanistan_.28642–1747.29 (accessed February 5, 2004).

6. Ewans, *Afghanistan*, 12–15.

7. Ibid., 15.

8. Ibid., 16–19.

9. McCauley, *Afghanistan and Central* Asia, 5; Ewans, *Afghanistan*, 26.

10. Ibid., 52.

11. For a more detailed discussion of the rise of Dost Mohammad, see Ewans, 32–61.

12. Ewans, *Afghanistan*, 52.

13. Larry P. Goodson, *Afghanistan's Endless War: State Failure, Regional Politics and the Rise of the Taliban* (Seattle: University of Washington Press, 2001), 33–35.

14. McCauley, *Afghanistan and Central Asia*, 5.

15. Goodson, *Afghanistan's Endless War*, 35.

16. Ewans, *Afghanistan*, 78.

17. Ibid., 78.

18. McCauley, 8–10.

19. Goodson, *Afghanistan's Endless War*, 49.

20. Ibid., 52.

21. Ibid., 52.

22. Goodson, *Afghanistan's Endless War*, 58.

23. McCauley, *Afghanistan and Central Asia*, 16–18.

24. Barnett Rubin, *The Fragmentation of Afghanistan: State Formation and Collapse in the International System* (New Haven: Yale University Press, 2002), 3.

25. McCauley, *Afghanistan and Central Asia*, 20–22.

26. Goodson, *Afghanistan's Endless War*, 104–127.

27. Norchi, "Blowback From Afghanistan," 11.

28. Ibid., 1.

29. Goodson, *Afghanistan's Endless War*, 126.

30. Ibid., 118.

31. Goodson, *Afghanistan's Endless War*, 94.

32. Sakena Yacoobi, phone interview with the Tanenbaum Center, October 17, 2003.

33. Mahnaz Afkhami, "Safe and Secure: Eliminating Violence Against Women and Girls in Muslim Societies." *Sisterhood is Global Institute* (1998), quoted in Sakena Yacoobi, "The Afghan Institute of Learning: Bringing Human Rights Education to Afghan Women," Hurights Osaka, http://www.hurights.or.jp/hreas/7/01Afghan.pdf, 1999 (accessed February 5, 2004).

34. Yacoobi, "The Afghan Institute of Learning," 3–4.

35. Yacoobi, interview.

36. Ibid.

37. Ibid.

38. Ibid.

39. Yacoobi, "The Afghan Institute of Learning," 7.

40. Ibid, 8.

41. Sakena Yacoobi, lecture, Tanenbaum Center's *Peacemakers in Action* Retreat, Amman, Jordan, May 4, 2004.

42. Yacoobi, interview.

43. Ibid.

44. Ibid.

45. Ibid.

46. Ibid.

47. Sakena Yacoobi, brief autobiographical document submitted to the Tanenbaum Center, August 25, 2003.

48. Yacoobi, interview.

49. Ibid.

50. Ibid.

51. *The CIA World Factbook Online*, http://www.cia.gov/cia/publications/factbook/geos/af.html (accessed on April 1, 2006).

13. Toward a Zone of Peace: The Rev. Dr. Benny Giay

1. The First and Original Online Library West Papua, Irian Jaya, "Detailed History," http://www.irja.org/history/papuanhistory.htm (accessed April 13, 2006).

2. BBC World Service, "Case Study: West Papua's Cultural Identity," http://www.bbc.co.uk/worldservice/people/features/ihavearightto/four_b/casestudy_art27.shtml (accessed April 13, 2006).

3. John Ryan, *The Hotland: Focus on New Guinea* (New York: St. Martin's Press, 1969), 5–6.

4. Ibid., 15.

5. Ibid., 19.

6. Australia West Papua Association, "West Papua Information Kit," http://www.cs.utexas.edu/users/cline/papua/intro.htm (accessed August 2, 2005).

7. Ibid.

8. Ibid.

9. Ibid.

10. J. M. Sutherland to D. Murray, "Foreign Office Southeast Asian Department," 30 April, 1968. PRO, FCO UK 15/162 DH1/7, cited in John Saltford, "Irian Jaya: United Nations Involvement with the Act of Self-Determination in West Irian (Indonesian West New Guinea), 1968 to 1969," http://www.angelfire.com/journal/issues/saltford.html (accessed August 2, 2005). For a more extended analysis, see John Saltford, *The United Nations and the Indonesian Takeover of West Papua, 1962–1969: The Anatomy of Betrayal* (London and New York: Routledge Curzon, 2002).

11. Australia West Papua Association, "West Papua Information Kit," http://www.cs.utexas.edu/users/cline/papua/intro.htm (accessed August 2, 2005).

12. Benny Giay, e-mail message to the Tanenbaum Center, March 4, 2004.

13. Benny Giay, phone interview with the Tanenbaum Center, November 16, 2004.

14. Giay, e-mail message.

15. Ibid.

16. Ibid.

17. Ibid.

18. Ibid.

19. Ibid.

20. Giay, phone interview, November 16, 2004.

21. Giay, e-mail message.

22. Ibid.

23. Giay, phone interview, November 16, 2004.

24. Ibid.

25. Ibid.

26. Ibid.

27. Benny Giay, "Zakheus Pakage and His Communities: Indigenous Religious Discourse, Sociopolitical Resistance, and an Ethnohistory of the Me of Irian Jaya" (Ph.D. diss., Department of Cultural Anthropology/Sociology of Development, Free University, Amsterdam, 1995).

28. Ibid.

29. Ibid.

30. Ibid.

31. Ibid.

32. Giay, phone interview, November 16, 2004.

33. Ibid.

34. Human Rights Watch, "Indonesia: Investigate Death of Papuan Leader," November 11, 2001, http://hrw.org/english/docs/2001/11/11/indone3347.htm.

35. Benedetti, "The Murder of Theys Hiyo Eluay, Leader of the Inter-Tribal Council and the PPC," WestPAN: Canada's West Papua Action Network, October 1, 2005, http://www.westpapua.ca/?q=node/123.

36. Benny Giay, phone interview with the Tanenbaum Center, July 9, 2004.

37. Thaha M. Alhamid, "West Papua: Calling for Justice and Peace," October 18, 2002.

38. Benny Giay, e-mail message.

39. Benny Giay, phone interview, July 9, 2004.

40. Brigham Golden, conversation with the Tanenbaum Center, April 21, 2006.

41. Benny Giay, phone interview, November 16, 2004.

42. Benny Giay, e-mail message.

43. Benny Giay, *Menuju Papua Baru: Beberapa Pokok Pikiran Sekitar Emansipasi Orang Papua* (Jayapura: Deiyai/Elsham, 2000).

44. Ibid.

45. Benny Giay, e-mail message.

46. Ibid.

47. Ibid.

48. Ibid.

49. Psalm 72:11–14.

50. Benny Giay, "Towards a New Papua: When They Hear the Sacred Texts of the

Church, Papuans See a Better Future," *Inside Indonesia*, July–September 2001, http://www.insideindonesia.org/edit67/giay.htm.

51. Ibid.

52. Ibid.

53. *CIA World Factbook Online*, http://www.cia.gov/cia/publications/factbook/geos/id.html (accessed April 1, 2006).

54. "Search for West Papua Ambushers," http://news.bbc.co.uk/2/hi/asia-pacific/2230489.stm (accessed October 29, 2004).

55. Prevention, "Building Human Security in Indonesia," Program on Humanitarian Policy and Conflict Research, http://www.preventconflict.org/portal/main/maps_wpapua_background_php (accessed August 23, 2005).

56. *Building Human Security in Indonesia*, s.v. "West Papua/ Irian Jaya," http://www.preventconflict.org/portal/main/maps_wpapua_overview_php (accessed October 29, 2004).

Bibliography

Africa

Earl Conteh-Morgan and Mac Dixon-Fyle, *Sierra Leone at the End of the Twentieth Century: History, Politics and Society* (New York: P. Lang, 1999)

J.E. Flint, ed., *The Cambridge History of Africa,* vol. 5, *c. 1790 c.–1870* (Cambridge: Cambridge University Press, 1976)

Abdel-Fatu Musah and J. Kayode Fayemi, eds., *Mercenaries: An African Security Dilemma* (London: Pluto Press, 2000)

Michael Jackson, *In Sierra Leone* (Durham, NC: Duke University Press, 2004)

The Nigerian Military: A Sociologican Analysis of Authority and Revolt (Cambridge: Cambridge University Press, 1971)

Imam Muhammad Ashafa and Pastor James Wuye, *The Pastor and the Imam – Responding to Conflict* (Lagos: Ibrash Press, 1999)

Leonard Thompson, *A History of South Africa* (New Haven: Yale University Press, 2001)

Ann Lesch, *Sudan: Contested National Identities* (Bloomington: Indiana University Press, 1998)

Francis Mading Deng, *War of Visions: Conflict of Identities in Sudan* (Washington, D.C., Brookings Institution Press, 1995)

P. M. Holt and M. W. Daly, *The History of Sudan: From the Coming of Islam to the Present Day* (London: Weidenfeld and Nicolson)

Gabriel Warburg, *Islam, Nationalism and Communism in a Traditional Society: The Case of Sudan* (London: Totowa: Frank Cass and Company Limited)

Gabriel Warburg, *Islam, Sectarianism and Politics in Sudan since the Mahdiyya* (Madison: The University of Wisconsin Press)

Abdel Salam Sidahmed and Aslir Sidahmed, *Sudan, Contemporary Middle East* (London; New York: Routledge, 2005)

Paul B. Henze, *Layers of Time: A History of Ethiopia* (New York: Palgrave Press, 2000)

Harold G. Marcus, *A History of Ethiopia* (Berkeley: University of California Press, 1994)

David Pool, *Guerillas to Government: The Eritrean People's Liberation Front* (Athens: Ohio University Press, 2001)

Central America

Federal Research Division of the Library of Congress, *El Salvador: A Country Study*, Richard A. Haggarty, ed., Washington, D.C.: U.S. Government Printing Office

Central Asia

Martin McCauley, *Afghanistan and Central Asia: A Modern History* (London: Pearson Education, 2002)

Martin Ewans, *Afghanistan: A Short History of Its People and Politics* (New York: Harper Collins Publishers, 2002)

Larry P. Goodson, *Afghanistan's Endless War: State Failure, Regional Politics and the Rise of the Taliban* (Seattle: University of Washington Press, 2001)

Barnett Rubin, *The Fragmentation of Afghanistan: State Formation and Collapse in the International System* (New Haven: Yale University Press, 2002)

Barnett Rubin, *The Search for Peace in Afghanistan: From Buffer State to Failed State* (New Haven: Yale University Press, 1995)

Amin Saikal, *Modern Afghanistan: A History of Struggle and Survival* (New York: I.B. Tauris, 2004)

Conflict Resolution

R. Scott Appleby, *The Ambivalence of the Sacred: Religion, Violence, and Reconciliation* (New York: Rowman & Littlefield Publishers, Inc., 1999)

Kevin Avruch, Peter W. Black, and Joseph A. Scimecca, eds., *Conflict Resolution: Cross-Cultural Perspectives* (New York: Greenwood Press, 1991)

J. I. Coffey and Charles T. Mathewes, eds., *Religion, Law and the Role of Force: A Study of Their Influence on Conflict and on Conflict Resolution* (Ardsley, NY: Transnational Publishers, 2002)

Marc Gopin, *Between Eden and Armageddon: The Future of World Religions, Violence, and Peacemaking* (New York: Oxford University Press, 2000)

Martin E Marty and R. Scott Appleby, eds., *Religion, Ethnicity, and Self-Identity: Nations in Turmoil* (Hanover, NH: University Press of New England, 1997)

Eugene Weiner, ed., *The Handbook of Interethnic Coexistence* (New York: Continuum Publishing Group, 1998)

East Asia

John Ryan, *The Hot Land: Focus on New Guinea* (New York: St. Martin's Press, 1969)

Ress Yassin, ed., *Irian Jaya: The Land of Challenges and Promises* (Jakarta: Laksmi Studio, 1987)

Eastern Europe

Noel Malcom, *Bosnia: A Short History* (London: Macmillan, 1994)

Noel Malcolm, *Kosovo: A Short History* (New York: Harper Perennial, 1999)

Khurshid Ahmad, ed., *Islam: Its Meaning and Message* (Leicester: The Islamic Foundation, 1980)

Neven Andjelic, *Bosnia-Herzegovina: The End of a Legacy* (London: Frank Cass, 2003)

Middle East

Mark Tessler, *A History of the Israeli-Palestinian Conflict* (Bloomington: Indiana University Press, 1994)

Mitchell Cohen, *Zion and State: Nation, Class and the Shaping of Modern Israel* (New York: Columbia University Press, 1992)

Michael J. Cohen, *The Origins and Evolution of the Arab-Zionist Conflict* (University of California Press, 1987)

Rabbi Joseph Telushkin, *Jewish Literacy: The Most Important Things to Know About the Jewish Religion, Its People and Its History* (New York: William Morrow and Company, Inc., 1991)

Donna E. Arzt, *Refugees Into Citizens: Palestinians and the End of the Arab-Israeli Conflict* (New York: Council on Foreign Relations, Inc., 1997)

Arthur Goldschmidt, Jr., *A Concise History of the Middle East* (Boulder, CO: Westview Press, 1996)

Baruch Kimmerling, *The Palestinian People: A History* (Cambridge, MA: Harvard University Press, 2003)

R. A. S. Macalister, *A History of Civilization in Palestine* (New York, G.P. Putnam's Sons, 1912)

Michael Oren, *Six Days of War: June 1967 and the Making of the Modern Middle East* (New York: Oxford University Press, 2002)

Thomas Friedman, *From Beirut to Jerusalem* (New York: Farrar, Straus, Giroux, 1989)

David Grossman, *The Yellow Wind* (New York: Noonday Press, 1998)

Marc Gopin, *Holy War, Holy Peace: How Religion Can Bring Peace to the Middle East* (New York: Oxford University Press, 2002)

Religion

Abdulaziz Sachedina, *The Islamic Roots of Democratic Pluralism* (New York: Oxford University Press, 2001)

Western Europe

Peter Fry and Fiona Somerset Fry, *A History of Ireland* (Oxford and New York: Routledge)

Mike Cronin, *A History of Ireland* (London: Palgrave Press, 2001)

R. F. Foster, *Modern Ireland, 1600–1972* (London: Penguin Press, 1988)

Patrick Geoghegan, "Act of Union," *The Encyclopedia of Ireland*, ed. Brian Lalor (New Haven: Yale University Press, 2003)

Paul Bew and Gordon Gillespie, *Northern Ireland: A Chronology of the Troubles 1968–1999* (Dublin: Gill and Macmillan, 1999)

Thomas Hennessey, *A History of Northern Ireland, 1920–1996* (Ireland: Macmillan Press, 1997)

Ilan Pappe, *A History of Modern Palestine: One Land, Two Peoples* (Cambridge; New York: Cambridge University Press, 2004)

Jacob de Haas, *History of Palestine: The Last Two Thousand Years* (New York: Macmillan, 1934)

Elias Chacour and Mary E. Jensen, *We Belong to the Land: The Story of a Palestinian Israeli who Lives for Peace and Reconciliation* (San Francisco: Harper Collins, 1990)

Elias Chacour, *Blood Brothers* (Grand Rapids, MI: Chosen Books, 2003)

Index

Abacha, General Sani, 254
Abbas, Mahmud, 320
Abd-Rabbo, Yasser, 319
Abdullah, Crown Prince, 319
Abidjan Peace Accord, 285–6
Abiola, Chief Moshood, 254
Abrahamic Faiths. *See specific denominations by name*
Abuja Agreements, 298
Academic Associate Peace Work (AAPW), 264, 267
Aceh, Indonesia, 402
"Act of Free Choice", 405, 413
Action Group (NG), 251
Ad Hoc Ethiopian Peace Committee (AHPC), 164–70, 171. *See also* elders as peacemaker tool
Adams, Gerry. *See also* Sinn Féin
  Hume and, 71–2, 73, 74, 77
  Mansergh and, 71, 72–3, 74, 77
  on Reid, 65–6, 77, 79
Addis Ababa Accord of Sudan (1972), 191–2
Addis Ababa Peace and Democracy Conference (1991), 169–70
Adifaris, Assefa, 164
Afghan Communist Party (PDPA), 387, 400
Afghan Institute of Learning (AIL). *See also* Yacoobi, Sakena
  boys' education, 395–6
  "Guide to Teaching Human Rights in the Afghan Classroom" (AIL), 393–4
  overview of, 13–14, 382, 391–6, 397

teaching methods and strategy of, 393–5
Afghanistan, 398–9. *See also* Taliban; Yacoobi, Sakena
  9/11 and, 382, 388, 389, 400
  Afghan Communist Party (PDPA), 387, 400
  al-Qaeda within, 388
  Anglo-Afghan War, 385–6
  anti-American sentiment within, 388
  Bin Laden sheltered by, 388
  demographics of, 383, 399–400
  economic overview of, 401
  fact sheet, 399–401
  fifth century BCE through late 19th centuries, 384–5
  geography of, 382–3, 399
  Great Britain and, 385–6
  historical overview of conflict, 382–3, 400–1
  India and, 386
  Islam within, 383, 384
  isolationism of, 385, 386
  Kabul, 384
  Karzai, Hamid, 401
  madrasas, 387
  mujahedin, 387
  National Assembly, 401. *See also* Karzai, Hamid
  Northern Alliance, 382, 388–9
  Soviet Union and, 386, 387
  U.S. and, 387, 388
  U.S. invasion of, 382, 389, 400
  Western imperialism vs., 385

475

Afkhami, Mahnaz, 391
AFRC (Armed Forces Revolution
    Council), 286
African Women's Peace Table, 235
Afrikaners, 216, 217, 219, 220. *See also*
    Boers; Nationalist Party of South
    Africa
agreement-making by peacemakers,
    443–4, 445–7
Ahmad Shah, 384–5
AHPC. *See* Ad Hoc Ethiopian Peace
    Committee
AIDS, 235
AIL. *See* Afghan Institute of Learning
Aksumite Empire, 152
Alas, José "Chencho", 31–49. *See also* El
    Salvador
    abduction of, 34–5
    alliances created by, 39–40
    Bible as peacemaker tool of, 25, 32, 34,
        46
    campesinos and, 32–3
    Chavez y Gonzalez, Archbishop Luis,
        25, 31, 33, 34–5
    community leaders trained by, 34
    Cursillo Movement founded by, 31–2
    exile of, 41–3
    Foundation for Self-Sufficiency in
        Central America, 47
    Institute for Technology, Environment
        and Self-Sufficiency, 44
    interfaith mobilization by, 47–8
    land reform focus of, 25
    Lempa River project, 38–9, 44
    Mesoamerican Peace Project, 47,
        48–9
    National Teacher's Strike, 35–7
    overview of, 25–6
    peacekeeping efforts by, 443
    priesthood left by, 43, 47–8
    pulpit as peacemaker tool, 11
    religious training of, 31–2
    as religiously motivated peacemaker,
        47–9
    risks taken for peacemaking, 434,
        435
    sermons as peacemaker tool of, 36
    Suchitoto, as priest of, 32–41
    Vatican II, effect upon, 30

    writings by, 14, 46–7, 48–9
    Zone of Peace and, 15, 25–6, 44–7
Albania. *See* Kosovo
Albright, Madeline, 137, 138
Alcalay, Rabbi Yehuda, 305
Alexander the Great, 303, 384
Alexandria Summit and Declaration,
    352–3
Algiers Peace Agreement, 176
All People's Congress (APC), 282–3
Alomang, Yosepha, 418
al-Qaeda, 388. *See also* Bin Laden,
    Osama; September 11, 2001
Alternative Peace Initiative (API), 112
Aman, General, 156
Amanullah Khan, 386
American nuns in El Salvador, 42
Amir, Yigal, 354
ANC (African National Congress). *See also*
    Mandela, Nelson
    armed struggle adopted by, 227
    ban against, 221, 224
    colonialism vs., 219
    Democratic Party and, 225
    founding of, 219
    Madlala-Routledge, Nozizwe and, 227,
        229
    PAC, split from, 221
    as Pan African Association, 219
    passive resistance by, 221
    post-apartheid era, 224, 225
    United Democratic Front (UDF), 222–3,
        227, 231
    United Party of South Africa, 220
    youth leagues, 220
Anglo-Afghan War, 385–6
Anglo-Irish Agreement (1985), 67–73,
    95
Anglo-Irish Treaty (1921), 58
Annan, Kofi, 3
Antiochus, King IV, 303
apartheid, 220, 221, 222–3, 224. *See also*
    South Africa
APC (All People's Congress), 282–3
API (Alternative Peace Initiative), 112
Appleby, R. Scott, 54
Apprentice Boys, 59
al-Aqsa Mosque, 304, 314, 319
The Arab League, 309, 319

"Arab Revolt" (1936), 308
Arafat, Chairman Yasser. *See also*
    Palestinian Authority
  as Chairman of Palestinian Authority,
    317–19
  death of, 320
  Froman and, 6, 342, 349–50, 356
  Oslo agreements and, 316, 318–19
Araujo, Arturo, 28–9
Armed Forces Revolution Council
    (AFRC), 286
Artemije, Bishop, 129, 131, 137, 138, 141
Arusha, 236
Ashafa, Imam Muhammad. *See also*
    Nigeria; Wuye, Pastor James
  debate as peacemaking tool, 12–13
  institution-and-capacity building by,
    445
  Interfaith Mediation Centre, 12–13,
    247–8
  as Kaduna native, 255
  Kaduna Peace Agreement and, 14, 272
  on manipulation of religion for
    violence, 430
  media as peacemaking partner, 267–8
  militant organizations, contact with,
    268–9
  as militant youth activist, 259–61
  Muslim-Christian Dialogue Forum
    (MCDF), 247–8, 264–9, 270, 271,
    272–3, 432
  Muslim-Christian Youth Dialogue
    Forum (MCYDF), 263–4
  National Council of Muslim Youth
    Organizations (NACOMYO), 260, 263
  overview of, 247–8, 432
  peacemakers trained by, 267
  personal awareness of, 8
  Qur'an as peacemaker tool of, 266, 267
  religious background, 262–3
  religious motivation for peacemaking,
    269–70
  secular peacemaking tools adapted by,
    18–19
  status as religious leaders, 271
  threats to religiously-motivated
    peacemaking, 270–2
  Wuye, Pastor James, becoming brothers
    with, 261–4

Zangon Kataf reconciliation efforts,
    265–6
Ashkenazi, Dalia, 358, 362, 363, 365, 367,
    369
Assab, 157
Austro-Hungarian Empire, 98
Azikiwe, Benjamin Nnamdi, 252

Babangida, General, 253–4
Babur, 384
Babylonians, 303
Baker, James, 333
Bakshi-Doron, Chief Rabbi Eliyahu,
    349–50, 353
Balfour Declaration, 306, 307, 308
Balkan War (1912), 125
Balkans. *See* Bosnia and Herzegovina
Ballestas, Ricardo Esquivia, 6
Bambayi riots, 230
Barak, Ehud, 318–19
Barrios, President, 27
al-Bashir, Omar Hassan, 209
Basotholand, 217–18, 228–30
Basque region, 19
Battle of Blood River, 217
The Beatitudes. *See* Sermon on the Mount
Begin, Menachem, 313, 315
Beilin, Yossi, 319
Belay, Dr. Haile Salassie, 168, 170–1
Belfast, 56–7. *See also* Ulster
Belfast Agreement (Good Friday
    Agreement), 53, 72, 73–82, 95
Berom people, 272
Besrat, Kassahun, 164
Bible as peacemaker tool. *See also*
    Christians and Christianity; Judaism;
    Qur'an
  Chacour, 323–4, 338–40
  Froman, 341–2, 346, 350, 351–2, 354
  Giay, 420–1
  Isaac, 161–2
  Janjic, 146
  Landau, 357, 363, 370, 373–4
  Lowrey, 207–8
  Madlala-Routledge, 239
  Magee, 84–5
  Wuye, 266, 267, 270
Biko, Steve, 222, 226
Bin Laden, Osama, 382, 388, 389, 400

Bio, Brigadier-General Julius Maada, 285

Biram, Palestine, 322, 331

birr, 174

Black Consciousness movement of South Africa, 222

Blood Brothers (Chacour), 336–7

Bloody Friday, 61

Bloody Sunday, 60–1

"blowback" theory, 388

Blue Nile, 152

Boers, 216, 217, 218, 245. *See also* Dutch colonialism

Bogside riots, 59

Bosnia and Herzegovina, 97–119. *See also* Markovic, Friar Ivo; Yugoslavia
  Balkan War (1912), 125
  Bosniak/Croat Federation, creation of, 121, 122
  Bosniaks, 121
  Bosnian Franciscan community, 108–9, 118
  Bosnian independence movement, 101–2
  Communist Yugoslavia, 99–100
  Croatia, 101, 104
  current entities of, 106
  Dayton Peace Agreement, 106, 121–2, 128, 149, 236
  demographics of, 101, 121
  disintegration of Yugoslavia, 100–1
  economic overview, 122
  EUFOR, 106, 122
  Greater Serbia, goals of, 121
  historical overview of conflict, 97, 98, 121
  independence, declarations of, 101–2
  independence, war for, 102–4
  legitimization of violence by religion, 106, 107–8, 115
  media in, 113–14
  NATO campaign, 106, 122, 442–3
  Republika Srpska (RS), 122
  Sarajevo, battle for, 103
  Slovenia, 101
  U.S. and, 104, 105, 106, 121–2, 128, 149, 236

Vance-Owen peace plan, 104, 105
  World Wars and, 99
  Yugoslav People's Army (JNA), 101, 102–3

Bosque, Pio Romero, 28

Botha, Louis, 218

Botha, Pieter Willem, 222–3

Bradford, Rev. Robert, 63–4

Brcko Districk, 106. *See also* Bosnia and Herzegovina

Britain. *See* Great Britain

British Council, 264

Broek, Father Theo Van den, 414, 418

B'Tselem, 318

Buddhism, 383

buildings, religious, 11

Bulgaria, 125

Burundi, 273

Bush, George W., 319–20, 354

"Bushmen" of South Africa, 215

Byzantine Empire, 98

CAMA (Compassion and Missionary Associates), 407–8

Cameroons (NCNC), 251

Camp David Accords (1978), 315

Camp David Summit (2000), 318–19

campesinos, 27, 32–3

Cape Colony, 218

Carey, George, 354

Carter, Jimmy, 105, 163

Casas, Bartholomew de las, 26

case studies as peacemaking technique, 391–2. *See also* storytelling as peacemaking technique

Catholic Church. *See also* Christians and Christianity
  Maronites,
  Melkites, 322, 323
  Second Vatican Council, 30, 32

Causaus y Torres, Bishop, 27

Caux, Switzerland, 167, 168

Central America. *See also specific countries by name*
  FSSCA (Foundation for Self-Sufficiency in Central America), 47
  as a zone of peace, 45–7

Chacour, Abuna Elias, 321–41. *See also*
    Israeli-Palestinian Conflict
1967 Six-Day War and, 330
background and religious upbringing,
    325
Bible as peacemaker tool of, 323–4,
    338–40
Blood Brothers written by, 336–7
components of identity of, 321–2
dialogue as peacemaking tool, 334–5,
    338–9
education used as peacemaker tool by,
    13–14, 331. *See also* MEEI
evolution of a peacemaker, 325–7
expulsion from home, 323
Galilee ministry and commitment to
    the Church, 327–32
Hebrew University, march on Knesset
    from, 331
Hebrew University studies of, 330
institution-and-capacity building by,
    444
interfaith mobilization by, 329–30, 333,
    337
international involvement in
    peacemaking, 336–8
kidnapping of, 332
on "living stones", 337
on manipulation of religion for
    violence, 430, 434
Mar Elias Educational Institution
    (MEEI), 13, 332–6, 341
Melkite Catholic Church and, 322, 323
overview of, 431
reflections on peacemaking methods,
    338–9
religious motivation for peacemaking,
    9, 324, 339–40
Chad, 213
Chavez y Gonzalez, Archbishop Luis, 25,
    31, 33, 34–5
"Chencho". *See* Alas, José "Chencho"
Christian Association of Nigeria (CAN),
    268, 269
Christian Association of Nigeria, Youth
    Wing (Youth CAN), 260, 263
Christian Council of Churches Sierra
    Leone, 279, 296–8

Christian Democratic Party of El
    Salvador, 29–30
Christian Maronites, 322
Christian Sisters, 329
Christians and Christianity. *See* Bible as
    peacemaker tool; Jesus Christ;
    Second Vatican Council; *specific
    denominations by name*
Church of the Holy Sepulcher, 314
Church World Service, 297–8
citizen diplomacy. *See* Track Two
    diplomacy
Clinton, Bill, 316, 318–19
Clonard Monastery, 59
Coalition of Ethiopian Democratic Forces
    (COEDF), 169
CODESA (Convention for a Democratic
    South Africa), 224
Cohen, Herman, 168, 177
Cold War, 356–7
Colony of Natal, 218
Combined Loyalist Military Command, 80
Committee for Ethiopian Literacy, 163
Communism. *See* Cold War; Soviet Union
community leaders
    Alas, trained by, 34
    elders as, 12, 151, 173–4, 175, 177, 182,
        193–4. *See also* Ad Hoc Ethiopian
        Peace Committee
    peacemakers as, 5
Compassion and Missionary Associates
    (CAMA), 407–8
Comprehensive Peace Agreement of
    Sudan, 187
Congress Alliance of South Africa, 221
Conteh-Morgan, Earl, 280
Convention for a Democratic South Africa
    (CODESA), 224
Coordinadora del Bajo Lempa, 44–7
Council of Chalcedon, 322
Council of Church's Relief and
    Rehabilitation Department, 287
Craig, William, 63
Creoles, 279, 280–2
criollos, 27
Croatia, 101, 104. *See also* Bosnia and
    Herzegovina
Cuban Missile Crisis, 356–7

cultural rituals and traditions as
peacemaker tools, 11–12, 19, 200,
202–3, 204, 208. *See also* elders as
peacemaker tool
cultures of peace. *See* Zone of Peace
Cursillo Movement, 31–2
"The Cybermonk". *See* Janjic, Father Sava
Cyrus, King, 303

Dalai Lama, H.H., 348
Dang, Telar, 210–11
Danhier, Nyuong, 202
Daoud, Mohammed, 387
Darfur, 186, 195, 210, 213. *See also* Sudan
Darius the Great, 384
David, King,
Dayan, Moshe, 315
Dayton Peace Agreement, 106, 121–2,
128, 149, 236
DDR (disarmament, demobilization, and
reintegration) program, 298
de Klerk, Frederik Willem, 224, 230–1
debate as peacemaker tool, 12–13
Decani Monastery, 128–9, 131–3, 135. *See
also* Janjic, Father Sava
"Declaration on the Future of Serbia",
137
Dejic, Father Vasilije, 139
Democratic Opposition of Serbia (DOS),
150
Democratic Party of South Africa, 225
Democratic Unionist Party (DUP), 95
Deng, Francis, 188
Dengel, Emperor Lebna, 153
Derg, the, 155–6, 166–9, 184. *See also*
Mengistu Haile-Mariam
Dhimmitude, 124–5
Dingane (Zulu warrior), 217
Dinka peoples of Sudan, 214. *See also*
Lowrey, Rev. Dr. William;
People-to-People Peace Process
Nuer-Dinka Chiefs and Church Leaders
Reconciliation Conference, 199
overview of conflict the Nuer, 194,
195
SPLM/A composed of, 192
Wunlit Dinka-Nuer West Bank Peace
and Reconciliation Conference,
200

Diplomacy. *See* Track One diplomacy;
Track Two diplomacy
Dixon-Fyle, Mac, 280
Dome of the Rock, 304, 314. *See also*
Al-Aqsa Mosque
DOS (Democratic Opposition of Serbia),
150
Dost Mohamed Khan, 385
Downing Street Declaration, 76–7
DUP (Democratic Unionist Party), 95
Durand Line, 386
Durrani dynasty, 384–5
Dutch colonialism. *See* Netherlands, The
Dutch East India Company, 216

East Jerusalem. *See* Jerusalem
East Timor, 402, 426
ECOMOG, 286
Ecuador, 32
educational initiatives by peacemakers,
13–14. *See also* Afghan Institute of
Learning; Mar Elias Educational
Institution
Egypt
1948 War with Israel, 311
1967 Six-Day War, 312
Camp David Accords, 315
Israel, ceasefire with, 313
Jordan, Iraq and, 312
Mamelukes, 304, 305
Sinai Campaign, 311
Straits of Tiran, 311, 312
Sudan and, 188, 189–91
Suez Canal, 311
War of Attrition, 314–15
Yom Kippur War,
El Salvador, 25–49. *See also* Alas, José
"Chencho"
Catholic Church within, 26, 27, 29, 31
death squads, 30–1, 35
economy and demographics, 27–8, 31,
43, 52
fact sheet, 50
Football War, 30
historical overview of conflict, 26–7,
51
independence of, 27–8
Lowrey, Rev. Dr. William in, 197
National Teacher's Strike (1971), 35–7

U.S. involvement in, 43, 51
U.S. nuns in El Salvador, violence
    against, 42
violence against activists, 40–1
elders as peacemaker tool, 12, 151, 173–4,
    175, 177, 182, 193–4. *See also* Ad Hoc
    Ethiopian Peace Committee; rituals
    as peacemaker tools
ELF (Eritrea Liberation Front), 155
Elizabeth, Queen (of England), 55
ELSHAM (Institute for Human Rights
    Studies and Advocacy), 409
Eluay, Theus, 413, 414–15
e-mail as peacemaker tool. *See* Janjic,
    Father Sava
emotional intelligence of peacemakers,
    7–8
empathetic detachment of peacemakers.
    See neutrality of peacemakers
Empey, Reg, 63
encomienda, 26
England. *See* Great Britain
Epistle of James, 196. *See also* Bible as
    peacemaker tool
EPLF. *See* Eritrean People's Liberation
    Front
EPRDF. *See* Ethiopian People's
    Revolutionary Democratic Front
Eritrea, 151
    Addis Ababa Peace and Democracy
        Conference and, 169
    currency conflict, 174–5
    Eritrea Liberation Front (ELF),
        155
    Eritrean People's Liberation Front
        (EPLF), 155, 156, 163–4, 168
    historical overview of conflict, 184
    Italy and, 154, 155
    Mengistu, fall of, 156–7
    national identity within Ethiopia,
        153–4
    postindependence disputes and
        reconciliation, 174–6
    referendum for independence, 174
    Selassie and, 155
Eshkol, Levi, 312
ETA (Basque region), 19
Ethiopia, 182–3. *See also* Isaac,
    Dr. Ephraim

Addis Ababa Peace and Democracy
    Conference and, 169–70
constitution, 173
currency conflict, 174–5
Derg, the, 155–6, 166–9, 184
early history of, 152–3
economic overview of, 184–5
elders as peacemaker tool in, 12, 151,
    173–4, 175, 177, 182. *See also* Ad Hoc
    Ethiopian Peace Committee
Eritrean identity within, 153–4
Ethiopian Coalition, 166, 169. *See also*
    Ethiopian People's Revolutionary
    Democratic Front
Ethiopian Jews, 166–8, 177
Ethiopian Orthodox Christianity,
    152–4
Ethiopian Orthodox Church, 170
Ethiopian People's Revolutionary
    Democratic Front (EPRDF), 156–7,
    168, 169, 184
Ethiopian People's Revolutionary Party
    (EPRP), 156
Ethiopian Socialist Party (MEISON),
    156, 169
fact sheet, 183–4
fall of Mengistu and, 156–7
famine of 1973–74, 155
historical overview of conflict, 151
international involvement in
    peacemaking, 176
Islam, beginnings of within, 153–4
Italian and, 154–5, 160
overview of, 151–2
port access of, 157
post-Eritrean independence disputes
    and reconciliation, 174–6
recent background, 184
Red Terror, 156
referendum for Eritrean independence
    and, 174
Selassie, Emperor Haile I, 154–5
separation of church and state, 173
socialist regime (1974–1989), 155–6
Sudanese People's Liberation
    Movement/Army (SPLM/A), aid to,
    192
ethnic cleansing. *See* Bosnia and
    Herzegovina; Kosovo

European Union (EU)
  in Bosnia and Herzegovina, 104, 105,
    106, 122
  in Ethiopia, 179–80
  EUFOR (European Union
    peacekeepers), 106, 122
Evangelical Church of West Papua. *See
  also* Giay, The Reverend Benny
  CAMA (Compassion and Missionary
    Associates), 407–8
  Educational Foundation for the
    Indonesian Evangelical Church, 412
  ELSHAM (Institute for Human Rights
    Studies and Advocacy), 409
  failures of, 408, 419
  human rights violations addressed by,
    409
Eynde, Johan van den, 414

Face to Face. *See* Oci u Oci Interreligious
    Service
faith as motivator. *See* religious
    motivation for peacemaking
Fanous, Michail, 362
FAPU (United Popular Action Front),
    39–40
Farabundo Martí National Liberation
    Front (FMLN), 51
Faraj (friend of Abuna Elias Chacour),
    326
Fasilides, Emperor, 153
Fatah, 317. *See also* Palestinian Authority
Federal Democratic Republic of Ethiopia.
    See Ethiopia
Federal Units of Yugoslavia, 128
Federated Socialist Republic of
    Yugoslavia, 99. *See also* Yugoslavia
Federation of Bosnia and Herzegovina,
    106. *See also* Bosnia and Herzegovina
fellaheen, 305–6
Ferdinand, Archduke Franz, 99,
    125–6
Fianna Fail. *See* Haughey, Charles;
    Mansergh, Dr. Martin
First *Intifada*, 316–17, 344–5
Flight of the Earls, 55
FMLN (Farabundo Martí National
    Liberation Front), 51
Football War, 30

Forum for Reconciliation of Irian Society
    (FORERI), 412, 416
Foundation for Self-Sufficiency in Central
    America (FSSCA), 47
France, 154, 189, 306, 311
Franciscan Church. *See* Markovic, Friar
    Ivo
Frazier, Robert, 167, 168, 177
Free Papua Movement (OPM), 404–5,
    413, 414
Freeport Mining Company, 406, 408
Freetown, Sierra Leone, 280. *See also*
    Sierra Leone
Froman, Rabbi Menachem, 341–56. *See
    also* Israeli-Palestinian Conflict
  advocacy for the "other", 348–52
  Alexandria Summit and Declaration,
    352–3
  Arafat meetings, 6, 342, 349–50, 356
  background, 342–5
  Bible as peacemaker tool of, 341–2, 346,
    350, 351–2, 354
  as community member, 6
  dialogue as peacemaking tool of, 355
  grassroots peacemaking by, 345–8
  hudna (ceasefire) proposal, 352
  humane state (*medina enoshit*)
    proposal, 345, 346, 350–1
  interfaith mobilization by, 16, 347–8,
    349–50, 352–3, 355, 356
  on Jerusalem, 350–1
  joint committee of sheikhs and rabbis
    proposal, 349–50
  on media, 355
  overview of peacemaking efforts, 341–2
  peacemaking via interreligious
    conferences, 352–3
  reflections on peacemaking methods,
    354–5
  on religious figures within the peace
    process, 442
  religiously motivated peacemaking of,
    355–6
  on Western leaders, 354
  on Zionism, 351
FSSCA (Foundation for Self-Sufficiency
    in Central America), 47
Fulani people, 248, 249, 250, 251, 255–7,
    272

Gabur, Abdul, 421
Gaelic population of Ireland, 55
Galawdewos, Negus of Ethiopia, 153
Galilee, 327–9, 330, 332
Gandhi, Mohandas, 228, 232, 238
Garang, Bishop Nathaniel, 203
Garang, John, 192, 209–10, 214. *See also* SPLM/A
Gaza. *See* Palestine and Palestinians
Gelbard, Robert S., 131
Genesis. *See* Bible as peacemaker tool
Geneva Accords (2003), 302, 319–20
Geneva Conventions (1949), 318
Genghis Khan, 384
George III, King (of England), 57
Germany, 403
Ghaznavids, 384
Giay, The Reverend Benny. *See also* West Papua
  background of, 406–22
  Belgian filmmakers' abduction and, 414
  Bible as peacemaker tool of, 420–1
  on CAMA (Compassion and Missionary Associates), 407–8
  case study of, 402–3
  on Church failures, 407–8, 419
  education, commitment to, 417–19
  Educational Foundation for the Indonesian Evangelical Church, 412
  ELSHAM (Institute for Human Rights Studies and Advocacy), 409
  evolution of a peacemaker, 402–3, 410–15
  Forum for Reconciliation of Irian Society (FORERI), 412
  global community as peacemaking tool, 17–18
  on heroes, 418
  Institute for Social and Pastoral Studies, 418–19
  interreligious and intercultural respect of, 440
  papers and books written by, 410–12, 417, 418, 421
  as Papua Peace Commission director, 416
  as Papuan Presidium Council member, 413
  reflections on peacemaking methods, 419–21
  religious motivation for peacemaking, 9, 406–7
  risks taken for peacemaking, 402, 410, 412, 414, 434–5
  Special Autonomy Rule for Papua, 412–13
  storytelling as technique of, 418
  S.T.T. Walter Post Theological Seminary, 408–9
  Tanenbaum Center's Peacemaker in Action award received by, 422
  zones of peace and, 15, 402, 416–17, 420
girls' education. *See* Afghan Institute of Learning
global community as peacemaker tool, 17–18. *See also* European Union; NATO; *specific countries by name*; United Nations
Golan Heights, 313
Goldstein, Baruch, 354
Good Friday Agreement (Belfast Agreement), 14, 53, 61, 72, 73–82, 95
Gospel. *See* New Testament
Gowon, General, 252–3
Grande, Fr. Rutilio, 40–1
Great Britain. *See also* Ireland, Northern
  Afghanistan and, 385–6
  India and, 386–7
  New Guinea and, 403
  Nigeria and, 249–50, 255–6
  Northern Ireland and, 54–6, 58, 59, 60–1, 63, 95
  Palestine and, 306–9, 310
  "regional stability" policy of, 154
  Sierra Leone and, 280, 300
  South Africa and, 216–18, 221, 245
  Sudan and, 154, 155, 190–1, 193
  Suez Canal and, 311
Great Depression, 219
Greater Serbia, 121, 149. *See also* Bosnia and Herzegovina; Serbia and Montenegro
Greece, 125, 303
Group Areas Act of South Africa, 220–1
group belonging vs. personal faith of peacemakers, 116

"Guide to Teaching Human Rights in the
    Afghan Classroom" (AIL), 393–4
Guidebook for Peacemakers (Alas), 46–7
Gul, Pari, 393
Gulf War (1990–1991), 362–3
Gumede, Archibald, 227
Gush Emunim, 361–2

Haganah, 308, 309, 310
The Hague, 176
Halevi, Yossi Klein, 374
Hamas, 320–1
Hamiti, Xhabir, 143
al-Haram al-Sharif (Temple Mount), 314
Hashemi family, 307
Haughey, Charles, 67, 71, 72
Hausa people, 248–9, 250, 251, 255–7
Heath, Edward, 61, 63
Hebrew Scripture. *See* Bible as
    peacemaker tool
Hebrew University, 330, 331
Hebrews. *See* Judaism
Henry VIII, King (of England), 55
Herceg-Bosna, 104. *See also* Bosnia and
    Herzegovina
hermeneutics of peace, 438
Hernandez, General Maximiliano, 29
Herzegovina. *See* Bosnia and Herzegovina
Herzl, Theodore, 305, 343
Hindu Kush Mountains, 382–3
Hinduism, 383
HIV/AIDS, 235
Hobbes, Thomas, 160
Hock, Klaus, 269, 460
Holland, Mary, 73
Holocaust, the, 186, 195, 309
Holy Spirit, 79. *See also* Jesus Christ
"homelands" of South Africa, 221, 223
Honduras, 30
"Hottentots" of South Africa, 215
hudna for Israeli-Palestinian conflict, 352
Hughes, Brendan, 65
Huguenots in South Africa, 216
humane state (*medina enoshit*), 345, 346,
    350–1
Hume, John, 53, 71–2, 73, 74, 77
Hungary, Kingdom of, 98
hunger strikes during The Troubles, 65–6

Hussein, Sharif, 306
el-Husseini, Abd el-Kader, 310
Husseini family, 308
Hut Tax War of 1898, 282

Ibillin, Galilee, 328–9, 330, 332
Ibo people, 248, 251, 252
IDF (Israel Defense Forces),
IFOR (NATO-led Implementation Force)
    in Bosnia, 122
IGAD (Intergovernmental Authority on
    Development), 209–10, 214
Ihejirika, Sam, 264, 461
IMF (International Monetary Fund), 283
India, 386
indigenous beliefs, 11–12. *See also* elders
    as peacemaker tool; rituals as
    peacemaker tools
Indonesia. *See also* West Papua
    Aceh, 402
    colonialization of, 425
    East Timor, secession from, 402, 426
    economic overview of, 426
    New Guinea, 403, 404
    Papuans, intra-conflict of, 402
    parliamentary delegation sent to Papua,
        421
    Republic of Indonesia, creation of, 404
    West Papua emigration, 425
Industrial and Commercial Workers'
    Union of South Africa, 219
Inkatha movement, 223, 229, 230
"insider-partial", 206–7
Institute for Social and Pastoral Studies,
    418–19
Institute for Technology, Environment
    and Self-Sufficiency (the "Institute"),
    44
institution-and-capacity building by
    peacemakers, 443, 444–5
intellect of peacemakers, 8
intelligence, emotional, 7–8
Interfaith Mediation Centre, 12–13,
    247–8. *See also* Ashafa, Imam
    Muhammad; Wuye, Pastor James
interfaith mobilization
    Alas, 47–8
    Chacour, 329–30, 333, 337

Froman, 347–8, 349–50, 352–3, 355, 356
Janjic, 133–4, 138
Landau, 371
Madlala-Routledge, 239
as peacemaker tools, 16
Reid, 86–7
Interfaith Prayer Day (Ethiopia), 172
Intergovernmental Authority on
    Development (IGAD), 209–10, 214
Interim Agreement. *See* Oslo Accords
international involvement in
    peacemaking. *See* European Union;
    NATO; *specific countries by name*; UN
International Monetary Fund (IMF), 283
International Rescue Committee (IRC),
    390
Internet as peacemaker tool. *See* Janjic,
    Father Sava, as "the Cybermonk"
Inter-Religious Council of Sierra Leone,
    16, 279, 287–8, 291, 294–5, 440–1. *See
    also* Koroma, Alimamy P.
Interreligious Service Oci u Oci (Face to
    Face), 16, 97, 111–12
Intifada. *See also* Israeli-Palestinian
    conflict
  First, 316–17, 344–5
  Second, 317–19, 348–65, 366, 370
IRA. *See* Irish Republican Army
Iraq, 236–7, 311, 312
Iraq War (1990–1991), 362–3
IRC (International Rescue Committee),
    390
Ireland, Northern, 91. *See also* Irish
    Republican Army (IRA); Magee, The
    Rev. Roy; Reid, Father Alex
  1641 massacre of Protestant settlers, 56
  1994 IRA ceasefire, 79–80
  Anglo-Irish Agreement (1985), 67–73,
    95
  Anglo-Irish Treaty (1921), 58
  Belfast, Catholic settlement within,
    56–7
  Bloody Friday, 61
  Bloody Sunday, 60–1
  economy and demographics, 82, 93, 452
  fact sheet, 92–3
  Good Friday Agreement (Belfast
    Agreement), 53, 61, 72, 73–82, 95

historical overview of conflict, 54–61, 94
Irish independence movement
    (1801–1921), 57–8
Irish War of Independence, 57–8
nationalists, overview of, 94
paramilitary organizations within,
    87–8, 95
"peace lines" of Northern Ireland, 59
Remembrance Day bombing (1987), 72
Republic of Ireland and, 58, 95, 96
Shankill Road bombing (1993), 75–6
The Troubles, 56–7, 73
Ulster, 55, 58, 94
Ulster Defense Association (UDA), 64,
    68–9, 95
Ulster Unionist Party (UUP), 95
Ulster Volunteer Force (UVF), 64, 74–5,
    95
United Kingdom (UK) and, 54–6, 58,
    59, 60–1, 63, 95
Irgun, 308, 309, 310
Irian Jaya, 405, 413
Irish Republican Army (IRA)
  1994 ceasefire by, 79–80
  Irish War of Independence and, 57–8
  overview of, 95
  Provisional IRA, formation of, 60
  Real IRA, 81
  Sinn Féin as political arm of, 94. *See
    also* Sinn Féin
Ironsi, Major-Gen. Aguyi, 252
Isaac, Dr. Ephraim, 157–82. *See also*
    Ethiopia; Israel
  Ad Hoc Ethiopian Peace Committee
    (AHPC), 164–70, 171
  Addis Ababa Peace and Democracy
    Conference, 169–70
  agreement-making by, 446–7
  background and early peacemaking by,
    151, 157–8, 162–4
  Committee for Ethiopian Literacy, 163
  early influences and encounters with
    violence, 158–61
  elders as peacemaker tool, 151, 175,
    177, 182
  emotional intelligence of, 8
  Eritrean referendum for independence,
    174

Isaac, Dr. Ephraim (*cont.*)
  father (Yeshaq Mesha), 159–60
  indigenous belief systems as
    peacemaker tool, 12, 173–4
  Interfaith Prayer Day (Ethiopia), 172
  on international involvement in
    peacemaking, 176
  interreligious and intercultural respect
    of, 439
  Italian occupation of Ethiopia and, 160
  London Peace Talks and, 166–9
  Messiah (Handel) translation by, 162
  on Middle East conflict, 178
  PDC Conference, 172, 175
  peacemaking techniques, 176–80
  post-Eritrean independence disputes
    and reconciliation, 174–6
  on reconciliation vs. peace, 176, 178
  religious motivation for peacemaking,
    161–2, 180–2
  Toronto Congress, 163
  as Yemenite Jew, 158
Isaias Afewerki, 157, 174, 175–6
Islam. *See also* Qur'an
  Afghanistan and, 383, 384, 388, 400. *See
    also* Taliban
  Bosniaks vs., 121
  Dhimmitude, 124–5
  within Ethiopia, beginnings of, 153–4
  founding of, 304. *See also* Muhammad,
    Prophet
  Israeli-Palestinian conflict and, 352
  Kosovo and, 124–5
  Nigeria and, 250, 253–4, 255, 256,
    257–8, 269. *See also* Zangon Kataf,
    market riots
  South Africa and, 216
  Sudan and, 189, 190, 192
  in West Papua, 415–17
Ismail (Ottoman Empire), 189
isolation of peacemakers, 6
Israel, State of, 375–7. *See also* Froman,
    Rabbi Menachem; Israeli-Palestinian
    conflict; Jerusalem; Landau, Yehezkel
  1982 War in Lebanon, 315–16
  declarations of independence, 310
  demographics of, 376–7
  early history of. *See* Palestine and
    Palestinians
  economic overview of, 377

fact sheet, 375–7
independence of, 323
Israel Defense Forces (IDF), 310
Jewish tradition for peace within,
  350–1
Operation Solomon, 166–8, 177
paramilitary factions, 308, 309, 310
Zionism and, 305–6, 351. *See also* Oz
  veShalom peace movement; World
  Zionist Organization
Israel Interfaith Association, 360
Israeli-Palestinian conflict, 302–21. *See
  also* Chacour, Abuna Elias; Froman,
  Rabbi Menachem; Israel, State of;
  Jerusalem; Landau, Yehezkel;
  Palestine and Palestinians
  1948 War, 310–11
  1967 Six-Day War, 312–13, 330, 342
  Camp David Accords, 315
  current situation/conflict, 319–21
  Disengagement Plan, 320
  early history of, 303
  Intifada, First, 316–17, 344–5
  Intifada, Second, 317–19, 348–65, 366,
    370
  Isaac, Dr. Ephraim on, 178
  Israeli settlements, 303, 313, 317,
    322–45, 351–2, 361–2, 376
  Israeli-Egyptian ceasefire, 313
  Jewish immigration to Palestine, 305–6,
    308
  Lowrey, Rev. Dr. William on, 207
  medina enoshit (humane state), 345,
    346, 350–1
  Oslo Accords, 316, 317–18, 319, 345–6
  Palestine, early history of. *See* Palestine
    and Palestinians
  Palestine Mandate, 307, 309
  refugee issue, 311, 312, 313, 318, 323,
    363, 365
  Road Map to Peace, 319–20
  Security Fence, 320
  Sinai Campaign, 311–12
  War of Attrition, 314–15
  Yom Kippur War,
Isseroff, Ami, 305
Italy, 151, 154, 155, 160
Iwanngin, Agu, 421

Jacadewa, Priscilla, 418

Jama'atu Nasril Islam (JNI), 259–60, 268, 269
James, Epistle of, 196
James II, King (of England), 56
Janjic, Father Sava. *See also* Kosovo; Serbian Orthodox Church; Yugoslavia
  ambivalence on use of force, 437
  Decani Monastery, 128–9, 131–3, 135
  emotional and physical exhaustion of, 123, 139
  enforcement as type of peacemaking by, 443
  evolution of a peacemaker, 128–9
  on forgiveness, 143
  global community as peacemaking tool, 17
  intellect of, 8
  interfaith mobilization by, 133–4, 138
  on Kosovo conflict and causes, 140–1
  on manipulation of religion for violence, 430
  marginalized by Milosevic, 141
  media, countering biased portrayals by, 17
  on moral obligation to protect all people, 133–4
  NATO and U.S. meetings, 137–9
  neutrality of, 141–3
  overview of, 123
  papers written by, 14, 137, 138, 143–5
  peacekeeping efforts of, 129–40, 443
  reflections on peacemaking methods, 141–5
  refugees helped by, 131–3, 135
  religious motivation for peacemaking, 9, 139–40, 145–6
  on responsibilities of religious communities, 143
  risks taken for peacemaking, 431, 434
  as "the Cybermonk", 17, 129, 141–2
Japan, 404
Javanese people, 425. *See also* Indonesia
Jehoshaphat, King, 351–2
Jerusalem. *See also* Israel, State of; Israeli-Palestinian conflict
  1950 annexation by Israel, 377
  as capital of Israel, 303, 377
  Froman on, 350–1
  Jordan and, 313
  Landau on, 368

Muslim holy sites within, 304, 314, 319
  overview of, 313–14
  Six-Day War and, 313
  Western Wall, 304
Jesus Christ. *See also* Christians and Christianity
  birth of, 303–4
  Chacour inspired by, 324
  Church of the Holy Sepulcher and, 314
  Lowrey inspired by, 208
  Magee inspired by, 84–5, 438
  natures of, 322
  Reid inspired by, 79, 84–5, 89–90, 438
  Sermon on the Mount (The Beatitudes), 324, 339–40
  Wuye inspired by, 263
The Jewish Agency for Palestine, 307
Jews. *See* Israel, State of; Judaism
Jikany clan, 194–5, 198. *See also* Nuer people
JNA (Yugoslav People's Army), 101, 102–3
JNI (*Jama'atu Nasril Islam*), 259–60, 268, 269
Johnson, David, 284
Johnson, Gregory G., 147
The Joint Declaration of Peace (Downing Street), 76–7
Jones, Sidney, 414
Jordan, 307, 311, 312, 313–14
Josephate, Mother, 329
journalists. *See* media
Judah (kingdom), 303. *See also* Israel, State of
Judaism. *See also* Israel, State of; Israeli-Palestinian Conflict; the Holocaust
  dhimma under Ottoman Empire, 124–5
  early history of, 303
  Ethiopian Jews, 166–8, 177
  peace, tradition for, 161, 350–1, 357, 363, 370. *See also* Bible as peacemaker tool
  Yemenites, 158
Zionism and, 305–6, 351. *See also* Oz veShalom peace movement; World Zionist Organization

Judea. *See* Israeli-Palestinian conflict, Israeli settlements

Kabbah, Amad Tejan, 285, 286, 290, 292, 298
Kabul, 384. *See also* Afghanistan
Kadima party, 321
Kaduna, 247. *See also* Nigeria
 Ashafa and Wuye within, 265–7, 271
 Kaduna Peace Agreement, 14, 272, 273–4
 Kafanchan, 260
 overview of conflict, 254–7
 Shari'a law enacted within, 257–8
 Zangon Kataf. *See also* Zangon Kataf
Kamic, Chief Kakeny, 210
Kano, Nigeria, 257–8, 266
Karzai, Hamid, 401
Kataf people of Nigeria, 255–7. *See also* Zangon Kataf
Kennedy, John F., 357
Kenya, American Embassy within, 388
Khalifa Abdallah, 190
Khan, Abdur Rahman, 386
Khartoum government, 187, 195. *See also* Sudan
Khartoum Peace Agreement, 192, 214
Al-Khayri family, 363, 365
Khoikhoi people, 215
Khoisan people, 215, 216
King, The Rev. Dr. Martin Luther, Jr., 232, 434
King, Tom, 68
King, Trevor, 80
King-Crane Commission, 307
KLA (Kosovo Liberation Army), 130–1, 136–7
Kook, HaRav Avraham Yitzchak HaCohen (the Elder), 342–3, 355–6
Kook, Rav Tzvi Yehuda, 343
Koroma, Alimamy P. *See also* Sierra Leone
 agreement-making by, 447
 background and early peacemaking by, 286–98
 Inter-Religious Council of Sierra Leone, 16, 279, 287–8, 291, 294–5, 440–1
 as local religious leadership, 4
 mediation of peace talks by, 291–5

 neutrality of, 288–91, 295, 440–1
 overview of, 278–9
 peacekeeping efforts by, 443
 post-conflict climate activities, 296–8
 reflections on peacemaking methods, 295–8
 RUF and, 289, 292–3
Koroma, Lt. Col. Johnny Paul, 286
Kosovo. *See also* Janjic, Father Sava; Serbia and Montenegro
 Albania and, 124, 125
 autonomy under UN Interim Administration Mission in Kosovo, 136
 Balkan War, 125
 conflict legitimized by religion in, 140–1
 Democratic Opposition of Serbia (DOS), 150
 demographics of, 123
 economic overview of, 150
 historical overview of conflict, 149–50
 international involvement within, 136, 150, 442–3
 Islamization of, 124–5
 Kosovo Liberation Army (KLA), 130–1, 136–7
 "Peace Accord" following Russo-Ottoman War, 125
 post-Tito, 127–8
 pre-World War history of, 123–5
 Rambouillet, 236
 under Tito, 126–7
 violence against religious institutions in, 136
 World Wars and, 125–6
Kostunica, Vojislav, 150
Kotel. *See* Western Wall
Kushans, 384
KwaZulu-Natal province, 225–6

Landau, Yehezkel, 356–74. *See also* Israeli-Palestinian conflict
 Ashkenazi and, 358, 362, 363, 365, 367, 369
 Bible as peacemaker tool of, 357, 363, 370, 373–4
 on conflict fed by religion, 429–30

direct approach to peacemaking, 368–9
evolution of a peacemaker, 360
holistic peacemaking, 370–1
interfaith mobilization by, 360, 371
on Jerusalem, 368
on media, 359, 372
Open House, 365, 368–9, 371, 374
overview of, 356–8, 431
Oz veShalom peace movement, 360, 362, 371
peace work in the United States, 9, 17, 365–7
reflections on peacemaking methods, 373
on religious figures in the peace process, 441–2
religious motivation for peacemaking, 370, 373–4
storytelling as peacemaking technique of, 363–5
"Three A's" philosophy and method to peacemaking, 369–73
Laskar Jihad, 415–17
Latin American Pastoral Institute (IPLA), 32
Lawrence, T.E., 306
League of Nations, 307
Lebanon, 307, 311, 315–16
Lederach, John Paul, 206
Lehi, 309, 310
Lekota, Mosiuoa, 235
Lempa River, 38–9, 44, 46, 47
Leninism. *See* socialism
Lesch, Ann, 187–8
Lesotho, 218–28
Liberia, 287. *See also* Taylor, Charles
Libya. *See* al-Qaddafi, Muammar
Limba people, 279
listening as peacemaker tool, 86
Little, David, 429–48
"living stones", 337
local leadership. *See* community leaders
Loki Accord, 199, 201–2, 210
Lomé Peace Accords, 286, 294–5, 298
London Peace Talks, 166–9
loneliness. *See* isolation of peacemakers
Longère, Father, 327
Lorde, Audre, 240

Lou clan, 194–5, 198, 200–1. *See also* Nuer people
Lower Lempa. *See* Lempa River
Lowrey, Rev. Dr. William, 196–211. *See also* People-to-People Peace Process; Sudan
agreement-making by, 445
background and early peacemaking by, 196–9
Christianity as inspiration for, 196, 204–5, 207–8
in El Salvador, 197
fair fighters connected by, 204–5
family of, 197–8
group by group peace efforts, 205
indigenous belief systems as peacemaker tool, 11–12
as insider-partial, 206–7
on interreligious and intercultural respect, 439–40
on leadership, 193
on Middle East conflict, 207
New Sudan Council of Churches (NSCC), 187, 198–9, 214
Nuer-Dinka relations and, 199, 211
overview of, 186–7
peacemaker efforts within U.S., 9
peacemaking techniques, 201–2
post-1998 peace conferences, 209–10
Presbyterian Hunger Program Committee, 197
pulpwood cutters, advocacy on behalf of, 197
spheres of brokenness/peacebuilding, 206
underground railway for Nuer leaders, 200
University of Southern Mississippi and, 196
Waat Lou Nuer Peace and Governance Conference, 200–1
World Vision International, 210
Wunlit Dinka-Nuer West Bank Peace and Reconciliation Conference, 200
Loyalist Volunteer Force (LVF), 95
Lucy (hominid fossil), 152
LVF. *See* Loyalist Volunteer Force

Machar, Riek, 192–3, 209–10, 214. *See also* SSIM/A
Madaki, Colonel, 258
Madlala-Routledge, Nozizwe, 225–40. *See also* South Africa
  African Women's Peace Table, 235
  ANC membership, 227
  antagonism generated by peacemaking of, 435
  on black-on-black violence, 229–30, 237–8
  Convention for a Democratic South Africa (CODESA) formed, 231
  as Deputy Minister of Health, 240
  early activism of, 226–8
  emotional intelligence of, 7–8
  Gandhi as inspiration for peacemaking, 228, 232, 238
  HIV/AIDS advocacy, 235
  intra-group peacemaking, 228
  Iraq war, opposition to, 236–7
  King Jr., The Rev. Dr. Martin Luther as inspiration of, 232
  as Member of Parliament, 231
  Ministry of Defense position, 231–4, 237
  Natal Organization of Women, 227
  neutrality of, 229, 441
  overview of, 215, 225–7
  as Quaker, 215, 225, 228, 232–3, 238–40, 436
  reflections on peacemaking methods, 237–8
  Routledge, Jeremy, 225, 228, 233
  SACP (South African Communist Party), 228
  solitary confinement of, 435
  spiritual motivation for peacemaking, 9, 226–7, 238–40
  women's rights and, 18, 230–1, 234–6, 432–3
  as Zulu, 225
madrasas of Afghanistan, 387
Magee, The Rev. Roy, 53–4. *See also* Ireland, Northern
  ambivalence on use of force, 436, 437
  on Anglo-Irish Agreement (1985), 68–70
  background and early efforts by, 61–4
  Church opposition to peacemaker efforts by, 69

current activities of, 91
  Good Friday Agreement and, 73–82
  on inclusive approach to peacemaking, 86–7
  IRA ceasefire, response to, 79–80
  Jesus Christ as inspiration for peacemaking of, 438
  on paramilitary organizations, 87–8
  pulpit as peacemaker tool, 11
  Reid, Father Alex and, 79
  on religiously motivated peacemaking, 82–90
  Tipperary International Peace Prize received by, 81
  Ulster Defense Association (UDA) and, 68–9
  use of religious texts as peacemaker tool, 10–11
Magok, Chief Isaac, 204
Mahdist rule, 190
Major, John, 77
Makarije, Father, 132–3
Makeny, Chief, 210
Mamelukes of Egypt, 304, 305
Mandela, Nelson, 222, 224, 225. *See also* ANC
Mansergh, Dr. Martin, 71, 73, 74, 77
Mar Elias Educational Institution (MEEI), 13, 332–6, 341. *See also* Chacour, Abuna Elias
Margai, Albert, 282
Margai, Milton, 282
Markovic, Friar Ivo. *See also* Bosnia and Herzegovina; Yugoslavia
  ambivalence on use of force, 436, 437
  Church opposition to peacemaking by, 118
  death of father, 110
  enforcement as type of peacemaking, 443
  humanitarian efforts by, 110
  institution-and-capacity building by, 444–5
  interfaith mobilization by, 16
  Interreligious Service Oci u Oci (Face to Face), 16, 97, 111–12
  on manipulation of religion for violence, 430, 434

media and, 113–14
"oasis of peace" created by, 109
overview of peacemaking efforts, 97–8, 107–13, 443
pacifism, rejection of, 117
Pale, visit to, 111
on peacemaking ideology, 115
Pontanima Choir and Chamber Orchestra, 16, 111–12
on religious symbols, 107
religious training and early peace efforts of, 106–8, 119
religiously motivated peacemaking of, 116–18
risks taken for peacemaking, 114–15, 431–2, 434
secular peacemaking tools adapted by, 19
writings by, 14–15
Maronite Catholic Church, 322
Marti, Agustin Farabundo, 28, 29
Marxism. See socialism
Massawa, 157
Masson, Charles, 385
Matiep, Paulino, 193, 209–10, 214
Maze Prison IRA, 65–6
Mbeki, Thabo, 224, 225, 231, 232
MCDF. See Muslim-Christian Dialogue Forum
MCYDF (Muslim-Christian Youth Dialogue Forum), 263–4
media
    Bosnia and Herzegovina and, 105, 113–14
    Ethiopia and, 165, 167
    Israeli-Palestinian conflict and, 355, 359, 372
    Kosovo and, 17, 129, 139
    Nigeria and, 267–8
    Northern Ireland and, 75
mediation skills of peacemakers. See peacemaker tools and approaches
Medillin documents, 32
medina enoshit (humane state), 345, 346, 350–1
MEEI. See Mar Elias Educational Institution
Meir, Golda, 314–15
MEISON. See Ethiopian Socialist Party

Melanesian Christians, 425
Melchior, Michael, 350
Melchizidek, Archbishop, 170–1
Meles Zenawi, 156, 157, 169, 175–6. See also Ethiopian People's Revolutionary Democratic Front
Melkite Catholic Church, 322, 323. See also Chacour, Abuna Elias
Melrose, Joseph, 294
Mende people of Sierra Leone, 279
Mengesha, Ras, 163
Mengistu Haile-Mariam, 156, 167, 192. See also the Derg
Mercaz HaRav Yeshiva, 342–3. See also Kook, HaRav Avraham Yitzchak HaCohen (the Elder)
Mesha, Yeshaq, 159–60
Mesoamerican Peace Project, 47, 48–9
Messiah (Handel), 162
mestizos, defined, 27
mfecane, 217
Middle East conflict. See Israeli-Palestinian Conflict
The Military Observer Group of the Economic Community of West African States (ECOMOG), 286
Milosevic, Slobodan, 100–1, 103–4, 127–8, 130–1, 134, 137, 140–1, 149
Miss World beauty pageant of 2002, 272
Mladic, Ratko, 103
Moghul Empire, 384
Mohammed, Brigadier Murtala Ramat, 253
Molina, Col. Armando, 38, 40
Momoh, General Joseph Saidu, 283
Montenegro. See Serbia and Montenegro
Montesinos, Antonio de, 26
Morazan, Francisco, 27
Morina, Qemajl, 142–3
Morning Star Flag, 404, 413
Moshoeshoe, King, 217
Muhammad, Prophet. See also Islam
    as founder of Islam, 304
    as inspiration for peacemakers, 262
    Miss World beauty pageant of 2002 and, 272
    portrayal in European newspapers, 272–3
Muhammad Ahmad, 190

Muhammad Ali (Ottoman Empire), 189
mujahedin in Afghanistan, 387
Mullins, John, 72
Musa, Idris, 262
music as peacemaking tool, 16, 111–12,
    203–4, 225
Muslim-Christian Dialogue Forum
    (MCDF), 247–8, 264–9, 270, 271,
    272–3, 432. *See also* Interfaith
    Mediation Centre
Muslim-Christian Youth Dialogue Forum
    (MCYDF), 263–4
Muslims. *See* Islam

NACOMYO (National Council of Muslim
    Youth Organizations), 260, 263
Nahal, 342
nakfa, 174–5
Napoleon, 189
Nasser, Gamal Abdel, 311, 312–13, 314
Natal, Colony of, 218
Natal Organization of Women (NOW),
    227
National Council of Muslim Youth
    Organizations (NACOMYO), 260, 263
National Council of Nigeria, 251
National Provisional Ruling Council
    (NPRC), 283
Nationalist Democratix Organization
    (ORDEN), 35
Nationalist Party of South Africa, 220,
    222, 223, 224, 225. *See also* de Klerk,
    Frederik Willem
NATO
    Bosnia and Herzegovina and, 105, 106,
        122, 442–3
    Kosovo campaign, 132, 134, 135–40,
        150, 442–3
Natshe, Mustafa, 347
Navarro, Alfonso, 41
NCNC (Cameroons), 251
NEPAD (New Partnership for Africa's
    Development), 235
NEPU (Northern Progressive Union), 251
Netherlands, the. *See also* Boers
    Dutch East India Company, 216
    Indonesia, colonialization of, 425
    New Guinea, colonialization of, 403,
        404, 405

neutrality of peacemakers
    of Ad Hoc Ethiopian Peace Committee,
        165
    Janjic, Father Sava, 141–3
    Koroma, 288–91, 295, 440–1
    Madlala-Routledge, 229, 441
    as peacemaker skill, 18
    Reid, 441
New Guinea, 403, 404. *See also* Indonesia
New Partnership for Africa's Development
    (NEPAD), 235
New Sudan Council of Churches (NSCC),
    187, 198–9, 214
New Testament. *See* Bible as peacemaker
    tool
NG (Action Group), 251
Nigeria, 274–5. *See also* Ashafa, Imam
    Muhammad; Kaduna; Wuye, Pastor
    James
    Christianity under British rule, 250
    Christian-Muslim clashes, 253
    civil war, 252
    colonial occupation of, 249–50
    current tensions, 272–3
    demographics of, 248, 275–6
    economic overview of, 276–7
    evolution of Islamic rule in Northern
        Nigeria, 248–9
    fact sheet, 275–6
    Fulani people, 248, 249, 250, 251,
        255–7, 272
    Hausa people, 248–9, 250, 251, 255–7
    historical overview of conflict, 276
    independence of, 250
    Indirect Rule by Britain, 249–50,
        255–6
    jihad within, 257
    missionary activity within, 250, 253
    overview of, 248
    political activism of Christian churches
        within, 256
    postindependence tensions, 250–4
    Republic of Biafra, 252
    Shari'a law within, 250, 253–4, 255,
        256, 257–8, 269
Nimeiry, Jafaar, 192
9/11 terror attacks. *See* September 11,
    2001
1948 War, 311, 312, 363

1967 Six-Day War, 312–13, 330, 342
1982 War in Lebanon, 315–16
Noble Sanctuary, 314. *See also* Dome of
    the Rock
nonpartisanship of peacemakers. *See*
    neutrality of peacemakers
Norchi, Charles H., 383, 388
Northern Alliance, 382, 388–9
Northern Ireland. *See* Ireland, Northern
Northern Ireland Civil Rights Association,
    58
Northern People's Congress (NPC) of
    Nigeria, 251, 252
Northern Progressive Union (NEPU) of
    Nigeria, 251
NOW (Natal Organization of Women),
    227
NPC. *See* Northern People's Congress
NPRC (National Provisional Ruling
    Council), 283
NSCC (New Sudan Council of Churches),
    187, 198–9, 214
Nubian kingdoms, 188, 189
Nuer peoples. *See also* Lowrey, Rev. Dr.
    William; People-to-People Peace
    Process; Sudan
  intra-tribal conflict, 187, 193, 194,
    200–1
  Nuer-Dinka Chiefs and Church Leaders
    Reconciliation Conference, 199
  overview of conflict with the Dinka,
    194, 195
  SSIM/A composed of, 192
  underground railway for leaders, 200
  Wunlit Dinka-Nuer West Bank Peace
    and Reconciliation Conference, 200
Nuns, American, 42

Obasanjo, Gen. Olusegun, 253, 254, 276
Occupied Territories of Palestine. *See*
    Israeli-Palestinian conflict
Oci u Oci (Face to Face) Interreligious
    Service, 16, 97, 111–12
October War. *See* Yom Kippur War
official diplomacy. *See* Track One
    diplomacy
Official IRA. *See* Irish Republican Army
    (IRA)
O'Fiaich, Cardinal, 65, 66

Okelo, Francis, 292
Old Testament. *See* Bible as peacemaker
    tool
Olmert, 321
Omagh bombing, 81
Open House, 365, 368–9, 371, 374
Operation Solomon, 166–8, 177
OPM (Free Papua Movement), 404–5,
    413, 414
Orange Free State, 217, 218. *See also*
    Boers
Orange Order, 56, 59
ORDEN (Nationalist Democratic
    Organization), 35
Organization for Security and
    Cooperation in Europe (OSCE),
    134–5, 137
Orjiako, H., 461
Oromo, Liberation Front, 163–4
OSCE (Organization for Security and
    Cooperation in Europe), 134–5, 137
Oslo Accords, 316, 317–18, 319, 345–6
Ottoman Empire
  Battle of Kosovo Polje, 124–5
  Bosnia and Herzegovina and, 98
  Ethiopia and, 153
  Palestine, control of, 304, 305–6
  Russo-Ottoman War, 125
  Sudan and, 189–90
Oz veShalom peace movement, 360, 362,
    371

PA (Palestinian Authority), 317. *See also*
    Arafat, Chairman Yasser
PAC (Pan-Africanist Congress), 221, 224
Pakage, Zakheus, 411–12
Pakistan, 386–7
Palestine and Palestinians. *See also* Arafat,
    Chairman Yasser; Chacour, Abuna
    Elias; Israeli-Palestinian conflict
  British Mandate period, 306–10
  Fatah faction, 317
  fellaheen, 305–6
  Gaza Strip, 378
  greater-Syrian Mandate, 307
  Hamas, 320–1
  under Israel occupation, 313
  Judah (kingdom), 303
  Palestinian Authority (PA), 317

Palestine and Palestinians (*cont.*)
  PLO (Palestinian Liberation
    Organization), 315–16
  refugees, 311, 312, 313, 318, 323, 363,
    365
  Roman Era, 303–5
  Sabra and Shatilla massacre, 316
  Transjordan and, 307
  uprising of. *See Intifada*
  West Bank, 313, 379–81
  World War I and, 306
  World War II years, 309
Palmah, 309, 310
pan-African network regional model, 273
Pan-Africanist Congress (PAC), 221, 224
Panjdeh Incident of 1895, 386
Papua. *See* Indonesia; West Papua
Paris Peace Conference, 386
parish leaders as peacemakers. *See* pulpit
    as peacemaker tool
Partisans of Yugoslavia,
Pass Laws of South Africa, 221, 223
The Pastor and the Imam (Ashafa and
    Wuye), 267
PAXnet, 210
PDC. *See* peacemaker tools and
    approaches
PDC (Christian Democratic Party) of El
    Salvador, 29–30
PDPA (Afghan Communist Party), 387,
    400
Peace and Development Committee
    (PDC), 171–2, 175, 178, 182
"peace lines" of Northern Ireland, 59
Peacebuilding and Advocacy Network,
    210
peacemaker tools and approaches, 9–19.
    See also Bible as peacemaker tool;
    interfaith mobilization; media;
    neutrality; storytelling; Zone of Peace
  agreement-making, 443–4, 445–7
  alliances, 180, 181–2
  communication skills, 14–15
  cultural rituals and traditions, 11–12,
    19, 200, 202–3, 204, 208. *See also*
    elders as peacemaker tool
  debate as, 12–13
  education, 13–14
  elders as, 12, 151, 173–4, 175, 177, 182,
    193–4. *See also* Ad Hoc Ethiopian

  Peace Committee; rituals as
    peacemaker tools
  enforcement, 442–3
  general lessons of, 437–8
  global community, 17–18
  group by group peace achievements,
    205
  institution-and-capacity building, 443,
    444–5
  listening, 86
  negotiation skills, 18
  new applications of religious
    peacemaking, 19
  peacekeeping, 443
  publicly-focused approach, 444
  pulpit as, 11, 36
  Qur'an as peacemaker tool, 10, 13–14,
    266, 267, 391, 392–3
  reconciliation vs. peace, 176, 178
  religious buildings as, 11
  religious symbols as, 107
  religiously focused approach, 10–19,
    441–2, 444
  respect, 85
  secular peacemaking tools adapted by,
    18–19
  shimagele-jarsa, 165–6
  spheres of brokenness and spheres of
    peacebuilding by Lowrey, 206
  theory and practice of religious
    peacemaking, 438–47
  training of other peacemakers, 267
  Western ideas as. *See* secular
    peacemaking
peacemakers. *See also* risks taken for
    peacemaking; *specific peacemakers by
    name*
  as community members, 5
  emotional intelligence of, 7–8
  intellect of, 8
  isolation of, 6
  misimpressions corrected by, 429–38
  neutrality of, 18, 440–1
  overview of, 3–9, 21
  personal faith of vs. group belonging,
    116
  religion and personal identities of, 7–9
  as vocation, 19–21
peasants, land reform and. *See* Alas, José
  "Chencho"

Pedi people, 216
Penn, William, 233. *See also* Quaker Faith
People-to-People Peace Process
  conference format, 201–2
  founding of, 199–204
  importance of, 211
  rituals of conferences, 19, 200, 202–3, 204, 208
Persian Empire, 303, 384
Peshawar region, 386
Phalangist militia, 316
Phoenix Settlement, 228
Pineda y Saldana, Bishop Tomas Miguel, 27
PIRA. *See* Irish Republican Army (IRA)
Pitt, William, 57
PLO (Palestinian Liberation Organization), 315–16. *See also* Palestine and Palestinians
Pontanima Choir and Chamber Orchestra, 16, 111–12
Population Registration Act (1950) of South Africa, 220
Portugal, 279–80
Potato Famine of Ireland (1845–49), 57
Powell, Colin L., 320
prayers, common. *See* interfaith mobilization
Presbyterian Hunger Program Committee, 197
Pristina University, 127
Protestant Reformation, 55
Provisional IRA. *See* Irish Republican Army (IRA)
Provisional Military Administration Council of Ethiopia. *See* the Derg
Provos. *See* Irish Republican Army (IRA)
publicly-focused approach to peacemaking, 444
pulpit as peacemaker tool, 11, 36

al-Qaddafi, Muammar, 284–5
Qadiriyya, Nigeria, 260
al-Qaeda, 388. *See also* Bin Laden, Osama; September 11, 2001
Qastel battle, 310
Quaker faith, 228, 238–43, 436
Quiñonez, Dr., 32–3
Qur'an as peacemaker tool. *See also* Islam
  Ashafa inspired by, 266, 267

Yacoobi inspired by, 10, 13–14, 391, 392–3

Rabin, Yitzhak, 316, 317
racial segregation. *See* apartheid
Rambouillet, 236
Ramle, 368–9. *See also* Open House
Raya, Joseph, 330–1
Reagan, Ronald, 43, 51
Real IRA, 81
Reali High School in Haifa, 342
Red Aid International (SRI), 28, 29
Red Terror, 156
Redemptorist order, 64, 70
Reid, Father Alex, 53–91. *See also* Ireland, Northern
  Adams-Hume dialogues, 74, 77
  Adams-Mansergh dialogues, 71, 77
  agreement-making by, 447
  background and early peacemaking by, 64–7
  on Belfast, 90
  ceasefire and, 67, 73–9, 82
  church support for peacemaking efforts, 70
  communication skills of, 14
  current activities of, 91
  exhaustion as result of efforts, 66–7
  Haughey and Hume, letter written to, 71
  as image of The Troubles, 73
  on inclusive approach to peacemaking, 86–7
  Jesus Christ as inspiration for peacemaking of, 438
  Magee, The Rev. Roy and, 79
  neutrality of, 441
  on paramilitary organizations, 87–8
  peacemaking in Basque region, 19
  position papers of, 72, 77, 88–90
  on religiously motivated peacemaking, 82–90
  spiritual motivation for peacemaking, 9
  as "the Sagart", 65–6, 79
  Tipperary International Peace Prize received by, 81
"Religion in Kosovo" (Janjic), 143–5
religious buildings as peacemaker tools, 11

religious motivation for peacemaking. *See individual peacemakers*; peacemaker tools and approaches; peacemakers
Religious Society of Friends. *See* Quaker faith
religious texts as peacemaker tool. *See* Bible; Qur'an
Remembrance Day bombing (1987), 72
Republic of Biafra, 252. *See also* Nigeria
Republic of Ireland, 58, 94, 95, 96. *See also* Ireland, Northern
Republika Srpska (RS), 106, 122. *See also* Bosnia and Herzegovina
respect as foundation of peacemaker relationships. *See also* interfaith mobilization
  Isaac on, 179–80
  Lowrey on, 204
  Madlala-Routledge on, 239
  Reid and Magee on, 85
Retief, Piet, 217
Revolutionary United Front (RUF)
  Abidjan Peace Accord, 285–6
  civil war started by, 283, 300
  demonstrations against by Koroma, Alimamy P., 289
  founding of, 284–5
  human rights violations by, 284–6
  Koroma meeting, 292–3
  Sankoh, Foday, 284–5, 286, 292–3, 294
  Taylor, Charles and, 294
Reynolds, Albert, 74, 77, 79–80
Riebeeck, Jan van, 216
Rig Veda, 383
The Rising of 1641, 56
risks taken for peacemaking
  Alas, 434, 435
  Giay, 402, 410, 412, 414, 434–5
  Janjic, 431, 434
  Markovic, 114–15, 431–2, 434
  Yacoobi, 396–7
rituals as peacemaker tools, 11–12, 19, 200, 202–3, 204, 208. *See also* elders as peacemaker tool
Road Map to Peace plan, 319–20
Roman rule of Judea, 303–5
Romero, Bishop Oscar, 39, 41, 42
Romero, Humberto, 40, 42
Routledge, Jeremy, 225, 228, 233

RS. *See* Republika Srpska
Ruaei, Chief William, 202
RUF. *See* Revolutionary United Front
Rumbiak, John, 409, 414, 416, 418
Russia. *See* Soviet Union
Ryacudu, Ryamizard, 415

Sabra and Shatilla massacre, 316, 319
SACP (South African Communist Party), 224, 228
Sadat, Anwar, 314–15. *See also* Egypt
Safe and Secure (case study), 391
"Sagart, the", 79. *See also* Reid, Father Alex
Salih, Sheikh Abu, 348, 352
San people of South Africa, 215
SANDF (South African National Defense Force), 234–7
Sands, Bobby, 65, 66
Sankoh, Foday, 284–5, 286, 292–3, 294
SANNC (South African Native National Congress), 219. *See also* ANC
Sarajevo, 103. *See also* Bosnia and Herzegovina
Sassey, Kadi, 292
Sava, Father. *See* Janjic, Father Sava
SDLP (Social Democratic and Labour Party), 94. *See also* Hume, John
Second Anglo-Afghan War, 385–6
Second *Intifada*, 317–19, 348–65, 366, 370. *See also* Israeli-Palestinian conflict
Second Vatican Council, 30, 32
secular peacemaking tools, adaptation of, 18–19
Security Fence of Israel, 320
segregation of races. *See* apartheid
Selassie, Emperor Haile I, 154–5, 184
Seleucus, 303
SEMA (Strategic Empowerment and Mediation Agency), 264, 267
Seminar on Trauma Awareness and Recovery (STAR), 297–8
separation of church and state in Ethiopia, 173
September 11, 2001. *See also* al-Qaeda
  "blowback" theory and, 388
  Chacour on, 336
  U.S. invasion of Afghanistan following, 382, 389, 400

West Papua and, 415
World Conference on Religion and
    Peace (WCRP) and, 352
Serbia and Montenegro. *See also* Bosnia
    and Herzegovina; Kosovo; Yugoslavia
Balkan War, 125
early history of Serbs, 124
fact sheet, 148–9
"Greater Serbia", 121, 149
historical overview of conflict, 149–50
international involvement in
    peacemaking, 150
Milosevic, Slobodan and, 103–4
Serbian Orthodox Church. *See also*
    Artemije, Bishop; Janjic, Father Sava
Decani Monastery, 128–9, 131–3, 135
destruction of property of, 139
dhimmitude for, 124
on peacemaking, 146
as voice of moderation in Kosovo, 141
Sermon on the Mount (The Beatitudes),
    324, 339–40. *See also* Jesus Christ
sermons. *See* pulpit as peacemaker tool
SFOR (NATO-led Stabilization Force) in
    Bosnia, 106, 122
Shaka (Zulu warrior), 217
"shalom society", 420–1
Shankill Butchers, 67
Shankill Road bombing (1993), 75–6
Shared Moral Commitment (Kosovo), 138
Shari'a
    in Afghanistan, 388, 400. *See also*
        Taliban
    hudna (ceasefire), 352
    in Nigeria, 250, 253–4, 255, 256, 257–8,
        269. *See also* Zangon Kataf, market
        riots
    in Sudan, 190, 192
Sharm-el-Sheikh summit, 348
Sharon, Ariel
    1982 War in Lebanon and, 315
    Disengagement Plan, 320
    election of, 319
    Kadima party, 321
    Sabra and Shatilla massacre, 316, 319
    Temple Mount visit, 319, 348, 349
Sheba, Queen of. *See* Solomonid dynasty
Shiism, 384
shimagele-jarsa, 165–6

Shonekan, Ernest, 254
Shuja, Shah, 385
shuttle diplomacy, 315
Sider, Sheikh Talal, 342, 349–50, 352, 353
Sierra Leone, 298–9. *See also* Koroma,
    Alimamy P.; Revolutionary United
    Front
Abidjan Peace Accord, 285–6
Abuja Agreements, 298
AFRC (Armed Forces Revolution
    Council), 286
APC (All People's Congress), 282–3
Christian Council of Churches Sierra
    Leone, 279, 296–8
civil war, 278, 283–4, 298, 300
Creoles, 279, 280–2
DDR (disarmament, demobilization,
    and reintegration) program, 286, 298
demographics of, 279, 299–300
early history of, 279–80, 282–3
fact sheet, 299–300
Freetown, 280
historical overview of conflict, 300
Hut Tax War of 1898, 282
independence from Great Britain, 300
international involvement in, 285–6
interreligious respect within, 278
Limba people, 279
Mende people, 279
NPRC (National Provisional Ruling
    Council), 283
SLPP (Sierra Leone People's Party), 282
Temne people, 279, 280, 281. *See also*
    All People's Party
trust in religious leaders within, 291
Truth and Reconciliation Commission
    of Sierra Leone, 298
Simon, Philippe, 414
Sinai Campaign, 311–12
singing as peacemaker tool, 16, 111–12,
    203–4, 225
Sinn Féin. *See also* Irish Republican Army
    (IRA)
    Adams and Hume, 71–2, 73, 74, 77
    Adams and Mansergh, 71, 72–3, 74, 77
    Adams on Reid, 65–6, 77, 79
    historical overview of, 57, 94
Sisulu, Walter, 222
Six-Day War, 312–13, 330, 342

The Slaughter, 29
Slavs, 124. *See also* Kosovo
Slovenia, 101. *See also* Yugoslavia
SLPP (Sierra Leone People's Party), 282
Sobukwe, Robert, 221–2. *See also* PAC
Socialism, 155–6
Society of Friends. *See* Quaker Faith
Society of United Irishmen, 56
SOKAPU (Southern Kaduna People
    Union), 258
Sokoto, Nigeria, 249, 257–8
"Soldiers of Destiny". *See* Fianna Fail
Solomon, King, 303
Solomonid dynasty, 152
Sotho people, 216
South Africa, 243–4. *See also*
    Madlala-Routledge, Nozizwe
  Afrikaners, 216, 217, 219, 220. *See also*
    Boers; Nationalist Party of South
    Africa
  ANC strikes, 219
  apartheid, 220, 221, 222–3, 224, 245
  Basotholand, 217–18, 228–30
  Black Consciousness movement, 222
  black-on-black violence, 230, 237–8
  Boers, 216, 217, 218, 245
  Cape Colony, 218
  Colony of Natal, 218
  Congress Alliance, 221
  Convention for a Democratic South
    Africa (CODESA), 224
  demographics of, 245
  economic overview of, 245–6
  European settlement, 216–18
  fact sheet, 244–5
  gold and diamonds, 218, 245
  Great Britain and, 216–18, 221, 245
  Group Areas Act of South Africa, 220–1
  "homelands", 221, 223
  as independent republic, 221
  Indian population of, 218
  Industrial and Commercial Workers'
    Union of South Africa, 219
  KwaZulu-Natal province, 225–6
  Lesotho, 218–28
  Mandela, Nelson, 222, 224, 225
  mfecane, 217
  missionary efforts within, 219

  Nationalist Party of South Africa, 220,
    222, 223, 224, 225
  Orange Free State, 217, 218
  overview of, 215–25, 245
  PAC (Pan-Africanist Congress), 221, 224
  Pass Laws of South Africa, 221, 223
  Population Registration Act (1950) of
    South Africa, 220
  post-apartheid era, 224–5
  slave economy of, 216, 218
  South Africa Indian Congress, 219
  South African National Defense Force
    (SANDF), 234–7
  South African Native Convention
    (1909), 218
  South African Native National Congress
    (SANNC), 219
  Soweto youth march, 222
  Transvaal, 217, 218
  Truth and Reconciliation Commission,
    224–5
  Union of South Africa, 218, 219–20,
    245
  United Democratic Front (UDF), 222–3,
    227, 231
  United Party of South Africa, 220
  women's movement within, 230–1
  World War I and, 219
  Xhosa people, 216, 217
  Zulu people, 216, 217, 223, 225–6
South Sudan Defense Force (SSDF),
    192–3, 209–10, 214
South Sudan Independence
    Movement/Army (SSIM/A), 192–3,
    194, 195, 200, 209–10, 214
South Sudan Unity Movement/Army
    (SSUM/A), 193, 209–10, 214
Southern Kaduna People Union
    (SOKAPU), 258
Soviet Union
  Afghanistan and, 385–6, 387, 390,
    400
  communism, collapse of, 128
  Russian Revolution, 219
  Russo-Ottoman War, 125
  Yugoslavia and, 100
Soweto youth march, 222
Spain, 19, 403

SPDF (Sudan People's Democratic Front), 214
Special Autonomy Rule for Papua, 412–13, 414, 421
SPLM/A. *See* Sudanese People's Liberation Movement/Army
SRI (Red Aid International), 28, 29
SSDF (South Sudan Defense Force), 192–3, 209–10, 214
SSIM/A. *See* South Sudan Independence Movement/Army
SSUM/A (South Sudan Unity Movement/Army), 193, 209–10, 214
STAR (Seminar on Trauma Awareness and Recovery), 297–8
Stevens, Siaka P., 282–3
Stojanovic, Milka, 132
storytelling
  by Giay, 418
  by Landau, 363–5
  by Lowrey, 208
  by Yacoobi, 391–2
Straits of Tiran, 311, 312
Strasser, Captain Valentine, 283
Strategic Empowerment and Mediation Agency (SEMA), 264, 267
S.T.T. Walter Post Theological Seminary, 408–9
Sudan, 212. *See also* Dinka peoples of Sudan; Lowrey, Rev. Dr. William; Nuer people
  Addis Ababa Accord, 191–2
  civil war, 191–3
  Closed District Ordinance, 190–1
  Comprehensive Peace Agreement, 187, 209–10, 213
  Darfur, 186, 195, 210, 213
  demographics of, 187–8, 212–13
  elders as peacemaker tool in, 193–4
  fact sheet, 212–13
  geography, 187–8, 212
  Great Britain and, 154–5
  historical overview of conflict, 213
  Holocaust, parallel to, 186
  independence of, 191
  Intergovernmental Authority on Development (IGAD), 209–10, 214
  Islamic influence in, 189

  Khartoum government, 187, 195
  Khartoum Peace Agreement (1997), 192, 214
  Loki Accord, 199, 201–2, 210
  Mahdist rule, 190
  mysticism within, 190
  New Sudan Council of Churches (NSCC), 187, 198–9, 214
  Nubian kingdom, 188
  oil as source of conflict, 193
  organizations and abbreviations, list of, 214
  overview of conflict, 186–7
  pre-independence history, 188–91
  relief efforts hindered by conflict, 195
  religious affiliations with militias, 188
  Shari'a law, 190, 192
  slave trade within, 189
  South and North reunited under colonial rule, 191
  South Sudan Defense Force (SSDF), 192–3, 214
  South Sudan Independence Movement/Army (SSIM/A), 214
  South Sudan Unity Movement/Army (SSUM/A), 193, 214
  Southern isolation from the North by British rule, 190–1
  Sudan People's Democratic Front (SPDF), 214
  Sudanese People's Liberation Movement/Army (SPLM/A), 192, 193, 194, 195, 209, 214
  Wunlit Dinka-Nuer Peace Conferences, 200, 201, 202, 203, 204, 209
Suez Canal, 311–12
Suharto, Mohammed, 405
Sukarno, President, 404, 405
Sumatran Muslims, 425
Sunnis, 384
Switzerland, 167, 168
Sykes-Picot Agreement, 306
symbolic acts. *See* rituals as peacemaker tools
symbolism, religious, 107
Syria, 307, 311, 312, 313, 315

Taliban. *See also* Afghanistan
  Islamic law under, 388, 400
  overthrow of, 382, 389, 443
  overview of, 400–1
  rise to power, 387–8, 400
  Yacoobi, Sakena on, 13–14, 396, 397
Tamerlane, 384
Tanenbaum Center for Interreligious
    Understanding, 3, 6–7, 273
Tanzania, American Embassy within, 388
Taylor, Charles, 284–5, 286, 293–4
techniques of peacemakers. *See*
    peacemaker tools and approaches
Tekoa, 343–5, 351–2
Temne people, 279, 280, 281. *See also* All
    People's Party
Temple, First (Solomon's), 303
Temple, Second, 303, 304. *See also*
    Western Wall
Temple Mount, 304, 314, 319. *See also*
    Western Wall
  Sharon visit to, 348, 349
texts, religious. *See* Bible as peacemaker
    tool; Qur'an as peacemaker tool
Thaha Al-Hamid, Muhammad, 416
Thatcher, Prime Minister Margaret, 66
theories of religious peacemaking. *See*
    peacemaker tools and approaches
Tigray People's Liberation Front, 163–4
Tijani, Sheikh Ahmad, 261
Tijaniyya, 260
Tinahoun, Dr., 170–1
Tipperary International Peace Prize, 81
Tito, Josip Broz, 99–100, 126–7, 149
tools of peacemakers. *See* peacemaker
    tools and approaches
Torah. *See* Bible as peacemaker tool
Toronto Congress, 163
Toynbee, Alfred, 383
Track One diplomacy, 20–1, 176, 443,
    446–7
Track Two diplomacy
  defined, 443
  in Ethiopia, 176
  for Israeli-Palestinian conflict, 354, 371
  Janjic, Father Sava and, 14, 144–5
  Lowrey, Rev. Dr. William as example of,
    446
  overview of, 20–1

traditions. *See* cultural rituals and
    traditions as peacemaker tools
Trajkovic, Morricilo, 131
Transjordan, 307
Transvaal, 217, 218. *See also* Boers
Treaty of Gandamak, 385–6
Treaty of Rawalpindi, 386
trekboers, 216
tribal leadership. *See* elders as
    peacemaker tool
Trimble, David, 53, 63
The Troubles, 56–7, 73. *See also* Ireland,
    Northern
Truth and Reconciliation Commission of
    Sierra Leone, 298
Truth and Reconciliation Commission of
    South Africa, 224–5
tsunami of 2004, 426
Tswana people, 216
Tudjman, President, 104
Turay, Thomas Mark, 290, 294–5
Tutu, Archbishop Desmond, 223
Tyrie, Andy, 64

UDA. *See* Ulster Defense Association
UDF (United Democratic Front), 222–3,
    227, 231. *See also* ANC
Ulster, 55, 58, 94. *See also* Ireland,
    Northern
Ulster Defense Association (UDA), 64,
    68–9, 95
Ulster Unionist Party (UUP), 95
Ulster Volunteer Force (UVF), 64, 74–5,
    95
UN. *See* United Nations
UNESCO, 45–7
Union of South Africa. *See* South Africa
Unionists of Northern Ireland, 94
United Democratic Front (UDF), 222–3,
    227, 231. *See also* ANC
United National Opposition (UNO), 30
United Nations
  Bosnia and Herzegovina and, 102,
    104–5
  ECOMOG, 286
  El Salvador and, 443
  Israeli-Palestinian conflict and, 309–12,
    314, 318, 319, 320
  Kosovo and, 136, 150

Sierra Leone and, 300, 443
South Africa and, 222
Sudan and, 195
UNESCO, 45–7
UNTEA, 404
women within peacemaking process
    resolution, 18, 235–6
zones of peace declared by, 416
United Party of South Africa, 220
United Popular Action Front (FAPU),
    39–40
United Religions (UR), 180
United States
    Afghanistan and, 382, 387, 388, 389, 400
    Bin Laden sought by, 389
    Bosnia and Herzegovina and, 104, 105,
        106, 121–2, 128, 149, 236
    embassy bombings in Kenya and
        Tanzania, 388
    Ethiopian Jews and, 166–8, 177
    Israeli-Palestinian conflict and, 307,
        311, 315, 366–7, 372–3
    Janjic, peacemaking efforts within,
        137–9
    Landau, peacemaking efforts within, 17
    New Guinea and, 404
    Salvadoran conflict and, 43, 51
    Taliban and, 382, 389
University of Southern Mississippi, 196
UNMIK (UN Interim Administration
    Mission in Kosovo), 136, 150
UNO (United National Opposition), 30
UNTEA (United Nations Temporary
    Executive Authority), 404
UR (United Religions), 180
Usman dan Fodio, 249
USSR. See Soviet Union
Ustasha movement, 99, 101
UUP (Ulster Unionist Party), 95
UVF (Ulster Volunteer Force), 64, 74–5, 95

Valdivieso, Bishop Antonio de, 26
Van der Merwe, H. W., 228
Vance-Owen peace plan, 104, 105
Vanguard movement, 63
Vatican II, 30, 32
Verwoerd, Hendrik Frensch, 220
Vick, Carl, 197
Vietnam War, 357

Waat Lou Nuer Peace and Governance
    Conference, 200–1
Wahid, Abdurrahman, 412–14
Wailing Wall. See Western Wall
Washington Post, 167
Wasley, Andrew, 141–2
WCRP (World Conference on Religion
    and Peace), 352. See also
    Inter-Religious Council of Sierra
    Leone
West Bank. See Palestine and Palestinians
West Jerusalem. See Jerusalem
West Papua, 422–3. See also Giay, The
    Reverend Benny; Indonesia
    "Act of Free Choice", 405
    demographics of, 423–5
    economy, 406, 426
    fact sheet, 423–5
    flag, 418
    Free Papua Movement (OPM), 404–5,
        413, 414
    historical overview of conflict, 403–6
    human rights violations, 408
    independence, desire for, 404–5, 426
    as Irian Jaya, 405, 413
    Javanese people, 425
    Melanesian Christians, 425
    missionary activity within, 419–21,
        425
    Morning Star Flag, 404, 413
    New Guinea Council, 404
    overview of conflict, 402, 425
    Papua Peace Commission, 402, 416–17
    Papuan People's Congress, 413–14
    Papuan Presidium Council (the
        "Council"), 413–14
    Papuans, history of, 402, 403
    post-9/11 climate, 415
    Special Autonomy Rule for Papua,
        412–13
    spiritual traditions of, 419–21
    Sumatran Muslims, 425
    violence against Papuan pastors, 410,
        412
Western media. See media
Western methods as peacemaking tools,
    18–19, 115
Western Wall, 304, 314. See also Temple
    Mount

White, Canon Andrew P.B., 6–7
White Huns, 384
White Paper, 308–9
William of Orange, 56, 59
women, education of. *See* Afghan
      Institute of Learning
Women for Peaceful Change Now
      (WPCN), 230
Women in International Security (WIS),
      236
women within peacemaking process, 18,
      86, 230, 235–6, 432–3, 437. *See also*
      Madlala-Routledge, Nozizwe;
      Yacoobi, Sakena
women's rights within South Africa
      military, 234–6
World Conference on Religion and Peace
      (WCRP), 352. *See also* Inter-Religious
      Council of Sierra Leone
World Vision International, 210
World War I
      Bosnia and Herzegovina history and, 99
      Kosovo and, 125–6
      South Africa and, 219
World War II
      Afghanistan and, 386
      Bosnia and Herzegovina and, 99
      Ethiopia and, 151
      Kosovo and, 125–6
      New Guinea and, 404
      South Africa and, 220
World Zionist Organization, 307
WPCN (Women for Peaceful Change
      Now), 230
Wunlit Dinka-Nuer Peace Conferences,
      200, 201, 202, 203, 204, 209
Wuye, Pastor James. *See also* Ashafa,
      Imam Muhammad; Nigeria
      Ashafa, Imam Muhammad, becoming
      brothers with, 261–4
      Bible as peacemaker tool of, 266, 267,
      270
      debate as peacemaking tool, 12–13
      on Indirect Rule by British, 255
      institution-and-capacity building by,
      445
      Interfaith Mediation Centre, 12–13,
      247–8

as Kaduna native, 255
Kaduna Peace Agreement and, 14,
      272
on manipulation of religion for
      violence, 430
media as peacemaking partner, 267–8
militant organizations, contact with,
      268–9
militant youth activist background,
      259–61
Muslim-Christian Dialogue Forum
      (MCDF), 247–8, 264–9, 270, 271,
      272–3, 432
Muslim-Christian Youth Dialogue
      Forum (MCYDF), 263–4
overview of, 247–8, 432
peacemakers trained by, 267
personal awareness of, 8
on political activism of Christians, 256
religious motivation for peacemaking,
      262–3, 269–70
secular peacemaking tools adapted by,
      19
status as religious leaders, 271
threats to religiously-motivated
      peacemaking, 270–2
Youth CAN, 260, 263
Zangon Kataf reconciliation efforts,
      256–7, 265–6

Xhosa people, 216, 217

Yacoobi, Sakena, 389–98. *See also* Afghan
      Institute of Learning (AIL);
      Afghanistan
      background of, 389–91
      clarity of purpose of, 8
      enforcement as type of peacemaking,
      443
      institution-and-capacity building by,
      445
      motivation, 396–8
      overview of, 382, 432–3
      peacekeeping efforts by, 390–1, 443
      Qur'an as peacemaker tool of, 391,
      392–3
      religious motivation, 397–8, 438
      risks taken, 396–7

storytelling, 391–2
on Taliban, 396, 397
teaching methods and strategy of,
393–5
Yassin, Sheikh Ahmad, 347
Yemenite Judaism, 158
Yom Kippur War, 315
Yoruba people, 248, 251
Youth Wing of the Christian Association
of Nigeria (Youth CAN), 260, 263
Yugoslav People's Army (JNA), 101, 102–3
Yugoslavia. *See also* Bosnia and
Herzegovina; Janjic, Father Sava;
Markovic, Friar Ivo; Serbia and
Montenegro
Balkan War (1912), 125
Communism of, 99–100
disintegration of, 100–1
economic policies of, 100
establishment of, 126
Federal Units of Yugoslavia,
disintegration of, 128
historical overview of conflict, 149–50
Kingdom of, 98
Milosevic, Slobodan, 100–1, 103–4,
127–8, 130–1, 134, 137, 140–1, 149

Yussef, General Nasser, 346–7

Zagreb, 104. *See also* Croatia
a-Zahar, Mahmoud, 347
"Zakheus Pakage and His Communities"
(Giay), 411–12
Zamfara, Nigeria, 257
Zangon Kataf. *See also* Kaduna; Shari'a
law in Nigeria
Ashafa and Wuye within, 265–7, 271
history of, 255
Kataf people of Nigeria, 255–7
market riots of, 256–7, 260–1, 266–7,
271
Zenawi, Ato Meles, 169, 174
Zionism, 305–6, 351. *See also* Israel, State
of; Oz veShalom peace movement;
World Zionist Organization
Zone of Peace
Alas and, 15, 25–6, 44–7
Central America as, 45–7
Giay and, 402, 416–17, 420
as peacemaker tool, 15
as UN technique, 18, 45–7
Zoroaster, 383
Zulu people, 216, 217, 223, 225–6